T0214747

Lecture Notes in Computer Science 12472

More information about this subseries at http://www.springer.com/series/7410

Willy Susilo · Robert H. Deng ·
Fuchun Guo · Yannan Li ·
Rolly Intan (Eds.)

Information Security

23rd International Conference, ISC 2020
Bali, Indonesia, December 16–18, 2020
Proceedings

 Springer

Editors
Willy Susilo ⓘ
Institute of Cybersecurity
and Cryptology
University of Wollongong
Wollongong, NSW, Australia

Fuchun Guo ⓘ
Institute of Cybersecurity
and Cryptology
University of Wollongong
Wollongong, NSW, Australia

Rolly Intan
Petra Christian University
Surabaya, Indonesia

Robert H. Deng ⓘ
Singapore Management University
Singapore, Singapore

Yannan Li ⓘ
Institute of Cybersecurity
and Cryptology
University of Wollongong
Wollongong, NSW, Australia

ISSN 0302-9743   ISSN 1611-3349   (electronic)
Lecture Notes in Computer Science
ISBN 978-3-030-62973-1   ISBN 978-3-030-62974-8   (eBook)
https://doi.org/10.1007/978-3-030-62974-8

LNCS Sublibrary: SL4 – Security and Cryptology

This Springer imprint is published by the registered company Springer Nature Switzerland AG
The registered company address is: Gewerbestrasse 11, 6330 Cham, Switzerland

Preface

On behalf of the Program Committee, it is our pleasure to present the proceedings of the 23rd Information Security Conference (ISC 2020), which was held online during December 16–18, 2020. There was no physical conference due to the COVID-19 global pandemic. ISC is an annual international conference covering research in theory and applications of information security. Both academic research with high relevance to real-world problems, as well as developments in industrial and technical frontiers fall within the scope of the conference.

The 23rd edition of ISC was organized by the Petra Christian University, Surabaya, Indonesia, and was held online. Professor Rolly Intan (Petra Christian University, Indonesia) served as the general chair, and Professor Willy Susilo (University of Wollongong, Australia) and Professor Robert H. Deng (Singapore Management University, Singapore) served as the program co-chairs. The Program Committee comprised 40 members from top institutions around the world. Out of 87 submissions, the Program Committee eventually selected 23 papers (2 of which were accepted after a shepherding process) for presentation in the conference and publication in the proceedings, resulting in an acceptance rate of 26.4%. The submission process was double-blind, and the review process was organized and managed through the Easychair online reviewing system, with all papers receiving at least three reviews. To manage the final version of the papers, we used the Springer's Online Conference Service (OCS). The final program was quite balanced in terms of topics, containing both theoretical/cryptography papers, as well as more practical/systems security papers. The Best Paper Award was selected based on the highest mark received during the review. The program co-chairs decided to present the Best Paper Award to "ELD: Adaptive Detection of Malicious Nodes under Mix-Energy-Depleting-Attacks Using Edge Learning in IoT Networks" by Zuchao Ma, Liang Liu, and Weizhi Meng. Beyond the research papers, the conference program also included five insightful keynote talks by Professor Reihaneh Safavi-Naini (University of Calgary, Canada), Dr. Melissa Chase (Microsoft Research Redmond, USA), Professor Dr.-Ing. Tibor Jager (Bergische Universität Wuppertal, Germany), Professor Yingjiu Li (University of Oregon, USA), and Dr. Tieyan Li (Huawei Technologies Co. Ltd., Singapore).

A successful conference is the result of the joint effort of many people. We would like to express our appreciation to the Program Committee members and external reviewers for the time spent reviewing papers, participating in the online discussion, and shepherding some of the papers to ensure the highest quality possible. We also deeply thank our invited speakers for their willingness to participate in the conference, especially during the difficult time in the middle of the global pandemic. We also express our appreciation to the publication chairs: Dr. Fuchun Guo (University of Wollongong, Australia), Dr. Yannan Li (University of Wollongong, Australia), and Dr. Henry Novianus Palit (Petra Christian University, Indonesia), and the financial chair Leo Willyanto Santoso (Petra Christian University, Indonesia). We would particularly like to express our gratitude to Dr. Yannan Li who managed the OCS system and handled all the issues with regards to the production of the final proceedings. Finally, we also thank Springer for publishing these proceedings as part of their LNCS series and allowing us to use their OCS system, and the ISC Steering Committee for their continuous support and assistance.

Finally, ISC 2020 would not have been possible without the authors who submitted their work and presented their contributions, as well as the attendees who came to the conference. We would like to thank them all, and we look forward to their future contributions to ISC.

December 2020   Willy Susilo
                                                        Robert H. Deng

Organization

Program Chairs

Willy Susilo — University of Wollongong, Australia
Robert H. Deng — Singapore Management University, Singapore

General Chair

Rolly Intan — Petra Christian University, Indonesia

Publication Chairs

Fuchun Guo — University of Wollongong, Australia
Yannan Li — University of Wollongong, Australia
Henry Novianus Palit — Petra Christian University, Indonesia

Steering Committee

Zhiqiang Lin — The Ohio State University, USA
Javier Lopez — University of Malaga, Spain
Masahiro Mambo — Kanazawa University, Japan
Eiji Okamoto — University of Tsukuba, Japan
Michalis Polychronakis — Stony Brook University, USA
Willy Susilo — University of Wollongong, Australia
Jianying Zhou — Singapore University of Technology and Design, Singapore

Financial Chair

Leo Willyanto Santoso — Petra Christian University, Indonesia

Program Committee

Masayuki Abe — Kyoto University, Japan
Joonsang Baek — University of Wollongong, Australia
Liqun Chen — University of Surrey, UK
Xiaofeng Chen — Xidian University, China
Yueqiang Cheng — Baidu, USA
Mauro Conti — University of Padua, Italy
Jorge Cuellar — Siemens AG, Germany
Josep Domingo-Ferrer — Universitat Rovira i Virgili, Spain
Dung Hoang Duong — University of Wollongong, Australia

Joaquin Garcia-Alfaro	Télécom Sudparis, France
Shoichi Hirose	University of Fukui, Japan
Tibor Jager	Bergische Universitat Wuppertal, Germany
Han Jinguang	University of Surrey, UK
Angelos D. Keromytis	Georgia Institute of Technology, USA
Florian Kerschbaum	University of Waterloo, Canada
Hiroaki Kikuchi	Meiji University, Japan
Hyoungshick Kim	Sungkyunkwan University, South Korea
Miroslaw Kutylowski	Wroclaw University of Science and Technology, Poland
Jooyoung Lee	Korea Advanced Institute of Science and Technology, South Korea
Joseph Liu	Monash University, Australia
Mark Manulis	University of Surrey, UK
Daniel Masny	University of California, Berkeley, USA
Khoa Nguyen	Nanyang Technological University, Singapore
Josef Pieprzyk	CSIRO Data 61, Australia
Vincent Rijmen	Katholieke Universiteit Leuven, Belgium
Reihaneh Safavi-Naini	University of Calgary, Canada
Ron Steinfield	Monash University, Australia
Atsushi Takayasu	The University of Tokyo, Japan
Huaxiong Wang	Nanyang Technological University, Singapore
Cong Wang	City University of Hong Kong, Hong Kong
Avishai Wool	Tel Aviv University, Israel
Toshihiro Yamauchi	Okayama University, Japan
Guomin Yang	University of Wollongong, Australia
Xun Yi	RMIT University, Australia
Yong Yu	Shaanxi Normal University, China
Mingwu Zhang	Hubei University of Technology, China

External Reviewers

Antonio Muñoz	Cailing Cai	Mingming Wang
Gang Shen	Andrei Kelarev	Przemysław Kubiak
Fadi Hassan	Sergio Martìnez	Jay Prakash
Viet Vo	Jun Shen	Hiroshi Onuki
David Jinwei Hu	Handong Cui	John Castellanos
Ankit Gangwal	Morshed Islam	Juan Rubio
Xianhui Lu	Alberto Blanco-Justicia	Luca Pajola
Saqib A. Kakvi	Lin Lyu	Yi Xie
Li Huilin	Jie Chen	David Niehues
Tadanori Teruya	Pengfei Sun	Matteo Cardaioli
Guohua Tian	Antonio Muñoz	Xiaoning Liu
Yanmei Cao	Chhagan Lal	Yuanyuan Zhang
Shen Hua	Fei Zhu	Alessandro Visintin

Haoran Yuan

Ruben Rios

Gareth T. Davies

Yonghui Chen

Shota Yamada

Xianrui Qin

Setareh Sharifian

Jixin Zhang

Zhi Zhang

Mingli Wu

Rami Haffar

Tomoki Moriya

Hanwen Feng

Huibo Wang

Flavio Toffalini

Xu Yang

Rahman Ziaur

Yanqi Zhao

Tianxu Han

Kai Gellert

Ahmad Salehi Shahraki

Zhe Xia

Sabyasachi Dutta

Tianhao Wang

Najeeb Jebreel

Yanhong Xu

Zhiqiang Gu

Junbin Shi

Ashneet Khandpur Singh

Mingzhe Zhai

Mengdie Huang

Yasuhiko Ikematsu

Xuechao Yang

Contents

Malware Analysis

Network and System Security

Blokchain

Security Applications

Public-Key Cryptography

Anonymous IBE from Quadratic Residuosity with Fast Encryption

Xiaopeng Zhao[1], Zhenfu Cao[1,2(✉)], Xiaolei Dong[1], and Jinwen Zheng[1]

[1] Shanghai Key Laboratory of Trustworthy Computing, East China Normal University, Shanghai, China
`52164500025@stu.ecnu.edu.cn`, `{zfcao,dongxiaolei}@sei.ecnu.edu.cn`,
`jinwen.zheng@foxmail.com`
[2] Cyberspace Security Research Center, Peng Cheng Laboratory, Shenzhen and Shanghai Institute of Intelligent Science and Technology, Tongji University, Shanghai, China

Abstract. We develop two variants of Cocks' identity-based encryption. One variant has faster encryption, where the most time-consuming part only requires several modular multiplications. The other variant makes the first variant anonymous under suitable complexity assumptions, while its decryption efficiency is about twice lower than the first one. Both the variants have ciphertext expansion twice more extensive than the original Cocks' identity-based encryption. To alleviate the issue of the second variant's large ciphertext expansion, we consider using it to construct a public-key encryption with keyword search scheme with a fast encryption algorithm by means of the transform in [1].

Keywords: Public-key cryptography · Quadratic residuosity · Identity-based encryption · Cocks' scheme · Anonymous encryption · Public-key encryption with keyword search

1 Introduction

The notion of identity-based cryptography was first proposed by Shamir [19] in 1984. This new paradigm of cryptography aims at solving the issue of managing and recovering the public-key certificate by simplifying the key management. For example, users' identification information such as email addresses or names rather than digital certificates can be used as their public key to encrypt or verify digital signature. Shamir constructed an identity-based signature scheme using the RSA function, but developing identity-based encryption (IBE) schemes turns out to be much harder. Until the year 2001, Shamir's open problem was solved by Boneh and Franklin [5] and Cocks [13] independently. Recently, lattice was considered as an emergent system for constructing IBE schemes (e.g., as in [15]). The Boneh-Franklin IBE scheme makes use of bilinear maps and is truly practical. Therefore, this work has attracted tons of attention from researchers over the years. However, Cocks' IBE scheme received less attention because of

W. Susilo et al. (Eds.): ISC 2020, LNCS 12472, pp. 3–19, 2020.
https://doi.org/10.1007/978-3-030-62974-8_1

the lack of algebraic structure. Although Cocks' IBE scheme is inefficient for large messages, it is simple, elegant, and secure under the standard quadratic residuosity (QR) assumption in the random oracle model. It can be used to encrypt short session keys in practice, e.g., a 128-bit symmetric key. Thus, the scheme was followed up by some researchers [2,6,7,10–12,14,17,20].

In 2016, Joye [17] made Cocks' scheme amenable to applications including electronic voting, auction systems, private information retrieval, or cloud computing; Joye proved that Cocks' scheme is homomorphic by considering Cocks' ciphertext as elements of a certain algebraic group. A similar conclusion can also be reached by considering Cocks' scheme over the polynomial quotient ring $\mathbb{Z}_N[x]/(x^2 - R_{\mathsf{id}})$ for which N is an RSA modulus and R_{id} is the IBE public key of an identity id [10,11]. Our two variants are based on the latter structure.

It is well-known that Cocks' scheme is not anonymous due to Galbraith's test [4]. The test has been well studied by several researchers [2,20]. Despite the test, some researchers [2,6,12,14,17] managed to propose anonymous variants of Cocks' scheme. In [14], the anonymization of Cocks' scheme was achieved for the first time, and a public-key encryption with keyword search (PEKS) scheme was proposed based on a variant of the quadratic residuosity problem. In this work, we mainly follow the approach of Joye in [17], which does not increase Cocks' ciphertext size or sacrifice its security.

In this work, we use the time-space tradeoff method to propose two variants of Cocks' IBE scheme [13] in the following two aspects:

1. Our first variant omits the computation of the Jacobi symbol $\left(\frac{a}{b}\right)$ for κ-bit integers a and b, which has $\mathcal{O}\left(M(\kappa)\log\kappa\right)^1$ time complexity [8], and the modular multiplicative inverse in Cocks' encryption. In detail, the ciphertext extension is increased by a factor of 2, but the most time-consuming part of the encryption in our variant only requires several modular multiplications of time complexity $\mathcal{O}\left(M(\kappa)\right)$ (see [9, Section 2.4]). The variant can also be proved semantic secure under a complexity assumption slightly stronger than the QR assumption, moreover, this improvement hardly affects the decryption speed.
2. Inspired by the anonymous variant of Cocks' scheme, without ciphertext expansion, proposed in [17, Section 6.2], our second variant makes the first variant anonymous under suitable complexity assumptions. This improvement does not affect the ciphertext expansion either. To alleviate the issue of the second variant's large ciphertext expansion, we consider using this variant to construct a PEKS scheme with a fast PEKS-encryption algorithm by means of the transform in [1].

The rest of the paper is organized as follows. In Sect. 2, we review the notion of semantic secure and the notion of anonymity. In Sect. 3, we describe our first variant and prove that it is semantic secure. In Sect. 4, we describe our second variant and prove that it is anonymous under reasonable complexity

---

[1] $M(\kappa)$ is the time to multiply κ-bit numbers.

assumptions. In Appendix A, we give a suitable application of our second variant. Concluding remarks are given in Sect. 5.

2   Preliminaries

We write $x \xleftarrow{R} X$ for sampling at random an element x from the set X. If $\mathcal{A}$ is an algorithm, then we write $x \leftarrow \mathcal{A}(y)$ to mean: "run $\mathcal{A}$ on input y and the output is assigned to x".

2.1   Identity-Based Encryption

An *identity-based encryption* (IBE) scheme is defined as a tuple of probabilistic polynomial time (PPT) algorithms (Setup, KeyGen, Enc, Dec):

Setup(1^κ) The setup algorithm Setup is a randomized algorithm that takes a security parameter 1^κ as input, and returns a tuple (mpk, msk), where mpk denotes the public parameters and msk denotes the master secret key. The message space is denoted by M.

KeyGen(msk, id) The key generation algorithm KeyGen takes msk and an identity id as inputs, and returns a decryption key sk$_{id}$ associated with the identity id.

Enc(mpk, id, m) The encryption algorithm Enc is a randomized algorithm that takes the public parameters mpk, an identity id and a message $m \in$ M as inputs, and returns a ciphertext C.

Dec(mpk, sk$_{id}$, C) The decryption algorithm Dec takes the public parameters mpk, a secret key sk$_{id}$ (corresponding to the identity id) and a ciphertext C as inputs, and returns a message m if C is a valid ciphertext, and $\perp$ otherwise.

For any identity id and all messages $m \in$ M, the *correctness* property requires that

$$\text{Dec} \left(\text{mpk}, \text{sk}_{id}, C \leftarrow \text{Enc}(\text{mpk}, \text{id}, m) \right) = m.$$

2.2   Security Notions

The following notions are consistent with the notions described in [17, Section 2.2].

Semantic Security. The semantic security property [16] states that it is infeasible for any adversary with the limited computation ability to get any information of a message given the corresponding ciphertext. The behaviors of an adversary $\mathcal{A}$ can be simulated by a pair of probabilistic PPT algorithms ($\mathcal{A}_1, \mathcal{A}_2$). The adversary is allowed to adaptively make private key extraction queries to the key-extraction oracle Extract(mpk, msk, ·). The game between an adversary and a challenger contains the following five successive phases:

INITIALIZATION PHASE: The challenger takes a security parameter κ as input and runs the algorithm Setup. It then gives the public parameters mpk to the adversary $\mathcal{A}$ while keeping the master secret key msk to itself.

THE FIRST QUERY PHASE: After receiving mpk, $\mathcal{A}_1$ adaptively chooses an identity subspace ID_1 in the identity space ID, and issues the key generation queries to $\mathsf{Extract}(\mathsf{mpk}, \mathsf{msk}, \cdot)$ and obtains the private key corresponding to each identity in ID_1.

CHALLENGE PHASE: $\mathcal{A}_1$ fixes a challenge identity $\mathsf{id}^* \notin \mathsf{ID}_1$ and two different messages m_0, $m_1 \in \mathsf{M}$ of equal length. It then returns them along with some state information s. The challenger chooses uniformly at random a bit b and encrypts m_b with mpk and id^*. It then returns the corresponding ciphertext C as the challenge ciphertext to $\mathcal{A}_2$.

THE SECOND QUERY PHASE: Just like THE FIRST QUERY PHASE, $\mathcal{A}_2$ can adaptively issue more key generation queries in the identity space $\mathsf{ID}_2 \subseteq \mathsf{ID}$ which does not contain id^*.

GUESS PHASE: The goal of $\mathcal{A}_2$ is to guess the bit b from C and s. It outputs a guess b' of b.

Formally, an IBE scheme is said to be semantically secure if the advantage

$\mathsf{Adv}_{\mathcal{A}}^{\mathsf{IND\text{-}ID\text{-}CPA}}(1^\kappa)$

$$= \left| \Pr \left[\begin{array}{l} (\mathsf{mpk}, \mathsf{msk}) \overset{R}{\leftarrow} \mathsf{Setup}(1^\kappa), \\ (\mathsf{id}^*, m_0, m_1, \mathsf{s}) \leftarrow \mathcal{A}_1^{\mathsf{Extract}(\mathsf{mpk},\mathsf{msk},\cdot)}, \\ b \overset{R}{\leftarrow} \{0, 1\}, \, C \leftarrow \mathsf{Enc}(\mathsf{mpk}, \mathsf{id}^*, m_b) \end{array} : \mathcal{A}_2^{\mathsf{Extract}(\mathsf{mpk},\mathsf{msk},\cdot)}(C, \mathsf{s}) = b \right] - \frac{1}{2} \right|$$

is negligible in the security parameter κ for any PPT adversary $\mathcal{A}$. The semantic security can also be called indistinguishable, chosen–identity, chosen–plaintext (IND-ID-CPA) security.

Anonymity. The notion of *anonymity* [3] is a strong requirement of privacy: it is infeasible for any adversary with the limited computation ability to get the identity of the recipient from the ciphertext. Anonymous IBE can be used for searchable encryption [1,4]. The behaviors of an adversary $\mathcal{A}$ can also be simulated by a pair of probabilistic PPT algorithms $(\mathcal{A}_1, \mathcal{A}_2)$. The game between an adversary and a challenger contains the following five successive phases:

INITIALIZATION PHASE: The same as that in Sect. 2.2.

THE FIRST QUERY PHASE: The same as that in Sect. 2.2.

CHALLENGE PHASE: The adversary chooses two distinct challenge identities $\mathsf{id}_0^*, \mathsf{id}_1^* \notin \mathsf{ID}_1$ and a message $m \in \mathsf{M}$. It then returns them along with some state information s. The challenger chooses a random bit b and encrypts m with mpk and id_b^*. It then sends the corresponding ciphertext C to $\mathcal{A}_2$.

THE SECOND QUERY PHASE: Just like THE FIRST QUERY PHASE, $\mathcal{A}_2$ can issue more key generation queries in the identity space $\mathsf{ID}_2 \subseteq \mathsf{ID}$ which does not contain id_0^* and id_1^*.

GUESS PHASE: The same as that in Sect. 2.2.

Formally, an IBE scheme is said to be *anonymous* if the advantage

$\mathsf{Adv}_{\mathcal{A}}^{\mathsf{ANO\text{-}ID\text{-}CPA}}(\kappa)$

$$= \left| \Pr \left[\begin{array}{l} (\mathsf{mpk}, \mathsf{msk}) \xleftarrow{R} \mathsf{Setup}(1^{\kappa}), \\ (\mathsf{id}_0^*, \mathsf{id}_1^*, m, \mathsf{s}) \leftarrow \mathcal{A}_1^{\mathsf{Extract}(\mathsf{mpk}, \mathsf{msk}, \cdot)}, \;\; : \;\; \mathcal{A}_2^{\mathsf{Extract}(\mathsf{mpk}, \mathsf{msk}, \cdot)} (\mathsf{s}, C) = b \\ b \xleftarrow{R} \{0, 1\}, \; C \leftarrow \mathsf{Enc}(\mathsf{mpk}, \mathsf{id}_b^*, m) \end{array} \right] - \frac{1}{2} \right|$$

is negligible in the security parameter κ for any PPT adversary $\mathcal{A}$.

2.3   Complexity Assumption

Let N be a product of two RSA primes p and q. Let $\mathbb{J}_N = \left\{ x \in \mathbb{Z}_N^* \;\middle|\; \left(\frac{x}{N} \right) = 1 \right\}$, i.e., the set of integers whose Jacobi symbols are 1. Let $\mathbb{QR}_N = \{ x \mid \exists y \in \mathbb{Z}_N^*, x \equiv y^2 \pmod{N} \}$. The following complexity assumption slightly modifies the QR assumption.

Definition 1 (Strong Quadratic Residuosity (SQR) Assumption). *Given a security parameter κ. A PPT algorithm RSAGen (1^{κ}) generates two RSA primes p and q such that $p \equiv -q \mod 4$ and their product $N = pq$. RSAGen (κ) also chooses $u \xleftarrow{R} \mathbb{J}_N \setminus \mathbb{QR}_N$. The strong quadratic residuosity assumption with respect to RSAGen (κ) asserts that the advantage $\mathsf{Adv}_{\mathcal{A}, \mathsf{RSAGen}}^{\mathsf{SQR}} (\kappa)$ defined as*

$$\left| \Pr \left[\mathcal{A} (N, u, x) = 1 \;\middle|\; x \xleftarrow{R} \mathbb{QR}_N \right] - \Pr \left[\mathcal{A} (N, u, x) = 1 \;\middle|\; x \xleftarrow{R} \mathbb{J}_N \setminus \mathbb{QR}_N \right] \right|$$

is negligible for any PPT adversary $\mathcal{A}$; the probabilities are taken over the experiment of running $(N, p, q, u) \leftarrow \mathsf{RSAGen}(\kappa)$ and choosing at random $x \in \mathbb{QR}_N$ and $x \in \mathbb{J}_N \setminus \mathbb{QR}_N$.

Remark 1. The only difference between the SQR assumption and the assumption on which Cocks' scheme relies is the choice of p and q. In the latter assumption, $N = pq$ where $p \equiv q \equiv 3 \pmod{4}$, and $-1 \in \mathbb{J}_N \setminus \mathbb{QR}_N$ is public. Hence, we believe that breaking one is as intractable as breaking the other.

3   A Variant of Cocks' IBE Scheme with Fast Encryption

Our first scheme can be viewed as a variant of the classical Cocks' scheme. Define the function

$$\mathcal{J}_N(x) = \begin{cases} \bot, & \text{if } \gcd(x, N) \neq 1; \\ i, & \text{if } \gcd(x, N) = 1 \text{ and } \left(\frac{x}{N} \right) = (-1)^i. \end{cases}$$

Our first scheme proceeds as follows.

Setup(1^κ) Given a security parameter κ, Setup generates two RSA primes p and q such that $p \equiv -q \mod 4$ and their product $N = pq$. Setup also samples an element $u \xleftarrow{R} \mathbb{J}_N \setminus \mathbb{QR}_N$. The public parameters is $\mathsf{mpk} = \{N, u, \mathsf{H}\}$ where H is a publicly available cryptographic hash function mapping an arbitrary binary string to $\mathbb{J}_N$. The master secret key is $\mathsf{msk} = \{p, q\}$.

KeyGen($\mathsf{mpk}, \mathsf{msk}, \mathsf{id}$) Using mpk and msk, KeyGen sets $R_{\mathsf{id}} = \mathsf{H}(\mathsf{id})$. If $R_{\mathsf{id}} \in \mathbb{QR}_N$, KeyGen computes $r_{\mathsf{id}} = R_{\mathsf{id}}^{1/2} \mod N$; otherwise it computes $r_{\mathsf{id}} = (uR_{\mathsf{id}})^{1/2} \mod N$. Finally, KeyGen returns $\mathsf{sk_{id}} = \{r_{\mathsf{id}}\}$ as user's private key.

Enc($\mathsf{mpk}, \mathsf{id}, m$) On inputting mpk, an identity id and a message $m \in \{0, 1\}$, Enc derives the hash value $R_{\mathsf{id}} = \mathsf{H}(\mathsf{id})$. Enc then chooses at random two polynomials $f(x), \overline{f}(x)$ of degree 1 from $\mathbb{Z}_N[x]$ and calculates

$$g(x) = f(x)^2 \mod (x^2 - R_{\mathsf{id}}) \quad \text{and} \quad \overline{g}(x) = \overline{f}(x)^2 \mod (x^2 - uR_{\mathsf{id}}).$$

The returned ciphertext is $C = ((-1)^m \cdot g(x), (-1)^m \cdot \overline{g}(x))$.

Dec($\mathsf{mpk}, \mathsf{sk_{id}}, C$) On inputting mpk, a secret key $\mathsf{sk_{id}} = \{r_{\mathsf{id}}\}$ and a ciphertext $C = (c(x), \overline{c}(x))$, Dec computes

$$m' = \begin{cases} \left(\dfrac{c(r_{\mathsf{id}})}{N} \right) & \text{if } r_{\mathsf{id}}^2 \equiv \mathsf{H}(\mathsf{id}) \pmod{N}; \\ \left(\dfrac{\overline{c}(r_{\mathsf{id}})}{N} \right) & \text{otherwise.} \end{cases}$$

and recovers the message m as $\mathcal{J}_N(m')$.

CORRECTNESS. The correctness of the decryption follows by noticing that when $r_{\mathsf{id}}^2 \equiv \mathsf{H}(\mathsf{id}) \pmod{N}$ we have

$$m' = \left(\frac{c(r_{\mathsf{id}})}{N} \right) = \left(\frac{(-1)^m f(r_{\mathsf{id}})^2}{N} \right) = (-1)^m,$$

and thus we can recover the message m by the function $\mathcal{J}_N$. When $r_{\mathsf{id}}^2 \equiv u\mathsf{H}(\mathsf{id}) \pmod{N}$, we can proceed similarly.

Remark 2. In the encryption, if we set $f(x) = ax + b$, we have

$$g(x) = f(x)^2 = (ax + b)^2 \equiv a^2 R_{\mathsf{id}} + b^2 + 2abx \pmod{x^2 - R_{\mathsf{id}}}.$$

Thus, calculating $g(x)$ needs two squares, two general multiplications and one addition modulo N. In the decryption, we need one more modular multiplication than Cocks' decryption. However, this hardly affects the decryption speed because computing one general 1024-bit Jacobi symbol is about 27 times slower than calculating one general 1024-bit modular multiplication according to the running times in [6, Table 1].

Before proving that the above scheme is semantic secure, we need the following theorem.

Theorem 1. *Let $t \in \mathbb{Z}_N^*$ and R an element in $\mathbb{J}_N \setminus \mathbb{QR}_N$. If $c(x) = \frac{f(x)^2}{t}$ mod $(x^2 - R)$ for some $f(x) \in \mathbb{Z}_N[x]$ is a polynomial of degree 1, then the sets*

$$\Omega_k = \left\{ g(x) \in \mathbb{Z}_N[x] \;\middle|\; \deg g(x) = 1, \; \frac{g(x)^2}{k} \text{ mod } (x^2 - R) = c(x) \right\}$$

are of the same size for each $k \in \mathbb{Z}_N^*$.

Proof. Consider the two sets $\Omega_t, \Omega_{\bar{t}}$, to prove the theorem, it suffices to prove that $\#\Omega_t = \#\Omega_{\bar{t}}$ for fixed t and any $\bar{t} \in \mathbb{Z}_N^*$. Suppose that $\left(\frac{t^{-1}\bar{t}}{p} \right) = (-1)^{i_t}$ and $\left(\frac{t^{-1}\bar{t}}{q} \right) = (-1)^{j_t}$ for $i_t, j_t \in \{0, 1\}$. Since

$$\left(\frac{R^{i_t}}{p} \right) = \left(\frac{t^{-1}\bar{t}}{p} \right) \quad \text{and} \quad \left(\frac{R^{j_t}}{q} \right) = \left(\frac{t^{-1}\bar{t}}{q} \right),$$

there exist $W_p \in \mathbb{Z}_p^*$ and $W_q \in \mathbb{Z}_q^*$ such that

$$W_p^2 R^{i_t} \equiv t^{-1}\bar{t} \pmod{p}$$
$$W_q^2 R^{j_t} \equiv t^{-1}\bar{t} \pmod{q}.$$

According to the Chinese Remainder Theorem, we have

$$\mathbb{Z}[x]/(N, x^2 - R) \cong \mathbb{Z}[x]/(p, x^2 - R) \oplus \mathbb{Z}[x]/(q, x^2 - R).$$

Therefore, the map $\phi : \Omega_t \to \Omega_{\bar{t}}$ given by $h(x) \mapsto g(x)$ where $h(x) \in \Omega_t, g(x) \in \Omega_{\bar{t}}$ and

$$g(x) \equiv W_p x^{i_t} h(x) \pmod{(p, x^2 - R)}$$
$$g(x) \equiv W_q x^{j_t} h(x) \pmod{(q, x^2 - R)}$$

is well defined. In the other direction, the inverse map $\psi : \Omega_{\bar{t}} \to \Omega_t$ is given by $g(x) \mapsto h(x)$ where

$$h(x) \equiv W_p^{-1} \left(R^{-1}x \right)^{i_t} g(x) \pmod{(p, x^2 - R)}$$
$$h(x) \equiv W_q^{-1} \left(R^{-1}x \right)^{j_t} g(x) \pmod{(q, x^2 - R)}$$

It is straightforward to verify that the composite map $\psi \circ \phi = 1_{\Omega_t}$ and $\phi \circ \psi = 1_{\Omega_{\bar{t}}}$ where 1_{Ω_t} and $1_{\Omega_{\bar{t}}}$ denote the identity maps on Ω_t and $\Omega_{\bar{t}}$ respectively. This establishes the bijection and completes the proof. □

Theorem 2. *Let $\mathcal{A} = (\mathcal{A}_1, \mathcal{A}_2)$ be an adversary against the IND-ID-CPA security of the scheme in Sect. 3, making q_H queries to the random oracle H that are not followed by (private key) extraction queries before the* CHALLENGE PHASE. *Then, there exists an adversary $\mathcal{B}$ against the SQR assumption such that*

$$\mathsf{Adv}_{\mathcal{A}}^{\mathsf{IND\text{-}ID\text{-}CPA}}(\kappa) = \frac{q_H}{2} \cdot \mathsf{Adv}_{\mathcal{B},\mathsf{RSAGen}}^{\mathsf{SQR}}(\kappa)$$

The security proof is obtained by following the proof of [17, Appendix A].

Proof. Suppose that $\mathcal{B}$ is given a tuple $(N, u) \leftarrow \mathsf{RSAGen}(\kappa)$ and a random element $w \in \mathbb{J}_N$, and is asked to determine whether $w \in \mathbb{J}_N \setminus \mathbb{QR}_N$. $\mathcal{B}$ sets $\mathsf{mpk} = \{N, u, \mathsf{H}\}$ and gives it to $\mathcal{A}_1$, who has oracle access to hash queries and extraction queries, i.e., asking the private key corresponding to each identity in the chosen set ID_1. $\mathcal{B}$ answers the oracle queries as follows:

Hash queries. Initially, $\mathcal{B}$ maintains a counter ctr initialized to 0 and a list $\mathcal{S}_{\mathsf{H}} \leftarrow \emptyset$ whose entry is in the form $(\mathsf{id}, R_{\mathsf{id}}, r_{\mathsf{id}})$. In addition, $\mathcal{B}$ selects $i^* \xleftarrow{R} \{1, 2, \ldots, q_{\mathsf{H}}\}$.

When $\mathcal{A}$ queries oracle H on an identity id, $\mathcal{B}$ increments ctr and checks whether there is an entry whose first component is id. If so, it returns R_{id}; otherwise,

1. If $ctr = i^*$, it returns w and appends the entry $(\mathsf{id}, w, \perp)$ to $\mathcal{S}_{\mathsf{H}}$.
2. Otherwise, it returns $h = u^{-j} r^2 \bmod N$ for which $r \xleftarrow{R} \mathbb{Z}_N$ and $j \xleftarrow{R} \{0, 1\}$, and appends the entry (id, h, r) to $\mathcal{S}_{\mathsf{H}}$.

Extraction queries. When $\mathcal{A}$ queries the secret key on id, $\mathcal{B}$ first checks whether there is an entry whose first component is id. If not, it invokes $\mathsf{H}(\mathsf{id})$ to generate such an entry $(\mathsf{id}, R_{\mathsf{id}}, r_{\mathsf{id}})$. Finally, if $r_{\mathsf{id}} = \perp$, it aborts; otherwise, it returns r_{id}.

Afterwards, $\mathcal{A}_1$ selects a challenge identity $\mathsf{id}^* \notin \mathsf{ID}_1$. If $\mathsf{H}(\mathsf{id}^*) \neq w$, $\mathcal{B}$ returns $b \xleftarrow{R} \{0, 1\}$; otherwise, $\mathcal{B}$ does the following process:

1. Choose at random two polynomials $f(x), \overline{f}(x)$ of degree 1 from $\mathbb{Z}_N[x]$ and $b \xleftarrow{R} \{0, 1\}$. Calculate

$$g(x) = f(x)^2 \bmod (x^2 - w)$$
$$\overline{g}(x) = \overline{f}(x)^2 \bmod (x^2 - uw)$$

The corresponding ciphertext is

$$C_b = \begin{cases} (g(x), -\overline{g}(x)), & \text{if } b = 0; \\ (-g(x), \overline{g}(x)), & \text{otherwise.} \end{cases}$$

2. Give C_b to $\mathcal{A}_2$. $\mathcal{A}_2$ may issue more hash queries and extraction queries on identities except for id^*. Finally, $\mathcal{A}_2$ returns a bit b'.
3. If $b = b'$ return 1; otherwise return 0.

We first analyze the subcase that $w \neq \mathsf{H}(\mathsf{id}^*)$. In this case $\mathcal{B}$ returns a random bit, regardless of what w is. Therefore, we have $\Pr[\mathcal{B}(N, u, w) = 1 \mid w \in \mathbb{QR}_N \wedge w \neq \mathsf{H}(\mathsf{id}^*)] = \Pr[\mathcal{B}(N, u, w) = 1 \mid w \in \mathbb{J}_N \setminus \mathbb{QR}_N \wedge w \neq \mathsf{H}(\mathsf{id}^*)] = 1/2$. We now consider the subcase that $w = \mathsf{H}(\mathsf{id}^*)$. If $w \in \mathbb{QR}_N$, according to the fact that $uw \in \mathbb{J}_N \setminus \mathbb{QR}_N$ and Theorem 1, we conclude that C_b is a valid ciphertext for b. For the same reason, if $w \in \mathbb{J}_N \setminus \mathbb{QR}_N$, we conclude that C_b is a valid ciphertext for $1 - b$; in this case, $\mathcal{B}$ returns 1 if and only if $\mathcal{A}$ loses the IND-ID-CPA game. Let $\epsilon = \Pr\left[\mathcal{B}\left(N, u, w\right) = 1 \mid w \in \mathbb{QR}_N \wedge w = \mathsf{H}(\mathrm{id}^*)\right]$, and hence $\Pr\left[\mathcal{B}\left(N, u, w\right) = 1 \mid w \in \mathbb{J}_N \setminus \mathbb{QR}_N \wedge w = \mathsf{H}(\mathrm{id}^*)\right] = 1 - \epsilon$. We have

$$
\begin{aligned}
&\Pr\left[\mathcal{B}\left(N, u, w\right) = 1 \mid w \in \mathbb{QR}_N\right] \\
&= \Pr\left[w = \mathsf{H}(\mathrm{id}^*)\right] \cdot \Pr\left[\mathcal{B}\left(N, u, w\right) = 1 \mid w \in \mathbb{QR}_N \wedge w = \mathsf{H}(\mathrm{id}^*)\right] \\
&\quad + \Pr\left[w \neq \mathsf{H}(\mathrm{id}^*)\right] \cdot \Pr\left[\mathcal{B}\left(N, u, w\right) = 1 \mid w \in \mathbb{QR}_N \wedge w \neq \mathsf{H}(\mathrm{id}^*)\right] \\
&= \frac{\epsilon}{q_\mathsf{H}} + \left(1 - \frac{1}{q_\mathsf{H}}\right) \cdot \frac{1}{2}
\end{aligned}
$$

and similarly,

$$
\begin{aligned}
&\Pr\left[\mathcal{B}\left(N, u, w\right) = 1 \mid w \in \mathbb{J}_N \setminus \mathbb{QR}_N\right] \\
&= \Pr\left[w = \mathsf{H}(\mathrm{id}^*)\right] \cdot \Pr\left[\mathcal{B}\left(N, u, w\right) = 1 \mid w \in \mathbb{J}_N \setminus \mathbb{QR}_N \wedge w = \mathsf{H}(\mathrm{id}^*)\right] \\
&\quad + \Pr\left[w \neq \mathsf{H}(\mathrm{id}^*)\right] \cdot \Pr\left[\mathcal{B}\left(N, u, w\right) = 1 \mid w \in \mathbb{J}_N \setminus \mathbb{QR}_N \wedge w \neq \mathsf{H}(\mathrm{id}^*)\right] \\
&= \frac{1 - \epsilon}{q_\mathsf{H}} + \left(1 - \frac{1}{q_\mathsf{H}}\right) \cdot \frac{1}{2}
\end{aligned}
$$

Consequently, we have

$$
\begin{aligned}
&\mathsf{Adv}_{\mathcal{B}, \mathsf{RSAGen}}^{\mathsf{SQR}}(\kappa) \\
&= \left| \Pr\left[\mathcal{B}\left(N, u, w\right) = 1 \mid w \in \mathbb{QR}_N\right] - \Pr\left[\mathcal{B}\left(N, u, w\right) = 1 \mid w \in \mathbb{J}_N \setminus \mathbb{QR}_N\right] \right| \\
&= \left| \frac{\epsilon}{q_\mathsf{H}} + \left(1 - \frac{1}{q_\mathsf{H}}\right) \cdot \frac{1}{2} - \left(\frac{1 - \epsilon}{q_\mathsf{H}} + \left(1 - \frac{1}{q_\mathsf{H}}\right) \cdot \frac{1}{2}\right) \right| \\
&= \frac{2}{q_\mathsf{H}} \cdot \left| \epsilon - \frac{1}{2} \right| \\
&= \frac{2}{q_\mathsf{H}} \mathsf{Adv}_{\mathcal{A}}^{\mathsf{IND\text{-}ID\text{-}CPA}}(\kappa).
\end{aligned}
$$

This completes the proof. $\square$

4   An Anonymous Variant of Cocks' IBE Scheme with Fast Encryption

Galbraith developed a *test* which shows that Cocks' scheme is not anonymous. It was rigorously proved in [2,20] that the test can distinguish the identity of the recipient from the ciphertext with overwhelming probability. It is not difficult to see that the scheme in Sect. 3 is also not anonymous when we simply modify *Galbraith's test* as:

$$
\mathcal{GT}_N(R_{\mathsf{id}}, C_i(x)) = \left(\frac{c_{i0}^2 - c_{i1}^2 \alpha_i R_{\mathsf{id}}}{N}\right), \quad i = 1, 2.
$$

where $\alpha_1 = 1, \alpha_2 = u$, and $C = (C_1(x), C_2(x)) = (c_{10} + c_{11}x, c_{20} + c_{21}x)$ represents the ciphertext (we still call it Galbraith's test in what follows). We should generate two types of ciphertexts whose Galbraith's tests are -1 and $+1$ separately to avoid this attack. Multiplying the ciphertext polynomial by a scalar does not work since the corresponding Galbraith's tests do not change. What about multiplying a polynomial? A polynomial x is feasible since

$$\mathcal{GT}_N(R_{\mathsf{id}}, C_i'(x) = xC_i(x)) = -\mathcal{GT}_N(R_{\mathsf{id}}, C_i(x)), \quad i = 1, 2.$$

Therefore, inspired by the anonymous variant of Cocks' scheme, without ciphertext expansion in [17, Section 6.2], we can construct the following anonymous variant of the scheme in Sect. 3, without ciphertext expansion. Our second scheme proceeds as follows.

Setup(1^κ) Given a security parameter κ, Setup generates two RSA primes p and q such that $p \equiv -q \mod 4$ and their product $N = pq$. Setup samples an element $u \xleftarrow{R} \mathbb{J}_N \setminus \mathbb{QR}_N$. The public parameters is $\mathsf{mpk} = \{N, u, \mathsf{H}\}$ where H is a publicly available cryptographic hash function mapping an arbitrary binary string to $\mathbb{J}_N$. The master secret key is $\mathsf{msk} = \{p, q\}$.

KeyGen($\mathsf{mpk}, \mathsf{msk}, \mathsf{id}$) Using mpk and msk, KeyGen sets $R_{\mathsf{id}} = \mathsf{H}(\mathsf{id})$. If $R_{\mathsf{id}} \in \mathbb{QR}_N$, KeyGen computes $r_{\mathsf{id}} = R_{\mathsf{id}}^{1/2} \mod N$; otherwise it computes $r_{\mathsf{id}} = (uR_{\mathsf{id}})^{1/2} \mod N$. Finally, KeyGen returns $\mathsf{sk}_{\mathsf{id}} = \{r_{\mathsf{id}}\}$ as user's private key.

Enc($\mathsf{mpk}, \mathsf{id}, m$) On inputting mpk, an identity id and a message $m \in \{0, 1\}$, Enc derives the hash value $R_{\mathsf{id}} = \mathsf{H}(\mathsf{id})$. Enc then chooses at random two polynomials f_1, f_2 of degree 1 from $\mathbb{Z}_N[x]$ and two bits $\beta_1, \beta_2 \xleftarrow{R} \{0, 1\}$. Set

$$g_1^{(0)}(x) = (-1)^m f_1(x)^2 \qquad \mod (x^2 - R_{\mathsf{id}})$$
$$g_1^{(1)}(x) = (-1)^m x \cdot f_1(x)^2 \quad \mod (x^2 - R_{\mathsf{id}})$$
$$g_2^{(0)}(x) = (-1)^m f_2(x)^2 \qquad \mod (x^2 - uR_{\mathsf{id}})$$
$$g_2^{(1)}(x) = (-1)^m x \cdot f_2(x)^2 \quad \mod (x^2 - uR_{\mathsf{id}})$$

The returned ciphertext is

$$C = \left(g_1^{(\beta_1)}(x), g_2^{(\beta_2)}(x) \right).$$

Dec($\mathsf{mpk}, \mathsf{sk}_{\mathsf{id}}, C$) On inputting mpk, a secret key $\mathsf{sk}_{\mathsf{id}} = \{r_{\mathsf{id}}\}$ and a ciphertext polynomial set $C = (C_1(x), C_2(x))$, if $r_{\mathsf{id}}^2 \equiv R_{\mathsf{id}} \pmod{N}$, Dec sets $h(x) = C_1(x)$ and computes $\sigma = \mathcal{GT}_N(R_{\mathsf{id}}, C_1(x))$; otherwise it sets $h(x) = C_2(x)$ and computes $\sigma = \mathcal{GT}_N(R_{\mathsf{id}}, C_2(x))$. Finally, Dec computes

$$m' = \begin{cases} \left(\frac{h(r_{\mathsf{id}})}{N} \right), & \text{if } \sigma = 1; \\ \left(\frac{r_{\mathsf{id}} h(r_{\mathsf{id}})}{N} \right), & \text{otherwise.} \end{cases}$$

and recovers the message m as $\mathcal{J}_N(m')$.

CORRECTNESS. According to the correctness proof of the scheme in Sect. 3, it is enough to show that the decryption is correct when $\sigma = -1$ and $r_{id}^2 \equiv R_{id}$ (mod N). In this case, we have $C_1(x) = g_1^{(1)}(x)$ and

$$m' = \left(\frac{r_{id} C_1(r_{id})}{N} \right) = \left(\frac{(-1)^m r_{id}^2 f_1(r_{id})^2}{N} \right) = (-1)^m.$$

Thus, the decryption works correctly.

Remark 3. The computation amount in the decryption is about twice times larger than that of the scheme in Sect. 3. However, the efficiency of the encryption and the size of the ciphertext expansion do not change.

It is easy to see that the above scheme is also IND-ID-CPA secure by comparing the ciphertexts between it and the scheme in Sect. 3: the ciphertext polynomials for the two schemes differ at most by a polynomial x. Therefore, assuming that there exists an IND-ID-CPA adversary $\mathcal{A}$ against the above scheme, we can construct an adversary $\mathcal{B}$ which can break the IND-ID-CPA security of the scheme in Sect. 3; given the ciphertext of the above scheme, $\mathcal{B}$ finds the original two polynomials $f_1(x)$ and $f_2(x)$ using Galbraith's test. Then $\mathcal{B}$ gives the ciphertext $C = (f_1(x), f_2(x))$ to $\mathcal{A}$. Finally, $\mathcal{B}$ returns whatever $\mathcal{A}$ returns.

The following theorem estimates the size of the first component of the scheme's ciphertext space when its encryption selects $\beta_1 = 0$.

Theorem 3. *With the notations in the above scheme, if we fix N and m, and assume without loss that $R_{id} = H(id) \in \mathbb{QR}_N$, then the set*

$$Z_{N,m,R_{id}} = \left\{ C_{a,b}(x) = (-1)^m (ax + b)^2 \bmod (x^2 - R_{id}) : a, b \xleftarrow{R} \mathbb{Z}_N^* \mid ar_{id} \pm b \in \mathbb{Z}_N^* \right\}$$

has size at least $\frac{\varphi(N)(p-3)(q-3)}{16}$ (φ denotes the Euler's totient function). Therefore, the set of the first component of the scheme's ciphertext has size at least $\frac{\varphi(N)(p-3)(q-3)}{8}$ when its encryption selects $\beta_1 = 0$.

Proof. We have by a simple calculation that

$$C_{a,b}(x) = (-1)^m (ax + b)^2 \equiv (-1)^m \left(a^2 R_{id} + b^2 + 2abx \right) \pmod{x^2 - R_{id}}.$$

Suppose that $C_{a_1,b_1}(x) = C_{a_2,b_2}(x)$, we have

$$a_1^2 R_{id} + b_1^2 \equiv a_2^2 R_{id} + b_2^2 \pmod{N}$$
$$2a_1 b_1 \equiv 2a_2 b_2 \pmod{N}$$

This is equivalent to

$$(a_1 r_{id} + b_1)^2 \equiv (a_2 r_{id} + b_2)^2 \pmod{N}$$
$$(a_1 r_{id} - b_1)^2 \equiv (a_2 r_{id} - b_2)^2 \pmod{N}$$

Fixing a_1 and b_1, if $a_1 r_{\mathsf{id}} + b_1 \in \mathbb{Z}_N^*$ and $a_1 r_{\mathsf{id}} - b_1 \in \mathbb{Z}_N^*$ (the latter means that $\mathcal{GT}_N(R_{\mathsf{id}}, C_{a_1,b_1}(x)) = 1$), then there are at most 16 choices of $a_2 \in \mathbb{Z}_N^*$ and $b_2 \in \mathbb{Z}_N^*$ for which $C_{a_1,b_1}(x) = C_{a_2,b_2}(x)$. The number of cases of $a_1 r_{\mathsf{id}} \pm b_1 \in \mathbb{Z}_N^*$ for $a_1, b_1 \in \mathbb{Z}_N^*$ is exactly $\varphi(N)(p-3)(q-3)$. This proves the first assertion. It is then clear that $Z_{N,0,R_{\mathsf{id}}} \cap Z_{N,1,R_{\mathsf{id}}} = \emptyset$ since the decryption algorithm can recover the original message. This proves the remaining assertion. □

Given an RSA modulus $N = pq$ and $\Delta \in \mathbb{Z}_N^*$, define the following sets:

- $\mathbb{S}_{N,\Delta} = \left\{ u \in \mathbb{Z}_N^* \mid \gcd(u^2 - \Delta, N) = 1 \right\}$
- $\mathbb{S}_{N,\Delta}^{[-1]} = \left\{ u \in \mathbb{Z}_N^* \mid \left(\frac{u^2 - \Delta}{N} \right) = -1 \right\}$
- $\mathbb{S}_{N,\Delta}^{[+1]} = \left\{ u \in \mathbb{Z}_N^* \mid \left(\frac{u^2 - \Delta}{N} \right) = 1 \right\}$
- $(\mathbb{S}_{N,\Delta})^2 = \left\{ u \in \mathbb{Z}_N^* \mid \left(\frac{u^2 - \Delta}{p} \right) = \left(\frac{u^2 - \Delta}{q} \right) = 1 \right\}$

For a prime p, let $\mathbb{QR}_p$ be the set of quadratic residues modulo p containing 0^2. Perron [18] proved that any r relatively prime to p the set $r + \mathbb{QR}_p$ contains k quadratic residues and k quadratic non-residues when $p = 4k - 1$, or $k + 1$ quadratic residues and k quadratic non-residues when $p = 4k + 1$ and $r \in \mathbb{QR}_p$. Now, we take $r = -\Delta = -R_{\mathsf{id}}$ and assume without loss that $p \equiv 3 \pmod 4$, $q \equiv 1 \pmod 4$ and $R_{\mathsf{id}} \in \mathbb{QR}_N$. There are $\left(\frac{p+1}{4} - 1 \right) \times 2 = \frac{p-3}{2}$ elements $u \in \mathbb{Z}_p^*$ for which $\left(\frac{u^2 - \Delta}{p} \right) = 1$. Similarly, there are $\left(\frac{q+3}{4} - 2 \right) \times 2 = \frac{q-5}{2}$ elements $u \in \mathbb{Z}_q^*$ for which $\left(\frac{u^2 - \Delta}{q} \right) = 1$. Thus the size of $(\mathbb{S}_{N,\Delta})^2$ equals $\frac{(p-3)(q-5)}{4}$ and the size of $\mathbb{S}_{N,\Delta}^{[+1]}$ equals $\frac{(p-3)(q-5)}{4} + \frac{(p-3)(q-1)}{4} = \frac{(p-3)(q-3)}{2}$ (See also [20, Corollary 3.4]). Consequently, the set

$$S_{N,\Delta}^{[+1]} = \left\{ a + bx : a, b \xleftarrow{R} \mathbb{Z}_N^* \mid \frac{a}{b} \in \mathbb{S}_{N,\Delta}^{[+1]} \right\}$$

has size $\frac{\varphi(N)(p-3)(q-3)}{2}$. We have proved that the set of the first component of the scheme's ciphertext has size at least $\frac{\varphi(N)(p-3)(q-3)}{8}$ when $\beta_1 = 0$. Since this set can not cover the set $S_{N,\Delta}^{[+1]}$, to prove that the scheme achieves anonymity, we need to make the following complexity assumption:

Assumption 1. *Given an identity* id, *the set* $\left\{ (f, g) \mid f \in S_{N,R_{\mathsf{id}}}^{[+1]}, \ g \in S_{N,uR_{\mathsf{id}}}^{[+1]} \right\}$ *is computationally equivalent to the scheme's ciphertext space when the identity of the recipient is* id, *and* $\mathsf{Enc}(\mathsf{PP}, \mathsf{id}, \cdot)$ *selects* $\beta_1 = \beta_2 = 0$.

When $\mathsf{Enc}(\mathsf{PP}, \mathsf{id}, \cdot)$ selects $\beta_1 = \beta_2 = 1$, it is clear that each component of the ciphertext space has size at least $\frac{\varphi(N)(p-3)(q-3)}{8}$. However, the set

$$S_{N,\Delta}^{[-1]} = \left\{ c + dx : c, d \xleftarrow{R} \mathbb{Z}_N^* \mid \frac{c}{d} \in \mathbb{S}_{N,\Delta}^{[-1]} \right\}$$

also has size $\frac{\varphi(N)(p-3)(q-3)}{2}$. Again, we shall make another assumption:

---

[2] Perron considered the integer 0 as a quadratic residue. We should deal with it carefully.

Assumption 2. *Given an identity* id, *the set* $\left\{(f,g) \mid f \in S_{N,R_{\text{id}}}^{[-1]}, \ g \in S_{N,uR_{\text{id}}}^{[-1]}\right\}$ *is computationally equivalent to the scheme's ciphertext space when the identity of the recipient is* id, *and* Enc(PP, id, ·) *selects* $\beta_1 = \beta_2 = 1$.

Theorem 4. *If Assumption 1 and 2 hold, the above scheme is anonymous.*

Proof. Let id_0^* and id_1^* be two distinct challenge identities. Without loss of generality, we assume that both $\text{H}(\text{id}_0^*)$ and $\text{H}(\text{id}_1^*)$ are in $\mathbb{QR}_N$. Letting $\Delta = R_{\text{id}^*} = \text{H}(\text{id}_r^*)$ for some $r \in \{0,1\}$, consider the following two distributions:

$$D_{0,r} = \left\{\{g_1^{(\beta_1)}(x), g_2^{(\beta_2)}(x)\} \ \leftarrow \ \text{Enc}\left(\text{mpk}, \text{id}_r^*, m\right) : \ m, \beta_1, \beta_2 \in \{0,1\}\right\}$$

$$D_{1,r} = \left\{\{a + bx, c + dx\} \ : \ a,b,c,d \xleftarrow{R} \mathbb{Z}_N^*, \ \frac{a}{b} \in \mathbb{S}_{N,\Delta}, \ \frac{c}{d} \in \mathbb{S}_{N,\Delta}\right\}$$

We claim that $D_{0,r}$ and $D_{1,r}$ are computationally indistinguishable with overwhelming probability. The first component of an element in $D_{0,r}$ can be written as

$$\begin{cases} a_1 + b_1 x \ : \ \frac{a_1}{b_1} \in (\mathbb{S}_{N,\Delta})^2, & \text{if } \beta_1 = 0; \\ a_2 + b_2 x \ : \ \frac{a_2}{b_2} \in \mathbb{S}_{N,\Delta}^{[-1]}, & \text{otherwise.} \end{cases}$$

If Assumption 1 holds, since $S_{N,\Delta}^{[+1]} \cup S_{N,\Delta}^{[-1]} = \left\{a + bx : a,b \in \mathbb{Z}_N^* \mid \frac{a}{b} \in \mathbb{S}_{N,\Delta}\right\}$ and β_1 is chosen at random, we deduce that the first component of an element in $D_{0,r}$ are computationally indistinguishable from that in $D_{1,r}$. If Assumption 2 holds, the similar arguments are valid for the second component, and hence we have proved the claim. Since $D_{1,0}$ and $D_{1,1}$ are also computationally indistinguishable with overwhelming probability, this proves that $D_{0,0}$ and $D_{0,1}$ are computationally indistinguishable with overwhelming probability, and hence the scheme is anonymous. □

5   Conclusion

The encryptions in known variants of Cocks' scheme are much slower than the corresponding decryptions, i.e., the scheme by Clear *et al.* [12] needs about 79 ms and 27 ms for encrypting a 128-bit message with a 1024-bit RSA modulus N. Our second variant features both anonymity and the best encryption compared with other variants (i.e., nearly 10 times faster than those in the same setting according to the running times in [6, Table 1]). Furthermore, they inherit the homomorphic property. These make schemes from quadratic residuosity more competitive in the fields of IBE.

Acknowledgements. This work was supported in part by the National Natural Science Foundation of China (Grant No.61632012 and 61672239), in part by the Peng Cheng Laboratory Project of Guangdong Province (Grant No. PCL2018KP004), and in part by the "Fundamental Research Funds for the Central Universities".

A   A Public-Key Encryption with Keyword Search Scheme from Quadratic Residuosity

Boneh *et al.* introduced the notion of *public-key encryption with keyword search* (PEKS) and gave a proper security model and a construction methodology in [4]. PEKS is a form of "searchable encryption" that performs a keyword search on data encrypted using a public-key system. A promising application of PEKS is that of intelligent email routing. One may consider that mails come through a gateway which tests whether a keyword (e.g., "urgent") exists in an email. Of course, any other information about the email can not be revealed. A PEKS scheme consists of four PPT algorithms (KeyGen, PEKS, Trapdoor, Test).

KeyGen(1^κ) The key generation algorithm KeyGen is a randomized algorithm that takes as input a security parameter 1^κ and generates a public/private key pair (pk, sk).

PEKS(pk, W) Given a public key pk and a keyword W, PEKS returns a searchable ciphertext S for W.

Trapdoor(sk, W) Given a private key sk and a keyword W, the trapdoor algorithm Trapdoor produces a trapdoor T_W for keyword W.

Test(pk, S, T_W) Given a public key pk, a searchable ciphertext $S \leftarrow$ PEKS (pk, W') and a trapdoor $T_W \leftarrow$ Trapdoor(sk, W), the test algorithm Test returns a bit b with 1 meaning "accept" or "yes" and 0 meaning "reject" or "no". It is required that $b = 1$ when $W = W'$.

In [1], the authors presented a new transform called new-ibe-2-peks that transforms any IND-ID-CPA-secure and anonymous IBE scheme into a PEKS-IND-CPA-secure and *computationally consistent* PEKS scheme. The resulting PEKS-encryption algorithm picks and encrypts a random message X and appends X to the ciphertext. We can naturally apply new-ibe-2-peks to the scheme of Sect. 4 and obtain the following PEKS scheme from quadratic residuosity.

KeyGen(1^κ) Given a security parameter κ, KeyGen defines a parameter k and generates two RSA primes p and q such that $p \equiv -q \mod 4$ and their product $N = pq$. KeyGen also samples an element $u \xleftarrow{R} \mathbb{J}_N \setminus \mathbb{QR}_N$. The public key is pk $= \{N, k, u, \mathsf{H}\}$ where H is a publicly available cryptographic hash function mapping an arbitrary binary string to $\mathbb{J}_N$. The secret key is sk $= \{p, q\}$.

PEKS(pk, W) Given a public key pk and a keyword W, PEKS selects a k-bit message $X = [x_{k-1}, x_{k-2}, \ldots, x_0]$ (with $x_i \in \{0, 1\}$) and computes $R = \mathsf{H}(W)$. For each $i = 0, 1, \ldots k - 1$, it chooses at random two polynomials $f_{i,1}, f_{i,2}$ of degree 1 from $\mathbb{Z}_N[x]$, and two bits $\beta_{i,1}, \beta_{i,2} \xleftarrow{R} \{0, 1\}$. Set

$$g_{i,1}^{(0)}(x) = (-1)^{x_i} f_{i,1}(x)^2 \qquad \mod (x^2 - R)$$

$$g_{i,1}^{(1)}(x) = (-1)^{x_i} x \cdot f_{i,1}(x)^2 \quad \mod (x^2 - R)$$

$$g_{i,2}^{(0)}(x) = (-1)^{x_i} f_{i,2}(x)^2 \qquad \mod (x^2 - uR)$$

$$g_{i,2}^{(1)}(x) = (-1)^{x_i} x \cdot f_{i,2}(x)^2 \quad \mod (x^2 - uR)$$

PEKS returns the searchable ciphertext

$$S = \left(g_{0,1}^{(\beta_{0,1})}(x), g_{0,2}^{(\beta_{0,2})}(x), g_{1,1}^{(\beta_{1,1})}(x), g_{1,2}^{(\beta_{1,2})}(x), \ldots, g_{k-1,1}^{(\beta_{k-1,1})}(x), g_{k-1,2}^{(\beta_{k-1,2})}(x), X \right).$$

Trapdoor(sk, W) Given a private key sk and a keyword W, the trapdoor algorithm Trapdoor computes $R = H(W)$. If $R \in \mathbb{QR}_N$, it computes $T_W = R^{1/2} \bmod N$; otherwise it computes $T_W = (uR)^{1/2} \bmod N$. Trapdoor returns T_W.

Test(pk, S, T_W) Given a public key pk, a searchable ciphertext

$$S = (C_{0,1}(x), C_{0,2}(x), C_{1,1}(x), C_{1,2}(x), \ldots, C_{k-1,1}(x), C_{k-1,2}(x), X)$$

where $C_{i,j}(x) = c_{i,j,0} + c_{i,j,1}x, \forall 0 \le i < k, \forall 1 \le j \le 2$, and a trapdoor $T_W \leftarrow$ Trapdoor(sk, W), the test algorithm Test computes $R = H(W)$. If $T_W^2 \equiv R \pmod{N}$, Test computes $\sigma_i = \left(\frac{c_{i,1,0}^2 - c_{i,1,1}^2 R}{N} \right)$ and sets $h_i(x) = C_{i,1}(x), \forall 0 \le i < k$; otherwise it computes $\sigma_i = \left(\frac{c_{i,2,0}^2 - c_{i,2,1}^2 uR}{N} \right)$ and sets $h_i(x) = C_{i,2}(x), \forall 0 \le i < k$. Finally, Test computes

$$x_i' = \begin{cases} \left(\frac{h_i(T_W)}{N} \right), & \text{if } \sigma_i = 1; \\ \left(\frac{T_W h_i(T_W)}{N} \right), & \text{otherwise.} \end{cases}$$

and recovers $X' = [\mathcal{J}_N(x_{k-1}'), \mathcal{J}_N(x_{k-2}'), \ldots, \mathcal{J}_N(x_0')]$. Test returns 1 if $X = X'$; and 0 otherwise.

For encrypting a message m with n keywords $W_1, W_2, \ldots, W_n$ with user's public key upk, Boneh $et\ al.$ in [4] suggested that the sender computes and sends the ciphertext

$$C = (\text{Enc}(\text{upk}, m), \text{PEKS}(\text{upk}, W_1), \text{PEKS}(\text{upk}, W_2), \ldots, \text{PEKS}(\text{upk}, W_n))$$

to a proxy given the trapdoor T_{W_i} for each keyword W_i. Then the proxy can test whether m contains some keyword W_i, but it learns nothing more about any other information about m.

References

1. Abdalla, M., et al.: Searchable encryption revisited: consistency properties, relation to anonymous IBE, and extensions. J. Cryptol. **21**(3), 350–391 (2008). https://doi.org/10.1007/s00145-007-9006-6
2. Ateniese, G., Gasti, P.: Universally anonymous IBE based on the quadratic residuosity assumption. In: Fischlin, M. (ed.) CT-RSA 2009. LNCS, vol. 5473, pp. 32–47. Springer, Heidelberg (2009). https://doi.org/10.1007/978-3-642-00862-7_3
3. Bellare, M., Boldyreva, A., Desai, A., Pointcheval, D.: Key-privacy in public-key encryption. In: Boyd, C. (ed.) ASIACRYPT 2001. LNCS, vol. 2248, pp. 566–582. Springer, Heidelberg (2001). https://doi.org/10.1007/3-540-45682-1_33

4. Boneh, D., Di Crescenzo, G., Ostrovsky, R., Persiano, G.: Public key encryption with keyword search. In: Cachin, C., Camenisch, J.L. (eds.) EUROCRYPT 2004. LNCS, vol. 3027, pp. 506–522. Springer, Heidelberg (2004). https://doi.org/10.1007/978-3-540-24676-3_30

5. Boneh, D., Franklin, M.: Identity-based encryption from the Weil pairing. In: Kilian, J. (ed.) CRYPTO 2001. LNCS, vol. 2139, pp. 213–229. Springer, Heidelberg (2001). https://doi.org/10.1007/3-540-44647-8_13

6. Boneh, D., Gentry, C., Hamburg, M.: Space-efficient identity based encryption without pairings. In: 48th Annual IEEE Symposium on Foundations of Computer Science (FOCS 2007), pp. 647–657. IEEE (2007)

7. Boneh, D., LaVigne, R., Sabin, M.: Identity-based encryption with e^{th} residuosity and its incompressibility. In: Autumn 2013 TRUST Conference. Washington DC (Oct 9–10, 2013), poster presentation (2013)

8. Brent, R.P., Zimmermann, P.: An $O(M(n) \log n)$ algorithm for the Jacobi symbol. In: Hanrot, G., Morain, F., Thomé, E. (eds.) ANTS 2010. LNCS, vol. 6197, pp. 83–95. Springer, Heidelberg (2010). https://doi.org/10.1007/978-3-642-14518-6_10

9. Brent, R.P., Zimmermann, P.: Modern Computer Arithmetic, vol. 18. Cambridge University Press, Cambridge (2010)

10. Clear, M., Hughes, A., Tewari, H.: Homomorphic encryption with access policies: characterization and new constructions. In: Youssef, A., Nitaj, A., Hassanien, A.E. (eds.) AFRICACRYPT 2013. LNCS, vol. 7918, pp. 61–87. Springer, Heidelberg (2013). https://doi.org/10.1007/978-3-642-38553-7_4

11. Clear, M., McGoldrick, C.: Additively homomorphic IBE from higher residuosity. In: Lin, D., Sako, K. (eds.) PKC 2019. LNCS, vol. 11442, pp. 496–515. Springer, Cham (2019). https://doi.org/10.1007/978-3-030-17253-4_17

12. Clear, M., Tewari, H., McGoldrick, C.: Anonymous IBE from quadratic residuosity with improved performance. In: Pointcheval, D., Vergnaud, D. (eds.) AFRICACRYPT 2014. LNCS, vol. 8469, pp. 377–397. Springer, Cham (2014). https://doi.org/10.1007/978-3-319-06734-6_23

13. Cocks, C.: An identity based encryption scheme based on quadratic residues. In: Honary, B. (ed.) Cryptography and Coding 2001. LNCS, vol. 2260, pp. 360–363. Springer, Heidelberg (2001). https://doi.org/10.1007/3-540-45325-3_32

14. Di Crescenzo, G., Saraswat, V.: Public key encryption with searchable keywords based on Jacobi symbols. In: Srinathan, K., Rangan, C.P., Yung, M. (eds.) INDOCRYPT 2007. LNCS, vol. 4859, pp. 282–296. Springer, Heidelberg (2007). https://doi.org/10.1007/978-3-540-77026-8_21

15. Gentry, C., Peikert, C., Vaikuntanathan, V.: Trapdoors for hard lattices and new cryptographic constructions. In: Dwork, C. (ed.) Proceedings of the 40th Annual ACM Symposium on Theory of Computing, 2008. pp. 197–206. ACM (2008). https://doi.org/10.1145/1374376.1374407

16. Goldwasser, S., Micali, S.: Probabilistic encryption. J. Comput. Syst. Sci. **28**(2), 270–299 (1984)

17. Joye, M.: Identity-based cryptosystems and quadratic residuosity. In: Cheng, C.-M., Chung, K.-M., Persiano, G., Yang, B.-Y. (eds.) PKC 2016. LNCS, vol. 9614, pp. 225–254. Springer, Heidelberg (2016). https://doi.org/10.1007/978-3-662-49384-7_9

18. Perron, O.: Bemerkungen über die verteilung der quadratischen reste. Math. Z. **56**(2), 122–130 (1952)

19. Shamir, A.: Identity-Based cryptosystems and signature schemes. In: Blakley, G.R., Chaum, D. (eds.) CRYPTO 1984. LNCS, vol. 196, pp. 47–53. Springer, Heidelberg (1985). https://doi.org/10.1007/3-540-39568-7_5
20. Tiplea, F.L., Iftene, S., Teseleanu, G., Nica, A.: On the distribution of quadratic residues and non-residues modulo composite integers and applications to cryptography. Appl. Math. Comput. **372** (2020). https://doi.org/10.1016/j.amc.2019.124993

Time-Specific Signatures

Masahito Ishizaka[✉] and Shinsaku Kiyomoto

KDDI Research, Inc., Saitama, Japan
{ma-ishizaka,kiyomoto}@kddi-research.jp

Abstract. In Time-Specific Signatures (TSS) parameterized by an integer $T \in \mathbb{N}$, a signer with a secret-key associated with a numerical value $t \in [0, T - 1]$ can anonymously, i.e., without revealing t, sign a message under a numerical range $[L, R]$ such that $0 \leq L \leq t \leq R \leq T - 1$. A direct application of TSS is anonymous questionnaire, where each user associated with a numerical value such as age, date, salary, geographical position (represented by longitude and latitude), etc., can anonymously fill in a questionnaire in an efficient manner.

In this paper, we propose two *polylogarithmically* efficient TSS constructions based on an asymmetric pairing with groups of prime order, which achieve different characteristics in efficiency. In the first one based on a forward-secure signatures scheme concretely obtained from a hierarchical identity-based signatures scheme proposed by Chutterjee and Sarker (IJACT'13), size of the master public-key, size of a secret-key and size of a signature are asymptotically $O(\log T)$, and size of the master secret-key is $O(1)$. In the second one based on a wild-carded identity-based ring signatures scheme obtained as an instantiation of an attribute-based signatures scheme proposed by Sakai, Attrapadung and Hanaoka (PKC'16), the sizes are $O(\log T)$, $O(1)$, $O(\log^2 T)$ and $O(\log T)$, respectively.

Keywords: Time-specific signatures · Forward-secure signatures · Wildcarded identity-based ring signatures · Co-computational Diffie-Hellman assumption · Symmetric external Diffie-Hellman assumption

1   Introduction

Time-Specific Encryption [17]. In a Time-Specific Encryption (TSE) system with total time periods $T \in \mathbb{T}$, each secret-key is associated with a time period $t \in [0, T - 1]$ and a plaintext is encrypted under a time interval $[L, R]$ such that $0 \leq L \leq R \leq T - 1$. A user who has a secret-key for t can correctly decrypt any ciphertext under $[L, R]$ if $t \in [L, R]$. Paterson and Quaglia [17] showed that a TSE scheme can be generically constructed from an identity-based encryption (IBE) [19] scheme or a broadcast encryption (BE) scheme [11]. Kasamatsu et al. [14] proposed a (direct) construction based on Boneh-Boyen-Goh hierarchical identity-based encryption (HIBE) scheme [7]. Ishizaka and Kiyomoto [13] proposed a generic construction from wildcarded identity-based encryption (WIBE) [1,5] w/o hierarchical key-delegatability.

TSE is less functional compared to functional encryption [8], (ciphertext-policy) attribute-based encryption [4] and etc. Because of that, we require a TSE scheme to be highly efficient. Specifically, in previous works [13, 14, 17], *polylogarithmic* efficiency

© Springer Nature Switzerland AG 2020
W. Susilo et al. (Eds.): ISC 2020, LNCS 12472, pp. 20–38, 2020.
https://doi.org/10.1007/978-3-030-62974-8_2

is required. For instance, by instantiating the IBE-based generic TSE construction by Waters IBE scheme [20], they obtain a TSE scheme, whose size of the master public-key $|mpk|$, that of a secret-key $|sk_t|$ for t and that of a ciphertext $|c_{[L,R]}|$ under $[L, R]$ are asymptotically $O(\log T)$. [14] proposed a direct construction with $(|mpk|, |sk_t|, |c_{[L,R]}|) = (O(\log T), O(\log^2 T), O(1))$. By instantiating the WIBE-based generic construction [13] by their original WIBE scheme based on [20], they obtained a TSE scheme with $(|mpk|, |sk_t|, |c_{[L,R]}|) = (O(\log T), O(1), O(\log^2 T))$.

Time-Specific Signatures. In [17], the authors left as an open problem an approach to realize Time-Specific Signatures (TSS), which are the digital signature analogue of TSE. In TSS system, a signer with a secret-key associated with a numerical value $t \in [0, T - 1]$ can correctly sign a message under a numerical range $[L, R]$ s.t. $0 \leq L \leq t \leq R \leq T - 1$. As attribute-based signatures (ABS) [6, 16, 18], we require TSS to be existentially unforgeable and perfectly private.

One typical application example of TSS is anonymous questionnaire. For instance, a company might need opinions from consumers in an age group which are useful to invent a product whose main target is the age group. In a situation where a city plans a development at a location point represented by longitude and latitude, the city might need to efficiently collect opinions from citizens living near the developed point[1].

Our Contributions. In this paper, we propose two polylogarithmically efficient TSS schemes, which have different characteristics in efficiency.

There has existed a folklore to obtain a time-specific cryptosystem from a forward-secure cryptosytem, which has actually contributed to realize TSE [14]. We attempt applying it to TSS. Let us introduce *backward*-secure signatures (BSS). In the forward-secure signatures (FSS) [2, 3], there exists a polynomial time one-way algorithm to evolve a secret-key for a time period $t \in [0, T - 1]$ into one for a future $t' > t$. On the other hand, in the BSS, we can evolve a secret-key for t into one for a past $t' < t$. It is possible to obtain a TSS scheme from FSS and BSS schemes since if we give a secret-key for a time period t, which is composed of secret-keys of the FSS and BSS schemes for the time period t, to a signer, the signer can generate a signature under a range $[L, R]$ s.t. $L \leq t \leq R$ by firstly generating a signature under the time period R from the FSS secret-key for t, secondly generating a signature under L from the BSS secret-key for t and finally combining the signatures in a proper manner. It has not been rigorously proven that this approach properly works in a general manner. We show that the approach actually works to the concrete FSS scheme obtained by applying the tree-based Canetti-Helevi-Katz transformation [9] to a HIBS scheme proposed by Chutterjee&Sarker [10]. As a result, we obtain a TSS scheme with a well-balanced efficiency. Specifically, its size of the master public-key, that of the master secret-key, that of a secret-key for t and that of a signature under $[L, R]$ are $(2 \log T + N + 3)(|g| + |\tilde{g}|)$, $|g|$, $O(\log T)|g|$ and $(2 \log T + 2)|g|$, respectively, where $N \in \mathbb{N}$ denotes bit length of a (signed-)message, and $|g|$ (resp. $|\tilde{g}|$) denotes bit length of an element in a bilinear group $\mathbb{G}$ (resp. $\tilde{\mathbb{G}}$) of prime order relative to an asymmetric pairing $e : \mathbb{G} \times \tilde{\mathbb{G}} \to \mathbb{G}_T$.

---

[1] Precisely, this is an application of *two-dimensional* TSS. It has been unknown whether one-dimensional TSS implies two-dimensional TSS. Two-dimensional TSS, or (more generally) multi-dimensional TSS, has still been left as an open problem.

[13] showed that there exists a generic approach to construct a TSE scheme with time periods T from a WIBE scheme whose length of a (wildcarded) identity is $\log T$ such that each secret-key for a time period $t \in [0, T - 1]$ consists of only one secret-key for identity $t \in \{0, 1\}^{\log T}$. Thus, we can obtain a TSE scheme with constant size secret-keys from a WIBE scheme with constant size secret-keys. We show that such an approach also works for TSS. We introduce wildcarded identity-based *ring* signatures (WIBRS)[2] scheme and show that a concrete scheme with constant size secret-keys is obtained as an instantiation of an ABS scheme (whose signer-policy is represented as a circuit) proposed in [18]. As a result, we obtain a TSS scheme such that size of the master public-key, that of the master secret-key, that of a secret-key for t and that of a signature under $[L, R]$ are $O(\log T)|\tilde{g}|$, $O(\log T)|g|$, $O(1)(|g| + |\tilde{g}|)$ and $O(\log^2 T)(|g| + |\tilde{g}|)$, respectively. A drawback is that size of a signature can be large. Precisely, we prove that the size is *loosely* upper-bounded by $(120 \log^2 T - 94 \log T - 34)(|g| + |\tilde{g}|)$.

Paper Organization. Section 2 is a section for preliminaries. In Sect. 3, we provide syntax and security definitions of TSS. In Sect. 4 and Sect. 5, we propose the FSS-based TSS scheme and the WIBRS-based TSS scheme, respectively. Section 6 is the concluding section.

2   Preliminaries

Notations. For $\lambda \in \mathbb{N}$, 1^λ denotes a security parameter. PPT_λ denotes a set of all probabilistic algorithms whose running time is polynomial in λ. A function $f : \mathbb{N} \to \mathbb{R}$ is negligible if for every $c \in \mathbb{N}$, there exists $x_0 \in \mathbb{N}$ such that for every $x \geq x_0$, $f(x) \leq x^{-c}$. NGL_λ denotes a set of all functions negligible in λ. Given a bit string $x \in \{0, 1\}^L$, for every $i \in [0, L - 1]$, let $x[i] \in \{0, 1\}$ denote its i-th bit. For $wID \in \{0, 1, *\}^L$, $|wID|_* \in [0, L]$ denotes number of wildcard symbol $*$ in wID, formally $\sum_{i \in [0, L-1] \; s.t. \; wID[i]=*} 1$.

Asymmetric Bilinear Groups of Prime Order. $\mathcal{G}_{BG}$ generates bilinear groups of prime order. Let $\lambda \in \mathbb{N}$. $\mathcal{G}_{BG}$ takes 1^λ and randomly generates $(p, \mathbb{G}, \tilde{\mathbb{G}}, \mathbb{G}_T, e, g, \tilde{g})$. p is a prime with bit length λ. $(\mathbb{G}, \tilde{\mathbb{G}}, \mathbb{G}_T)$ are multiplicative groups of order p. $(g, \tilde{g})$ are generators of $\mathbb{G}$ and $\tilde{\mathbb{G}}$, respectively. $e : \mathbb{G} \times \tilde{\mathbb{G}} \to \mathbb{G}_T$ is an asymmetric function which is computable in polynomial time and satisfies the following conditions: (1) Bilinearity: For every $a, b \in \mathbb{Z}_p$, $e(g^a, \tilde{g}^b) = e(g, \tilde{g})^{ab}$, (2) Non-degeneracy: $e(g, \tilde{g}) \neq 1_{\mathbb{G}_T}$, where $1_{\mathbb{G}_T}$ denotes the unit element of $\mathbb{G}_T$.

Definition 1. *Co-Computational Diffie-Hellman (Co-CDH) assumption holds if* $\forall \lambda \in \mathbb{N}$, $\forall \mathcal{A} \in \text{PPT}_\lambda$, $\exists \epsilon \in \text{NGL}_\lambda$ *s.t.* $\text{Adv}_{\mathcal{A}}^{Co\text{-}CDH}(\lambda) := \Pr[g^{\alpha\beta} \leftarrow \mathcal{A}(p, \mathbb{G}, \tilde{\mathbb{G}}, g, \tilde{g}, g^\alpha, g^\beta, \tilde{g}^\beta)] < \epsilon$, *where* $(p, \mathbb{G}, \tilde{\mathbb{G}}, g, \tilde{g}) \leftarrow \mathcal{G}(1^\lambda)$ *and* $\alpha, \beta \xleftarrow{U} \mathbb{Z}_p$.

Definition 2. *Computational Diffie-Hellman (CDH) assumption on* $\mathbb{G}$ *(resp.* $\tilde{\mathbb{G}}$*) holds if* $\forall \lambda \in \mathbb{N}$, $\forall \mathcal{A} \in \text{PPT}_\lambda$, $\exists \epsilon \in \text{NGL}_\lambda$ *s.t.* $\text{Adv}_{\mathcal{A}}^{CDH}(\lambda) := \Pr[g^{\alpha\beta} \leftarrow \mathcal{A}(p, \mathbb{G}, \tilde{\mathbb{G}}, g, \tilde{g}, h^\alpha, h^\beta)] < \epsilon$, *where* $(p, \mathbb{G}, \tilde{\mathbb{G}}, g, \tilde{g}) \leftarrow \mathcal{G}(1^\lambda)$, $\alpha, \beta \xleftarrow{U} \mathbb{Z}_p$ *and* $h := g$ *(resp.* $h := \tilde{g}$*).*

---

[2] In WIBRS, a signer (with an identity) chooses multiple wildcarded identities, (at least) one of which is satisfied by the identity of the signer.

$Expt^{\text{EUF-CMA}}_{\Sigma_{\text{TSS}},\mathcal{A}}(1^\lambda, T)$:

  $(mpk, msk) \leftarrow \text{Setup}(1^\lambda, T).\ (\sigma^*, m^*, [L^*, R^*]) \leftarrow \mathcal{A}^{\mathfrak{Reveal}, \mathfrak{Sign}}(mpk)$, where

  - $\mathfrak{Reveal}(t_\iota \in [0, T-1])$: **Rtrn** $sk_\iota \leftarrow \text{KGen}(msk, t_\iota)$.

  - $\mathfrak{Sign}(t_\theta \in [0, T-1], m_\theta \in \{0, 1\}^*, L_\theta \in [0, T-1], R_\theta \in [0, T-1])$:

    $sk_\theta \leftarrow \text{KGen}(msk, t_\theta)$. **Rtrn** $\sigma_\theta \leftarrow \text{Sig}(sk_\theta, m_\theta, [L_\theta, R_\theta])$.

  Rtrn 1 if $1 \leftarrow \text{Ver}(\sigma^*, m^*, [L^*, R^*]) \bigwedge_{\iota=1}^{q_r} t_\iota \notin [L^*, R^*] \bigwedge_{\theta=1}^{q_s} (m_\theta, L_\theta, R_\theta) \neq (m^*, L^*, R^*)$. **Rtrn** 0.

$Expt^{\text{PP}}_{\Sigma_{\text{TSS}},\mathcal{A},0}(1^\lambda, T)$:	$Expt^{\text{PP}}_{\Sigma_{\text{TSS}},\mathcal{A},1}(1^\lambda, T)$:
$(mpk, msk) \leftarrow \text{Setup}(1^\lambda, T)$	$(mpk, msk') \leftarrow \text{Setup}'(1^\lambda, T)$
Rtrn $b \leftarrow \mathcal{A}^{\mathfrak{Reveal}, \mathfrak{Sign}}(mpk, msk)$, where	**Rtrn** $b \leftarrow \mathcal{A}^{\mathfrak{Reveal}, \mathfrak{Sign}}(mpk, msk)$, where
- $\mathfrak{Reveal}(t_\iota)$: **Rtrn** $sk_\iota \leftarrow \text{KGen}(msk, t_\iota)$.	- $\mathfrak{Reveal}(t_\iota)$: **Rtrn** $sk_\iota \leftarrow \text{KGen}'(msk', t_\iota)$.
- $\mathfrak{Sign}(\iota \in [1, q_r], m, L, R)$:	- $\mathfrak{Sign}(\iota \in [1, q_r], m, L, R)$:
Rtrn $\perp$ if $t_\iota \notin [L, R]$.	**Rtrn** $\perp$ if $t_\iota \notin [L, R]$.
Rtrn $\sigma \leftarrow \text{Sig}(sk_\iota, m, L, R)$.	**Rtrn** $\sigma \leftarrow \text{Sig}'(msk', m, L, R)$.

Fig. 1. Top: Experiment for (adaptive) existential unforgeability w.r.t. a TSS scheme Σ_{TSS}. Bottom: Experiments for perfect privacy w.r.t. Σ_{TSS}. Note: $\iota \in [1, q_r]$ and $\theta \in [1, q_s]$ for $q_r, q_s \in \mathbb{N}$.

Definition 3. *Symmetric External (Computational) Diffie-Hellman (SXDH) assumption holds if the CDH assumption holds on both $\mathbb{G}$ and $\hat{\mathbb{G}}$ hold.*

3 Time-Specific Signatures (TSS)

Syntax. Time-specific signatures (TSS) consist of following 4 polynomial time algorithms, where Ver is deterministic and the others are probabilistic. Let $T \in \mathbb{N}$ denote total number of numerical values, which means that $[0, T-1]$ is the space of numerical values. **Setup** algorithm Setup takes $(1^\lambda, T)$ as input then outputs a master public-key mpk and a master secret-key msk. Concisely, we write $(mpk, msk) \leftarrow \text{Setup}(1^\lambda, T)$. Note that all the other three algorithms implicitly take mpk as input. **Key-generation** algorithm KGen takes msk and a numerical value $t \in [0, T-1]$, then outputs a secret-key sk_t for the time period. Concisely, $sk_t \leftarrow \text{KGen}(msk, t)$. **Signing** algorithm Sig takes a secret-key sk_t for $t \in [0, T-1]$, a message $m \in \{0, 1\}^*$, and a numerical range $[L, R]$ s.t. $0 \leq L \leq R \leq T-1$, then outputs a signature σ. Concisely, $\sigma \leftarrow \text{Sig}(sk_t, m, [L, R])$. **Verifying** algorithm Ver takes σ, $m \in \{0, 1\}^*$, and $[L, R]$ s.t. $0 \leq L \leq R \leq T-1$, then outputs 1 or 0. Concisely, $1/0 \leftarrow \text{Ver}(\sigma, m, [L, R])$.

We require every TSS scheme to be correct. A TSS scheme $\Sigma_{\text{TSS}} = \{\text{Setup}, \text{KGen}, \text{Sig}, \text{Ver}\}$ is correct, if $\forall \lambda \in \mathbb{N}, \forall T \in \mathbb{N}, \forall (mpk, msk) \leftarrow \text{Setup}(1^\lambda, T), \forall t \in [0, T-1], \forall sk_t \leftarrow \text{KGen}(msk, t), \forall m \in \{0, 1\}^*, \forall L \in [0, T-1]$ s.t. $L \leq t, \forall R \in [0, T-1]$ s.t. $t \leq R, \forall \sigma \leftarrow \text{Sig}(sk_t, m, [L, R]), 1 \leftarrow \text{Ver}(\sigma, m, [L, R])$.

Existential Unforgeability [16, 18]. For a TSS scheme Σ_{TSS} and a probabilistic algorithm $\mathcal{A}$, we consider an experiment for (adaptive) existential unforgeability in Fig. 1.

Definition 4. *A TSS scheme Σ_{TSS} is (adaptively) existentially unforgeable, if $\forall \lambda \in \mathbb{N}$, $\forall T \in \mathbb{N}, \forall \mathcal{A} \in \text{PPT}_\lambda, \exists \epsilon \in \text{NGL}_\lambda, Adv^{\text{EUF-CMA}}_{\Sigma_{\text{TSS}},\mathcal{A},T}(\lambda) := \Pr[1 \leftarrow Expt^{\text{EUF-CMA}}_{\Sigma_{\text{TSS}},\mathcal{A}}(1^\lambda, T)] < \epsilon$.*

Perfect (Signer) Privacy [6]. For a TSS scheme Σ_{TSS} and a probabilistic algorithm $\mathcal{A}$, we consider experiments for perfect privacy in Fig. 1.

Definition 5. Σ_{TSS} *is perfectly private, if for every* $\lambda, T \in \mathbb{N}$ *and every probabilistic algorithm* $\mathcal{A}$, *there exist probabilistic polynomial time algorithms* $\{\text{Setup}', \text{KGen}', \text{Sig}'\}$ *s.t.* $Adv^{PP}_{\Sigma_{\text{TSS}}, \mathcal{A}, T}(\lambda) := |\sum_{b=0}^{1}(-1)^b \Pr[1 \leftarrow Expt^{PP}_{\Sigma_{\text{TSS}}, \mathcal{A}, b}(1^\lambda, T)]| = 0.$

4   TSS Based on Forward-Secure Signatures

We propose a TSS scheme w. well-balanced efficiency from *forward-secure signatures*.

It is easy for us to suggest an intuitive idea to obtain a TSS scheme from a forward-secure signatures (FSS) scheme. As we might have already known, in a FSS system, there exists a one-way algorithm which transforms a secret-key for a time period t into one for a future one $t' > t$. As a related primitive, we consider *backward*-secure signatures (BSS), where there exists a one-way algorithm which transforms a secret-key for t into one for a past $t' < t$. A secret-key for $t \in [0, T-1]$ consists of (sk_F, sk_B), where sk_F (resp. sk_B) is a secret-key for t generated under the pair of keys (mpk_F, msk_F) (resp. (mpk_B, msk_B)) on the FSS (resp. BSS) scheme. A secret-key $sk_t = (sk_F, sk_B)$ generates a signature under $[L, R]$ s.t. $0 \leq L \leq t \leq R \leq T-1$ by firstly generating a signature under time period $R \geq t$ by using the secret-key sk_F, secondly generating a signature under $L \leq t$ by using sk_B, then adequately combining the signatures.

As far as we know, there has not existed a generic approach to obtain a TSS scheme from FSS and BSS schemes[3] whose security is guaranteed by a rigorous proof. In this section, we show that the approach actually works on the concrete FSS scheme obtained by applying the Canetti-Halevi-Katz transformation [9] to a hierarchical identity-based signatures (HIBS) scheme in [10].

4.1   Construction

We consider the *second* HIBS scheme proposed in [10]. It adopts an asymmetric bilinear pairing $e : \mathbb{G} \times \tilde{\mathbb{G}} \to \mathbb{G}_T$, where order of the groups is a prime p. Let g (resp. $\tilde{g}$) denote a generator of $\mathbb{G}$ (resp. $\tilde{\mathbb{G}}$). Let $h - 1$ (for $h \in \mathbb{N}$) denote the maximum hierarchical length of an identity. Let $H : \{0, 1\}^* \to \{0, 1\}^N$ (with $N \in \mathbb{N}$) denote a collision-resistant hash function. At the setup phase, $h + N + 2$ integers $\alpha, \alpha_0, \cdots, \alpha_h, \beta_0, \cdots, \beta_{N-1} \xleftarrow{U} \mathbb{Z}_p$ are randomly chosen. The master public-key is set as $(g, \tilde{g}, g_1, g_2, \{u_i, \tilde{u}_i \mid i \in [0, h]\}, \{v_i, \tilde{v}_i \mid i \in [0, N-1]\})$, where $g_1 \xleftarrow{U} \mathbb{G}$, $g_2 := \tilde{g}^\alpha$, $u_i := g^{\alpha_i}$, $\tilde{u}_i := \tilde{g}^{\alpha_i}$, $v_i := g^{\beta_i}$ and $\tilde{v}_i := \tilde{g}^{\beta_i}$. The master secret-key is set as g_1^α. A secret-key for an identity $ID_0 \| \cdots \| ID_i$ with hierarchical length $i \in [0, h-1]$, where $ID_0, \cdots, ID_i \in \{0, 1\}^*$, is set as $(g_1^\alpha \prod_{j \in [0, i]} (u_j \prod_{k \in [0, N-1]} v_k^{d_i[k]})^{r_j}, g^{r_0}, \cdots, g^{r_i})$, where $r_j \xleftarrow{U} \mathbb{Z}_p$ and $d_j[0] \| \cdots \| d_j[N-1] \leftarrow H(0 \| ID_j)$. Obviously, we can transform a secret-key for an identity into a secret-key for any descendant identity of the identity. By the secret-key, a signature on a message m is generated as $(g_1^\alpha \prod_{j \in [0, i+1]} (u_j \prod_{k \in [0, N-1]} v_k^{d_i[k]})^{r_j}, g^{r_0}, \cdots, g^{r_i})$, where $r_{i+1} \xleftarrow{U} \mathbb{Z}_p$ and $d_{i+1}[0] \| \cdots \| d_{i+1}[N-1] \leftarrow H(1 \| m)$.

---

[3] Or, only a FSS scheme, since a BSS scheme is obtained from a FSS scheme.

Let us apply the CHK transformation [9] to the HIBS scheme with the maximum hierarchical length $h = \log T \in \mathbb{N}$ to obtain a FSS scheme with total time periods $T \in \mathbb{N}$. We consider a (complete) binary tree with depth $\log T \in \mathbb{N}$. The master secret-key and the master public-key are described as g_1^α and $(g, \tilde{g}, g_1, g_2, \{u_i, \tilde{u}_i \mid i \in [0, \log T]\}, \{v_i, \tilde{v}_i \mid i \in [0, N-1]\})$, respectively. A secret-key for a time period $t \in [0, T-1]$ is described as $(sk_{t[0]\|\cdots\|t[\log T-1]}, \{sk_{t[0]\|\cdots\|t[i-1]\|1} \mid i \in [0, \log T-1] \text{ s.t. } t[i] = 0\})$, where sk_x (with $x \in \{0,1\}^{\leq \log T}$) is a randomly-generated secret-key for an identity x by using the secret-key generation algorithm of the HIBS scheme. By the secret-key for t, a signature for a time period $t' \geq t$ on a message m is generated as a signature for an identity $t'[0]\|\cdots\|t'[\log T-1]$ on m by using the signing algorithm of the HIBS scheme. Note that $t \leq t'$ implies that a secret-key for t certainly includes a secret-key for an ancestral identity of the identity t', thus, the signature generation always succeeds.

Based on the approach to obtain a TSS scheme from FSS and BSS schemes explained earlier, we construct a TSS scheme Π_{TSS} as shown in Fig. 2.

The master secret-key and the master public-key for the FSS scheme part is normally generated. Thus, they are g_1^α and $(g, \tilde{g}, g_1, g_2, \{u_i, \tilde{u}_i \mid i \in [0, \log T]\}, \{v_i, \tilde{v}_i \mid i \in [0, N-1]\})$, respectively. The variables prepared for the BSS scheme part are $\{w_i, \tilde{w}_i \mid i \in [0, \log T-1]\}$ (whose roles are analogous to those of $\{u_i, \tilde{u}_i \mid i \in [0, \log T-1]\}$ for the FSS scheme part), and the other variables are shared by both parts.

A secret-key sk_t for a numerical value $t \in [0, T-1]$ consists of the FSS part sk_r and the BSS part sk_l, and they are expressed as $(sk_{t[0]\|\cdots\|t[\log T-1]}, \{sk_{t[0]\|\cdots\|t[i-1]\|1} \mid i \in [0, \log T-1] \text{ s.t. } t[i] = 0\})$ and $(sk_{t'[0]\|\cdots\|t'[\log T-1]}, \{sk_{t'[0]\|\cdots\|t'[i-1]\|1} \mid i \in [0, \log T-1] \text{ s.t. } t'[i] = 0\})$, respectively, where $t' := T - 1 - t$. Each element in sk_r and each element in sk_l are generated from the *pseudo* master secret-key $g_1^\alpha g^\delta$ and $g^{-\delta}$, respectively, where $\delta \in \mathbb{Z}_p$ is a randomly chosen integer. $sk_{t[0]\|\cdots\|t[\log T-1]}$ (resp. $sk_{t'[0]\|\cdots\|t'[\log T-1]}$) which includes $\log T$ random variables is *normally* generated by choosing $\log T$ fresh random variables then using them and the pseudo master secret-key $g_1^\alpha g^\delta$ (resp. $g^{-\delta}$). On the other hand, each element $sk_{t[0]\|\cdots\|t[i-1]\|1}$ for $i \in [0, \log T-1]$ s.t. $t[i] = 0$ which includes $i + 1$ random variables is generated by choosing only one fresh random variable (for depth i) then using the variable, already chosen $i - 1$ random variables (for depth $0, \cdots, i-1$) in $sk_{t[0]\|\cdots\|t[\log T-1]}$ and the pseudo master secret-key. Likewise, each element in sk_l is generated. The reason why we have introduced such a technique is to reduce size of a secret-key from $O(\log^2 T)|g|$ to $O(\log T)|g|$.

A secret-key sk_t for $t \in [0, T-1]$ signs a message m under a range $[L, R]$ s.t. $t \in [L, R]$ as follows. Let $L' := T - 1 - L$. Note that $t \in [L, R]$ implies $t \leq R \wedge t' \leq L'$, which implies $\exists i_r, i_l \in [0, \log T]$ s.t. $\bigwedge_{i \in [0, i_r-1]} t[i] = R[i]] \bigwedge [i_r \neq \log T \implies t[i_r] = 0 \wedge R[i_r] = 1] \bigwedge_{i \in [0, i_l-1]} t'[i] = L'[i]] \bigwedge [i_l \neq \log T \implies t'[i_l] = 0 \wedge L'[i_l] = 1]$. The key-generation algorithm guarantees that secret-key for the identity $R[0]\|\cdots\|R[i_r]$ (or $R[0]\|\cdots\|R[\log T-1]$ if $i_r = \log T$) (resp. $L'[0]\|\cdots\|L'[i_l]$ (or $L'[0]\|\cdots\|L'[\log T-1]$ if $i_l = \log T$)) exists in sk_r (resp. sk_l) in sk_t. Obviously, the secret-key derives a secret-key for the identity $R[0]\|\cdots\|R[\log T-1]$ (resp. $L'[0]\|\cdots\|L'[\log T-1]$), which is expressed as $(g_1^\alpha g^\delta \prod_{i \in [0, \log T-1]} (u_i v_0^{R[i]})^{r_i}, g^{r_0}, \cdots, g^{r_{\log T-1}})$ (resp. $(g^{-\delta} \prod_{i \in [0, \log T-1]} (w_i v_0^{L'[i]})^{s_i}, g^{s_0}, \cdots, g^{s_{\log T-1}})$) with $r_0, \cdots, r_{\log T-1} \in \mathbb{Z}_p$ (resp. $s_0, \cdots, s_{\log T-1} \in \mathbb{Z}_p$). From the two secret-keys, we obtain a signature $(g_1^\alpha \prod_{i \in [0, \log T-1]} (u_i v_0^{R[i]})^{r_i} (w_i v_0^{L'[i]})^{s_i} (u_{\log T} \prod_{i \in [0, N-1]} v_i^{m[i]})^{r_{\log T}}, g^{r_0}, \cdots, g^{r_{\log T-1}}, g^{s_0},$

$\cdots, g^{s_{\log T-1}}, g^{r_{\log T}})$ with $r_{\log T} \in \mathbb{Z}_p$. As shown in Fig. 2, we actually *re-randomize* the $i_r + i_l + 1$ random variables $r_0, \cdots, r_{i_r}, s_0, \cdots, s_{i_l}$ to make the TSS scheme achieve perfect privacy under Definition 5.

4.2 Unforgeability

Existential unforgeability of the scheme Π_{TSS} in Fig. 2 is guaranteed by Theorem 1.

Theorem 1. *Π_{TSS} is existentially unforgeable under the co-CDH assumption.*

Proof. Let $\mathcal{A} \in \mathbb{PPT}_\lambda$ denote a PPT algorithm which behaves as an adversary in existential unforgeability experiment for our TSS scheme Π_{TSS}. Let $t_{\mathcal{A}} \in \mathbb{N}$ denote running time of $\mathcal{A}$ (which is polynomial in λ). We prove that there exists another PPT algorithm $\mathcal{B} \in \mathbb{PPT}_\lambda$ which uses $\mathcal{A}$ as a black-box and breaks the co-CDH assumption with

$$\mathsf{Adv}_{\mathcal{B}}^{\text{co-CDH}}(\lambda) \geq \frac{1}{2\{2(\log T \cdot q_r + q_s)(N+1)\}^{2\log T+1}} \cdot \mathsf{Adv}_{\Pi_{TSS},\mathcal{A},N,T}^{\text{EUF-CMA}}(\lambda). \qquad (1)$$

$\mathcal{B}$ behaves as follows. $\mathcal{B}$ is given $(g, \tilde{g}, g^\beta, g^\alpha, \tilde{g}^\alpha)$ as an instance of the co-CDH assumption. $\mathcal{B}$ sets $g_1 := g^\beta$ and $g_2 := \tilde{g}^\alpha$. $\mathcal{B}$ chooses an integer n s.t. $n(N+1) < p$. $\mathcal{B}$ randomly chooses: $\{k_i, s_i \overset{U}{\leftarrow} [0,N], x_i, z_i \overset{U}{\leftarrow} \mathbb{Z}_n, x_i', z_i' \overset{U}{\leftarrow} \mathbb{Z}_p \mid i \in [0, \log T - 1]\}$, $k_{\log T} \overset{U}{\leftarrow} [0,N], x_{\log T} \overset{U}{\leftarrow} \mathbb{Z}_n, x_{\log T}' \overset{U}{\leftarrow} \mathbb{Z}_p$, and $\{y_i \overset{U}{\leftarrow} \mathbb{Z}_n, y_i' \overset{U}{\leftarrow} \mathbb{Z}_p \mid i \in [0, N-1]\}$.

$\mathcal{B}$ sets: $\{u_i := (g^\alpha)^{p-nk_i+x_i} \cdot g^{x_i'}, \tilde{u}_i := (\tilde{g}^\alpha)^{p-nk_i+x_i} \cdot \tilde{g}^{x_i'} \mid i \in [0, \log T]\}$, $\{w_i := (g^\alpha)^{p-ns_i+z_i} \cdot g^{z_i'}, \tilde{w}_i := (\tilde{g}^\alpha)^{p-ns_i+z_i} \cdot \tilde{g}^{z_i'} \mid i \in [0, \log T - 1]\}$, and $\{v_i := (g^\alpha)^{y_i} \cdot g^{y_i'}, \tilde{v}_i := (\tilde{g}^\alpha)^{y_i} \cdot \tilde{g}^{y_i'} \mid i \in [0, N-1]\}$.

$\mathcal{B}$ gives $mpk := \big(p, \mathbb{G}, \tilde{\mathbb{G}}, \mathbb{G}_T, e, g, \tilde{g}, g_1, g_2, \{u_i, \tilde{u}_i, w_i, \tilde{w}_i \mid i \in [0, \log T - 1]\}, u_{\log T},$ $\tilde{u}_{\log T}, \{v_i, \tilde{v}_i \mid i \in [0, N-1]\}\big)$ to $\mathcal{A}$. Before defining how $\mathcal{B}$ behaves when $\mathcal{A}$ issues a query to $\mathfrak{Reveal}$ or $\mathfrak{Sign}$, we define some functions as follows.

For a bit $b \in \{0, 1\}$ and an integer $i \in [0, \log T]$,

$$\mathbf{F}_i(b) := p - nk_i + x_i + y_0 b, \quad \mathbf{J}_i(b) := x_i' + y_0' b, \quad \mathbf{L}_i(b) := x_i + y_0 b \bmod n,$$

$$\mathbf{H}_i(b) := p - ns_i + z_i + y_0 b, \quad \mathbf{Q}_i(b) := z_i' + y_0' b, \quad \mathbf{R}_i(b) := z_i + y_0 b \bmod n,$$

$$\mathbf{K}_i(b) := \begin{cases} 0 & \text{if } \mathbf{L}_i(b) = 0, \\ 1 & \text{otherwise.} \end{cases}, \quad \mathbf{U}_i(b) := \begin{cases} 0 & \text{if } \mathbf{R}_i(b) = 0, \\ 1 & \text{otherwise.} \end{cases}$$

For $m \in \{0, 1\}^N$,

$$\mathbf{F}_{\log T}(m) := p - nk_{\log T} + x_{\log T} + \sum_{i \in [0, N-1]} y_i m[i], \quad \mathbf{J}_{\log T}(m) := x_{\log T}' + \sum_{i \in [0, N-1]} y_i' m[i],$$

$$\mathbf{L}_{\log T}(m) := x_{\log T} + \sum_{i \in [0, N-1]} y_i m[i] \bmod n, \quad \mathbf{K}_{\log T}(m) := \begin{cases} 0 & \text{if } \mathbf{L}_{\log T}(m) = 0, \\ 1 & \text{otherwise.} \end{cases}$$

$\text{TSS.Setup}\left(1^{\lambda}, N, T\right)$:

$(p, \mathbb{G}, \tilde{\mathbb{G}}, \mathbb{G}_T, e, g, \tilde{g}) \leftarrow \mathcal{G}_{BG}(1^{\lambda})$. $\alpha \xleftarrow{U} \mathbb{Z}_p$, $g_2 := \tilde{g}^{\alpha}$. $g_1 \xleftarrow{U} \mathbb{G}$.

For every $i \in [0, \log T - 1]$, $x_i, z_i \xleftarrow{U} \mathbb{Z}_p$, $u_i := g^{x_i}$, $\tilde{u}_i := \tilde{g}^{x_i}$, $w_i := g^{z_i}$, $\tilde{w}_i := \tilde{g}^{z_i}$.

$x_{\log T} \xleftarrow{U} \mathbb{Z}_p$, $u_{\log T} := g^{x_{\log T}}$, $\tilde{u}_{\log T} := \tilde{g}^{x_{\log T}}$.

For every $i \in [0, N - 1]$, $y_i \xleftarrow{U} \mathbb{Z}_p$, $v_i := g^{y_i}$, $\tilde{v}_i := \tilde{g}^{y_i}$.

Rtrn (mpk, msk), where $msk := g_1^{\alpha}$ and $mpk := \big(p, \mathbb{G}, \tilde{\mathbb{G}}, \mathbb{G}_T, e, g, \tilde{g}, g_1, g_2,$
$\{u_i, \tilde{u}_i, w_i, \tilde{w}_i \mid i \in [0, \log T - 1]\}, u_{\log T}, \tilde{u}_{\log T}, \{v_i, \tilde{v}_i \mid i \in [0, N - 1]\}\big)$.

$\text{TSS.KGen}\,(msk, t \in [0, T - 1])$:

$\delta \xleftarrow{U} \mathbb{Z}_p$. $\tilde{t} := T - 1 - t$.

$\mathbb{J}_r := \{i \in [0, \log T - 1] \text{ s.t. } t[i] = 0\}$. $\mathbb{J}_l := \{i \in [0, \log T - 1] \text{ s.t. } \tilde{t}[i] = 0\}$.

For every $i \in [0, \log T - 1]$, do: $r_i \xleftarrow{U} \mathbb{Z}_p$. If $t[i] = 0$, $r_i' \xleftarrow{U} \mathbb{Z}_p$.

$sk_r := \Big(g_1^{\alpha} g^{\delta} \prod_{i \in [0, \log T - 1]} \big(u_i v_0^{t[i]}\big)^{r_i}, g^{r_0}, \cdots, g^{r_{\log T - 1}},$
$\Big\{g_1^{\alpha} g^{\delta} \prod_{i \in [0, j-1]} \big(u_i v_0^{t[i]}\big)^{r_i} \big(u_j v_0\big)^{r_j'}, g^{r_j'} \mid j \in \mathbb{J}_r \Big\}\Big)$.

For every $i \in [0, \log T - 1]$, do: $s_i \xleftarrow{U} \mathbb{Z}_p$. If $\tilde{t}[i] = 0$, $s_i' \xleftarrow{U} \mathbb{Z}_p$.

$sk_l := \Big(g^{-\delta} \prod_{i \in [0, \log T - 1]} \big(w_i v_0^{\tilde{t}[i]}\big)^{s_i}, g^{s_0}, \cdots, g^{s_{\log T - 1}},$
$\Big\{g^{-\delta} \prod_{i \in [0, j-1]} \big(w_i v_0^{\tilde{t}[i]}\big)^{s_i} \big(w_j v_0\big)^{s_j'}, g^{s_j'} \mid j \in \mathbb{J}_l \Big\}\Big)$.

Rtrn $sk_t := (sk_l, sk_r)$

$\text{TSS.Sig}\left(sk_t, m \in \{0, 1\}^N, L \in [0, T - 1], R \in [0, T - 1]\right)$:

Parse sk_t as (sk_l, sk_r). $\tilde{t} := T - 1 - t$. $\tilde{L} := T - 1 - L$.

Parse sk_r as $\Big(D_{\log T}, d_0, \cdots, d_{\log T - 1}, \big\{D_j, d_j' \mid j \in [0, \log T - 1] \text{ s.t. } t[j] = 0\big\}\Big)$.

Parse sk_l as $\Big(E_{\log T}, e_0, \cdots, e_{\log T - 1}, \big\{E_j, e_j' \mid j \in [0, \log T - 1] \text{ s.t. } \tilde{t}[j] = 0\big\}\Big)$.

$t \in [L, R] \implies$

$\exists i_r \in [0, \log T] \text{ s.t. } \bigwedge_{i \in [0, i_r - 1]} [t[i] = R[i]] \bigwedge [i_r \neq \log T \implies t[i_r] = 0 \wedge R[i_r] = 1]$
$\bigwedge \exists i_l \in [0, \log T] \text{ s.t. } \bigwedge_{i \in [0, i_l - 1]} \big[\tilde{t}[i] = \tilde{L}[i]\big] \bigwedge \big[i_l \neq \log T \implies \tilde{t}[i_l] = 0 \wedge \tilde{L}[i_l] = 1\big]$.

For every $i \in [0, i_r]$, $\tilde{r}_i \xleftarrow{U} \mathbb{Z}_p$. For every $i \in [i_r + 1, \log T - 1]$, $r_i^* \xleftarrow{U} \mathbb{Z}_p$.

For every $i \in [0, i_l]$, $\tilde{s}_i \xleftarrow{U} \mathbb{Z}_p$. For every $i \in [i_l + 1, \log T - 1]$, $s_i^* \xleftarrow{U} \mathbb{Z}_p$. $r_{\log T} \xleftarrow{U} \mathbb{Z}_p$.

Rtrn $\sigma := \Big(D_{i_r} \prod_{i \in [0, i_r]} \big(u_i v_0^{R[i]}\big)^{\tilde{r}_i} \prod_{i \in [i_r + 1, \log T - 1]} \big(u_i v_0^{R[i]}\big)^{r_i^*} E_{i_l} \prod_{i \in [0, i_l]} \big(w_i v_0^{\tilde{L}[i]}\big)^{\tilde{s}_i}$

$\cdot \prod_{i \in [i_l + 1, \log T - 1]} \big(w_i v_0^{\tilde{L}[i]}\big)^{s_i^*} \Big(u_{\log T} \prod_{j \in [0, N - 1]} v_j^{m[j]}\Big)^{r_{\log T}},$

$\{d_i g^{\tilde{r}_i} \mid i \in [0, i_r - 1]\}, d_{i_r}' g^{\tilde{r}_{i_r}}, \{g^{r_i^*} \mid i \in [i_r + 1, \log T - 1]\},$

$\{e_i g^{\tilde{s}_i} \mid i \in [0, i_l - 1]\}, e_{i_l}' g^{\tilde{s}_{i_l}}, \{g^{s_i^*} \mid i \in [i_l + 1, \log T - 1]\}, g^{r_{\log T}}\Big)$.

$\text{TSS.Ver}\left(\sigma, m \in \{0, 1\}^N, L \in [0, T - 1], R \in [0, T - 1]\right)$:

Parse σ as $\big(U, V_0, \cdots, V_{\log T - 1}, V_0', \cdots, V_{\log T - 1}', V_{\log T}\big)$. $\tilde{L} := T - 1 - L$.

Rtrn 1 if

$(U, \tilde{g}) = e(g_1, g_2) \cdot \prod_{i \in [0, \log T - 1]} e\big(V_i, \tilde{u}_i \tilde{v}_0^{R[i]}\big) e\big(V_i', \tilde{w}_i \tilde{v}_0^{\tilde{L}[i]}\big) \cdot e\big(V_{\log T}, \tilde{u}_{\log T} \prod_{j \in [0, N - 1]} \tilde{v}_j^{m[j]}\big)$.

Rtrn 0, otherwise.

Fig. 2. Our TSS scheme Π_{TSS}, where $N, T \in \mathbb{N}$.

When $\mathcal{A}$ issues $t_\iota \in [0, T-1]$, where $\iota \in [1, q_r]$, as a query to $\mathfrak{Reveal}$, $\mathcal{B}$ takes different actions in the following three cases:

(R1) $$\bigvee_{i \in [0, \log T-1] \text{ s.t. } t_\iota[i]=1} \left[K_i(1) = 1 \bigwedge \left[i \neq 0 \implies \bigwedge_{j \in [0, i-1] \text{ s.t. } t_\iota[j]=0} K_j(1) = 1 \right] \right],$$

(R2) $$\bigvee_{i \in [0, \log T-1] \text{ s.t. } \tilde{t}_\iota[i]=1} \left[U_i(1) = 1 \bigwedge \left[i \neq 0 \implies \bigwedge_{j \in [0, i-1] \text{ s.t. } \tilde{t}_\iota[j]=0} U_j(1) = 1 \right] \right],$$

(R3) Otherwise,

where $\tilde{t}_\iota := T - 1 - t_\iota$. Specifically, $\mathcal{B}$ behaves as follows in each case.

$\mathcal{B}$'s behaviour for the case R1: Let $k \in [0, \log T - 1]$ denote the integer i which satisfies the condition which appeared in the definition of the case R1. Note that it is implied that $t_\iota[k] = 1 \bigwedge F_k(1) \neq 0 \bigwedge [k \neq 0 \implies \bigwedge_{j \in [0, k-1] \text{ s.t. } t_\iota[j]=0} F_j(1) \neq 0]$.

Let $\delta \xleftarrow{U} \mathbb{Z}_p$. For $i \in [0, k]$, let $r_i \xleftarrow{U} \mathbb{Z}_p$. $\mathcal{B}$ computes: $d_k := g_1^{-1/F_k(1)} g^{r_k}$, $d_i := g^{r_i}$ (for $i \in [0, k-1]$), $\Delta_k := g_1^{-J_k(1)/F_k(1)} (g^\alpha)^{r_k F_k(1)} g^{r_k J_k(1)}$, and $\Delta_i := (u_i v_0^{t_\iota[i]})^{r_i}$ (for $i \in [0, k-1]$).

For every $i \in [k+1, \log T - 1]$, $r_i \xleftarrow{U} \mathbb{Z}_p$ and $d_i := g^{r_i}$. Let $D_{\log T} := g^\delta \cdot \prod_{i \in [0,k]} \Delta_i \cdot \prod_{i \in [k+1, \log T-1]} (u_i v_0)^{r_i}$. Note that $(D_{\log T}, d_0, \cdots, d_{\log T-1})$ correctly distribute since $d_k = g^{r_k - \beta/F_k(1)} =: g^{\tilde{r}_k}$, where $\tilde{r}_k := r_k - \beta/F_k(1)$, and

$$\Delta_k = g_1^\alpha g_1^{-\alpha F_k(1)/F_k(1)} g^{-J_k(1)/F_k(1)} g^{r_k(\alpha F_k(1)+J_k(1))} = g_1^\alpha g^{-\frac{\beta}{F_k(1)}(\alpha F_k(1)+J_k(1))} g^{r_k(\alpha F_k(1)+J_k(1))}$$

$$= g_1^\alpha g^{(r_k - \frac{\beta}{F_k(1)})(\alpha F_k(1)+J_k(1))} = g_1^\alpha g^{\tilde{r}_k(\alpha F_k(1)+J_k(1))} = g_1^\alpha g^{\tilde{r}_k(\alpha(p-nk_k+x_k+y_0)+x_k'+y_0')}$$

$$= g_1^\alpha \left((g^\alpha)^{p-nk_k+x_k} g^{x_k'} (g^\alpha)^{y_0} g^{y_0'} \right)^{\tilde{r}_k} = g_1^\alpha (u_k v_0)^{\tilde{r}_k}.$$

For every $i \in [k+1, \log T - 1]$ s.t. $t_\iota[i] = 0$, $\mathcal{B}$ chooses $r_i' \xleftarrow{U} \mathbb{Z}_p$ and computes $d_i' := g^{r_i'}$ and $D_i' := g^\delta \prod_{j \in [0,k]} \Delta_j \prod_{j \in [k+1, i-1]} (u_j v_0^{t_\iota[j]})^{r_j} (u_i v_0)^{r_i'}$.

If $k \neq 0 \bigwedge \exists i \in [0, k-1]$ s.t. $t_\iota[i] = 0$ is logically true, then for every $j \in [0, k-1]$ s.t. $t_\iota[j] = 0$, $\mathcal{B}$ behaves as follows. We remind us that $F_j(1) \neq 0$. $\mathcal{B}$ computes: $d_j' := g_1^{-1/F_j(1)} g^{r_j'}$ and $D_j := g_1^{-J_j(1)/F_j(1)} (g^\alpha)^{r_j' F_j(1)} g^{r_j' J_j(1)} g^\delta \prod_{i \in [0, j-1]} (u_i v_0^{t_\iota[i]})^{r_i}$.

Note that for every $i \in [0, j-1]$, $r_i \in \mathbb{Z}_p$ has already been chosen and known by $\mathcal{B}$. The fact that d_j' and D_j correctly distribute can be verified in the same manner as (d_k, Δ_k).

$\mathcal{B}$ sets sk_r to $(D_{\log T}, d_0, \cdots, d_{\log T-1}, \{D_i, d_i' \mid i \in [0, \log T-1] \text{ s.t. } t_\iota[i] = 0\})$.

Next, $\mathcal{B}$ generates sk_l as follows. For every $i \in [0, \log T - 1]$, $s_i \xleftarrow{U} \mathbb{Z}_p$. For every $i \in [0, \log T - 1]$ s.t. $\tilde{t}_\iota[i] = 0$, $s_i' \xleftarrow{U} \mathbb{Z}_p$. sk_l is set as $(E_{\log T}, e_0, \cdots, e_{\log T-1}, \{E_i, e_i' \mid i \in [0, \log T - 1] \text{ s.t. } \tilde{t}_\iota[i] = 0\})$, where $E_{\log T} := g^{-\delta} \prod_{i \in [0, \log T-1]} (w_i v_0^{\tilde{t}_\iota[i]})^{s_i}$, $e_i := g^{s_i}$ (for $i \in [0, \log T - 1]$), $E_i := g^{-\delta} \prod_{j \in [0, i-1]} (w_j v_0^{\tilde{t}_\iota[j]})^{s_j} (w_i v_0)^{s_i'}$ (for $i \in [0, \log T - 1]$ s.t. $\tilde{t}_\iota[i] = 0$), and $e_i' := g^{s_i'}$ (for $i \in [0, \log T - 1]$ s.t. $\tilde{t}_\iota[i] = 0$).

Finally, $\mathcal{B}$ returns $sk_\iota := (sk_l, sk_r)$ to $\mathcal{A}$.

R2: $\mathcal{B}$'s behaviour in this case is analogous to the one in the case R1.
R3: $\mathcal{B}$ aborts the simulation.

When $\mathcal{A}$ issues $(t_\theta, L_\theta, R_\theta, m_\theta)$, where $\theta \in [1, q_s]$, as a query to $\mathfrak{Sign}$, $\mathcal{B}$ acts differently in the 4 cases: (S1) $\bigvee_{i \in [0, \log T - 1]} \mathbf{K}_i(R_\theta[i]) = 1$, (S2) $\bigvee_{i \in [0, \log T - 1]} \mathbf{U}_i(\tilde{L}_\theta[i]) = 1$, (S3) $\mathbf{K}_{\log T}(m_\theta) = 1$ and (S4) Otherwise, where $\tilde{L}_\theta := T - 1 - L_\theta$.

$\underline{\mathcal{B}\text{'s behaviour for the case S1:}}$ Let i_θ denote the integer $i \in [0, \log T - 1]$ satisfying $\mathbf{K}_i(R_\theta[i]) = 1$. Note that $\mathbf{K}_{i_\theta}(R_\theta[i_\theta]) = 1$ implies that $\mathbf{F}_{i_\theta}(R_\theta[i_\theta]) \neq 0$.

For every $i \in [0, \log T - 1]$, $r_i, s_i \xleftarrow{U} \mathbb{Z}_p$. $r_{\log T} \xleftarrow{U} \mathbb{Z}_p$. $\mathcal{B}$ computes:
$$U := g_1^{-\mathbf{J}_{i_\theta}(R_\theta[i_\theta])/\mathbf{F}_{i_\theta}(R_\theta[i_\theta])} (g^\alpha)^{r_{i_\theta} \mathbf{F}_{i_\theta}(R_\theta[i_\theta])} g^{r_{i_\theta} \mathbf{J}_{i_\theta}(R_\theta[i_\theta])} \prod_{i \in [0, \log T - 1] \setminus \{i_\theta\}} \left(u_i v_0^{R_\theta[i]} \right)^{r_i}$$
$\prod_{i \in [0, \log T - 1]} \left(w_i v_0^{\tilde{L}_\theta[i]} \right)^{s_i} \left(u_{\log T} \prod_{i \in [0, N-1]} v_i^{m_\theta[i]} \right)^{r_{\log T}}$, $V_i := g^{r_i}$ (for $i \in [\log T - 1] \setminus \{i_\theta\}$),
$V_{i_\theta} := g_1^{-1/\mathbf{F}_{i_\theta}(R_\theta[i_\theta])} g^{r_{i_\theta}}$, $V_i' := g^{s_i}$ (for $i \in [\log T - 1]$), and $V_{\log T} := g^{r_{\log T}}$.

$\mathcal{B}$ sets $\sigma_\theta := (U, V_0, \cdots, V_{\log T - 1}, V_0', \cdots, V_{\log T - 1}', V_{\log T})$ and returns it to $\mathcal{A}$. We can verify that it correctly distributes as we did in the case R1.

$\underline{\text{S2:}}$ This is analogous to the case S1.

$\underline{\text{S3:}}$ Note that $\mathbf{K}_{\log T}(m_\theta) = 1$ implies $\mathbf{F}_{\log T}(m_\theta) \neq 0$.

Let $r_{\log T} \xleftarrow{U} \mathbb{Z}_p$. $\mathcal{B}$ computes: $d_{\log T} := g_1^{-1/\mathbf{F}_{\log T}(m_\theta)} g^{r_{\log T}}$, and $\Delta_{\log T} :=$
$g_1^{-\mathbf{J}_{\log T}(m_\theta)/\mathbf{F}_{\log T}(m_\theta)} (g^\alpha)^{r_{\log T} \mathbf{F}_{\log T}(m_\theta)} g^{r_{\log T} \mathbf{J}_{\log T}(m_\theta)}$.

For every $i \in [0, \log T - 1]$, $r_i, s_i \xleftarrow{U} \mathbb{Z}_p$. $\mathcal{B}$ computes: $U := \Delta_{\log T} \cdot$
$\prod_{i \in [0, \log T - 1]} \left(u_i v_0^{R_\theta[i]} \right)^{r_i} \prod_{i \in [0, \log T - 1]} \left(w_i v_0^{\tilde{L}_\theta[i]} \right)^{s_i}$, $V_i := g^{r_i}$ (for $i \in [\log T - 1]$), $V_i' := g^{s_i}$
(for $i \in [\log T - 1]$), $V_{\log T} := d_{\log T}$.

$\mathcal{B}$ sets $\sigma_\theta := (U, V_0, \cdots, V_{\log T - 1}, V_0', \cdots, V_{\log T - 1}', V_{\log T})$ and returns it to $\mathcal{A}$. It correctly distributes since $d_{\log T} = g^{r_{\log T} - \beta/\mathbf{F}_{\log T}(m_\theta)} =: g^{\tilde{r}_{\log T}}$, where $\tilde{r}_{\log T} := r_{\log T} - \beta/\mathbf{F}_{\log T}(m_\theta)$, and

$$\begin{aligned}
\Delta_{\log T} &= g_1^\alpha g_1^{-\alpha \frac{\mathbf{F}_{\log T}(m_\theta)}{\mathbf{F}_{\log T}(m_\theta)} - \frac{\mathbf{J}_{\log T}(m_\theta)}{\mathbf{F}_{\log T}(m_\theta)}} g^{r_{\log T}(\alpha \mathbf{F}_{\log T}(m_\theta) + \mathbf{J}_{\log T}(m_\theta))} \\
&= g_1^\alpha g^{-\frac{\beta}{\mathbf{F}_{\log T}(m_\theta)}(\alpha \mathbf{F}_{\log T}(m_\theta) + \mathbf{J}_{\log T}(m_\theta))} g^{r_{\log T}(\alpha \mathbf{F}_{\log T}(m_\theta) + \mathbf{J}_{\log T}(m_\theta))} \\
&= g_1^\alpha g^{(r_{\log T} - \frac{\beta}{\mathbf{F}_{\log T}(m_\theta)})(\alpha \mathbf{F}_{\log T}(m_\theta) + \mathbf{J}_{\log T}(m_\theta))} = g_1^\alpha g^{\tilde{r}_{\log T}(\alpha \mathbf{F}_{\log T}(m_\theta) + \mathbf{J}_{\log T}(m_\theta))} \\
&= g_1^\alpha g^{\tilde{r}_{\log T} \{\alpha(p - nk_{\log T} + x_{\log T} + \sum_{i \in [0, N-1]} y_i m_\theta[i]) + x_{\log T}' + \sum_{i \in [0, N-1]} y_i' m_\theta[i]\}} \\
&= g_1^\alpha \{(g^\alpha)^{p - nk_{\log T} + x_{\log T}} g^{x_{\log T}'} \prod_{i \in [0, N-1]} (g^\alpha)^{y_i m_\theta[i]} g^{y_i' m_\theta[i]}\}^{\tilde{r}_{\log T}} = g_1^\alpha (u_{\log T} \prod_{i \in [0, N-1]} v_i^{m_\theta[i]})^{\tilde{r}_{\log T}}.
\end{aligned}$$

$\underline{\text{S4:}}$ $\mathcal{B}$ aborts the simulation.

When $\mathcal{A}$ finally outputs a forged signature σ^* for (m^*, L^*, R^*), $\mathcal{B}$ takes different actions in the following two cases: (F1) $\bigwedge_{i \in [0, \log T - 1]} \mathbf{F}_i(R^*[i]) = 0 \bigwedge_{i \in [0, \log T - 1]} \mathbf{H}_i(\tilde{L}^*[i]) = 0 \bigwedge \mathbf{F}_{\log T}(m^*) = 0$ and (F2) Otherwise, where $\tilde{L}^* := T - 1 - L^*$.

$\underline{\mathcal{B}\text{'s behaviour for the case F1:}}$ If σ^* is a correct signature, it is described as
$(g_1^\alpha \prod_{i \in [0, \log T - 1]} (u_i v_0^{R^*[i]})^{r_i} \prod_{i \in [0, \log T - 1]} (w_i v_0^{\tilde{L}^*[i]})^{s_i} (u_{\log T} \prod_{i \in [0, N-1]} v_i^{m^*[i]})^{r_{\log T}}, g^{r_0}, \cdots,$
$g^{r_{\log T - 1}}, g^{s_0}, \cdots, g^{s_{\log T - 1}}, g^{r_{\log T}})$, where $r_0, \cdots, r_{\log T - 1}, s_0, \cdots, s_{\log T - 1}, r_{\log T} \in \mathbb{Z}_p$. Let σ^* be denoted by $(U, V_0, \cdots, V_{\log T - 1}, V_0', \cdots, V_{\log T - 1}', V_{\log T})$.

F1 implies that $\bigwedge_{i \in [0, \log T - 1]} u_i v_0^{R^*[i]} = g^{\alpha \mathbf{F}_i(R^*[i]) + \mathbf{J}_i(R^*[i])} = g^{\mathbf{J}_i(R^*[i])}$, $\bigwedge_{i \in [0, \log T - 1]} w_i v_0^{\tilde{L}^*[i]} = g^{\alpha \mathbf{H}_i(\tilde{L}^*[i]) + \mathbf{Q}_i(\tilde{L}^*[i])} = g^{\mathbf{Q}_i(\tilde{L}^*[i])}$, and $u_{\log T} \prod_{i \in [0, N-1]} v_i^{m^*[i]} = g^{\alpha \mathbf{F}_{\log T}(m^*) + \mathbf{J}_{\log T}(m^*)} = g^{\mathbf{J}_{\log T}(m^*)}$.

$\mathcal{B}$ outputs U/W, where $W := V_{\log T}^{\mathbf{J}_{\log T}(m^*)} \prod_{i \in [0, \log T - 1]} V_i^{\mathbf{J}_i(R^*[i])} V_i'^{\mathbf{Q}_i(\check{L}^*[i])}$, as an answer for the co-CDH problem. If σ^* is a correct signature, $U/W = g_1^\alpha = g^{\alpha\beta}$.

F2: $\mathcal{B}$ aborts the simulation.

$\mathcal{B}$ behaves as above. Let **Abort** denote the event where $\mathcal{B}$ aborts. Let $\neg$**Abort** denote the event where $\mathcal{B}$ does not abort. We obtain $\mathsf{Adv}_{\mathcal{B}}^{\text{co-CDH}}(\lambda) = \Pr[g^{\alpha\beta} \leftarrow \mathcal{B} \wedge \mathbf{Abort}] + \Pr[g^{\alpha\beta} \leftarrow \mathcal{B} \wedge \neg\mathbf{Abort}] \geq \Pr[g^{\alpha\beta} \leftarrow \mathcal{B} \wedge \neg\mathbf{Abort}] = \Pr[g^{\alpha\beta} \leftarrow \mathcal{B} \mid \neg\mathbf{Abort}] \Pr[\neg\mathbf{Abort}]$. Since, in the case where $\mathcal{B}$ does not abort the simulation, $\mathcal{B}$ perfectly simulates the existential unforgeability experiment for $\mathcal{A}$, and $\mathcal{B}$ correctly answers if (and only if) $\mathcal{A}$ behaves to make the experiment output 1, the last term is equal to $\Pr[1 \leftarrow \mathbf{Expt}_{\Pi_{\text{TSS}}, \mathcal{A}}^{\text{EUF-CMA}}(1^\lambda, N, T)] \Pr[\neg\mathbf{Abort}]$. Hence, $\mathbf{Abort}_{\mathcal{B}}^{\text{co-CDH}}(\lambda) \leq \mathsf{Adv}_{\Pi_{\text{TSS}}, \mathcal{A}, N, T}^{\text{EUF-CMA}}(\lambda) \cdot \Pr[\neg\mathbf{Abort}]$.

Finally, we analyse $\Pr[\neg\mathbf{Abort}]$. Let $\mathbf{H}$ denote the event where $\mathcal{B}$ has not aborted the simulation until $\mathcal{A}$ outputs the forged signature. Let $\mathbf{F}$ denote the event where $\mathcal{B}$ does not abort after $\mathcal{A}$ outputs the forged signature. Obviously, it holds $\Pr[\neg\mathbf{Abort}] = \Pr[\mathbf{H}]\Pr[\mathbf{F} \mid \mathbf{H}] = \Pr[\mathbf{F}]\Pr[\mathbf{H} \mid \mathbf{F}]$.

Let $\mathbf{R}_\iota$ denote the event where, on the ι-th query to $\mathfrak{Reveal}$, $\mathcal{B}$ does not abort. Likewise, let $\mathbf{S}_\theta$ denote the event where, on the θ-th query to $\mathfrak{Sign}$, $\mathcal{B}$ does not abort. For $\mathbf{X} \in \{\mathbf{H}, \mathbf{R}_\iota, \mathbf{S}_\theta\}$, let $\neg\mathbf{X}$ denote the negation of $\mathbf{X}$. We present three Lemmata 1, 2, 3. Proofs for them are omitted because of the strict page limitation, but described in the full paper. The proofs for Lemmata 1, 2 are analogous to one for *Proposition 5* in [10]. The proof for Lemma 3 is analogous to one for *Proposition 1* in [10]. Finally, we obtain $\Pr[\neg\mathbf{Abort}] = (1 - \Pr[\neg\mathbf{H} \mid \mathbf{F}])\Pr[\mathbf{F}] = (1 - \Pr[\bigvee_{\iota \in [1, q_r]} \neg\mathbf{R}_\iota \bigvee_{\theta \in [1, q_s]} \neg\mathbf{S}_\theta \mid \mathbf{F}])\Pr[\mathbf{F}] \geq (1 - \sum_{\iota \in [1, q_r]} \Pr[\neg\mathbf{R}_\iota \mid \mathbf{F}] - \sum_{\theta \in [1, q_s]} \Pr[\neg\mathbf{S}_\theta \mid \mathbf{F}])\Pr[\mathbf{F}]$. The last term is equal to $\Pr[\neg\mathbf{Abort}] \geq \{1 - \frac{1}{n}(\log T \cdot q_r + q_s)\} \frac{1}{\{n(N+1)\}^{2\log T + 1}}$, because of Lemmata 1, 2, 3. Hence, we obtain $\Pr[\neg\mathbf{Abort}] \geq \frac{1}{2} \frac{1}{\{2(\log T \cdot q_r + q_s)(N+1)\}^{2\log T + 1}}$, because of $n := 2(\log T \cdot q_r + q_s)$.

By the above inequalities for $\mathbf{Abort}_{\mathcal{B}}^{\text{co-CDH}}(\lambda)$ and $\Pr[\neg\mathbf{Abort}]$, we obtain (1). □

Lemma 1. *For every* $\iota \in [1, q_r]$, $\Pr[\neg\mathbf{R}_\iota \mid \mathbf{F}] \leq (\log T)/n$.

Lemma 2. *For every* $\theta \in [1, q_s]$, $\Pr[\neg\mathbf{S}_\theta \mid \mathbf{F}] \leq 1/n$.

Lemma 3. $\Pr[\mathbf{F}] \geq 1/\{n(N+1)\}^{2\log T + 1}$.

4.3 Perfect Privacy

Let us prove that our TSS scheme Π_{TSS} is perfectly private. We define $(\text{Setup}', \text{KGen}', \text{Sig}')$ used in $\mathbf{Expt}_{\Pi_{\text{TSS}}, \mathcal{A}, 1}^{\text{PP}}$ as follows. The first two are the same as the original ones of Π_{TSS}. Sig' *directly* generates a signature under $[L, R]$ from msk. From $\mathcal{A}$'s view point, the two experiments identically distribute. Thus, we obtain

Theorem 2. *Our TSS scheme* Π_{TSS} *is perfectly private under Definition 5.*

4.4 Efficiency Analysis

mpk has $2\log T + N + 3$ elements from $\mathbb{G}$ and the same number of elements from $\tilde{\mathbb{G}}^4$. Thus, $|mpk| = (2\log T + N + 3)(|g| + |\tilde{g}|)$. Size of msk is $|msk| = |g|$. Size of a

---

[4] We have ignored information about the pairing (i.e., p, $\mathbb{G}$, $\tilde{\mathbb{G}}$ and e) included in mpk.

signature under any $[L, R]$ is $|\sigma_{[L,R]}| = (2 \log T + 2)|g|$. For size $|sk_t|$, let us independently analyse the first part sk_r and the second part sk_l of sk_t. The maximum size of sk_r is $((\log T + 1) + 2 \log T)|g| = (3 \log T + 1)|g|$ when $t = 0$. The maximum size of sk_l is also $(3 \log T + 1)|g|$ when $t = T - 1$. Thus, $|sk_t|$ is at most $(6 \log T + 2)|g|$. Thus, asymptotically, $|sk_t| = O(\log T)|g|$. Table 1 in Sect. 6 compares our two TSS schemes.

5   TSS Based on Wildcarded Identity-Based Ring Signatures

We propose another TSS scheme with constant-size secret-keys based on *wildcarded identity-based ring signatures*.

IBE-based TSE [17]. In [17], the authors generically constructed a TSE scheme from an IBE scheme. For the TSS scheme, a (complete) binary tree with T leaf nodes is introduced. Each leaf node corresponds to each time period $t \in [0, T - 1]$. Let $anc(t)$ denote a set composed of ancestor nodes of t and the node t itself. Let $sk_{ID=str}$ denote a (randomly-generated) secret-key for a bit string $str \in \{0, 1\}^*$ (as an identity) on the underlying IBE scheme. The secret-key for $t \in [0, T-1]$ is $sk_t = \{sk_{ID=str} \mid str \in anc(t)\}$.

To encrypt a message m under $[L, R]$, a set of nodes $\mathbb{T}_{[L,R]}$ which *covers* the range is chosen. For a node $str \in \{0, 1\}^{\leq \log T}$, let $dec(str)$ denote a set of leaf nodes any one of which is descendant of the node. The set $\mathbb{T}_{[L,R]}$ is chosen to satisfy that $[\bigcup_{str \in \mathbb{T}_{[L,R]}} dec(str) = [L, R]] \bigwedge_{str, str' \in \mathbb{T}_{[L,R]} \text{ s.t. } str \neq str'} [dec(str) \bigcap dec(str') = \emptyset] \bigwedge [\text{The cardinality } |\mathbb{T}_{[L,R]}| \text{ is the } minimum]$. For the formal algorithm (denoted by Cover in this paper) where we choose $\mathbb{T}_{[L,R]}$, refer to *Algorithm 1* in [17]. Then, a ciphertext for m under $[L, R]$ is set as a set of ciphertexts $\{ct_{ID=str} \mid str \in \mathbb{T}_{[L,R]}\}$, where $ct_{ID=str}$ denotes a (randomly-generated) ciphertext for the message m under str (as an identity) on the underlying IBE scheme. A secret-key sk_t for $t \in [0, T - 1]$ can correctly decrypt a ciphertext $ct_{[L,R]}$ under $[L, R]$ s.t. $t \in [L, R]$ since $t \in [L, R]$ implies that there must exist only one node $str \in \{0, 1\}^{\leq \log T}$ which is included in both $anc(t)$ and $\mathbb{T}_{[L,R]}$, i.e., $anc(t) \bigcup \mathbb{T}_{[L,R]} = \{str\}$.

WIBE-based TSE [13]. One disadvantage of the IBE-based TSE construction is that size of secret-keys is linearly dependent on $\log T$, thus cannot be constant. The authors in [13] showed that by using wildcarded identity-based encryption (WIBE) [1,5] (w/o hierarchical key-delegatability) instead of the IBE in the IBE-based TSE, we can obtain a TSE scheme with contant-size secret-keys. In the WIBE-based TSE, each node $str \in \{0, 1\}^{\leq \log T}$ in the binary tree with T leafs is added $\log T - |str|$ wildcarded symbols $*^{\log T - |str|}$ from right, thus it is changed into $str||*^{\log T - |str|} \in \{0, 1, *\}^{\log T}$. The set of identities $\mathbb{T}_{[L,R]}$ is wildcarded, which means $\mathbb{T}_{[L,R]}^* := \{str||*^{\log T - |str|} \mid str \in \mathbb{T}_{[L,R]}\}$. A secret-key for $t \in \{0, 1\}^{\log T}$ can correctly decrypt a ciphertext under $[L, R]$ since $t \in [L, R]$ implies that there must exist only one wildcarded identity $wID \in \{0, 1, *\}^{\log T}$ in $\mathbb{T}_{[L,R]}^*$ which is satisfied by t. Each secret-key for $t \in [0, T - 1]$ consists of a single secret-key for $t \in \{0, 1\}^{\log T}$ on the underlying WIBE scheme, which implies that if the WIBE scheme is with constant-size secret-keys, the obtained TSS scheme is also with.

Our Approach. Analogously, we consider WIBS-based TSS. From the *standard* WIBS[5] scheme, we cannot (or at least need a sophisticated methodology to) obtain an expected result. We introduce wildcarded identity-based *ring* signatures (WIBRS). Its syntax and security definition are in Subsect. 5.1. It is parameterized by $n \in \mathbb{N}$. It makes each signer choose $l \le n$ number of wildcarded identities $wID_1, \cdots, wID_l \in \{0, 1, *\}^L$ such that the signer's identity $ID \in \{0, 1\}^L$ satisfies at least one wID among the l wIDs. We show that a TSS scheme can be generically constructed by a WIBRS scheme with $L = \log T$ and $n = 2 \log T - 2$ in Subsect. 5.2. We instantiate an attribute-based signatures (ABS) scheme [18] to obtain a WIBRS scheme with constant-size secret-keys in Subsect. 5.3. We rigorously evaluate the efficiency of the TSS scheme instantiated by the WIBRS scheme in Subsect. 5.4.

Remark. In [13], another sophisticated TSE construction from WIBE (w. ciphertexts of smaller size) was also proposed. We can analogously consider a sophisticated WIBRS-based TSS construction, which can shorten size of a signature. However, we only consider the simple WIBRS-based TSS construction because of its simplicity.

5.1 Wildcarded Identity-Based Ring Signatures (WIBRS)

Syntax. Wildcarded Identity-Based Ring Signatures (WIBRS) consist of following 4 polynomial time algorithms, where Ver is deterministic and the others are probabilistic. Let $n \in \mathbb{N}$ denote the maximum cardinality of a *ring* of wildcarded identities. **Setup** algorithm Setup takes $(1^\lambda, L, n)$ as input, then outputs a master public-key mpk and a master secret-key msk. Concisely, we write $(mpk, msk) \leftarrow$ Setup$(1^\lambda, L, n)$. **Key-generation** algorithm KGen takes msk and an identity $ID \in \{0, 1\}^L$, then outputs a secret-key sk for the identity. Concisely, we write $sk \leftarrow$ KGen(msk, ID). **Signing** algorithm Sig takes a secret-key sk for $ID \in \{0, 1\}^L$, a message $m \in \{0, 1\}^*$, and wildcarded identities $(wID_1, \cdots, wID_l)$ s.t. $l \le n \bigwedge_{i=1}^{l} wID_i \in \{0, 1, *\}^L$, then outputs a signature σ. Concisely, we write $\sigma \leftarrow$ Sig$(sk, m, wID_1, \cdots, wID_l)$. **Verifying** algorithm Ver takes σ, $m \in \{0, 1\}^*$, and $(wID_1, \cdots, wID_l)$, then outputs a bit $1/0$. Concisely, we write $1/0 \leftarrow$ Ver$(\sigma, m, wID_1, \cdots, wID_l)$.

We introduce a deterministic polynomial-time Boolean algorithm verifying whether an ID satisfies a wildcarded ID. The algorithm Match_L takes $ID \in \{0, 1\}^L$ and $wID \in \{0, 1, *\}^L$, and outputs 1 iff $\forall i \in [0, L-1]$ s.t. $wID[i] \ne *, ID[i] = wID[i]$.

We require every WIBRS scheme to be correct. A scheme $\Sigma_{\text{WIBRS}} = \{\text{Setup}, \text{KGen}, \text{Sig}, \text{Ver}\}$ is correct, if $\forall \lambda, L, n \in \mathbb{N}$, $\forall (mpk, msk) \leftarrow$ Setup$(1^\lambda, L, n)$, $\forall ID \in \{0, 1\}^L$, $\forall sk \leftarrow$ KGen(msk, ID), $\forall m \in \{0, 1\}^*$, $\forall l \in \mathbb{N}$ s.t. $l \le n$, $\forall (wID_1, \cdots, wID_l)$ s.t. $\bigwedge_{i=1}^{l} wID_i \in \{0, 1, *\}^L \bigwedge \bigvee_{j=1}^{l} 1 \leftarrow \text{Match}_L(ID, wID_j)$, $\forall \sigma \leftarrow$ Sig$(sk, m, wID_1, \cdots, wID_l)$, $1 \leftarrow$ Ver$(\sigma, m, wID_1, \cdots, wID_l)$.

Existential Unforgeability and Perfect Privacy. For a WIBRS scheme Σ_{WIBRS} and a probabilistic algorithm $\mathcal{A}$, we consider experiments in Fig. 3.

Definition 6. Σ_{WIBRS} *is existentially unforgeable, if* $\forall \lambda \in \mathbb{N}$, $\forall L \in \mathbb{N}$, $\forall n \in \mathbb{N}$, $\forall \mathcal{A} \in \text{PPT}_\lambda$, $\exists \epsilon \in \text{NGL}_\lambda$, $Adv_{\Sigma_{\text{WIBRS}}, \mathcal{A}, L, n}^{EUF\text{-}CMA}(\lambda) := \Pr[1 \leftarrow Expt_{\Sigma_{\text{WIBRS}}, \mathcal{A}}^{EUF\text{-}CMA}(1^\lambda, L, n)] < \epsilon$.

---

[5] The digital signature analogue of the WIBE.

$Expt^{\text{EUF-CMA}}_{\Sigma_{\text{WIBRS}},\mathcal{A}}(1^\lambda, L, n)$:

  $(mpk, msk) \leftarrow \text{Setup}(1^\lambda, L, n). (\sigma^*, m^*, wID_1^*, \cdots, wID_{l^*}^*) \leftarrow \mathcal{A}^{\text{Reveal,Sign}}(mpk)$, where
  - $\text{Reveal}(ID_\iota \in \{0,1\}^L)$, where $\iota \in [1, q_r]$: **Rtrn** $sk_\iota \leftarrow \text{KGen}(msk, ID_\iota)$.
  - $\text{Sign}(ID_\theta \in \{0,1\}^L, m_\theta \in \{0,1\}^*, wID_{1,\theta}, \cdots, wID_{l_\theta,\theta} \in \{0,1,*\}^L)$, where $\theta \in [1, q_s]$:
    $sk_\theta \leftarrow \text{KGen}(msk, ID_\theta)$. **Rtrn** $\sigma_\theta \leftarrow \text{Sig}(sk_\theta, m_\theta, wID_{1,\theta}, \cdots, wID_{l_\theta,\theta})$.
  Rtrn 1 if $1 \leftarrow \text{Ver}(\sigma^*, m^*, wID_1^*, \cdots, wID_{l^*}^*) \bigwedge_{\iota=1}^{q_r} \bigwedge_{i \in [1, l^*]} 0 \leftarrow \text{Match}_L(ID_\iota, wID_i^*)$
  $\bigwedge_{\theta=1}^{q_s} (m_\theta, wID_{1,\theta}, \cdots, wID_{l_\theta,\theta}) \neq (m^*, wID_1^*, \cdots, wID_{l^*}^*)$. **Rtrn** 0 otherwise.

$Expt^{\text{PP}}_{\Sigma_{\text{WIBRS}},\mathcal{A},0}(1^\lambda, L, n)$:	$Expt^{\text{PP}}_{\Sigma_{\text{WIBRS}},\mathcal{A},1}(1^\lambda, L, n)$:
$(mpk, msk) \leftarrow \text{Setup}(1^\lambda, L, n)$	$(mpk, msk') \leftarrow \text{Setup}'(1^\lambda, L, n)$
Rtrn $b \leftarrow \mathcal{A}^{\text{Reveal,Sign}}(mpk, msk)$, where	**Rtrn** $b \leftarrow \mathcal{A}^{\text{Reveal}',\text{Sign}'}(mpk, msk)$, where
- $\text{Reveal}(ID_\iota)$, where $\iota \in [1, q_r]$:	- $\text{Reveal}'(ID_\iota)$, where $\iota \in [1, q_r]$:
Rtrn $sk_\iota \leftarrow \text{KGen}(msk, ID_\iota)$.	**Rtrn** $sk_\iota \leftarrow \text{KGen}'(msk, ID_\iota)$.
- $\text{Sign}(\iota \in [1, q_r], m, wID_1, \cdots, wID_l)$:	- $\text{Sign}'(\iota \in [1, q_r], m, wID_1, \cdots, wID_l)$:
Rtrn $\perp$ if $\bigwedge_{i=1}^l 0 \leftarrow \text{Match}_L(ID_\iota, wID_i)$.	**Rtrn** $\perp$ if $\bigwedge_{i=1}^l 0 \leftarrow \text{Match}_L(ID_\iota, wID_i)$.
Rtrn $\sigma \leftarrow \text{Sig}(sk_\iota, m, wID_1, \cdots, wID_l)$.	**Rtrn** $\sigma \leftarrow \text{Sig}'(msk', m, wID_1, \cdots, wID_l)$.

Fig. 3. Top: Experiment for (adaptive) existential unforgeability w.r.t. a WIBRS scheme Σ_{WIBRS}. Bottom: Experiments for perfect privacy w.r.t. a WIBRS scheme Σ_{WIBRS}

$\text{Setup}(1^\lambda, T)$:	$\text{Sig}(sk_t, m, L, R)$:
Rtrn $(mpk, msk) \leftarrow \text{Setup}'(1^\lambda, \log T, 2\log T - 2)$	$\mathbb{T}_{[L,R]} \leftarrow \text{Cover}_{\log T}(L, R)$.
$\text{KGen}(msk, t)$: Parse t as $t[0]\|\cdots\|t[\log T - 1]$.	$\mathbb{T}^*_{[L,R]} := \{ID\|*^{\log T - |ID|} \mid ID \in \mathbb{T}_{[L,R]}\}$.
Rtrn $sk_t \leftarrow \text{KGen}'(msk, t)$.	$t \in [L, R] \implies \exists wID \in \mathbb{T}^*_{[L,R]}$
$\text{Ver}(\sigma_{[L,R]}, m, L, R)$: $\mathbb{T}_{[L,R]} \leftarrow \text{Cover}_{\log T}(L, R)$.	s.t. $1 \leftarrow \text{Match}_{\log T}(t, wID)$
$\mathbb{T}^*_{[L,R]} := \{ID\|*^{\log T - |ID|} \mid ID \in \mathbb{T}_{[L,R]}\}$.	**Rtrn** $\sigma_{[L,R]} \leftarrow \text{Sig}'(sk, m, \mathbb{T}^*_{[L,R]})$.
Rtrn $1 / 0 \leftarrow \text{Ver}'(\sigma_{[L,R]}, m, \mathbb{T}^*_{[L,R]})$.	

Fig. 4. A generic TSS construction from a WIBRS scheme $\Sigma_{\text{WIBRS}} = \{\text{Setup}', \text{KGen}', \text{Sig}', \text{Ver}'\}$

Definition 7. Σ_{WIBRS} *is perfectly private, if for every* $\lambda, L, n \in \mathbb{N}$ *and every probabilistic algorithm* $\mathcal{A}$, *there exist probabilistic polynomial time algorithms* $\{\text{Setup}', \text{KGen}', \text{Sig}'\}$ *s.t.* $Adv^{\text{PP}}_{\Sigma_{\text{WIBRS}},\mathcal{A},L,n}(\lambda) := |\sum_{b=0}^{1}(-1)^b \Pr[1 \leftarrow Expt^{\text{PP}}_{\Sigma_{\text{WIBRS}},\mathcal{A},b}(1^\lambda, L, n)]| = 0.$

5.2 A TSS Scheme from WIBRS Scheme with $L = \log T$ and $n = 2\log T - 2$

A TSS scheme is generically constructed from a WIBRS scheme parameterized by $L = \log T$ and $n = 2\log T - 2$ as described in Fig. 4. Theorem 3 guarantees that security of the TSS scheme is reduced to that of the underlying WIBRS scheme. We omit a proof for the theorem since it is almost obvious.

Theorem 3. *If the underlying WIBRS scheme is existentially unforgeable (resp. perfectly private), then the TSS scheme is existentially unforgeable (resp. perfectly private).*

5.3 A WIBRS Scheme as an Instantiation of ABS Scheme [18]

ABS with a Signer-Policy Represented as a Circuit. In [18], an ABS scheme, where signer-policy is described as a circuit $\phi : \{0,1\}^L \rightarrow \{0,1\}$, is proposed. Each secret-key

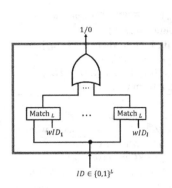

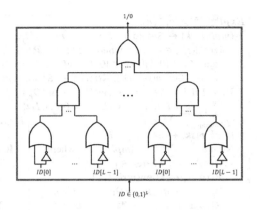

Fig. 5. A circuit representing a disjunctive signer-policy defined on $l(\leq n)$ wildcarded identities $wID_1, \cdots, wID_l \in \{0, 1, *\}^L$.

Fig. 6. A circuit representing a disjunctive signer-policy defined on n (non-)wildcarded identities $wID_1, \cdots, wID_n$ s.t. $\bigwedge_{i=1}^{n} wID_i = *^L$.

is associated with an attribute $x \in \{0, 1\}^L$. A signer with a secret-key for x, who chooses a circuit ϕ as a signer-policy, can correctly sign a message if the attribute satisfies the circuit, i.e., $\phi(x) = 1$. Each circuit is assumed to be constructed by only NAND gates with fan-in 2. Their ABS scheme is built by a structure-preserving signatures (SPS) scheme [15], a non-interactive witness-indistinguishable (NIWI) proof system [12] and a collision-resistant hash function. A secret-key for an attribute $x \in \{0, 1\}^L$ is a signature θ_x of the SPS scheme on a message $(g^0, g^{x[0]}, \cdots, g^{x[L-1]})$, where g is a generator of $\mathbb{G}$ of an asymmetric pairing $e : \mathbb{G} \times \tilde{\mathbb{G}} \to \mathbb{G}_T$ with prime order. A signer with $x \in \{0, 1\}^L$ signs a message m under a circuit ϕ by proving on NIWI proof system that x satisfies ϕ and θ_x is a correct signature on $(g^0, g^{x[0]}, \cdots, g^{x[L-1]})$, where the message m is inserted into the circuit ϕ in an adequate way.

A circuit representing a disjunctive signer-policy defined on $l \leq n$ wildcarded identities $wID_1, \cdots, wID_l \in \{0, 1, *\}^L$ is described as shown in Fig. 5.

Universality of NAND Gates with Fan-in 2. We commonly know that an AND gate with fan-in 2 (resp. an OR gate with fan-in 2, a NOT gate) can be constructed by two (resp. three, two) NAND gates with fan-in 2. Thus, $\text{AND}(A, B) = \text{NAND}(\text{NAND}(A, B), \text{NAND}(A, B))$, $\text{OR}(A, B) = \text{NAND}(\text{NAND}(A, A), \text{NAND}(B, B))$ and $\text{NOT}(A) = \text{NAND}(A, A)$.

We can easily prove that an AND (resp. OR) gate with fan-in $L \in \mathbb{N}$ can be constructed by $L - 1$ AND (resp. OR) gates with fan-in 2, which implies that it can be constructed by $2(L - 1)$ (resp. $3(L - 1)$) NAND gates with fan-in 2.

Efficiency and Security of the WIBRS Scheme. mpk has a common reference string crs on NIWI proof system [12], a verification key vk on structure-preserving signature scheme [15] and a hash key hk of a collision-resistant hash function. vk includes $L + 7$ elements in $\tilde{\mathbb{G}}$, and crs and hk are independent of L. Thus, $|mpk| = O(L)|\tilde{g}|$. msk is the signing key on the signature scheme [15] itself. It includes $2L + 8$ elements in $\mathbb{G}$, which means $|msk| = O(L)|g|$. A secret-key for $ID \in \{0, 1\}^L$ is a signature on the signature scheme [15]. The signature is generated by considering the ID as a message. Thus, $|sk_{ID}| = 6|g| + 2|\tilde{g}|$, which is asymptotically $O(1)(|g| + |\tilde{g}|)$.

As we explain below, size of a signature for a ring $(wID_1, \cdots, wID_l)$ (where $l \leq n$) is asymptotically $|\sigma| = O(nL)(|g| + |\tilde{g}|)$. According to [18], size of a signature for a circuit is determined by total number of input wires N_{in} of the circuit and that of NAND-gates N_{ga} in the circuit. Precisely, it is described as $|\sigma| = (6N_{in} + 10N_{ga} + 16)(|g| + |\tilde{g}|)$. For the WIBRS scheme, it is (almost) obvious that both N_{in} and N_{ga} are maximized when the signer-policy is a disjunctive policy defined on n number of wildcarded identities $wID_1, \cdots, wID_n$, every one of which is $*^L$ [6]. The signer-policy is described as a circuit shown in Fig. 6. The circuit takes $N_{in} = L$ input wires. The circuit includes nL NOT gates, nL OR gates with fan-in 2, n AND gates with fan-in L, and one OR gate with fan-in n. Hence, the circuit includes $N_{ga} = 6nL + n - 3$ NAND gates with fan-in 2. We conclude that size of a signature is *loosely* upper-bounded by $(6N_{in} + 10N_{ga} + 16)(|g| + |\tilde{g}|) = (60nL + 6L + 10n - 14)(|g| + |\tilde{g}|)$. Asymptotically, $O(nL)$.

Its security is reduced to that of the original [18].

Theorem 4. *If the ABS scheme [18] is existentially unforgeable (resp. perfectly private) under Definition 8 (resp. Definition 9 [7]), then the WIBRS scheme is existentially unforgeable (resp. perfectly private) under Definition 6 (resp. Definition 7).*

5.4 Analyzing Efficiency of the TSS Scheme

Our TSS scheme is obtained from the WIBRS scheme in the last subsection parameterized by $L = \log T$ and $n = 2 \log T - 2$. The reason why $n = 2 \log T - 2$ is that among every range $[L, R]$, the maximum number of wildcarded identities for the range is $|\mathbb{T}_{[L,R]}| = 2 \log T - 2$ when $[L, R] = [1, T - 2]$.

Spatial efficiency of the TSS scheme is rigolously analyzed as follows. mpk, msk and sk_t are unchanged from the WIBRS scheme. Thus, $|mpk| = O(\log T)|\tilde{g}|$, $|msk| = O(\log T)|g|$ and $|sk_t| = 6|g| + 2|\tilde{g}| = O(1)(|g| + |\tilde{g}|)$. In the last subsection, we explained that a loose upper bound for the size of a signature of the WIBRS scheme is $(60nL + 6L + 10n - 14)(|g| + |\tilde{g}|)$. By substituting $\log T$ and $2 \log T - 2$ for L and n, respectively, we obtain $(120 \log^2 T - 94 \log T - 34)(|g| + |\tilde{g}|)$ as a loose upper bound for the size of a signature of the TSS scheme. Asymptotically, it is $O(\log^2 T)(|g| + |\tilde{g}|)$.

6 Conclusion

In this paper, we proposed two TSS schemes, each of which is polylogarithmically efficient, based on an asymmetric bilinear pairing with prime order, and secure, i.e., existentially unforgeable and perfectly private, under standard assumption. Their characteristics are summarized in Table 1. The first one achieves a well-balanced efficiency. The second one has secret-keys of constant size, but has signatures of large size.

---

[6] In other words, for every possible signer-policy (or ring of wildcarded identities), N_{in} and N_{ga} are smaller than or equal to the *largest* N_{in} and N_{ga}, respectively.

[7] Although the definition of perfect privacy used in [18] is different from Definition 9, it has been shown by Blömer et al. [6] that the ABS scheme [18] is perfectly private under Definition 9.

Table 1. Comparison of Our TSS Schemes

TSS Scheme	$|mpk|$	$|msk|$	$|sk_\iota|$	$|\sigma_{[L,R]}|$	Assumpt.
FSS-based	$(2\log T + N + 3)(|g| + |\breve{g}|)$	$|g|$	$O(\log T)|g|$	$(2\log T + 2)|g|$	co-CDH
WIBRS-based	$O(\log T)|\breve{g}|$	$O(\log T)|g|$	$O(1)(|g| + |\breve{g}|)$	$O(\log^2 T)(|g| + |\breve{g}|)$	SXDH

For a data a, $|a|$ denotes its bit length. For FSS-based TSS scheme, $N \in \mathbb{N}$ denotes bit length of an message. $|g|$ (resp. $|\breve{g}|$) denotes bit length of an element in bilinear group $\mathbb{G}$ (resp. $\breve{\mathbb{G}}$).

A   Attribute-Based Signatures (ABS) for Circuits

Syntax. Attribute-based signatures (ABS) for circuits [18] consist of following 4 polynomial time algorithms, where Ver is deterministic and the others are probabilistic. Let $L \in \mathbb{N}$ denote length of an attribute. Setup takes $(1^\lambda, L)$ as input then outputs mpk and msk. We write $(mpk, msk) \leftarrow \text{Setup}(1^\lambda, L)$. KGen takes msk and an attribute $x \in \{0, 1\}^L$, then outputs a sk_x for the attribute. We write $sk_x \leftarrow \text{KGen}(msk, x)$. Sig takes a sk_x for $x \in \{0, 1\}^L$, a message $m \in \{0, 1\}^*$, and a signer-policy $\phi : \{0, 1\}^L \rightarrow \{0, 1\}$ s.t. $1 \leftarrow \phi(x)$, then outputs a signature σ. We write $\sigma \leftarrow \text{Sig}(sk_x, m, \phi)$. Ver takes σ, $m \in \{0, 1\}^*$, and ϕ, then outputs a bit $1/0$. We write $1/0 \leftarrow \text{Ver}(\sigma, m, \phi)$.

We require every ABS scheme to be correct. A scheme $\Sigma_{\text{ABS}} = \{\text{Setup}, \text{KGen}, \text{Sig}, \text{Ver}\}$ is correct, if $\forall \lambda \in \mathbb{N}$, $\forall L \in \mathbb{N}$, $\forall (mpk, msk) \leftarrow \text{Setup}(1^\lambda, L)$, $\forall x \in \{0, 1\}^L$, $\forall sk_x \leftarrow \text{KGen}(msk, x)$, $\forall m \in \{0, 1\}^*$, $\forall \phi$ s.t. $1 \leftarrow \phi(x)$, $\forall \sigma \leftarrow \text{Sig}(sk_x, m, \phi)$, $1 \leftarrow \text{Ver}(\sigma, m, \phi)$.

Existential Unforgeability and Perfect Privacy. For an ABS scheme Σ_{ABS} and a probabilistic algorithm $\mathcal{A}$, we consider experiments in Fig. 7.

$\boldsymbol{Expt}^{\text{EUF-CMA}}_{\Sigma_{\text{ABS}}, \mathcal{A}}(1^\lambda, L)$:
  $(mpk, msk) \leftarrow \text{Setup}(1^\lambda, L)$. $(\sigma^*, m^*, \phi^*) \leftarrow \mathcal{A}^{\mathfrak{Reveal}, \mathfrak{Sign}}(mpk)$, where

  - $\mathfrak{Reveal}(x_\iota \in \{0, 1\}^L)$: **Rtrn** $sk_\iota \leftarrow \text{KGen}(msk, x_\iota)$.
  - $\mathfrak{Sign}(x_\theta \in \{0, 1\}^L, m_\theta \in \{0, 1\}^*, \phi_\theta)$: $sk_\theta \leftarrow \text{KGen}(msk, x_\theta)$. **Rtrn** $\sigma_\theta \leftarrow \text{Sig}(sk_\theta, m_\theta, \phi_\theta)$.

  Rtrn 1 if $1 \leftarrow \text{Ver}(\sigma^*, m^*, \phi^*) \bigwedge_{\iota=1}^{q_r} 0 \leftarrow \phi^*(x_\iota) \bigwedge_{\theta=1}^{q_s} (m_\theta, \phi_\theta) \neq (m^*, \phi^*)$. **Rtrn** 0 otherwise.

$\boldsymbol{Expt}^{\text{PP}}_{\Sigma_{\text{ABS}}, \mathcal{A}, 0}(1^\lambda, L)$: | $\boldsymbol{Expt}^{\text{PP}}_{\Sigma_{\text{TSS}}, \mathcal{A}, 1}(1^\lambda, L)$:
  $(mpk, msk) \leftarrow \text{Setup}(1^\lambda, L)$ | $(mpk, msk') \leftarrow \text{Setup}'(1^\lambda, L)$
  Rtrn $b \leftarrow \mathcal{A}^{\mathfrak{Reveal}, \mathfrak{Sign}}(mpk, msk)$, where | **Rtrn** $b \leftarrow \mathcal{A}^{\mathfrak{Reveal}, \mathfrak{Sign}}(mpk, msk)$, where

  - $\mathfrak{Reveal}(x_\iota)$, where $\iota \in [1, q_r]$: | - $\mathfrak{Reveal}(x_\iota)$, where $\iota \in [1, q_r]$:
    Rtrn $sk_\iota \leftarrow \text{KGen}(msk, x_\iota)$. | **Rtrn** $sk_\iota \leftarrow \text{KGen}'(msk, x_\iota)$.
  - $\mathfrak{Sign}(\iota \in [1, q_r], m, \phi)$: **Rtrn** $\bot$ if $0 \leftarrow \phi(x_\iota)$. | - $\mathfrak{Sign}(\iota \in [1, q_r], m, \phi)$: **Rtrn** $\bot$ if $0 \leftarrow \phi(x_\iota)$.
    Rtrn $\sigma \leftarrow \text{Sig}(sk_\iota, m, \phi)$. | **Rtrn** $\sigma \leftarrow \text{Sig}'(msk', m, \phi)$.

Fig. 7. Top: Experiment for (adaptive) existential unforgeability w.r.t. an ABS scheme Σ_{ABS}. Bottom: Experiments for perfect privacy w.r.t. an ABS scheme Σ_{ABS}.

Definition 8. Σ_{ABS} *is existentially unforgeable, if* $\forall \lambda \in \mathbb{N}$, $L \in \mathbb{N}$, $\forall \mathcal{A} \in \text{PPT}_\lambda$, $\exists \epsilon \in \text{NGL}_\lambda$, $Adv^{EUF\text{-}CMA}_{\Sigma_{\text{ABS}}, \mathcal{A}, L}(\lambda) := \Pr[1 \leftarrow \boldsymbol{Expt}^{EUF\text{-}CMA}_{\Sigma_{\text{ABS}}, \mathcal{A}}(1^\lambda, L)] < \epsilon$.

Definition 9. Σ_{ABS} *is perfectly private, if for every* $\lambda, L \in \mathbb{N}$ *and every probabilistic algorithm* $\mathcal{A}$, *there exist probabilistic polynomial time algorithms* {Setup′, KGen′, Sig′} *s.t.* $Adv^{PP}_{\Sigma_{ABS},\mathcal{A},L}(\lambda) := |\sum_{b=0}^{1}(-1)^b \Pr[1 \leftarrow Expt^{PP}_{\Sigma_{ABS},\mathcal{A},b}(1^\lambda, L)]| = 0.$

References

1. Abdalla, M., Catalano, D., Dent, A.W., Malone-Lee, J., Neven, G., Smart, N.P.: Identity-based encryption gone wild. In: Bugliesi, M., Preneel, B., Sassone, V., Wegener, I. (eds.) ICALP 2006. LNCS, vol. 4052, pp. 300–311. Springer, Heidelberg (2006). https://doi.org/10.1007/11787006_26

2. Anderson, R.: Two remarks on public key cryptology (1997). http://www.cl.cam.ac.uk/users/rja14

3. Bellare, M., Miner, S.K.: A forward-secure digital signature scheme. In: Wiener, M. (ed.) CRYPTO 1999. LNCS, vol. 1666, pp. 431–448. Springer, Heidelberg (1999). https://doi.org/10.1007/3-540-48405-1_28

4. Bethencourt, J., Sahai, A., Waters, B.: Ciphertext-policy attribute-based encryption. In: 2007 IEEE Symposium on Security and Privacy (SP 2007), pp. 321–334. IEEE (2007)

5. Birkett, J., Dent, A.W., Neven, G., Schuldt, J.C.N.: Efficient chosen-ciphertext secure identity-based encryption with wildcards. In: Pieprzyk, J., Ghodosi, H., Dawson, E. (eds.) ACISP 2007. LNCS, vol. 4586, pp. 274–292. Springer, Heidelberg (2007). https://doi.org/10.1007/978-3-540-73458-1_21

6. Blömer, J., Eidens, F., Juhnke, J.: Enhanced security of attribute-based signatures. In: Camenisch, J., Papadimitratos, P. (eds.) CANS 2018. LNCS, vol. 11124, pp. 235–255. Springer, Cham (2018). https://doi.org/10.1007/978-3-030-00434-7_12

7. Boneh, D., Boyen, X., Goh, E.-J.: Hierarchical identity based encryption with constant size ciphertext. In: Cramer, R. (ed.) EUROCRYPT 2005. LNCS, vol. 3494, pp. 440–456. Springer, Heidelberg (2005). https://doi.org/10.1007/11426639_26

8. Boneh, D., Sahai, A., Waters, B.: Functional encryption: definitions and challenges. In: Ishai, Y. (ed.) TCC 2011. LNCS, vol. 6597, pp. 253–273. Springer, Heidelberg (2011). https://doi.org/10.1007/978-3-642-19571-6_16

9. Canetti, R., Halevi, S., Katz, J.: A forward-secure public-key encryption scheme. In: Biham, E. (ed.) EUROCRYPT 2003. LNCS, vol. 2656, pp. 255–271. Springer, Heidelberg (2003). https://doi.org/10.1007/3-540-39200-9_16

10. Chatterjee, S., Sarkar, P.: Practical hybrid (hierarchical) identity-based encryption schemes based on the decisional bilinear diffie-hellman assumption. Int. J. Appl. Cryptography (IJACT) **3**(1), 47–83 (2013)

11. Fiat, A., Naor, M.: Broadcast encryption. In: Stinson, D.R. (ed.) CRYPTO 1993. LNCS, vol. 773, pp. 480–491. Springer, Heidelberg (1994). https://doi.org/10.1007/3-540-48329-2_40

12. Groth, J., Sahai, A.: Efficient non-interactive proof systems for bilinear groups. In: Smart, N. (ed.) EUROCRYPT 2008. LNCS, vol. 4965, pp. 415–432. Springer, Heidelberg (2008). https://doi.org/10.1007/978-3-540-78967-3_24

13. Ishizaka, M., Kiyomoto, S.: Time-specific encryption with constant size secret-keys secure under standard assumption. Cryptology ePrint Archive: Report 2020/595 (2020)

14. Kasamatsu, K., Matsuda, T., Emura, K., Attrapadung, N., Hanaoka, G., Imai, H.: Time-specific encryption from forward-secure encryption. In: Visconti, I., De Prisco, R. (eds.) SCN 2012. LNCS, vol. 7485, pp. 184–204. Springer, Heidelberg (2010). https://doi.org/10.1007/978-3-642-32928-9_11

15. Kiltz, E., Pan, J., Wee, H.: Structure-preserving signatures from standard assumptions, revisited. In: Gennaro, R., Robshaw, M. (eds.) CRYPTO 2015. LNCS, vol. 9216, pp. 275–295. Springer, Heidelberg (2015). https://doi.org/10.1007/978-3-662-48000-7_14

16. Maji, H.K., Prabhakaran, M., Rosulek, M.: Attribute-based signatures. In: Kiayias, A. (ed.) CT-RSA 2011. LNCS, vol. 6558, pp. 376–392. Springer, Heidelberg (2011). https://doi.org/10.1007/978-3-642-19074-2_24

17. Paterson, K.G., Quaglia, E.A.: Time-specific encryption. In: Garay, J.A., De Prisco, R. (eds.) SCN 2010. LNCS, vol. 6280, pp. 1–16. Springer, Heidelberg (2010). https://doi.org/10.1007/978-3-642-15317-4_1

18. Sakai, Y., Attrapadung, N., Hanaoka, G.: Attribute-based signatures for circuits from bilinear map. In: Cheng, C.-M., Chung, K.-M., Persiano, G., Yang, B.-Y. (eds.) PKC 2016. LNCS, vol. 9614, pp. 283–300. Springer, Heidelberg (2016). https://doi.org/10.1007/978-3-662-49384-7_11

19. Shamir, A.: Identity-based cryptosystems and signature schemes. In: Blakley, G.R., Chaum, D. (eds.) CRYPTO 1984. LNCS, vol. 196, pp. 47–53. Springer, Heidelberg (1985). https://doi.org/10.1007/3-540-39568-7_5

20. Waters, B.: Efficient identity-based encryption without random oracles. In: Cramer, R. (ed.) EUROCRYPT 2005. LNCS, vol. 3494, pp. 114–127. Springer, Heidelberg (2005). https://doi.org/10.1007/11426639_7

Compatible Certificateless and Identity-Based Cryptosystems for Heterogeneous IoT

Rouzbeh Behnia[1]([envelope]), Attila Altay Yavuz[1], Muslum Ozgur Ozmen[2], and Tsz Hon Yuen[3]

[1] University of South Florida, Tampa, FL, USA
{behnia,attilaayavuz}@usf.edu
[2] Purdue University, West Lafayette, IN, USA
mozmen@purdue.edu
[3] The University of Hong Kong, Pokfulam, Hong Kong
thyuen@cs.hku.hk

Abstract. Certificates ensure the authenticity of users' public keys, however their overhead (e.g., certificate chains) might be too costly for some IoT systems like aerial drones. Certificate-free cryptosystems, like identity-based and certificateless systems, lift the burden of certificates and could be a suitable alternative for such IoTs. However, despite their merits, there is a research gap in achieving compatible identity-based and certificateless systems to allow users from different domains (identity-based or certificateless) to communicate seamlessly. Moreover, more efficient constructions can enable their adoption in resource-limited IoTs.

In this work, we propose new identity-based and certificateless cryptosystems that provide such compatibility and efficiency. This feature is beneficial for heterogeneous IoT settings (e.g., commercial aerial drones), where different levels of trust/control is assumed on the trusted third party. Our schemes are more communication efficient than their public key based counterparts, as they do not need certificate processing. Our experimental analysis on both commodity and embedded IoT devices show that, only with the cost of having a larger system public key, our cryptosystems are more computation and communication efficient than their certificate-free counterparts. We prove the security of our schemes (in the random oracle model) and open-source our cryptographic framework for public testing/adoption.

Keywords: Identity-based cryptography · Certificateless cryptography · IoT systems · Lightweight cryptography

1 Introduction

Mobile and heterogeneous IoT applications harbor large quantities of resource-limited and non-stationary IoT devices, each with different capabilities, con-

---

M. O. Ozmen—Work done in part when Muslum Ozgur Ozmen was at the University of South Florida.

W. Susilo et al. (Eds.): ISC 2020, LNCS 12472, pp. 39–58, 2020.
https://doi.org/10.1007/978-3-030-62974-8_3

figurations, and user domains. For instance, emerging commercial aerial drone network protocols[1] need a near real-time communication and processing over a bandwidth-limited network. There are multiple hurdles of relying on traditional PKI for such systems: (i) The maintenance of PKI for such IoT networks demands a substantial infrastructure investment [25]. (ii) PKI requires transmission and verification of certificate chains at the sender's/verifier's side. This communication and computation overhead could create a major bottleneck for mobile IoT devices (e.g., aerial drones [21]) that potentially need to interact with a number of devices. In certain cases, these certificate chains might be larger than the actual measurements/commands being transmitted and therefore, might be the dominating cost for these applications. Figure 1-a depicts a high-level illustration of traditional PKI for mobile IoT applications.

Identity-based (IDB) and certificateless (CL) cryptosystems offer implicit certification [1,9,25], and therefore can mitigate the aforementioned hurdles. In IDB, the user's public key is derived from their identifying information, and the system relies on a fully-trusted third party (TTP), called the private key generator (PKG), to issue users' private keys. The top portion of Fig. 1-b depicts IDB encryption, wherein the user authenticates itself to the PKG and receives a private key corresponding to its identity D_1. The sender can use D_1 as the public key to run encryption. IDB is potentially suitable for applications where the system setup is done and managed by a trusted centralized entity. In CL systems [1] the trust on the TTP is lowered by allowing the private key of the user to consist of two parts. One is computed by the user and the other is by the TTP (called the KGC). The bottom portion of Fig. 1-b outlines CL encryption, where the user computes its key pair and then works as in IDB to receive the other part of the private key from the KGC. CL cryptosystems are suitable for architectures that might not assume a fully trusted third party where the trust level on the KGC is similar to traditional certification authorities.

IDB and CL cryptosystems have their own merits and drawbacks, and therefore might be used in different IoT applications. Hence, it is expected that there will be different user groups who rely on IDB and CL cryptosystems initiated in different domains/systems. For example, Amazon's Prime Air[2] would require drones, under the complete control of Amazon, to interact with other drones (e.g., personal) to ensure safe operation. By employing IDB cryptography on its drones, Amazon can have complete control over the operations of its delivery drones while avoiding the overheads of traditional PKI. However, it is a strong assumption that other drones, outside Amazon's network, will adopt a similar cryptographic setting to ensure safe and secure operations. For instance, personal users rarely trust any third party to have complete control and knowledge of their drones' activity. To the best of our knowledge, there is a significant research gap in enabling a seamless communication between users who are registered under different domains (e.g., IDB and CL). This is a potential obstacle to widely deploy efficient certificate-free solutions in heterogeneous environments.

---

[1] https://github.com/mavlink/mavlink.
[2] https://www.amazon.com/Amazon-Prime-Air/b?ie=UTF8&node=8037720011.

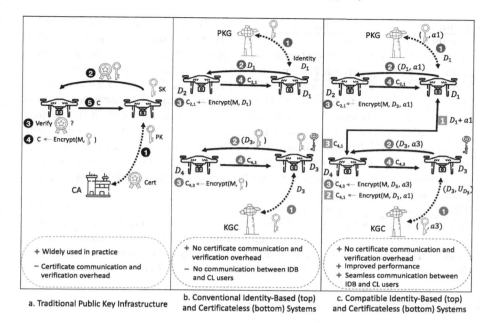

Fig. 1. Proposed IDB and CL cryptosystems and alternatives (high-level)

This limitation is mentioned in Fig. 1-b. Moreover, it is important to further improve the computational efficiency of IDB and CL techniques to offer a low end-to-end delay that is needed by delay-aware IoT applications.

Our Contribution. We propose a new series of public key encryption, digital signature, and key exchange schemes that permit users from different domains (IDB or CL) to communicate seamlessly. To our knowledge, this is the first set of certificate-free cryptosystems that achieve such compatibility and efficiency, and therefore a suitable alternative for resource-limited IoT systems such as commercial aerial drones. The idea behind our constructions is to create special key generation algorithms that harness the additive homomorphic property of the exponents and cover-free functions to enable the users to incorporate their private keys into the one provided by the TTP without falsifying it. As detailed in Sect. 4, this special design is applicable across our IDB and CL algorithms, and therefore it permits a seamless communication between our IDB and CL cryptosystems. This strategy also reduces the cost of online operations and enables our schemes to achieve a lower end-to-end delay compared to their counterparts. We elaborate on some desirable properties of our schemes as below.

- Compatible IDB and CL Schemes: Figure 1.c outlines the concept of *compatible* IDB and CL schemes where the users from different domains (and trust-levels) can use identical encryption, signature, and key exchange algorithms to communicate without any additional overhead.

- **Computation & Communication Efficiency:** Based on our analysis, new schemes offer performance advantages over their counterparts: (i) Similar to other IDB/CL cryptosystems, our schemes lift the hurdle of certificate transmission and verification, and therefore offer significant communication efficiency over some of the most efficient PKI-based schemes. This advantage grows proportional to the size of the certificate chain. (ii) Our schemes outperform their certificate-free counterparts on the vast majority of the performance metrics. For instance, the end-to-end delay in our IDB/CL encryption schemes is ≈25% lower than our most efficient counterpart in [29]. Our signature schemes achieve up to %52 faster end-to-end delay as compared to our counterparts. We also achieve a 65% lower end-to-end delay for our key exchange schemes.
- **Open-Sourced Implementation:** We implemented our schemes on a commodity hardware and an 8-bit AVR microprocessor, and compared their performance with a variety of their counterparts capturing some of the most efficient traditional PKI, IDB and CL schemes (see Sect. 6 for details). We open-source our implementations for broad testing, benchmarking, and adoption purposes.

2 Preliminaries

Notation. Given two primes p and q, we define a finite field $\mathbb{F}_p$ and a group $\mathbb{Z}_q$. We work on $E(\mathbb{F}_p)$ as an elliptic curve (EC) over $\mathbb{F}_p$, where $P \in E(\mathbb{F}_p)$ is the generator of the points on the curve. We denote a scalar and a point on a curve with small and capital letters, respectively. $x \xleftarrow{\$} S$ denotes a random uniform selection of x from a set S. We define the bit-length of a variable as $|x|$ (i.e., $|x| = \log_2 x$). EC scalar multiplication is denoted as xP, and all EC operations use an additive notation. Hash functions are $H_1 \colon E(\mathbb{F}_p) \times E(\mathbb{F}_p) \to \{0,1\}^\gamma$, $H_2 \colon \{0,1\}^n \times \{0,1\}^* \to \mathbb{Z}_q, H_3 \colon E(\mathbb{F}_p) \to \{0,1\}^n$ $H_4 \colon \{0,1\}^n \to \{0,1\}^n$ and $H_5 \colon \{0,1\}^n \times E(\mathbb{F}_p) \to \mathbb{Z}_q$, where all hash functions are random oracles [6]. FourQ [12] is a special EC that is defined by the complete twisted Edwards equation $\mathcal{E}/F_{p^2} \colon -x^2 + y^2 = 1 + dx^2 y^2$. FourQ is known to be one of the fastest elliptic curves that admits 128-bit security level [12]. Moreover, with extended twisted Edwards coordinates, FourQ offers the fastest EC addition algorithms [12], that is extensively used in our optimizations. All of our schemes are realized on FourQ.

Definitions. We first give our intractability assumptions followed by the definitions of identity-based and certificateless encryption and signature schemes.

Definition 1. *Given points $P, Q \in E(\mathbb{F}_p)$, the Elliptic Curve Discrete Logarithm Problem (ECDLP) asks to find a, if it exists, such that $aP(\bmod p) = Q$.*

Definition 2. *Given $P, aP, bP \in E(\mathbb{F}_p)$, the Computational Diffie-Hellman (CDH) problem asks to compute abP.*

Definition 3. *An identity-based encryption scheme is consisted of four algorithms* IBE = {Setup, Extract, Enc, Dec}.

$(msk, params) \leftarrow$ IBE.Setup(1^κ): *Given the security parameter* κ, *the PKG selects master secret key* msk, *computes master public key* mpk *and system parameters* $params$ *(an implicit input to all the following algorithms).*

$(sk_{ID}, Q_{ID}) \leftarrow$ IBE.Extract(ID, msk): *Given an identity* ID *and* msk, *the PKG computes the commitment value* Q_{ID} *and the private key* sk_{ID}.

$c \leftarrow$ IBE.Enc(m, ID, Q_{ID}): *Given a message* m *and* (ID, Q_{ID}), *the sender computes the ciphertext* c.

$m \leftarrow$ IBE.Dec(sk_{ID}, c): *Given the ciphertext* c *and the private key of the receiver* sk_{ID}, *the receiver returns either the corresponding plaintext* m *or* $\perp$ *(invalid).*

Definition 4. *An identity-based signature scheme is defined by four algorithms* IBS $= \{$Setup, Extract, Sig, Ver$\}$.

$(msk, mpk, params) \leftarrow$ IBS.Setup(1^κ): *As in* IBE.Setup *in Definition 3.*

$(sk_{ID}, Q_{ID}) \leftarrow$ IBS.Extract(ID, msk): *As in* IBE.Extract *in Definition 3.*

$\sigma \leftarrow$ IBS.Sign(m, sk_{ID}): *Given a message* m *and* sk_{ID}, *returns a signature* σ.

$d \leftarrow$ IBS.Verify(m, ID, Q_{ID}, σ): *Given* m, σ *and* (ID, Q_{ID}) *as input, if the signature is valid, it returns* $d = 1$, *else* $d = 0$.

Definition 5. *A certificateless encryption scheme is defined by six algorithms* CLE $= \{$KGCSetup, UserSetup, PartKeyGen, UserKeyGen, Enc, Dec$\}$.

$(msk, mpk, params) \leftarrow$ CLE.KGCSetup(1^κ): *Give the security parameter* κ, *the KGC generates master secret key* msk, *master public key* mpk *and the system parameters* $params$ *(an implicit input to all the following algorithms).*

$(\alpha, U) \leftarrow$ CLE.UserSetup$(\cdot)$: *The user* ID *computes her secret value* α *and its corresponding commitment* U.

$(w, Q_{ID}) \leftarrow$ CLE.PartKeyGen(ID, U, msk): *Given* ID, U, *and* msk, *the KGC computes partial private key* w *and its corresponding public commitment* Q_{ID}.

$x_{ID} \leftarrow$ CLE.UserKeyGen(w, α): *Given* (w, α), *the user* ID *computes* x_{ID}.

$c \leftarrow$ CLE.Enc(m, ID, Q_{ID}): *Given* (m, ID, Q_{ID}), *sender computes ciphertext* c.

$m' \leftarrow$ CLE.Dec(x_{ID}, c): *Given the ciphertext* c *and the private key of the receiver* x_{ID}, *the receiver returns either corresponding plaintext* m *or* $\perp$ *(invalid).*

Definition 6. *A certificateless signature scheme is defined by six algorithms* CLS $= \{$KGCSetup, UserSetup, PartKeyGen, UserKeyGen, Sig, Ver$\}$. *The definition of algorithms are as in Definition 5 except for* (CLS.Sig, CLS.Ver).

$\sigma \leftarrow$ CLS.Sig(m, x_{ID}): Given a message m, and the signer's private key x_{ID}, it returns a signature σ.

$d \leftarrow$ CLS.Ver(m, ID, Q_{ID}, σ): Given m, σ and (ID, Q_{ID}) as input, if the signature is valid, it returns $d = 1$, else $d = 0$.

3 Security Model

The security model of identity-based schemes is slightly stronger than those for traditional PKI based schemes. More specifically, the adversary can query for the private key of any user ID, except for the target user ID^*. In this paper, we constructed our schemes by following the security model of Identity-based systems proposed in [9]. In certificateless systems, the private key of the users consists of two parts: (i) user secret key α, which is selected by the user, and

(ii) partial private key w, which is supplied to the user by the KGC. Therefore, following [1], it is natural to consider two types of adversaries for such systems.

A Type-I adversary $\mathcal{A}_I$ does not have access to msk or the user's partial private key w but is able to replace any user's public key U with public key of its choice U'. However, in our security model, since we adopt the binding method [1], replacing the public key will result in falsifying the partial private key (and evidently the private key). Therefore, following [2], we allow $\mathcal{A}_I$ to query for the secret key of the user via $\alpha \leftarrow \mathcal{O}_{\mathtt{SecKey}}(ID)$. Note that our model can also be extended to allow $\mathcal{A}_I$ to replace the public key of the user (see Sect. 5). A Type-II adversary $\mathcal{A}_{II}$ is assumed to be a malicious KGC. Having knowledge on msk, $\mathcal{A}_{II}$ can query the partial private key of the user via $w \leftarrow \mathcal{O}_{\mathtt{PartKey}}(ID)$. Following [1], we allow the adversary $\mathcal{A} \in \{\mathcal{A}_I, \mathcal{A}_{II}\}$ to extract private key of users' private keys via the $x_{ID} \leftarrow \mathcal{O}_{\mathtt{Corrupt}}(ID)$. We note that inspired by [3], many improvements on the security models of certificateless systems have been suggested (e.g., [2,3,17]). In this paper, we provide our proof in the original model proposed in [1,3], but note that many of those stronger security requirements can be enforced if needed.

Definition 7. *The indistinguishability of a* CLE *under chosen ciphertext attack (IND-CLE-CCA) experiment* $Expt_{\mathcal{A}}^{IND\text{-}CLE\text{-}CCA}$ *is defined as follows.*

- $\mathcal{C}$ runs CLE.KGCSetup(1^κ) and returns mpk and $params$ to $\mathcal{A}$.
- $(ID^*, m_0, m_1) \leftarrow \mathcal{A}^{\mathcal{O}_{\mathtt{PartKey}}, \mathcal{O}_{\mathtt{SecKey}}, \mathcal{O}_{\mathtt{Corrupt}}, \mathcal{O}_{\mathtt{Dec}}}(mpk, params)$
- $\mathcal{C}$ picks $b \xleftarrow{\$} \{0,1\}$, $c_b \leftarrow$ CLE.Enc($m_b, ID^*, params$) and returns c_b to $\mathcal{A}$.
- $\mathcal{A}$ performs the second series of queries, with a restriction of querying ID^* or c_b to Corrupt($\cdot$) or CLE.Dec($\cdot$), respectively. Finally, $\mathcal{A}$ outputs a bit b'.

$\mathcal{A}$ wins the above experiment if $b = b'$ and the following conditions hold: (i) ID^* was never submitted to $\mathcal{O}_{\mathtt{Corrupt}}$. (ii) If $\mathcal{A} = \mathcal{A}_I$, ID^* was never submitted to $\mathcal{O}_{\mathtt{PartKey}}$. (iii) If $\mathcal{A} = \mathcal{A}_{II}$, ID^* was never submitted to $\mathcal{O}_{\mathtt{SecKey}}$. The IND-CLE-CCA advantage of $\mathcal{A}$ is $\Pr[b = b'] \leq \frac{1}{2} + \epsilon$, for a negligible ϵ.

Definition 8. *The existential unforgeability under chosen message attack (EU-CLS-CMA) experiment* $Expt_{\mathcal{A}}^{EU\text{-}CLS\text{-}CMA}$ *for a certificateless signature* CLS *is defined as follows.*

- $\mathcal{C}$ runs CLS.KGCSetup(1^κ) and returns mpk and $params$ to $\mathcal{A}$.
- $(ID^*, m^*, \sigma^*) \leftarrow \mathcal{A}^{\mathcal{O}_{\mathtt{PartKey}}, \mathcal{O}_{\mathtt{SecKey}}, \mathcal{O}_{\mathtt{Corrupt}}, \mathcal{O}_{\mathtt{Sign}}}(mpk, params)$

$\mathcal{A}$ wins the above experiment if $1 \leftarrow$ CLS.Ver(m^*, σ^*, ID), and the following conditions hold: (i) ID^* was never submitted to $\mathcal{O}_{\mathtt{Corrupt}}$. (ii) If $\mathcal{A} = \mathcal{A}_I$, ID^* was never submitted to $\mathcal{O}_{\mathtt{PartKey}}$. (iii) If $\mathcal{A} = \mathcal{A}_{II}$, ID^* was never submitted to $\mathcal{O}_{\mathtt{SecKey}}$. The EU-CLS-CMA advantage of $\mathcal{A}$ is $\Pr[Expt_{\mathcal{A}}^{EU\text{-}CLS\text{-}CMA} = 1]$

4 Proposed Schemes

4.1 Proposed Identity-Based Cryptosystem

Most of pairing-free IDB schemes rely on the classical signatures (e.g., [24]) in their key generation to provide implicit certification. The use of such signatures

---

Algorithm 1. Identity-Based Encryption

$(msk, params) \leftarrow$ IBE.Setup(1^κ):
1: Select primes p and q and $(t, k) \in \mathbb{N}$ where $t >> k$.
2: **for** $i = 1, \ldots, t$ **do**
3: $\quad v_i \xleftarrow{\$} \mathbb{Z}_q$, $V_i \leftarrow v_i P \bmod p$
4: **return** $msk \leftarrow (v_1, \ldots, v_t)$, $mpk \leftarrow (V_1, \ldots, V_t)$ and $params \leftarrow (\text{H}_1, \text{H}_2, \text{H}_3, \text{H}_4, p, q, k, t, mpk)$

$(w, Q) \leftarrow$ IBE.Extract(ID, U, msk):
1: $\beta \xleftarrow{\$} \mathbb{Z}_q$, $Q \leftarrow \beta P \bmod p$
2: $(j_1, \ldots, j_k) \leftarrow \text{H}_1(ID, Q)$ where for all $i = 1, \ldots, t$, $1 < j_i < |t|$
3: $y \leftarrow \sum_{i=1}^k v_{j_i} \bmod q$
4: $x \leftarrow y + \beta \bmod q$
5: **return** (x, Q)

$c \leftarrow$ IBE.Enc(m, ID_a, Q_a):   Bob encrypts message $m \in \{0, 1\}^n$.

1: $\sigma \xleftarrow{\$} \{0, 1\}^n$, $r \leftarrow \text{H}_2(\sigma, m)$, $R \leftarrow rP \bmod p$
2: $(j_1, \ldots, j_k) \leftarrow \text{H}_1(ID_a, Q_a)$, $Y_a \leftarrow \sum_{i=1}^k V_{j_i} \bmod p$
3: $u \leftarrow \text{H}_3(r(Y_a + Q_a) \bmod p) \oplus \sigma$, $v \leftarrow \text{H}_4(\sigma) \oplus m$
4: **return** $c = (R, u, v)$

$m \leftarrow$ IBE.Dec(x_a, c):   Alice decrypts the ciphertext c.

1: $\sigma' \leftarrow \text{H}_3(x_a R \bmod p) \oplus u$
2: $m' \leftarrow v \oplus \text{H}_4(\sigma')$, $r' \leftarrow \text{H}_2(\sigma', m)$
3: **if** $r'P \pmod p = R$ **then** **return** m'
4: **else return** $\bot$

---

to construct IDB schemes usually require several expensive operations (e.g., scalar multiplication), and therefore may incur a non-negligible computation overhead. To reduce this cost, we exploit the message encoding technique and subset resilient functions (similar to [23]) along with the exponent product of powers property to generate keys. This permits an improved efficiency for both the PKG and user since it only requires a hash call and a few point additions.

Our IDB schemes use similar IBE.Setup and IBE.Extract functions whose key steps are outlined as follows. In the IBE.Setup, the PKG selects t values $v_i \leftarrow \mathbb{Z}_q$, and computes their commitments as $V_i \leftarrow v_i P \bmod p$, for $i = 1, \ldots, t$, it then sets the master secret key $msk \leftarrow (v_1, \ldots, v_t)$ and the system-wide public key $mpk \leftarrow (V_1, \ldots, V_t)$. This is similar to the scheme in [23], where EC scalar multiplication is used as the one-way function. In IBE.Extract, the PKG picks a nonce $\beta \leftarrow \mathbb{Z}_q$ and computes its commitments $Q \leftarrow \beta P \bmod p$. The PKG then derives indexes $(j_1, \ldots, j_k) \leftarrow \text{H}_1(ID, Q)$, which select k-out-of-t elements from the master secret key v_{j_i} for $i = 1, \ldots, k$. Note that Q is implicitly authenticated by being included in input of $\text{H}_1(\cdot)$, this is similar to the technique used in other pairing-free identity-based and certificateless systems [3,15]. In Steps 3–4, unlike the scheme in [23], where secret keys are exposed, we use the additive homomorphic property in the exponent to mask the one-time signature y (Step 3) via the nonce β (in line with [4,5]). The PKG will then sends (x, Q) to the user via a secure channel.

Identity-Based Encryption Scheme: In IBE.Enc (Algorithm 1, Step 2), the indexes obtained from H_1 are used to retrieve the components V_{j_i} from the system-wide public key mpk. The input of H_3 is the ephemeral key, which given the ciphertext $c = (R, u, v)$, can be recomputed by the receiver in the IBE.Dec algorithm. σ and r are computed in-line with the transformation proposed in [14].

Algorithm 2. Identity-Based Signature

$(msk, params) \leftarrow$ IBS.Setup (1^κ): Description identical to IBE.Setup in Algorithm 1, except that only the description of H_1 and H_5 is included in $params$.	1: $r \xleftarrow{\$} \mathbb{Z}_q$, $R \leftarrow rP \bmod p$ 2: $e \leftarrow H_5(m, R)$ 3: $s \leftarrow r - e \cdot x_a \bmod q$ 4: **return** (s, e)

$(w, Q) \leftarrow$ IBS.Extract(ID, U, msk):   As in IBE.Extract in Algorithm 1.

$(s, e) \leftarrow$ IBS.Sign(m, x_a):   Alice ID_a signs message m.

$\{0,1\} \leftarrow$ IBS.Verify$(m, ID_a, Q_a, \langle s, e \rangle)$:   Bob verifies the signature (s, e).   1: $(j_1, \ldots, j_k) \leftarrow H_1(ID_a, Q_a)$ 2: $Y_a \leftarrow \sum_{i=1}^{k} V_{j_i} \bmod p$ 3: $R' \leftarrow sP + e(Y_a + Q_a) \bmod p$ 4: **if** $e = H_5(m, R')$ **then return** 1   5: **else return** 0

Identity-Based Signature Scheme: In IBS.Verify, the public key of the user Y_a is computed from $V_{j_i} \in mpk$ via the indexes retrieved from the output of H_1. The key generation is as in Algorithm 1. The rest of the signing and verification steps are akin to Schnorr signatures [24].

Identity-Based Key Exchange Scheme: For the key exchange scheme, we run IBE.Setup and then let both parties, Alice and Bob, obtain (x_A, Q_A) and (x_B, Q_B) via the IBE.Extract algorithm, respectively. Alice then picks $z_A \xleftarrow{\$} \mathbb{Z}_q$, computes its commitment $M_A \leftarrow z_A P \bmod p$, and sends (M_A, Q_A) to Bob. Bob does the same and sends (M_B, Q_B) to Alice. Alice then computes $(j_1, \ldots, j_k) \leftarrow H_1(ID_b, Q_b)$ and $Y_b \leftarrow \sum_{i=1}^{k} V_{j_i} \bmod p$ and outputs the shared secret key as $K_a \leftarrow x_a(Y_b + Q_b) + z_a M_b \bmod p$. Bob works similarly, and outputs the shared key as $K_b \leftarrow x_b(Y_a + Q_a) + z_b M_a \bmod p$.

4.2   Proposed Certificateless Cryptosystem

For our CL schemes to achieve the same trust level (Level 3) [16] on the third party (KGC), as in traditional PKI, we use the binding method [1] in the CLE.PartKeyGen and CLS.PartKeyGen algorithms. Note that the same secure channel which is used for user authentication (e.g., SSL/TLS), can be used to send the user commitment U to the KGC. This permits an implicit certification of U, and therefore any changes of U, will falsify the private key.

The CLE.KGCSetup algorithm is as in IBE.Setup in Algorithm 1. The CLE.PartKeyGen algorithm is similar to the IBE.Extract in Algorithm 1, with the difference that the user commitment U is used to compute Q. In CLE.UserKeyGen, the correctness of the partial private key is checked first before the private key x is computed.

Certificateless Encryption Scheme: Note that the CLE.Enc and CLE.Dec algorithms are identical to IBE.Enc and IBE.Dec algorithms in Algorithm 1.

Certificateless Signature Scheme: The setup and key generation algorithms are as in Algorithm 3, and the CLS.Sign and CLS.Verify algorithms are as in IBS.Sign and IBS.Verify in Algorithm 2, respectively.

Algorithm 3. Certificateless Encryption

$(msk, params) \leftarrow$ CLE.KGCSetup(1^κ):
As in IBE.Setup in Alg. 1.

$(\alpha, U) \leftarrow$ CLE.UserSetup($\cdot$):

1: $\alpha \xleftarrow{\$} \mathbb{Z}_q, U \leftarrow \alpha P \bmod p$
2: **return** (α, U)

$(w, Q) \leftarrow$ CLE.PartKeyGen(ID, U, msk):

1: $\beta \xleftarrow{\$} \mathbb{Z}_q, W \leftarrow \beta P \bmod p$
2: $Q = U + W \bmod p$
3: $(j_1, \ldots, j_k) \leftarrow$ H$_1(ID, Q)$ where for all $i = 1, \ldots, t, \ 1 < j_i < |t|$
4: $y \leftarrow \sum_{i=1}^{k} v_{j_i} \bmod q$
5: $w \leftarrow y + \beta \bmod q$
6: **return** (w, Q)

$x \leftarrow$ CLE.UserKeyGen(w, α):

1: $(j_1, \ldots, j_k) \leftarrow$ H$_1(ID, Q), \ Y \leftarrow \sum_{i=1}^{k} V_{j_i} \bmod p$
2: $W' \leftarrow Q - U \bmod p, W'' := wP - Y \bmod p$

3: **if** $W' = W''$ **then return** $x \leftarrow w + \alpha \bmod q$ **else return** $\perp$

$c \leftarrow$ CLE.Enc(m, ID_a, Q_a): Bob encrypts message $m \in \{0, 1\}^n$.

1: $\sigma \xleftarrow{\$} \{0, 1\}^n, \ r \leftarrow$ H$_2(\sigma, m), R \leftarrow rP \bmod p$
2: $(j_1, \ldots, j_k) \leftarrow$ H$_1(ID_a, Q_a), \ Y_a \leftarrow \sum_{i=1}^{k} V_{j_i} \bmod p$
3: $u \leftarrow$ H$_3(r(Y_a + Q_a) \bmod p) \oplus \sigma$, $v \leftarrow$ H$_4(\sigma) \oplus m$
4: **return** $c = (R, u, v)$

$m \leftarrow$ CLE.Dec(x_a, c): Alice decrypts the ciphertext c.

1: $\sigma' \leftarrow$ H$_3(x_a R \bmod p) \oplus u$
2: $m' \leftarrow v \oplus$ H$_4(\sigma'), r' \leftarrow$ H$_2(\sigma', m)$
3: **if** $r'P \ (\bmod \ p) = R$ **then return** m'
4: **else return** $\perp$

Algorithm 4. Certificateless Digital Signature

$(msk, params) \leftarrow$ CLS.KGCSetup(1^κ):
As in CLE.KGCSetup in Alg. 3, except that H$_1$ and H$_5$ are in *params*.

$(\alpha, U) \leftarrow$ CLS.UserSetup($params$):
As in CLE.UserSetup in Alg. 3.

$(w, Q) \leftarrow$ CLS.PartKeyGen(ID, U, msk):
As in CLE.PartKeyGen in Alg. 3.

$x \leftarrow$ CLS.UserKeyGen($params, \alpha, w$):
As in CLE.UserKeyGen in Alg. 3.

$(s, e) \leftarrow$ CLS.Sign(m, x_a): Alice ID_a signs message m.

1: $r \xleftarrow{\$} \mathbb{Z}_q, R \leftarrow rP \bmod p$
2: $e \leftarrow$ H$_5(m, R)$
3: $s \leftarrow r - e \cdot x_a \bmod q$
4: **return** (s, e)

$\{0, 1\} \leftarrow$ CLS.Verify($m, Q_a, \langle s, e \rangle$):
Bob verifies the signature (s, e).

1: $(j_1, \ldots, j_k) \leftarrow$ H$_1(ID_a, Q_a)$
2: $Y_a \leftarrow \sum_{i=1}^{k} V_{j_i} \bmod p$
3: $R' \leftarrow sP + e(Y_a + Q_a) \bmod p$
4: **if** $e =$ H$_5(m, R')$ **then return** 1
5: **else return** 0

Certificateless Key Exchange Scheme: Given the compatibility of our IDB and CL schemes, after the initial algorithms (system setup and key generation) take place as in Algorithm 3, the CL key exchange will be identical to the one proposed in the identity-based key exchange scheme above.

4.3 Compatibility of Identity-Based and Certificateless Schemes

In our CL schemes, we utilize the additive homomorphic property of the exponents (i.e., w) when the KGC includes the addition of commitments (W and

U) in the H_1. After receiving w, the user exploits the homomorphic property to modify the key without falsifying it and obtain x. For instance, we observed that our counterparts (e.g., [1,9]) do not offer such a compatibility, since the partial private key is the KGC's commitment to the (hash of) user identity, without a homomorphic property. Moreover, the KGC does not output any auxiliary value to incorporate the user commitment with it.

As shown above, our IDB and CL schemes are compatible, thanks to the special design of their key generation algorithms (i.e., `Extract` in IDB, `UserSetup` and `PartKeyGen` in CL). Therefore, after the users computed/obtained their keys from the third party, the interface of the main cryptographic functions (e.g., encrypt, decrypt, sign, etc.) are identical in both systems, therefore, the users can communicate with uses in different domains seamlessly. For instance, ciphertext $c = (R, u, v)$ outputted by the `CLE.Enc` in Algorithm 1, can be decrypted by a user in the identity-based setting by the `IBE.Dec` algorithm in Algorithm 1. This also applies to the signature and the key exchange schemes proposed above.

5   Security Analysis

Theorem 1. *If an adversary $\mathcal{A}_I$ can break the IND-CLE-CCA security of the encryption scheme proposed in Algorithm 3 after q_{H_i} queries to random oracles H_i for $i \in \{1, 2, 3, 4\}$, q_D queries to the decryption oracle and q_{sk} to the private key extraction oracle with probability ϵ. There exists another algorithm $\mathcal{C}$ that runs $\mathcal{A}_I$ as subroutine and breaks a random instance of the CDH problem (P, aP, bP) with probability ϵ' where: $\epsilon' > \frac{1}{q_{H_3}} \left(\frac{2\epsilon}{e(q_{sk}+1)} - \frac{q_{H_2}}{2^n} - \frac{q_D(q_{H_2}+1)}{2^n} - \frac{2q_D}{p} \right)$.*

Proof. Our proof technique is similar to the one in [3]. $\mathcal{C}$ *simulates* the real environment for $\mathcal{A}_I$. It knows the t secret values $v_i's$ in the scheme, and tries to embed a random instance of the CDH problem (P, aP, bP). $\mathcal{C}$ sets aP as a part of the target user's (ID^*) public key (i.e., $Q_{ID^*} \leftarrow aP$) and bP as a part of the challenge ciphertext (i.e., $R^* \leftarrow bP$). $\mathcal{C}$ uses four lists, namely List_{H_1}, List_{H_2}, List_{H_3}, and List_{H_4}, to keep track of the random oracle responses and following the IND-CLE-CCA experiment $Expt_{\mathcal{A}}^{IND\text{-}CLE\text{-}CCA}$ (Definition 7), $\mathcal{C}$ responds to $\mathcal{A}_I$ queries as follows.

Queries to $H_1(ID_i, Q_i)$: If the entry $(\langle ID_i, Q_i \rangle, h_{1,i})$ exists in List_{H_1}, $\mathcal{C}$ returns $h_{1,i}$, otherwise, it chooses $h_{1,i} \xleftarrow{\$} \gamma$, and inserts $(\langle ID_i, Q_i \rangle, h_{1,i})$ in List_{H_1}.

Queries to $H_2(\sigma_i, m_i)$: If the entry $(\langle \sigma_i, m_i \rangle, h_{2,i})$ exists in List_{H_2}, $\mathcal{C}$ returns $h_{2,i}$, otherwise, it chooses $h_{2,i} \xleftarrow{\$} \mathbb{Z}_q$, and inserts $(\langle \sigma_i, m_i \rangle, h_{2,i})$ in List_{H_2}.

Queries to $H_3(K_i)$: If the entry $(K_i, h_{3,i})$ exists in List_{H_3}, $\mathcal{C}$ returns $h_{3,i}$, otherwise, it chooses $h_{3,i} \xleftarrow{\$} \{0,1\}^n$, and inserts $(K_i, h_{3,i})$ in List_{H_3}.

Queries to $H_4(\sigma_i)$: If the entry $(\sigma_i, h_{4,i})$ exists in List_{H_4}, $\mathcal{C}$ returns $h_{4,i}$, otherwise, it chooses $h_{4,i} \xleftarrow{\$} \{0,1\}^n$, and inserts $(\sigma_i, h_{4,i})$ in List_{H_4}.

Public key request: Upon receiving a public key request on ID_i, $\mathcal{C}$ works as follows. If $(\langle ID_i, U_i, Q_i \rangle, \zeta_i)$ exists in List_{PK}, then it returns (ID_i, U_i, Q_i). Else, it flips a fair coin where $\Pr[\zeta = 0] = \delta$, and works as follows (δ will be determined later in the proof). If $\zeta = 0$, it runs the partial key extraction oracle below first, update List_{PK} and then output (ID_i, U_i, Q_i). If $\zeta = 1$, pick $t \xleftarrow{\$} \mathbb{Z}_q$, set $Q_i \leftarrow aP \mod p$, adds $(ID_i, U_i, \langle \perp, Q_i \rangle)$ to $\text{List}_{\text{PartialSK}}$ and adds $(\langle ID_i, U_i, Q_i \rangle, \zeta_i)$ to List_{PK}, before outputting (ID_i, U_i, Q_i).

Partial Key Extraction: Upon receiving a partial key extraction query on (ID_i, U_i), $\mathcal{C}$ works as follow:

- If $(ID_i, U_i, \langle w_i, Q_i \rangle) \in \text{List}_{\text{PartialSK}}$, return (w_i, Q_i).
- Else,
  - $w_i \xleftarrow{\$} \mathbb{Z}_q$, $Z_i \leftarrow w_i P \mod p$, $(j_1, \ldots, j_k) \xleftarrow{\$} [1, \ldots, t]$, $Q_i \leftarrow Z_i - \sum_{i=1}^{k} V_{j_i} + U_i \mod p$.
  - If $(ID_i, Q_i, \ldots) \in \text{List}_{\text{H}_1}$, aborts. Else, adds $(\langle ID_i, Q_i \rangle, h_{1,i})$ to List_{H_1}, where $h_{1,i} \leftarrow (j_1, \ldots, j_k)$ and output the partial private key as (w_i, U_i, Q_i) after adding it to $\text{List}_{\text{PartialSK}}$.

Secret Key Request: Upon receiving a secret key request on ID_i, $\mathcal{C}$ checks if there exists a pair $(ID_i, u_i, U_i) \in \text{List}_{\text{SecretKey}}$, it returns u_i. Otherwise, selects $u_i \xleftarrow{\$} \mathbb{Z}_q$, computes $U_i \leftarrow u_i P \mod p$ and inserts (ID_i, u_i, U_i) in $\text{List}_{\text{SecretKey}}$.

Private Key Request: To answer a private key request on (ID_i, U_i), $\mathcal{C}$ runs the public key request oracle above to get $(\langle ID_i, U_i, Q_i \rangle, \zeta_i) \in \text{List}_{PK}$ and finds (ID_i, u_i, U_i) in $\text{List}_{\text{SecretKey}}$. If $\zeta = 0$, finds $((ID_i, U_i, \langle w_i, Q_i \rangle) \in \text{List}_{\text{PartialSK}}$ and returns $w_i + u_i$ as the response. Otherwise, it aborts.

Decryption Query: Upon receiving a decryption query on $(ID_i, Q_i, c_i = \langle R_i, u_i, v_i \rangle)$, $\mathcal{C}$ works as follows.

- Searches List_{PK} for an entry $(\langle ID_i, U_i, Q_i \rangle, \zeta_i)$. If $\zeta = 0$, works as follows.
  - Searches $\text{List}_{\text{PartialSK}}$ for a tuple $(ID_i, U_i, \langle w_i, Q_i \rangle)$ and searches for $(ID, \langle w, Q \rangle)$ in $\text{List}_{\text{PartialSK}}$, set $\sigma' \leftarrow \text{H}_3((w + \alpha)R \mod p) \oplus u$, $m' = v \oplus \text{H}_4(\sigma')$, $r' := \text{H}_2(\sigma', m)$.
  - Checks if $R = r'P \mod p$ holds, outputs m'
- Else, if $\zeta = 1$, works as follows.
  - Runs the oracle for H_1 to get $h_{1,i}$ (to compute the public key Y_i) and checks lists List_{H_2}, List_{H_3} and List_{H_4} for tuples $(\langle \sigma_i, m_i \rangle, h_{2,i})$, $(K_i, h_{3,i})$, and $(\sigma_i, h_{4,i})$, such that $R_i = h_{2,i}P \mod p$, $u = h_{3,i} \oplus \sigma_i$ and $v = h_{4,i} \oplus m_i$ exists. Checks if $K_i = r_i(Y_i + Q_i)$ holds, outputs m_i, else, aborts.

After the first round of queries, $\mathcal{A}_I$ outputs ID^* and two messages m_0 and m_1 on which it wishes to be challenged on. We assume that ID^* has been already queried to H_1 and was not submitted to the *private key request oracle*. $\mathcal{C}$ checks $(\langle ID^*, U^*, Q^* \rangle, \zeta) \in \text{List}_{PK}$ if $\zeta = 0$, it aborts. Otherwise, it computes the challenge ciphertext as follows. $\beta^* \xleftarrow{\$} \{0, 1\}$, $\sigma^* \xleftarrow{\$} \{0, 1\}^*$, $u^* \leftarrow \{0, 1\}^n$, $b \xleftarrow{\$} \{0, 1\}$. $R^* \leftarrow aP$ (this implicitly implies that $a = \text{H}_2(\sigma^*, m_b)$), $\text{H}_3(K_{ID^*}) \leftarrow u^* \oplus \sigma^*$ and $v^* \leftarrow \text{H}_4(\sigma^*) \oplus m_b$. Return (R^*, u^*, v^*).

$\mathcal{A}_I$ initiates the second round of queries similar as above, with the restrictions defined in Definition 5. When $\mathcal{A}_I$ outputs its decision bit b', $\mathcal{C}$ returns a set $\Lambda = \{K_i - R_i^{y_i}$, where K_is are the input queries to $\text{H}_3\}$.

Notice that if $\mathcal{C}$ does not abort, and $\mathcal{A}_I$ outputs its decision bit b', then the public key must have the $Q_{ID^*} = aP$, and given how the challenge ciphertext is formed (e.g., $R^* = bP$), $K_{ID^*} = y_{ID^*}abP$ should hold, where y_{ID^*} is known to $\mathcal{C}$. Hence, the answer to a random instance of the CDH problem (P, aP, bP), can be derived from examining the $\mathcal{A}_I$'s choice of public key and H_3 queries.

Here, we provide an indistinguishability argument for the above simulation. First we look at the simulation of the decryption algorithm. If $\zeta = 0$, we can see that the simulation is perfect. For $\zeta = 1$, an error might occur in the event that c_i is valid, but (σ_i, m_i), K_i, and σ_i were never queried to H_2, H_3, and H_4, respectively. For the first two hash functions, the probability that the c_i is valid, given a query to H_3 was never made, considers the query to H_2 as well (not considering the checking phase in the simulation). Therefore, the probability that this could occur is $\frac{q_{H_2}}{2^n} + \frac{1}{p}$. When considering H_4, this probability is $\frac{1}{2^n} + \frac{1}{p}$. Given the number of decryption queries q_D, we have the probability of decryption error $\frac{q_D(q_{H_2}+1)}{2^n} + \frac{2q_D}{p}$.

$\mathcal{C}$ will also fail in simulation during the partial key extraction queries if the entry $(ID_i, Q_i, \dots)$ already exists in List_{H_1}. This will happen with probability $\frac{q_{H_1}}{2^\gamma}$.

The probability that $\mathcal{C}$ does not abort in the simulation is $\delta^{q_{sk}}(1 - \delta)$ which is maximized at $\delta = 1 - \frac{1}{q_{sk}+1}$. Therefore, the probability that $\mathcal{C}$ does not abort is $\frac{1}{e(q_{sk}+1)}$, where e is the base of natural logarithm. Given the argument above, we know that if (σ^*, m_b), (K^*) were never queried to H_2 and H_3 oracles, then $\mathcal{A}_I$ cannot gain any distinguishing advantage more than $\frac{1}{2}$. Given all the above arguments, the probability that K_{ID^*} has been queried to H_3 is $\geq \frac{2\epsilon}{e(q_{sk}+1)} - \frac{q_{H_2}}{2^n} - \frac{q_D(q_{H_2}+1)}{2^n} - \frac{2q_D}{p}$.

Therefore, if the above probability occurs, $\mathcal{C}$ can solve the CDH problem by finding and computing $K_{ID^*} = y_{ID^*}abP$ from the list Λ. Given the size of the list Λ (i.e., q_{H_3}), the probability for $\mathcal{C}$ to be successful in solving CDH is:
$$\epsilon' > \frac{1}{q_{H_3}}\left(\frac{2\epsilon}{e(q_{sk}+1)} - \frac{q_{H_2}}{2^n} - \frac{q_D(q_{H_2}+1)}{2^n} - \frac{2q_D}{p}\right).$$

Theorem 2. *If an adversary $\mathcal{A}_{II}$ can break the IND-CLE-CCA security of the encryption scheme proposed in Algorithm 3 after q_{H_i} queries to random oracles H_i for $i \in \{1, 2, 3, 4\}$, q_D queries to the decryption oracle and q_{sk} to the secret key extraction oracle with probability ϵ. There exists another algorithm $\mathcal{C}$ that runs $\mathcal{A}_{II}$ as subroutine and breaks a random instance of the CDH problem (P, aP, bP) with probability ϵ' where: $\epsilon' > \frac{1}{q_{H_3}}\left(\frac{2\epsilon}{e(q_{sk}+1)} - \frac{q_{H_2}}{2^n} - \frac{q_D(q_{H_2}+1)}{2^n} - \frac{2q_D}{p}\right).$*

Proof (Sketch). Having access to random oracles, and by keeping lists similar to above, the challenger $\mathcal{C}$ can simulate an indistinguishable environment for $\mathcal{A}_{II}$ and respond to its queries similar to the above proof. Note that following Definition 7, $\mathcal{A}_{II}$ can query for the secret key of all the users, except for the target user ID^*.

$\mathcal{C}$ knows the t private values $v_i's$ in the scheme, and tries to embed a random instance of the CDH problem (P, aP, bP). By flipping a fair coin, as in the *public key request* query above, $\mathcal{C}$ defines the probability to embed aP in the target U_{ID^*} value. $\mathcal{C}$ sets bP as a part of the challenge ciphertext (i.e., $R^* \leftarrow bP$).

After the $\mathcal{A}_{II}$ outputs a forgery, $\mathcal{C}$ can extract the solution to the CDH problem since it has knowledge over the t secret values and β^*.

Lemma 1. *A public key replacement attack by $\mathcal{A}_I$ is not practical since it will falsify the private key.*

Proof. Note that if $\mathcal{A}_I$ replaces U with a new value $\overset{\bullet}{U'}$ (which it might know the corresponding secret key), then the existing Q will be falsified since $Q = U + W$ and this will also falsify the current partial private key component y since it is computed based on the indexes that are obtained by computing $\mathtt{H}_1(ID, Q)$. Also note that, if $\mathcal{A}_I$ can obtain the original (α, U), given Q is public, it can compute W, however, W is merely the commitment of β and it does not disclose any information about β. The public key replacement attack in our security proof is possible if $\mathcal{A}_I$ requests a new partial private key for each new U' .

Lemma 2. *If an adversary $\mathcal{A}_I$ can break the EU-CMA security of the signature scheme proposed in Algorithm 4 , then one can build another algorithm $\mathcal{C}$ that runs $\mathcal{A}_I$ as subroutine and breaks a random instance of the ECDLP (P, aP).*

Proof. Due to the space constraint, here we give the high level idea of our proof. We let $\mathcal{A}_I$ be as in Definition 8, then we can build another algorithm $\mathcal{C}$ that uses $\mathcal{A}_I$ as a subroutine, and upon $\mathcal{A}_I$'s successful forgery, solves a random instance of the ECDLP (P, aP). $\mathcal{C}$ knows the t secret values v_i's and, similar to the proof of Theorem 1, it sets aP as a part of the target user's public key (i.e., $Q_{ID^*} \leftarrow aP$). Most of the simulation steps are like the ones in the proof of Theorem 1. At the end of the simulation phase, $\mathcal{A}_I$ outputs a forgery signature (s_1^*, e_1^*), the proof then uses the forking lemma [22] to run the adversary again to obtain a second forgery (s_2^*, e_2^*), using the same random tape. Our proof will follow the same approach as in [15] which is very similar to the proof in [24]. Given two forgeries and the knowledge of $\mathcal{C}$ on the $v_i's$ and α_{ID}^*, $\mathcal{C}$ can compute a and solve the ECDLP. Note that similar to Schnorr [24] the security of the scheme will be non-tight due to the forking lemma.

Parameters Selection for (t, k). Parameters (t, k) should be selected such that the probability $\frac{q_{\mathtt{H}_1} \cdot k!}{2^\gamma}$ is negligible. Considering that $\gamma = k \log_2 t$ (since k indexes that are $\log_2 t$-bit long are selected with the hash output), this gives us $\frac{q_{\mathtt{H}_1} \cdot k!}{2^{k|t|}}$. We further elaborate on some choices of (t, k) along with their performance implications in Sect. 6.

6   Performance Analysis and Comparison

We first present the analytical and then experimental performance analysis and comparison of our schemes with their counterparts. We focus on the *online* operations (e.g., encryption, signing, key exchange) for which both our IDB and CL schemes have the same algorithms, rather than one-time (offline) processes like setup and key generation. Since the online operations are identical in IDB and CL systems in our case, we refer to them as "Our Schemes" in the following

Table 1. Analytical comparison of public key encryption schemes

Scheme	sk	Enc	Comm.	Dec	PK	mpk	System Type	$\kappa^\dagger$
ECIES [26]	$\lvert q \rvert$	$2\,m_{EC} + dm_{EC}$	$2\lvert p\rvert + b + d + CF$	m_{EC}	$\lvert p\rvert$	–	TD	128
BF [9]	$\lvert p\rvert$	$bp + m_{EC} + ex$	$\lvert p\rvert + b + \lvert M\rvert$	$bp + m_{EC}$	$\lvert p\rvert$	$\lvert p\rvert$	IB	80
AP [1]	$\lvert p\rvert$	$3\,bp + m_{EC} + ex$	$\lvert p\rvert + b + \lvert M\rvert$	$bp + m_{EC}$	$2\lvert p\rvert$	$\lvert p\rvert$	CL	80
BSS [3]	$2\lvert q\rvert$	$4\,ex + m$	$\lvert p\rvert + b + \lvert M\rvert$	$3\,ex$	$2\lvert p\rvert$	$\lvert p\rvert$	CL	128
WSB [29]	$\lvert p\rvert + \lvert q\rvert$	$3\,m_{EC} + 2\,a_{EC}$	$2\lvert q\rvert + \lvert c\rvert$	$2\,m_{EC}$	$2\lvert p\rvert$	$\lvert p\rvert$	CL	128
Our Schemes	$\lvert p\rvert$	$2\,m_{EC} + k\,a_{EC}$	$\lvert p\rvert + b + \lvert M\rvert$	$2\,m_{EC}$	$\lvert p\rvert$	$t\lvert p\rvert$	IB/CL	128

†Denotes the security bit. **Enc**, **Dec**, and **Comm.** represent encryption, decryption, and communication load (bi-directional), respectively. m_{EC}, a_{EC}, and dm_{EC} denote the costs of EC scalar multiplication, EC addition, and double scalar multiplication over modulus p, respectively. m, ex and bp denote multiplication, exponentiation and pairing operation, respectively. k is the BPV parameter that shows how many precomputed pairs are selected in the online phase. b, d and CF denote block/key size for symmetric key encryption, message digest (i.e., MAC) size and size of the certificate, respectively. M denotes message space size. TD, IDB, and CL represent traditional public key cryptography, identity-based cryptography, and certificateless cryptography, respectively.

Table 2. Analytical comparison of digital signature schemes

Scheme	sk	Sign	Comm.	Verify	PK	mpk	System Type	κ
Schnorr [24]	$\lvert q\rvert$	m_{EC}	$2\lvert q\rvert + CF$	$2dm_{EC}$	$\lvert p\rvert$	–	TD	128
GG [15]	$\lvert q\rvert$	m_{EC}	$2\lvert p\rvert + \lvert q\rvert$	$2\,dm_{EC}$	$\lvert p\rvert$	$\lvert p\rvert$	IDB	128
AP [1]	$\lvert p\rvert$	$2\,m_{EC} + a_{EC} + bp$	$\lvert q\rvert + \lvert p\rvert$	$4\,bp + ex$	$2\lvert p\rvert$	$\lvert p\rvert$	CL	80
KIB [18]	$\lvert q\rvert$	m_{EC}	$\lvert q\rvert + \lvert p\rvert$	$3\,m_{EC}$	$3\lvert p\rvert$	$2\lvert p\rvert$	CL	128
Our Schemes	$\lvert q\rvert$	m_{EC}	$2\lvert q\rvert$	$dm_{EC} + k\,a_{EC}$	$\lvert p\rvert$	$t\lvert p\rvert$	IDB/CL	128

tables/discussions. We consider the cost of certificate verification for schemes in traditional PKI. We only consider the cost of verifying and communicating the cost of one certificate, which is highly conservative since in practice (i.e., X.509) there are at minimum two certificates in a certificate chain. This number could be as high as ten certificates in some scenarios.

Analytical Performance Analysis and Comparison We present a detailed analytical performance comparison of our schemes with their counterparts for public key encryption/decryption, digital signature and key exchange in Table 1, Table 2 and Table 3, respectively.

Our schemes have significantly lower communication overhead than their PKI-based counterpart in all cryptosystems as they do not require the transmission of certificates. As discussed above and also elaborated in Sect. 6, this translates into substantial bandwidth gain as well as computational efficiency since the certification verification overhead is also lifted. Moreover, in almost all instances, our schemes also offer a lower end-to-end computational overhead compared to their PKI-based counterparts. Our schemes also offer a lower end-to-end computational delay than that of all of their IDB and CL counterparts in all cryptosystems, with generally equal private and public key sizes. However, the master public key size of our scheme is larger than all of their counterparts.

Table 3. Analytical comparison of key exchange schemes

Scheme	sk	User Comp.	Comm.	PK	mpk	System Type
Ephemeral ECDH [13]	$|q|$	$2m_{EC}$	$2|p|+CF$	$|p|$	–	TD
ECHMQV [19]	$|q|$	$3\,m_{EC}$	$2|p|+CF$	$|p|$	–	TD
TFNS [28]	$|p|$	$bp+5\,m_{EC}$	$|p|$	$|p|$	$|p|$	IDB
AP [1]	$|p|$	$4\,bp+ex$	$3|p|$	$2|p|$	$|p|$	CL
YT [30]	$2|q|+|p|+|s|^{\dagger}$	$3\,dm_{EC}+5\,m_{EC}$	$3|p|+|s|$	$2|p|+|s|$	$2|p|$	CL
Our Scheme	$|q|$	$3\,m_{EC}+(k+1)\,a_{EC}$	$2|p|$	$|p|$	$t|p|$	IDB/CL

User Comp. denotes user computation.

$\dagger|s|$ denotes the output of a signature scheme that the authors in [30] use in their scheme

Table 4. Public key encryption schemes on commodity hardware

Scheme	sk	Enc	Comm.	Dec	PK	mpk	E2E Delay
ECIES [26]	32	55	$690^{\dagger}+|M|$	21	32	–	76
BF [9]	32	$\approx$2000	$48+|M|$	$\approx$2000	32	32	$\approx$4000
AP [1]	32	$\approx$6000	$48+|M|$	$\approx$2000	64	32	$\approx$8000
BSS [3]	64	73	$64+|M|$	53	64	32	126
WSB [29]	64	53	$64+|M|$	41	64	32	94
Our Schemes	32	39	$48+|M|$	33	32	32K	72

All sizes are in Bytes, and all computations are in microseconds.

$\dagger$We assume the certificate size is 578 Bytes, the size is given in RFC 5280 [11].

Table 5. Digital signature schemes on commodity hardware

Scheme	sk	Sign	Comm.	Verify	PK	mpk	E2E Delay
Schnorr [24]	32	12	642	44	32	–	56
GG [15]	32	12	96	44	32	32	56
AP [1]	32	$\approx$2000	64	$\approx$8000	64	32	$\approx$10000
KIB [18]	32	20	64	61	96	64	81
Our Schemes	32	12	64	27	32	32K	39

All sizes are in Bytes, and all computations are in microseconds.

Experimental Performance Analysis and Comparison: We now further elaborate on the details of our performance analysis and comparison with experimental results. We conduct experiments on both commodity hardware and low-end embedded devices that are typically found in IoT systems to objectively assess the performance of our schemes as well as their counterparts. Our open-sourced implementation is available via the following link.

https://github.com/Rbehnia/CertFreeSystems

Table 6. Key exchange schemes on commodity hardware

Scheme	sk	User Comp.	Comm.	PK	mpk	E2E Delay
Ephemeral ECDH [13]	32	55	642	32	–	110
ECHMQV [19]	32	74	642	32	–	148
TFNS [28]	32	≈2000	32	32	32	≈4000
AP [1]	32	≈8000	96	64	32	≈16000
YT† [30]	160	157	160	128	64	314
Our Scheme	32	57	64	32	32K	114

All sizes are in Bytes, and all computations are in microseconds.
†The signature size is considered as 64 bytes.

Table 7. Public key encryption schemes on 8-bit AVR processor

Scheme	sk	Enc	Comm.	Dec	PK	mpk
ECIES [26]	32	17 950 967	$610 + |c|$	6 875 861	32	–
BF [9]	32	60 802 555	$48 + |c|$	56 278 012	32	32
AP [1]	32	166 213 087	$48 + |c|$	58 912 609	64	32
BSS [3]	64	22 791 835	$64 + |M|$	16 590 321	64	32
WSB [29]	64	17 091 636	$64 + |c|$	13 631 755	64	32
Our Schemes	32	11 789 632	$48 + |c|$	9 883 161	32	32K

All sizes are in Bytes, and all computations are in CPU Cycles.

• *Experiments on Commodity Hardware:* We used an i7 Skylake laptop equipped with a 2.6 GHz CPU and 12 GB RAM in our experiments. We implemented our schemes on the FourQ curve [12] which offers fast elliptic curve operations for $\kappa = $ 128-bit security. We instantiated our random oracles with blake2 hash function[3], which offers high efficiency and security. For our parameters, we selected $k = 18$ and $t = 1024$. We conservatively estimated the costs of our counterparts based on the microbenchmarks on our evaluation setup of (i) FourQ curve for schemes that do not require pairing and (ii) PBC library[4] on a curve with $\kappa = $ 80-bit security (we used the most efficient alternative for them) for schemes that require pairing.

As depicted in Table 4, the encryption and decryption algorithms of our schemes are more efficient than their counterparts in the identity-based and certificateless settings. More specifically, the end-to-end delay of our schemes is ≈25% lower than that in [29], which is specifically suitable for aerial drones. One could also notice how the communication overhead is lower in certificateless and identity-based schemes since there is no need for certificate transmission.

As shown in Table 5, our schemes enjoy from the fastest verification algorithms among all its counterparts. This is again due to the novel way the user

---

[3] http://131002.net/blake/blake.pdf.
[4] https://crypto.stanford.edu/pbc/.

Table 8. Digital signature schemes on 8-bit AVR processor

Scheme	sk	Sign	Comm.	Verify	PK	mpk
Schnorr [24]	32	4 263 298	642	17 902 958	32	–
GG [15]	32	4 263 298	96	17 902 958	32	32
AP [1]	32	62 487 032	64	221 226 015	64	32
KIB [18]	32	7 025 861	64	20 617 583	96	64
Our Schemes	32	4 263 298	64	10 955 369	32	32K

All sizes are in Bytes, and all computations are in CPU Cycles.

keys are derived and results in 30% and 52% faster end-to-end delay as compared to its most efficient identity-based [15] and certificateless [18] counterparts, respectively. *One may notice that although schemes in [15, 18, 24], along with our schemes, all require a scalar multiplication in their signature generation (see Table 2), their experimental costs differ. The reason for this discrepancy is the fact that the cost of scalar multiplication over the generator P is faster than the scalar multiplication over any curve points, and these differences are considered in the experimental evaluations.*

As shown in Table 6, our schemes' performance is similar to that in their counterparts in traditional PKI setting [13, 19]. However, they outperform the most efficient counterpart in certificateless setting [30] by having 65% lower end-to-end delay and 60% smaller load for communication.

• *Experiments on Low-End Device:* We used an 8-bit AVR ATmega 2560 microprocessor to evaluate the costs of our schemes on an IoT device. AVR ATmega 2560 is a low-power microprocessor with 256 KB flash, 8 KB SRAM, 4 KB EEP-ROM, and operates at 16 MHz frequency. We used the 8-bit AVR library of the FourQ curve presented in [20]. For our counterparts, we again conservatively estimated their costs based on microbenchmarks in (i) FourQ curve 8-bit AVR implementation [20], and (ii) NanoECC [27], that implements a curve that supports pairings on 8-bit AVR microprocessors and offers $\kappa = 80$-bit security.

As depicted in Table 7, our schemes outperform all of their identity-based and certificateless counterparts and have a more efficient encryption algorithm than [26]. Our decryption algorithms, while being more efficient than all of their identity-based and certificateless counterparts, are slightly less efficient than the one in [26]. Similar to the trend in the analytical performance, our signature schemes outperform their counterparts. As Table 8 shows, our schemes' signing algorithm are amongst the most efficient ones, while the verification algorithm outperforms all the counterparts with similar communication overhead.

Limitations: The main limitation of our schemes is the size of the master public key. Note that if there are different TTP in different domains and users often communicate with the users in those domains, it would make sense to store different *mpk*. Otherwise, the users only need to store *mpk* for their own systems. We can reduce the size of the *mpk* in exchange for a small performance loss. For instance, with $k = 32$, we can reduce the size of the *mpk* by four times.

7   Related Work

There is a comprehensive literature covering different aspects of IDB and CL systems. Remark that most of the closely related works have been discussed in Sect. 3 and 5 in terms of security models and performance metrics. Overall, the main difference in our work is to focus on the achievement of inter-compatibility between IDB and CL with a high efficiency, with respect to existing alternatives.

The idea of IDB cryptography was proposed by Shamir [25]. However, the first practical instance of such schemes was proposed later by Boneh and Franklin [9] using bilinear pairing. To get the full adaptive-identity, chosen-ciphertext security guarantees without sacrificing performance, Boyen [10] described an augmented versions of the scheme in [8] in the random-oracle model. However, the augmented version also requires multiple pairing computations in the decryption algorithm. Following [7], several pairing-free signature scheme were proposed. Galindo and Garcia [15] proposed a lightweight IDB signature scheme based on [24] with reduction to the discrete logarithm problem (Table 9).

Table 9. Key exchange schemes on 8-bit AVR processor

Scheme	sk	User Comp.	Comm.	PK	mpk
Ephemeral ECDH [13]	32	18 039 710	642	32	–
ECHMQV [19]	32	24 601 857	642	32	–
TFNS [28]	32	82 356 781	32	32	32
AP [1]	32	221 226 015	96	64	32
YT [30]	160	54 212 824	160	128	64
Our Scheme	32	18 015 493	64	32	32K

All sizes are in Bytes, and all computations are in CPU Cycles.

CL cryptography [1] was proposed to address the private key escrow problem in IDB systems. In the same paper, the authors proposed an IND-CCA encryption scheme along with a signature and key exchange schemes. Following their work, Baek et al. [3] proposed the first IND-CCA secure certificateless encryption scheme without pairing. The scheme is constructed using Schnorr-like signatures in partial private key generation algorithm. Recently Won et al. [29] proposed another efficient IND-CCA encryption scheme that is specifically used for key encapsulation mechanisms. There has been a number of works that focus on the security models of certificateless systems. In most of the proposed models (e.g., [1]) a Type-II adversary is assumed to generate the keys honestly, and initiate the attacks only after the setup phase.

Acknowledgments. This work is supported by the Department of Energy Award DE-OE0000780 and NSF Award #1652389.

References

1. Al-Riyami, S.S., Paterson, K.G.: Certificateless public key cryptography. In: Laih, C.-S. (ed.) ASIACRYPT 2003. LNCS, vol. 2894, pp. 452–473. Springer, Heidelberg (2003). https://doi.org/10.1007/978-3-540-40061-5_29
2. Au, M.H., Mu, Y., Chen, J., Wong, D.S., Liu, J.K., Yang, G.: Malicious KGC attacks in certificateless cryptography. In: 2nd ACM Symposium on Information, Computer and Communications Security, pp. 302–311. ASIACCS (2007)
3. Baek, J., Safavi-Naini, R., Susilo, W.: Certificateless public key encryption without pairing. In: Zhou, J., Lopez, J., Deng, R.H., Bao, F. (eds.) ISC 2005. LNCS, vol. 3650, pp. 134–148. Springer, Heidelberg (2005). https://doi.org/10.1007/11556992_10
4. Behnia, R., Ozmen, M.O., Yavuz, A.A.: ARIS: authentication for real-time IoT systems. In: IEEE International Conference on Communications (ICC), ICC, pp. 1855–1867. ACM, New York (2019)
5. Behnia, R., Ozmen, M.O., Yavuz, A.A., Rosulek, M.: TACHYON: fast signatures from compact knapsack. In: Proceedings of the 2018 ACM SIGSAC Conference on Computer and Communications Security, CCS 2018, pp. 1855–1867. ACM, New York (2018)
6. Bellare, M., Rogaway, P.: Random oracles are practical: a paradigm for designing efficient protocols. In: Proceedings of the 1st ACM conference on Computer and Communications Security, CCS 1993, pp. 62–73. ACM, New York (1993)
7. Bellare, M., Namprempre, C., Neven, G.: Security proofs for identity-based identification and signature schemes. J. Cryptol. **22**(1), 1–61 (2009). https://doi.org/10.1007/s00145-008-9028-8
8. Boneh, D., Boyen, X.: Efficient selective-ID secure identity-based encryption without random oracles. In: Cachin, C., Camenisch, J.L. (eds.) EUROCRYPT 2004. LNCS, vol. 3027, pp. 223–238. Springer, Heidelberg (2004). https://doi.org/10.1007/978-3-540-24676-3_14
9. Boneh, D., Franklin, M.: Identity-based encryption from the Weil pairing. In: Kilian, J. (ed.) CRYPTO 2001. LNCS, vol. 2139, pp. 213–229. Springer, Heidelberg (2001). https://doi.org/10.1007/3-540-44647-8_13
10. Boyen, X.: A tapestry of identity-based encryption: practical frameworks compared. IJACT **1**(1), 3–21 (2008)
11. Cooper, D., Santesson, S., Farrell, S., Boeyen, S., Housley, R., Polk, W.: Internet X. 509 public key infrastructure certificate and certificate revocation list (CRL) profile. RFC 5280, RFC Editor, May 2008
12. Costello, C., Longa, P.: FourℚQ: four-dimensional decompositions on a ℚ-curve over the Mersenne prime. In: Iwata, T., Cheon, J.H. (eds.) ASIACRYPT 2015. LNCS, vol. 9452, pp. 214–235. Springer, Heidelberg (2015). https://doi.org/10.1007/978-3-662-48797-6_10
13. Diffie, W., Hellman, M.: New directions in cryptography. IEEE Trans. Inf. Theory **IT-22**, 644–654 (1976)
14. Fujisaki, E., Okamoto, T.: Secure integration of asymmetric and symmetric encryption schemes. In: Wiener, M. (ed.) CRYPTO 1999. LNCS, vol. 1666, pp. 537–554. Springer, Heidelberg (1999). https://doi.org/10.1007/3-540-48405-1_34
15. Galindo, D., Garcia, F.D.: A Schnorr-like lightweight identity-based signature scheme. In: Preneel, B. (ed.) AFRICACRYPT 2009. LNCS, vol. 5580, pp. 135–148. Springer, Heidelberg (2009). https://doi.org/10.1007/978-3-642-02384-2_9

16. Girault, M.: Self-certified public keys. In: Davies, D.W. (ed.) EUROCRYPT 1991. LNCS, vol. 547, pp. 490–497. Springer, Heidelberg (1991). https://doi.org/10.1007/3-540-46416-6_42
17. Huang, X., Mu, Y., Susilo, W., Wong, D.S., Wu, W.: Certificateless signature revisited. In: Pieprzyk, J., Ghodosi, H., Dawson, E. (eds.) ACISP 2007. LNCS, vol. 4586, pp. 308–322. Springer, Heidelberg (2007). https://doi.org/10.1007/978-3-540-73458-1_23
18. Karati, A., Islam, S.H., Biswas, G.: A pairing-free and provably secure certificateless signature scheme. Inf. Sci. **450**, 378–391 (2018)
19. Krawczyk, H.: HMQV: a high-performance secure Diffie-Hellman protocol. In: Shoup, V. (ed.) CRYPTO 2005. LNCS, vol. 3621, pp. 546–566. Springer, Heidelberg (2005). https://doi.org/10.1007/11535218_33
20. Liu, Z., Longa, P., Pereira, G.C.C.F., Reparaz, O., Seo, H.: FourQ on embedded devices with strong countermeasures against side-channel attacks. In: Fischer, W., Homma, N. (eds.) CHES 2017. LNCS, vol. 10529, pp. 665–686. Springer, Cham (2017). https://doi.org/10.1007/978-3-319-66787-4_32
21. Ozmen, M.O., Behnia, R., Yavuz, A.A.: IoD-crypt: a lightweight cryptographic framework for internet of drones. CoRR abs/1904.06829 (2019). http://arxiv.org/abs/1904.06829
22. Pointcheval, D., Stern, J.: Security proofs for signature schemes. In: Maurer, U. (ed.) EUROCRYPT 1996. LNCS, vol. 1070, pp. 387–398. Springer, Heidelberg (1996). https://doi.org/10.1007/3-540-68339-9_33
23. Reyzin, L., Reyzin, N.: Better than BiBa: short one-time signatures with fast signing and verifying. In: Batten, L., Seberry, J. (eds.) ACISP 2002. LNCS, vol. 2384, pp. 144–153. Springer, Heidelberg (2002). https://doi.org/10.1007/3-540-45450-0_11
24. Schnorr, C.: Efficient signature generation by smart cards. J. Cryptol. **4**(3), 161–174 (1991). https://doi.org/10.1007/BF00196725
25. Shamir, A.: Identity-based cryptosystems and signature schemes. In: Blakley, G.R., Chaum, D. (eds.) CRYPTO 1984. LNCS, vol. 196, pp. 47–53. Springer, Heidelberg (1985). https://doi.org/10.1007/3-540-39568-7_5
26. Shoup, V.: A proposal for an ISO standard for public key encryption. Cryptology ePrint Archive, Report 2001/112 (2001). https://eprint.iacr.org/2001/112
27. Szczechowiak, P., Oliveira, L.B., Scott, M., Collier, M., Dahab, R.: NanoECC: testing the limits of elliptic curve cryptography in sensor networks. In: Verdone, R. (ed.) EWSN 2008. LNCS, vol. 4913, pp. 305–320. Springer, Heidelberg (2008). https://doi.org/10.1007/978-3-540-77690-1_19
28. Tomida, J., Fujioka, A., Nagai, A., Suzuki, K.: Strongly secure identity-based key exchange with single pairing operation. In: Sako, K., Schneider, S., Ryan, P.Y.A. (eds.) ESORICS 2019. LNCS, vol. 11736, pp. 484–503. Springer, Cham (2019). https://doi.org/10.1007/978-3-030-29962-0_23
29. Won, J., Seo, S., Bertino, E.: Certificateless cryptographic protocols for efficient drone-based smart city applications. IEEE Access **5**, 3721–3749 (2017)
30. Yang, G., Tan, C.H.: Strongly secure certificateless key exchange without pairing. In: Proceedings of the 6th ACM Symposium on Information, Computer and Communications Security, pp. 71–79. ASIACCS, ACM, New York (2011)

Public-PEZ Cryptography

Soma Murata[1], Daiki Miyahara[1,3(✉)], Takaaki Mizuki[2],
and Hideaki Sone[2]

[1] Graduate School of Information Sciences, Tohoku University,
6-3-09 Aramaki-Aza-Aoba, Aoba-ku, Sendai 980-8578, Japan
{soma.murata.p5,daiki.miyahara.q4}@dc.tohoku.ac.jp
[2] Cyberscience Center, Tohoku University, 6-3 Aramaki-Aza-Aoba,
Aoba-ku, Sendai 980-8578, Japan
mizuki+lncs@tohoku.ac.jp
[3] National Institute of Advanced Industrial Science and Technology,
2-3-26, Aomi, Koto-ku, Tokyo 135-0064, Japan

Abstract. Secure multiparty computation (MPC) is a cryptographic technique that enables us to evaluate a predetermined function over players' private inputs while hiding information about the inputs. MPC can be conducted using a "private PEZ protocol," that uses PEZ candies and a dispenser. Specifically, in a private PEZ protocol, players first fill a predetermined sequence of candies in a dispenser. Then, each player in turn privately pops out a number of candies, wherein the number depends on their private input (without anybody else knowing how many candies pop out). The next candy to be popped out of the dispenser indicates the output value of the function. Thus, private PEZ protocols are fun and useful. One drawback would be that every player must pop out candies from the dispenser secretly, implying that a private PEZ protocol is vulnerable to dishonest players, for example, a player could peep the candies inside the dispenser. To overcome this drawback, we herein propose MPC protocols that do not need private actions such as secretly popping out candies after the setup (although each player rearranges the candies secretly in a setup phase, any illegal actions can be caught). That is, we construct a computational model of "public-PEZ cryptography," where any protocol within the model can be publicly executed. Especially, the proposed public-PEZ AND protocol, which uses only five candies and two dispensers, is simple and easy for conducting a secure computation of the AND function.

Keywords: Secure multiparty computations · Recreational cryptography · Private PEZ protocols · Card-based cryptography

1 Introduction

1.1 Background

Secure multiparty computation (MPC) is a cryptographic technique for evaluating a predetermined function over players' private inputs while hiding information about the inputs. Interestingly, MPC can be performed using not only

© Springer Nature Switzerland AG 2020
W. Susilo et al. (Eds.): ISC 2020, LNCS 12472, pp. 59–74, 2020.
https://doi.org/10.1007/978-3-030-62974-8_4

Fig. 1. PEZ candies, packages, and a dispenser.

Fig. 2. A deck of cards.

computers but also everyday objects. Some examples are *private PEZ protocols* using PEZ candies and a dispenser (as shown in Fig. 1) and *card-based protocols* using a deck of physical cards (as shown in Fig. 2). Using such physical cryptographic protocols, we can visually understand what MPC is and how secure the protocols are. Thus, they attract not only cryptographers but also non-experts, such as high school students, and they can be effectively used as educational tools.

Private PEZ protocols were first introduced in 2003 by Balogh *et al.* [2], and their results were improved recently by Abe *et al.* [1] in 2019. In a private PEZ protocol, players first fill in a dispenser with a predetermined sequence of candies whose order depends on the function that they want to securely compute. Subsequently, each player privately pops out a number of candies such that the number depends on their private input. Finally, the remaining topmost candy left in the dispenser becomes the output of the function. Thus, private PEZ protocols are fun and useful. One drawback is that every player must take out candies from the dispenser secretly, implying that a private PEZ protocol is vulnerable to dishonest players. For example, when a player pops out candies secretly, they could maliciously peep the candies inside the dispenser or replace them with another sequence of candies as per their preference.

1.2 Contributions

In this paper, to overcome the drawback of the above-mentioned private PEZ protocols, which require players' private actions, we consider a new usage of PEZ candies and dispensers by borrowing the ideas behind card-based protocols. That is, we design novel PEZ protocols that can be publicly executed. Specifically, we first propose a secure AND protocol using five PEZ candies and two dispensers; it allows Alice and Bob to compute the AND value of their private inputs without revealing them. Carrying the idea behind this protocol further, we construct a computational model of *public-PEZ cryptography*. Following this model, we present the formal description of our AND protocol. We also discuss some implementation issues.

1.3 Related Work

As mentioned above, we borrow the ideas and techniques from card-based protocols. The first card-based protocol was proposed by den Boer [3] in 1989; his famous protocol called the "five-card trick" performs a secure computation of the AND function. Our constructions are inspired by the card-based AND protocols [16,21] that use a shuffling operation called a "random bisection cut." In card-based protocols, all players first place a pair of cards face-down on a table whose order depends on their private input. Subsequently, they perform MPC by publicly shuffling and turning over the sequence of cards to obtain the output. A formal computational model of card-based protocols was presented (and was then reviewed) in the literature [11,19,20,31]. Based on the computational model, Koch *et al.* [11], Francis *et al.* [7], Kastner *et al.* [9], and Koch *et al.* [10] provided tight lower bounds on the number of required cards. In addition to simple MPCs, there are card-based protocols for zero-knowledge proof [4,6,12,15,28,29] and secure comparison [13,14,30]. Furthermore, there is another direction of card-based cryptography that relies on private actions [24–27,33]. Protocols using other everyday objects have been proposed, such as those using a dial lock [17], the 15-puzzle [18], envelopes [8], tamper-evident seals [23], and a visual secret sharing scheme [5].

1.4 Outline

The remainder of this paper is organized as follows. In Sect. 2, we present a simple and easy-to-implement AND protocol using five PEZ candies and two dispensers. In Sect. 3, we define each operation appearing in public-PEZ protocols and obtain a computational model. In Sect. 4, we formally describe the AND protocol introduced in Sect. 2 based on the model shown in Sect. 3. In Sect. 5, we discuss the feasibility of implementing the shuffling operations of public-PEZ protocols. The concluding statements are presented in Sect. 6.

2 Public-PEZ AND Protocol

In this section, we present a simple and easy-to-implement AND protocol using five PEZ candies and two dispensers.

Assume that Alice and Bob hold private input bits $a \in \{0, 1\}$ and $b \in \{0, 1\}$, respectively. They want to learn $a \wedge b$, namely the AND value of their inputs, without revealing the input values more than necessary. They only require two packages of PEZ candies (of different flavors) and two identical dispensers[1]. We assume that all candies are indistinguishable in terms of appearance, *i.e.*, they have the same color and shape; the PEZ candies sold in Japan satisfy this condition, *i.e.*, the lemon and orange candies appear identical, as shown in Fig. 3. We also assume that one cannot distinguish two candies of different flavors by their smells[2].

---

[1] Two identical dispensers can be easily obtained by buying two sets of the same product.
[2] This holds true at least for the authors' sense of smell.

Fig. 3. The PEZ candies sold in Japan; the lemon and orange candies are all white and indistinguishable.

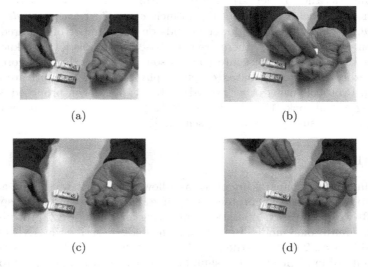

(a)

(b)

(c)

(d)

Fig. 4. How to prepare two candies of different flavors on Alice's palm.

Let us consider how a Boolean value can be encoded by a flavor of the candy: Let the lemon flavor be denoted by 0, and let the orange flavor be denoted by 1. As shown in Fig. 3, candies with the same flavor are packed in the same package. Let Alice take a lemon candy and an orange candy from the packages publicly and place the two candies with different flavors on her palm, as shown in Fig. 4. Next, let Alice arrange the two candies inside her hand (without Bob knowing their order), as shown in Fig. 5, according to her input bit $a \in \{0, 1\}$, as follows. If $a = 0$, she rearranges the two candies in the order of lemon, and then, orange, *i.e.*, 0 to 1; otherwise, in the order of orange to lemon, *i.e.*, 1 to 0. Subsequently, she takes the two candies from her palm and places them on the table so that the order satisfies

Fig. 5. Rearrange the two candies in Alice's hand without Bob knowing its order.

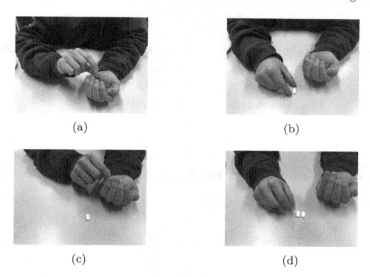

(a)   (b)

(c)   (d)

Fig. 6. Place the candies (whose order matches Alice's private bit) on the table without Bob knowing the order.

as shown in Fig. 6. In this manner, Alice can prepare two candies (of different flavors) corresponding to her private bit $a \in \{0, 1\}$ and its negation $\overline{a}$ without Bob knowing its value. Note that Alice and Bob face each other, and Bob watches Alice's behavior during the entire process. Therefore, Alice has no choice but to place two candies of different flavors on the table; if Alice acts maliciously, such an illegal action will be always identified.

We are now ready to present our protocol; it is based on the idea behind the card-based AND protocol proposed in [16]. Our protocol proceeds as follows.

1. As described above, Alice prepares two candies corresponding to a and $\overline{a}$. Similarly, Bob prepares two candies that correspond to b and $\overline{b}$. A sequence of candies is arranged on a table as follows:

Remember that the candies are indistinguishable from each other; for example, Alice does not know how the third candy tastes (unless she bites it to confirm its flavor).

2. Alice replaces the candy corresponding to $\bar{a}$ with a candy corresponding to 0, *i.e.*, she discards (or eats) the candy corresponding to $\bar{a}$ and places a candy there corresponding to 0, which is taken from the lemon package:

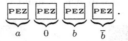

3. Alice and Bob fill the four candies into two identical dispensers as follows.

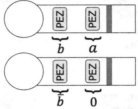

4. Shuffle the two dispensers. The resulting state can be described as follows.

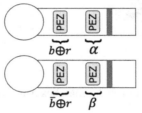

Here, $r \in \{0, 1\}$ is a uniformly distributed random bit, and α and β are defined as follows: if $r = 0$, $(\alpha, \beta) = (a, 0)$; if $r = 1$, $(\alpha, \beta) = (0, a)$. That is, $r = 0$ indicates that the shuffle has not swapped the two dispensers, and $r = 1$ means that the shuffle has swapped them. Moreover, if $b \oplus r = 0$, we have $a \wedge b = a \wedge r = \beta$ because $a \wedge 0 = 0$ and $a \wedge 1 = a$; if $b \oplus r = 1$, we have $a \wedge b = a \wedge \bar{r} = \alpha$ because $a \wedge \bar{0} = a$ and $a \wedge \bar{1} = 0$.

5. Pop out the candy from each dispenser and then bite them[3]. If the candy $b \oplus r$ popped out of the top dispenser corresponds to 0, the candy remaining in the bottom dispenser β represents the output $a \wedge b$; if $b \oplus r$ corresponds to 1, the candy remaining in the top dispenser α represents the output $a \wedge b$.

This is our AND protocol, using five candies and two dispensers along with one shuffle. Note that the shuffle and popping out candies can be done publicly. It should be also noted that in Step 1, hidden operations shown in Fig. 5 are required to prepare players' private inputs; this is inevitable for MPC and, as mentioned before, both players cannot place any pair of candies that deviates from the encoding rule.

---

[3] Alice and Bob may want to bite the candy simultaneously after splitting it for the purpose of preventing anyone from lying about the flavor.

After Step 5, the players obtain a candy corresponding to $a \wedge b$:

If they bite it, they can know the value of $a \wedge b$. Instead, this candy can be used as an input to another computation: that is, if Carol prepares two candies according to her private bit $c \in \{0, 1\}$, starting the AND protocol again with

generates a candy corresponding to $a \wedge b \wedge c$:

Thus, a secure AND computation of more than two inputs can be easily performed.

3 Formalizing Public-PEZ Protocols

In this section, by elaborating the idea behind our AND protocol shown in Sect. 2, we formally define each operation on PEZ candies and dispensers and provide a computational model of public-PEZ protocols that publicly perform MPC using PEZ candies and dispensers. We borrow the ideas and terms from the computational model of card-based protocols [19].

3.1 Sequence of Candies

There are various flavors of PEZ candies, such as lemon and orange; however, as assumed before, all candies have the same appearance so that they are indistinguishable (unless they are eaten). Considering all available candies, we denote the multiset of them by $\mathcal{B}$, which we call a *box*. Any element $c \in \mathcal{B}$ represents a flavor, such as $c \in [\texttt{lemon}, \texttt{lemon}, \texttt{orange}, \texttt{orange}, \texttt{grape}, \cdots]$. For simplicity, hereinafter, we consider only two flavors and denote them by 0 or 1. Therefore, for instance, the AND protocol presented in Sect. 2 works on the box

$$\mathcal{B} = [\, 0, 0, 0, 1, 1 \,] = [\, 3 \cdot 0, 2 \cdot 1 \,]$$

because it uses three lemon candies and two orange candies. Generally, if a protocol requires k candies corresponding to 0 and ℓ candies corresponding to 1, the box is expressed as

$$\mathcal{B} = [\, k \cdot 0, \ell \cdot 1 \,].$$

Next, we consider a "sequence" of candies. When a player takes a candy from a package, its flavor is publicly known. For instance, if there are three lemon candies and two orange candies taken from the packages, the order of which is

$$\underbrace{\text{PEZ}}_{0}\ \underbrace{\text{PEZ}}_{1}\ \underbrace{\text{PEZ}}_{0}\ \underbrace{\text{PEZ}}_{1}\ \underbrace{\text{PEZ}}_{0},$$

we write this sequence as $(0, 1, 0, 1, 0)$. Given such a sequence $(0, 1, 0, 1, 0)$, let both Alice and Bob (holding input bits a and b, respectively) rearrange two candies inside their hand as in the AND protocol, shown in Sect. 2; then, we have

$$\underbrace{\text{PEZ}}_{a}\ \underbrace{\text{PEZ}}_{\bar{a}}\ \underbrace{\text{PEZ}}_{b}\ \underbrace{\text{PEZ}}_{\bar{b}}\ \underbrace{\text{PEZ}}_{0},$$

where the flavors of the left-most four candies become publicly unknown. If the flavor of candy $c \in \mathcal{B}$ is unknown to the public, we denote it by $\frac{?}{c}$. Therefore, for example, when $a = 1$ and $b = 0$, the sequence above can be written as

$$\left(\frac{?}{1}, \frac{?}{0}, \frac{?}{0}, \frac{?}{1}, 0\right).$$

Now, consider a situation where players eat the first candy; then, the flavor, 1, becomes public while the candy has disappeared. We use expression $\frac{c}{\epsilon}$ with $c \in \mathcal{B}$ to represent a candy whose flavor is known to the public, but the candy itself does not exist. Therefore, the resulting sequence (from eating the left-most candy) can be written as

$$\left(\frac{1}{\epsilon}, \frac{?}{0}, \frac{?}{0}, \frac{?}{1}, 0\right).$$

For $c \in \mathcal{B}$, we define $\mathsf{atom}(c) = \mathsf{atom}(\frac{?}{c}) = \mathsf{atom}(\frac{c}{\epsilon}) = c$. For example, $\mathsf{atom}(1) = 1$, $\mathsf{atom}(\frac{?}{0}) = 0$, and $\mathsf{atom}(\frac{1}{\epsilon}) = 1$. For the box $\mathcal{B}$ with $|\mathcal{B}| = m$, we call $\Gamma = (\alpha_1, \alpha_2, \ldots, \alpha_m)$ a *sequence* from the box $\mathcal{B}$ if $\alpha_i \in \{0, 1, \frac{?}{0}, \frac{?}{1}, \frac{0}{\epsilon}, \frac{1}{\epsilon}\}$ for every i, $1 \leq i \leq m$, and $[\mathsf{atom}(\alpha_1), \mathsf{atom}(\alpha_2), \ldots, \mathsf{atom}(\alpha_m)] = \mathcal{B}$.

We define the set of all sequences from $\mathcal{B}$ as $\mathsf{Seq}^{\mathcal{B}}$:

$$\mathsf{Seq}^{\mathcal{B}} = \{\Gamma \mid \Gamma \text{ is a sequence from } \mathcal{B}\}.$$

3.2   Action

Next, we define four actions appearing in public-PEZ protocols. Assume that we have a sequence $\Gamma = (\alpha_1, \alpha_2, \ldots, \alpha_m)$.

Suppose that players want to check the flavors of some candies $\frac{?}{c}$. In this case, the players must bite them to determine their flavor, and the eaten candies will disappear. We denote this action by (bite, T) for a set $T \subseteq \{1, 2, \ldots, m\}$ such that $\alpha_i = \frac{?}{0}$ or $\frac{?}{1}$ for every $i \in T$, where every candy in T is eaten and disappears. That is, the resulting sequence becomes $(\beta_1, \beta_2, \ldots, \beta_m)$ such that

$$\beta_i = \begin{cases} \frac{\mathsf{atom}(\alpha_i)}{\epsilon} & \text{if } i \in T \\ \alpha_i & \text{otherwise} \end{cases}$$

for every i, $1 \leq i \leq m$. For instance, for a sequence $(\frac{?}{1}, \frac{?}{0}, \frac{?}{1}, \frac{?}{1}, \frac{?}{0})$, applying (bite, T) with a set $T = \{1, 3, 5\}$ results in $(\frac{1}{\epsilon}, \frac{?}{0}, \frac{1}{\epsilon}, \frac{?}{1}, \frac{0}{\epsilon})$.

Suppose that players want to rearrange the order of sequence Γ. We denote this action by (permute, π) for a permutation $\pi \in S_m$, where S_m is the symmetric group of degree m. That is, the resulting sequence becomes $(\alpha_{\pi^{-1}(1)}, \alpha_{\pi^{-1}(2)}, \ldots, \alpha_{\pi^{-1}(m)})$.

Suppose that players want to perform a shuffling action such as shuffling the two dispensers, seen in Sect. 2. We denote this type of action by (shuffle, $\Pi, \mathcal{F}$) for a subset $\Pi \subseteq S_m$ and a probability distribution $\mathcal{F}$ on Π. That is, defining $\mathsf{fixed}(\Pi) = \{j \mid 1 \leq j \leq m, \forall \sigma \in \Pi \; \sigma(j) = j\}$, the resulting sequence becomes $(\beta_1, \beta_2, \ldots, \beta_m)$ such that

$$\beta_i = \begin{cases} \alpha_i & \text{if } i \in \mathsf{fixed}(\Pi) \\ \frac{?}{\mathsf{atom}(\alpha_{\pi^{-1}(i)})} & \text{if } i \notin \mathsf{fixed}(\Pi) \end{cases}$$

for every i, $1 \leq i \leq m$, where π is drawn from Π according to $\mathcal{F}$. When $\mathcal{F}$ is uniform, we write (shuffle, Π) by omitting it. Note that when an action (shuffle, $\Pi, \mathcal{F}$) is applied to a sequence $(\alpha_1, \alpha_2, \ldots, \alpha_m)$, it should hold that $i \in \mathsf{fixed}(\Pi)$ for every i such that $\alpha_i = \frac{c}{\epsilon}$ for some c.

Herein, we introduce two shuffles that are also often used in card-based protocols. The first one is a "random cut" that shuffles a sequence cyclically. For instance, if a random cut is applied to a sequence of four candies, one of the following sequences is obtained. The probability of each occurrence is 1/4.

This shuffle is formally expressed as (shuffle, $\{\mathsf{id}, (1\,2\,3\,4), (1\,2\,3\,4)^2, (1\,2\,3\,4)^3\}$) where id is the identity permutation. The second one is a "random bisection cut," which was implicitly seen in Sect. 2. Here, a sequence of candies is divided in half and the two sub-sequences are shuffled. For instance, applying a random bisection cut to a sequence of four candies results in

$$
\begin{array}{cccc}
1 & 2 & 3 & 4 \\
\fbox{PEZ}\fbox{PEZ}\fbox{PEZ}\fbox{PEZ}
\end{array}
\rightarrow
\begin{array}{cccc}
1 & 2 & 3 & 4 \\
\fbox{PEZ}\fbox{PEZ}\fbox{PEZ}\fbox{PEZ} \\
3 & 4 & 1 & 2 \\
\fbox{PEZ}\fbox{PEZ}\fbox{PEZ}\fbox{PEZ},
\end{array}
$$

where each result occurs with a probability of $1/2$. This shuffle is formally expressed as $(\mathsf{shuffle}, \{\mathsf{id}, (1\,3)(2\,4)\})$.

Finally, we define an action used at the end of a protocol. We use (result, p) for $p \in \{1, 2, \cdots, m\}$ to represent that the protocol is terminated and its output is the p-th candy.

3.3 Computational Model of Public-PEZ Protocols

In this subsection, we define a computational model of public-PEZ protocols via an abstract machine.

Let $\mathcal{B}$ be a box. Depending on the players' input, an initial sequence Γ_0 (from $\mathcal{B}$) is determined. By $U \subseteq \mathsf{Seq}^{\mathcal{B}}$, we denote the set of all possible input sequences.

Next, we define a visible sequence that represents all public information with regard to the flavors of the candies. Consequently, we define $\mathsf{top}(\frac{?}{c}) = ?$ and $\mathsf{top}(c) = \mathsf{top}(\frac{c}{\epsilon}) = c$ for $c \in \mathcal{B}$, which is based on the fact that when players bite a candy, the candy will disappear but its flavor will be memorized by all players. Then, we define $\mathsf{vis}(\Gamma)$ of a sequence $\Gamma = (\alpha_1, \alpha_2, \ldots, \alpha_m)$ as

$$
\mathsf{vis}((\alpha_1, \alpha_2, \ldots, \alpha_m)) = (\mathsf{top}(\alpha_1), \mathsf{top}(\alpha_2), \ldots, \mathsf{top}(\alpha_m)).
$$

For instance,

$$
\mathsf{vis}\left(\left(\frac{1}{\epsilon}, 0, \frac{?}{1}, \frac{0}{\epsilon}, \frac{1}{\epsilon}, \frac{?}{0}, 1\right)\right) = (1, 0, ?, 0, 1, ?, 1).
$$

Furthermore, we define the set $\mathsf{Vis}^{\mathcal{B}}$ of all visible sequences as

$$
\mathsf{Vis}^{\mathcal{B}} = \{\mathsf{vis}(\Gamma) \mid \Gamma \in \mathsf{Seq}^{\mathcal{B}}\}.
$$

We are now ready to formally define a public-PEZ protocol. A *protocol* is a 4-tuple $\mathcal{P} = (\mathcal{B}, U, A, Q)$ such that

- $\mathcal{B}$ is a box;
- $U \subseteq \mathsf{Seq}^{\mathcal{B}}$ is a set of input sequences;
- Q is a set of states, containing the initial state q_0 and final state q_f;
- $A : (Q - \{q_f\}) \times \mathsf{Vis}^{\mathcal{B}} \to Q \times \texttt{Action}$ is an action function, where $\texttt{Action}$ is the set of all possible actions (bite, T), $(\mathsf{permute}, \pi)$, $(\mathsf{shuffle}, \Pi, \mathcal{F})$, and (result, p).

A protocol $\mathcal{P} = (\mathcal{B}, U, A, Q)$ proceeds as imagined; starting with an initial sequence $\Gamma_0 \in U$ and initial state q_0, it changes the sequence and state based on the output of the action function. When the state becomes q_f, the protocol $\mathcal{P}$ terminates with an action (result, p) for some p.

4 Formal Description of Our AND Protocol and Another One

In this section, we formally describe our AND protocol presented in Sect. 2 based on the computational model of public-PEZ protocols defined in Sect. 3, which can be described as follows.

The five-candy AND protocol _____
Box:
$$\mathcal{B} = [\,3 \cdot 0, 2 \cdot 1\,]$$

Input:

$$U = \left\{ \left(\frac{?}{0}, \frac{?}{0}, \frac{?}{1}, \frac{?}{0}, \frac{?}{1}\right), \left(\frac{?}{0}, \frac{?}{0}, \frac{?}{1}, \frac{?}{1}, \frac{?}{0}\right), \left(\frac{?}{0}, \frac{?}{1}, \frac{?}{0}, \frac{?}{0}, \frac{?}{1}\right), \left(\frac{?}{0}, \frac{?}{1}, \frac{?}{0}, \frac{?}{1}, \frac{?}{0}\right) \right\}$$

Steps:

1. (permute, $(1\,3)$)
2. (shuffle, $\{id, (2\,3)(4\,5)\}$)
3. (bite, $\{4\}$)
4. if visible seq.$= (?, ?, ?, 0, ?)$ then (result, 3)
5. else if visible seq.$= (?, ?, ?, 1, ?)$ then (result, 2)

_____

Next, to display another formal protocol, we describe the XOR protocol based on the card-based XOR protocol [22].

The XOR protocol based on [22] _____
Box:
$$\mathcal{B} = [\,7 \cdot 0, 7 \cdot 1\,]$$

Input:

$$U = \left\{ \left(\frac{?}{0}, \frac{?}{1}, \frac{?}{0}, \frac{?}{1}, \frac{?}{0}, \frac{?}{1}, \frac{?}{0}, \frac{?}{1}, \frac{?}{0}, \frac{?}{1}, 0, 0, 1, 1\right), \right.$$
$$\left(\frac{?}{0}, \frac{?}{1}, \frac{?}{1}, \frac{?}{0}, \frac{?}{0}, \frac{?}{1}, \frac{?}{0}, \frac{?}{1}, \frac{?}{0}, \frac{?}{1}, 0, 0, 1, 1\right),$$
$$\left(\frac{?}{1}, \frac{?}{0}, \frac{?}{0}, \frac{?}{1}, \frac{?}{0}, \frac{?}{1}, \frac{?}{0}, \frac{?}{1}, \frac{?}{0}, \frac{?}{1}, 0, 0, 1, 1\right),$$
$$\left. \left(\frac{?}{1}, \frac{?}{0}, \frac{?}{1}, \frac{?}{0}, \frac{?}{0}, \frac{?}{1}, \frac{?}{0}, \frac{?}{1}, \frac{?}{0}, \frac{?}{1}, 0, 0, 1, 1\right) \right\}$$

Steps:

1. (shuffle, $\{\mathsf{id}, (7\,8\,9\,10), (7\,8\,9\,10)^2, (7\,8\,9\,10)^3\}$)
2. (shuffle, $\{\mathsf{id}, (1\,2\,3\,4), (1\,2\,3\,4)^2, (1\,2\,3\,4)^3\}$)
3. (shuffle, $\{\mathsf{id}, (5\,6\,7\,8), (5\,6\,7\,8)^2, (5\,6\,7\,8)^3\}$)
4. (shuffle, $\{\mathsf{id}, (1\,5)\}$)
5. (bite, $\{1, 5\}$)
6. if visible seq.$= (0, ?, ?, ?, 0, ?, ?, ?, \cdots)$ then (permute, $(1\,11)(5\,12)$)
   go to step 2
   else if visible seq.$= (1, ?, ?, ?, 1, ?, ?, ?, \cdots)$ then (permute, $(1\,13)(5\,14)$)
   go to step 2
   else if visible seq.$= (0, ?, ?, ?, 1, ?, ?, ?, \cdots)$ or $(1, ?, ?, ?, 0, ?, ?, ?, \cdots)$
   go to step 7
7. (bite, $\{3, 7\}$)
8. if visible seq.$= (c, ?, 0, ?, \overline{c}, ?, 1, ?, \cdots)$ or $(c, ?, 1, ?, \overline{c}, ?, 0, ?, \cdots)$
   for some $c \in \{0, 1\}$ then (result, 9)
   else if visible seq.$= (c, ?, 0, ?, \overline{c}, ?, 0, ?, \cdots)$ or $(c, ?, 1, ?, \overline{c}, ?, 1, ?, \cdots)$
   for some $c \in \{0, 1\}$ then (result, 10)

We describe the above XOR protocol as an example. However, we do not intend to use this practically because it is relatively complicated, has a loop, and is a Las Vegas algorithm. (Actually, we can obtain a simple finite-runtime XOR protocol based on the four-card XOR protocol in [21].) Note that the number of available candies is finite, *i.e.*, the box $\mathcal{B}$ has exactly seven lemon candies and seven orange candies. Therefore, if there is no candy available in Step 6, the protocol fails. This is a big difference between card-based protocols and public-PEZ protocols; the Las Vegas algorithm does not work well in public-PEZ cryptography.

5   Implementations of Shuffles of Candies

In this section, we discuss the feasibility of shuffling actions in public-PEZ protocols. It is more difficult to shuffle a sequence of candies using the players' hands, compared to shuffling a sequence of cards. Therefore, we consider using the following special tools to implement a random bisection cut and random cut on a sequence of candies.

Random Bisection Cut. As already seen in Sect. 2, we use two identical dispensers. First, the two divided sequences of candies are packed into the two dispensers without changing the orders. Then, we shuffle the two dispensers, take out the candies from each of the dispensers, and arrange them.
   The operation of shuffling the two dispensers must be implemented so that nobody knows how many times they are switched. The previous research [32]

proposed a secure implementation method for a random bisection cut in card-based protocols using a Styrofoam ball. This method can be used in public-PEZ protocols as well. Specifically, two dispensers are placed in a Styrofoam ball (the contents of which cannot be seen from the outside). Then, the ball is thrown up to shuffle the dispensers inside the ball.

Random cut. We consider using a hose as shown in Fig. 7. First, we place the candies (to be shuffled) in the hose while maintaining the order, and tape its inlet and outlet. Then, we move the candies by rotating the hose. Finally, we take out the candies from the hose, while maintaining the order, and arrange them. The diameter of the hose must be tight enough that the order of the candies inside the hose does not change when it is rotated.

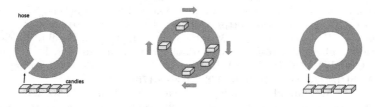

(a) Put candies in a hose.   (b) Rotate the hose.   (c) Take out the candies.

Fig. 7. How to implement a random cut.

6   Conclusion

In this study, we designed public-PEZ cryptography. We constructed its computational model and presented a few protocols within the model. Further, we discussed the feasibility of shuffling actions for a sequence of PEZ candies. As public-PEZ protocols do not require private actions, players can perform MPC more securely and easily. In particular, we believe that our AND protocol presented in Sect. 2 is practical enough to be utilized in daily activities.

People might assume that this paper would just replace "cards" in card-based cryptography with "candies and dispensers," *i.e.*, public-PEZ cryptography is a type of re-implementation of card-based cryptography, and thus, there would not be much novelty. However, we believe that this is not the case. As already demonstrated, unlike a deck of cards, one cannot turn a candy face down and a candy disappears after one confirms its value; therefore, we need novel and careful treatment to construct a rigorous model. In addition, public-PEZ cryptography is simple, which is a virtue.

Acknowledgement. We thank the anonymous referees, whose comments have helped us to improve the presentation of the paper. This work was supported in part by JSPS KAKENHI Grant Number JP19J21153.

References

1. Abe, Y., Iwamoto, M., Ohta, K.: Efficient private PEZ protocols for symmetric functions. In: Hofheinz, D., Rosen, A. (eds.) TCC 2019. LNCS, vol. 11891, pp. 372–392. Springer, Cham (2019). https://doi.org/10.1007/978-3-030-36030-6_15
2. Balogh, J., Csirik, J.A., Ishai, Y., Kushilevitz, E.: Private computation using a PEZ dispenser. Theoret. Comput. Sci. **306**(1), 69–84 (2003). https://doi.org/10.1016/S0304-3975(03)00210-X. http://www.sciencedirect.com/science/article/pii/S030439750300210X
3. Boer, B.: More efficient match-making and satisfiability *the five card trick*. In: Quisquater, J.-J., Vandewalle, J. (eds.) EUROCRYPT 1989. LNCS, vol. 434, pp. 208–217. Springer, Heidelberg (1990). https://doi.org/10.1007/3-540-46885-4_23
4. Bultel, X., et al.: Physical zero-knowledge proof for Makaro. In: Izumi, T., Kuznetsov, P. (eds.) SSS 2018. LNCS, vol. 11201, pp. 111–125. Springer, Cham (2018). https://doi.org/10.1007/978-3-030-03232-6_8
5. D'Arco, P., Prisco, R.D.: Secure computation without computers. Theoret. Comput. Sci. **651**, 11–36 (2016). https://doi.org/10.1016/j.tcs.2016.08.003
6. Dumas, J.-G., Lafourcade, P., Miyahara, D., Mizuki, T., Sasaki, T., Sone, H.: Interactive physical zero-knowledge proof for Norinori. In: Du, D.-Z., Duan, Z., Tian, C. (eds.) COCOON 2019. LNCS, vol. 11653, pp. 166–177. Springer, Cham (2019). https://doi.org/10.1007/978-3-030-26176-4_14
7. Francis, D., Aljunid, S.R., Nishida, T., Hayashi, Y., Mizuki, T., Sone, H.: Necessary and sufficient numbers of cards for securely computing two-bit output functions. In: Phan, R.C.-W., Yung, M. (eds.) Mycrypt 2016. LNCS, vol. 10311, pp. 193–211. Springer, Cham (2017). https://doi.org/10.1007/978-3-319-61273-7_10
8. Heather, J., Schneider, S., Teague, V.: Cryptographic protocols with everyday objects. Formal Aspects Comput. **26**(1), 37–62 (2013). https://doi.org/10.1007/s00165-013-0274-7
9. Kastner, J., et al.: The minimum number of cards in practical card-based protocols. In: Takagi, T., Peyrin, T. (eds.) ASIACRYPT 2017. LNCS, vol. 10626, pp. 126–155. Springer, Cham (2017). https://doi.org/10.1007/978-3-319-70700-6_5
10. Koch, A., Schrempp, M., Kirsten, M.: Card-based cryptography meets formal verification. In: Galbraith, S.D., Moriai, S. (eds.) ASIACRYPT 2019. LNCS, vol. 11921, pp. 488–517. Springer, Cham (2019). https://doi.org/10.1007/978-3-030-34578-5_18
11. Koch, A., Walzer, S., Härtel, K.: Card-based cryptographic protocols using a minimal number of cards. In: Iwata, T., Cheon, J.H. (eds.) ASIACRYPT 2015. LNCS, vol. 9452, pp. 783–807. Springer, Heidelberg (2015). https://doi.org/10.1007/978-3-662-48797-6_32
12. Lafourcade, P., Miyahara, D., Mizuki, T., Sasaki, T., Sone, H.: A physical ZKP for Slitherlink: how to perform physical topology-preserving computation. In: Heng, S.H., Lopez, J. (eds.) Information Security Practice and Experience. Lecture Notes in Computer Science, vol. 11653, pp. 135–151. Springer, Cham (2019). https://doi.org/10.1007/978-3-030-34339-2_8
13. Miyahara, D., Hayashi, Y., Mizuki, T., Sone, H.: Practical and easy-to-understand card-based implementation of yao's millionaire protocol. In: Kim, D., Uma, R.N., Zelikovsky, A. (eds.) COCOA 2018. LNCS, vol. 11346, pp. 246–261. Springer, Cham (2018). https://doi.org/10.1007/978-3-030-04651-4_17
14. Miyahara, D., Hayashi, Y., Mizuki, T., Sone, H.: Practical card-based implementations of Yao's millionaire protocol. Theoret. Comput. Sci. **803**, 207–221 (2020). https://doi.org/10.1016/j.tcs.2019.11.005

15. Miyahara, D., et al.: Card-based ZKP protocols for Takuzu and Juosan. In: Farach-Colton, M., Prencipe, G., Uehara, R. (eds.) 10th International Conference on Fun with Algorithms (FUN 2020). Leibniz International Proceedings in Informatics (LIPIcs), vol. 157, pp. 1–21. Schloss Dagstuhl-Leibniz-Zentrum für Informatik, Dagstuhl, Germany (2020). https://drops.dagstuhl.de/opus/volltexte/2020/12781

16. Mizuki, T.: Card-based protocols for securely computing the conjunction of multiple variables. Theoret. Comput. Sci. **622**, 34–44 (2016). https://doi.org/10.1016/j.tcs.2016.01.039

17. Mizuki, T., Kugimoto, Y., Sone, H.: Secure multiparty computations using a dial lock. In: Cai, J.-Y., Cooper, S.B., Zhu, H. (eds.) TAMC 2007. LNCS, vol. 4484, pp. 499–510. Springer, Heidelberg (2007). https://doi.org/10.1007/978-3-540-72504-6_45

18. Mizuki, T., Kugimoto, Y., Sone, H.: Secure multiparty computations using the 15 puzzle. In: Dress, A., Xu, Y., Zhu, B. (eds.) COCOA 2007. LNCS, vol. 4616, pp. 255–266. Springer, Heidelberg (2007). https://doi.org/10.1007/978-3-540-73556-4_28

19. Mizuki, T., Shizuya, H.: A formalization of card-based cryptographic protocols via abstract machine. Int. J. Inf. Secur. **13**(1), 15–23 (2013). https://doi.org/10.1007/s10207-013-0219-4

20. Mizuki, T., Shizuya, H.: Computational model of card-based cryptographic protocols and its applications. IEICE Trans. Fundam. Electron. Commun. Comput. Sci. **E100**(A(1)), 3–11 (2017). https://doi.org/10.1587/transfun.E100.A.3

21. Mizuki, T., Sone, H.: Six-card secure and and four-card secure XOR. In: Deng, X., Hopcroft, J.E., Xue, J. (eds.) FAW 2009. LNCS, vol. 5598, pp. 358–369. Springer, Heidelberg (2009). https://doi.org/10.1007/978-3-642-02270-8_36

22. Mizuki, T., Uchiike, F., Sone, H.: Securely computing XOR with 10 cards. Australas. J. Comb. **36**, 279–293 (2006)

23. Moran, T., Naor, M.: Basing cryptographic protocols on tamper-evident seals. Theoret. Comput. Sci. **411**(10), 1283–1310 (2010)

24. Nakai, T., Shirouchi, S., Iwamoto, M., Ohta, K.: Four cards are sufficient for a card-based three-input voting protocol utilizing private permutations. In: Shikata, J. (ed.) ICITS 2017. LNCS, vol. 10681, pp. 153–165. Springer, Cham (2017). https://doi.org/10.1007/978-3-319-72089-0_9

25. Nakai, T., Tokushige, Y., Misawa, Y., Iwamoto, M., Ohta, K.: Efficient card-based cryptographic protocols for millionaires' problem utilizing private permutations. In: Foresti, S., Persiano, G. (eds.) CANS 2016. LNCS, vol. 10052, pp. 500–517. Springer, Cham (2016). https://doi.org/10.1007/978-3-319-48965-0_30

26. Ono, H., Manabe, Y.: Efficient card-based cryptographic protocols for the millionaires' problem using private input operations. In: 2018 13th Asia Joint Conference on Information Security (AsiaJCIS), pp. 23–28, Aug 2018. DOIurl https://doi.org/10.1109/AsiaJCIS.2018.00013

27. Ono, H., Manabe, Y.: Card-based cryptographic protocols with the minimum number of rounds using private operations. In: Pérez-Solà, C., Navarro-Arribas, G., Biryukov, A., Garcia-Alfaro, J. (eds.) DPM/CBT -2019. LNCS, vol. 11737, pp. 156–173. Springer, Cham (2019). https://doi.org/10.1007/978-3-030-31500-9_10

28. Ruangwises, S., Itoh, T.: Physical zero-knowledge proof for Numberlink. In: Farach-Colton, M., Prencipe, G., Uehara, R. (eds.) 10th International Conference on Fun with Algorithms (FUN 2020). Leibniz International Proceedings in Informatics (LIPIcs), vol. 157, pp.1–11. Schloss Dagstuhl-Leibniz-Zentrum für Informatik, Dagstuhl, Germany (2020). https://drops.dagstuhl.de/opus/volltexte/2020/12783

29. Sasaki, T., Miyahara, D., Mizuki, T., Sone, H.: Efficient card-based zero-knowledge proof for Sudoku. Theoret. Comput. Sci. **839**, 135–142 (2020). https://doi.org/10.1016/j.tcs.2020.05.036

30. Takashima, K., et al.: Card-based secure ranking computations. In: Li, Y., Cardei, M., Huang, Y. (eds.) COCOA 2019. LNCS, vol. 11949, pp. 461–472. Springer, Cham (2019). https://doi.org/10.1007/978-3-030-36412-0_37

31. Takashima, K., Miyahara, D., Mizuki, T., Sone, H.: Card-based protocol against actively revealing card attack. In: Martín-Vide, C., Pond, G., Vega-Rodríguez, M.A. (eds.) Theory and Practice of Natural Computing. Lecture Notes in Computer Science, vol. 11949, pp. 95–106. Springer International Publishing, Cham (2019)

32. Ueda, I., Miyahara, D., Nishimura, A., Hayashi, Y., Mizuki, T., Sone, H.: Secure implementations of a random bisection cut. Int. J. Inf. Secur. **19**(4), 445–452 (2019). https://doi.org/10.1007/s10207-019-00463-w

33. Yasunaga, K.: Practical card-based protocol for three-input majority. IEICE Transactions on Fundamentals of Electronics, Communications and Computer Sciences pp. 1–3 (to appear). DOI: 10.1587/transfun.2020EAL2025

Two-Server Verifiable Homomorphic Secret Sharing for High-Degree Polynomials

Xin Chen[1,2,3] and Liang Feng Zhang[1(✉)]

[1] School of Information Science and Technology, ShanghaiTech University,
Shanghai, China
{chenxin3,zhanglf}@shanghaitech.edu.cn
[2] Shanghai Institute of Microsystem and Information Technology,
Chinese Academy of Sciences, Shanghai, China
[3] University of Chinese Academy of Sciences, Beijing, China

Abstract. Homomorphic secret sharing (HSS) allows multiple input clients to secret-share their data among multiple servers such that each server is able to locally compute a function on its shares to obtain a partial result and all partial results enable the reconstruction of the function's value on the outsourced data by an output client. The existing HSS schemes for *high-degree* polynomials either *require a large number of servers* or *lack verifiability*, which is essential for ensuring the correctness of the outsourced computations. In this paper, we propose a two-server verifiable HSS (VHSS) model and construct a scheme that supports the computation of high-degree polynomials. The degree of the outsourced polynomials can be as high as a polynomial in the system's security parameter. Despite of using only 2 servers, our VHSS ensures that each single server learns no information about the outsourced data and no single server is able to persuade the client to output a wrong function value. Our VHSS is significantly more efficient. When computing degree-7 polynomials, our scheme could be 3–10 times faster than the previously best construction.

Keywords: Homomorphic secret sharing · Verifiable computation · Nearly linear decryption

1 Introduction

In the context of outsourcing computations, the outsourced data may be leaked and the servers may be hijacked or return incorrect results for economic reasons (such as saving the computing resources). How to ensure the *privacy* of the outsourced data and the *integrity* of the outsourced computations are two top security issues.

A general method of protecting the privacy of the data in outsourcing computation is by using the homomorphic encryption (HE), which allows the cloud

© Springer Nature Switzerland AG 2020
W. Susilo et al. (Eds.): ISC 2020, LNCS 12472, pp. 75–91, 2020.
https://doi.org/10.1007/978-3-030-62974-8_5

servers to compute a function f on the ciphertexts $\mathsf{Enc}(x_1), \ldots, \mathsf{Enc}(x_n)$ to get a ciphertext of the function value $y = f(x_1, \ldots, x_n)$. The early HE schemes [19,26] only support degree-1 computations on the encrypted data. Gentry [18] proposed the first fully homomorphic encryption (FHE) scheme that allows the computation of any boolean circuits on encrypted data. Although the efficiency of FHE has been significantly improved in [7,11] during the past years, FHE is still impractical from the performance perspective [25]. As a multi-server counterpart of HE that is more efficient, the HSS of Boyle et al. [6] allows the input clients to secret-share their data among multiple servers such that upon request each server is able to compute a partial result and all partial results suffice to reconstruct the correct function value by an output client. Most of the existing HSS schemes are designed for computing specific functions, such as the affine functions [2], the point functions [5], the selection functions [15,17], and the depth-2 boolean circuits [8]. Recent works [4,9,13,16,21] have focused on the construction of HSS schemes that support high-degree polynomial computations.

While HE and HSS provide easy solutions to the data privacy problem in outsourcing of computations, they cannot help the output client verify whether the servers have done their computations correctly. Tsaloli et al. [29] proposed the notion of verifiable HSS (VHSS) which additionally add verifiability of the servers' results to the HSS schemes. Unfortunately, their construction only supports the product computations over a multiplicative Abelian group and has been proved to be insecure [20]. Yoshida and Obana [30] constructed verifiably multiplicative secret sharing schemes that enable the computation of polynomials over the shared data. However, the degrees of their polynomials cannot exceed the number of servers.

Therefore, if we restrict our attention to HSS schemes for high-degree polynomial computations, the state of the art offers either the construction [9] that has no verifiability or the constructions [30] that require a very large number of servers. In this paper, we shall focus on the construction of *two-server verifiable* HSS schemes that allow *high-degree* polynomial computations.

1.1   Our Contributions

In this paper, we propose a two-server verifiable homomorphic secret sharing (2SVHSS) model. Our model involves three kinds of parties: a set of *input clients*, a set of *servers*, and an *output client*. Each input client uses a public key to encrypt its data as shares to the servers; upon the request of computing a function on the outsourced data, each server performs a computation on its own shares and produces a partial result; finally, the output client reconstructs the function value from all partial results. A 2SVHSS scheme in our model should satisfy the properties of *correctness, semantic security, verifiability, context hiding* and *compactness*. The correctness property requires that whenever the scheme is correctly executed, the output client will always reconstruct the correct function value. The semantic security requires that each server learns no information about the outsourced data. The verifiability requires that no malicious server is able to persuade the output client to reconstruct a wrong function value. The context hiding property requires that the output client learns no more information about the outsourced data than what is implied by the function value. This property is specifically interesting when the output client is not one of the input clients. The compactness property requires that the output client's workload in a protocol execution should be substantially less than that required by the native computation of the function. This property is essential for HSS's applications in outsourcing computation. In the proposed model we construct a 2SVHSS scheme that allows the computation of polynomials over the outsourced data. The degrees of these polynomials can be as *high* as a polynomial in the system's security parameter. Achieving *verifiability* in two-server HSS for *high-degree* polynomials allows us to distinguish between this work and the existing ones.

1.2 Our Techniques

Our construction is based on the HSS of [9]. The core technique of the HSS scheme of [9] is a public-key encryption scheme supporting nearly linear decryption (PKE-NLD). Let $R = \mathbb{Z}[X]/(x^N + 1)$, where $p, q \in \mathbb{N}$, $p|q$ and $1 \ll p \ll q$. Informally, a public-key encryption scheme supports nearly linear decryption for a message $x \in R_p$ if the secret key is $\mathbf{s} = (s_1, s_2) = (1, s) \in R_p^2$, and for any ciphertext $\mathbf{c} \in R_q^2$ encrypting x, $\langle \mathbf{s}, \mathbf{c} \rangle = (q/p) \cdot x + e \mod q$ for some "small" noise $e \in R$. The input clients use PKE-NLD and the public key pk to encrypt $x \cdot \mathbf{s}$ as $\mathbf{C}^x = (\mathbf{c}^{x \cdot 1}, \mathbf{c}^{x \cdot s}) \in R_q^{2 \times 2}$, without knowing the secret key $\mathbf{s}$. In order to implement homomorphic computation on the ciphertext, they randomly split the secret key $\mathbf{s}$ into a pair of evaluation keys $(\mathsf{ek}_1, \mathsf{ek}_2) \in R_q^{2 \times 2}$ such that $\mathbf{s} = (\mathsf{ek}_1 + \mathsf{ek}_2) \mod q$. For every $b \in \{1, 2\}$, the server b uses ek_b to compute a share $\mathbf{t}_b^x$ of $x \cdot \mathbf{s}$, and returns it to the output client. It is clear that for $i \in \{1, 2\}$, $\langle \mathbf{t}_0^x, \mathbf{c}^{x' \cdot s_i} \rangle + \langle \mathbf{t}_1^x, \mathbf{c}^{x' \cdot s_i} \rangle = \langle x \cdot \mathbf{s}, \mathbf{c}^{x' \cdot s_i} \rangle \approx (q/p) \cdot xx' \cdot s_i$ over R_q.

The HSS of [9] supports the computation of restricted multiplication straightline programs [6,14]. To enable the computation of polynomials, we added homomorphic multiplication by known constants to [9] as follows. For every $b \in \{1, 2\}$, the server b computes the secret share $\mathbf{t}_b^{c \cdot x}$ (in fact, $\mathbf{t}_b^{c \cdot x} = c \cdot \mathbf{t}_b^x$) of $c \cdot x \cdot \mathbf{s}$ (where $c \in R_p$) by using $c \cdot \mathsf{ek}_b$. The correctness of the computation can be established as follows: $\mathbf{t}_1^{c \cdot x} + \mathbf{t}_2^{c \cdot x} = c \cdot (\mathbf{t}_1^x + \mathbf{t}_2^x) = (cx \cdot 1, cx \cdot s)$. To achieve verifiability, we add a verification key and a pair of additional evaluation keys. More precisely, the verification key $\mathsf{vk} = (\hat{s}, \hat{s} \cdot s)$ is obtained by multiplying the secret key $\mathbf{s} = (1, s)$ with a randomly chosen value $\hat{s} \in R_p$; and the additional evaluations keys $(\hat{\mathsf{ek}}_1, \hat{\mathsf{ek}}_2)$ are additive shares of vk, i.e., $\mathsf{vk} = (\hat{\mathsf{ek}}_1 + \hat{\mathsf{ek}}_2) \mod q$. With the additional evaluation keys, the servers can manage to compute $\tau = \hat{s} \cdot f(x_1, \dots, x_n)$. The output client can decide whether $f(x_1, \dots, x_n)$ is computed correctly by verifying the equation $\tau = \hat{s} \cdot f$. A successful attack of the verifiability by a malicious server requires that server to guess $\hat{s}$ correctly. However, that will happen with at most a negligible probability, because $\hat{s}$ is randomly split into two additive shares and sent to two servers respectively, a single server cannot obtain effective information about $\hat{s}$. Our verification process only needs to perform a fixed number of additions and multiplications on R and does not need to perform decryption (including modular exponentiation) like [4,13,21]. Therefore, our verification process consumes few resources which is very friendly to the output clients with limited computing power.

1.3   Applications

Our scheme has interesting applications in many scenarios such as secure computation [3,6], private manipulation of remote databases [12], and generating correlated random variables [3]. In addition, it can be used in industry.

Deep Neural Networks: The scheme of [31] has been using uses FHE to enable the evaluation of deep neural networks over the private data. Our scheme can provide an efficient alternative to FHE, and our scheme is verifiable and ensures the users to get the correct results from untrusted servers.

Smart Grid Network: Smart grid networks are envisioned to be the next generation power supply networks. The smart grid deploys sensors on the consumers to collect real-time data which will be uploaded to the servers. The control center requires the servers to perform some computations on the collected data for further analysis, such as regulating the supply of power. Khurana et al. [23] pointed out that the data stored on the servers will reveal their private information. A more serious problem is that the servers may be hijacked which will cause the control center to make a wrong judgment and cause catastrophic consequences. Such security problems can be solved by our scheme, which can preserve the privacy of the consumers by encrypting the collected data and allow the control center to verify the result.

Our scheme can be used to provide both data privacy, results verification and efficient computation in many other systems such as the healthcare systems [27] and the industrial control systems [28].

1.4   Related Work

Recent works [4,13,21] are to transform the level-k HE scheme to support the computation of high-degree polynomials. Informally, if an HE scheme can support computations of degree $\leq k$, we call it a level-k HE scheme. Although [4,13,21] achieve the purpose of computing polynomials through level-k HE, their constructions do not support verification and are only effective for low-degree polynomials. Some works [16,30] constructed multi-server schemes with verifiability. However, the degree of their polynomials can not exceed the number of servers.

Table 1 shows the comparisons between our scheme and some existing representative schemes for n input clients, m servers, and degree-d polynomials, where "$n = *$" means that the number of allowed input clients is unbounded. Compared with these representative works, our scheme satisfies all properties in comparison and supports polynomials of highest degree.

Table 1. Comparisons with Existing HSS Schemes

	n	m	d	Semantic security	Verifiability	Context hiding	Compactness
[13]	*	2	$2k$	✓	×	✓	✓
[4]	1	1	$2k$	✓	×	✓	×
[21]	*	m	$(k+1)m-1$	✓	×	✓	✓
[30]	*	m	$< m$	✓	✓	✓	✓
[16]	1	m	m	✓	✓	✓	×
Ours	*	2	$\mathsf{poly}(\lambda)$	✓	✓	✓	✓

1.5 Organization

In Sect. 2 we introduce the techniques that will be used in our construction. In Sect. 3 we formally define 2SVHSS. In Sect. 4 we give both construction and analysis of our 2SVHSS. In Sect. 5 we implement our scheme and compare with the best existing schemes in terms of efficiency. Finally, Sect. 6 contains our concluding remarks.

2 Preliminaries

We denote with $\lambda \in \mathbb{N}$ a security parameter, and use $\mathsf{poly}(\lambda)$ to denote any function bounded by a *polynomial* in λ. We say that a function is *negligible* in λ if it vanishes faster than the inverse of any polynomial in λ, and denote a negligible function by negl. We use PPT for probabilistic polynomial-time. For a positive integer n, we denote by $[n]$ the set $\{1, 2, \ldots, n\}$. For a real number $x \in \mathbb{R}$, by $\lfloor x \rceil \in \mathbb{Z}$ we denote the integer closest to x. Let $R = \mathbb{Z}[X]/(X^N + 1)$, where $N \in \mathbb{N}$ with $N \leq \mathsf{poly}(\lambda)$ is a power of 2. For $x \in R$ with coefficients $x_1, \ldots, x_N$, the *infinity norm* of x is defined as $\|x\|_\infty := \max_{i=1}^N |x_i|$. For $p \in \mathbb{N}$, by R_p we denote R/pR. We agree that the coefficients of any element in R_p are in the interval $(-\lfloor p/2 \rfloor, \ldots, \lfloor (p-1)/2 \rfloor]$. We define the *size* of a polynomial as the total number of multiplication and addition operations it contains. The size of the polynomial f is denoted as $\mathsf{size}(f)$. Let X, Y be two probability distributions over the same sample space U. We define the *statistical distance* between X and Y as $\mathsf{SD}[X, Y] := \frac{1}{2} \sum_{u \in U} |\Pr[X = u] - \Pr[Y = u]|$.

2.1 Public-Key Encryption with Nearly Linear Decryption

Boyle et al. [9] gave an instantiation of PKE-NLD that satisfies the following properties: First, it allows anyone to encrypt certain key-dependent messages without the secret key. Second, it allows distributed decryption of ciphertexts.

The PKE-NLD of [9] was instantiated with Ring-LWE [10,22] and parametriz-ed by modulus values $p, q \in \mathbb{N}$, and bounds $B_{\mathsf{sk}}, B_{\mathsf{ct}} \in \mathbb{N}$, where $p|q$, $p \geq \lambda^{\omega(1)}$, $q/p \geq \lambda^{\omega(1)}$ and $B_{\mathsf{sk}}, B_{\mathsf{ct}} \leq \mathsf{poly}(\lambda)$, as well as a ring $R =$

$\mathbb{Z}[X]/(X^N+1)$, where N is a power of 2. The secret key $\mathbf{s}$ satisfies $\|\mathbf{s}\|_\infty \le B_{\mathsf{sk}}$. The error e satisfies $\|e\|_\infty \le B_{\mathsf{ct}}$.

In the PKE-NLD instantiation of [9], $\mathcal{D}_{\mathsf{sk}}$ is a secret-key distribution such that each coefficient of the secret key s is uniformly distributed over $\{0, \pm 1\}$, subject to the constraint that h_{sk} out of the coefficients of s are non-zero. $\mathcal{D}_{\mathsf{err}}$ is an error distribution where each coefficient is a rounded Gaussian with a parameter σ, which gives $B_{\mathsf{err}} = 8\sigma$ as a high-probability bound on the l_∞ norm of samples from $\mathcal{D}_{\mathsf{sk}}$, with failure probability about 2^{-49}. The instantiation of PKE-NLD can be described as follows:

- PKE.Gen(1^λ) : Sample $a \leftarrow R_q$, $s \leftarrow \mathcal{D}_{\mathsf{sk}}$, $e \leftarrow \mathcal{D}_{\mathsf{err}}$ and compute $b = a \cdot s + e$ in R_q. Let $\mathbf{s} = (1, s)$ and output $\mathsf{pk} = (a, b)$, $\mathsf{sk} = \mathbf{s}$.
- PKE.Enc(pk, m) : To encrypt $m \in R_p$, sample $v \leftarrow \mathcal{D}_{\mathsf{sk}}$, $e_0, e_1 \leftarrow \mathcal{D}_{\mathsf{err}}$. Output the ciphertext $(c_0, c_1) \in R_q^2$, where $c_1 = -av + e_0$ and $c_0 = bv + e_1 + (q/p) \cdot m$.
- PKE.**OKDM**(pk, m) : Compute $\mathbf{c}^0 = \mathsf{PKE.Enc}(0)$ and $\mathbf{c}^m = \mathsf{PKE.Enc}(m)$. Output the tuple $(\mathbf{c}^m, \mathbf{c}^0 + (0, (q/p) \cdot m))$ as an encryption of $m \cdot \mathbf{s}$.
- PKE.DDec($b, \mathbf{t}_b, \mathbf{c}^x$) : Given $b \in [2]$, a ciphertext $\mathbf{c}^x = (c_0, c_1)$ and a share $\mathbf{t}_b = (t_{b,0}, t_{b,1})$ of $m \cdot \mathbf{s}$. Output $d_b = (\lfloor (p/q) \cdot (c_0 \cdot t_{b,0} + c_1 \cdot t_{b,1}) \rceil \mod p) \mod q$.

Without accessing the secret key, anyone can compute the encryption of any linear function of the secret key through key-dependent message (KDM) oracle.

Nearly Linear Decryption to the Message $x \cdot s_j$: for any $\lambda \in \mathbb{N}$, for any $(\mathsf{pk}, \mathbf{s}) \leftarrow \mathsf{PKE.Gen}(1^\lambda)$, and for any $\mathbf{c}_j \leftarrow \mathsf{PKE.OKDM}(\mathsf{pk}, x, j)$, it holds $\langle \mathbf{s}, \mathbf{c}_j \rangle = (q/p) \cdot (x \cdot s_j) + e \mod q$ for some $e \in R$ with $\|e\|_\infty \le B_{\mathsf{ct}}$, where $j \in [2]$.

Security: for any $\lambda \in \mathbb{N}$ and any PPT adversary $\mathcal{A}$, $\mathbf{Adv}_{\mathcal{A},\mathsf{PKE.OKDM}}^{\mathsf{kdm-ind}}(\lambda) := \left| \Pr\left[\mathbf{Exp}_{\mathcal{A},\mathsf{PKE.OKDM}}^{\mathsf{kdm-ind}}(\lambda) = 1\right] - 1/2 \right| \le \mathsf{negl}(\lambda)$, where $\mathbf{Exp}_{\mathcal{A},\mathsf{PKE.OKDM}}^{\mathsf{kdm-ind}}(\lambda)$ is defined as follows:

$$\mathbf{Exp}_{\mathcal{A},\mathsf{PKE.OKDM}}^{\mathsf{kdm-ind}}(\lambda):$$

(pk, sk) ← PKE.Gen(1^λ)
$\beta \leftarrow \{0, 1\}$
$\beta' \leftarrow \mathcal{A}^{\mathcal{O}_{\mathsf{KDM}}(\cdot,\cdot)}(1^\lambda, \mathsf{pk})$
If $\beta = \beta'$ return 1.
Else return 0.

$\mathcal{O}_{\mathsf{KDM}}(x, j):$
If $\beta = 0$ return PKE.OKDM(pk, x, j).
Else return PKE.Enc($\mathsf{pk}, 0$).

By PKE.**OKDM**(pk, x) we denote the KDM oracle that returns a componentwise encryption of $x \cdot \mathbf{s}$, i.e. the matrix $(\mathsf{PKE.OKDM}(\mathsf{pk}, x, 1), \mathsf{PKE.OKDM}(\mathsf{pk}, x, 2)) \in R_q^{2\times2}$.

The second property that PKE-NLD needs to satisfy is that it allows two non-communicating servers to perform decryption distributively.

Distributed Decryption of Sums of Ciphertexts: Let $B_{\mathsf{add}} \in \mathbb{N}$ be a polynomial in λ. Then there exists a deterministic polynomial time decryption procedure PKE.DDec with the following properties: for all $x \in R_p$ with $p/\|x\|_\infty \ge \lambda^{\omega(1)}$ and $q/(p \cdot \|x\|_\infty) \ge \lambda^{\omega(1)}$, for all $(\mathsf{pk}, \mathbf{s})$, for all messages

$m_1, \ldots, m_{B_{\mathsf{add}}} \in R_p$, for all encryption $\mathbf{c}_i$ of m_i that are either output of PKE.Enc or PKE.OKDM (in that case we have $m_i = x_i \cdot s_j$ for some $x_i \in R_p$ and $j \in [2]$), for the shares $\mathbf{t}_1, \mathbf{t}_2 \in R_q^2$ that were randomly chosen subject to $\mathbf{t}_1 + \mathbf{t}_2 = x \cdot \mathbf{s} \mod q$, for $\mathbf{c} := \sum_{i=1}^{B_{\mathsf{add}}} \mathbf{c}_i$ and $m := \sum_{i=1}^{B_{\mathsf{add}}} m_i$, PKE.DDec$(1, \mathbf{t}_1, \mathbf{c}) +$ PKE.DDec$(2, \mathbf{t}_2, \mathbf{c}) = x \cdot m \mod q$ with probability at least

$$1 - N \cdot (N \cdot B_{\mathsf{add}} \cdot \|x\|_\infty \cdot B_{\mathsf{ct}} \cdot p/q + \|x \cdot m\|_\infty/p + p/q + 1/p) \geq 1 - \lambda^{-\omega(1)}$$

over the randomly choice of the shares $\mathbf{t}_1, \mathbf{t}_2$. For $\mathbf{C} = (\mathbf{c}_1 | \mathbf{c}_2) \in R_p^{2 \times 2}$ by $\mathbf{m} \leftarrow$ PKE.**DDec**$(b, \mathbf{t}_b, \mathbf{C})$, we denote the componentwise decryption $\mathbf{m} \leftarrow$ (PKE.DDec$(b, \mathbf{t}_b, \mathbf{c}_1)$, PKE.DDec$(b, \mathbf{t}_b, \mathbf{c}_2)) \in R_p^2$.

3   Two-Server Verifiable Homomorphic Secret Sharing

A two-server verifiable homomorphic secret sharing (2SVHSS) scheme involves three kinds of parties: multiple input clients, two non-communicating servers and an output client. In a 2SVHSS scheme, any client that gets the public key can encrypt input value as ciphertexts and share between the two servers. The output client asks servers to compute the result and uses the verification key to verify the result.

Definition 1 (Two-server verifiable homomorphic secret sharing). *A 2S-VHSS scheme 2SVHSS for a function family $\mathcal{F}$ over a ring R with input space $\mathcal{I} \subseteq R$ consists of four PPT algorithms* (2SVHSS.Gen, 2SVHSS.Enc, 2SVHSS.Eval, 2SVHSS.Ver) *with the following syntax:*

- 2SVHSS.Gen(1^λ): *On input a security parameter 1^λ, the key generation algorithm outputs a public key* pk, *a verification key* vk *and a pair of evaluation keys* (ek$_1$, ek$_2$).
- 2SVHSS.Enc(pk, x): *On input a public key* pk *and an input value $x \in \mathcal{I}$, the encryption algorithm outputs a ciphertext* ct $\in \mathcal{C}$, *where $\mathcal{C}$ is the cipher space.*
- 2SVHSS.Eval$(b, \mathsf{ek}_b, (\mathsf{ct}^{(1)}, \ldots, \mathsf{ct}^{(n)}), f)$: *On input a server index $b \in [2]$, an evaluation key* ek$_b$, *a vector of n ciphertexts, a function $f \in \mathcal{F}$ with n input values, the homomorphic evaluation algorithm outputs a partial result y_b.*
- 2SVHSS.Ver$(\mathsf{vk}, (y_1, y_2))$: *On input a verification key* vk, *a pair of partial results (y_1, y_2), the verification algorithm outputs a result y (which is believed to be the correct computation result) or an error symbol $\perp$ (to indicate that one of the servers is cheating).*

All parties run the 2SVHSS scheme as follows. First, the output client runs 2SVHSS.Gen(1^λ) to generate $(\mathsf{pk}, \mathsf{vk}, (\mathsf{ek}_1, \mathsf{ek}_2))$. Next, the input clients will run 2SVHSS.Enc(pk, x_i) to generate ciphertext $\mathsf{ct}^{(i)}$ of x_i and upload $\mathsf{ct}^{(i)}$ to all servers. Then, in order to evaluate a function $f(x_1, \ldots, x_n)$, the output client simply sends f to all servers, and the server b runs 2SVHSS.Eval$(b, \mathsf{ek}_b, (\mathsf{ct}^{(i)})_i, f)$ to generate a partial result y_b and returns it to the output client. Finally, the output client runs 2SVHSS.Ver$(\mathsf{vk}, (y_1, y_2))$ to reconstruct and verify the value of $f(x_1, \ldots, x_n)$.

A 2SVHSS scheme should satisfy the following properties: *correctness, semantic security, verifiablility, context hiding* and *compactness*.

Definition 2 (Correctness). *The scheme* 2SVHSS *is said to correctly evaluate a function family* $\mathcal{F}$ *if for all honestly generated keys* $(\mathsf{pk}, \mathsf{vk}, (\mathsf{ek}_1, \mathsf{ek}_2)) \leftarrow$ 2SVHSS.Gen(1^λ), *for all* $x_1, \ldots, x_n \in \mathcal{I}$, *for all ciphertexts* $\mathsf{ct}^{(1)}, \ldots, \mathsf{ct}^{(n)} \in \mathcal{C}$, *where* $\mathsf{ct}^{(i)} \leftarrow$ 2SVHSS.Enc(pk, x_i) *for* $i \in [n]$, *for any function* $f \in \mathcal{F}$, $\Pr_{\mathsf{2SVHSS}, (x_i)_i, f}^{\mathsf{cor}}(\lambda) := \Pr[\mathsf{2SVHSS.Ver}(\mathsf{vk}, (y_1, y_2)) = f(x_1, \ldots, x_n)] \geq 1 - \lambda^{-\omega(1)}$, *where* $y_b \leftarrow$ 2SVHSS.Eval$(b, \mathsf{ek}_b, (\mathsf{ct}^{(i)})_i, f)$ *for* $b \in [2]$ *and the probability is taken over all the algorithms' random choices.*

Definition 3 (Semantic Security). *We define the experiment* $\mathbf{Exp}_{\mathcal{A}, \mathsf{2SVHSS}}^{\mathsf{SS}}(1^\lambda)$ *with a security parameter* $\lambda \in \mathbb{N}$ *and a PPT adversary* $\mathcal{A}$ *as follows:*

$\mathbf{Exp}_{\mathcal{A}, \mathsf{2SVHSS}}^{\mathsf{SS}}(1^\lambda)$:
$(b, x_0, x_1, \mathsf{state}) \leftarrow \mathcal{A}(1^\lambda); \beta \leftarrow \{0, 1\}$
$(\mathsf{pk}, \mathsf{vk}, (\mathsf{ek}_1, \mathsf{ek}_2)) \leftarrow$ 2SVHSS.Gen(1^λ)
$\mathsf{ct} \leftarrow$ 2SVHSS.Enc(pk, x_β)
$\mathsf{input}_b := (\mathsf{state}, \mathsf{pk}, \mathsf{ek}_b, \mathsf{ct})$
$\beta' \leftarrow \mathcal{A}(\mathsf{input}_b)$
If $\beta' = \beta$ *return 1. Else return 0.*

We define the advantage of $\mathcal{A}$ *as* $\mathbf{Adv}_{\mathcal{A}, \mathsf{2SVHSS}}^{\mathsf{SS}}(\lambda) := \Pr[\mathbf{Exp}_{\mathcal{A}, \mathsf{2SVHSS}}^{\mathsf{SS}}(1^\lambda) = 1]$. *Then we say that* 2SVHSS *is* semantically secure *if for all PPT adversary* $\mathcal{A}$ *it holds* $\mathbf{Adv}_{\mathcal{A}, \mathsf{2SVHSS}}^{\mathsf{SS}}(\lambda) \leq \mathsf{negl}(\lambda)$.

Definition 4 (Verifiability). *We define the experiment* $\mathbf{Exp}_{\mathcal{A}, \mathsf{2SVHSS}}^{\mathsf{Ver}}(1^\lambda)$ *with a security parameter* $\lambda \in \mathbb{N}$ *and a PPT adversary* $\mathcal{A}$ *as follows:*

- Setup. *The challenger runs the* 2SVHSS.Gen(1^λ) *to generate a public key* pk, *a verification key* vk, *a pair of evaluation keys* $(\mathsf{ek}_1, \mathsf{ek}_2)$, *and gives* pk *to* $\mathcal{A}$. *If* $\mathcal{A}$ *plays the role of a malicious server* b *the challenger gives* ek_b *to* $\mathcal{A}$.
- Verification Queries. $\mathcal{A}$ *adaptively issues verification queries. Let* $(f, (x_i)_i, (\mathsf{ct}^{(i)})_i, y_b')$ *be a query from* $\mathcal{A}$, *where* y_b' *is a modified partial result and* $\mathsf{ct}^{(i)} \leftarrow$ 2SVHSS.Enc(pk, x_i) *for all* $i \in [n]$. *Given the verification query, the challenger proceeds as follows: for each* $i \in [n]$ *compute* $y_{3-b} \leftarrow$ 2SVHSS.Eval$(3 - b, \mathsf{ek}_{3-b}, (\mathsf{ct}^{(i)})_i, f)$; *compute and respond with* $y' \leftarrow$ 2SVHSS.Ver$(\mathsf{vk}, (y_b', y_{3-b}))$. *In the process of verification queries, if the event* $y' \notin \{f(x_1, \ldots, x_n), \bot\}$ *occurs,* $\mathcal{A}$ *terminates the queries and the experiment outputs 1. If the event never occurs, the experiment outputs 0.*

We define the advantage of $\mathcal{A}$ *as* $\mathbf{Adv}_{\mathcal{A}, \mathsf{2SVHSS}}^{\mathsf{Ver}}(\lambda) := \Pr[\mathbf{Exp}_{\mathcal{A}, \mathsf{2SVHSS}}^{\mathsf{Ver}}(1^\lambda) = 1]$. *We say that* 2SVHSS *is* verifiable under adaptive chosen message and query verification attack, *if for all PPT adversary* $\mathcal{A}$ *it holds* $\mathbf{Adv}_{\mathcal{A}, \mathsf{2SVHSS}}^{\mathsf{Ver}}(\lambda) \leq \mathsf{negl}(\lambda)$.

Definition 5 (Context Hiding). *We say that the scheme* 2SVHSS *satisfies* context hiding *for a function family* $\mathcal{F}$ *if there exists a PPT simulator* Sim *such that the following holds: for any* $\lambda \in \mathbb{N}$, *any* $(\mathsf{pk}, \mathsf{vk}, (\mathsf{ek}_1, \mathsf{ek}_2)) \leftarrow$ 2SVHSS.Gen(1^λ), *any function* $f \in \mathcal{F}$, *any input values* $x_1, \ldots, x_n \in \mathcal{I}$, *any ciphertexts* $\mathsf{ct}^{(1)}, \ldots, \mathsf{ct}^{(n)} \in \mathcal{C}$, *where* $\mathsf{ct}^{(i)} \leftarrow$ 2SVHSS.Enc(pk, x_i) *for* $i \in [n]$, *and* $y_b \leftarrow$ 2SVHSS.Eval$(b, \mathsf{ek}_b, (\mathsf{ct}^{(i)})_i, f)$ *for* $b \in [2]$, *it holds* $\mathsf{SD}[(y_1, y_2), \mathsf{Sim}(1^\lambda, \mathsf{vk}, \mathsf{pk}, f(x_1, \ldots, x_n))] \leq \mathsf{negl}(\lambda)$.

Definition 6 (Compactness). *We say that the scheme* 2SVHSS *compactly evaluates a function family* $\mathcal{F}$ *if the running time of* 2SVHSS.Ver *is bounded by a fixed polynomial in* λ.

4 A Construction of 2SVHSS

In this section, we present a construction of 2SVHSS scheme, which allows the clients to outsource the computation of any polynomials $f(x_1, \ldots, x_n)$ with poly(λ) degree, where λ is the security parameter. We use the PKE-NLD instantiation in Sect. 2 to encrypt input values and perform homomorphic computation.

In our construction, an evaluation key consists of two parts: one part is the additive share of the secret key sk, and the other part is the additive share of the verification key $\mathsf{vk} = \hat{s} \cdot \mathsf{sk}$ (where $\hat{s}$ is randomly choose from the secret key distribution). The evaluation algorithm uses the additive share of sk to compute the additive share of the output y, and uses the additive share of vk to compute the additive share of the authentication tag τ of the output y. The verification algorithm uses these additive shares to reconstruct the output y and its tag τ, and then use $\hat{s}$ to verify the output y by checking the equation $\tau = \hat{s} \cdot y$.

In our construction, the evaluation algorithm consists of 6 subroutines: Load, Add$_1$, Add$_2$, cMult, Mult, Output. To compute f the servers need to execute these subroutines poly(λ) times, and each time these subroutines are executed, there is a unique identifier $\mathsf{id} \in \mathbb{N}$ corresponding to this execution.

Our scheme 2SVHSS = (2SVHSS.Gen, 2SVHSS.Enc, 2SVHSS.Eval, 2SVHSS.Ver) can be described as follows:

- 2SVHSS.Gen(1^λ): Generate a key pair $(\mathsf{pk}, \mathsf{sk}) \leftarrow$ PKE.Gen(1^λ) for encryption where $\mathsf{sk} = \mathbf{s} = (1, s) \in R_q^2$. Randomly choose $\hat{s} \leftarrow \mathcal{D}_{\mathsf{sk}}$ and let verification key $\mathsf{vk} = \hat{s} \cdot \mathbf{s} = (\hat{s}, \hat{s} \cdot s)$. Randomly choose $\mathbf{s}_{1,1} \leftarrow R_q^2$ and $\mathbf{s}_{1,2} \leftarrow R_q^2$. Define $\mathbf{s}_{2,1} = \mathsf{sk} - \mathbf{s}_{1,1} \mod q$, $\mathbf{s}_{2,2} = \mathsf{vk} - \mathbf{s}_{1,2} \mod q$. Draw two keys $K_1, K_2 \leftarrow \mathcal{K}^2$ for a pseudorandom function PRF : $\mathcal{K} \times \mathbb{N} \rightarrow R_q^2$. Output pk, vk and $(\mathsf{ek}_1, \mathsf{ek}_2)$, where $\mathsf{ek}_b = (K_1, K_2, \mathbf{s}_{b,1}, \mathbf{s}_{b,2})$ for $b = 1, 2$.
- 2SVHSS.Enc$(1^\lambda, \mathsf{pk}, x)$: Compute and output $\mathbf{C}^x \leftarrow$ PKE.**OKDM**(pk, x).
- 2SVHSS.Eval$(b, \mathsf{ek}_b, (\mathbf{C}^{x_1}, \ldots, \mathbf{C}^{x_n}), f)$:
  - Load: On input $(\mathsf{id}, \mathbf{C}^x)$ compute $\mathbf{t}_b^x \leftarrow$ PKE.**DDec**$(b, \mathbf{s}_{b,1}, \mathbf{C}^x) + (3 - 2b) \cdot$ PRF$(K_1, \mathsf{id}) \mod q$, $\tau_b^x \leftarrow$ PKE.**DDec**$(b, \mathbf{s}_{b,2}, \mathbf{C}^x) + (3 - 2b) \cdot$ PRF$(K_2, \mathsf{id}) \mod q$, and return $\mathbf{T}_b^x = (\mathbf{t}_b^x, \tau_b^x) \in R_q^{2 \times 2}$.
  - Add$_1$: On input $(\mathsf{id}, \mathbf{T}_b^x, \mathbf{T}_b^{x'})$ compute $\mathbf{t}_b^{x+x'} \leftarrow \mathbf{t}_b^x + \mathbf{t}_b^{x'} + (3 - 2b) \cdot$ PRF$(K_1, \mathsf{id}) \mod q$, $\tau_b^{x+x'} \leftarrow \tau_b^x + \tau_b^{x'} + (3 - 2b) \cdot$ PRF$(K_2, \mathsf{id}) \mod q$, and return $\mathbf{T}_b^{x+x'} = (\mathbf{t}_b^{x+x'}, \tau_b^{x+x'})$.
  - Add$_2$: On input $(\mathsf{id}, \mathbf{C}^x, \mathbf{C}^{x'})$ compute $\mathbf{C}^{x+x'} \leftarrow \mathbf{C}^x + \mathbf{C}^{x'} \mod q$, and return $\mathbf{C}^{x+x'}$.

- cMult: On input $(\mathsf{id}, c, \mathbf{C}^x)$ compute $\mathbf{t}_b^{c \cdot x} \leftarrow \mathsf{PKE.DDec}(b, c \cdot \mathbf{s}_{b,1}, \mathbf{C}^x) + (3 - 2b) \cdot \mathsf{PRF}(K_1, \mathsf{id}) \mod q$, $\boldsymbol{\tau}_b^{c \cdot x} \leftarrow \mathsf{PKE.DDec}(b, c \cdot \mathbf{s}_{b,2}, \mathbf{C}^x) + (3 - 2b) \cdot \mathsf{PRF}(K_2, \mathsf{id}) \mod q$, and return $\mathbf{T}_b^{c \cdot x} = (\mathbf{t}_b^{c \cdot x}, \boldsymbol{\tau}_b^{c \cdot x})$.
- Mult: On input $(\mathsf{id}, \mathbf{T}_b^x, \mathbf{C}^{x'})$ compute $\mathbf{t}_b^{x \cdot x'} \leftarrow \mathsf{PKE.DDec}(b, \mathbf{t}_b^x, \mathbf{C}^{x'}) + (3 - 2b) \cdot \mathsf{PRF}(K_1, \mathsf{id}) \mod q$, $\boldsymbol{\tau}_b^{x \cdot x'} \leftarrow \mathsf{PKE.DDec}(b, \boldsymbol{\tau}_b^x, \mathbf{C}^{x'}) + (3 - 2b) \cdot \mathsf{PRF}(K_2, \mathsf{id}) \mod q$, and return $\mathbf{T}_b^{x \cdot x'} = (\mathbf{t}_b^{x \cdot x'}, \boldsymbol{\tau}_b^{x \cdot x'})$.
- Output: On input $(\mathsf{id}, \mathbf{T}_b^x)$ parses $\mathbf{T}_b^x = (\mathbf{t}_b^x, \boldsymbol{\tau}_b^x) = ((t_b, \hat{t}_b), (\tau_b, \hat{\tau}_b))$ for some $t_b, \hat{t}_b, \tau_b, \hat{\tau}_b \in R_q$ and output partial result $y_b = (t_b, \tau_b) \mod r$.

- 2SVHSS.Ver$(\mathsf{vk}, (y_0, y_1))$: On input verification key $\mathsf{vk} = (\hat{s}, \hat{s} \cdot s)$ and two partial results (y_1, y_2), compute $y = t_1 + t_2 \mod r$ and $\tau = \tau_1 + \tau_2 \mod r$. If $\tau = \hat{s} \cdot y$, output y, otherwise, output $\perp$.

Theorem 1. *For all $\lambda \in \mathbb{N}$, for all inputs $x_1, \ldots, x_n \in R_r$, for all polynomials f which satisfy: f is of size $\mathsf{size}(f) \leq \mathsf{poly}(\lambda)$; the plaintexts upper bound $B_{\max}$ with $B_{\max} \geq r$, $p/B_{\max} \geq \lambda^{\omega(1)}$ and $q/(B_{\max} \cdot p) \geq \lambda^{\omega(1)}$; f has maximum number of input addition instructions P_{inp_+}, for $(\mathsf{pk}, \mathsf{vk}, (\mathsf{ek}_1, \mathsf{ek}_2)) \leftarrow 2\mathsf{SVHSS.Gen}(1^\lambda)$, for $\mathbf{C}^{x_i} \leftarrow 2\mathsf{SVHSS.Enc}(1^\lambda, \mathsf{pk}, x_i)$, there exists a PPT adversary $\mathcal{B}$ on the pseudorandom function PRF such that $\Pr_{2\mathsf{SVHSS}, (x_i)_i, f}^{\mathsf{cor}}(\lambda) \geq 1 - \mathbf{Adv}_{\mathsf{PRF}, \mathcal{B}}^{\mathsf{prf}}(\lambda) - N \cdot (B_{\max} + 1)/q - 4 \cdot \mathsf{size}(f) \cdot N^2 \cdot P_{\mathsf{inp}_+} \cdot B_{\max} \cdot (B_{\mathsf{ct}} \cdot p/q + B_{\mathsf{sk}}^2/p) - 4 \cdot \mathsf{size}(f) \cdot N \cdot (p/q + 1/p).$*

Proof. First, let $\epsilon_0 = \Pr_{2\mathsf{SVHSS}, (x_i)_i, f}^{\mathsf{cor}}(\lambda)$. Our goal is to prove that for all inputs $x_1, \ldots, x_n \in R_r$ and for all polynomials f, the probability $|1 - \epsilon_0| \leq \mathsf{negl}(\lambda)$. And, let $\epsilon_1 = \Pr_{2\mathsf{SVHSS}, (x_i)_i, f}^1(\lambda)$ denote the probability that evaluation yields the correct output, where we replace every evaluation of the PRF by inserting a value $\mathbf{r} \leftarrow R_q^2$ chosen at random. Boyle et al. [9] proved that $|\epsilon_0 - \epsilon_1| \leq \mathbf{Adv}_{\mathsf{PRF}, \mathcal{B}}^{\mathsf{prf}}(\lambda)$.

Next, we give a lower bound of the probability ϵ_1. It is for this reason that we prove that with overwhelming probability over the choice of $\mathbf{r} \leftarrow R_q^2$ all shares $(\mathbf{T}_1^x, \mathbf{T}_2^x)$ computed during homomorphic evaluation of f satisfy $\mathbf{t}_1^x + \mathbf{t}_2^x = x \cdot \mathbf{s} = (x, x \cdot s) \mod q$ (1), $\boldsymbol{\tau}_1^x + \boldsymbol{\tau}_2^x = x \cdot \hat{s} \cdot \mathbf{s} = (x \cdot \hat{s}, x \cdot \hat{s} \cdot s) \mod q$ (2). For $m \in R$ and $z_1, z_2 \in R_q$ be random, $z_1 + z_2 = m$ over R_r with probability at least $1 - N \cdot (B_{\max} + 1)/q \geq 1 - \lambda^{-\omega(1)}$, which has proved in [9]. Therefore assuming (1) and (2) are true, $t_1 + t_2 = x$ and $\tau_1 + \tau_2 = x \cdot \hat{s}$ over R_r with probability at least $1 - N \cdot (B_{\max} + 1)/q$. It is left to prove that indeed (1) and (2) hold true during homomorphic evaluation of f. PKE.DDec is the procedure for distributed decryption. Under the assumption that distributed decryption is always successful, we prove that the subroutines of evaluation algorithm and verification algorithm preserves correctness. Because addition of input values and the output of a memory value does not affect share, we ignore them.

- Consider input $(\mathsf{id}, \mathbf{C}^x)$ for $b \in [2]$. We have $\mathbf{t}_1^x + \mathbf{t}_2^x = \mathsf{PKE.DDec}(1, \mathbf{s}_{1,1}, \mathbf{C}^x) + \mathbf{r} + \mathsf{PKE.DDec}(2, \mathbf{s}_{2,1}, \mathbf{C}^x) - \mathbf{r} \mod q = x \cdot \mathbf{s} \mod q$, $\boldsymbol{\tau}_1^x + \boldsymbol{\tau}_2^x = \mathsf{PKE.DDec}(1, \mathbf{s}_{1,2}, \mathbf{C}^x) + \mathbf{r} + \mathsf{PKE.DDec}(2, \mathbf{s}_{2,2}, \mathbf{C}^x) - \mathbf{r} \mod q = x \cdot \hat{s} \cdot \mathbf{s} \mod q$.
- Consider input $(\mathsf{id}, \mathbf{T}_b^x, \mathbf{T}_b^{x'})$ for $b \in [2]$. We have $\mathbf{t}_1^{x+x'} + \mathbf{t}_2^{x+x'} = \mathbf{t}_1^x + \mathbf{t}_1^{x'} + \mathbf{r} + \mathbf{t}_2^x + \mathbf{t}_2^{x'} - \mathbf{r} \mod q = x \cdot \mathbf{s} + x' \cdot \mathbf{s} \mod q = (x + x') \cdot \mathbf{s} \mod q$, $\boldsymbol{\tau}_1^{x+x'} + \boldsymbol{\tau}_2^{x+x'} = \boldsymbol{\tau}_1^x + \boldsymbol{\tau}_1^{x'} + \mathbf{r} + \boldsymbol{\tau}_2^x + \boldsymbol{\tau}_2^{x'} - \mathbf{r} \mod q = x \cdot \hat{s} \cdot \mathbf{s} + x' \cdot \hat{s} \cdot \mathbf{s} \mod q = (x + x') \cdot \hat{s} \cdot \mathbf{s} \mod q$.

- Consider input $(id, c, \mathbf{C}^x)$ for $b \in [2]$. We have $t_1^{c \cdot x} + t_2^{c \cdot x} = \mathsf{PKE.DDec}(1, c \cdot \mathbf{s}_{1,1}, \mathbf{C}^x) + \mathbf{r} + \mathsf{PKE.DDec}(2, c \cdot \mathbf{s}_{2,1}, \mathbf{C}^x) - \mathbf{r} \mod q = (c \cdot \mathbf{s}) \cdot x \mod q = (c \cdot x) \cdot \mathbf{s} \mod q$, $\tau_1^{c \cdot x} + \tau_2^{c \cdot x} = \mathsf{PKE.DDec}(1, c \cdot \mathbf{s}_{1,2}, \mathbf{C}^x) + \mathbf{r} + \mathsf{PKE.DDec}(2, c \cdot \mathbf{s}_{2,2}, \mathbf{C}^x) - \mathbf{r} \mod q = (c \cdot \hat{s} \cdot \mathbf{s}) \cdot x \mod q = (c \cdot x) \cdot \hat{s} \cdot \mathbf{s} \mod q$.
- Consider input $(id, \mathbf{T}_b^x, \mathbf{C}^{x'})$ for $b \in [2]$. Assuming correctness holds for shares $(\mathbf{T}_1^x, \mathbf{T}_2^x)$ and distributed decryption it holds $t_1^{x \cdot x'} + t_2^{x \cdot x'} = \mathsf{PKE.DDec}(1, t_1^x, \mathbf{C}^{x'}) + \mathbf{r} + \mathsf{PKE.DDec}(2, t_2, \mathbf{C}^{x'}) - \mathbf{r} \mod q = (x \cdot \mathbf{s}) \cdot x' \mod q = (x \cdot x') \cdot \mathbf{s} \mod q$, $\tau_1^{x \cdot x'} + \tau_2^{x \cdot x'} = \mathsf{PKE.DDec}(1, \tau_1^x, \mathbf{C}^{x'}) + \mathbf{r} + \mathsf{PKE.DDec}(2, \tau_2, \mathbf{C}^{x'}) - \mathbf{r} \mod q = (x \cdot \hat{s} \cdot \mathbf{s}) \cdot x' \mod q = (x \cdot x') \cdot \hat{s} \cdot \mathbf{s} \mod q$.

From above all, for verification algorithm output $y_b = (t_b, \tau_b) \mod r$ $(b \in [2])$ it holds $\tau = \tau_1 + \tau_2 = \hat{s} \cdot t_1 + \hat{s} \cdot t_2 = \hat{s} \cdot (t_1 + t_2) = \hat{s} \cdot y$. As the equality $\tau = \hat{s} \cdot y$ is always satisfied, the verification algorithm will output $y = f(x_1, \ldots, x_n)$ with probability 1.

Last, we need to bound the probability that distributed decryption fails. By Sect. 2.1, the distributed decryption fails with probability at most $N^2 \cdot P_{\mathsf{inp}+} \cdot \|x\|_\infty \cdot B_{\mathsf{ct}} \cdot p/q + N \cdot \|x \cdot m\|_\infty / p + N \cdot (p/q + 1/p)$. Throughout the evaluation of f we are guaranteed $\|x\| \le B_{\mathsf{max}}$ for all intermediary values $x \in R$. We need to give the upper bound of $\|x \cdot m\|_\infty$. For the messages $m_i = x_i \cdot s_{j_i}$ we have $\|x \cdot \sum_{i=1}^{P_{\mathsf{inp}+}} x_i \cdot s_{j_i}\|_\infty \le \sum_{i=1}^{P_{\mathsf{inp}+}} \|x \cdot x_i \cdot s_{j_i}\|_\infty \le P_{\mathsf{inp}+} \cdot N \cdot B_{\mathsf{max}} \cdot B_{\mathsf{sk}}$. For the messages $m_i = x_i \cdot \hat{s} \cdot s_{j_i}$ we have $\|x \cdot \sum_{i=1}^{P_{\mathsf{inp}+}} x_i \cdot \hat{s} \cdot s_{j_i}\|_\infty \le \sum_{i=1}^{P_{\mathsf{inp}+}} \|x \cdot x_i \cdot \hat{s} \cdot s_{j_i}\|_\infty \le P_{\mathsf{inp}+} \cdot N \cdot B_{\mathsf{max}} \cdot B_{\mathsf{sk}}^2$.

Finally, applying a union bound over all $4 \cdot \mathsf{size}(f)$ decryptions (one homomorphic multiplication corresponds to 4 decryptions) yields $\epsilon_1 \ge 1 - N \cdot (B_{\mathsf{max}} + 1)/q - 4 \cdot \mathsf{size}(f) \cdot N^2 \cdot P_{\mathsf{inp}+} \cdot B_{\mathsf{max}} \cdot (B_{\mathsf{ct}} \cdot p/q + B_{\mathsf{sk}}^2/p) - 4 \cdot \mathsf{size}(f) \cdot N \cdot (p/q + 1/p)$. $\square$

Theorem 2. *The scheme* 2SVHSS *is semantically secure.*

The proof for the semantic security of our 2SVHSS is quite similar to that of [9]. In order to avoid duplication we only provide a proof sketch.

Proof Sketch. We prove that for every PPT adversary $\mathcal{A}$ on the semantic security of 2SVHSS there exists a PPT adversary $\mathcal{B}$ on the security of PKE.OKDM such that $\mathbf{Adv}_{\mathcal{A}, 2\mathsf{SVHSS}}^{\mathsf{ss}}(\lambda) \le \mathbf{Adv}_{\mathcal{B}, \mathsf{PKE.OKDM}}^{\mathsf{kdm-ind}}(\lambda)$. Boyle et al. [9] have proved $\mathbf{Adv}_{\mathcal{A}, \mathsf{HSS}}^{\mathsf{ss}}(\lambda) \le \mathbf{Adv}_{\mathcal{B}, \mathsf{PKE.OKDM}}^{\mathsf{kdm-ind}}(\lambda)$. Next we will explain that $\mathbf{Adv}_{\mathcal{A}, 2\mathsf{SVHSS}}^{\mathsf{ss}}(\lambda) = \mathbf{Adv}_{\mathcal{A}, \mathsf{HSS}}^{\mathsf{ss}}(\lambda)$. The ciphertexts of 2SVHSS are generated in the same way as HSS of [9]. But the information obtained by the adversary $\mathcal{A}$ in 2SVHSS is different from HSS, because the evaluation key in 2SVHSS is not exactly the same as the evaluation key in HSS, more specifically, the latter has more random numbers than the former. But the extra random numbers in the evaluation key of 2SVHSS does not provide any additional information about the input value to the adversary $\mathcal{A}$, therefore we have that $\mathbf{Adv}_{\mathcal{A}, 2\mathsf{SVHSS}}^{\mathsf{ss}}(\lambda) = \mathbf{Adv}_{\mathcal{A}, \mathsf{HSS}}^{\mathsf{ss}}(\lambda) \le \mathbf{Adv}_{\mathcal{B}, \mathsf{PKE.OKDM}}^{\mathsf{kdm-ind}}(\lambda)$. $\square$

Theorem 3. *The scheme* 2SVHSS *is verifiable.*

Proof. Let A be the event that $\mathbf{Exp}_{\mathcal{A},\text{2SVHSS}}^{\text{Ver}}(1^\lambda)$ outputs 1. Let A_j be the event that the $\mathbf{Exp}_{\mathcal{A},\text{2SVHSS}}^{\text{Ver}}(1^\lambda)$ outputs 1 after j verification queries. Let Q be the upper bound on the number of verification queries requested by the adversary. To prove the theorem we only need to prove $\Pr[A] \leq \mathsf{negl}(\lambda)$.

We first give the probability of event A_j happening. In the j-th verification query, the adversary $\mathcal{A}$ sends $(f, (x_i)_i, (\text{ct}^{(i)})_i, y_b')$ (where $b \in [2]$, if $\mathcal{A}$ plays the role of a malicious first server $b = 1$, otherwise $b = 2$) to the challenger, where $y_b' = (t_b', \tau_b')$. The challenger computes $y_{3-b} \leftarrow \text{2SVHSS.Eval}(3 - b, \text{ek}_{3-b}, (\text{ct}^{(i)})_i, f)$ for all $i \in [n]$, where $y_{3-b} = (t_{3-b}, \tau_{3-b})$. Next, the challenger runs 2SVHSS.Ver(vk, (y_1, y_2)) to compute $y' = t_b' + t_{3-b}$ and $\tau' = \tau_b' + \tau_{3-b}$.

Denote y and τ as the correct value when all participants honestly evaluate f, and let $\Delta_y = y' - y$ and $\Delta_\tau = \tau' - \tau$. Then the event A_i occurs if $\Delta_y \neq 0$ and $\tau' = \hat{s} \cdot y'$, that is, $\hat{s} \cdot \Delta_y = \Delta_\tau$. $\mathcal{A}$ can choose Δ_y and Δ_τ by modifying $y_b' = (t_b', \tau_b')$. Hence, the only way for $\mathcal{A}$ to let the challenger accept a wrong result is to guess $\hat{s}$. Since $\hat{s}$ is a polynomial of degree N and its coefficients are uniform in $\{0, \pm 1\}$, subject to the constraint that only $h_{\text{sk}} = N/2$ coefficients are non-zero, then there are $P = 2^{h_{\text{sk}}} \binom{N}{h_{\text{sk}}} = 2^{h_{\text{sk}}} \frac{\prod_{i=0}^{h_{\text{sk}}-1}(N-i)}{h_{\text{sk}}!} = 2^{h_{\text{sk}}} \prod_{i=0}^{h_{\text{sk}}-1} \frac{N-i}{h_{\text{sk}}-i} \geq 2^{h_{\text{sk}}} \prod_{i=0}^{h_{\text{sk}}-1} \frac{N}{h_{\text{sk}}} = 2^N$ possible values for $\hat{s}$. After $j - 1$ queries $\mathcal{A}$ can exclude $j - 1$ impossible values of $\hat{s}$, which means the number of possible values for $\hat{s}$ is $P - (j - 1)$. So $\Pr[A_i] = \frac{1}{P-(j-1)} = \frac{1}{P-j+1}$.

From above all, we have $\Pr[A] = \Pr[\bigcup_{j=1}^Q A_i] \leq \sum_{j=1}^Q \Pr[A_i] = \sum_{j=1}^Q \frac{1}{P-j+1} \leq \sum_{j=1}^Q \frac{1}{P-Q+1} \leq \frac{Q}{P-Q}$. Because $N > \lambda$ when choosing parameters (see Table 2 for more information), $P \geq 2^N > 2^\lambda$, and $Q = \mathsf{poly}(\lambda)$, $\frac{Q}{P-Q} \leq \mathsf{negl}(\lambda)$. □

Theorem 4. *The scheme* 2SVHSS *satisfies context hiding.*

Proof. We show how to construct a simulator Sim that can generate (y_1', y_2') with negligible statistical distance from (y_1, y_2), where $y_b = (t_b, \tau_b)$ for $b \in [2]$.

We give the description of simulator Sim: on input the security parameter 1^λ, the verification key vk $= (\hat{s}, \hat{s} \cdot s)$, the public key pk and the $y = f(x_1, \ldots, x_n)$, the simulator Sim chooses $t_1' \leftarrow R_q$ and $\tau_1' \leftarrow R_q$ at random, and let $t_2' = y - t_1' \mod q$, $\tau_2' = \hat{s} \cdot y - \tau_1' \mod q$. The simulator Sim outputs (y_1', y_2'), where $y_b' = (t_b', \tau_b')$ for $b \in [2]$. It is straightforward to see that (y_1, y_2) is indistinguishable from the (y_1', y_2'). □

5 Performance Analysis

In this section, we implemented our scheme and got the running time of our scheme, and compared our scheme with the LMS scheme [21] in terms of efficiency.

5.1 Evaluating 2SVHSS

We have implemented the scheme 2SVHSS in a Ubuntu 18.04.2LTS 64-bit operating system with Intel® Xeon(R) Gold 5218 2.30 GHZ × 64 processors and

160 GB RAM. We choose the PRF as the standard AES with 128-bit secret key from the library OpenSSL 1.0.2g and realize all large integer related mathematical computations based on the C libraries GMP 6.1.2 and FLINT 2.5.2.

According to the method of selecting parameters provided by [9], we first choose the plaintexts upper bound B_{max} and let $r = B_{max}$. r can take any integer in $[2, B_{max}]$, in order to maximize the input space $\mathcal{I} = R_r$ we let $r = B_{max}$. Next we choose $B_{err} = 8\sigma$, $\sigma = 8$ for the noise distribution, a statistical security parameter $\kappa = 40$, the number non-zero entries in the secret key $h_{sk} = N/2$, the number of homomorphic additions of inputs $P_{inp+} = 1$, and $B_{sk} = 1$. We choose the parameters so that each multiplication has a failure probability no more than $2^{-\kappa}$. To ensure this holds we set $p = N \cdot B_{max} \cdot h_{sk} \cdot 2^{\kappa+2}$ and $q \geq 2^{-\kappa+3} \cdot p \cdot N^2 \cdot B_{max} \cdot B_{ct}$, where $B_{ct} = B_{err}(2h_{sk} + 1)$ proved by [9]. The security parameters are obtained through the LWE estimator tool [32] by Albrecht et al. [1]. The parameters corresponding to different B_{max} and the running time of 6 subroutines in 2SVHSS.Eval algorithm are listed in Table 2.

Table 2. The Running Time(in milliseconds) of 6 Subroutines in 2SVHSS.Eval

B_{max}	N	$\lg p$	$\lg q$	Security	Load	Add_1	Add_2	cMult	Mult	Output
2	4096	66	153	117.1	106	13	<1	105	105	<1
2^{16}	4096	81	183	86.5	114	13	<1	115	114	<1
2^{32}	8192	99	220	198.7	276	29	<1	275	274	<1
2^{64}	8192	131	284	128.9	315	29	<1	320	318	<1
2^{128}	16384	197	417	214.0	1623	67	<1	1633	1630	<1
2^{256}	16384	325	673	96.7	2049	69	<1	2016	2012	<1

5.2 Comparisons with LMS [21]

We compare the efficiency of the scheme 2SVHSS with the LMS scheme [21] which supports polynomials of highest degree among all existing works, when the same number of servers are used. Because LMS is based on the k-HE assumption, we choose the homomorphic encryption scheme SH [10] to implement LMS. The reason for choosing the scheme SH is to achieve a fair comparison, because the scheme PKE in 2SVHSS is also based on SH. Under different B_{max} and the degree of the polynomials to be computed, the parameters N, q and security parameters of LMS are different. We set those parameters according to the method of [24], and use the LWE estimator tool [1,32] to estimate the corresponding security parameters. The parameters of 2SVHSS and LMS [21] are shown in Table 3. It is fair to compare the two schemes under the same security parameters. But in the case of using LWE estimator tool to estimate the safety parameters, it is difficult to ensure that the safety parameters are exactly the same. To avoid

Table 3. The Parameters of LMS and 2SVHSS

B_{max}		N	lg q	Security	B_{max}		N	lg q	Security
2^{32}	LMS deg-5	4096	151	119.5	2^{128}	LMS deg-5	8192	441	62.8
	LMS deg-7	4096	202	73.5		LMS deg-7	8192	589	42.3
	LMS deg-9	8192	258	151.9		LMS deg-9	16384	742	82.6
	LMS deg-11	8192	311	111		LMS deg-11	16384	892	62
	2SVHSS	8192	220	198.7		2SVHSS	16384	417	214.0
2^{64}	LMS deg-5	4096	246	53.6	2^{256}	LMS deg-5	16384	827	69.5
	LMS deg-7	8192	334	99		LMS deg-7	16384	1104	46.1
	LMS deg-9	8192	417	69.6		LMS deg-9	32768	1387	92.2
	LMS deg-11	8192	502	51.5		LMS deg-11	32768	1665	69.5
	2SVHSS	8192	284	128.9		2SVHSS	16384	673	96.7

Table 4. The Running Time (in seconds) of LMS and 2SVHSS

Server-Side								
The degree	deg-5		deg-7		deg-9		deg-11	
B_{max}	LMS	2SVHSS	LMS	2SVHSS	LMS	2SVHSS	LMS	2SVHSS
2^{32}	0.458	1.145	6.230	1.710	124.592	2.295	1016.660	2.831
2^{64}	0.588	1.152	19.230	1.849	159.609	2.700	1618.510	3.256
2^{128}	2.288	2.931	58.317	4.559	874.877	5.683	7620.583	6.905
2^{256}	14.941	10.761	214.354	14.392	3787.569	18.532	31097.442	22.527
Client-Side								
2^{256}	0.129	0.0024	0.427	0.0024	1.497	0.0024	2.134	0.0024

the suspicion of deliberately exaggerating the efficiency of 2SVHSS we let the security parameters of 2SVHSS larger than those of LMS under the same B_{max}.

Theoretical Analysis. On the server-side, to compute a degree-d term, LMS needs two servers to compute 2^{d-1} degree-d terms respectively, which will cause LMS to be very slow when computing high degree polynomials. 2SVHSS does not have this problem. On the client-side, for LMS, as the polynomial degree increases, the ciphertext size will also become larger (Table 3 shows this intuitively), which makes the time spent by LMS in decryption will increase as the degree of polynomials increases. 2SVHSS does not have the problem of ciphertext size increase, so the time spent by 2SVHSS is fixed.

Experimental Results. Table 4 shows the server-side and client-side running time of LMS and 2SVHSS computing one degree-d term for $d \in \{5, 7, 9, 11\}$, where server-side time is the average running time of the two servers to execute the evaluation algorithm.

It is easy to find out from Table 4 that when computing low-degree polynomials with a small B_{max}, LMS has trivial advantage on server-side. But 2SVHSS has a enormous advantage when computing polynomials higher than degree-7.

A large amount of server-side running time of LMS causes the client to wait a long time to obtain the result, which makes LMS difficult to apply in practice.

The advantage of 2SVHSS on the client-side is obvious. The cost of computing the degree-5 term LMS scheme is about 54 times that of 2SVHSS. And as the degree of polynomial increases, this advantage becomes more obvious, which consistent with our theoretical analysis.

6   Concluding Remarks

In order to solve the problem that the clients cannot compute and verify high-degree polynomial functions over outsourced data on a small number of servers, we proposed a two-server verifiable secret sharing model and constructed a scheme in this model. Our scheme allows the clients to efficient compute and verify the value of polynomials that may have a degree as high as a polynomial in the security parameter. In addition, 2SVHSS can protect outsourced data from leaking to the servers and the output client. In practical applications, 2SVHSS is better than the current best scheme LMS in computing high-degree polynomial functions.

Acknowledgments. The research was supported by Singapore Ministry of Education under Research Grant RG12/19 and National Natural Science Foundation of China (No. 61602304).

References

1. Albrecht, M.R., Player, R., Scott, S.: On the concrete hardness of learning with errors. J. Math. Crypt. **9**(3), 169–203 (2015)
2. Benaloh, J.C.: Secret sharing homomorphisms: keeping shares of a secret secret (Extended Abstract). In: Odlyzko, A.M. (ed.) CRYPTO 1986. LNCS, vol. 263, pp. 251–260. Springer, Heidelberg (1987). https://doi.org/10.1007/3-540-47721-7_19
3. Boyle, E., Couteau, G., Gilboa, N., Ishai, Y., Orrù, M.: Homomorphic secret sharing: optimizations and applications. In: ACM CCS 2017. ACM Press, October/November 2017
4. Barbosa, M., Catalano, D., Fiore, D.: Labeled homomorphic encryption: scalable and privacy-preserving processing of outsourced data. IACR Cryptol. ePrint Arch. **2017**, 326 (2017)
5. Boyle, E., Gilboa, N., Ishai, Y.: Function secret sharing. In: Oswald, E., Fischlin, M. (eds.) EUROCRYPT 2015. LNCS, vol. 9057, pp. 337–367. Springer, Heidelberg (2015). https://doi.org/10.1007/978-3-662-46803-6_12
6. Boyle, E., Gilboa, N., Ishai, Y.: Breaking the circuit size barrier for secure computation under DDH. In: Robshaw, M., Katz, J. (eds.) CRYPTO 2016. LNCS, vol. 9814, pp. 509–539. Springer, Heidelberg (2016). https://doi.org/10.1007/978-3-662-53018-4_19
7. Brakerski, Z., Gentry, C., Vaikuntanathan, V.: (Leveled) fully homomorphic encryption without bootstrapping. TOCT **6**(3), 13 (2014)
8. Beimel, A., Ishai, Y., Kushilevitz, E., Orlov, I.: Share conversion and private information retrieval. IEEE Conf. Comput. Complex. **2012**, 258–268 (2012)

9. Boyle, E., Kohl, L., Scholl, P.: Homomorphic secret sharing from lattices without FHE. In: Ishai, Y., Rijmen, V. (eds.) EUROCRYPT 2019. LNCS, vol. 11477, pp. 3–33. Springer, Cham (2019). https://doi.org/10.1007/978-3-030-17656-3_1

10. Brakerski, Z., Vaikuntanathan, V.: Fully homomorphic encryption from ring-LWE and security for key dependent messages. In: Rogaway, P. (ed.) CRYPTO 2011. LNCS, vol. 6841, pp. 505–524. Springer, Heidelberg (2011). https://doi.org/10.1007/978-3-642-22792-9_29

11. Brakerski, Z., Vaikuntanathan, V.: Efficient fully homomorphic encryption from (standard) LWE. In: 2011 IEEE 52nd Annual Symposium on Foundations of Computer Science, pp. 97–106, October 2011

12. Corrigan-Gibbs, H., Boneh, D., Mazières, D.: Riposte: an anonymous messaging system handling millions of users. In: Symposium on Security and Privacy (2015)

13. Catalano, D., Fiore, D.: Using linearly-homomorphic encryption to evaluate degree-2 functions on encrypted data. In: CCS 2015 (2015)

14. Cleve, R.: Towards optimal simulations of formulas by bounded-width programs. Comput. Complex. 1(1), 91–105 (1991). https://doi.org/10.1007/BF01200059

15. Cachin, C., Micali, S., Stadler, M.: Computationally private information retrieval with polylogarithmic communication. In: Stern, J. (ed.) EUROCRYPT 1999. LNCS, vol. 1592, pp. 402–414. Springer, Heidelberg (1999). https://doi.org/10.1007/3-540-48910-X_28

16. Chen X., Zhang L. F.: Two-Server Delegation of Computation on Label-Encrypted Data. IEEE Transactions on Cloud Computing (2019)

17. Efremenko, K.: 3-query locally decodable codes of subexponential length. Proc. STOC **2009**, 39–44 (2009)

18. Gentry, C.: Fully homomorphic encryption using ideal lattices. In: STOC 2009, pp. 169–178. ACM, New York (2009)

19. Goldwasser, S., Micali, S.: Probabilistic encryption. J. Comput. Syst. Sci. **28**(2), 270–299 (1984)

20. He, Y., Zhang, L.F.: Cheater-identifiable homomorphic secret sharing for outsourcing computations. J. Ambient Intell. Humanized Comput. 1–11 (2020). https://doi.org/10.1007/s12652-020-01814-5

21. Lai, R.W.F., Malavolta, G., Schröder, D.: Homomorphic secret sharing for low degree polynomials. In: Peyrin, T., Galbraith, S. (eds.) ASIACRYPT 2018. LNCS, vol. 11274, pp. 279–309. Springer, Cham (2018). https://doi.org/10.1007/978-3-030-03332-3_11

22. Lyubashevsky, V., Peikert, C., Regev, O.: A toolkit for ring-LWE cryptography. In: Johansson, T., Nguyen, P.Q. (eds.) EUROCRYPT 2013. LNCS, vol. 7881, pp. 35–54. Springer, Heidelberg (2013). https://doi.org/10.1007/978-3-642-38348-9_3

23. Khurana, H., Hadley, M., Lu, N., et al.: Smart-grid security issues. IEEE Symp. Secur. Priv. **8**(1), 81–85 (2010)

24. Lauter, K., Naehrig, M., Vaikuntanathan, V.: Can homomorphic encryption be practical? In: CCSW, pp. 113–124. ACM (2011)

25. Martins, P., Sousa, L., Mariano, A.: A survey on fully homomorphic encryption: an engineering perspective. ACM Comput. Surv. **50**(6), 83:1–83:33 (2017)

26. Paillier, P.: Public-key cryptosystems based on composite degree residuosity classes. In: Stern, J. (ed.) EUROCRYPT 1999. LNCS, vol. 1592, pp. 223–238. Springer, Heidelberg (1999). https://doi.org/10.1007/3-540-48910-X_16

27. Sharma, S., Chen, K., Sheth, A.: Towards practical privacy-preserving analytics for IoT and cloud based healthcare systems. IEEE Internet Comput. **22**(2), 42–51 (2018)

28. Sadeghi, A.R., Wachsmann, C., Waidner, M.: Security and privacy challenges in industrial internet of things. In: Annual Design Automation Conference. ACM (2015)
29. Tsaloli, G., Liang, B., Mitrokotsa, A.: Verifiable homomorphic secret sharing. In: ProvSec, pp. 40–55 (2018)
30. Yoshida, M., Obana, S.: Verifiably multiplicative secret sharing. In: Shikata, J. (ed.) ICITS 2017. LNCS, vol. 10681, pp. 73–82. Springer, Cham (2017). https:// doi.org/10.1007/978-3-319-72089-0_5
31. Zheng L., Chen C., Liu Y., et al.: Industrial scale privacy preserving deep neural network. arXiv preprint arXiv:2003.05198 (2020)
32. LWE estimator tool Homepage. https://bitbucket.org/malb/lwe-estimator. Accessed 8 Jul 2020

Symmetric-Key Cryptography
and Lattice

Searching for Balanced S-Boxes with High Nonlinearity, Low Differential Uniformity, and Improved DPA-Resistance

Youle Xu and Qichun Wang[✉]

School of Computer Science and Technology, Nanjing Normal University,
Nanjing, China
euler_x@qq.com, qcwang@fudan.edu.cn

Abstract. Substitution boxes (S-boxes) are one of the most crucial primitives in the field of block ciphers. Recently, differential power analysis (DPA), a very powerful technique which targets implementations of block ciphers, causes the modern block ciphers to be much more vulnerable than ever before. Up to now, the revised transparency order is one of the best metrics to assess the resistance of S-boxes against DPA attacks. In this paper, we present an efficient algorithm to search for cryptographically significant S-boxes with improved DPA-Resistance. Applying our developed algorithm, we generate an 8×8 balanced S-box with algebraic degree 7, nonlinearity 112, differential uniformity 4, absolute indicator 32, revised transparency order 6.8820 (whereas the Rijndael S-box has revised transparency order 6.9161) and thereby improved resistance towards DPA attacks. Moreover, many other balanced S-boxes with a much better trade-off of cryptographic characteristics than previous works (e.g. S-boxes given by B. Mazumdar and D. Mukhopadhyay in IEEE Trans. Computers 2017) are also captured. The comparison between ours and previous results manifests that our S-boxes are more secure and robust.

Keywords: Differential power analysis · S-boxes · Nonlinearity · Revised transparency order · Differential uniformity.

1 Introduction

S-boxes, also called vectorial Boolean functions, play an extremely important role in the symmetric-key cryptography, since the S-boxes are the only nonlinear components of block ciphers. Therefore the security and the strength of these cryptosystems deeply relies on the cryptographic characteristics of the S-boxes, such as nonlinearity, differential uniformity, algebraic degree. Ideally, it is fundamental for a practical S-box to be balanced. Generally, a practical S-boxes

This work was partly supported by National Natural Science Foundation of Jiangsu Province (Application No. SBK2020021060) and National Natural Science Foundation of China (No. 61572189).

W. Susilo et al. (Eds.): ISC 2020, LNCS 12472, pp. 95–106, 2020.
https://doi.org/10.1007/978-3-030-62974-8_6

must possess high nonlinearity, low differential uniformity, and not low algebraic degree in order to protect S-boxes against *linear cryptanalysis* [14], *differential attacks* [1] and *high order algebraic attacks* [10], respectively. Besides, to provide good diffusion properties, a low absolute indicator of S-boxes will be regarded to be good.

Recently, there are a large number of literature exploring the *side-channel attacks* (SCA), which was firstly introduced by Kocher [11]. In this class of the side-channel attacks, *differential power analysis* [12] is one of the most powerful and efficient attacks. The side-channel attacks including DPA attacks cause the cryptosystems to become much more vulnerable than ever before. Some countermeasures thereby have been proposed to resist DPA attacks, for example, masking and hiding schemes[13]. However, these countermeasures integrated into the hardware implementation are impractical for those areas constrained device. Thus, researchers have been making an effort to design DPA-resistant algorithms by selecting pertinent S-boxes, as updating the cryptographic properties of S-boxes can reduce the complexity to improve the resistance to DPA attacks.

Signal-to-Noise Ratio, an attempt to assess the behaviour of S-boxes against side-channel attacks was firstly investigated in 2004 [8]. Prouff then exhibited some properties of S-boxes on which DPA attacks depended and presented the notion of *transparency order* to quantify the resistance of S-boxes to DPA attacks [23]. Since then, a lot of works referring to the original transparency order have been explored. Next, Fei introduced confusion coefficient[6,7]. Very recently, Chakraborty et al. [4] found that the original definition has inadequacies, and contributed a refined definition of the transparency order. Moreover, [4] has verified practically that the revised transparency order has a marked impact on the resistance of the S-boxes against side-channel attacks. Specifically, low transparency order and low signal-to-noise ratio can be regarded as good.

The transparency order is one of the most significant properties and has received a lot of interest. In this paper, we mainly consider the notion of the revised transparency order as the cryptographic criteria to quantify the resilience of S-boxes against DPA attacks. In general, these criteria to evaluate S-box resistance towards DPA attacks cannot be good with the nonlinearity at the same time. Therefore, finding highly nonlinear balanced S-boxes with low differential uniformity, relatively low revised transparency order is a challenging problem.

1.1   Related Work

After the transparency order was provided, Carlet showed that some highly nonlinear S-boxes constructed using power maps have very bad transparency orders and hence low DPA resistance [2]. Since 2013, some constructed S-boxes with lower transparency order than AES S-box have been obtained using searching algorithm, such as [5,15–17,21,22,24]. However, the nonlinearity of those S-boxes in [5,15–17,21,22,24] is not very high, and the differential uniformity is incompetent. Hence, the security of those S-boxes is not adequate. In addition, the transparency order for Boolean functions has been explored recently, e.g. [9, 20, 25, 26].

Many explorations have investigated the transparency order on S-boxes and Boolean functions, and have obtained some cryptographically interesting results. However, there are still few results on the revised transparency order of S-boxes, in which cross-correlation is taken into consideration and thereby the better metric for assessing the resistance of S-boxes to DPA attacks is provided.

1.2 Our Contribution

In this paper, we take the revised transparency order into the primary account, and develop an efficient algorithm. We then apply our algorithm to search S-boxes with relatively good cryptographic properties. As a result, some S-boxes with very high nonlinearity, low differential uniformity, relatively good absolute indicator, lower signal-to-noise ratio and much better revised transparency order are captured. In addition, we make a comparison in terms of the revised transparency order of ours and previous works, which manifests our proposed S-boxes have a much better trade-off between important cryptographic properties of S-boxes.

We organize the rest of this paper as follows. In Sect. 2, we introduce the notations and preliminaries on cryptographic properties of S-boxes. Section 3 presents the search strategy. We then exhibit some cryptographically significant S-boxes we constructed, and give some comparisons in Sect. 4. Finally, Sect. 5 briefly summarizes the findings of this paper.

2   Preliminaries

Let n, m be two positive integers. We denote by $\mathbb{F}_2^n$ the n-dimensional vector space over $\mathbb{F}_2$, where $\mathbb{F}_2$ is the Galois field with two elements. The addition in $\mathbb{F}_2$ will be denoted by $\oplus$. For any vector $v \in \mathbb{F}_2^n$, the *Hamming weight* of v denoted by $w_H(v)$, is the number to the non-zero positions in the vector.

Any $n \times m$ S-box is a function from $\mathbb{F}_2^n$ into $\mathbb{F}_2^m$. The form of S-box F can be described as $F(x) = (f_1(x), f_2(x) \ldots, f_m(x))$, which is a combination of m Boolean functions $f_i : \mathbb{F}_2^n \to \mathbb{F}_2$ for $i = \{1, 2, \ldots, m\}$. These Boolean functions are called *coordinate functions* of F.

Here we briefly review some important cryptographic properties of the S-boxes. Any $n \times m$ S-box F has a unique representation of multivariate polynomial over $\mathbb{F}_2^m$, called *algebraic normal form* (ANF), that is,

$$F(x_1, x_2, \ldots, x_n) = \sum_{u \in \mathbb{F}_2^n} a_u \prod_{i=1}^{n} x_i^{u_i},$$

where $a_u \in \mathbb{F}_2^m$. The *algebraic degree* $deg(F)$ of F equals the maximum Hamming weight of u such that $a_u \neq 0$.

An S-box F is said to be balanced if it takes every value of $\mathbb{F}_2^m$ the same value 2^{n-m} of times. Particularly, an $n \times n$ S-box is balanced if it is a permutation on $\mathbb{F}_2^n$.

The *Walsh spectrum* of an $n \times m$ S-box F with respect to two vectors $u, v \in \mathbb{F}_2^n$ is defined by

$$\mathcal{W}_F(u, v) = \sum_{x \in \mathbb{F}_2^n} (-1)^{u \cdot F(x) \oplus x \cdot v},$$

where $u \cdot F$ for all $u \in \mathbb{F}_2^{n*}$ are called *component functions* and "." is an inner product over $\mathbb{F}_2$, for instance, $u \cdot F(x) = u_1 f_1(x) \oplus u_2 f_2(x) \oplus, \ldots, \oplus u_m f_m(x)$.

The nonlinearity of an $n \times m$ S-box is defined as the minimum *Hamming distance* between all non-zero component functions of F and all n-variable affine Boolean functions [3], which can be determined in terms of the Walsh spectrum, that is,

$$\mathcal{N}_F = 2^{n-1} - \frac{1}{2} \max_{u \in \mathbb{F}_2^n, v \in \mathbb{F}_2^{m*}} |\mathcal{W}_F(u, v)|.$$

Here, the hamming distance between two Boolean function f, g equals $w_H(f \oplus g)$. Ideally, a cryptographically significant S-box should have high nonlinearity to possess good confusion characteristics.

The derivative of S-box F with regard to vector $a \in \mathbb{F}_2^n$ is the function $\mathcal{D}_F(x, a) = F(x \oplus a) \oplus F(x)$. Let $\delta_F(a, b)$ denote the number of the solutions to the equation $\mathcal{D}_F(x, a) = F(x \oplus a) \oplus F(x) = b$, namely,

$$\delta_F(a, b) = |\{x \in \mathbb{F}_2^n | F(x) \oplus F(x \oplus a) = b\}|.$$

An $n \times m$ S-box F is called *differentially δ_F-uniform* [19], if there exist at most δ_F solutions to the equation for every non-zero $a \in \mathbb{F}_2^n$ and every $b \in \mathbb{F}_2^m$, i.e.,

$$\delta_F = \max_{a \in \mathbb{F}_2^{n*}, b \in \mathbb{F}_2^m} \delta_F(a, b).$$

The *autocorrelation function* of S-box F is defined as

$$\Delta_F(u, w) = \sum_{x \in \mathbb{F}_2^n} (-1)^{u \cdot (F(x) \oplus F(x \oplus w))},$$

where $w \in \mathbb{F}_2^n$. The maximum absolute value in the autocorrelation spectra, except that $w, u = (0, 0, \ldots, 0)$, of an $n \times m$ F is referred to as the *absolute indicator* of the *global avalanche characteristics (GAC)* [27], and is expressed as,

$$\Delta_F = \max_{u \in \mathbb{F}_2^{n*}, w \in \mathbb{F}_2^{n*}} |\Delta_F(u, w)|.$$

The *signal-to-noise ratio* of an $n \times m$ S-box F is formulated in terms of the Walsh spectrum as below [8]. In a way, a low signal-to-noise ratio suggests that S-boxes have good resistance towards DPA.

$$SNR(F) = m2^n \left(\sum_{u \in \mathbb{F}_2^n} \left(\sum_{v \in \mathbb{F}_2^m, w_H(v) = 1} \mathcal{W}_F(u, v) \right)^4 \right)^{-\frac{1}{2}}.$$

The revised transparency order of S-boxes was given by [4], and has been confirmed experimentally that S-boxes with low revised transparency order indeed have much better DPA resistance than those with high revised transparency order. The revised transparency order is depicted as below.

$$
\tau_F = \max_{\beta \in \mathbb{F}_2^m} \left(m - \frac{1}{2^{2n} - 2^n} \right.
$$

$$
\left. \sum_{\alpha \in \mathbb{F}_2^*} \sum_{j=1}^{m} \left| \sum_{i=1}^{m} (-1)^{\beta_i \oplus \beta_j} \mathcal{C}_{f_i, f_j}(\alpha) \right| \right),
$$

where $\mathcal{C}_{f_i, f_j}(\alpha) = \sum_{x \in \mathbb{F}_2^n} (-1)^{f_i(x) \oplus f_j(x \oplus \alpha)}$ is the crosscorrelation function between the coordinate functions f_i and f_j of F.

3   Search Strategy

It is observed that altering a few bits of a given S-box, the cryptographic properties, such as nonlinearity, differential uniformity, and revised transparency order, of the given S-box would change only a little. Based on this fact, we develop an efficient algorithm to construct S-boxes with very high nonlinearity, low differential uniformity and low revised transparency order.

3.1   Search Algorithm

The search algorithm our developed is described roughly as Algorithm 1 shows. We are concerned with not all of the bits in the truth table of a given S-box can be altered. Thus, we first generate a candidate pool (denoted as $\mathcal{P}_F$), which consists of optional bits to yield new S-boxes corresponding to the given S-box. The addition of such a pool can narrow the search space, and enhance the search algorithm efficiency.

At each iteration, we select some bits in the candidate pool. It is worth noting that all bits in the pool belong to the same coordinate functions. Plus the number of altered bits, denoted as b, must be even. The hamming weight of vector v_b must be 2^{b-1}, where v_b is constructed by bits of these b outputs. The reason that why we set these restrictions is that we want to restrict the search space to the balanced S-boxes classes. Technically, $0 \leq b \leq 2^n$. It is clear that the value of b has a direct effect on the search space, i.e., the greater the value of b is, the larger the search space is. Hence, the value of b should be set to be a pertinent value. In our experiment, we set b to be 2 as the initial one. It is noted that the value of b may be changed in a restrained way, if the search algorithm gets stuck in a local optimum.

The algorithm accordingly yields one new S-box (denoted by F') by altering b bits of the original S-box (denoted by F). In our experiment, the algorithm aims to find the S-boxes with the minimum value of the *cost functions*. We calculate a cost function associated with the F' and thereafter put F' and its corresponding

---

Algorithm 1. Developed algorithm to search for highly-nonlinear S-boxes with improved DPA-resistance

---

Require: An $n \times n$ balanced S-box (F_0), MAX_ITER
Ensure: generated $n \times n$ balanced S-boxes with the best desired cryptographic characteristics (F_{best})
1: $F \leftarrow F_0$
2: $max_{walsh} \leftarrow CAL_{walsh}(F)$
3: $min_{tof} \leftarrow CAL_{tof}(F)$
4: $mindu \leftarrow CAL_{du}(F)$
5: Insert F into the set $\mathcal{S}_{input}$
6: **for** $i \rightarrow 1$ **to** MAX_ITER **do**
7:     $cost_{min} = $ MIN_COST
8:     *Generate a pool ($\mathcal{P}_F$) of altered positions corresponding to F*
9:     **for** $j \rightarrow 1$ **to** $\mathcal{P}_F.size$ **do**
10:        *Select b bits in the candidate pool*
11:        *Generate a new S-box F' by altering selected bits while holding F' balanced*
12:        $max_{walsh} = CAL\_new\_walsh(F')$
13:        $\mathcal{N}_F(F') = 2^{n-1} - \frac{1}{2}max_{walsh}$
14:        **if** $\mathcal{N}_F(F') \geq$ NL **then**
15:            $\tau_F = CAL\_new\_tof(F')$
16:            $\delta_F = CAL\_new\_du(F')$
17:            $cost = \mathcal{C}_2(F')$
18:        **else**
19:            $cost = \mathcal{C}_1(F')$
20:        **end if**
21:        *Insert F' and its corresponding value of cost into the Hash_Map $\mathcal{H}_F$*
22:        **if** $cost \leq cost_{min}$ **then**
23:            $cost_{min} = cost$
24:        **end if**
25:    **end for**
26:    *Sort the Hash_Map $\mathcal{H}_F$ by its cost* in non-increasing order
27:    **while** $\mathcal{S}_{input}.find(\mathcal{H}_F.last())$ *equals* TRUE **do**
28:        $\mathcal{H}_F.remove(\mathcal{H}_F.last())$
29:    **end while**
30:    **if** $\mathcal{H}_F.empty()$ *equals* TRUE **then**
31:        **Return** F_{best}
32:        ▷*Algorithm terminates*
33:    **else**
34:        $F = \mathcal{H}_F.last()$
35:    **end if**
36:    Insert F into Set $\mathcal{S}_{input}$
37:    **if** F' has better cryptographic properties than F_{best} **then**
38:        $F_{best} = F'$
39:    **end if**
40: **end for**
41: **Return** F_{best}

---

value of cost function into a data structure (denoted as $\mathcal{H}_F$). When the candidate pool $\mathcal{P}_F$ associated with F yields all possible S-boxes, we choose one generated S-box, which minimizes the cost functions, as the input of the next iteration. In order to prevent the algorithm from resulting in a bad loop, we also provide a set (denote as $\mathcal{S}_{input}$) to store the input that has been selected. If current selected S-box has been in set $\mathcal{S}_{input}$, we remove it from $\mathcal{H}_F$. Subsequently, we rechoose one S-box with the minimum value of the cost function in $\mathcal{H}_F$, and repeat the process mentioned above until the selected S-box is a unique one. Otherwise, the algorithm will terminate.

3.2   Cost Function

A low algebraic degree of balanced S-boxes can be easily transformed to be high. Hence, we do not take the algebraic degree as the main component of designing the cost functions. The essential components of the cost functions are mainly nonlinearity, differential uniformity, and revised transparency order. The lower value of cost implies the better cryptographic properties in terms of nonlinearity, differential uniformity and DPA resistance. In our experiment, the cost functions are defined as follows.

$$C_1(F) = \sum_{u \in \mathbb{F}_2^{n*}} \left(\sum_{v \in \mathbb{F}_2^n} \left(\mathcal{W}_F^2(u, v) - 2^n \right)^R \right)$$
$$+ \frac{1}{2^{2n} - 2^n} \sum_{a \in \mathbb{F}_2^{n*}, b \in \mathbb{F}_2^n} N_{g4}(\delta_F(a, b)) + \frac{1}{n}\tau_F.$$

It's easily observed that,

- the first term of the cost function $C_1(F)$ is to restrict all component functions of the given S-box F the squared distance to Bent functions with respect to Walsh spectra. Therefore, this term can improve the nonlinearity of S-boxes to be closed to that of Bent functions. The parameter R is a small positive number, and is set to be 3–5 in our experiment
- the second term $\sum_{a \in \mathbb{F}_2^{n*}, b \in \mathbb{F}_2^n} N_{g4}(\delta_F(a, b))$ is to restrict the spread of differential spectra of the given S-box F, where $N_{g4}(\delta_F(a, b))$ represents the number of $\delta_F(a, b) > 4$. This term aims to find S-boxes having more potential to be converted to S-boxes with differential uniformity 4
- the third term of the cost function $C_1(F)$ is designed for searching S-boxes with lower revised transparency order. In our experiment, we investigate that the higher value of the third term is, the higher revised transparency order will be. This term plays a slightly important and necessary role in the cost function $C_1(F)$

In addition, the second cost function will be employed, if nonlinearity of generated S-boxes accords with the requirement, and is defined as

$$C_2(F) = \alpha \times \tau_F + \delta_F,$$

where α is a parameter to balance the differential uniformity and revised transparency order.

Table 1. Comparison of cryptographic properties between our proposed S-boxes and those of the AES S-box and the known S-boxes in the literatures

	$\mathcal{N}_F$	δ_F	τ_F	$deg(F)$	Δ_F	SNR
AES Rijndael	112	4	6.9160	7	32	9.6000
Proposed S-box #1	**112**	**4**	**6.8820**	**7**	**32**	**9.1092**
Proposed S-box #2	**110**	**4**	**6.8754**	**7**	**40**	**9.0664**
Proposed S-box #3	**108**	**4**	**6.8711**	**7**	**48**	**8.8466**
Proposed S-box #4	**106**	**4**	**6.8662**	**7**	**48**	**8.8421**
Proposed S-box #5	**104**	**6**	**6.7636**	**7**	**48**	**7.2775**
Proposed S-box #6	**104**	**8**	**6.7414**	**7**	**64**	**7.4703**
Ref.[17]	102	8	6.6898	7	98	7.4181
	102	10	6.7627	7	64	5.5173
	102	12	6.8466	7	64	7.1316
Proposed S-box #7	**102**	**8**	**6.3784**	**7**	**64**	**5.8804**
Ref.[22]	100	10	6.815	7	104	−
	98	14	6.67	7	96	−
	92	12	6.869	7	96	−

4   Experimental Results

We define the profile of an S-box as its nonlinearity, differential uniformity, algebraic degree, revised transparency order, signal-to-noise ratio, and absolute indicator. In Table 1, we exhibit the profiles of the major proposed S-boxes using our devloped algorithm. We first employ the reverse function as the initial input of our search algorithm. As a result, the algorithm generates an 8×8 balanced S-box with the profile (112, 4, 7, **6.8820**, **9.1092**, 32), which is much better than AES S-box with revised transparency order 6.9161 and signal-to-noise ratio 9.6000. This noticeable improvement can provide S-boxes much more DPA-resistance than AES S-box. The S-box with the profile (112, 4, 7, 6.8820, 9.1092, 32) is the proposed S-box in Table 1, and its truth table is given below (in decimal format):

[69, 133, 252, 61, 136, 19, 155, 145, 88, 120, 172, 123, 103, 54, 43, 144, 27, 72, 161, 142, 113, 112, 151, 210, 231, 81, 165, 163, 10, 202, 92, 63, 143, 206, 158, 247, 119, 208, 253, 99, 108, 170, 106, 164, 236, 194, 159, 127, 140, 153, 39, 132, 101, 110, 73, 86, 241, 177, 16, 18, 60, 117, 149, 20, 40, 128, 240, 118, 135, 204, 93, 7, 116, 89, 179, 239, 4, 70, 152, 31, 48, 176, 0, 71, 147, 100, 137, 34, 28, 97,

9, 134, 214, 173, 209, 201, 53, 250, 76, 59, 189, 190, 69, 1, 230, 192, 162, 180, 58, 229, 167, 114, 55, 29, 249, 216, 83, 25, 215, 233, 24, 105, 80, 238, 111, 183, 218, 227, 222, 181, 50, 44, 37, 67, 237, 32, 90, 47, 255, 21, 51, 139, 141, 244, 64, 157, 13, 197, 196, 3, 219, 213, 95, 166, 96, 154, 87, 251, 198, 188, 45, 5, 33, 207, 12, 182, 195, 6, 248, 11, 148, 191, 168, 35, 221, 184, 171, 175, 121, 160, 17, 205, 187, 224, 23, 107, 232, 62, 178, 85, 156, 125, 203, 57, 46, 102, 146, 56, 91, 79, 199, 169, 245, 109, 211, 8, 217, 226, 186, 52, 26, 84, 94, 124, 2, 104, 98, 82, 235, 246, 49, 174, 223, 78, 234, 38, 22, 64, 228, 75, 36, 150, 77, 185, 122, 14, 66, 242, 74, 131, 42, 220, 15, 30, 130, 138, 254, 129, 212, 41, 200, 193, 243, 225, 115, 126]

We also generate some cryptographically significant S-boxes with nonlinearity level of 104–110 and good revised transparency order (there is no known S-box of this nonlinearity level with good revised transparency order). Moreover, the developed algorithm captures some noteworthy improved results based on recent work of B. Mazumdar and D. Mukhopadhyay [17]. The best achieved nonlinear S-boxes given by [17] have the nonlinearity 102, whose profiles are (102, 8, 7, 6.6898, 7.4181, 98), (102, 10, 7, 6.7627, 7.4181, 64), and (102, 12, 6.8466, 7.1316, 64), respectively. As a comparison, our proposed S-box #7 has much better revised transparency order **6.3784**, signal-to-noise ratio **5.8804** and absolute indicator **64**, while possessing the same nonlinearity, differential uniformity and algebraic degree. The proposed S-boxes has a substantial enhancement in terms of DPA-resistance. We give the truth table of proposed S-box #7 as below. In addition, more other proposed S-boxes can be found in the Appendix section.

[255, 73, 146, 195, 5, 217, 148, 205, 74, 67, 194, 154, 9, 107, 27, 82, 148, 137, 132, 233, 71, 213, 103, 3, 66, 245, 210, 234, 54, 147, 44, 249, 41, 104, 51, 159, 13, 36, 219, 147, 142, 129, 251, 18, 107, 103, 2, 22, 53, 222, 225, 116, 173, 199, 213, 85, 108, 156, 38, 178, 88, 60, 243, 112, 82, 116, 144, 218, 98, 125, 191, 204, 18, 10, 144, 217, 167, 241, 39, 14, 29, 95, 128, 124, 247, 26, 4, 110, 214, 48, 206, 169, 4, 184, 44, 188, 104, 95, 29, 93, 211, 64, 136, 70, 91, 59, 143, 39, 171, 128, 138, 55, 216, 48, 121, 84, 220, 226, 100, 119, 184, 60, 112, 25, 231, 178, 224, 190, 166, 160, 184, 198, 33, 109, 180, 41, 76, 244, 254, 129, 126, 116, 25, 252, 48, 207, 4, 203, 32, 1, 179, 11, 79, 35, 98, 160, 94, 25, 28, 56, 58, 46, 191, 103, 133, 76, 250, 39, 239, 62, 247, 39, 8, 95, 92, 90, 169, 172, 32, 35, 157, 242, 127, 155, 8, 42, 113, 187, 88, 220, 105, 159, 146, 99, 246, 212, 123, 64, 170, 252, 229, 228, 129, 133, 213, 113, 140, 28, 150, 49, 78, 195, 31, 171, 203, 47, 87, 145, 73, 197, 21, 253, 46, 175, 177, 234, 96, 63, 242, 194, 234, 78, 157, 193, 205, 151, 160, 230, 238, 199, 101, 156, 33, 7, 240, 10, 115, 251, 239, 129, 165, 245, 195, 158, 79, 16]

Since some known S-boxes, e.g., [5, 15, 16, 21, 24], do not provide the revised transparency order of S-boxes they attained, we cannot make a direct comparison. But the nonlinearity of those work is not high, the differential uniformity is too high. From Table 1, it is clear to see that our S-boxes have the best trade-off between all the important cryptographic criteria, among all currently known S-boxes of [5, 15–17, 21, 22, 24].

5   Conclusion

In this paper, we propose a novel and efficient algorithm to search for S-boxes with very high nonlinearity, low differential uniformity, and improved resistance against DPA attacks. Some resitrictions are employed to restrict the search space of the balanced S-boxes classes. We also apply some approaches to narrow the search space. As a result, we generate a balanced S-box with profile $(112, 4, 7, 6.8820, 9.1092)$ using our devloped algorithm. The proposed S-boxes possess much better revised transparency order and signal-to-noise ratio, which are the best guidance (up to now) to quantify the resistance of S-boxes against DPA attacks. We list some of the best constructed S-boxes and give a comprehensive comparison, which shows that our proposed S-boxes have the best trade-off than those of previous works.

Appendices

Proposed S-box #2: nlf $= 110, \tau_F = 6.8754$
[69, 82, 172, 84, 3, 4, 188, 93, 88, 52, 252, 246, 251, 135, 213, 152, 27, 169, 165, 102, 67, 214, 244, 137, 231, 57, 161, 109, 139, 147, 32, 209, 125, 69, 205, 58, 106, 30, 143, 41, 224, 167, 85, 189, 158, 193, 108, 220, 184, 215, 182, 111, 16, 64, 140, 185, 6, 218, 35, 83, 39, 14, 241, 38, 116, 157, 240, 154, 174, 136, 104, 43, 40, 166, 179, 197, 124, 103, 78, 155, 28, 181, 0, 21, 8, 113, 79, 92, 48, 47, 9, 44, 56, 10, 226, 151, 129, 159, 225, 119, 76, 62, 230, 175, 126, 253, 138, 236, 162, 160, 53, 107, 150, 149, 242, 101, 249, 191, 24, 5, 131, 73, 75, 60, 80, 207, 55, 11, 21, 248, 238, 33, 228, 117, 74, 86, 105, 45, 216, 148, 66, 110, 36, 20, 250, 23, 180, 121, 130, 194, 115, 99, 192, 171, 59, 232, 243, 208, 254, 127, 217, 210, 146, 202, 134, 50, 176, 90, 91, 63, 91, 112, 71, 255, 97, 222, 223, 145, 94, 54, 239, 13, 128, 95, 2, 144, 49, 19, 118, 96, 217, 64, 177, 234, 132, 122, 168, 25, 195, 227, 153, 77, 18, 22, 12, 183, 221, 233, 170, 42, 247, 200, 178, 190, 187, 114, 206, 212, 164, 15, 17, 229, 156, 1, 237, 201, 51, 100, 142, 245, 81, 203, 141, 34, 37, 173, 163, 46, 72, 199, 219, 31, 87, 204, 61, 235, 120, 186, 198, 7, 196, 70, 123, 26, 133, 98]

Proposed S-box #3: nlf $= 108, \tau_F = 6.8711$

[69, 82, 172, 84, 3, 4, 188, 93, 88, 52, 252, 246, 251, 135, 213, 152, 27, 169, 165, 102, 67, 214, 244, 137, 231, 49, 161, 109, 139, 147, 32, 209, 125, 73, 205, 58, 106, 30, 143, 41, 224, 163, 85, 189, 158, 193, 108, 220, 184, 215, 182, 111, 16, 64, 140, 185, 6, 218, 35, 87, 39, 14, 241, 38, 116, 157, 240, 154, 174, 136, 104, 43, 40, 166, 179, 197, 124, 103, 78, 155, 28, 181, 0, 21, 8, 113, 79, 92, 48, 47, 9, 44, 56, 10, 226, 151, 129, 159, 225, 119, 76, 62, 230, 175, 126, 253, 138, 236, 162, 160, 53, 107, 150, 149, 242, 101, 249, 191, 24, 5, 131, 73, 75, 60, 80, 207, 55, 11, 29, 248, 238, 33, 228, 117, 74, 86, 105, 45, 216, 148, 66, 110, 36, 20, 250, 23, 180, 121, 130, 194, 119, 99, 192, 171, 59, 232, 243, 208, 254, 127, 217, 210, 146, 202, 134, 50, 176, 90, 91, 63, 211, 112, 67, 255, 97, 222, 223, 145, 94, 54, 239, 13, 128, 95, 2, 144, 49, 19, 118, 96, 89, 64, 177, 234, 132, 122, 168, 25, 195, 227, 153, 77, 18,

22, 12, 183, 221, 233, 170, 42, 247, 200, 178, 190, 187, 114, 206, 212, 164, 15, 17, 229, 156, 1, 237, 201, 51, 100, 142, 245, 81, 203, 141, 34, 37, 173, 167, 46, 72, 199, 219, 31, 87, 204, 61, 235, 120, 186, 198, 7, 196, 70, 123, 26, 133, 98]

References

1. Biham, E., Shamir, A.: Differential cryptanalysis of DES-like cryptosystems. In: Menezes, A.J., Vanstone, S.A. (eds.) CRYPTO 1990. LNCS, vol. 537, pp. 2–21. Springer, Heidelberg (1991). https://doi.org/10.1007/3-540-38424-3_1
2. Carlet, C.: On highly nonlinear s-boxes and their inability to thwart DPA attacks. In: Maitra, S., Veni Madhavan, C.E., Venkatesan, R. (eds.) INDOCRYPT 2005. LNCS, vol. 3797, pp. 49–62. Springer, Heidelberg (2005). https://doi.org/10.1007/11596219_5
3. Carlet, C.: Vectorial Boolean Functions for Cryptography, Encyclopedia of Mathematics and its Applications, Cambridge University Press, pp. 398–470. (2010). https://doi.org/10.1017/CBO9780511780448.012
4. Chakraborty, K., Sarkar, S., Maitra, S., Mazumdar, B., Mukhopadhyay, D., Prouff, E.: Redefining the transparency order. Des. Codes Crypt. **82**(1), 95–115 (2016). https://doi.org/10.1007/s10623-016-0250-3
5. Evci, M.A., Kavut, S.: DPA resilience of rotation-symmetric s-boxes. In: Yoshida, M., Mouri, K. (eds.) IWSEC 2014. LNCS, vol. 8639, pp. 146–157. Springer, Cham (2014). https://doi.org/10.1007/978-3-319-09843-2_12
6. Fei, Y., Ding, A.A., Lao, J., Zhang, L.: A statistics-based fundamental model for side-channel attack analysis. IACR Cryptology ePrint Archive **2014**, 152 (2014). http://eprint.iacr.org/2014/152
7. Fei, Y., Luo, Q., Ding, A.A.: A statistical model for DPA with novel algorithmic confusion analysis. In: Prouff, E., Schaumont, P. (eds.) CHES 2012. LNCS, vol. 7428, pp. 233–250. Springer, Heidelberg (2012). https://doi.org/10.1007/978-3-642-33027-8_14
8. Guilley, S., Hoogvorst, P., Pacalet, R.: Differential power analysis model and some results. In: Quisquater, J.-J., Paradinas, P., Deswarte, Y., El Kalam, A.A. (eds.) CARDIS 2004. IIFIP, vol. 153, pp. 127–142. Springer, Boston, MA (2004). https://doi.org/10.1007/1-4020-8147-2_9
9. Jain, A., Chaudhari, N.S.: Evolving highly nonlinear balanced Boolean functions with improved resistance to DPA attacks. NSS 2015. LNCS, vol. 9408, pp. 316–330. Springer, Cham (2015). https://doi.org/10.1007/978-3-319-25645-0_21
10. Knudsen, L.R.: Truncated and higher order differentials. In: Preneel, B. (ed.) FSE 1994. LNCS, vol. 1008, pp. 196–211. Springer, Heidelberg (1995). https://doi.org/10.1007/3-540-60590-8_16
11. Kocher, P.C.: Timing attacks on implementations of Diffie-Hellman, RSA, DSS, and other systems. In: Koblitz, N. (ed.) CRYPTO 1996. LNCS, vol. 1109, pp. 104–113. Springer, Heidelberg (1996). https://doi.org/10.1007/3-540-68697-5_9
12. Kocher, P., Jaffe, J., Jun, B.: Differential power analysis. In: Wiener, M. (ed.) CRYPTO 1999. LNCS, vol. 1666, pp. 388–397. Springer, Heidelberg (1999). https://doi.org/10.1007/3-540-48405-1_25
13. Mangard, S., Oswald, E., Popp, T.: Power Analysis Attacks - Revealing the Secrets of Smart Cards. Springer, New York (2007)
14. Matsui, M.: Linear cryptanalysis method for DES cipher. In: Helleseth, T. (ed.) EUROCRYPT 1993. LNCS, vol. 765, pp. 386–397. Springer, Heidelberg (1994). https://doi.org/10.1007/3-540-48285-7_33

15. Mazumdar, B., Mukhopadhyay, D., Sengupta, I.: Constrained search for a class of good bijective s-boxes with improved DPA resistivity. IEEE Trans. Inf. Forensics Secur. **8**(12), 2154–2163 (2013). https://doi.org/10.1109/TIFS.2013.2285522

16. Mazumdar, B., Mukhopadhyay, D., Sengupta, I.: Design and implementation of rotation symmetric s-boxes with high nonlinearity and high DPA resilience. In: 2013 IEEE International Symposium on Hardware-Oriented Security and Trust (HOST), pp. 87–92 (June 2013). https://doi.org/10.1109/HST.2013.6581571

17. Mazumdar, B., Mukhopadhyay, D.: Construction of rotation symmetric s-boxes with high nonlinearity and improved DPA resistivity. IEEE Trans. Comput. **66**(1), 59–72 (2017)

18. Messerges, T.S., Dabbish, E.A.: Investigations of power analysis attacks on smartcards. In: Guthery, S.B., Honeyman, P. (eds.) Proceedings of the 1st Workshop on Smartcard Technology, Smartcard 1999, Chicago, Illinois, USA, 10–11 May 1999. USENIX Association (1999). https://www.usenix.org/conference/usenix-workshop-smartcard-technology/investigations-power-analysis-attacks-smartcards

19. Nyberg, K.: Differentially uniform mappings for cryptography. In: Helleseth, T. (ed.) EUROCRYPT 1993. LNCS, vol. 765, pp. 55–64. Springer, Heidelberg (1994). https://doi.org/10.1007/3-540-48285-7_6

20. Picek, S., Batina, L., Jakobovic, D.: Evolving DPA-resistant Boolean functions. In: Bartz-Beielstein, T., Branke, J., Filipič, B., Smith, J. (eds.) PPSN 2014. LNCS, vol. 8672, pp. 812–821. Springer, Cham (2014). https://doi.org/10.1007/978-3-319-10762-2_80

21. Picek, S., Ege, B., Batina, L., Jakobovic, D., Chmielewski, Ł., Golub, M.: On using genetic algorithms for intrinsic side-channel resistance: the case of AES s-box. In: Proceedings of the First Workshop on Cryptography and Security in Computing Systems. p. 13–18. CS2 2014, Association for Computing Machinery, New York, NY, USA (2014). https://doi.org/10.1145/2556315.2556319

22. Picek, S., Mazumdar, B., Mukhopadhyay, D., Batina, L.: Modified transparency order property: solution or just another attempt. In: Chakraborty, R.S., Schwabe, P., Solworth, J. (eds.) SPACE 2015. LNCS, vol. 9354, pp. 210–227. Springer, Cham (2015). https://doi.org/10.1007/978-3-319-24126-5_13

23. Prouff, E.: DPA attacks and s-boxes. In: Gilbert, H., Handschuh, H. (eds.) FSE 2005. LNCS, vol. 3557, pp. 424–441. Springer, Heidelberg (2005). https://doi.org/10.1007/11502760_29

24. Spain, M., Varia, M.: Evolving s-boxes with reduced differential power analysis susceptibility. IACR cryptology ePrint Arch. **2016,** 1145 (2016). http://eprint.iacr.org/2016/1145

25. Wang, Q., Stănică, P.: Transparency order for Boolean functions: analysis and construction. Des. Codes Crypt. **87**(9), 2043–2059 (2019). https://doi.org/10.1007/s10623-019-00604-1

26. Xu, Y., Wang, Q.: Searching for highly nonlinear DPA-resistant balanced Boolean functions in the rotation symmetric class. In: 2019 IEEE International Symposium on Information Theory (ISIT), pp. 1212–1216 (July 2019). https://doi.org/10.1109/ISIT.2019.8849385

27. Zhang, X.M., Zheng, Y.: GAC the criterion for global avalanche characteristics of cryptographic functions. In: Maurer, H., Calude, C., Salomaa, A. (eds.) J. UCS The Journal of Universal Computer Science, pp. 320–337. Springer, Berlin (1996). https://doi.org/10.1007/978-3-642-80350-5_30

Integerwise Functional Bootstrapping on TFHE

Hiroki Okada[1](✉)(iD), Shinsaku Kiyomoto[1], and Carlos Cid[2,3]

[1] KDDI Research, Inc., Saitama, Japan
ir-okada@kddi-research.jp
[2] Royal Holloway, University of London, Egham, UK
[3] Simula UiB, Bergen, Norway

Abstract. We propose a new technique for implementing an arbitrary 1-variable function during a bootstrapping procedure based on an *integerwise* variant of the fully homomorphic encryption scheme TFHE. The integerwise TFHE was implicit in the original TFHE paper (Asiacrypt' 2016), and Bourse *et al.* provided an explicit form (CRYPTO' 2018). However, the modified integerwise TFHE scheme can perform only the homomorphic evaluations of the integer addition and the sign function, and thus, the application of the scheme is restricted.

Our scheme has diverse functionalities of the integerwise TFHE scheme. Based on our bootstrapping procedure, we propose several useful basic functions: homomorphic equality testing, multiplication by a binary number and a division algorithm. We also derive empirical results that show that our division algorithm is approximately 3.4x faster than the fastest division algorithm in the literature based on fully homomorphic encryption schemes, with a runtime less than 1 s for each 4-bit integer division task.

Keywords: Fully homomorphic encryption · Secure computation · Secure division · LWE · TFHE

1 Introduction

Fully homomorphic encryption (FHE) provides a method for performing computations on encrypted data without the requirement of decryption. The first construction of FHE was introduced by Gentry in 2009 [19, 20], with numerous improvements [4–6, 15–17, 21, 22, 31–33] having been proposed since, resulting in a variety of new features and underlying hardness assumptions. The applications of FHE are widespread, and one of the most remarkable applications is privacy-preserving delegated computation, such as privacy-preserving machine learning as a service (MLaaS) [2, 23]. Users of such a service require that their sensitive data to be hidden from the server, and the server may not want to send their cognitive models to users. FHE enables this scenario elegantly, with non-interactivity; methods based on secure multi-party computation (MPC) require

© Springer Nature Switzerland AG 2020
W. Susilo et al. (Eds.): ISC 2020, LNCS 12472, pp. 107–125, 2020.
https://doi.org/10.1007/978-3-030-62974-8_7

more interactions, and often, users need to be online during the computation. However, because of the inefficiency of the existing FHE schemes, most applications are constructed by avoiding operations considered to be *non-FHE friendly*, such as comparison, division, and various nonlinear functions.

FHE schemes feature *integerwise* or *bitwise* encryption. In bitwise encryption the plaintext space is $\mathbb{Z}_2$, and in integerwise encryption the plaintext space is $\mathbb{Z}_p$ for some $p > 2$. Several studies [11,12,34] have been performed on basic integer arithmetic. The proposed algorithms are primarily for bitwise encryption, and they simply leverage the classical algorithms for logical circuits, such as the full adder, long multiplication, and nonrestoring division methods. Although the bitwise integer comparison algorithm is efficient [9], bitwise integer addition and multiplication are not practical. In the case of integer addition, for example, a full adder needs to perform homomorphic multiplication l times for an l-bit integer. Since integer multiplication calls integer addition approximately l times, homomorphic multiplication must be performed approximately l^2 times [34]. In contrast, integerwise FHE schemes can perform integer addition and multiplication efficiently, since the implementation of homomorphic addition (multiplication) is merely integer addition (multiplication). Based on this fact, recent works [1,2,23,25] on privacy-preserving MLaaS have used integerwise homomorphic encryption. However, the typical algorithms considered in these applications avoid arithmetic operations such as division and comparison, which are considered to be inefficient. Although concrete algorithms for secure integerwise comparison [27] and integerwise division [29] have recently been proposed, they are still not efficient enough to be considered practical. Efficient algorithms for basic arithmetic operations are required to increase the overall efficiency of higher-level applications.

There are many open source implementations for homomorphic encryption, e.g., HELib [24], HEAAN [13], PALISADE [28], SEAL [10] and TFHE [15–17]. For the purposes of our work, we consider the TFHE scheme and its associated library. TFHE is an improved variant of the FHEW scheme [18], which can perform the bootstrapping procedure in less than 0.1 s. The bootstrapping procedure is the bottleneck of FHE constructions, and thus, the TFHE scheme has attracted attention from researchers and implementers as one of the fastest FHE schemes. However, TFHE does not (explicitly) support integerwise arithmetic. As noted above, although bitwise integer addition and multiplication are not practical since they need to perform bootstrapping as many times as the number of bits, integerwise addition and multiplication only need to perform bootstrapping once. Although Bourse *et al.* [2] modified TFHE to enable integerwise encryption, the modified scheme can only perform integer addition and the sign function.

1.1   Our Contribution

The modified TFHE scheme from Bourse *et al.* [2] enables integerwise encryption, but can only perform integer addition and the sign function. In this paper, we propose a technique to perform an arbitrary function of one variable during a bootstrap procedure on the integerwise TFHE scheme. The technique is, basically, the generalization of the constant variable "testvector" in TFHE bootstrapping.

We apply our modified bootstrapping procedure to several homomorphic evaluations of fundamental arithmetic by showing the specific setting of the value of the testvector. We propose, on integerwise TFHE bootstrapping, a homomorphic equality test (Eq, Algorithm 4), a homomorphic equality test between a ciphertext and a plaintext (ConstEq, Algorithm 5), homomorphic multiplication with a binary number (MultbyBin, Algorithm 6), and homomorphic division with a constant plaintext (DivbyConst, Algorithm 7). Using these algorithms as building blocks, we also construct a homomorphic division algorithm on integerwise TFHE (Div, Algorithm 8). We derive empirical results that show that our division algorithm is approximately 3.4x faster than the current state-of-the-art division algorithms. We also show that our homomorphic division algorithm can be generalized to a *homomorphic calculation of an arbitrary 2-variable function*.

2   Preliminaries

2.1   Background on TFHE

Notations. We denote the security parameter as λ. The torus of real numbers modulo 1 $\mathbb{R}/\mathbb{Z}$ is denoted by $\mathbb{T}$. For any ring $\mathcal{R}$, $\mathcal{R}[X]$ denotes polynomials of the variable X with coefficients in $\mathcal{R}$. We denote $\mathbb{R}[X]/(X^N + 1)$ by $\mathbb{R}_N[X]$, and $\mathbb{Z}[X]/(X^N + 1)$ by $\mathbb{Z}_N[X]$, and we write their quotient as $\mathbb{T}_N[X] = \mathbb{R}_N[X]/\mathbb{Z}_N[X]$, which is the ring of polynomials in X with quotient $X^N + 1$ and real coefficients modulo 1. We write the set $\{0, 1\}$ as $\mathbb{B}$. We write vectors in bold. We use $\mathbf{s} \xleftarrow{U} \mathcal{S}$ to denote the process of sampling $\mathbf{s}$ uniformly at random over $\mathcal{S}$, and $e \leftarrow \chi$ denotes the process of sampling e according to the probability distribution χ.

Learning with Errors. The learning with errors (LWE) problem was introduced by Regev [30]. In this work we define LWE over the torus, as in [14,15]. Let n be a positive integer and χ be a probability distribution over $\mathbb{R}$. For a secret vector $\mathbf{s} \in \mathbb{B}^n$, we define the LWE distribution as $\mathsf{LWE}_{n,\mathbf{s},\chi} := \{(\mathbf{a}, b) \mid \mathbf{a} \xleftarrow{U} \mathbb{T}^n, e \leftarrow \chi, b = \mathbf{a} \cdot \mathbf{s} + e \in \mathbb{T}\}$. Search-LWE is the problem of recovering the vector $\mathbf{s}$ from a collection $\{(\mathbf{a}_i, \mathbf{a}_i \cdot \mathbf{s} + e_i)\}_{i=1}^m$ of the samples drawn according to $\mathsf{LWE}_{n,\mathbf{s},\chi}$. Decision-LWE is the problem of distinguishing whether samples $\{(\mathbf{a}_i, \mathbf{s} \cdot \mathbf{a}_i + e_i)\}_{i=1}^m$ are drawn from the LWE distribution $\mathsf{LWE}_{n,\mathbf{s},\chi}$ or uniformly from $\mathbb{T}^{n+1}$.

For the distribution of the error, the *sub-Gaussian* distribution is used in the TFHE. A distribution χ_σ over $\mathbb{R}$ is σ-sub-Gaussian if and only if it satisfies $\forall t \in \mathbb{R}, E(e^{tX}) \leq e^{\sigma^2 t^2/2}$. Let χ and χ' be two independent σ- and σ'-sub-Gaussian stochastic variables. Then, for all $k, l \in \mathbb{R}$, $k\chi + l\chi'$ is $\sqrt{k^2\sigma^2 + l^2\sigma'^2}$-sub-Gaussian.

Encryption from LWE. We outline Regev's bitwise encryption scheme [30], which is used in TFHE. Let $m \in \mathbb{B}$ be a plaintext. Then, the scheme is described as follows: On inputting the security parameter λ, the public parameters are fixed as $n = n(\lambda)$, $\sigma = \sigma(\lambda)$, and the setup algorithm $\mathsf{Setup}(\lambda)$ samples $\mathbf{s} \xleftarrow{U} \mathbb{B}^n$ and outputs $\mathbf{s}$. The encryption algorithm $\mathsf{Enc}(\mathbf{s}, m)$ samples $\mathbf{a} \xleftarrow{U} \mathbb{T}^n$ and $e \leftarrow \mathcal{D}_{\mathbb{T}_N[X], \sigma}$, which is a Gaussian distribution with noise parameter σ, then outputs $(\mathbf{a}, b)$, where $b = \mathbf{a} \cdot \mathbf{s} + e + m/2$. The decryption algorithm $\mathsf{Dec}(\mathbf{s}, (\mathbf{a}, b))$ returns $\lceil 2(b - \mathbf{a} \cdot \mathbf{s}) \rfloor$. Under the condition that the noise e is bounded as

$$|e| < 1/4, \tag{1}$$

decryption works by multiplying by 2 and rounding because $2(b - \mathbf{a} \cdot \mathbf{s}) = 2e + m$, and $|2e| < \frac{1}{2}$; therefore $\lceil 2(b - \mathbf{a} \cdot \mathbf{s}) \rfloor = m$. This scheme can be extended to encrypt nonbinary values as we will explain in Sect. 2.3.

TLWE. TLWE is a generalization of LWE and ring-LWE [26], which is the analog on the torus of the general-LWE problem of [3]. Let $k \geq 1$ be an integer, N is a power of 2 and χ is an error distribution over $\mathbb{R}_N[X]$. A TLWE secret key $\overline{\mathbf{s}} \in \mathbb{B}_N[X]^k$ is a vector of k polynomials over $\mathbb{Z}_N[X]$ with binary coefficients. Given a message encoded as a polynomial $\mu \in \mathbb{T}_N[X]$, a fresh TLWE encryption of μ under the key $\overline{\mathbf{s}}$ is a sample $(\overline{\mathbf{a}}, \overline{b}) \in \mathbb{T}_N[X]^k \times \mathbb{T}_N[X]$, with $\overline{\mathbf{a}} \leftarrow \mathbb{T}_N[X]^k$ and $\overline{b} = \overline{\mathbf{s}} \cdot \overline{\mathbf{a}} + \mu + e$, where $e \leftarrow \chi$.

From a TLWE encryption $(\overline{\mathbf{a}}, \overline{b})$ of a polynomial $\mu \in \mathbb{T}_N[X]$ under a TLWE key $\overline{\mathbf{s}} \in \mathbb{B}_N[X]^k$, we can extract an LWE encryption of the constant term of μ with $\mathsf{SampleExtract}$, which is a simple procedure of extracting the coefficients of the TLWE sample. We denote the extracted LWE encryption by $(\mathbf{a}', b') := \mathsf{SampleExtract}((\overline{\mathbf{a}}, \overline{b}))$, where $\mathbf{a}' = (\mathsf{coefs}(\overline{a}_1(1/X)), \ldots, \mathsf{coefs}(\overline{a}_k(1/X)))$ and b' is the constant term of $\overline{b}$, under an extracted key $\mathbf{s}' = \mathsf{KeyExtract}(\overline{s}) := (\mathsf{coefs}(\overline{s}_1(X)), \ldots, \mathsf{coefs}(\overline{s}_k(X))) \in \mathbb{Z}^{kN}$, and $\mathsf{coefs}(a(X))$ denotes a vector of coefficients of $a \in \mathbb{T}_N(X)$.

Choosing a large N and $k = 1$ corresponds to the classical (binary) ring-LWE. When $N = 1$ and k is large, TLWE is simply binary LWE. In the TFHE library [7], N and k are set to $N = 1024$ and $k = 1$ as default parameters; TLWE is used as ring-LWE in the library, i.e., the TLWE samples are simply ring-LWE samples $(a, b) \in \mathbb{T}_N[X] \times \mathbb{T}_N[X]$.

TGSW. TGSW is a generalized version of the GSW FHE scheme [22]. TGSW can be seen as the matrix equivalent of TLWE, as GSW can be seen as the matrix equivalent of LWE. Each row in the TGSW sample is a TLWE sample. Following [15], we also define an external product $\boxdot$, that performs the mapping $\boxdot : \mathsf{TGSW} \times \mathsf{TLWE} \to \mathsf{TLWE}$. Basically, the external product of the TGSW encryption of a polynomial $\mu_1 \in \mathbb{T}_N[X]$ and a TLWE encryption of a polynomial $\mu_2 \in T_N[X]$ is a TLWE encryption of $(\mu_1 \cdot \mu_2) \in T_N[X]$. More details can be found in [15].

Algorithm 1: TFHE bootstrapping [15] for binary arithmetic

Input: An LWE sample $(\mathbf{a}, b) \in \mathsf{LWE_s}(m_{\mathrm{in}})$ whose plaintext $m_{\mathrm{in}} \in \{0, 1\}$, a
constant $m_{\mathrm{set}} \in \{0, 1\}$, a bootstrapping key $\mathsf{BK_{s \to s'', \alpha}}$, and a
keyswitching key $\mathsf{KS_{s' \to s, \gamma}}$, where $\mathbf{s}' = \mathsf{KeyExtract}(\mathbf{s}'')$.

Output: An LWE sample $\mathsf{LWE_s}(m_{\mathrm{out}})$, where $m_{\mathrm{out}} = m_{\mathrm{in}} \cdot m_{\mathrm{set}}$.

1 $\mu := \frac{m_{\mathrm{set}}}{2} \in \mathbb{T}$, $\mu' = \frac{\mu}{2} \in \mathbb{T}$

2 $\overline{b} := \lceil 2Nb \rfloor$, $\overline{a_i} := \lceil 2Na_i \rfloor$ for each $i \in [1, n]$

3 $\mathsf{testv} := (1 + X + \cdots + X^{N-1}) \cdot X^{\frac{N}{2}} \cdot \mu' \in \mathbb{T}_N[X]$

4 $\mathsf{ACC} \leftarrow X^{\overline{b}} \cdot (0, \mathsf{testv}) \in \mathbb{T}_N[X] \times \mathbb{T}_N[X]$

5 **for** $i = 1$ **to** n **do** $\mathsf{ACC} \leftarrow [\mathbf{h} + (X^{-\overline{a_i}} - 1) \cdot \mathsf{BK}_i] \boxdot \mathsf{ACC}$

6 $\mathbf{u} := (0, \mu') + \mathsf{SampleExtract}(\mathsf{ACC})$

7 **return** $\mathsf{KeySwitch_{KS}}(\mathbf{u})$

2.2 Overview of TFHE Bootstrapping

This section revisits the TFHE bootstrapping proposed in [15] to introduce the rest of the paper. Algorithm 1 shows the bootstrapping algorithm.

As already stated, in the default setting of the TFHE library [7], the dimension of the TLWE sample k is set to $k = 1$. In this setting, TLWE samples are simply ring-LWE samples $(\overline{a}, \overline{b}) \in \mathbb{T}_N[X] \times \mathbb{T}_N[X]$. Thus, in the rest of this paper, we assume that $k = 1$, and we consider a TLWE sample $(a, b) \in \mathbb{T}_N[X] \times \mathbb{T}_N[X]$, for simplicity.

Input. The input of the bootstrapping procedure is an LWE sample $(\mathbf{a}, b) \in \mathbb{T}^n \times \mathbb{T}$, where $b = \mathbf{a} \cdot \mathbf{s} + e + \frac{m_{\mathrm{in}}}{2}$. Here, the required condition to ensure that decryption of LWE encryption succeeds is $|e| < \frac{1}{4}$.

Rounding (line 2). After line 2 of rounding, we obtain an LWE sample over integers $(\overline{\mathbf{a}}, \overline{b}) \in \mathbb{Z}_{2N}^n \times \mathbb{Z}_{2N}$, which satisfies

$$\overline{b} - \overline{\mathbf{a}} \cdot \mathbf{s} = \lceil 2Nb \rfloor - \sum_{i=1}^{n} \lceil 2Na_i \rfloor s_i = 2Nb + \xi_0 - \sum_{i=1}^{n}(2Na_i + \xi_i)s_i$$
$$= 2N(e + m_{\mathrm{in}}/2) + e_{\mathsf{ACC}}, \tag{2}$$

where $e_{\mathsf{ACC}} := \xi_0 - \sum_{i=1}^{n} \xi_i s_i$ and $\xi_0, \ldots \xi_n$ are rounding errors that are uniformly distributed in $(-\frac{1}{2}, \frac{1}{2})$. Please note that $e_{\mathsf{ACC}} = 0$ if the coefficients $(\mathbf{a}, b) \in \frac{1}{2N}\mathbb{Z}/\mathbb{Z}$, and thus we can ignore e_{ACC} in the TFHE library when we use its default parameter $N = 1024$.

BlindRotate (line 4 and line 5). At the beginning of iteration $i = 1$, ACC is a trivial TLWE ciphertext $(0, X^{\overline{b}} \cdot \mathsf{testv}) \in \mathbb{T}_N[X] \times \mathbb{T}_N[X]$, so $\|\mathsf{Err}(\mathsf{ACC}_1)\|_\infty = 0$. At the end of rotation, from Theorem 4.6 in [15] we obtain

$$\|\mathsf{Err}(\mathsf{ACC}_n)\|_\infty \le 2n(k+1)lN\beta\alpha_{\mathsf{BK}} + n(1 + kN)\epsilon, \tag{3}$$

where $\beta = B_g/2$ and $\epsilon = 1/2B_g^l$ are precision parameters of the gadget decomposition and $l \in \mathbb{N}$ and $B_g \in \mathbb{N}$. α_{BK} is a noise parameter of the bootstrapping key BK. After the iteration, the message of ACC is a polynomial $X^{\overline{b}-\overline{\mathbf{a}}\mathbf{s}} \cdot \mathsf{testv}$. From (2) and $e_{\mathsf{ACC}} = 0$, we obtain $\varphi((\overline{\mathbf{a}}, \overline{b})) := \overline{b} - \overline{\mathbf{a}} \cdot \mathbf{s} = 2N(e + m_{\mathrm{in}}/2)$. Recall that $X^{\overline{b}-\overline{\mathbf{a}}\mathbf{s}} \cdot \mathsf{testv} = X^{\overline{b}-\overline{\mathbf{a}}\mathbf{s}+\frac{N}{2}} \cdot (1 + X^{-1} + \cdots + X^{-(N-1)}) \cdot \mu'$. Here, $\overline{b} - \overline{\mathbf{a}} \cdot \mathbf{s} + \frac{N}{2} = 2Ne + \frac{N}{2} + Nm_{\mathrm{in}}$, and from (1) we obtain $0 < 2Ne + \frac{N}{2} < N$. Thus, $\overline{b} - \overline{\mathbf{a}} \cdot \mathbf{s} + \frac{N}{2} \in (0, N)$ if $m_{\mathrm{in}} = 0$, $\overline{b} - \overline{\mathbf{a}} \cdot \mathbf{s} + \frac{N}{2} \in (N, 2N)$ if $m_{\mathrm{in}} = 1$. Then, we obtain that the constant term of $X^{\overline{b}-\overline{\mathbf{a}}\mathbf{s}} \cdot \mathsf{testv}$ is μ' and if $m_{\mathrm{in}} = 0$, $-\mu'$ if $m_{\mathrm{in}} = 1$. (Recall that $X^N + 1 \equiv 0$, and $X^{-i} \equiv -X^{N+i}$.)

Extract (line 6). $\mathsf{SampleExtract}$ simply extracts the coefficients of the TLWE sample. After $\mathsf{SampleExtract}$, we obtain an LWE sample over the torus $(\mathbf{a}', b') := (\mathsf{coefs}(a''(X)), b_0'') \in \mathbb{T}^N \times \mathbb{T}$, where $\mathsf{coefs}(a''(X))$ is a vector of coefficients of $a'' \in \mathbb{T}_N(X)$ and $b_0'' \in \mathbb{T}$ is a constant term of $b'' \in \mathbb{T}_N(X)$. The message of the extracted sample $\mathsf{msg}((\mathbf{a}', b'))$ is the constant term of $(X^{\overline{b}-\overline{\mathbf{a}}\mathbf{s}} \cdot \mathsf{testv})$, which is μ' if $m_{\mathrm{in}} = 0$ and $-\mu'$ if $m_{\mathrm{in}} = 1$. Thus, $\mathsf{msg}(\mathbf{u}) = \mu' + \mathsf{msg}(\mathsf{SampleExtract}(\mathsf{ACC})$ is $2\mu'$ if $m_{\mathrm{in}} = 0$ and 0 if $m_{\mathrm{in}} = 1$; i.e., $\mathsf{msg}(\mathbf{u}) = \mu \cdot m_{\mathrm{in}}$. Since $\mathsf{Extract}$ adds no extra noise, the size of the error of $(\mathbf{a}', b')$ remains to be $\|\mathsf{Err}(\mathsf{ACC})\|_\infty$.

KeySwitch (line 7). After $\mathsf{KeySwitch}$, we obtain a TLWE ciphertext $(\mathbf{a}, b) \in \mathbb{T}^n \times \mathbb{T}$ under the secret key $\mathbf{s}$, whose message is $\frac{m_{\mathrm{out}}}{2} \in \mathbb{T}$. We denote this TLWE ciphertext by $\mathsf{LWE}_{\mathbf{s}}(m_{\mathrm{out}})$ for simplicity. We use the same $\mathsf{KeySwitch}$ procedure as in [15]. Here, $\mathsf{KS}_{\mathbf{s}' \to \mathbf{s}, \gamma, t}$ is a keyswitching key, where $\mathsf{KS}_{i,j} \in \mathsf{LWE}_{\mathbf{s}, \gamma}(s_i' \cdot 2^{-j})$ for $i \in [1, N]$ and $j \in [1, t]$. $\gamma \in \mathbb{R}$ is a noise parameter that satisfies $\|\mathsf{Err}(\mathsf{KS}_{i,j})\|_\infty \leq \gamma$, and $t \in \mathbb{N}$ is a precision parameter. From Lemma 4.3 in [15], we obtain $\varphi_{\mathbf{s}}(\mathbf{a}, b) = \varphi_{\mathbf{s}}(\mathbf{0}, b') - \sum_{i=1}^N \sum_{j=1}^t a_{i,j}' \varphi_{\mathbf{s}}(\mathsf{KS}_{i,j}), = \varphi_{\mathbf{s}'}(\mathbf{a}', b') - \sum_{i=1}^N \sum_{j=1}^t a_{i,j}' \mathsf{Err}(\mathsf{KS}_{i,j}) + \sum_{i=1}^N (a_i' - \overline{a}_i') s_i'$. Thus, we obtain the bound on the noise as $\|\mathsf{Err}(\mathbf{a}, b)\|_\infty \leq \|\mathsf{Err}(\mathsf{ACC})\|_\infty + Nt\gamma + N2^{-(t+1)} \leq 2n(k+1)lN\beta\alpha_{\mathsf{BK}} + n(1 + kN)\epsilon + Nt\gamma + N2^{-(t+1)}$, where a second inequality is derived by using (3). We can ensure that the output of the bootstrapping procedure is a "fresh" LWE sample by selecting the parameters that satisfy the upper bound from (1) as follows:

$$2n(k+1)lN\beta\alpha_{\mathsf{BK}} + n(1 + kN)\epsilon + Nt\gamma + N2^{-(t+1)} < 1/4. \qquad (4)$$

2.3   Integerwise LWE Encryption

As in [2], we use a variant of the Regev encryption scheme that supports a nonbinary message space. Let $B \in \mathbb{N}$, and let plaintext $m_{\mathrm{in}} \in \{-B, \ldots, B-1\}$. Then, the integerwise LWE encryption scheme is described as follows:

$\mathsf{Setup}(\lambda)$: for a security parameter λ, fix $n = n(\lambda)$ and $\sigma = \sigma(\lambda)$; return $\mathbf{s} \xleftarrow{U} \mathbb{B}^n$.

$\mathsf{Enc}(\mathbf{s}, m)$: samples $\mathbf{a} \xleftarrow{U} \mathbb{T}^n$ and $e \leftarrow \mathcal{D}_{\mathbb{T}_N[X], \sigma}$, which is a Gaussian distribution with noise parameter σ, and return $(\mathbf{a}, b)$, where $b = \mathbf{a} \cdot \mathbf{s} + e + \frac{m}{2B}$.

$\mathsf{Dec}(\mathbf{s}, (\mathbf{a}, b))$: return $\lceil (b - \mathbf{a} \cdot \mathbf{s}) \cdot 2B \rfloor$.

Algorithm 2: General functional bootstrapping procedure

Input: A ciphertext $C_{m_{in}} :=$ An LWE sample $(\mathbf{a}, b) \in \mathsf{LWE_s}(m_{in})$, where its plaintext $m_{in} \in \{-B, \ldots, B-1\}$, a bootstrapping key $\mathsf{BK}_{\mathbf{s} \to \mathbf{s}'', \alpha}$, a keyswitching key $\mathsf{KS}_{\mathbf{s}' \to \mathbf{s}, \gamma}$, where $\mathbf{s}' = \mathsf{KeyExtract}(\mathbf{s}'')$, a constant function $f : \{0, \ldots, B-1\} \to \{-B, \ldots, B-1\}$, and a set of coefficients $\{\mu_0, \ldots, \mu_{N-1}\}$ of the testvector which corresponds to the function f.

Output: An LWE sample $\mathsf{LWE_s}(m_{out}) := \mathsf{Bootstrap}(C_{m_{in}}, f)$, where

$$m_{out} = f'(m_{in}) := \begin{cases} f(m_{in}) & (m_{in} \in \{0, \ldots, B-1\}), \\ -f(B+m_{in}) & (m_{in} \in \{-B, \ldots, -1\}). \end{cases} \quad (6)$$

1   $\bar{b} := \lceil 2Nb \rfloor$, $\overline{a_i} := \lceil 2Na_i \rfloor$ for each $i \in [1, n]$
2   $\mathsf{testv} := \mu_0 + \mu_1 X^{-1} + \cdots + \mu_{N-1} X^{-(N-1)} \in \mathbb{T}_N[X]$
3   $\mathsf{ACC} \leftarrow X^{\bar{b}} \cdot (0, \mathsf{testv}) \in \mathbb{T}_N[X] \times \mathbb{T}_N[X]$
4   **for** $i = 1$ to n **do** $\mathsf{ACC} \leftarrow [\mathbf{h} + (X^{-\overline{a_i}} - 1) \cdot \mathsf{BK}_i] \boxdot \mathsf{ACC}$
5   $\mathbf{u} := \mathsf{SampleExtract}(\mathsf{ACC})$
6   **return** $\mathsf{KeySwitch}_{\mathsf{KS}}(\mathbf{u})$

Under the condition that the noise e is bounded as

$$|e| < 1/4B, \quad (5)$$

decryption works by multiplying by $2B$ and rounding because $(b - \mathbf{a} \cdot \mathbf{s}) \cdot 2B = \left(e + \frac{m}{2B}\right) \cdot 2B = m + 2Be$ and $|2Be| < \frac{1}{2}$ holds from (5).

3   Integerwise General Functional Bootstrapping

We propose a modified variant of TFHE that encrypts integer plaintext and can perform arbitrary functions during bootstrapping. On top of the integerwise LWE encryption Sect. 2.3, we propose a general functional bootstrapping procedure in Sect. 3.1. We discuss the security of our scheme in Sect. 3.2.

3.1   General Functional Bootstrapping

We propose a general functional bootstrapping procedure in Algorithm 2. The difference from Algorithm 1 is the test vector, which is used in BlindRotate. In addition, the input of the bootstrapping procedure is the ciphertext of the integer, which enables integerwise homomorphic evaluation.

Input. The input of the bootstrapping procedure is an LWE sample $(\mathbf{a}, b) \in \mathbb{T}^n \times \mathbb{T}$, where $b = \mathbf{a} \cdot \mathbf{s} + e + m_{in}/2B$. Here, the required condition to ensure that the decryption of the LWE encryption succeeds is (5).

Rounding (line 1). After rounding, we obtain an LWE sample over integers $(\bar{\mathbf{a}}, \bar{b}) \in \mathbb{Z}_{2N}^n \times \mathbb{Z}_{2N}$. Similar to (2), we obtain

$$\bar{b} - \bar{\mathbf{a}}\mathbf{s} = 2N(e + m_{in}/2B) + e_{\mathsf{ACC}}, \quad (7)$$

and when $N = 1024$ we also obtain $e_{\mathsf{ACC}} = 0$ as explained in Sect. 2.2.

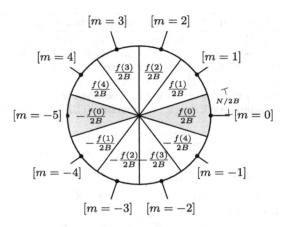

Fig. 1. Illustration of the slices for plaintext and bootstrapping (when $B = 5$)

BlindRotate (lines 3 and 4). At the beginning of the iteration $i = 1$, ACC is a trivial TLWE ciphertext $(0, X^{\overline{b}} \cdot \text{testv}) \in \mathbb{T}_N[X] \times \mathbb{T}_N[X]$, As with the original TFHE bootstrapping procedure, after the iteration, the message of ACC is a polynomial $X^{\overline{b}-\overline{\mathbf{a}}\mathbf{s}} \cdot \text{testv}$. From (7) and $e_{\text{ACC}} = 0$, we obtain $\varphi((\overline{\mathbf{a}}, \overline{b})) := \overline{b} - \overline{\mathbf{a}}\mathbf{s} = 2N\left(e + \frac{m_{\text{in}}}{2B}\right)$, and from (5), we obtain $-\frac{N}{2B} < 2Ne < \frac{N}{2B}$. Moreover, note that the value of testv is different from that in the original TFHE bootstrapping. The test vector is defined as $\text{testv} := \mu_0 + \mu_1 X^{-1} + \cdots + \mu_{N-1}X^{-(N-1)} \in \mathbb{T}_N[X]$ in our scheme. In the rest of this paragraph, we explain how to homomorphically evaluate the input constant function f during bootstrapping by setting the value of the coefficients of testv. See also Fig. 1, which illustrates our setting.

When $m_{\text{in}} = 0$, we obtain $\varphi((\overline{\mathbf{a}}, \overline{b})) = 2Ne$, thus $(\overline{\mathbf{a}}, \overline{b}) \in \{-\lfloor\frac{N}{2B}\rfloor, \ldots, \lfloor\frac{N}{2B}\rfloor\}$. Then, the constant term of

$$X^{\varphi((\overline{\mathbf{a}}, \overline{b}))} \cdot \text{testv} = X^{\varphi((\overline{\mathbf{a}}, \overline{b}))} \cdot (\mu_0 + \mu_1 X^{-1} + \cdots + \mu_{N-1}X^{-(N-1)})$$
$$= X^{\varphi((\overline{\mathbf{a}}, \overline{b}))} \cdot (\cdots - \mu_{N-1}X^1 + \mu_0 + \mu_1 X^{-1} \ldots)$$

is in $\{-\mu_{N-\lfloor\frac{N}{2B}\rfloor}, \ldots, -\mu_{N-1}, \mu_0, \mu_1, \ldots, \mu_{\lfloor\frac{N}{2B}\rfloor}\} := \mathcal{M}_0$. For all $\mu \in \mathcal{M}_0$, we define its value as $\mu := \frac{f(0)}{2B} \in \mathbb{T}$. Note that now we have $X^N + 1 \equiv 0 \Leftrightarrow X^{-i} \equiv -X^{N-i} \Leftrightarrow X^i \equiv -X^{-(N-i)}$.

When $m_{\text{in}} = -B$, similar to the case when $m_{\text{in}} = 0$, the constant term of $X^{\varphi((\overline{\mathbf{a}}, \overline{b}))} \cdot \text{testv}$ is in $\{\mu_{N-\lfloor\frac{N}{2B}\rfloor}, \ldots, \mu_{N-1}, -\mu_0, -\mu_1, \ldots, -\mu_{\lfloor\frac{N}{2B}\rfloor}\} := \mathcal{M}_{-B}$, elements of which are the sign inversions of those of $\mathcal{M}_0$. Thus, note that all values of $\mu \in \mathcal{M}_{-B}$ are already defined as $\mu := \frac{-f(0)}{2B} \in \mathbb{T}$.

When $m_{\text{in}} \in \{1, \ldots, B-1\}$, we obtain $\varphi((\overline{\mathbf{a}}, \overline{b})) = 2N\left(e + \frac{m_{\text{in}}}{2B}\right)$. Since $-\frac{N}{2B} < 2Ne < \frac{N}{2B}$ holds from (5), we have $\frac{N}{2B} < (m_{\text{in}} - \frac{1}{2})\frac{N}{B} < \varphi((\overline{\mathbf{a}}, \overline{b})) < (m_{\text{in}} + \frac{1}{2})\frac{N}{B} < N$. Thus, we obtain $\varphi((\overline{\mathbf{a}}, \overline{b})) \in \{\lceil(m_{\text{in}} - \frac{1}{2})\frac{N}{B}\rceil, \ldots, \lfloor(m_{\text{in}} + \frac{1}{2})\frac{N}{B}\rfloor\}$, and the

constant term of $X^{\varphi((\overline{\mathbf{a}},\overline{b}))} \cdot \mathsf{testv}$ is in $\{\mu_{\lceil (m_{\mathrm{in}} - \frac{1}{2})\frac{N}{B}\rceil}, \cdots, \mu_{\lfloor (m_{\mathrm{in}} + \frac{1}{2})\frac{N}{B}\rfloor}\} := \mathcal{M}_{m_{\mathrm{in}}}$.
For all $\mu \in \mathcal{M}_{m_{\mathrm{in}}}$, we define its value as $\mu := \frac{f(m_{\mathrm{in}})}{2B} \in \mathbb{T}$.

When $m_{\mathrm{in}} \in \{-(B-1), \ldots, -1\}$, we have $-N < (m_{\mathrm{in}} - \frac{1}{2})\frac{N}{B} < \varphi((\overline{\mathbf{a}},\overline{b})) < (m_{\mathrm{in}} + \frac{1}{2})\frac{N}{B} < -\frac{N}{2B}$. Therefore, $\varphi((\overline{\mathbf{a}},\overline{b})) \in \{\lceil (m_{\mathrm{in}} - \frac{1}{2})\frac{N}{B}\rceil, \ldots, \lfloor (m_{\mathrm{in}} + \frac{1}{2})\frac{N}{B}\rfloor\}$, then the constant term of $X^{\varphi((\overline{\mathbf{a}},\overline{b}))} \cdot \mathsf{testv}$ is in $\{-\mu_{N+\lceil (m_{\mathrm{in}} - \frac{1}{2})\frac{N}{B}\rceil}, \ldots, -\mu_{N+\lfloor (m_{\mathrm{in}} + \frac{1}{2})\frac{N}{B}\rfloor}\}$. Note that these values are the sign inversions of the previously defined $\mu \in \mathcal{M}_{m_{\mathrm{in}}}$, for $m_{\mathrm{in}} \in \{1, \ldots, B-1\}$.

Extract (line 5). The message of the extracted sample $\mathsf{msg}((a', b'))$ is the constant term of $(X^{\overline{b} - \overline{\mathbf{a}}\mathbf{s}} \cdot \mathsf{testv})$. By our construction of BlindRotate, its value becomes $\mu = \frac{m_{\mathrm{out}}}{2B} = \frac{f'(m_{\mathrm{in}})}{2B} \in \mathbb{T}$, where f' is defined in (6).

KeySwitch (line 7). After KeySwitch, we obtain a TLWE ciphertext $(\mathbf{a}, b) \in \mathbb{T}^n \times \mathbb{T}$ under the secret key $\mathbf{s}$, whose message is $\frac{m_{\mathrm{out}}}{2B} \in \mathbb{T}$. We denote this TLWE ciphertext by $\mathsf{LWE}_{\mathbf{s}}(m_{\mathrm{out}})$ for simplicity. Similar to (4), we can ensure that the output of the bootstrapping procedure is a "fresh" LWE sample by selecting the parameters that satisfy the upper bound from (5) as follows:

$$2n(k+1)lN\beta\alpha_{\mathsf{BK}} + n(1 + kN)\epsilon + Nt\gamma + N2^{-(t+1)} < 1/4B. \qquad (8)$$

3.2   Security

The security of the scheme basically relies on the original TFHE scheme since our modification is performed only on the setting of the testvector, except for the change in the bound of the noise given in (8). While the bound of TFHE is fixed as $1/4$ as shown in (4), it is $1/4B$ in our scheme. Thus, the larger the plaintext we use is, the lower the bound becomes, which leads to the need to use smaller noise in the TLWE sample if (8) does not hold. Conversely, after we fix the security parameters and noise size, if we select B that satisfies (8), then the security of our scheme solely relies on the original TFHE scheme. We use the same security parameters and noise as the original TFHE scheme and set the value of B that satisfies (8) in our experiments later in Sect. 5. Additionally, note that the bound given in (8) does not depend on the function f; thus, we can perform arbitrary functions at the same cost.

4   Applications

In this section, we introduce several applications of our general TFHE bootstrapping scheme (Algorithm 2):

Algorithm 3: Homomorphic evaluation of sign function

Input: A ciphertext $C_{m_{\text{in}}}$, where $m_{\text{in}} \in \{-B, \ldots, B-1\}$.
Output: $C_{m_{\text{out}}} := \text{Sign}(C_{m_{\text{in}}})$, where $m_{\text{out}} = -1$ if $m_{\text{in}} \in \{-B+1, \ldots, -1\}$, 0
 if $m_{\text{in}} \in \{-B, 0\}$, and 1 if $m_{\text{in}} \in \{1, \ldots, B-1\}$.

1 **return** $\text{Bootstrap}(C_{m_{\text{in}}}, f_{\text{sign}})$, where $f_{\text{sign}}(x) := 1$ if $x \in \{1, \ldots B-1\}$, 0 if
 $x = 0$.

- $C_{\text{sign}(a)} = \text{Sign}(C_a)$: Sign function (Algorithm 3)
- $C_{(a=b)} = \text{Eq}(C_a, C_b)$: Equality test (Algorithm 4)
- $C_{(a=b)} = \text{ConstEq}(C_a, b)$: Equality test with a plaintext (Algorithm 5)
- $C_{a \cdot b} = \text{MultbyBin}(C_a, C_b)$: Multiplication with a binary number (Algorithm 6)
- $C_{\lfloor a/d \rfloor} = \text{DivbyConst}(C_a, d)$: Division by a plaintext (Algorithm 7)
- $C_{\lfloor a/d \rfloor} = \text{Div}(C_a, C_d)$: Division (Algorithm 8)

Sign() is the homomorphic evaluation of the sign, which was proposed in [2]. We show how to perform Sign() in our scheme, to clarify that our general framework includes the homomorphic function. Note that the original integerwise TFHE proposed in [2] can perform only sign() bootstrapping, and it cannot perform multiplication of the integer ciphertexts.

We propose Eq and ConstEq in Sect. 4.2, MultbyBin in Sect. 4.3, and DivbyConst in Sect. 4.4; then, based on these functions, we propose Div in Sect. 4.5.

4.1 Homomorphic Evaluation of Sign()

We show our homomorphic evaluation of the sign function in Algorithm 3. This algorithm is constructed by using Bootstrap as sign bootstrapping with an input function sign. Specifically, we express f_{sign} by defining the coefficients $\mu_0, \ldots, \mu_{N-1} \in \mathbb{T}$ of the testvector as follows:

$$
\begin{cases}
\mu_0, \ldots, \mu_{\lfloor \frac{N}{2B} \rfloor} & := 0, \\
\mu_{\lfloor \frac{N}{2B} \rfloor + 1}, \ldots, \mu_{N - \lfloor \frac{N}{2B} \rfloor - 1} & := \frac{1}{2B}, \\
\mu_{N - \lfloor \frac{N}{2B} \rfloor}, \ldots, \mu_{N-1} & := 0.
\end{cases}
$$

We can confirm, from (6), that $m_{\text{out}} = f'(m_{\text{in}}) = f_{\text{sign}}(m_{\text{in}}) = 1$ for $m_{\text{in}} \in \{1, \ldots, B-1\}$, $m_{\text{out}} = f'(m_{\text{in}}) = -f_{\text{sign}}(B + m_{\text{in}}) = -1$ for $m_{\text{in}} \in \{-B+1, \ldots, -1\}$, $m_{\text{out}} = f'(m_{\text{in}}) = 0$ for $m_{\text{in}} = 0$, and $m_{\text{out}} = f'(m_{\text{in}}) = -f_{\text{sign}}(B + m_{\text{in}}) = 0$ for $m_{\text{in}} = -B$. Note that the output of the function is tricky in the case of $m_{\text{in}} = -B$. The plaintext of the output with $m_{\text{in}} = -B$ becomes the same as that of $m_{\text{in}} = 0$ by construction. If needed, it is easy to avoid this feature by restricting the input plaintext space as $m \in \{-B+1, \ldots, B-1\}$.

4.2 Homomorphic Equality Test

We show that our general bootstrapping framework includes the homomorphic evaluation of the equality test. Also, note that for our equality tests (Algorithms 4 and 5), we require that the input plaintexts m_1 and m_2 to be in $\{0, \ldots, B-1\}$ (or in $\{-B, \ldots, -1\}$). The restriction is needed because if $m_2 = B + m_1$, then $m_2 - m_1 = B$ and the output becomes *true* although $m_1 \neq m_2$.

Algorithm 4: Homomorphic equality test

Input: Two ciphertexts C_{m_1} and C_{m_2}, where $m_1, m_2 \in \{0, \ldots, B-1\}$.
Output: $C_{m_{\text{out}}} := \mathsf{Eq}(C_{m_1}, C_{m_2})$, where $m_{\text{out}} = B$ if $m_0 = m_1$, 0 else.
1 **return** $\mathsf{Bootstrap}(C_{m_1} - C_{m_2}, f_{\text{ztest}})$, where $f_{\text{ztest}}(x) := B$ if $x = 0$,
$f_{\text{ztest}}(x) := 0$ otherwise.

Algorithm 5: Homomorphic equality test with a constant

Input: A ciphertext C_{m_1} and plaintext m_2, where $m_1, m_2 \in \{0, \ldots, B-1\}$.
Output: $C_{m_{\text{out}}} := \mathsf{ConstEq}(C_{m_1}, m_2)$, where $m_{\text{out}} = B$ if $m_1 = m_2$, 0 else.
1 Encode $m_2 \in \{0, \ldots, B-1\}$ to $\nu_{m_2} := \frac{m_2}{2B} \in \mathbb{T}$.
2 **return** $\mathsf{Bootstrap}(C_{m_1} - (\mathbf{0}, \nu_{m_2}), f_{\text{ztest}})$, where $f_{\text{ztest}}(x) := B$ if $x = 0$,
$f_{\text{ztest}}(x) := 0$ else.

In other FHE schemes, such as HElib, the integerwise homomorphic equality test is typically performed based on Fermat's little theorem [8]. For example, in HElib (i.e., in the BGV FHE scheme [3]), the plaintext space is $\mathbb{Z}_p$ for some prime number p, and the homomorphic equality test is constructed based on the fact that $(x - y)^{p-1} \equiv 1 \bmod p$ if $x - y \not\equiv 0$, and 0 if $x - y \equiv 0$. However, this algorithm is inefficient since it needs to perform homomorphic multiplication for approximately $\log(p)$ times, and some bootstrapping is required to deal with the noise growth caused by multiplication. Our equality test bootstrapping on integerwise TFHE is efficient since it can be performed with only one bootstrapping procedure.

We show an equality test of two ciphertexts in Algorithm 4. This algorithm is constructed by using $\mathsf{Bootstrap}$ as a "zero test" bootstrapping with the input function f_{ztest}. Specifically, we express f_{ztest} by defining the coefficients $\mu_0, \ldots, \mu_{N-1} \in \mathbb{T}$ of the testvector as follows:

$$\begin{cases} \mu_0, \ldots, \mu_{\lfloor \frac{N}{2B} \rfloor} & := \frac{B}{2B} = \frac{1}{2}, \\ \mu_{\lfloor \frac{N}{2B} \rfloor + 1}, \ldots, \mu_{N - \lfloor \frac{N}{2B} \rfloor - 1} & := 0, \\ \mu_{N - \lfloor \frac{N}{2B} \rfloor}, \ldots, \mu_{N-1} & := \frac{-B}{2B} = -\frac{1}{2}. \end{cases}$$

The equality test can also be performed between a ciphertext and a plaintext. We show the algorithm in Algorithm 5. The only difference is that the second argument is a plaintext m_1, and it is encoded as a trivial $(\mathbf{0}, \nu_{m_1})$ LWE sample.

4.3   Homomorphic Multiplication with a Binary Number

We propose homomorphic multiplication with a binary number ($\mathsf{MultbyBin}$) in Algorithm 6. As we stated earlier, integerwise TFHE cannot perform a very basic calculation: the multiplication of integer ciphertexts. $\mathsf{MultbyBin}$ enables us to homomorphically multiply a ciphertext of an integer message by a ciphertext of a binary message. This algorithm is called later in the homomorphic division algorithm Div (Algorithm 8). We illustrate how the $\mathsf{MultbyBin}$ algorithm works in Fig. 2. Note that this algorithm requires B to be an odd number, and we restrict $m_{\text{in}} \in \{0, \ldots, B-1\}$, the details of which are explained later in this subsection.

Algorithm 6: Homomorphic multiplication by binary number

Input: Ciphertexts $C_{m_{\text{int}}}, C_{m_{\text{bin}}}$, where $m_{\text{int}} \in \{0, \ldots, B-1\}$, $m_{\text{bin}} \in \{B, 0\}$.
Output: $C_{m_{\text{out}}} := \text{MultbyBin}(C_{m_{\text{int}}}, C_{m_{\text{bin}}}) = C_{m_{\text{int}}}$ if $m_{\text{bin}} = B$, C_0 else.
1 $C_{\text{tmp}} = \text{Bootstrap}(C_{m_{\text{int}}} + C_{m_{\text{bin}}} + (\mathbf{0}, \frac{B}{2B}), f_{\text{id}})$
2 **return** $\text{Bootstrap}(C_{m_{\text{int}}} + C_{\text{tmp}}, f_{\text{half}})$

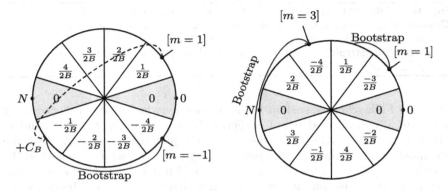

Fig. 2. Illustration of MultbyBin when $(m_{\text{int}}, m_{\text{bin}}) = (1, 0)$. Left: line 1. Right: line 2.

To construct MultbyBin, we define 2 functions f_{id} and f_{half} to be used as an argument of Bootstrap. The function $f_{\text{id}} : \{0, \ldots, B-1\} \rightarrow \{0, \ldots, B-1\}$ is defined as $f_{\text{id}}(x) := x$. For f_{id}, we define the coefficients $\mu_0, \ldots, \mu_{N-1} \in \mathbb{T}$ of the testvector as follows:

$$\begin{cases} \mu_0, \ldots, \mu_{\lfloor \frac{N}{2B} \rfloor} & := \frac{f_{\text{id}}(0)}{2B} = 0, \\ \mu_{\lfloor \frac{(2i-1)N}{2B} \rfloor + 1}, \ldots, \mu_{\lfloor \frac{(2i+1)N}{2B} \rfloor} & := \frac{f_{\text{id}}(i)}{2B} = \frac{i}{2B}, \text{ for } i = 1, \cdots, B-1, \\ \mu_{N - \lfloor \frac{N}{2B} \rfloor}, \ldots, \mu_{N-1} & := \frac{-f_{\text{id}}(0)}{2B} = 0. \end{cases}$$

The function f_{half} is defined as $f_{\text{half}}(x) := \frac{x}{2}$ if x is even, $-\frac{x+1}{2} - \frac{B-1}{2}$ otherwise. For f_{half}, we define the coefficients $\mu_0, \ldots, \mu_{N-1} \in \mathbb{T}$ of the testvector as follows:

$$\begin{cases} \mu_0, \ldots, \mu_{\lfloor \frac{N}{2B} \rfloor} & := \frac{f_{\text{half}}(0)}{2B} = 0, \\ \mu_{\lfloor \frac{(2i-1)N}{2B} \rfloor + 1}, \ldots, \mu_{\lfloor \frac{(2i+1)N}{2B} \rfloor} & := \frac{f_{\text{half}}(i)}{2B}, \text{ for } i = 1, \cdots, B-1, \\ \mu_{N - \lfloor \frac{N}{2B} \rfloor}, \ldots, \mu_{N-1} & := \frac{-f_{\text{half}}(0)}{2B} = 0. \end{cases}$$

Now, we explain how Algorithm 6 works. In line 1, we homomorphically add $C_{m_{\text{bin}}}$, which is a ciphertext of a binary value in $\{B, 0\}$, and a trivial (noiseless) ciphertext $(\mathbf{0}, \frac{B}{2B})$ to $C_{m_{\text{int}}}$ and the output of the bootstrapping procedure with f_{id} is stored as C_{tmp}. If $C_{m_{\text{bin}}}$ is a ciphertext of 0 (*false*), then $C_{m_{\text{bin}}} + (\mathbf{0}, \frac{B}{2B})$ is C_B (a ciphertext of B), so the phase of $C_{m_{\text{int}}}$ is rotated to a position symmetrical about the origin, as illustrated by the dashed arrow in the left image of Fig. 2. Then, the phase of the ciphertext is rotated to the position symmetrical about the x-axis after the bootstrapping with f_{id}; C_{tmp} becomes a ciphertext of $-m_{\mathrm{int}}$. If $C_{m_{\mathrm{bin}}}$ is a ciphertext of B (true), then $C_{m_{\mathrm{bin}}} + (\mathbf{0}, \frac{B}{2B})$ is C_0 (a ciphertext of 0), so C_{tmp} remains as a ciphertext of m_{int}. Thus, in line 2, $C_{m_{\mathrm{int}}} + C_{\mathrm{tmp}} = C_{m_{\mathrm{int}}} + C_{m_{\mathrm{int}}}$ when $m_{\mathrm{bin}} = B$, and $C_{m_{\mathrm{int}}} + C_{\mathrm{tmp}} = C_0$ when $m_{\mathrm{bin}} = 0$. After bootstrapping with f_{half}, $C_{m_{\mathrm{int}}} + C_{m_{\mathrm{int}}}$ is converted to $C_{m_{\mathrm{int}}}$, and C_0 remains as C_0, as illustrated in Fig. 2. Finally, we obtain $C_{m_{\mathrm{out}}} = C_{m_{\mathrm{int}}}$ when $m_{\mathrm{bin}} = B$, and C_0 when $m_{\mathrm{bin}} = 0$.

Algorithm 7: Homomorphic division by a constant

Input: A ciphertext $C_{m_{\mathrm{in}}}$, where $m_{\mathrm{in}} \in \{0, \ldots, B-1\}$, and a constant plaintext $m_d \in \{1, \ldots, B-1\}$.
Output: $C_{m_{\mathrm{out}}} := \mathsf{DivbyConst}(C_{m_{\mathrm{in}}}, m_d) := C_{\lfloor m_{\mathrm{in}}/m_d \rfloor}$
1 **return** $\mathsf{Bootstrap}(C_{m_{\mathrm{in}}}, f_{\mathrm{div}, m_d})$

As we noted before, we restrict that B must be odd. If B is even, when $m_{\mathrm{int}} = \frac{B}{2}$ and $m_{\mathrm{bin}} = B$, the ciphertext in line 2 $C_{m_{\mathrm{int}}} + C_{\mathrm{tmp}} = C_{m_{\mathrm{int}}} + C_{m_{\mathrm{int}}}$ is converted to C_0, but we want it to remains as $C_{\frac{B}{2}}$. Thus, the restriction is needed to perform bootstrapping with f_{half} as we intended. In addition, we restrict the input m_{int} to be in $\{0, \ldots, B-1\}$, because we cannot[1] perform multiplication with binary on negative inputs $m_{\mathrm{int}} \in \{-B+1, \ldots, -1\}$ with $\mathsf{MultbyBin}$. In the case of $m_{\mathrm{int}} \in \{-B+1, \ldots, -1\}$, if m_{bin} is B (*true*), the plaintext of C_{tmp} in line 1 becomes $-(B + m_{\mathrm{int}})$, and then the output becomes $m_{\mathrm{out}} = 0$ since $C_{\mathrm{tmp}} + C_{m_{\mathrm{bin}}} = C_B$ for all $m_{\mathrm{int}} \in \{-B+1, \ldots, -1\}$, while m_{bin} is *true*. If m_{bin} is 0, in line 1 the plaintext of C_{tmp} is $B - m_{\mathrm{int}}$, and then the output becomes $m_{\mathrm{out}} = -B + m_{\mathrm{int}}$. Thus, the outputs of $\mathsf{MultbyBin}$ for $m_{\mathrm{int}} \in \{-B+1, \ldots, -1\}$ are not those of multiplication with binary and we need the restriction.

4.4 Homomorphic Division by a Constant

We propose an algorithm for homomorphic division by a constant ($\mathsf{DivbyConst}$) in Algorithm 7. The inputs of this algorithm are a ciphertext $C_{m_{\mathrm{in}}}$ and a plaintext m_d, and the output is a ciphertext of $C_{\lfloor m_{\mathrm{in}}/m_d \rfloor}$. Note that we restrict the input as $m_{\mathrm{in}} \in \{0, \ldots, B-1\}$ and $m_d \in \{1, \ldots, B-1\}$.

Bitwise integer division by 2 on TFHE was proposed in [16]. However, the algorithm corresponds to a right shift over the bits; thus, the dividend is restricted to be a power of two. In [29], homomorphic division by a constant was proposed based on HElib, i.e., the BGV FHE scheme [3]. This algorithm is based on polynomial interpolation, which needs to calculate the list powers of the ciphertexts $\{C_a, C_a^2, C_a^3, \ldots, C_a^{p-1}\}$, where p is the modulo of the plaintext space $\mathbb{Z}_p$. Thus, homomorphic multiplication needs to be performed $p-1$ times, which is not efficient. In contrast, our algorithm for homomorphic division by a constant on integerwise TFHE is efficient since it can be performed with only one bootstrapping procedure.

---

[1] Precisely, although we can perform binary multiplication on $m_{\mathrm{int}} = -B$ or B, which is equivalent to $m_{\mathrm{int}} = 0$, we omit $-B$ from the space of input m_{int} for simplicity.

Algorithm 8: Homomorphic division

Input: Ciphertexts $C_{m_{\text{in}}}$ and C_{m_d}, where $m_{\text{in}} \in \{0, \ldots, B-1\}$ and
    $m_d \in \{1, \ldots, B-1\}$.
Output: $C_{m_{\text{out}}} := \text{Div}(C_{m_{\text{in}}}, C_{m_d}) := C_{\lfloor m_{\text{in}}/m_d \rfloor}$
1 $C_{\text{sum}} := C_0$ (noiseless TLWE sample of 0)
2 **for** $i = 1$ to $(B-1)$ **do**
3 | $C_{\lfloor m_{\text{in}}/i \rfloor} = \text{DivbyConst}(C_{m_{\text{in}}}, i)$,
4 | $C_{(m_d=i)} = \text{ConstEq}(C_{m_d}, i)$
5 | $C_{\text{sum}} = \text{Bootstrap}(C_{\text{sum}} + \text{MultbyBin}(C_{\lfloor m_{\text{in}}/i \rfloor}, C_{(m_d=i)}), f_{\text{id}})$
6 **end**
7 **return** C_{sum}

The function $f_{\text{div},d} : \{0, \ldots, B-1\} \to \{0, \ldots, B-1\}$ is defined as $f_{\text{div},d}(x)$ $:= \lfloor x/d \rfloor$ for $d \in \{1, \ldots, B-1\}$, i.e., the output is the quotient of the integer division (x/d). For $f_{\text{div},d}$, we define the coefficients $\mu_0, \ldots, \mu_{N-1} \in \mathbb{T}$ of the testvector as follows:

$$\begin{cases} \mu_0, \ldots, \mu_{\lfloor \frac{N}{2B} \rfloor} & := \frac{f_{\text{div},d}(0)}{2B} = 0, \\ \mu_{\lfloor \frac{(2i-1)N}{2B} \rfloor + 1}, \ldots, \mu_{\lfloor \frac{(2i+1)N}{2B} \rfloor} & := \frac{f_{\text{div},d}(i)}{2B} = \frac{\lfloor i/d \rfloor}{2B}, \text{ for } i = 1, \cdots, B-1, \quad (9) \\ \mu_{N-\lfloor \frac{N}{2B} \rfloor}, \ldots, \mu_{N-1} & := \frac{-f_{\text{div},d}(0)}{2B} = 0. \end{cases}$$

Note that we need to store a set of $\{\mu_0, \ldots, \mu_{N-1}\}$ for each $d \in \{0, \ldots, B-1\}$. Thus we need to store NB values in $\mathbb{T}$ as precomputed constants. We need to restrict the input m_{in} to be in $\{0, \ldots, B-1\}$ since we cannot perform division for $m_{\text{in}} \in \{-B, \ldots, -1\}$ as the output m_{out} becomes $- \lfloor (B - m_{\text{in}})/m_d \rfloor$.

4.5 Homomorphic Division

Finally, we present a homomorphic division algorithm Div in Algorithm 7. This algorithm calls DivbyConst, ConstEq and MultbyBin. Since the subalgorithms need the input m_{in} to be in $\{0, \ldots, B-1\}$, Div also follows this restriction.

Now, we explain how Div works. In line 1, we initialize a ciphertext $C_{\text{sum}} = C_0$ as a trivial TLWE sample with a message of 0, i.e., $(\mathbf{0}, 0)$. While in the for loop in lines 2–6, we first calculate a ciphertext of $\lceil a/i \rceil$, $C_{\lceil a/i \rceil}$ with DivbyConst. Then, we homomorphically check if the iteration index i equals d, which is the plaintext of the input ciphertext C_d with ConstEq, and output the ciphertext of the Boolean value $C_{(d=i)}$. In line 5, we obtain $\text{MultbyBin}(C_{\lfloor a/i \rfloor}, C_{(i=d)}) = C_{\lfloor a/d \rfloor}$ if $i = d$, C_0 otherwise. Thus, at the end of this loop, $C_{\text{sum}} = C_0 + \cdots + C_{\lfloor a/d \rfloor} + \cdots + C_0 = C_{\lfloor a/d \rfloor}$.

Algorithm 9: Homomorphic evaluation of a 2-variable function

Input: Ciphertexts C_{m_1} and C_{m_2}, where $m_1, m_2 \in \{0, \ldots, B-1\}$, a 2-variable
function $f(x, y) : \{0, \ldots, B-1\} \times \{0, \ldots, B-1\} \to \{0, \ldots, B-1\}$, and
sets of coefficients $\{\mu_{0,y}, \ldots, \mu_{N-1,y}\}$ of the testvector which corresponds
to 1-variable functions $f_y(x) := f(x, y)$, for all fixed $y \in \{0, \ldots, B-1\}$.

Output: $C_{m_{\mathrm{out}}} := \mathsf{Func}(C_{m_1}, C_{m_2}) := C_{f(m_1, m_2)}$

1 $C_{\mathsf{sum}} := C_0$ (noiseless TLWE sample of 0)
2 **for** $i = 0$ to $(B-1)$ **do**
3 $\quad C_{f_i(m_1)} = \mathsf{Bootstrap}(C_{m_{\mathrm{in}}}, f_i),$
4 $\quad C_{(m_2=i)} = \mathsf{ConstEq}(C_{m_2}, i)$
5 $\quad C_{\mathsf{sum}} = \mathsf{Bootstrap}(C_{\mathsf{sum}} + \mathsf{MultbyBin}(C_{f_i(m_1)}, C_{(m_2=i)}), f_{\mathrm{id}})$
6 **end**
7 **return** C_{sum}

Generalization to the 2-variable function. We show that the homomorphic division algorithm can be generalized to a homomorphic evaluation of the arbitrary 2-variable function $\mathsf{Func}(C_{m_1}, C_{m_2})$ in Algorithm 9. The algorithm takes two ciphertexts C_{m_1} and C_{m_2}, a 2-variable function $f(x, y)$ and sets of coefficients $\{\mu_{0,y}, \ldots, \mu_{N-1,y}\}$ of the testvector, which corresponds to a 1-variable function $f_y(x) := f(x, y)$ for all fixed $y \in \{0, \ldots, B-1\}$. Then, the algorithm outputs $C_{f(m_1, m_2)}$. This algorithm generalizes Div by replacing DivbyConst with $\mathsf{Bootstrap}(C_{m_{\mathrm{in}}}, f_y)$, which homomorphically evaluates the 1-variable function $f_y(x) := f(x, y)$ over a ciphertext C_x.

5 Results of Homomorphic Division

We implemented our homomorphic division algorithm based on the TFHE library [7]. Our parameters settings follow the default values given in the library, which are as follows:

- The degree of the polynomials in the ring: $N = 1024$.
- The dimension of the LWE and TLWE sample: $n = 500$ and $k = 1$.
- Decomposition basis and length for TGSW ciphertexts: $B_g = 2^{10}$ and $l = 2$.
- Decomposition basis and length for KeySwitch: 2^l and $t = 8$.
- Standard deviation of the noise in the keyswitching keys: $\sigma_{\mathsf{KS}} = 2.44 \cdot 10^{-5}$.
- Standard deviation of the noise in the bootstrapping keys: $\sigma_{\mathsf{BK}} = 7.18 \cdot 10^{-9}$.

As discussed in [15], these choices of parameters achieve a minimum security level of 128 bits. Our single bootstrapping procedure takes approximately 10 ms with a 3.4-GHz Intel Core i5 CPU. We implemented homomorphic division to calculate a 4-bit integer, which is the same target as that of existing works on homomorphic division algorithms [11,12,29,34]. To encrypt the 4-bit integer in our scheme, we set $B = 17$.

In Table 1, we show our results and refer to the values given in the existing works on homomorphic division. We ran Div (Algorithm 8) 1000 times and calculated the average. Our method is approximately 3.4x faster than the fastest

Table 1. Results: comparison with existing homomorphic division implementations.

Method	FHE lib	Type	Bits	Time [sec]	Security λ [bits]
[12]	HElib	Bitwise	4	67.94	>128
[34]	HElib	Bitwise	4	14.63	>128
[11]	HElib	Bitwise	4	7.74	>80
[29]	HElib	Integerwise	4	3.15	>80
Ours (Div)	TFHE	Integerwise	4	0.93	>128
Nonrestoring division	TFHE	Bitwise	4	2.05	>128

Table 2. A breakdown of the running time of our Div (Algorithm 8)

Functions	# of bootstrap	Time [msec]	# Of calls	Mean [msec]
MultbyBin (line 5)	2	346.0 (37.2%)	$B - 1 = 16$	21.6
ConstEq (line 4)	1	174.8 (18.8%)	$B - 1 = 16$	10.9
DivbyConst (line 3)	1	175.8 (18.9%)	$B - 1 = 16$	11.0
Bootstrap$(\cdot, f_{\mathrm{id}})$ (line 5)	1	173.9 (18.7%)	$B - 1 = 16$	10.9

method given in the table, despite achieving a higher level of security ($\lambda > 128$) than that of the existing methods. To make a fair comparison, we also implemented the nonrestoring division algorithm on the original (bitwise) TFHE library with the same parameters that we used in our algorithm. The nonrestoring division algorithm is a classic bitwise algorithm for integer division, which is used in the existing works on integer division [11,12,34]. We can confirm in Table 1 that our method is approximately 2.2x faster than the nonrestoring division.

As a reference, in Table 2, we show the breakdown of the running time of our Div, which was performed in 0.93 s. We show the running time cost for each of MultbyBin, ConstEq, DivbyConst, and Bootstrap$(\cdot, f_{\mathrm{id}})$ in line 5 of Algorithm 8. We can confirm that the costs of these functions accounts for almost the whole running time. Moreover, since the single bootstrapping procedure takes approximately 10 ms with our PC, we can also confirm that the running time of these functions is dominated by the cost of bootstrapping. Our functions can be performed without extra costs over single bootstrapping.

Limitation in the Correctness. In the parameter setting showed in the beginning of this section, the standard deviation of the final error after bootstrapping is $\sigma = 0.00961$ as described in [15]. The probability that the noise amplitude after the bootstrapping is larger than $1/16$, i.e., the probability of the decryption error, is upper bounded by $\mathrm{erf}(1/16\sqrt{2}\sigma) < 2^{-32}$. This condition is enough for the original bitwise TFHE scheme. However, for our scheme, decryption fails if the noise amplitude after the bootstrapping is larger than $1/4B$, as shown in (8). The probability of decryption error is upper-bounded by $\mathrm{erf}(1/4B\sqrt{2}\sigma) < 2^{-4.06}$ for our scheme. This upper-bound seems large, but we actually observed in our experiment that the decryption error rate is approximately 0.08% (4 decryption errors in 5000 bootstrapping). In other words, our scheme has a trade-off between the size of the plaintext space B and the decryption error rate. For 5-bit integers, i.e., for $B = 33$, the upper bound of the probability of decryption error becomes rapidly higher, to approximately 30%. Thus, our scheme is practical for ≤ 4 bit integers input, for this parameter setting of the original TFHE. Please note that, although decryption error rate of our scheme becomes higher as B grows, it does not affect the security of the scheme, since the size of B does not change the size of noise σ [2].

6   Conclusion

In this paper, we proposed a technique for realizing general functional bootstrapping on the integerwise variant of TFHE by generalizing the test vector used in bootstrapping and showing the concrete setting of the value of the test vector. Based on our general functional bootstrapping, we extended the functionality of the integerwise TFHE scheme to construct several useful functions on our scheme, such as homomorphic equality testing, multiplication by a binary number and a division algorithm. As an example of the improvements derived from our FHE scheme, we implemented our division algorithm and showed that its runtime is less than 1 s, and is approximately 3.4x faster than the fastest division algorithm. Efficient algorithms for basic arithmetic operations will undoubtedly be needed to increase options for optimizing high-level applications of secure computations, and we believe that our bootstrapping method can be used to develop a diversity of homomorphic calculation algorithms.

Acknowledgements. We would like to thank Benjamin Curtis and Rachel Player for their comments on early versions of the paper.

References

1. Bost, R., Popa, R.A., Tu, S., Goldwasser, S.: Machine learning classification over encrypted data. In: NDSS Symposium 2015 (2015). https://doi.org/10.14722/ndss.2015.23241
2. Bourse, F., Minelli, M., Minihold, M., Paillier, P.: Fast homomorphic evaluation of deep discretized neural networks. In: Shacham, H., Boldyreva, A. (eds.) CRYPTO 2018. LNCS, vol. 10993, pp. 483–512. Springer, Cham (2018). https://doi.org/10.1007/978-3-319-96878-0_17
3. Brakerski, Z., Gentry, C., Vaikuntanathan, V.: (Leveled) fully homomorphic encryption without bootstrapping. In: ITCS 2012, pp. 309–325. ACM (2012). https://doi.org/10.1145/2090236.2090262
4. Brakerski, Z., Vaikuntanathan, V.: Efficient fully homomorphic encryption from (standard) LWE. In: FOCS 2011, pp. 97–106. IEEE (2011). https://doi.org/10.1109/FOCS.2011.12

5. Brakerski, Z., Vaikuntanathan, V.: Fully homomorphic encryption from ring-LWE and security for key dependent messages. In: Rogaway, P. (ed.) CRYPTO 2011. LNCS, vol. 6841, pp. 505–524. Springer, Heidelberg (2011). https://doi.org/10.1007/978-3-642-22792-9_29
6. Brakerski, Z., Vaikuntanathan, V.: Lattice-based FHE as secure as PKE. In: ITCS 2014, pp. 1–12. ACM (2014). https://doi.org/10.1145/2554797.2554799
7. Carpov, S., Chillotti, I., Gama, N., Georgieva, M., Izabachene, M.: TFHE: Fast fully homomorphic encryption over the torus (2019). https://tfhe.github.io/tfhe/. Accessed Jun 2020
8. Çetin, G.S., Doröz, Y., Sunar, B., Martin, W.J.: Arithmetic using word-wise homomorphic encryption. Cryptology ePrint Archive, Report 2015/1195 (2015). https://eprint.iacr.org/2015/1195
9. Çetin, G.S., Doröz, Y., Sunar, B., Savaş, E.: Depth optimized efficient homomorphic sorting. In: Lauter, K., Rodríguez-Henríquez, F. (eds.) LATINCRYPT 2015. LNCS, vol. 9230, pp. 61–80. Springer, Cham (2015). https://doi.org/10.1007/978-3-319-22174-8_4
10. Chen, H., et al.: Microsoft SEAL: Fast and easy-to-use homomorphic encryption library (2019). https://www.microsoft.com/en-us/research/project/microsoft-seal/ Accessed Jun 2020
11. Chen, J., Feng, Y., Liu, Y., Wu, W.: Faster binary arithmetic operations on encrypted integers. In: WCSE 2017, pp. 956–960 (2017). https://doi.org/10.18178/wcse.2017.06.166
12. Chen, Y., Gong, G.: Integer arithmetic over ciphertext and homomorphic data aggregation. IEEE CNS **2015**, 628–632 (2015). https://doi.org/10.1109/CNS.2015.7346877
13. Cheon, J.H., Han, K., Kim, A., Kim, M., Song, Y.: Bootstrapping for approximate homomorphic encryption. In: Nielsen, J.B., Rijmen, V. (eds.) EUROCRYPT 2018. LNCS, vol. 10820, pp. 360–384. Springer, Cham (2018). https://doi.org/10.1007/978-3-319-78381-9_14
14. Cheon, J.H., Stehlé, D.: Fully homomophic encryption over the integers revisited. In: Oswald, E., Fischlin, M. (eds.) EUROCRYPT 2015. LNCS, vol. 9056, pp. 513–536. Springer, Heidelberg (2015). https://doi.org/10.1007/978-3-662-46800-5_20
15. Chillotti, I., Gama, N., Georgieva, M., Izabachène, M.: Faster fully homomorphic encryption: bootstrapping in less than 0.1 seconds. In: Cheon, J.H., Takagi, T. (eds.) ASIACRYPT 2016. LNCS, vol. 10031, pp. 3–33. Springer, Heidelberg (2016). https://doi.org/10.1007/978-3-662-53887-6_1
16. Chillotti, I., Gama, N., Georgieva, M., Izabachène, M.: Faster packed homomorphic operations and efficient circuit bootstrapping for TFHE. In: Takagi, T., Peyrin, T. (eds.) ASIACRYPT 2017. LNCS, vol. 10624, pp. 377–408. Springer, Cham (2017). https://doi.org/10.1007/978-3-319-70694-8_14
17. Chillotti, I., Gama, N., Georgieva, M., Izabachène, M.: TFHE: fast fully homomorphic encryption over the torus. J. Cryptology **33**(1), 34–91 (2019). https://doi.org/10.1007/s00145-019-09319-x
18. Ducas, L., Micciancio, D.: FHEW: bootstrapping homomorphic encryption in less than a second. In: Oswald, E., Fischlin, M. (eds.) EUROCRYPT 2015. LNCS, vol. 9056, pp. 617–640. Springer, Heidelberg (2015). https://doi.org/10.1007/978-3-662-46800-5_24
19. Gentry, C.: A fully homomorphic encryption scheme. Ph.D. thesis, Stanford University (2009). crypto.stanford.edu/craig
20. Gentry, C.: Fully homomorphic encryption using ideal lattices. In: STOC 2009, pp. 169–178. ACM (2009). https://doi.org/10.1145/1536414.1536440

21. Gentry, C., Halevi, S., Smart, N.P.: Homomorphic evaluation of the AES circuit. In: Safavi-Naini, R., Canetti, R. (eds.) CRYPTO 2012. LNCS, vol. 7417, pp. 850–867. Springer, Heidelberg (2012). https://doi.org/10.1007/978-3-642-32009-5_49

22. Gentry, C., Sahai, A., Waters, B.: Homomorphic encryption from learning with errors: conceptually-simpler, asymptotically-faster, attribute-based. In: Canetti, R., Garay, J.A. (eds.) CRYPTO 2013. LNCS, vol. 8042, pp. 75–92. Springer, Heidelberg (2013). https://doi.org/10.1007/978-3-642-40041-4_5

23. Gilad-Bachrach, R., Dowlin, N., Laine, K., Lauter, K., Naehrig, M., Wernsing, J.: CryptoNets: applying neural networks to encrypted data with high throughput and accuracy. In: ICML 2016, vol. 48, pp. 201–210. PMLR (2016). https://doi.org/10.5555/3045390.3045413

24. Halevi, S., Shoup, V.: HElib - An implementation of homomorphic encryption (2019). https://github.com/shaih/HElib/. Accessed Jun 2020

25. Juvekar, C., Vaikuntanathan, V., Chandrakasan, A.: GAZELLE: a low latency framework for secure neural network inference. In: USENIX Security 2018, pp. 1651–1669 (2018)

26. Lyubashevsky, V., Peikert, C., Regev, O.: On ideal lattices and learning with errors over rings. In: Gilbert, H. (ed.) EUROCRYPT 2010. LNCS, vol. 6110, pp. 1–23. Springer, Heidelberg (2010). https://doi.org/10.1007/978-3-642-13190-5_1

27. Narumanchi, H., Goyal, D., Emmadi, N., Gauravaram, P.: Performance analysis of sorting of FHE data: integer-wise comparison vs bit-wise comparison. In: AINA 2017, pp. 902–908. IEEE (2017). https://doi.org/10.1109/AINA.2017.85

28. New Jersey Institute of Technology: PALISADE. https://git.njit.edu/palisade/PALISADE (2019)

29. Okada, H., Cid, C., Hidano, S., Kiyomoto, S.: Linear depth integer-wise homomorphic division. In: Blazy, O., Yeun, C.Y. (eds.) WISTP 2018. LNCS, vol. 11469, pp. 91–106. Springer, Cham (2019). https://doi.org/10.1007/978-3-030-20074-9_8

30. Regev, O.: On lattices, learning with errors, random linear codes, and cryptography. J. ACM 56(6), 34:1–34:40 (2009). https://doi.org/10.1145/1568318.1568324

31. Smart, N.P., Vercauteren, F.: Fully homomorphic encryption with relatively small key and ciphertext sizes. In: 2010, pp. 420–443 (2010). https://doi.org/10.1007/978-3-642-13013-7_25

32. Stehlé, D., Steinfeld, R.: Faster fully homomorphic encryption. In: Abe, M. (ed.) ASIACRYPT 2010. LNCS, vol. 6477, pp. 377–394. Springer, Heidelberg (2010). https://doi.org/10.1007/978-3-642-17373-8_22

33. van Dijk, M., Gentry, C., Halevi, S., Vaikuntanathan, V.: Fully homomorphic encryption over the integers. EUROCRYPT **2010**, 24–43 (2010). https://doi.org/10.1007/978-3-642-13190-5_2

34. Xu, C., Chen, J., Wu, W., Feng, Y.: Homomorphically encrypted arithmetic operations over the integer ring. In: Bao, F., Chen, L., Deng, R.H., Wang, G. (eds.) ISPEC 2016. LNCS, vol. 10060, pp. 167–181. Springer, Cham (2016). https://doi.org/10.1007/978-3-319-49151-6_12

Attacks and Cryptanalysis

Rotational Cryptanalysis of Salsa Core Function

Ryoma Ito[✉]

National Institute of Information and Communications Technology,
4-2-1, Nukui-Kitamachi, Koganei, Tokyo 184-8795, Japan
itorym@nict.go.jp

Abstract. This paper presents rotational cryptanalysis of the Salsa core function, and warns designers of symmetric-key primitives not to incorporate the Salsa core function into other encryption schemes. The core functions of Serpent, ChaCha, and AES are actually incorporated into SOSE-MANUK, BLAKE2, and SNOW-V, respectively. We first construct a toy model of the Salsa core function, and observe the rotational characteristics in the toy model by conducting an experiment. Since our experimental observations differ from the theoretical results presented by Khovratovich et al. at FSE 2010 and FSE 2015, we provide their proofs. In addition, we then demonstrate the rotational distinguishers for the Salsa and ChaCha permutations, and compare their results. While the rotational distinguisher for the ChaCha permutation performs properly only up to 8 rounds with a probability of approximately $2^{-489.6}$, the rotational distinguisher for the Salsa permutation performs properly up to 32 rounds with a probability of approximately $2^{-506.752}$. Consequently, our study clarifies how weak the Salsa permutation is to rotational cryptanalysis. Finally, we remark that our results do not affect the security of Salsa.

Keywords: ARX · Stream cipher · Salsa · Rotational cryptanalysis

1 Introduction

The Addition-Rotation-XOR (ARX) construction is becoming the mainstream of design for symmetric-key primitives. Actually, numerous ARX-based primitives have been proposed, such as stream ciphers Salsa and ChaCha, block ciphers SPECK and CHAM, hash functions BLAKE2 and Skein, message authentication code (MAC) algorithm Chaskey, and submissions for the National Institute of Standards and Technology's (NIST) lightweight cryptography standardization SNEIK and SPARKLE. This is because the ARX-based primitives can achieve good confusion, diffusion, and performance with only the following three simple operations: modular addition, left/right rotation, and XOR.

Consequently, one can infer that the ARX-based primitives have become hot cryptanalysis targets. In particular, differential and linear cryptanalysis, which are the two most powerful generic attacks for symmetric-key primitives, have been applied to numerous ARX-based primitives [4,5,7,9,16,20]. In addition,

© Springer Nature Switzerland AG 2020
W. Susilo et al. (Eds.): ISC 2020, LNCS 12472, pp. 129–145, 2020.
https://doi.org/10.1007/978-3-030-62974-8_8

a specific cryptanalysis, which is called *rotational cryptanalysis*, for the ARX-based primitives has also been proposed [1,8,10–14,17–19].

Related Works. The beginning of rotational cryptanalysis can be traced back to the Ph.D. thesis of Daum submitted in 2005 [6]. The author analyzed the relationship between modular addition and bit rotation in details, and proved that one modular addition preserves the propagation of the so-called *rotational pair* with a probability of up to $2^{-1.415}$.

Khovratovich and Nikolić [10] applied the propagation characteristic of a rotational pair (so-called *rotational characteristic*) in modular addition to the rotational cryptanalysis for the ARX-based primitives. The authors established a new technique of a generic attack. Additionally, they focused on the rotational characteristics in both rotation and XOR, which are preserved with a probability of one, and demonstrated that the rotational cryptanalysis for the ARX-based primitives performs properly based on the Markov cipher assumption, which is often utilized in differential cryptanalysis. In particular, by simply counting the number of modular additions, we can obtain rotational characteristics throughout the ARX-based primitives. Rotational cryptanalysis mainly performed with hash functions, such as Keccak [19], BLAKE2 [8], and Skein [12,13].

Khovratovich et al. [11] demonstrated that not all the ARX-based primitives can be assumed to be Markov ciphers. When the output of a modular addition becomes the input of another, rotational characteristic in the latter differs from that presented in [10]. They refer to the structure, where modular addition is connected like a chain, as a *chained modular addition*. After verifying the above fact using two toy models with the same number of modular additions but different rotational characteristics, they proved the rotational characteristic of a chained modular addition and applied it to BLAKE2 and Skein, which have the structure of a chained modular addition.

Afterward, several applications of rotational cryptanalysis for the ARX-based block ciphers and MAC algorithm Chaskey have been reported in [1,14,17,18].

Motivations. This paper discusses the rotational cryptanalysis of the Salsa core function, which is also called the round function in general. Salsa is an ARX-based stream cipher designed by Bernstein in 2005 and has been accepted as one of the finalists for the eSTREAM software portfolio [3]. Although differential cryptanalysis for Salsa has been reported to attack only up to 8 rounds (out of 20 rounds in the original version of Salsa) [5], no study has yet applied rotational cryptanalysis to ARX-based stream ciphers including ChaCha [2], which is a variant of Salsa.

As discussed in [10, Section 3], it is noteworthy that *all inputs to the ARX-based primitive must be a rotational pair for the rotational cryptanalysis to perform well*. Since both Salsa and ChaCha utilize constants as one of their inputs, it is practically difficult for adversaries to obtain a rotational pair of constants. Therefore, we cannot apply rotational cryptanalysis to the ARX-based stream cipher.

From a different viewpoint, it is often the case that the core function of one encryption scheme is implemented in another to design symmetric-key primitives. The core functions of Serpent, ChaCha, and AES are actually implemented in SOSEMANUK, BLAKE2, and SNOW-V, respectively. If there exists a fatal weakness in the core function, then the encryption scheme that implemented its core function may also have weakness. It is undeniable that the Salsa core function may be implemented in another encryption scheme in the future. Therefore, it is important to clarify whether the Salsa core function has a weakness to rotational cryptanalysis.

Our Contributions. We first construct a toy model of the Salsa core function, and observe rotational characteristics in the toy model by conducting an experiment. Our experimental observation demonstrates that the rotational pair in the toy model propagates with a higher probability than the theoretical value presented in [10,11]. Additionally, we analyze the toy model in details, and clarify that its structure in Salsa, where one of the inputs to two consecutive modular additions has the same value, affects the rotational characteristics in the toy model. The details of our contributions can be summarized as follows.

- Lemma 3 presents a rotational characteristic in the toy model including the first two consecutive modular additions. While the rotational pair in the toy model propagates with a probability of $2^{-2.246}$, the theoretical values studied in [10] and [11] are $2^{-2.8}$ and $2^{-3.6}$, respectively.
- Lemma 4 analyzes a rotational characteristic in the toy model including the first three consecutive modular additions. While the rotational pair in the toy model propagates with a probability of $2^{-3.247}$, the theoretical values explored in [10] and [11] are $2^{-4.2}$ and $2^{-6.3}$, respectively.
- Theorem 2 examines the rotational characteristic in the toy model including the first four consecutive modular additions, that is, the full Salsa core function. While the rotational pair in the toy model propagates with a probability of $2^{-4.248}$, the theoretical values considered in [10] and [11] are $2^{-5.6}$ and $2^{-9.3}$, respectively.

Furthermore, we predict that the Salsa-type ARX primitive is a Markov cipher in the Salsa core function units. By simply counting the number of the Salsa core functions, this prediction facilitates our rough estimation of rotational characteristics for the Salsa-type ARX primitives.

Based on our theorem and prediction, we demonstrate that rotational distinguisher for the Salsa permutation, which has the same construction as the original version and allows us to set the arbitrary input values, performs properly up to 32 rounds with a probability of approximately $2^{-506.752}$ although the number of rounds in the original version of Salsa is 20. According to the theoretical value explored in [11], we similarly demonstrate that a rotational distinguisher for the ChaCha permutation performs properly only up to 8 rounds with a probability of approximately $2^{-489.6}$.

Therefore, it is clear from these results that the Salsa permutation is weaker to the rotational cryptanalysis than the ChaCha permutation. Consequently, we do not recommend incorporating the Salsa core function into the design of new encryption schemes. Finally, we remark that our results do not affect the security of Salsa.

Organization of This Paper. The rest of this paper is organized as follows. Section 2 briefly describes Salsa, and it also describes some useful theorem and lemmas, which are used in our cryptanalysis and discussion, introduced in some previously conducted studies. Section 3 analyzes our experimental observations for rotational characteristics in the toy model, provides new results and their proofs, and demonstrates the accuracy of our results through experiments. In Sect. 4, we compare the rotational characteristics between the Salsa and ChaCha permutations; we show that the Salsa permutation is weak to rotational cryptanalysis. Section 5 concludes this paper.

2   Preliminaries

2.1   Description of Salsa

The ARX-based stream cipher Salsa [3] involves three steps to generate a keystream block of 16 words, where each word size is 32 bits.

The first step is to initialize the internal state matrix of order 4×4 from a 256-bit secret key $k = (k_0, k_1, \ldots, k_7)$, a 64-bit nonce $v = (v_0, v_1)$, a 64-bit block counter $t = (t_0, t_1)$, and four 32-bit constants, $c_0 = \text{0x61707865}$, $c_1 = \text{0x3320646}e$, $c_2 = \text{0x79622}d32$, and $c_3 = \text{0x6}b206574$. After the initialization, we have the following initial state matrix:

$$X^{(0)} = \begin{pmatrix} x_0^{(0)} & x_1^{(0)} & x_2^{(0)} & x_3^{(0)} \\ x_4^{(0)} & x_5^{(0)} & x_6^{(0)} & x_7^{(0)} \\ x_8^{(0)} & x_9^{(0)} & x_{10}^{(0)} & x_{11}^{(0)} \\ x_{12}^{(0)} & x_{13}^{(0)} & x_{14}^{(0)} & x_{15}^{(0)} \end{pmatrix} = \begin{pmatrix} c_0 & k_0 & k_1 & k_2 \\ k_3 & c_1 & v_0 & v_1 \\ t_0 & t_1 & c_2 & k_4 \\ k_5 & k_6 & k_7 & c_3 \end{pmatrix}.$$

Then, the next step is to execute the core function, which is called **quarter-round** function in Salsa, and update a vector $(x_a^{(r)}, x_b^{(r)}, x_c^{(r)}, x_d^{(r)})$ by sequentially computing

$$\begin{cases} x_b^{(r+1)} = ((x_a^{(r)} + x_d^{(r)}) \lll 7) \oplus x_b^{(r)}, \\ x_c^{(r+1)} = ((x_b^{(r+1)} + x_a^{(r)}) \lll 9) \oplus x_c^{(r)}, \\ x_d^{(r+1)} = ((x_c^{(r+1)} + x_b^{(r+1)}) \lll 13) \oplus x_d^{(r)}, \\ x_a^{(r+1)} = ((x_d^{(r+1)} + x_c^{(r+1)}) \lll 18) \oplus x_a^{(r)}, \end{cases}$$

where the symbols '+', '$\lll$', and '$\oplus$' represent word-wise modular addition, bit-wise left rotation, and bit-wise XOR, respectively. In odd number rounds, which are called **columnrounds**, the **quarterround** function is applied to the following four column vectors: $(x_0^{(r)}, x_4^{(r)}, x_8^{(r)}, x_{12}^{(r)})$, $(x_5^{(r)}, x_9^{(r)}, x_{13}^{(r)}, x_1^{(r)})$, $(x_{10}^{(r)}, x_{14}^{(r)}, x_2^{(r)}, x_6^{(r)})$, and $(x_{15}^{(r)}, x_3^{(r)}, x_7^{(r)}, x_{11}^{(r)})$. In even number rounds, which are called rowrounds, the quarterround function is applied to the following four row vectors: $(x_0^{(r)}, x_1^{(r)}, x_2^{(r)}, x_3^{(r)})$, $(x_5^{(r)}, x_6^{(r)}, x_7^{(r)}, x_4^{(r)})$, $(x_{10}^{(r)}, x_{11}^{(r)}, x_8^{(r)}, x_9^{(r)})$, and $(x_{15}^{(r)}, x_{12}^{(r)}, x_{13}^{(r)}, x_{14}^{(r)})$.

Besides, the final round is denoted by R, where the original version of Salsa is $R = 20$ rounds. After the final round, we have the following final state matrix:

$$X^{(R)} = \begin{pmatrix} x_0^{(R)} & x_1^{(R)} & x_2^{(R)} & x_3^{(R)} \\ x_4^{(R)} & x_5^{(R)} & x_6^{(R)} & x_7^{(R)} \\ x_8^{(R)} & x_9^{(R)} & x_{10}^{(R)} & x_{11}^{(R)} \\ x_{12}^{(R)} & x_{13}^{(R)} & x_{14}^{(R)} & x_{15}^{(R)} \end{pmatrix}.$$

The final step is to obtain a keystream block Z by computing the following equation:

$$Z = X^{(0)} + X^{(R)}.$$

2.2   Rotational Cryptanalysis

Khovratovich and Nikolić [10] investigated the propagation of a *rotational pair* $(X, X \lll r)$ throughout the ARX-based primitives, and designed a new technique called *rotational cryptanalysis*. As described in Lemma 1, the technique of rotational cryptanalysis is based on the *rotational probability* of modular addition presented in the Ph.D. thesis of Daum [6].

Lemma 1 ([6, Corollary 4.12]).

1. *If we suppose an n-bit word A to be fixed and an n-bit word B to be chosen uniformly at random, then we obtain*

$$\Pr[(A + B) \lll r = (A \lll r) + (B \lll r)] = 2^{-n}(2^{n-r} - A_R)(2^r - A_L),$$

   where $A_L = (a_{n-1}, \ldots, a_{n-r})$ and $A_R = (a_{n-r-1}, \ldots, a_0)$ for A.
2. *If we suppose two n-bit words A and B to be chosen uniformly at random, then we obtain*

$$\Pr[(A + B) \lll r = (A \lll r) + (B \lll r)] = \frac{1}{4}(1 + 2^{r-n} + 2^{-r} + 2^{-n}).$$

For $n = 8$ and $r = 1$, we obtain the rotational probabilities of the first and second types of modular addition in Lemma 1 as $2^{-1.245}$ and $2^{-1.404}$, respectively. Moreover, we obtain the rotational probabilities of rotation and XOR as

$$\Pr[(x \lll r_1) \lll r_2 = (x \lll r_2) \lll r_1] = 1, \tag{1}$$

$$\Pr[(x \oplus y) \lll r = (x \lll r) \oplus (y \lll r)] = 1. \tag{2}$$

Since only modular addition has a rotational probability of less than one, Khovratovich and Nikolić described that a rotational probability throughout the ARX-based ciphers can be obtained by simply counting the number of the second type of modular addition in Lemma 1, as described in the following theorem.

Theorem 1 ([10, Theorem 2]. *Let q be the number of modular additions in an ARX-based primitive that has an arbitrary number of rotations and XORs. Then, the rotational probability of the ARX-based primitive is p_+^q, where p_+ denotes the rotational probability of modular addition depending on the word size n and the rotation amount r.*

They observed that **all** inputs to the ARX-based primitive must be rotational pair for the rotational cryptanalysis to perform well.

Theorem 1 holds based on the assumption that an ARX-based primitive is a Markov cipher (refer to [15, Section 3] for details). However, when the output of modular addition becomes the input of another, Khovratovich et al. [11] demonstrated that the rotational probability of the second modular addition cannot be obtained from Theorem 1. The authors referred to the structure, where modular addition is connected like a chain, as a *chained modular addition*. As described in Lemma 2, they provided a rotational probability of the chained modular addition.

Lemma 2 ([11, Lemma 2]. *Let $a_1, \ldots, a_k$ be n-bit words chosen at random and let r be a positive integer such that $0 < r < n$. Then, we have*

$$\Pr([(a_1 + a_2) \lll r = (a_1 \lll r) + (a_2 \lll r)]$$
$$\wedge [(a_1 + a_2 + a_3) \lll r = (a_1 \lll r) + (a_2 \lll r) + (a_3 \lll r)]$$
$$\wedge \ldots$$
$$\wedge [(a_1 + a_2 + \cdots + a_k) \lll r = (a_1 \lll r) + (a_2 \lll r) + \ldots (a_k \lll r)]$$
$$= \frac{1}{2^{nk}} \binom{k + 2^r - 1}{2^r - 1} \binom{k + 2^{n-r} - 1}{2^{n-r} - 1}.$$

Khovratovich et al. applied rotational cryptanalysis to BLAKE2 and Skein, which are the ARX-based hash functions that include chained modular additions. Consequently, rotational distinguishers for the permutation of BLAKE2 and Skein perform properly up to 7 (out of 12) rounds with a rotational probability of approximately $2^{-1015.2}$ and 28 (out of 72) rounds with a rotational probability of approximately $2^{-507.6}$, respectively.

3   Rotational Cryptanalysis of the Salsa Core Function

3.1   Experimental Observations

To investigate the accurate rotational probability of the Salsa core function, we construct a toy model of the Salsa core function with a word size of eight bits, as illustrated in Fig. 1. This is because the rotational probability of the toy model can be obtained from all the input/output rotational pairs with 2^{32} trials, which is the number of trails that can execute an exhaustive search.

The function family f_i is defined by $f_i(a, b, c, r) = ((a + b) \lll r) \oplus c$, where i denotes a sequential number. Then, the toy model updates a vector (a, b, c, d) by sequentially computing

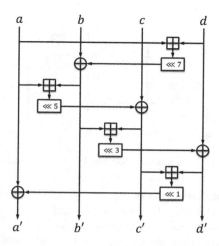

Fig. 1. A toy model of the Salsa core function.

Table 1. A comparison between the rotational probabilities ($\log_2$) of the toy model obtained by the conducted experiments (experimental observations) and those obtained based on the assumption that the toy model is a Markov cipher (Markov assumption).

Rotational probabilities	# of modular additions			
	1	2	3	4
Experimental observation	−1.404	−2.246	−3.241	−4.197
Markov assumption		−1.404	−2.808	−4.212	−5.616

$$\begin{cases} b = f_1(a, d, b, 7) = ((a + d) \lll 7) \oplus b, \\ c = f_2(b, a, c, 5) = ((b + a) \lll 5) \oplus c, \\ d = f_3(c, b, d, 3) = ((c + b) \lll 3) \oplus d, \\ a = f_4(d, c, a, 1) = ((d + c) \lll 1) \oplus a. \end{cases}$$

From the above sequential computation of the function family f_i, we further define the function family F_i as follows:

$$F_1 = f_1, \quad F_2 = f_2 \circ f_1, \quad F_3 = f_3 \circ f_2 \circ f_1, \quad F_4 = f_4 \circ f_3 \circ f_2 \circ f_1,$$

where i denotes the sequential number (the number of modular additions in the function). Now, we obtain the following four rotational probabilities of the toy model through our conducted experiment:

$$\Pr[\overleftarrow{F_1(a, b, c, d)} = F_1(\overleftarrow{a}, \overleftarrow{b}, \overleftarrow{c}, \overleftarrow{d})], \tag{3}$$

$$\Pr[\overleftarrow{F_2(a, b, c, d)} = F_2(\overleftarrow{a}, \overleftarrow{b}, \overleftarrow{c}, \overleftarrow{d})], \tag{4}$$

$$\Pr[\overleftarrow{F_3(a, b, c, d)} = F_3(\overleftarrow{a}, \overleftarrow{b}, \overleftarrow{c}, \overleftarrow{d})], \tag{5}$$

$$\Pr[\overleftarrow{F_4(a, b, c, d)} = F_4(\overleftarrow{a}, \overleftarrow{b}, \overleftarrow{c}, \overleftarrow{d})], \tag{6}$$

where symbol '←' represents the left rotation by one bit.

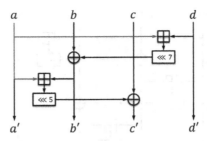

Fig. 2. Function F_2 of the toy model. (Color figure online)

Table 1 shows a comparison between the rotational probabilities of the toy model obtained by conducting the experiment and those obtained based on the assumption that the toy model is a Markov cipher (hence, we can refer to Theorem 1). It is noteworthy that we obtain a rotational probability of the second type of modular addition in Lemma 1 as $2^{-1.404}$ for $n = 8$ and $r = 1$. Thus, we can observe from the table that the rotational probabilities of the toy model obtained by the conducted experiment are higher than those obtained based on Theorem 1. To the best of our knowledge, no study has analyzed such rotational probabilities in details. Therefore, it is important to clarify the rotational characteristic of the Salsa core function.

In the sequel, we analyze the rotational probabilities of the toy model in detail, and provide their proofs in Sect. 3.2. Afterword, Sect. 3.3 presents the experimental verifications to confirm the accuracy of the theoretical results.

3.2   Proofs

Rotational Probability of Function. F_2**.** We first analyze function F_2 of the toy model in details, and then explain the following two characteristics of the Salsa core function.

1. One variable remains the same and becomes the input of the two consecutive modular additions. In the case of function F_2, variable a corresponds to it (see red arrows shown in Fig. 2).
2. The rotational probability throughout the function matches the one after the output of the last modular addition. This is clear from Eqs. (1) and (2). In the case of function F_2, Eq. (4) can be rewritten as follows:

$$\Pr[\overleftarrow{(((a + d) \lll 7) \oplus b) + a} = (((\overleftarrow{a} + \overleftarrow{d}) \lll 7) \oplus \overleftarrow{b}) + \overleftarrow{a}]. \qquad (7)$$

Based on the above characteristics of the Salsa core function, we discuss the rotational probability of function F_2 in Lemma 3, and prove this lemma.

Lemma 3. *Let $P(\cdot, n, r)$ be a rotational probability of the first type of modular addition in Lemma 1, that is, $P(A, n, r) = 2^{-n}(2^{n-r} - A_R)(2^r - A_L)$. Then, the rotational probability of function F_2 is given as follows:*

$$\Pr[\overleftarrow{F_2(a,b,c,d)} = F_2(\overleftarrow{a},\overleftarrow{b},\overleftarrow{c},\overleftarrow{d})] = 2^{-n} \sum_{a\in\{0,1\}^n} P(a,n,1) \cdot P(a,n,1),$$

where symbol '$\leftarrow$' represents the left rotation by one bit, and thus the rotation amount is $r = 1$.

Proof. As mentioned in Sect. 2.2, **all** the inputs to the ARX-based primitive must be a rotational pair for the rotational cryptanalysis to perform properly. Besides, the inputs to the second modular addition in function F_2, which are 'a' and "$((a+d) \lll 7) \oplus b$", must be rotational pairs. Since variable a is always a rotational pair, we should consider only whether the following equation is satisfied:

$$\overleftarrow{((a+d) \lll 7) \oplus b} = ((\overleftarrow{a}+\overleftarrow{d}) \lll 7) \oplus \overleftarrow{b}. \tag{8}$$

If Eq. (8) holds, then Eq. (7) can be further rewritten as follows:

$$\Pr[\overleftarrow{(((a+d) \lll 7) \oplus b) + a} = \overleftarrow{(((a+d) \lll 7) \oplus b)} + \overleftarrow{a}]. \tag{9}$$

Based on the condition that Eq. (8) holds, Eq. (9) implies that the rotational probability of function F_2 can be obtained by utilizing Lemma 1.

It is noteworthy that variable a remains the same and becomes the inputs of the two consecutive modular additions. Thus, variable a should not be considered to be uniform at random in terms of the same input of the two consecutive modular additions. Therefore, to obtain the rotational probability of function F_2, we cannot employ the rotational probability of the second type of modular addition in Lemma 1.

Now, we assume that variable a is fixed. Once the value of variable a is naturally determined, the input value of the first and second modular additions corresponding to variable a is always constant. Therefore, we can consider the assumption to be correct. To obtain the rotational probability of function F_2, we follow the rotational probability of the first type of modular addition in Lemma 1. This implies that the probability that Eq. (8) holds, and the probability that Eq. (9) holds under the condition that Eq. (8) holds can be obtained based on the rotational probability of the first type of modular addition in Lemma 1.

Let $P(\cdot, n, r)$ be the rotational probability of the first type of modular addition in Lemma 1, that is, $P(A, n, r) = 2^{-n}(2^{n-r} - A_R)(2^r - A_L)$. Let E_1 and E_2 be the events represented by Eqs. (8) and (9), respectively. Then, we have the following equations:

$$\Pr[\mathsf{E}_1] = 2^{-n} \sum_{a\in\{0,1\}^n} P(a,n,r), \tag{10}$$

$$\Pr[\mathsf{E}_2 \mid \mathsf{E}_1] = 2^{-n} \sum_{a\in\{0,1\}^n} P(a,n,r), \tag{11}$$

where variable a is chosen uniformly at random from 0 to $2^n - 1$. We note the following two points.

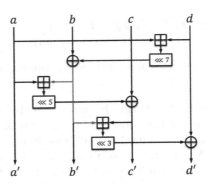

Fig. 3. Function F_3 of the toy model.

1. Eq. (10) is valid only when considering the event E_2. When the event E_2 is not considered, the probability of the event E_1 follows the rotational probability of the second type of modular addition in Lemma 1.
2. The events E_1 and $[E_2 \mid E_1]$ should be considered to occur simultaneously since one of the inputs to the first and second modular additions is the same.

In conclusion, we have the rotational probability of function F_2 as follows:

$$\Pr[\overleftarrow{F_2(a,b,c,d)} = F_2(\overleftarrow{a}, \overleftarrow{b}, \overleftarrow{c}, \overleftarrow{d})] = \Pr[E_2 \mid E_1] \cdot \Pr[E_1]$$
$$= 2^{-n} \sum_{a \in \{0,1\}^n} P(a,n,1) \cdot P(a,n,1),$$

where symbol '$\leftarrow$' represents the left rotation by one bit. Thus, the rotation amount is $r = 1$. $\qquad\square$

Rotational Probability of Functions. F_3 **and** F_4**.** We next analyze function F_3 of the toy model in details, and then explain the following three characteristics of the Salsa core function:

1. The output value of a function remains the same and becomes the input of two consecutive modular additions. In the case of function F_3, function $f_1(a,d,b,7)$ corresponds to it (see red arrows shown in Fig. 3).
2. A difference between functions F_2 and F_3 is whether or not to execute function f_3. Similarly, a difference between functions F_1 and F_2 is whether or not to execute function f_2.
3. The function family f_i has various parameters, but the calculation procedure is the same. Thus, we can observe that the above two differences have a common relationship whether or not to execute function f_i.

Based on the above characteristics of the Salsa core function, we present the rotational probability of function F_3 as Lemma 4, and prove this lemma.

In the following lemma and its proof, we utilize the following six events as notations:

E_3: $\overleftarrow{f_1(a,d,b,7)} = f_1(\overleftarrow{a},\overleftarrow{d},\overleftarrow{b},7)$

E_4: $\overleftarrow{f_2(b,a,c,5)} = f_2(\overleftarrow{b},\overleftarrow{a},\overleftarrow{c},5)$

E_5: $\overleftarrow{f_3(c,b,d,3)} = f_3(\overleftarrow{c},\overleftarrow{b},\overleftarrow{d},3)$

E_6: $\overleftarrow{F_1(a,b,c,d)} = F_1(\overleftarrow{a},\overleftarrow{b},\overleftarrow{c},\overleftarrow{d})$

E_7: $\overleftarrow{F_2(a,b,c,d)} = F_2(\overleftarrow{a},\overleftarrow{b},\overleftarrow{c},\overleftarrow{d})$

E_8: $\overleftarrow{F_3(a,b,c,d)} = F_3(\overleftarrow{a},\overleftarrow{b},\overleftarrow{c},\overleftarrow{d})$

It is noteworthy that the event E_3 is the same as the event E_1 in the proof of Lemma 3.

Lemma 4. *The rotational probability of function F_3 is given by*

$$\Pr[E_8] = \frac{\Pr[E_7]}{\Pr[E_3]} \cdot \Pr[E_7],$$

where $\Pr[E_7]$ is given by Lemma 3 and $\Pr[E_3]$ is given by $\Pr[E_1]$ in the proof of Lemma 3.

Proof. As mentioned in Sect. 2.2, **all** the inputs to the ARX-based primitive must be a rotational pair for the rotational cryptanalysis to perform properly. Therefore, based on the proof of Lemma 3, the rotational probability of function F_3 can be calculated as follows:

$$\Pr[E_8] = \Pr[E_5 \wedge E_4 \wedge E_3] = \Pr[E_5 \mid E_4 \wedge E_3] \cdot \Pr[E_4 \wedge E_3], \tag{12}$$

where $\Pr[E_7] = \Pr[E_4 \wedge E_3]$ is given by Lemma 3. It is easy to calculate $\Pr[E_4 \wedge E_3]$ according to Lemma 3, whereas it is difficult to calculate $\Pr[E_5 \mid E_4 \wedge E_3]$. We note that the following equation holds:

$$\Pr[E_8 \wedge E_7] = \Pr[E_5 \wedge E_4 \wedge E_3 \wedge E_4 \wedge E_3] = \Pr[E_5 \wedge E_4 \wedge E_3] = \Pr[E_8]. \tag{13}$$

Since Eq. (13) always holds, Eq. (12) can be rewritten as follows:

$$\Pr[E_8] = \Pr[E_8 \wedge E_7] = \Pr[E_8 \mid E_7] \cdot \Pr[E_7]. \tag{14}$$

Now, we calculate $\Pr[E_8 \mid E_7]$ as the target. As mentioned concerning the characteristics of the Salsa core function, we can consider that the two differences, which are (F_1, F_2) and (F_2, F_3) pairs, have a common relationship whether or not to execute function f_i. Consequently, we observe that the following equation holds:

$$\Pr[E_8 \mid E_7] = \Pr[E_7 \mid E_6]. \tag{15}$$

The fact that the event E_8 occurs based on the condition that the event E_7 occurs essentially means that the event E_5 occurs. Similarly, the fact that the event E_7 occurs based on the condition that the event E_6 occurs basically means that the event E_4 occurs. The difference is whether the event E_5 or E_4 occurs. The events E_5 and E_4 have different parameters, but the calculation procedure is the same.

Therefore, when each precondition is satisfied, the probabilities of the event E_5 and E_4 can be considered to be the same, and thus Eq. (15) holds.

Now, we calculate $Pr[E_7 \mid E_6]$ as the target; then, we have

$$Pr[E_7 \mid E_6] = \frac{Pr[E_7 \wedge E_6]}{Pr[E_6]} = \frac{Pr[E_4 \wedge E_3 \wedge E_3]}{Pr[E_3]} = \frac{Pr[E_4 \wedge E_3]}{Pr[E_3]} = \frac{Pr[E_7]}{Pr[E_3]}, \quad (16)$$

where $Pr[E_7]$ is given by Lemma 3, and $Pr[E_3]$ is given by $Pr[E_1]$ in the proof of Lemma 3.

In conclusion, we have the rotational probability of function F_2 as follows:

$$Pr[E_8] = Pr[E_8 \mid E_7] \cdot Pr[E_7] = Pr[E_7 \mid E_6] \cdot Pr[E_7] = \frac{Pr[E_7]}{Pr[E_3]} \cdot Pr[E_7].$$

$\square$

In a similar way as in the proof of Lemma 4, we present the rotational probability of function F_4 as Theorem 2, and therefore the proof is omitted.

In the Theorem 2, we employ the following event as notation:

$$E_9: \overleftarrow{F_4(a,b,c,d)} = F_4(\overleftarrow{a}, \overleftarrow{b}, \overleftarrow{c}, \overleftarrow{d})$$

Theorem 2. *The rotational probability of function F_4 is given by*

$$Pr[E_9] = \frac{Pr[E_7]}{Pr[E_3]} \cdot Pr[E_8],$$

where $Pr[E_8]$ is given by Lemma 4, $Pr[E_7]$ is given by Lemma 3, and $Pr[E_3]$ is given by $Pr[E_1]$ in the proof of Lemma 3.

3.3   Experimental Verifications

We have conducted an experiment to confirm the accuracy of the theoretical values in our lemmas and theorem. Our experimental environment is given as follows: Intel(R) Core(TM) i7-7567U CPU with 3.50 GHz, 16.0 GB memory, gcc 9.3.0 compiler, and C language.

We apply the toy model designed in Sect. 3.1. As mentioned in Sect. 3.1, the rotational probability of the toy model can be obtained from all the input/output rotational pairs with 2^{32} trials, which is the number of trails that can execute an exhaustive search.

Further, we utilize the percentage of the relative error ϵ of the theoretical values compared with the experimental values:

$$\epsilon = \frac{|\text{experimental value} - \text{theoretical value}|}{\text{experimental value}} \times 100(\%).$$

Table 2 shows a comparison between the experimental and theoretical values for the toy model. It can be observed that ϵ is sufficiently small when the number of modular additions is both two and three. Therefore, we can confirm the accuracy

Table 2. A comparison between the experimental and theoretical values ($\log_2$) for the toy model when the rotation amount is $r = 1$. The value in parentheses is the predicted value based on Prediction 1.

# of modular additions	1	2	3	4	5	6
Experimental value	−1.404	−2.246	−3.241	−4.197	−5.309	−6.510
Theoretical value	−1.404	−2.246	−3.247	−4.248	−	−
ϵ (%)	0.000	0.000	0.446	3.463	−	−
# of modular additions	7	8	9	10	11	12
Experimental value	−7.528	−8.486	−9.618	−10.820	−11.851	−12.807
Theoretical value	−	(−8.496)	−	−	−	(−12.744)
ϵ (%)	−	(0.668)	−	−	−	(4.454)
# of modular additions	13	14	15	16	17	18
Experimental value	−13.943	−15.150	−16.187	−17.142	−18.286	−19.482
Theoretical value	−	−	−	(−16.992)	−	−
ϵ (%)	−	−	−	(10.945)	−	−
# of modular additions	19	20	21	22	23	24
Experimental value	−20.566	−21.518	−22.703	−23.860	−24.945	−26.046
Theoretical value	−	(−21.240)	−	−	−	(−25.488)
ϵ (%)	−	(21.249)	−	−	−	(51.782)

of the theoretical values in Lemmas 3 and 4. Moreover, when the number of modular additions is four, it can be also observed that ϵ is slightly large such as $\epsilon = 3.463$ (%). Although we can reduce the relative error by analyzing function F_4 of the toy model in details (we have not actually analyzed it), we can consider it to be sufficiently accurate as a rough estimation. Therefore, we can confirm the accuracy of the theoretical values in Theorem 2 as a rough estimation.

As described in Prediction 1, we then predict the rotational probabilities when the number of modular additions is greater than four.

Prediction 1 *Let q be the number of the Salsa core functions that has four modular additions. Then, the rotational probability of the Salsa-type ARX primitive is p_+^q, where p_+ denotes the rotational probability of the Salsa core function that depends on the word size n and the rotational amount r.*

Besides, we assume that the Salsa-type ARX primitive is a Markov cipher in the Salsa core function units. If our prediction is correct, we can easily analyze the rotational characteristics of the Salsa-type ARX primitive.

In Table 2, we substitute the predicted theoretical values in parentheses based on Prediction 1; then, we also substitute the percentage of the relative error ϵ in parentheses corresponding to the predicted values. According to Prediction 1, we can observe from this table that most of ϵ obtained are large, but they are also considered to be sufficiently accurate as rough estimations. Therefore, our prediction can be considered to be correct in terms of a rough estimation.

Finally, we have conducted an experiment with 2^{32} trials to obtain the rotational probability of the original version of the Salsa core function, which has a

Table 3. A comparison between the experimental and theoretical values ($\log_2$) for the original version of the Salsa core function when the rotation amount is $r = 1$. The value in parentheses is the predicted value based on Prediction 1.

# of modular additions	1	2	3	4	5	6
Experimental value	−1.415	−2.263	−3.263	−4.206	−5.169	−6.126
Theoretical value	−1.415	−2.263	−3.111	−3.959	−	−
ϵ (%)	0.000	0.000	11.111	18.713	−	−
# of modular additions	7	8	9	10	11	12
Experimental value	−7.086	−8.043	−9.000	−9.959	−10.918	−11.875
Theoretical value	−	(−7.918)	−	−	−	(−11.877)
ϵ (%)	−	(9.056)	−	−	−	(0.132)
# of modular additions	13	14	15	16	17	18
Experimental value	−12.831	−13.790	−14.753	−15.712	−16.669	−17.634
Theoretical value	−	−	−	(−15.836)	−	−
ϵ (%)	−	−	−	(8.206)	−	−
# of modular additions	19	20	21	22	23	24
Experimental value	−18.580	−19.530	−20.495	−21.446	−22.417	−23.415
Theoretical value	−	(−19.795)	−	−	−	(−23.754)
ϵ (%)	−	(16.784)	−	−	−	(20.578)

word size of 32 bits. Table 3 illustrates a comparison between the experimental and theoretical values for the original version of the Salsa core function based on our lemmas, theorem, and prediction. According to our lemmas, theorem, and prediction, it can be observed that most of the relative errors ϵ obtained are large. It is noteworthy that the experimental values are not always correct because we could not execute an exhaustive search. Therefore, they are also considered to be sufficiently accurate as rough estimations. We apply this result in the next section.

4   A Weakness of the Salsa Permutation

As mentioned in Sect. 2.2, **all** the inputs to the ARX-based primitive must be a rotational pair for the rotational cryptanalysis to perform properly. Since the input values of Salsa use a 256-bit secret key, a 64-bit nonce, a 64-bit block counter, and four 32-bit constants, it is impossible to make all the input values into a rotational pair. Therefore, the rotational cryptanalysis of Salsa does not perform properly.

It is often the case that the core function of one encryption scheme is implemented in another. The core functions of Serpent, ChaCha, and AES are actually implemented in SOSEMANUK, BLAKE2, and SNOW-V, respectively. If there exists a fatal weakness in the core function, the encryption scheme that implemented this core function might also have this weakness. Particularly, since Salsa itself is a highly secure encryption scheme for which only up to 8 rounds (out of the 20 rounds in the original version) can be attacked [5], its core function

Table 4. A comparison of the rotational probabilities ($\log_2$) of the Salsa and ChaCha permutations when the rotation amount is $r = 1$. The rotational probability of the Salsa permutation is based on our lemmas, theorem, and prediction, while the rotational probability of the ChaCha permutation is based on Lemma 2.

# of rounds	1	2	3	4	5	6
Salsa permutation	-15.836	-31.672	-47.508	-63.344	-79.180	-95.016
ChaCha permutation	-28.800	-74.400	-130.400	-192.800	-261.600	-333.600
# of rounds	7	8	9	10	11	12
Salsa permutation	-110.852	-126.688	-142.524	-158.630	-174.196	-190.032
ChaCha permutation	-410.400	-489.600	-571.200	-656.000	-743.200	-832.000

may be incorporated into the design of new encryption schemes (since ChaCha is considered to be a more secure encryption scheme than Salsa, we believe that it is more likely to incorporate the ChaCha core function instead of the Salsa core function into the design of new encryption schemes). Now, we argue that there can be weakness to incorporate the Salsa core function into the design of new encryption schemes.

To confirm the weakness in the Salsa permutation, which has the same construction as the original version of Salsa that can allow us to set the arbitrary input values (the ChaCha permutation is also similar), we compare the rotational probabilities of the Salsa and ChaCha permutations. Table 4 demonstrates a comparison of the rotational probabilities of the Salsa and ChaCha permutations when the rotational amount is $r = 1$. From Theorem 2 and Prediction 1, the rotational probability of the Salsa permutation can be obtained as a rough estimation. Specifically, by simply counting the number of the Salsa core functions, the rotational probability of the Salsa permutation can be calculated based on Prediction 1 since $p_+ = 2^{-3.959}$ from Theorem 2. It is noteworthy that the Salsa permutation comprises four Salsa core functions in each round; therefore, we obtain the rotational probability of the Salsa permutation as listed in Table 4. In addition, the rotational probability of the ChaCha permutation can be obtained from Lemma 2. Particularly, since the ChaCha core function is implimented in BLAKE2, the rotational probability of the ChaCha permutation can be similarly calculated as the rotational cryptanalysis of BLAKE2 permutation proposed by Khovratovich et al. in [11]. According to the study in [11], the ChaCha permutation has exactly 8 chains of $2R$ modular additions in each chain over R rounds. Consequently, as demonstrated in Table 4, we obtain the rotational probability of the ChaCha permutation.

From Table 4, it can be observed that the rotational distinguisher for the ChaCha permutation performs properly only up to 8 rounds (out of the 20 rounds in the original version of ChaCha) since 9-round ChaCha permutation (with 8 chains of 18 modular additions each) has a rotational probability of $(2^{-71.4})^8 = 2^{-571.2} < 2^{-512.0}$. Moreover, the rotational distinguisher for the Salsa permutation performs properly up to 32 rounds (although the number of rounds in the original version of Salsa is 20) since 32-round Salsa permutation (with 128 Salsa core functions) has a rotational probability of $(2^{-3.959})^{128} = 2^{-506.752} > 2^{-512.0}$.

In conclusion, it is clear from the above discussion that the Salsa permutation is weaker to the rotational cryptanalysis than the ChaCha permutation. Therefore, we do not recommend incorporating the Salsa core function into the design of new encryption schemes. Finally, we remark that the rotational cryptanalysis of the Salsa permutation does not affect the security of Salsa.

5   Conclusion

This study has provided some theoretical results of rotational characteristics in the Salsa core function. Although the rotational probability of the Salsa core function is $2^{-5.6}$ based on the theoretical values presented in [10], we proved herein that it is actually $2^{-4.248}$. Furthermore, we clarified how the weakness of the Salsa permutation is to rotational cryptanalysis. Since the rotational distinguisher for the Salsa permutation performs properly up to 32 rounds with a probability of approximately $2^{-506.752}$, we do not recommend incorporating the Salsa core function into the design of new encryption schemes from the perspective of efficiency.

As mentioned in Sect. 1, since both Salsa and ChaCha use *constants* as one of their inputs, it is practically difficult for adversaries to obtain a rotational pair of constants. Additionally, Ashur and Liu [1] investigated how the rotational cryptanalysis is affected when *constants* are injected into the internal state. by investigating how rotational cryptanalysis is affected when *constants* are used as the inputs, we may similarly apply the rotational cryptanalysis to the ARX-based stream ciphers including Salsa and ChaCha. In the future, we hope to extend this study in the above direction.

References

1. Ashur, T., Liu, Y.: Rotational cryptanalysis in the presence of constants. IACR Trans. Symmetric Cryptology **2016**(1), 57–70 (2016)
2. Bernstein, D.J.: ChaCha, a variant of Salsa20. In: Workshop Record of SASC, vol. 8 (2008)
3. Bernstein, D.J.: The Salsa20 family of stream ciphers. In: Robshaw, M., Billet, O. (eds.) New Stream Cipher Designs. LNCS, vol. 4986, pp. 84–97. Springer, Heidelberg (2008). https://doi.org/10.1007/978-3-540-68351-3_8
4. Biryukov, A., Velichkov, V., Le Corre, Y.: Automatic search for the best trails in ARX: application to block cipher SPECK. In: Peyrin, T. (ed.) FSE 2016. LNCS, vol. 9783, pp. 289–310. Springer, Heidelberg (2016). https://doi.org/10.1007/978-3-662-52993-5_15
5. Arka Rai Choudhuri and Subhamoy Maitra: Significantly improved multi-bit differentials for reduced round Salsa and ChaCha. IACR Trans. Symmetric Cryptology **2016**(2), 261–287 (2017)
6. Daum, M.: Cryptanalysis of Hash functions of the MD4-family. PhD thesis, Ruhr-Universität Bochum, Universitätsbibliothek (2005)

7. Fu, K., Wang, M., Guo, Y., Sun, S., Hu, L.: MILP-based automatic search algorithms for differential and linear trails for speck. In: Peyrin, T. (ed.) FSE 2016. LNCS, vol. 9783, pp. 268–288. Springer, Heidelberg (2016). https://doi.org/10.1007/978-3-662-52993-5_14

8. Guo, J., Karpman, P., Nikolić, I., Wang, L., Wu, S.: Analysis of BLAKE2. In: Benaloh, J. (ed.) CT-RSA 2014. LNCS, vol. 8366, pp. 402–423. Springer, Cham (2014). https://doi.org/10.1007/978-3-319-04852-9_21

9. Huang, M., Wang, L.: Automatic tool for searching for differential characteristics in ARX ciphers and applications. In: Hao, F., Ruj, S., Sen Gupta, S. (eds.) INDOCRYPT 2019. LNCS, vol. 11898, pp. 115–138. Springer, Cham (2019). https://doi.org/10.1007/978-3-030-35423-7_6

10. Khovratovich, D., Nikolić, I.: Rotational cryptanalysis of ARX. In: Hong, S., Iwata, T. (eds.) FSE 2010. LNCS, vol. 6147, pp. 333–346. Springer, Heidelberg (2010). https://doi.org/10.1007/978-3-642-13858-4_19

11. Khovratovich, D., Nikolić, I., Pieprzyk, J., Sokołowski, P., Steinfeld, R.: Rotational cryptanalysis of ARX revisited. In: Leander, G. (ed.) FSE 2015. LNCS, vol. 9054, pp. 519–536. Springer, Heidelberg (2015). https://doi.org/10.1007/978-3-662-48116-5_25

12. Khovratovich, D., Nikolić, I., Rechberger, C.: Rotational rebound attacks on reduced skein. In: Abe, M. (ed.) ASIACRYPT 2010. LNCS, vol. 6477, pp. 1–19. Springer, Heidelberg (2010). https://doi.org/10.1007/978-3-642-17373-8_1

13. Khovratovich, D., Nikolić, I., Rechberger, C.: Rotational rebound attacks on reduced skein. J. Cryptology 27(3), 452–479 (2013). https://doi.org/10.1007/s00145-013-9150-0

14. Kraleva, L., Ashur, T., Rijmen, V.: Rotational cryptanalysis on MAC algorithm chaskey. IACR cryptology ePrint archive 2020, 538 (2020)

15. Lai, X., Massey, J.L., Murphy, S.: Markov ciphers and differential cryptanalysis. In: Davies, D.W. (ed.) EUROCRYPT 1991. LNCS, vol. 547, pp. 17–38. Springer, Heidelberg (1991). https://doi.org/10.1007/3-540-46416-6_2

16. Liu, Y., Wang, Q., Rijmen, V.: Automatic search of linear trails in ARX with applications to SPECK and chaskey. In: Manulis, M., Sadeghi, A.-R., Schneider, S. (eds.) ACNS 2016. LNCS, vol. 9696, pp. 485–499. Springer, Cham (2016). https://doi.org/10.1007/978-3-319-39555-5_26

17. Liu, Y., De Witte, G., Ranea, A., Ashur, T.: Rotational-XOR cryptanalysis of reduced-round SPECK. IACR Trans. Symmetric Cryptology 2017(3), 24–36 (2017)

18. Jinyu, L., Liu, Y., Ashur, T., Sun, B., Li, C.: Rotational-XOR cryptanalysis of simon-like block ciphers. IACR Cryptology ePrint Arch. 2020, 486 (2020)

19. Morawiecki, P., Pieprzyk, J., Srebrny, M.: Rotational cryptanalysis of round-reduced KECCAK. In: Moriai, S. (ed.) FSE 2013. LNCS, vol. 8424, pp. 241–262. Springer, Heidelberg (2014). https://doi.org/10.1007/978-3-662-43933-3_13

20. Zhang, Y., Sun, S., Cai, J., Hu, L.: Speeding up MILP aided differential characteristic search with matsui's strategy. In: Chen, L., Manulis, M., Schneider, S. (eds.) ISC 2018. LNCS, vol. 11060, pp. 101–115. Springer, Cham (2018). https://doi.org/10.1007/978-3-319-99136-8_6

Analyzing the Chain of Trust Model Based on Entity Dependence

Ge Cheng⬤, Hui Xie⁽✉⁾⬤, and Dongliang Zhang⬤

School of Computer Science & School of Cyberspace Science, Xiangtan University,
Xiangtan 41105, China
chengge@xtu.edu.cn, {201821562162,201821562061}@smail.xtu.edu.cn

Abstract. This paper provides a chain of trust model in line with the
TCG trust concepts. This model gives a formal definition and proof
of trust state, trust root and trust measurement and chain of trust by
the concept of Smith's entity dependence and the assumption that the
authenticity can measure the entity's conduct with accuracy. The model
is universal, which can provide a theoretical basis for assessing the existing trusted computing platform, and provide theoretical support for the
future research on how to build a more reasonable chain of trust.

Keywords: Trusted computing · Logic of secure system · Chain of
trust · Entity dependence · LVMM

1 Introduction

Building a trusted computing environment which meets the definition of TCG
needs the support of software and hardware. Trusted Computing Platform
(TCP) is the term the community has used for the implementation of the trusted
components based on the TCG's specifications. Trusted computing platform is
the hardware foundation of building a trusted computing environment. There are
two ways to accomplish the trusted computing platform; one is only to depend
on the hardware protection, for example, IBM4758 platform and smart card, the
other is based on trusted hardware, extended by the software, for example, the
computing platform that is based on AMD or Intel dynamic root of trust for
measurement (DRTM). The main difference between the two implementations
is that their computing platforms have a different division of labour on their
required software and hardware in accordance with the security protection and
resource consumption. Therefore, each trusted computing environment is made
up of a series of interactive entities and modules. The core idea of construction and transitivity of chain of trust is that the whole system is decomposed
into a series of related entities, allowing some entities to measure other entities. However, how to decompose the configuration, how to measure the entity,
which one entity is to measure another, and why we need to trust these entities
are still some of the issues associated with the software and hardware architecture of trusted computing platform. Different trusted computing platforms have
different implementations.

© Springer Nature Switzerland AG 2020
W. Susilo et al. (Eds.): ISC 2020, LNCS 12472, pp. 146–159, 2020.
https://doi.org/10.1007/978-3-030-62974-8_9

At present, in the field of trusted computing, the development of advanced technology is ahead of its theoretical research. The existing main theoretical research is the trustworthy computing, trust management and formalized description of the specific trusted computing environment. The existing main theoretical researches have several differences and therefore cannot serve as the basis of building trusted computing environment. In case of formalized description of the specific trusted computing environment, its theory has great limitations, so it's difficult to be widely used in the current trusted computing field.

To solve above problems, this paper proposes a new chain of trust model with general emphasis on entity dependence and logic of secure system [8]. This model solves problems of: how to decompose the configuration, how to measure an entity, which entity is to measure the other, and why we need to trust these entities? This model gives a formal definition and proof of trust state, trust root and trust measurement by the assumption that the authenticity can measure the entity's conduct with accuracy.

The rest of the document is organized as follows; Section 2 discusses the recent research related to this paper. Section 3 discusses the status and chain of trust. We talk about the analysis of the existing chain of trust of trusted computing platform in section 4. Section 5 discusses the new mechanism and prototype of building chain of trust. Finally, Sect. 6 gives the conclusion.

2   Related Work

2.1   Model Based on Trustworthy Computing Context

Trustworthy computing originated from fault-tolerant computing, which was mainly used to resolve availability, reliability and survivability [3,10,20] of the entire life cycle of a computer hardware and software system from development to use. LIN et al. [15,16] proposed trustworthy research based on network, as well as trustworthy study based on virtualization technology and SOA. The former mainly researches service failure model and fault model of the stochastic Petri net system, the latter mainly is trustworthy research of virtualized SOV system of service-oriented. Because their theory and theory of trusted computing are quite different in content, their theory is difficult to be widely used in current field of trusted computing.

2.2   Trusted and Trusted Measurement Model Based on Trusted Management Context

Blaze et al. [5] who first proposed the idea of trusted management, and Jøsang et al. [12–14] first put forward trusted measurement mode based on subjective logic. They defined the concept of the proof space and concept space in detail, and described how to measure trusted relationship. Trusted is divided into two categories by Beth [4]: one is the recommended trusted, the other is direct trusted. He proposed a method to calculate the probability of an entity being trusted or not, and assumed that the probability value is proportional to the credibility of the entity, in addition, his paper describes the constraint rules and the way of trusted deduction and calculation. Wu et al. [21] proposed P2P trusted system evaluation model based on probability theory, which utilizes subjective experience and feedback information to control the strategic deception and dishonest recommendation. Xu et al. [9] proposed a new P2P network trusted model based on probability statistics, which mainly utilizes some methods of probability and statistics to calculate the credibility of node, and improves the success rate of network transactions. Its theory is used in the permissions management and access control of network transactions. Therefore, they cannot serve as theoretical guidance of building a trusted computing environment, and it is very difficult to be widely used in the field of trusted computing.

2.3 Specific Trusted Computing Platform Model

Chen et al. [7] formally described the process of security startup based on predicate logic. On the basis of IBM's secure coprocessor, Smith [23] put forward authentication model, which gives the formalization definition of trusted based on the dependent relationship between the entities and trusted set, and proved the completeness and reliability of the model. Zhou et al. [24] proposed a VM trusted measurement model under the cloud computing environment. The measurement process was separated into management domain measurement and user domain measurement, and it improves the scalability of measurement model. Chang et al. [6] put forward a kind of trust chain analysis based on the extended trusted virtual platform, which mainly deals with the analysis issue of chain of trust of trusted virtual platform. For specific trusted computing platform models, they only formally described some trusted characteristics of the platform, which don't have general meaning. Therefore, it is difficult to be widely used in the construction of trusted computing environment.

In the existing research literature, the research of this paper is similar in content to Smith's external authentication model, but Smith's external authentication model still has a lot of limitations. The external authentication model is based on the security coprocessor of IBM4758, and the trusted computing environment built is located within the scope of physical protection. However, current trusted computing platforms require that the built trusted computing environment extends to the outside of the physical protection platform. For example, the trusted computing platform that is on the basis of TCG/TPM or DRTM. So Smith's model leaves a lot desired to meet the requirements of the trusted computing platform.

3 Status and Chain of Trust

3.1 The Dependence Relationship Between Entities

This paper assumes that there is only one area of memory used to store software in the trusted computing environment system, and the software stored in the memory will not be changed by external sources outside the trusted computing environment system.

Described in this paper, the trusted computing environment is not limited to a specific trusted computing platform. The trusted computing platform is based on secure coprocessor of IBM4758 and the TCG/TPM or DRTM, both of which conform to the above assumptions.

Definition 1. *Let $\hat{p}(t)$ denote a program p in a trusted computing environment, at some time t, loaded into system and running. We call $\hat{p}(t)$ an entity.*

Note 1. Program p refers to the code that has computing power in the trusted computing environment system, or the encapsulation of its associated storage data, or a random sequence, operating system, or even a particular module, etc.

Note 2. Entity as defined herein and program are two different concepts. Entity is associated with the time the program and its container are loaded into system; if the program is loaded into the system at different times or is contained in different containers, and then it is considered to be a different entity.

At time t, the status of a trusted computing environment S_t is associated with the thread set $\{I_1, I_2, \cdots, I_n\}$ executing at the moment in the trusted computing environment and the entity's action sequence $seq\,(\hat{p}(t_1), \hat{p}(t_2), \cdots, \hat{p}(t_n))$. This paper assumes that the operation of the loader is atomic; meaning that only one thread at a time can load a program.

Definition 2. *At time t, with the encapsulation of all the entities in the trusted system to represent the state of system at time t, we let S_t denote it, where $seq\,(\hat{p}(t_1), \hat{p}(t_2), \cdots, \hat{p}(t_n))$.*

Note 1. The formula $Mem\,(m, \hat{p}(t_1), \hat{p}(t_2), \cdots, \hat{p}(t_n))\,@t$ denotes that there is an entity sequence $\hat{p}(t_1), \hat{p}(t_2), \cdots, \hat{p}(t_n)$ in the system memory at time t.

Note 2. When the system starts a thread to load a new entity, the state of the system will change accordingly. At some time, the state of the system is determined by the status of system of previous time and new entity loaded by thread at that time.

There are different interactions between the different entities, wherein some entities can control or read and write other entities, there is dependency between the entities.

Definition 3. *(Dependency)For entity $\hat{p}(t_1), \hat{p}(t_2)$, if the entity $\hat{p}(t_1)$ can read or write or control related data or program of the entity $\hat{p}(t_2)$, then the entity $\hat{p}(t_2)$ depends on the entity $\hat{p}(t_1)$. We let $\hat{p}(t_2)\,Dep\,\hat{p}(t_1)$ denote it.*

Note 1. Typically, new loaded entity depends on the existing entity.

Note 2. Entity dependency can be further divided into data dependency and control dependency, they are collectively known as rely-on in this paper, there is no further discussion of the distinction, but readers who are interested in it can refer to [4].

Corollary 1. *According to Definition 3, the following properties hold:*

1) Idempotence $\hat{p}(t_1)\, Dep\, \hat{p}(t_1)$;
2) Transitivity If $\hat{p}(t_2)\, Dep\, \hat{p}(t_1)$ and $\hat{p}(t_3)\, Dep\, \hat{p}(t_2)$, then $\hat{p}(t_3)\, Dep\, \hat{p}(t_1)$.

Note 1. Let $\rightarrow$ denote the transitive closure of dependency, $Dep\, \hat{p}(t) = \{\hat{q}(t) : (\hat{p}(t) \rightarrow \hat{q}(t))@t\}$ denotes the set of all entities which can affect the correctness of behavior of the entity $\hat{p}(t)$ at time t.

3.2   Trusted Set

Definition 4. *Relier R refers to an external entity of trusted computing environment or a platform user, let $Tset(R)$ denote it.*

Theorem 1. *The trusted computing environment loads an entity $\hat{p}(t)$ at time t, if $(Dep\, \hat{p}(t) \subseteq Tset(R))@t$ holds, then the relier R confirms that the entity $\hat{p}(t)$ is trusted at time t.*

Proof. From Corollary 1 we can confirm the credibility of the entity $\hat{p}(t)$ within the trusted computing environment depending on $Dep\, \hat{p}(t)$, at time t. Therefore, the relier R confirms the credibility of the entity $\hat{p}(t)$ basing on the credibility of all entities, so the above theorem can be proved by the known condition $(Dep\, \hat{p}(t) \subseteq Tset(R))@t$ and Definition 4.

Corollary 2. *Suppose relier R confirms that one entity $\hat{p}(t-1)$ of trusted computing environment is trusted at time $t-1$, if $(Dep\, \hat{p}(t-1) = Dep\, \hat{p}(t))@t$ holds, then the relier R also confirms that the entity $\hat{p}(t)$ is trusted at time t.*

Corollary 3. *At time t, $\forall \hat{p}(t_s)$ and $(\hat{p}(t_s) \in S_t)@t$, then $(Dep\, \hat{p}(t_s) \subseteq Tset(R))@t$ holds, which is the necessary and sufficient condition that the state S_t of the trusted computing environment is trusted.*

Note 1. Corollary 3 can be used as a gist of confirming the credibility of the state of the trusted computing environment.

3.3   Root of Trust and Trusted Measurement

Definition 5. *Trusted record refers to the evidence set of proving the credibility of the entity $\hat{p}(t)$ behavior; the relier R trusts any evidence of the set and confirms that the entity $\hat{p}(t)$ is trusted. Let $Tproof(\hat{p}(t))$ denote it in this paper.*

Theorem 2. *If for entity $\hat{p}(t)$ within a trusted computing environment, $(Dep\, \hat{p}(t) - \{\hat{p}(t)\} \subseteq Tset(R)@t) \wedge \exists \hat{p}(t') \in S_{t-1}, (Dep\, \hat{p}(t') \subseteq Tset(R))@t \wedge (v(\hat{p}(t'), \hat{p}(t)) \subset Tproof(\hat{p}(t)))@t$ holds, and then the relier R confirms that the entity $\hat{p}(t)$ is trusted.*

Proof. Since at time t, $\exists \hat{p}(t') \in S_{t-1}$, $(Dep\ \hat{p}(t') \subseteq Tset(R)@t) \wedge (v(\hat{p}(t'), \hat{p}(t)) \subset Tproof(\hat{p}(t)))@t$ combined with Definition 4 and Definition 5, we can confirm that $(\hat{p}(t) \in Tset(R))@t$ holds. At the same time, due to $(Dep\ \hat{p}(t) - \{\hat{p}(t)\} \subseteq Tset(R)@t$, we can confirm that $(Dep\ \hat{p}(t) \subseteq Tset(R))@t$ holds. Therefore, the Theorem 2 can be proved by above condition and Theorem 1.

Corollary 4. *For entity $\hat{p}(t)$ within trusted computing environment, $(\hat{p}(t) \in Tset(R))@(t-1)$ holds. If $(S_t - S_{t-1} = \{\hat{p}(t')\})@t \wedge \exists \hat{p}(t'') \in S_{t-1}$, $(Dep\ \hat{p}(t'') \subseteq Tset(R))@t \wedge (v(\hat{p}(t''), \hat{p}(t')) \subset Tproof(\hat{p}(t')))@t$, then $(\hat{p}(t) \in Tset(R))@t$ holds.*

Definition 6. *In a trusted system, $\forall R, t$, if $(\hat{r}(t_0) \in Tset(R))@t \wedge (Dep\ \hat{r}(t_0) = \{\hat{r}(t_0)\})@t$ holds, then we denote $\hat{r}(t_0)$ as the root of trust.*

Note 1. $\hat{r}(t_0)$ refers to a root of trust entity; for any relier at any time, $\hat{r}(t_0)$ is trusted. That is, its credibility is objective and not subject to conditions.

Theorem 3. $\hat{r}(t_0)$ *is a root of trust entity of trusted computing environment, for any reliers, if system state satisfies the following two conditions:*

(1) $S_1 \vdash Mem(m, \hat{r}(t_0))@t_0$;
(2) *For* $1 < k < t$, $S_{k+1} - S_k \vdash Mem(m, \hat{p}(t_k))@t_k \wedge \exists \hat{p}(t') \in S_k$, $(v(\hat{p}(t'), \hat{p}(t_k)) \subset Tproof(\hat{p}(t_k)))@t_k$, *then the system state is trusted at time t.*

Proof. For the system state sequence $S_1, S_2, \cdots, S_{t-1}, S_t$:

When $N = 1$, $S_1 \vdash Mem(m, \hat{r}(t_0))@t_0$. Since r is the root of trust, the system state S_1 can be proved to be trusted by $(\hat{r}(t_0) \in Tset(R))@t \wedge (Dep\ \hat{r}(t_0) = \{\hat{r}(t_0)\})@t$ and Definition 6;

When $N = k$, we suppose that S_k is trusted;

When $N = k + 1$, $S_{k+1} - S_k \vdash Mem(m, \hat{p}(t_k))@t_k$ holds. Since S_k is trusted, according to the condition (2) and Corollary 4, $\forall \hat{p}(t') \in S_k$, $(\hat{p}(t') \in Tset(R))@t'$ holds, such that S_{k+1} is trusted by Corollary 4.

In summary, the conclusion is proved.

3.4 Chain of Trust Model

Definition 7. *In the trusted system, if there is an entity set $\hat{P} = \{\hat{p}(t_1), \hat{p}(t_2), \cdots, \hat{p}(t_k)\} \subseteq S_t$ at time t, where $0 < t_0 < \cdots < t_k < t$, then*

$$Dep\ \hat{p}(t_k) - \{\hat{p}(t_k)\} = Dep\ \hat{p}(t_{k-1})$$
$$\wedge Dep\ \hat{p}(t_{k-1}) - \{\hat{p}(t_{k-1})\} = Dep\ \hat{p}(t_{k-2})$$
$$\wedge Dep\ \hat{p}(t_{k-2}) - \{\hat{p}(t_{k-2})\} = Dep\ \hat{p}(t_{k-3})$$
$$\cdots$$
$$\wedge Dep\ \hat{p}(t_1) - \{\hat{p}(t_1)\} = Dep\ \hat{p}(t_0),$$

and $\forall \hat{p}(t') \in \hat{P} - \{\hat{r}(t_0)\}$, $\exists \hat{p}(t'') \in \hat{P}$, $(Dep(\hat{p}(t'')) \subseteq Tset(R))@t \wedge (v(\hat{p}(t'), \hat{p}(t'')) \in Tproof(\hat{p}(t'')))@t$ *holds, we conclude that there is a chain of trust in the system from the root of trust $\hat{r}(t_0)$ to the entity $\hat{r}(t_k)$.*

Theorem 4. *Let $0 \leq t_0 < t_n < t$, if there is a chain of trust from the root of trust entity $\hat{r}(t_0)$ to the entity $\hat{p}(t_n)$ at time t, then the relier R confirms that the entity $\hat{p}(t_n)$ is trusted at time t.*

Proof. we can know by the Definition 7, if there is a chain of trust from the root of trust entity $\hat{r}(t_0)$ to the entity $\hat{p}(t_n)$ at time t, then

$$Dep\, \hat{p}\,(t_k) - \{\hat{p}\,(t_k)\} = Dep\, \hat{p}\,(t_{k-1})$$
$$\wedge Dep\, \hat{p}\,(t_{k-1}) - \{\hat{p}\,(t_{k-1})\} = Dep\, \hat{p}\,(t_{k-2})$$
$$\wedge Dep\, \hat{p}\,(t_{k-2}) - \{\hat{p}\,(t_{k-2})\} = Dep\, \hat{p}\,(t_{k-3})$$
$$\cdots$$
$$\wedge Dep\, \hat{p}\,(t_1) - \{\hat{p}\,(t_1)\} = \{\hat{r}(t_0)\},$$

where $0 < t_0 < \cdots < t_k < t$, so $Dep\ \hat{p}(t_n) \subseteq \hat{P}$ holds, where $\hat{P} = \{\hat{p}(t_1), \hat{p}(t_2), \cdots, \hat{p}(t_n)\}$.

$\forall \hat{p}(t'), \exists \hat{p}(t'') \in \hat{P} : (v(\hat{p}(t'), \hat{p}(t'')) \in Tproof(R))@t$ holds, so $(Dep\ \hat{p}(t_n) \subseteq \hat{P} \subseteq Tset(R))@t$ can be proved by the Theorem 2.

Finally, the conclusion is proved by Theorem 1.

4   Analysis of the Existing Chain of Trust of Trusted Computing Platform

4.1   SRTM-Based Trusted Computing Platform

TCG has developed a set of trusted boot standards that describe how to build and transfer the chain of trust based on integrity measurement and proof. First, trusted measurement of TCG starts from the time the system is powered on, and transfers the control to a piece of code of BIOS. Secondly, the root of trust uses the same method to measure the remaining portion of BIOS, then control is transferred to the measured program or module and so on; this process will continue until the operating system boots. Measurements produced during the process are stored in platform configuration register (PCR) of TPM.

Theorem 3 of this paper describes a kind of method of building and transferring chain of trust. The trusted boot, defined by TCG, is a special case of the theorem. So this theorem can be used to prove the credibility of building and transferring the chain of trust during the process of trusted boot defined by TCG. The trusted boot defined by TCG starts with root of trust. One level measures and certifies another, a layer trusts another, and this type of credibility is extended to the whole system of the computer. However, the method of building and transferring chain of trust during the process of trusted boot defined by TCG constrains condition 2 of Theorem 3 about how to select an entity.

Similarly, Theorem 3 can also prove the credibility of building and transferring chain of trust of the IBM's IMA [22] and the BEAR [17,18] system of Dartmouth University. First, for building and transferring chain of trust, these systems are based on the method of trusted boot defined by TCG, which is extended to the whole operating system. Then, the control is transferred to the operating system. The operating system will measure the next entity. As shown in Fig. 1, the user can load the follow-up entity on the basis of their needs, which is different from the trusted boot defined by TCG whose entity must be loaded according to a fixed sequence. However, Theorem 3 does not require that an entity to be loaded according to a fixed sequence. So the above two systems in building and transferring chain of trust both are in line with condition of Theorem 3.

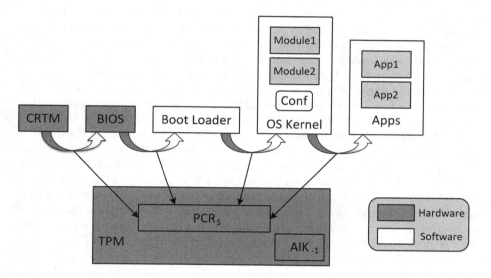

Fig. 1. IMA's SRTM-based chain of trust

4.2 DRTM-Based Trusted Computing Platform

DRTM-based trusted computing platform does not require system reboot, which allows the system to build a chain of trust at any untrusted moment as a starting point, but DRTM requires the support of CPU. AMD and Intel have proposed DRTM technology independently. They are AMD's Secure Virtual Machine (SVM) and Intel's Trusted eXecution Technology (TXT).

Theorem 3 is also a special case of Theorem 4, that is to say, on power-up of the system, the root of trust for measurement is loaded, and from $\hat{r}(t_0)$ to $\hat{p}(t_n)$, there is a chain of trust consisting of all entities loaded. Theorem 4 shows that the relier is only concerned about the credibility of interaction entities, without the need to ensure that trusted computing environment system is trusted. This is due to the fact that Definition 7 gives a method of building dynamic chain of trust. We can select a true subset that contains DRTM from entities of trusted computing environment, and build a chain of trust based on the true subset. DRTM does not need to start at time $t_0 = 0$, it can load at any time where

$0 \leq t_0 < t_n < t$. However, it requires that the entity of true subset selected is not affected by any entity outside trusted computing platform.

Theorem 4 can be used to confirm the credibility of chain of trust which is based on DRTM in the trusted computing environment. For example, the Flicker [19] system, due to the newly added DRTM extended command can provide isolation with the system. The system utilizes extended command to execute a piece of code. In this system, it is assumed that DRTM entity was loaded at time t_0 and the entity $\hat{p}(t_1)$ of executed codes was loaded at time t_1, and another entity was not loaded between t_0 and t_1. In this system, extended commands of supporting DRTM can take advantage of the way of suspending the original system to ensure that the entity $\hat{p}(t_1)$ does not depend on other entity which was loaded before time t_0. In addition, the system will delete the entity $\hat{p}(t_1)$ before time t_n when operating system begins to restart, which can ensure that the entity $\hat{p}(t_1)$ does not depend on other entity which was loaded after the time t_n. The credibility of building and transfer chain of trust of this system can be proved by Definition 7 and Theorem 4.

Flicker achieves its secure execution environment by suspending the original operating system and application software which are running on it. However, the security architecture of Intel's TXT [1] and the security architecture of Flicker are different. The security architecture of Intel's TXT is a type of architecture of trusted computing environment based on enhanced security coprocessor, which allows the protected code and unsafe code to simultaneously run on the trusted computing platform. In order to prevent other programs to access or modify data of protected programs, the security architecture of Intel's TXT provides a secure execution environment. When the processor is transferred to safe mode, the enhanced security coprocessor that has a safe mode utilizes a method of encrypting data to achieve the isolation between other entities and itself. But, Intel TXT does not have a safe mode. Through the Theorem 4, when DRTM is loaded, in order to ensure safe programs and unsafe programs to run simultaneously on the trusted computing platform, we need some software to isolate them. The isolation provided by virtualization technology can achieve this purpose, and most of processors that support DRTM also support hardware-assisted virtualization technology. Figure 2 is security architecture of Intel's TXT. Virtual Machine Monitor (VMM) can isolate operation environments that have different needs to different virtual domains. It is similar to Terrer architecture, but the difference between the two is: According to the building of Intel's TXT, VMM can dynamically load without restarting operating system based on its protection needs, and TPM1.2 can provide the proof to chain of trust from DRTM of Intel's TXT to VMM. Microsoft's Next-Generation Secure Computing Base (NGSCB) [2] is a particular implementation of security architecture of Intel's TXT. VMM divides hardware resources into two parts, where the remaining original operating system runs on the left and the right is a Micro Secure Kernel called nexus. Agent refers to an application that runs on the nexus, which runs in isolated address space and uses certified primitives. Nexus and VMM provide agent with a secure running architecture that is consistent with architecture of

Intel's TXT. The secure architecture of Intel's TXT and the design of Microsoft's NGSCB both satisfy condition of Definition 7. Assuming the DRTM entity $\hat{r}(t_0)$ is loaded at time t_0 and the VMM entity $\hat{p}(t_1)$ is loaded at time t_1, and there is no other entity to be loaded between t_0 and t_1, DRTM can ensure the isolation between the entity $\hat{r}(t_0)$ and the entity $\hat{p}(t_1)$ from t_0 to t_n, so that it ensures that the above entity does not depend on the entity that was loaded before the time t_0. Virtualization technology provides the isolation between running-state VMM and trusted domain, which ensures that these entities do not rely on the entity that was loaded after the time t_n. The built chain of trust meets Definition 7.

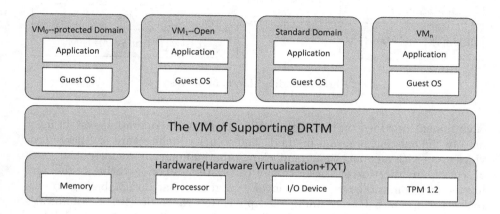

Fig. 2. The security architecture of Intel's TXT

5 New Mechanism and Prototype of Building Chain of Trust

From Fig. 1 and Theorem 3, we can appreciate that building a chain of trust of SRTM-based requires all entities that were loaded into trusted computing environment are trusted during the period from the time when the system loads root of chain to confirmation time in the process of building a chain of trust, which makes it very difficult to build a trusted computing environment through static chain of trust. For example, to build a trusted computing environment of a windows-based machine, we need to measure the whole operating system and all procedures that run on it. Moreover, there are a lot of measurements of trusted software that are generated during the process, and they need to be stored and managed. However, even without considering the performance issue of measuring in the process, it is very difficult to achieve.

Flicker takes the DRTM as a trusted base that has a shorter chain of trust. However, to achieve this, Flicker needs to pause the operating system and all software running on it. We can deduce that the method of building a chain of trust of Flicker system is correct basing on Theorem 4. But the isolated running

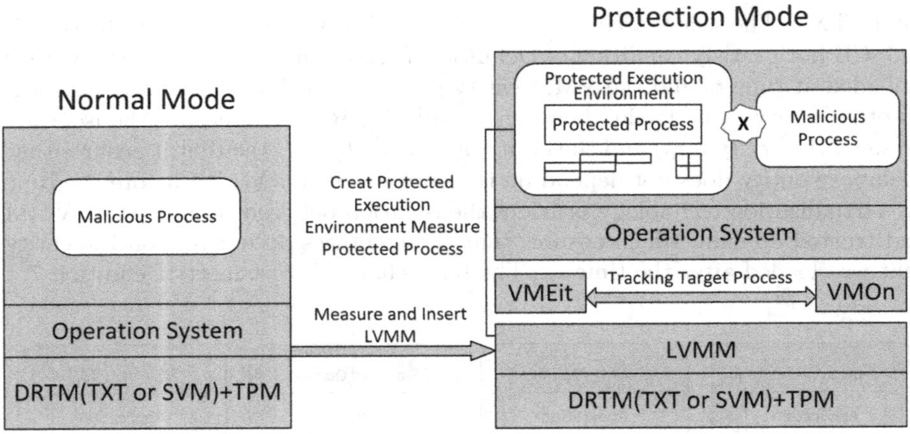

Fig. 3. Building the chain of trust

environment provided by the method of suspending the operating system must modify the existing program method. The security architecture of Flicker provides users with an approximate unlocking programming environment, the codes of security architecture of Flicker cannot call system call of operating system and library function, moreover cannot invoke programs that do not belong to current session, which largely limits the application range of Flicker. Microsoft's NGSCB and Intel's TXT both achieve dynamic virtualization through DRTM, but their trusted computing environment was built on the isolated domains that are similar to running environment of operating system. According to Theorem 4, although Microsoft's NGSCB and Intel's TXT are able to utilize DRTM and hardware-assisted virtualization technology to exclude the host operation system outside trusted base, the chain of trust built on the isolated domain is similar to the traditional static chain of trust, which cannot solve the problem of managing a large number of hash values. This paper introduces a lightweight virtual machine monitor (LVMM) to implement a new mechanism of building chain of trust. That is to say, in the running operating system environment, this paper utilizes hardware virtualization technology and DRTM to load a trusted LVMM. LVMM creates and maintains the protected execution environment for objective programs, and monitors the access to memory pages of objective programs located in PEX. LVMM ensures that one can operate sensitive resources only in the PEX.

As shown in Fig. 3. Cherub [11] takes advantage of extended instructions provided by hardware virtualization technology in the running operating system to load LVMM and moves the operating system to a VM. Dynamic DRTM technology can make the LVMM start with a kind of trusted way. TPM provides integrity proof of lightweight virtual machine that can measure the integrity of protected code and data of PEX.

In the running phase, Cherub utilizes shadow page mechanism to hidden LVMM and page table of safety function module from operating system and protects them from malicious DMA's attack by I/O hardware virtualization technology. It marks protected codes and data of the target program in the shadow page table of LVMM so that LVMM can check the legitimacy of access to these memory pages. Meanwhile, when the control of the processor is transferred to the code outside PEX, LVMM will encrypt the page where the codes and data of PEX are located. When the control returns to PEX, LVMM will decrypt these pages. LVMM also depends on the I/O hardware virtualization to protect PEX against DMA's malicious attacks. When system does not need the defensive function provided by LVMM, Cherub can easily uninstall LVMM. Then operating system will consequently control all system resources. Dynamically loading and unloading LVMM and Cherub are more flexible than other all-purpose security architectures that are based on VM monitor software, which have significant performance disadvantage.

TPM and DRTM can ensure the credibility and integrity of safety function module and LVMM from the time DRTM is loaded to the time the operating system is restated, which ensures that above-mentioned entities do not depend on any entity that was loaded by trusted computing platform before the initial time. The integrity protection of the safety function module and LVMM is able to ensure that these entities do not rely on any entity that was loaded after the time when operating system restarted. Therefore, the built chain of trust model conforms to Definition 7 and the condition of Theorem 4.

6   Conclusion

At present, the existing theoretical study of trusted computing lacks theoretical content on building trusted computing environment. Moreover, some related theory is difficult to be widely used in the construction of trusted computing environment. To solve these problems, this paper gives the formalisation description of chain of trust model defined by TCG based on entity dependence and safety logic system. The model has universal significance, and this paper utilizes it to assess existing trusted computing platforms that are based on SRTM or DRTM. At the same time, the theory of the model can provide other scholars to further study chain of trust and trusted computing environment with theoretical reference.

Acknowledgements. This work is supported by the Youth Project of the National Natural Science Foundation of China under Grant No.61202397.

References

1. Intel® Trusted Execution Technology (Intel® TXT) Overview, https://www.intel.com/content/www/us/en/support/articles/000025873/technologies.html, library Catalog: www.intel.com

2. At WinHEC, Microsoft Discusses Details of Next-Generation Secure Computing Base, May 2003.https://news.microsoft.com/2003/05/07/at-winhec-microsoft-discusses-details-of-next-generation-secure-computing-base/, library Catalog: news.microsoft.com Section: Feature Stories
3. Arlat, J., Costes, A., Crouzet, Y., Laprie, J.C., Powell, D.: Fault injection and dependability evaluation of fault-tolerant systems. IEEE Trans. Comput. **42**(8), 913–923 (1993). https://doi.org/10.1109/12.238482
4. Beth, T., Borcherding, M., Klein, B.: Valuation of trust in open networks. In: Gollmann, D. (ed.) ESORICS 1994. LNCS, vol. 875, pp. 1–18. Springer, Heidelberg (1994). https://doi.org/10.1007/3-540-58618-0_53
5. Blaze, M., Feigenbaum, J., Lacy, J.: Decentralized trust management. In: Proceedings 1996 IEEE Symposium on Security and Privacy, pp. 164–173. IEEE (1996). https://doi.org/10.3724/10.1109/SECPRI.1996.502679
6. Chang, D.X., Feng, D.G., Qin, Y., Zhang, Q.Y.: Analyzing the trust chain of trusted virtualization platform based on the extended ls (2). J. China Inst. Commun. **34**(5), 31–41 (2013). http://ir.iscas.ac.cn/handle/311060/15629
7. Chen, S., Wen, Y., Zhao, H.: Formal analysis of secure bootstrap in trusted computing. In: Xiao, B., Yang, L.T., Ma, J., Muller-Schloer, C., Hua, Yu. (eds.) ATC 2007. LNCS, vol. 4610, pp. 352–360. Springer, Heidelberg (2007). https://doi.org/10.1007/978-3-540-73547-2_37
8. Datta, A., Franklin, J., Garg, D., Kaynar, D.: A logic of secure systems and its application to trusted computing. In: 2009 30th IEEE Symposium on Security and Privacy, pp. 221–236. IEEE (2009). https://doi.org/10.1109/SP.2009.16
9. Hai-mei, X., Shou-qing, Q., Xian-liang, L., Hong, H.: A novel trust model of p2p networks based on theory of probability and statistics. J. Electron. Inf. Technol. **33**(6), 1314–1318 (2011). https://doi.org/10.3724/SP.J.1146.2010.00179
10. Isermann, R.: Process fault detection based on modeling and estimation methods–a survey. Automatica **20**(4), 387–404 (1984). https://doi.org/10.1016/0005-1098(84)90098-0
11. Jin, H., Cheng, G., Zou, D., Zhang, X.: Cherub: fine-grained application protection with on-demand virtualization. Comput. Math. Appl. **65**(9), 1326–1338 (2013). https://doi.org/10.1016/j.camwa.2012.02.001
12. Josang, A.: Trust-based decision making for electronic transactions. In: Proceedings of the 4th Nordic Workshop on Secure Computer Systems (NORDSEC 1999), pp. 496–502. Citeseer (1999)
13. Jøsang, A.: A logic for uncertain probabilities. Int. J. Uncertainty, Fuzziness Knowl. Based Syst. **9**(03), 279–311 (2001)
14. Jøsang, A., Knapskog, S.J.: A metric for trusted systems. In: Proceedings of the 21st National Security Conference, NSA. Citeseer (1998)
15. Lin, C., Kong, X.Z., Zhou, H.: Enhance the dependability of computing systems: integration of virtualization and SOA. J. Softw. **7** (2009). https://doi.org/10.3724/SP.J.1001.2009.03549
16. Lin, C., Wang, Y.Z., Yang, Y., Qu, Y.: Research on network dependability analysis methods based on stochastic petri net. Dianzi Xuebao(Acta Electronica Sinica) **34**(2), 322–332 (2006)
17. MacDonald, R., Smith, S., Marchesini, J., Wild, O.: Bear: an open-source virtual secure coprocessor based on TCPA. Computer Science Technical Report TR2003-471, Dartmouth College (2003)
18. Marchesini, J., Smith, S., Wild, O., MacDonald, R.: Experimenting with TCPA/TCG hardware, or: how i learned to stop worrying and love the bear. Computer Science Technical Report TR2003-476, Dartmouth College (2003)

19. McCune, J.M., Parno, B.J., Perrig, A., Reiter, M.K., Isozaki, H.: Flicker: an execution infrastructure for TCB minimization. In: Proceedings of the 3rd ACM SIGOPS/EuroSys European Conference on Computer Systems 2008, pp. 315–328 (2008). https://doi.org/10.1145/1352592.1352625

20. Meyer, J.F.: On evaluating the performability of degradable computing systems. IEEE Trans. Comput. **29**(8), 720–731 (1980). https://doi.org/10.1109/TC.1980.1675654

21. Peng, W., Guoxin, W., Qun, F.: A ruputation-based trust model based on probability and statistics for P2P systems. J. Comput. Res. Dev. **45**(3), 408–416 (2008)

22. Qu, W., Li, M., Weng, C.: An active trusted model for virtual machine systems. In: 2009 IEEE International Symposium on Parallel and Distributed Processing with Applications, pp. 145–152. IEEE (2009). https://doi.org/10.1109/ISPA.2009.68

23. Smith, S.W.: Outbound authentication for programmable secure coprocessors. In: Gollmann, D., Karjoth, G., Waidner, M. (eds.) ESORICS 2002. LNCS, vol. 2502, pp. 72–89. Springer, Heidelberg (2002). https://doi.org/10.1007/3-540-45853-0_5

24. Zhou, Z., Wu, L., Hong, Z., et al.: Trustworthiness measurement model of virtual machine for cloud computing. J. Southeast Univ. (Natural Science Edition) **441**, 45–50 (2014). https://doi.org/10.3969/j.issn.1001-0505.2014.01.009

Evaluation on the Security of Commercial Cloud Container Services

Yifei Wu[1,2], Lingguang Lei[1,2(✉)], Yuewu Wang[1,2], Kun Sun[3],
and Jingzi Meng[1,2]

[1] State Key Laboratory of Information Security, Institute of Information
Engineering, Chinese Academy of Sciences, Beijing, China
{wuyifei,wuyifei,wangyuewu,mengjingzi}@iie.ac.cn
[2] School of Cyber Security, University of Chinese Academy of Sciences,
Beijing, China
[3] Center for Secure Information Systems, George Mason University, Fairfax, USA
ksun3@gmu.edu

Abstract. With the increasing adoption of the container mechanism in the industrial community, cloud vendors begin to provide cloud container services. Unfortunately, it lacks a concrete method to evaluate the security of cloud containers, whose security heavily depends on the security policies enforced by the cloud providers. In this paper, we first derive a metric checklist that identifies the critical factors associated with the security of cloud container services against the two most severe threats, i.e., the privilege escalation and container escaping attacks. Specifically, we identify the metrics which directly reflect the working conditions of the attacker. We also extract the metrics essential to achieve privilege escalation and container escaping attacks by investigating the feasible methods for breaking the security measures, including KASLR, SMEP and SMAP, etc. Since memory corruption vulnerabilities are frequently adopted in the privilege escalation attacks, we collect a dataset of the publicly released memory corruption vulnerabilities to assist the evaluation. Then, we develop a tool to collect the metric data listed in the checklist from inside the cloud containers and perform security inspection on five in-service commercial cloud container services. The results show that some containers are enforced with weak protection mechanisms (e.g., with the Seccomp mechanism being disabled), and the KASLR could be bypassed on all five cloud containers. However, even after obtaining ROOT privilege in a container, attackers still can hardly escape from the container on the public cloud platforms, since the necessary files for crafting or compiling a loadable kernel module for the host OS are inaccessible to the container. Finally, we provide some suggestions to improve the security of the cloud container services.

Keywords: Container · Privilege escalation · Kernel security
mechanisms · CPU Protection Mechanisms · Container escape

© Springer Nature Switzerland AG 2020
W. Susilo et al. (Eds.): ISC 2020, LNCS 12472, pp. 160–177, 2020.
https://doi.org/10.1007/978-3-030-62974-8_10

1   Introduction

Container technology is increasingly adopted by the industrial community [38]. The primary reason is the flexibility introduced by the container orchestration tools such as Docker [11] and Kubernetes [15], which facilitate the deployment, scaling, and management of the containerized applications. The cloud vendors also begin to provide container services, e.g., Amazon Fargate [7], Google GKE (Google Kubernetes Engine) [12], etc. As a lightweight alternative to the traditional virtual-machine based cloud service, the cloud container service allows the container instances from different tenants to be executed on the same physical or virtual server.

As an OS-level virtualization technology implemented in the Linux kernel, all containers running on one host share the same Linux kernel. There is a consensus that the container mechanism is less secure than the traditional virtualization technology like Xen [17] and KVM [35], etc., due to its kernel-sharing feature. However, it lacks a concrete method to evaluate the security of the cloud container services. Existing studies mainly focus on analyzing the security of the containers running on the local platforms [16,19,27,37]. For example, XinLin et al. [27] provide a measurement study on the security of local Docker container systems, where the processes inside the container are granted with default Docker container permissions. Also, it assumes the attackers could configure portions of the underlying execution environment (e.g., they can select to install a vulnerable kernel system and obtain the image file and the source code of the kernel system). However, execution environment of the remote cloud containers is configured by the service providers and uncontrollable to the attackers. Therefore, security evaluation on the local container platforms could not completely reflect the security of various remote cloud containers, which are deployed with a dedicated kernel system and protection policies.

In this paper, we provide a metric-based method to evaluate the security of cloud container services against the privilege escalation attack (i.e., obtaining ROOT privilege from inside the container) and the container escaping attack, which will seriously damage or even invalid the isolation provided by container mechanism. We first investigate the critical factors associated with the security of a cloud container service and derive a metric checklist to facilitate the security inspection. Specifically, we identify the essential metrics associated with the cloud containers' execution environment, which directly reflect the working conditions of the attackers, including version and updating time of the underlying kernel system (they partially illustrate vulnerability of the underlying kernel system), permissions assigned to the container tenants, and the protection policies configured by the service provider (e.g., whether security measures including Seccomp [10], MAC, KASLR [21], SMEP [4] and SMAP [20] are enabled). We also extract the metrics critical to achieve privilege escalation by investigating the feasible methods for breaking the security measures, which are commonly adopted to defend against privilege escalation [27]. To aid our analysis, we collect a dataset of publicly released memory corruption vulnerabilities, which are necessary for the privilege escalation attacks. Meanwhile, we analyze the procedure to achieve container escaping and identify the related critical metrics.

Then, we develop a tool to examine the identified metrics listed in the checklist and perform a detailed evaluation on the security of five popular cloud container services[1]. We first explore the execution environment of the cloud container services, and the results show that kernel systems of four container services are last updated in 2019. However, we find two cloud container services have assigned ROOT privilege to the container tenants (i.e., ccs4 and ccs5 in Table 1). The CPU mechanisms (i.e., SMEP and SMAP) are enabled by almost all container services, while the kernel protection mechanisms (i.e., MAC, Seccomp, and KASLR) are not effectively leveraged. For example, Seccomp and MAC are both enabled by only one service, and the KASLR is enabled by two services.

Investigation on the possibility of privilege escalation attack is performed on the containers that are not assigned ROOT privilege (i.e., containers provided by cloud services ccs1, ccs2 and cc3 in Table 1). The results show that KASLR could be successfully bypassed on all services. However, since the underlying kernel system of the three cloud containers was updated recently, we fail to find feasible memory corruption vulnerabilities (and exploits) to bypass SMEP and SMAP on ccs1, cc2 and ccs3. Experiments on the container escaping attacks show that container escaping is difficult on the public cloud platforms even after the attackers obtain ROOT privilege. Since there are no user-space APIs (e.g., system calls) for a process to transfer from one container to another container, container escaping should be achieved by modifying the kernel data. The most generic method to get into the kernel is through a kernel module. However, the Linux system only allows a matching kernel module (e.g., the module compiled with the same header files and symbol table as the running system) to be loaded. In our experiments, container escaping fails on the cloud containers, since the necessary files for crafting or compiling a loadable kernel module are inaccessible to the attackers inside the containers.

We have reported our findings to five cloud service providers, and received responses from most of the providers. After our suggestion, cp2 disabled the Intel TSX (Transactional Synchronization Extensions) [13] mechanism on the ccs2 service to prevent the bypassing of KASLR, and cp5 replied that they would constrain the tenant's capability and enable the KASLR to enhance the security of ccs5.

In summary, we make the following contributions:

- We present a metric-based method and design a tool to evaluate the security of cloud container services against the privilege escalation and container escaping attacks.

---

[1] As per requirement of some service providers, we use cp1, cp2, cp3, cp4, cp5 to represent the five cloud providers, and ccs1, ccs2, ccs3, ccs4, ccs5 to represent the five cloud container services in the evaluation results.

- We construct a dataset of memory corruption vulnerabilities which are usually necessary when achieving privilege escalation from inside the container to support the work of our evaluation tool.
- We evaluate the security of five in-service cloud container services in detail, and identify the major obstacles for the attackers to escape from public cloud containers. We also provide the suggestions to improve the security of the cloud container services based on our evaluation.

2 Background

2.1 Container Mechanism

Container [28] is a lightweight OS-level virtualization technology implemented in Linux kernel, which provides isolation for one or more Linux processes. The processes running inside a container feel like they own the entire system, although containers running on the same host share the same Linux kernel. Isolation between the containers is achieved through two kernel mechanisms, i.e., Namespace [9] and Cgroup [6]. There are seven types of namespaces, i.e., user, uts, net, pid, mnt, ipc and cgroup. Each namespace isolates a specific kernel resource for one container. For example, the mnt namespace provides an isolated file system for a container through isolating the file system mount points. After isolation, the files in different mnt namespaces are not visible to each other and cannot affect each other. Compared to the Namespace mechanism that concerns kernel data isolation, the Cgroup mechanism focuses more on performance isolation by limiting the amount of resources (e.g., CPU, memory, devices, etc.) that a container can use. Docker [32] is a pervasively used container engine that facilitates the management of the containers, such as container creating, deleting, starting and stopping, etc. Popular cloud providers also begin to provide the multi-tenancy cloud container services, such as Amazon Fargate [7], Google GKE (Google Kubernetes Engine) [12], etc. The underlying technology of these services is the container mechanism. Therefore, several tenants might share the same Linux kernel.

2.2 Linux Kernel Security Mechanisms

Isolation enforced by the container mechanism is invalid, if a process inside the container compromises the kernel or escapes the container boundary to enter another container. Therefore, several Linux kernel security mechanisms are adopted to constrain the capability of the processes inside the containers, such as Kernel Address Space Layout Randomization (KASLR) [21], Capability [8], Seccomp [10] and Mandatory Access Control (MAC) mechanisms. The KASLR mechanism makes the Linux kernel boot up at a random base address rather than at a fixed base address. As such, the attackers could not obtain addresses of critical kernel functions, which are usually necessary to compromise the kernel. Capability is a privilege decentralized mechanism, which divides the superuser privilege (i.e., ROOT privilege) into 38 units, known as capabilities. Each capability represents a permission to operate some specific kernel resources. The Seccomp mechanism constrains the system calls a process can invoke. SELinux [30], AppArmor [1] are two MAC mechanisms frequently used to enforce mandatory access control on the kernel resources.

2.3   CPU Protection Mechanisms

Two CPU protection mechanisms are also frequently used to protect the Linux kernel, i.e., Supervisor Mode Access Prevention (SMAP) and Supervisor Mode Execution Prevention (SMEP) [4]. SMAP prevents supervisor mode programs from accessing user-space memory, while SMEP prevents supervisor mode programs from executing user-space code. SMAP and SMEP could be enabled by setting the 21st and 20th bits of the CR4 register, respectively.

3   Metric Checklist for Container Security Evaluation

Before performing the security evaluation, we first derive a metric checklist that identifies the critical factors associated with the security of cloud container services. As a technology implemented in the Linux kernel, isolation introduced by container will be seriously damaged or even invalid, if the processes inside a container could obtain the ROOT privilege or escape the container boundary. Therefore, we focus on investigating the security of cloud container services against these two most severe threats, i.e., the possibility to achieve privilege escalation and container escaping from inside the container. Specifically, we first identify the metrics which directly reflect the cloud container's execution environment. Then, we investigate and summarize the feasible methods for breaking the security measures including KASLR, SMEP and SMAP, which are commonly adopted to defend against privilege escalation [27]. Finally, we extract the metrics essential to achieve container escaping.

3.1   Execution Environment Related Metrics

Security of the container services heavily depends on the execution environment, including version and updating time of the underlying kernel system, permissions assigned to the container tenants, and the protection policies configured by the service providers. Version and updating time of the underlying kernel system impact not only the probability of finding feasible memory corruption vulnerabilities, but also the possibility to obtain a matching kernel image, both of which are frequently leveraged in privilege escalation attacks [27]. Thus they are very important to the security of container services. The permission information directly reflects the ability of an attacker, which means the capabilities assigned to container processes on Linux platforms. The protection policies signify the difficulty of launching the attacks, which includes the configuration of both the Linux kernel (see Sect. 2.2) and CPU protection (see Sect. 2.3) mechanisms, i.e., Seccomp, MAC, KASLR, SMEP and SMAP. As such, we introduce eight execution-environment-related metrics into the checklist, i.e., kernel version and updating time; capabilities assigned to a container tenant; and the policies of Seccomp, MAC, KASLR, SMEP and SMAP.

3.2 Privilege Escalation Related Metrics

The key security mechanisms against privilege escalation are KASLR, SMEP and SMAP [27]. KASLR prevents the attackers from guessing the kernel functions addresses (e.g., *commit_creds()* and *prepare_kernel_cred()* are two kernel functions frequently used in privilege escalation attacks). SMAP and SMEP can prevent the hijacked control flow from accessing the user-space data and executing the user-space code (shellcode). An attacker must bypass these mechanisms to achieve privilege escalation from inside the container [27]. In the following, we summarize the methods which could be used to bypass the KASLR, SMEP and SMAP, and extract the critical factors for achieving the bypassing.

1) Bypassing KASLR. The KASLR mechanism has been introduced since Linux kernel 3.14, which makes the kernel image decompress itself at a random location during the booting time. It can be enabled by setting the CONFIG_RANDOMIZE_BASE option when compiling the kernel, and it has been enabled by default since kernel 4.12. Without KASLR, the base address of the kernel code will be configured at $0 \times$ FFFFFFFF81000000. In theory, the number of slots available to the KASLR mechanism for achieving base address randomization is 256 on the $\times$ 86-32 platforms and 512 on the $\times$ 86-64 platforms [21]. In general, there are mainly two approaches to achieve KASLR bypassing, i.e., reading sensitive files and launching cache-based side-channel attacks.

a) *Bypassing KASLR through Reading Sensitive File.* Two types of files might be used to bypass KASLR. First, the dmesg file under the directory of /var/log may contain kernel-address related sensitive information (e.g., the kernel's base address might be obtained by searching the keywords such as "Freeing SMP" or "Freeing unused" in the dmesg file). However, we might not be able to obtain exact addresses of the critical kernel functions (e.g., *native_write_cr4()*) with only the kernel's base address, since the offsets of the kernel functions (to the base address) vary when the kernel images are compiled with different compilers (e.g., the gcc compilers of different versions) or different compiling options (e.g., the options defined in the .config file). Therefore, in order to obtain the exact addresses, kernel images of the running systems are also necessary. Second, the address of each kernel function could be obtained directly from the /proc/kallsyms file, if it is set as readable to the user.

b) *Bypassing KASLR through Cache-based Side-channel Attacks.* Since the low entropy of the KASLR's implementation, cache-based side-channel attacks are also frequently used to bypass KASLR. Basically, the attacks are launched based on the observation that it takes less time to access a content residing in the cache than the one in the memory. And the most effective cache-based side-channel attack for bypassing KASLR is called TLB-cache-based [23,24] side-channel attack.

TLB-cache-based side-channel attacks are also known as double-page fault attacks [23,24], and they are accomplished based on a feature of some Intel CPUs. When a user program accesses a privileged kernel address, the processing procedure will be slightly different for the mapped and unmapped addresses. As illustrated in Fig. 1, when a mapped address is accessed, a TLB entry will be created in the TLB cache before the kernel delivers a segment fault signal to the user program (since the privilege check fails). But for an unmapped address, no TLB entry will be created. Therefore, the attackers can deduce whether a kernel address is mapped or not, by accessing the same address twice and comparing the time duration of receiving the segment fault signal. As such, the base address of the kernel image could be obtained by probing the whole region of the kernel space. However, the time to execute segment fault handler function is also counted into the duration (i.e., t1 and t2), and it is usually far longer than the difference caused by TLB hit or miss. For obtaining stable results, it is better to reduce the noise caused by the segment fault handler as far as possible. Yeongjin Jang et al. [24] proposed a highly stable solution (named DrK) by leveraging the Intel TSX (Transactional Synchronization Extensions) instructions. With TSX, the CPU will directly inform the segment fault to the user program without the attendance of Linux kernel, as such the noise caused by segment fault handler is omitted.

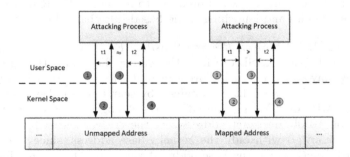

Fig. 1. TLB-cache based side-channel attack to bypass KASLR. ① Access a kernel address p; ② Receive a segment fault signal (since the privileged check fails) and record the time duration for obtaining the signal (t1); ③ Access p again; ④ Record the time duration for the second access (t2). When accessing a mapped address, a TLB entry will be created in step ②, and t2 will be smaller than t1 (since the TLB hit). Or else, no TLB entry will be created, then t2 and t1 will be almost the same.

2) Bypassing SMEP and SMAP. SMEP and SMAP are introduced into the Linux kernel since version 3.0 and 3.7, respectively. In general, the attackers can disable SMEP and SMAP by redirecting a corrupted kernel pointer to the *native_write_cr4()* function through memory corruption vulnerabilities. For example, with parameter 0x407f0, *native_write_cr4()* will set the 20th and 21st bits of the CR4 register as zero (i.e., disabling the SMEP and SMAP). However, this method requires to leverage a memory corruption vulnerability in Linux kernel, i.e., seeking out (and overwriting) a corrupted kernel pointer that points to a function taking one and only one parameter. SMAP is sometimes disabled by default, then the SMEP could be disabled similarly but with loosen requirement of the corrupted kernel pointer (i.e., no additional requirement on the parameters). Specifically, the attackers can craft a malicious Return Oriented Programming (ROP) chain by concatenating exploitable kernel gadgets, and the chain realizes the similar function of *native_write_cr4()* (i.e., setting CR4 register). Then, they store the ROP chain as user-space data and redirect a corrupted kernel pointer to execute a "stack pivot" instruction, which will put the address of the ROP chain to the esp (Extended Stack Pointer) register and thereby make the ROP chain being executed. Although stored as user-space data, the chain could be read from kernel since SMAP is disabled. Also, the chain could be successfully executed since it is constructed by concatenating exploitable gadgets in the kernel space. However, the attackers need to bypass KASLR and obtain the kernel image of the running system (which is necessary for obtaining the accurate addresses of the exploitable kernel gadgets), before crafting a usable ROP chain.

On the whole, five factors are critical in compromising KASLR, SMEP and SMAP, which are the accessibility of dmesg and /proc/kallsyms, availability of the TSX instructions, and the possibility to find feasible memory corruption exploits and matching kernel images for the underlying Linux kernel system. These privilege-escalation-associated metrics are also introduced into the checklist.

3.3   Container Escaping Related Metrics

Although container escaping is easy on the local platforms after the attackers obtain the ROOT privilege, it is not an easy task on the public cloud platforms. There are no user-space APIs (e.g., system calls) for transferring a process from one container to another container, and a process' container attribute is defined through the data field (i.e., *nsproxy*) of the kernel data structure (i.e., *task_struct*). Therefore, container escaping could be achieved by modifying the kernel data. In general, there are two ways to get into the kernel from user-space after obtaining the ROOT privilege, i.e., finding and exploiting a feasible kernel memory corruption vulnerability, and crafting a loadable kernel module. The former needs a feasible vulnerability. The later needs a compiling environment for a kernel module or needs to bypass the verification of loading a kernel module.

Two verification will be performed before loading a kernel module, i.e., whether the module contains a Vermagic value matching the running kernel system, and whether the kernel functions and structures utilized in the module are attached with correct CRC (Cyclic Redundancy Check) values [40]. `Vermagic` is a unique string that identifies the version of the kernel system on which the module is compiled. A kernel module could be successfully loaded when both checks pass. Therefore, the attackers can craft a loadable kernel module by either compiling it on the running systems (corresponding files such as kernel symbol table and kernel header files, etc. should be accessible), or compiling an incorrect kernel module and substituting the `Vermagic` and CRCs values with the correct ones. And kernel address of the memory accommodating each kernel function's (or structure's) CRC value usually could be obtained by reading the `/proc/kallsyms` file. For example, the address of kernel function A's CRC value is marked as `_kcrctab_A` in the `/proc/kallsyms` file. And the `Vermagic` value could be derived from an existing loadable kernel module. As such, the attackers could craft a loadable kernel module if they can find an existing loadable kernel module and obtain the `_kcrctab_*` values.

Based on the analysis above, we introduce three container-escaping-associated metrics into the checklist, which are the availability of the header files, `Vermagic` value and CRC value associated with the underlying Linux kernel system.

3.4   Memory Corruption Vulnerabilities

As illustrated in Sect. 3.2, when performing privilege escalation attack, the attackers need to overwrite certain kernel memory through memory corruption vulnerabilities in the Linux kernel, such as UAF (Use-After-Free), race condition, improper verification, buffer overflow, etc. It is pretty unlikely to patch all vulnerabilities considering the large code size of the Linux kernel. Distribution of memory corruption vulnerabilities partially reflects the possibility to achieve privilege escalation from inside the containers. Therefore, we provide a statistic analysis on the emerging and fixing pattern of the memory corruption vulnerabilities in this section.

1) Dataset. We collect a memory corruption vulnerability dataset by manually analyzing the vulnerabilities published on the National Vulnerability Database (NVD) between 2008 and 2018 [3]. NVD is the U.S. government repository of standards based vulnerability management data. Each vulnerability is assigned with a Common Vulnerabilities and Exposures (CVE) ID. First, we pick out all vulnerabilities used to compromise Linux kernel by investigating the vulnerability description on the NVD website. Then, we further find out the vulnerabilities which could be exploited to corrupt kernel memory. On one way, we will include all vulnerabilities which are explicitly stated the consequences of overwriting kernel memory or gaining privileges (through memory corruption), e.g., the vulnerabilities which use vulnerable system calls to generate UAF (Use-After-Free), race condition, buffer overflow, integer overflow, etc.

For the vulnerabilities without explicit statements of overwriting kernel memory, we analyze the work principles of the vulnerabilities to check whether they could be exploited to corrupt kernel memory. For example, the descriptions of the vulnerabilities with ID CVE-2011-0709 and CVE-2017-8890 only state that they will cause DoS (Denial of Service) attacks through NULL pointer dereference and DF (double free), respectively. Since dereferencing of a NULL kernel pointer and double freeing of kernel memory have a high possibility of being exploited to cause kernel memory corruption [5], so they are also counted. To achieve a more accurate analysis, besides the descriptions on the NVD website, we also refer to the reports associated with the vulnerabilities on other websites, such as "SecurityFocus" [39] and "Red Hat Bugzilla" [14] (both websites are utilized by the technical communities to track bugs and discuss the details of the bugs).

Since our goal is to evaluate the possibility of launching attacks from inside containers, we exclude those vulnerabilities which are difficult to be exploited inside the container. For example, the vulnerabilities requiring the capabilities (e.g.,CAP_SYS_ADMIN) or system calls (e.g., ptrace(), bpf(), keyctl(), clone(), etc.) or operations (e.g., mounting a file system or image files) which are not available in the containers.

2) Number of Memory Corruption Vulnerabilities. In total, we find 374 kernel memory corruption vulnerabilities, and the number of each year is illustrated in Fig. 2. 54% (202) of vulnerabilities are explicitly stated that they could be exploited to corrupt kernel memory, while other 172 are identified by analyzing the vulnerabilities' work principle. On average, there are 34 memory corruption vulnerabilities each year. In addition, target kernel versions of the vulnerabilities change synchronously along with the updating of the Linux kernel. For example, the vulnerabilities published between 2012 and 2014 mainly target at Linux kernel 3.x, while the ones published in 2018 mainly focus on Linux kernel whose version is higher than 4.14. This shows that the memory corruption vulnerabilities are hardly to be cleared up even Linux kernel is continually

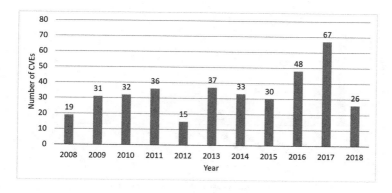

Fig. 2. Number of the memory corruption vulnerabilities

updated. Therefore, there is always a possibility to achieve kernel memory over-writing through kernel vulnerabilities.

As shown in Fig. 2, the number in 2017 is higher than others, and it is about twice of the average value. It is possible due to the dramatic increase of the total reported vulnerabilities in 2017 [31]. After further analysis, we find the reasons for the surge of the vulnerabilities in 2017 are mainly two-fold. First, the assignment process of CVE numbers was improved in 2017, where the CVE numbers could be assigned in a matter of hours or days through filling a web form. But before 2017, the assigning process is more tedious, and it takes far more time. Therefore, the higher number of vulnerabilities in 2017 does not necessarily mean that more vulnerabilities are discovered this year, but more researchers apply for and get CVE numbers successfully. Second, with the popularization of cloud computing, mobile Internet, and IoT devices in 2017, the generalization of cyberspace attacks and the lack of security awareness lead to an increase in the number of vulnerabilities [41].

3) Release Time of the Patches. Besides the vulnerability number, the time duration for an exposed vulnerability to be patched is also critical to the attackers. Therefore, we also analyze the patch release time for the 374 kernel memory corruption vulnerabilities identified. Normally, the patch for each vulnerability is also published on the NVD website, along with the vulnerability. In the situation when more than one patches are released for a vulnerability, the earliest release time will be utilized. Figure 3 depicts the statistics results of the patch release time, which shows more than 97% of vulnerabilities are patched within 5 months after the CVE numbers are assigned. And we are not able to find patches for 4 vulnerabilities, i.e., the ones labeled as "Unknown" in Fig. 3. We find patches of about 52% of vulnerabilities are released before the CVE numbers are assigned. The reasons might be two-fold. First, it takes a long time for the CVE number to be reviewed and assigned, so there is a lag. The researchers who discover

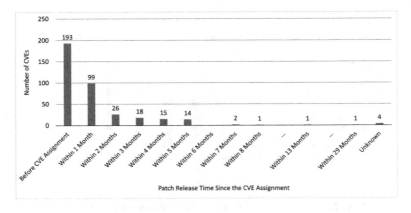

Fig. 3. Statistics on the patch release time since the CVE assignment

the vulnerability (or those who are aware of the vulnerability) have developed and published a patch before the CVE number is assigned. Second, the CVE assignment is intentionally delayed, as such the attackers could not utilize the published vulnerability to launch zero-day attacks.

4   Evaluation and Analysis

In this section, we perform an evaluation on five popular cloud container services, which are increasingly utilized to deploy industrial applications [36]. Particularly, we develop a tool to facilitate the collection of metric data listed in the checklist from inside the cloud containers. Most metric data could be obtained through existing Linux commands, e.g., the capabilities assigned to a container process could be fetc.hed through the `getpcaps` command, the kernel version could be obtained through the `uname -a` command. We investigate the availability of memory corruption vulnerability by checking the underlying kernel version against the dataset collected from NVD (see Sect. 3.4). To explore whether the kernel image and header files of the underlying kernel system are available, we collect a repository which includes kernel image files and header files downloaded both from the virtual machines of these cloud service providers and the Linux Kernel Archives [2].

All container services have the concept of regions, i.e., the containers might be deployed on servers located at different physical regions. For example, ccs5 allows a user to apply for a container from one of the three regions. As such, we randomly select three regions for each container service and investigate whether the configuration varies for the containers deployed on servers located at different physical regions. The results show that containers deployed in different regions share the same configuration. Therefore, we evaluate one representative container for each service. All data associated with the container services were collected in August 2019.

4.1   Container Execution Environment Detection

Table 1. Execution Environment of the Cloud Containers

Cloud container service	Kernel version		Permissions	Protection mechanisms				
	Version	Update date	No of Caps	Seccomp	MAC	KASLR	SMEP	SMAP
ccs1	4.14	2019/06	14	√	×	×	√	×
ccs2	4.14	2019/06	14	×	√	√	√	√
ccs3	4.15	2019/05	14	×	×	√	√	√
ccs4	3.10*	2018/04	37†	×	×	×	√	√
ccs5	4.1.51	2019/02	38	×	×	×	√	√

√ represents the protection mechanism is enabled, and × means it is disabled.
* The underlying kernel system is Red Hat.
† Since CAP_AUDIT_READ is not supported in this kernel system, 37 capabilities represent ROOT privilege.

Execution environments of the cloud containers are illustrated in Table 1. First, kernel systems of all container services except ccs4 are last updated in 2019. However, we find ccs4 and ccs5 have already assigned ROOT privilege to the container tenants. The CPU mechanisms (i.e., SMEP&SMAP) are enabled by almost all container services, while the kernel protection mechanisms are not effectively leveraged. For example, Seccomp and MAC are both enabled by only one service, and the KASLR is enabled by two services. A study of the privilege escalation vulnerabilities [27] shows that 11 exploits are blocked by Seccomp and MAC. Furthermore, KASLR is a necessary step for privilege escalation. Improperly setting of these mechanisms might let pass a series of exploits.

4.2   Privilege Escalation Evaluation

Table 2 depicts the possibility to achieve privilege escalation from inside the cloud containers. Since ROOT privilege has already been assigned to the container tenants of ccs4 and ccs5 as illustrated in Table 1, we investigate the possibility of privilege escalation attacks on the other three cloud container services. As illustrated before, the essential problems for achieving privilege escalation are bypassing KASLR, SMEP and SMAP. From Table 2 we can see that the KASLR could be successfully bypassed on all services through either reading the `/proc/kallsyms` file or conducting TLB-cache based side-channel attacks with the help of Intel TSX mechanism (The `/proc/kallsyms` file is also accessible on the containers provided by ccs4 and ccs5). As for the bypassing of SMEP and SMAP, we can obtain the feasible kernel images to craft an ROP chain for the containers provided by ccs1 and ccs2, since both services utilize the same kernel images for the virtual machines and containers. However, since kernel systems of the three container services were updated recently, we fail to find feasible memory corruption vulnerabilities (and exploits) to bypass SMEP and SMAP.

Table 2. Results of Privilege Escalation Attacks on the Cloud Containers[*]

Cloud Container Service	Bypassing KASLR				Bypassing SMEP&SMAP		
	dmesg	/proc/kallsyms	TSX	Success	Feasible Exploits	Kernel Image	Success
ccs1	√	√	×	Y	×	√	N
ccs2	√	×	√	Y	×	√	N
ccs3	√	×	√	Y	×	×	N

√ represents the item is accessible (or available) to the attackers, and × means it is inaccessible (or unavailable).
* "ccs4" and "ccs5" are not illustrated, since the containers of these two services have already been assigned ROOT privilege.

4.3   Container Escaping Evaluation

Table 3. Results of Container Escaping on the Cloud Containers*

Cloud Container Service	Compiling Environment	Bypassing Verification	
	header files	Vermagic(loadable module)	CRC(_kcrctab_*)
ccs4	×	√	×
ccs5	×	×	√

√ represents the item is accessible (or available) to the attackers, and × means it is inaccessible (or unavailable).
* "ccs1" , "ccs2" and "ccs3" are not illustrated, since lacks of feasible vulnerability for the containers of these three services.

The results of container escaping are shown in Table 3. Due to the lacking of feasible vulnerability, we use the second method to get into the kernel. Because ccs4 and ccs5 have already assigned the container tenants ROOT privilege, we have the capability to load module. We find the kernel header files are inaccessible to the containers for both services, so we could not directly compile a loadable kernel module. Meanwhile, we find the _kcrctab_* values are absent on the containers of ccs4 (although the /proc/kallsyms file is accessible), while no existing loadable kernel modules could be found in the containers provided by ccs5.

5   Discussion and Future Work

We give some suggestions to enhance the security of cloud container services from the following aspects. First, the kernel mechanisms including Seccomp, Capabilities and MAC should be enabled and set with as strict policies as possible, which might block a series of exploits. For example, in the study performed by XinLin et al. [27], 67.57% of exploits are blocked by these kernel mechanisms. Second, the KASLR mechanism should be effectively utilized by not only being enabled, but also with the sensitive files (including dmesg, and /proc/kallsyms etc.) set as inaccessible for the container tenants. Third, vulnerabilities in the underlying kernel system should be patched as soon as possible, which will increase the difficulty for the attackers to seek out a usable exploit. Fourth, it is better to use the kernel images of different versions in the virtual machines from the ones in the containers, if the service provider allows the tenants to apply for both virtual machines and containers. This can prevent the attackers from crafting a feasible ROP chain for bypassing SMEP, and also raise the bar to achieve container escape. We have supplied these suggestions to the cloud service providers.

It is more challenging to achieve privilege escalation on the public cloud platforms than on local Docker platforms, since the lack of available exploits on the specific underlying kernel systems. However, according to our research, tens of memory corruption vulnerabilities are published each year, and there is a lag for the vulnerabilities to be patched. Therefore, by continuously collecting the emerging exploits and tracking the updating states of the cloud container services' underlying kernel systems, it is possible for attackers to obtain ROOT privilege from inside the containers. Security of the cloud container services heavily depends on whether a vulnerable kernel system is updated in time and how long is the lag. However, the problem has not been well studied yet. Also, more persuasive evaluation could be obtained if the memory corruption vulnerability dataset could be greatly enlarged. We leave them as our future work.

6   Related Work

There are a line of research works on the security of the container mechanism. For example, M. Ali Babar et al. [16] compared the security between the containers based on different OS-level virtualization implementations, i.e., Rkt, Docker and LXD. Thanh Bui et al. [19] compared the architecture between hypervisor-based virtualization and container-based virtualization briefly, and they mainly analyzed the docker internal security. XinLin et al. [27] used the vulnerabilities to measure the security of the local container, and they analyzed the influence of different capabilities on container vulnerability exploitation. Reshetova et al. [37] theoretically analyzed the security of different OS-level virtualization implementations, i.e., FreeBSD Jails, Linux-VServer, Solaris Zones, OpenVZ, LxC and Cells. Z Jian et al. [25] summarized two approaches to achieve container escape and evaluated the proposed defense tool with 11 CVE vulnerabilities. A. Martin et al. [29] classified the vulnerabilities of the container to five categories and performed a vulnerability assessment based on the security architecture and use cases of Docker. A. Mouat et al. [33] provided an overview of some container vulnerabilities, such as kernel exploits, container breakouts and secret leakage. Different from these works, we focus more on the security of the remote cloud containers, which is more complicated and varies on different cloud container platforms.

Many researchers also investigate the security of cloud container orchestration tools [18,34]. Alexander et al. proposed a method to detect the container environment [26], i.e., comparing the number of processes returned by the *sysinfo()* system call and the "ps -ef" command. Xing Gao et al. [22] proposed that the leaked host information will seriously threaten the security of the cloud server. They also introduced a leakage channel detection method based on the context and listed the leakage channels.

7   Conclusion

Cloud container service is widely used, so its security is particularly important. In this paper, we provide a concrete method to evaluate the security of cloud container services. We also perform a detailed evaluation of five in-service cloud container services, i.e., whether the user can achieve privilege escalation from inside the cloud containers, and the possibility to achieve the cloud container escaping. We find some incorrect configurations in them (e.g., two cloud container services have assigned ROOT privilege to their container tenants by default). Moreover, the KASLR mechanism could be successfully bypassed on all five cloud containers. However, even after obtaining ROOT privilege in a container, attackers still can hardly escape from the container on the public cloud platforms. Finally, we give some suggestions to improve the security of the cloud container services.

Acknowledgment. We thank the anonymous reviewers for their insightful comments on improving our work. This work is partially supported by National Key R&D Program of China under Award No. 2018YFB0804402, the National Natural Science Foundation of China under GA No. 61802398, the National Cryptography Development Fund under Award No. MMJJ20180222 and the NSF grant CNS-1815650.

References

1. Apparmor security profiles for docker. https://docs.docker.com/engine/security/apparmor/
2. The linux kernel archives. https://www.kernel.org
3. National vulnerability database. https://nvd.nist.gov/
4. Supervisor mode execution prevention. https://en.wikipedia.org/wiki/Control_register#SMEP
5. Cve-2016-2384 (2016). https://xairy.github.io/blog/2016/cve-2016-2384
6. Cgroup_namespaces-overview of linux cgroup namespaces (2017). https://www.man7.org/linux/man-pages/man7/cgroup_namespaces.7.html
7. Aws fargate (2018). https://aws.amazon.com/fargate
8. Overview of linux capabilities (2018). http://man7.org/linux/man-pages/man7/capabilities.7.html
9. Overview of linux namespaces (2018). http://man7.org/linux/man-pages/man7/namespaces.7.html
10. Seccomp security profiles for docker (2018). https://docs.docker.com/engine/security/seccomp/
11. What is docker (2018). https://www.docker.com/what-docker
12. Google kubernetes engine (2019). https://cloud.google.com/kubernetes-engine/
13. Intel transactional synchronization extensions (intel tsx) overview (2019). https://software.intel.com/en-us/cpp-compiler-developer-guide-and-reference-intel-transactional-synchronization-extensions-intel-tsx-overview
14. Red hat bugzilla (2019). https://bugzilla.redhat.com/
15. Authors, T.K.: Production-grade container orchestration (2018). https://kubernetes.io/
16. Babar, M.A., Ramsey, B.: Understanding container isolation mechanisms for building security-sensitive private cloud. Technical Report, CREST, University of Adelaide, Adelaide, Australia (2017)
17. Barham, P., et al.: Xen and the art of virtualization. SIGOPS Oper. Syst. Rev. **37**(5), 164–177 (2003)
18. Bernstein, D.: Containers and cloud: from LXC to docker to kubernetes. IEEE Cloud Comput. **1**(3), 81–84 (2014)

19. Bui, T.: Analysis of docker security. CoRR abs/1501.02967 (2015)
20. Corbet, J.: Supervisor mode access prevention (2012). https://lwn.net/Articles/517475/
21. Edge, J.: Kernel address space layout randomization (2013), https://lwn.net/Articles/569635/
22. Gao, X., Gu, Z., Kayaalp, M., Pendarakis, D., Wang, H.: Containerleaks: emerging security threats of information leakages in container clouds. In: 47th Annual IEEE/IFIP International Conference on Dependable Systems and Networks, DSN 2017, Denver, CO, USA, June 26–29, 2017. pp. 237–248 (2017)
23. Hund, R., Willems, C., Holz, T.: Practical timing side channel attacks against kernel space ASLR. In: 2013 IEEE Symposium on Security and Privacy, pp. 191–205, May 2013
24. Jang, Y., Lee, S., Kim, T.: Breaking kernel address space layout randomization with intel TSX. In: Proceedings of the 2016 ACM SIGSAC Conference on Computer and Communications Security, Vienna, Austria, October 24–28, 2016, pp. 380–392 (2016)
25. Jian, Z., Chen, L.: A defense method against docker escape attack. In: Proceedings of the 2017 International Conference on Cryptography, Security and Privacy, ICCSP 2017, Wuhan, China, March 17–19, 2017, pp. 142–146 (2017)
26. Kedrowitsch, A., Yao, D.D., Wang, G., Cameron, K.: A first look: Using linux containers for deceptive honeypots. In: Proceedings of the 2017 Workshop on Automated Decision Making for Active Cyber Defense, pp. 15–22. ACM (2017)
27. Lin, X., Lei, L., Wang, Y., Jing, J., Sun, K., Zhou, Q.: A measurement study on linux container security: attacks and countermeasures. In: Proceedings of the 34th Annual Computer Security Applications Conference, pp. 418–429. ACSAC 2018, ACM, New York, NY, USA (2018)
28. Ltd, C.: Lxc introduction (2018). https://linuxcontainers.org/lxc/introduction/
29. Martin, A., Raponi, S., Combe, T., Pietro, R.D.: Docker ecosystem - vulnerability analysis. Comput. Commun. **122**, 30–43 (2018)
30. McCarty, B.: Selinux: Nsa's open source security enhanced linux, vol. 238. O'Reilly (2005). http://www.oreilly.de/catalog/selinux/index.html
31. Ángel Mendoza, M.: Vulnerabilities reached a historic peak in 2017 (2018). https://www.welivesecurity.com/2018/02/05/vulnerabilities-reached-historic-peak-2017/
32. Merkel, D.: Docker: lightweight linux containers for consistent development and deployment. Linux J. **2014**(239), 2 (2014)
33. Mouat, A.: Docker security using containers safely in production (2015). https://www.oreilly.com/content/docker-security/
34. Pahl, C., Brogi, A., Soldani, J., Jamshidi, P.: Cloud container technologies: a state-of-the-art review. In: IEEE Transactions on Cloud Computing (2017)
35. Qumranet, A., Qumranet, Y., Qumranet, D., Qumranet, U., Liguori, A.: KVM: the linux virtual machine monitor. In: Proceedings Linux Symposium, vol. 15 (2007)
36. Reports, H.C.R.: Containers as a service market research report - global forecast 2023 (2019). https://www.marketresearchfuture.com/reports/containers-as-a-service-market-4611
37. Reshetova, E., Karhunen, J., Nyman, T., Asokan, N.: Security of OS-Level virtualization technologies. In: Bernsmed, K., Fischer-Hübner, S. (eds.) NordSec 2014. LNCS, vol. 8788, pp. 77–93. Springer, Cham (2014). https://doi.org/10.1007/978-3-319-11599-3_5
38. Sconway: Kubernetes continues to move from development to production (2017). https://www.cncf.io/blog/2017/12/06/cloud-native-technologies-scaling-production-applications/

39. SecurityFocus: Securityfocus (2019). https://www.securityfocus.com/
40. Stoler, N.: How i hacked play-with-docker and remotely ran code on the host (2019). https://www.cyberark.com/threat-research-blog/how-i-hacked-play-with-docker-and-remotely-ran-code-on-the-host/
41. Vertical, horizontal data: Inventory of cyber security vulnerabilities in 2017: The number of vulnerabilities has grown unprecedentedly and may occur at all levels (2017), https://news.zoneidc.com/679.html

Walls Have Ears: Eavesdropping User Behaviors via Graphics-Interrupt-Based Side Channel

Haoyu Ma[1,2], Jianwen Tian[1], Debin Gao[1], and Chunfu Jia[3(✉)]

[1] Singapore Management University, Singapore 188065, Singapore
{hyma,jwtian,dbgao}@smu.edu.sg
[2] Xidian University, Xi'an 710126, People's Republic of China
[3] Nankai University, Tianjin 300350, People's Republic of China
cfjia@nankai.edu.cn

Abstract. Graphics Processing Units (GPUs) are now playing a vital role in many devices and systems including computing devices, data centers, and clouds, making them the next target of side-channel attacks. Unlike those targeting CPUs, existing side-channel attacks on GPUs exploited vulnerabilities exposed by application interfaces like OpenGL and CUDA, which can be easily mitigated with software patches. In this paper, we investigate the lower-level and native interface between GPUs and CPUs, i.e., the graphics interrupts, and evaluate the side channel they expose. Being an intrinsic profile in the communication between a GPU and a CPU, the pattern of graphics interrupts typically differs from one GPU workload to another, allowing a spy process to monitor interrupt statistics as a robust side channel to infer behavior of other processes. We demonstrate the practicality of such side-channel exploitations in a variety of attacking scenarios ranging from previously explored tasks of fingerprinting the document opened and the application launched, to distinguishing processes that generate seemingly identical displays. Our attack relies on system-level footprints rather than API-level ones and does not require injecting any payload into the GPU resource space to cause contentions. We evaluate our attacks and demonstrate that they could achieve high accuracy in the assumed attack scenarios. We also present in-depth studies to further analyze the low-level rationale behind such effectiveness.

Keywords: Side-channel attacks · GPU · Graphics interrupts · Machine learning

1 Introduction

Graphics Processing Units (GPUs) have become increasingly important components for today's computing devices, not only because applications may involve

W. Susilo et al. (Eds.): ISC 2020, LNCS 12472, pp. 178–195, 2020.
https://doi.org/10.1007/978-3-030-62974-8_11

heavy graphics and multi-media workloads, but also because of the capability of GPUs in accelerating applications in domains such as security, computational finance, and bio-informatics [9]. Such development naturally makes GPUs a tempting target to attacks aiming to leak user privacy.

Several vulnerabilities have already been demonstrated in GPU security [13,15,18,19,23,32], most of which focused on vulnerabilities caused by defective memory management and privacy-leaking APIs from GPU-related frameworks OpenGL, OpenCL, and CUDA. This includes the latest work on GPU side channel attacks [19] which demonstrated the practicability of exploiting resource tracking APIs provided by the aforementioned frameworks to leak user privacy. These previous attacks typically require injecting an attack process into the same GPU where the victim process resides, and running it in parallel with the victim process in order to capture any footprints it leaves. Although not having been explicitly admitted in existing work, such an attack strategy is not subtle enough considering that a defense opponent could potentially be able to detect the attacks by identifying the existence of their co-residing attack processes. In addition, with the GPU side-channel attacks drawing people's attention, corresponding defense approaches against GPU memory leakage were also proposed [21,29]. Manufacturers like Nvidia were also reported to be taking actions to mitigate the resource tracking vulnerability [20].

In this paper, we consider a less demanding threat model and identify the statistics of graphics interrupts as another source for side-channel attacks on GPUs. Graphics interrupt statistics are available to non-privileged processes on Linux-based systems, which are typically readable at /proc/interrupt. The key insight is that footprints of the graphics stack exist not only within the GPU resource space (exploited by existing work) but also at the interface between a CPU and a GPU (interrupts as exploited in this paper). Specifically, a GPU sends interrupt requests (IRQs) to signal key events like completion of a graphics command or reporting a GPU error. Consequently, when handling different GPU workloads, it is likely for the CPU to capture relevant IRQs in different temporal patterns. As modern operating systems provide statistics of interrupts captured at runtime, a malicious party may use the graphics interrupt statistics as signatures to infer the exact workload that is being processed by the GPU. Such an attack, unlike the existing ones, operates completely in a passive manner, i.e., it does not require any payload to be co-resident with the victim process inside the GPU resource space to cause contentions of any kind.

To demonstrate that graphics interrupts are indeed exploitable, we implemented several side-channel attacks under various attacking scenarios, including webpage fingerprinting, application inferencing, and distinguishing processes that output seemingly identical displays, on two common graphics adapters of Nvidia's and Intel's. Our attack periodically samples counts of graphics interrupts and uses the pattern of increments as a time-series signature to identify the target workloads with a machine learning model. Evaluations showed that our attacks demonstrated comparable accuracy with the latest GPU side-channel attacks based on memory APIs and performance counters [19] in webpage fin-

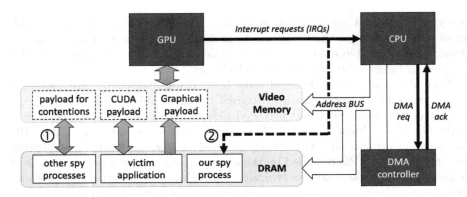

Fig. 1. Conventional GPU-related attacks and our attack strategy.

gerprinting. Experiments also demonstrated accuracy as high as 99.8% in GUI-application fingerprinting. Last but not least, we found our application finger-printing attack being capable of identifying different types of graphics workloads which present the same visual perception. Experiments on this aspect demon-strated a high accuracy in distinguishing different video players when playing the same video, or detecting differences in playing the same video encoded with different codec.

2   Related Work

GPU-Based Side Channels. Existing GPU side-channel attacks focused on disclosing the webpage loaded and sensitive workload on cryptographic algorithms [13,15,18,19,23,32]. Most of them exploited GPU vulnerabilities related to insecure memory management, e.g., not initializing newly allocated blocks [13,32] and vulnerabilities in the CUDA driver [23]. Recently, Naghibi-jouybari et al. [19] studied the practicability of exploiting GPU resource tracking APIs.

These existing GPU side-channel attacks work according to an intrusive model in which contentions are introduced inside the GPU resource space. Figure 1 demonstrates this attacking strategy with the payload being deployed in the GPU memory. This strategy is not only intrusive to the victim process but also easy to defeat by simple countermeasures of software patching. For exam-ple, most browsers have now reduced the timer resolution and thus eliminated the timing signal used by the attacks. GPU manufacturers have also noticed the potential vulnerability caused by the resource tracking APIs and expressed plans to fix the problem with updates to OpenGL and CUDA. In this paper, we pro-pose a novel GPU side-channel attack which works by collecting graphics-related interrupt footprints. Our approach operates passively rather than being intru-sive to its victims, making it more stealthy than the existing attack strategies while being able to achieve similar effectiveness.

Interrupts. Interrupts have been exploited in privacy leakage scenarios. Diao et al. [3] reported using interrupts to infer unlock patterns on Android devices. Tang et al. [25] further suggested that patterns of interrupt increment could be exploited to identify hardware related sensitive behaviors of Android apps. Another study demonstrated inferencing of instruction-granular execution states from hardware-enforced enclaves by measuring the latency of carefully timed interrupts [26]. There were also researches suggesting that attackers could establish covert channels based on the CPU time used for handling interrupts [6,16]. In this paper, we focus specifically on using statistics of graphics interrupts as a side channel to infer GPU related activities, and study the potential risk of privacy leakage that can be caused by such an attack.

Webpage Fingerprinting. Early approaches for webpage fingerprinting include measuring web access time to exploit browser caching [5], measuring memory footprints [11], and analyzing network traffic [7,22]. The relationship between webpage loading and graphics displaying behaviors was also proposed for webpage fingerprinting. For example, previous researches had proposed using display-related features of browsers to construct cross-origin timing attacks [12,27]. Kotcher et al. [12] found that after applying CSS filters to a framed document, its rendering time becomes dependent on its content.

Proc Filesystem. The proc filesystem on Linux-based systems is another leakage vector that was used by side-channel attacks for inferring application UI status [2], keystrokes [30], TCP sequence numbers [24], and user identities [31].

3   Our Idea

3.1   Graphics Interrupts

Communication between CPUs and GPUs is critical to a computer's graphics pipeline; see Fig. 1. Important components of such communication include DMA requests and acknowledgment to enable buffer sharing, the command FIFO between CPUs and GPUs, as well as interrupts from the GPU to CPU when certain events need to be processed immediately (IRQs as shown in Fig. 1). These IRQs are reflections of the corresponding workload being processed.

Table 1 lists all IRQs defined in a popular open-source graphics driver on Linux, namely the drm/i915 Intel GFX Driver. Each of these interrupt types is either about a specific engine of the GPU, including the RCS (rendering), BCS (blitter copy), VCS (video en/decoding), and VECS (video enhancement) engine, or about basic events (such as vertical blanking). For example, displaying a PNG picture only involves rendering static frames which will be done by the RCS engine, while playing an MKV video may require the VCS engine to perform decoding throughout the process. This suggests that graphics interrupts are good reflections of content of the document being displayed. By the same token, the user interface of an application needs to be rendered and refreshed, which could be reflected on the corresponding graphics interrupts.

Table 1. Interrupt Request Definitions in drm/i915 Driver.

Name of IRQ	Description
GEN8_DE_MISC_IRQ	Miscellaneous interrupt raised by graphics system events (GSE) and panel self refresh events (PSR)
GEN8_DE_PORT_IRQ	The display engine port interrupt, related to AUX DDI A done event and hotplug events
GEN8_PIPE_VBLANK	Related to vertical blanking events
GEN8_PIPE_CDCLK_CRC_DONE	This displays core clock (CDCLK)
GEN8_PIPE_FIFO_UNDERRUN	Related to GPU's command FIFO when running into a buffer underrun
GEN8_DE_PCH_IRQ	The south display engine interrupt, also deals with hotplug interruption and ambus events
GEN8_GT_RCS_IRQ	Interrupt of the RCS engine which performs computing and rendering
GEN8_GT_BCS_IRQ	Interrupt of the Blitter COPY engine
GEN8_GT_VCS0_IRQ	Interrupt of the VCS engine used in processing videos where it performs encoding and decoding
GEN8_GT_VCS1_IRQ	Same as the previous one
GEN8_GT_VECS_IRQ	Interrupt of the video enhancement engine
GEN8_GT_PM_IRQ	Related to power management events
GEN8_GT_GUC_IRQ	Related to microprocess interruptions of the graphics microcontroller (GuC)

3.2 Threat Model and Our Idea

Different from existing side-channel attacks on GPUs, our proposal considers a lower level interface which works completely in a passive manner by capturing only statistical interrupt information provided by the OS kernel. As illustrated in Fig. 1, unlike existing attacks which intrusively cause contentions in the GPU resource space (as highlighted by ① in the figure), our attack does not access GPU resources but instead reads interrupt statistics from the OS (as highlighted by ②). Although such a spy process could potentially exploit other system side channels (e.g., CPU cache and network related ones) to launch data-driven leakage attacks, our investigation here focuses on the leakage of GUI-related private information, which is more directly reflected over graphics interrupts.

Specifically, our threat model assumes a (non-privileged) spy process which periodically reads the aggregated graphics interrupt counts reported by the operating system, and uses a sliding window to extract subsequences of the collected time series of interrupt statistics. We then use a trained machine learning model to determine the task being processed by the GPU.

3.3 Challenges and Experiments

Although modern operating systems like Linux report graphics interrupt statistics to any unprivileged user process via the proc filesystem (procfs), the specific types of graphics interrupts (e.g., those reported in Table 1) are aggregated in the report. It is therefore not clear whether such coarse grained reporting of graphics interrupt reveals GUI-related private information. In this paper, we evaluate the extent to which such aggregated graphics interrupt information masks or reveals workloads on the GPU, and the extent to which such masking/revealing of workload leaks private information of victim processes.

We experimented with the graphics interrupts on two different microarchitectures, namely an Nvidia GeForce GTX 760M (with Nvidia driver version 340.107) and an Intel HD Graphics 520 GT2 (with drm/i915 driver integrated in Linux kernel 5.4.2). The Nvidia unit is chosen due to its popularity and potential use in general-purpose computing. The Intel unit is chosen because it is controlled by an open-source driver integrated in the Linux kernel, which allows us to observe the low-level details of the collected graphics interrupt patterns to make our experimental results explainable. The experiments were conducted on an Ubuntu 18.04 machine with an Intel i7-4700MQ Processor and 8 GB RAM, where interrupt statistics are obtained by reading /proc/interrupt. Note that in case of Windows, information of IRQs are managed by the interrupt descriptor table (IDT). Although there had not been software (via legitimate APIs or hacking techniques) reported specifically designed for extracting interrupt statistics on Windows, documentations suggest that it can be done in a similar way in which system call information is extracted with a kernel driver overwriting the system service descriptor table (SSDT) [10, 14].

4   Attack Scenario I: Webpage Fingerprinting

Our first attack implements webpage fingerprinting as it has been targets of many existing attack strategies (see Sect. 2). We make a comparative study with one of the latest attacks using GPU side channels [19]. To this end, we tested our attack on the same Alexa top 200 websites [1] with the Chrome browser and used the same basic machine learning models as in Naghibijouybari et al. for our classification, namely Gaussian Naive Bayes (NB), K-Nearest Neighbor with 3 neighbors (KNN-3), and Random Forest with 100 estimators (RF). We additionally included a state-of-the-art deep learning model on time series classification, the Residual Neural Network (ResNet) [8,28]. This is because a previous research on time series classification [4] suggested that deep learning methods typically outperform conventional statistics-based models because they do not require pre-processing the input data to extract feature vectors. Our ResNet model used the same hyperparameters as in the original proposal [28] with 3 residual blocks each built by stacking 3 convolutional blocks consisting of a convolutional layer followed by a batch normalization layer and a ReLU activation layer. The number of filters in the residual blocks are, respectively, set to 64, 128, and 128, with the convolution operation fulfilled by three 1-D filters of sizes 9, 5, and 3 without striding.

We automatically load each webpages 100 times with a script while having the timestamp of each events logged. Upon each webpage loading, we pick up 100 continuous samples of (aggregated) graphics interrupt counts collected by our spy process to form a time series corresponding to the event, with the value of each sample indicating the increment of graphics interrupts since the previous sampling. We use a sampling interval of 50 ms for negligible performance overhead. Note that in such a side-channel attack, data sampling of the spy process and the targeted sensitive events are supposed to be asynchronous for mimicking a practical attacking scenario. Therefore, we start establishing a time series using the last interrupt count collected before the timestamp of its corresponding web-page loading event as its first sample. Finally, we used 10 fold cross validation to measure the accuracy of the corresponding machine learning models.

Result and Analysis: As shown in Table 2, conventional machine learning models could no longer provide effective classification on side-channel leakage of graphics interrupts. Out of the three such learning methods tested, only random forest could maintain a precision of around 85% and 79%, respectively, on the Intel and Nvidia GPU. However, the state-of-the-art deep learning model on time series classification, namely ResNet, demonstrated much better accuracy on the Nvidia GPU (88.2% F-measure) and even better on the Intel GPU (92.0% F-measure). Although our results are not as good as those reported by Naghibijouybari et al. [19] when using the same conventional machine learning classifiers, we remind readers that our results are achieved without injecting GPU payload or causing contention in the GPU resource space, unlike those in Naghibijouybari et al. [19]. Such results suggest that graphics interrupts provide a valid privacy leakage vector to support side-channel attacks in the scenario of website fingerprinting, with an unprivileged spy process reading only aggregated graphics interrupts from /proc/interrupt.

Table 2. Performance of webpage fingerprinting: average and standard deviation.

		F-Measure	Precision	Recall
Graphics Interrupt (on Intel)	NB	46.3% (7.51)	48.7% (10.6)	49.7% (8.26)
	KNN-3	32.4% (6.12)	36.5% (8.72)	34.1% (5.12)
	RF	83.1% (7.02)	85.5% (5.78)	83.9% (5.47)
	ResNet	92.0% (1.35)	93.4% (1.27)	92.2% (1.31)
Graphics Interrupt (on Nvidia)	NB	46.7% (1.76)	49.0% (2.96)	50.1% (2.02)
	KNN-3	29.3% (1.12)	31.9% (1.26)	30.5% (1.41)
	RF	76.5% (0.56)	79.3% (0.65)	77.2% (0.66)
	ResNet	88.2% (0.51)	89.9% (0.31)	88.3% (0.44)
Naghibijouybari et al. [19] (on Nvidia)	NB	83.1% (13.5)	86.7% (20.0)	81.4% (13.5)
	KNN-3	84.6% (14.6)	85.7% (15.7)	84.6% (14.6)
	RF	89.9% (11.1)	90.4% (11.4)	90.0% (12.5)

To better understand the results, we dive into the low-level details of the interrupt handling process by hooking the IRQ handlers of the drm/i915 driver to gain more detailed logs on the graphics interrupts captured, which enabled us to investigate the interrupt counts for each IRQ listed in Table 1 Note that an unprivileged attacker (main threat model used in our paper) could not obtain such information. We do this solely for the purpose of better understanding our attacking capability behind the scene. Figure 2 demonstrates such detailed interrupt patterns on opening four webpages (homepages of Google, Facebook, Amazon, and Tencent) using three browsers (**Chrome**, **Falkon**, and **Firefox**). Our analysis reveals two interesting observations.

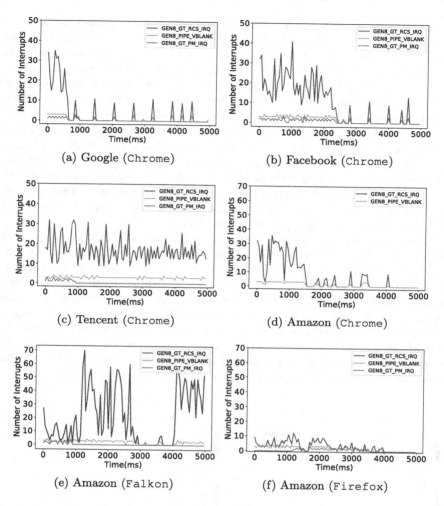

Fig. 2. Interrupt patterns (Intel) of different webpages (and the corresponding browser). Missing lines correspond to zero readings of IRQ types.

First, Google's homepage has the simplest layout and correspondingly, the GEN8_GT_RCS_IRQ interrupt boost (indicating events signaled by the rendering engine) of its loading was the shortest among the four webpages (for around 1.2 s, while those for Amazon and Facebook were respectively around 2.0 s and 3.7 s). In addition, all the tested webpages are static except that of Tencent which contains animation effects. As a result, we can see that the RCS interrupt pattern of Tencent's corresponds to continuous refreshing of the webpage, unlike what happened to the other tested webpages. These confirm our intuition (see Sect. 3) that graphics interrupts reflect layouts and objects of the display.

Second, we found that on opening the same webpage, different browsers resulted in distinct graphics interrupt patterns (see Fig. 2.d, 2.e and 2.f). This suggests that the detailed implementation of GPU acceleration in different browser engines also has a significant impact on our side-channel attacks. At this moment, we did not dig deeper into source code of the browsers to find out the decisive answer on how the implementation of different engines affects website-related graphics interrupt patterns. A reasonable guess on this is that each browser has a unique strategy with regard to the type and amount of data to be submitted to the GPU for processing, which will translate to different number of GEN8_GT_RCS_IRQ interrupts per sampling. We believe this is why browsing with Firefox causes significantly smaller amount of rendering-related interrupts on average compared with Falkon and Chrome. This also suggests that graphics interrupts could not only be used to fingerprint data (e.g., webpages) processed, but also for fingerprinting applications; see Sect. 5.

We also note that modern web browsers utilize the GPU to accelerate their rendering processes. Many webpages now contain optimized frontend/backend code to take advantage of it [17]. As a result, it is likely for different webpages to have adopted different acceleration techniques including server- and client-side rendering, rehydration, and prerendering, which also leads to differences in their resulting graphics interrupt patterns. To confirm this intuition, we used an open-source prerendering tool, pre-render[1], to convert a simple Vue webpage into its pre-rendered variant[2], and recorded the corresponding graphics interrupts when the two pages were loaded and displayed in Chrome. Figure 3 showed noticeable differences between the interrupt patterns on the two instances.

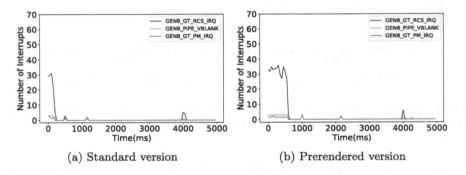

(a) Standard version   (b) Prerendered version

Fig. 3. Interrupt patterns (Intel) of two versions of a same Vue webpage, with and without pre-rendering.

---

[1] https://github.com/kriasoft/pre-render.
[2] The tested webpage can be accessed via http://pay.his.cat/app.html (original version) and http://pay.his.cat/index.html (prerendered version).

5   Attack Scenario II: GUI Application Fingerprinting

Our second attack attempts to fingerprint GUI applications with the same spy process monitoring graphics interrupts. Application fingerprinting has implications not only on revealing end user activities (e.g., which application is launched), but also on picking the best machine learning model for webpage fingerprinting. This is especially important since different browsers result in different graphics interrupt patterns even for the same webpages (see Sect. 4). With an effective application fingerprinting, it could then be possible to first identify the specific web browser being used and then pick the suitable machine learning model for webpage fingerprinting to achieve optimized accuracy.

We downloaded 20 popular applications on Ubuntu as test subjects (see Table 3 for the list of selected applications), and launched each of them 100 times with our scripts. Note that to demonstrate the connection between this attack and webpage fingerprinting, we included two web browsers, Firefox and Brave, into the test set. Since the goal of this attack is to infer the application launched, we did not further use them to process any input. Again, each time a subject application is launched, 100 samples (with sampling interval at 50 ms) of interrupt count were collected to form the corresponding time series.

Table 3. Subjects for our application fingerprinting attack.

Application	Category	Application	Category
Inkscape	graphics editor	libreoffice	text editor
GIMP		Notepadqq	
Krita		ClamTk	antivirus
atril	doc viewer	Deluge	download
Thunderbird	e-mail	Audacity	multimedia
Geary		Clementine	
Pidgin	social	Kdenlive	
Corebird		VLC	
Neofetc.h	system management	Firefox	web browser
Synaptic		Brave	

Result: Our attack on application fingerprinting demonstrated very high accuracy with all tested machine learning models on both Nvidia and Intel GPUs (as shown in Table 4). This suggests that graphics interrupts could effectively leak information about the running desktop applications, indicating good generality of our application fingerprinting attack. We believe that this is due to the higher degree of flexibility in the design of GUI of desktop applications, compared to the design of webpages which is governed by the html protocol.

Table 4. Results of application fingerprinting, average and standard deviation.

		F-Measure	Precision	Recall
Intel	NB	98.7% (0.26)	98.8% (0.19)	98.7% (0.26)
	KNN-3	91.4% (3.53)	91.9% (2.99)	91.5% (3.51)
	RF	99.6% (0.07)	99.7% (0.06)	99.7% (0.07)
	ResNet	99.5% (1.09)	99.5% (0.91)	99.6% (1.11)
Nvidia	NB	97.9% (3.09)	98.2% (1.91)	97.9% (3.31)
	KNN-3	95.4% (3.62)	95.6% (2.89)	95.5% (3.51)
	RF	99.3% (1.58)	99.4% (1.17)	99.3% (1.71)
	ResNet	99.8% (0.08)	99.8% (0.07)	99.8% (0.08)

6   Attack Scenario III: Beyond Visual Perception

In our attack scenarios I and II, webpage and application fingerprinting are both targeting objects that present unique visual perception to human users. The idea is that each unique GUI or view of the webpages correspond to unique work-load on the GPU, resulting in classifiable graphics interrupts. In this section, we investigate a more challenging problem in using aggregated graphics interrupt to differentiate objects with the same visual perception, i.e., can we differentiate something even a human being cannot differentiate with visual inspection? Such a capability has a strong implication on the research of human factors in security, e.g., in assisting human to detect phishing websites, to detect re-packaged applications, and in digital forensics.

As a first step in evaluating such a capability, we take video playback as an example. Specifically, we consider the following two experimental settings:

- Same video clip encoded with the same codec, played back with different video players, in which we played back a video clip in FLV format using four different video players (VLC, SMPlayer, TOTEM, and MPV);
- Same video clip encoded with different codec and played back with the same video player, in which we encoded a video using four codec (H264, MPEG4, WMV2, and XIVD) and had them played back using the VLC player.

Time series of graphics interrupt counts in this experiment were collected from the 2nd to the 6th seconds into the subject video[3] to avoid potential noise from setting up GUI of the video players. We repeated the experiment 100 times and performed a 10 fold validation over the collected data as usual. Unlike the previous experiments, here we only used ResNet as the classifier since it outperformed the other tested models (especially in webpage fingerprinting).

Result and Analysis: Table 5 shows the performance of our attack in the two settings listed above. We found that in the scenario of distinguishing different

---

[3] The video used can be found at https://www.dropbox.com/sh/vqd8ffi7eer8urd/AAAU9MYDg1bKkTtsSzjkpUp5a.

video players, our attack worked accurately without a single misclassification. While in the scenario of distinguishing different codec, the attack on the Nvidia GPU outperformed that on the Intel (86.3% vs. 70.2%).

Table 5. Distinguishing video playback events with ResNet: average and standard deviation.

		F-Measure	Precision	Recall
Diff players	Intel	100% (0)	100% (0)	100% (0)
	Nvidia	100% (0)	100% (0)	100% (0)
Diff codecs	Intel	70.2% (37.0)	76.0% (46.8)	72.0% (31.0)
	Nvidia	86.3% (24.4)	90.0% (19.4)	87.0% (21.0)

To further understand the low-level details behind such results, we again leveraged the hooked drm/i915 driver to demonstrate the IRQ-specific patterns of the tested events (as was done in Sect. 4). Figure 4 demonstrates such detailed patterns for six tested events (three for each setting). We can see that all demonstrated interrupt patterns show typical features of stream displaying, making different patterns appear to be similar to a certain extent. We believe this is the main contribution to the relatively low accuracy of our attack on the Intel GPU. On top of this, there are still two observations worth noting.

First, we found that different video player engines use different rendering techniques. Figure 4.a, 4.b, and 4.c show that when playing the same FLV video, VLC, SMPlayer, and TOTEM used different GPU engines. Specifically, SMPlayer relied purely on the basic RCS engine, while both VLC and TOTEM used the VCS engine (VCS engine is for video encoding and decoding). This means that SMPlayer resorts to a pure software solution while VLC and TOTEM utilized hardware acceleration. Furthermore, we observed that TOTEM additionally leveraged the BCS engine, i.e., the blitter engine, to accelerate 2D rendering. We believe that such differences on the implementation details are the main factors that make the tested video players distinguishable from one another.

Secondly, the same video player also behaves differently when decoding videos of different codec. In the case of VLC playing the H264 videos, patterns of GEN8_GT_VCS1_IRQ interrupts can be observed, indicating that hardware accelerated decoding were leveraged. However, the other cases, i.e., VLC playing the XVID, MPEG4 and WMV videos, only involved the RCS engine, indicating pure software-level decoding. To demonstrate how such implementation details affect effectiveness of our attack, we present the heatmap for classification results of distinguishing the aforementioned 4 types of codec on the Intel GPU in Fig. 5, where we can see that our attack never misclassified any event of playing back the H264 video—unlike the playback of other clips where a certain level of ambiguity existed.

7   Additional Experiments, Discussion, and Limitation

7.1   Tradeoff Between Accuracy and Timeliness

When considering an attack scenario with on-the-fly monitoring of GPU usage, classifications are expected to be made in real time. As discussed in Sect. 3, our spy process uses a sliding window to feed its machine learning model subsequences of the interrupt time series. Intuitively, a larger sliding window (corresponding to longer inputs to our deep learning model and better accuracy) will result in longer latencies, given that classification only happens after the subse-

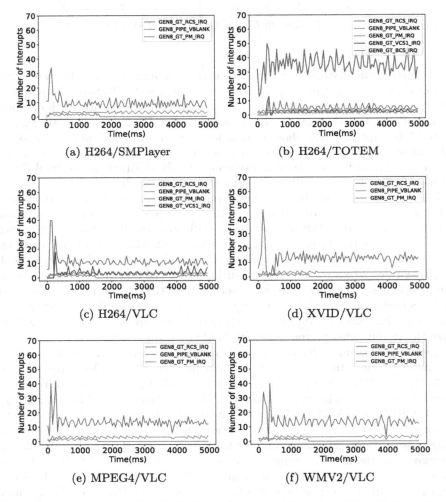

Fig. 4. Interrupt patterns (Intel) of playing the same video using different video players and codec. Missing lines correspond to zero readings of the IRQ types.

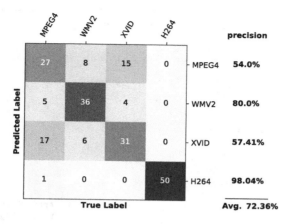

Fig. 5. Classifying (using ResNet) video playback of different codec using the same video player.

quences are collected. Therefore, in this subsection, we investigate the impact of reducing the length of such subsequences on the effectiveness of our attack.

We changed the length of subsequences with 10 different settings to train new machine learning models and observe the accuracy of them. Note that the sampling rate remains at 50 ms to minimize workload of our spy process. As presented in Fig. 6, the shortest interrupt time series length for reaching 99% accuracy in application fingerprinting was 50 samples, while that for reaching 80% accuracy in webpage fingerprinting was 60 (or 80 if we wish to reach 85% accuracy). This difference implies that launching applications splashes differently from the very beginning while loading webpages with the same browser splashes differently within a slightly longer period. Also, such result suggests that using time series of 60 to 80 samples, which translates to 3 to 4 s, would be good hyperparameter configurations to optimize the accuracy and timeliness tradeoff.

7.2   Robustness Against Noise

Since interrupt statistics is a fine-grained measurement, attacks based on such information could be interfered by other events which trigger screen refreshing or redrawing. The most typical example of such noise source is the movement of mouse cursor, in which areas at the past and present locations of the cursor have to be redrawn. Another possible scenario is when a multitasking user is conducting more than one screen redrawing activities at the same time, e.g., reading a document while playing a video simultaneously. We tested the robustness of our webpage fingerprinting attacks by collecting a group of new interrupt time series from the Nvidia GPU, in which the experiments involved manually moving the mouse cursor during the process of webpage loading, or having a random movie being played throughout the experiment. The test was conducted on the top 50 websites (given by Alexa) and repeated 100 times for each webpage. Two

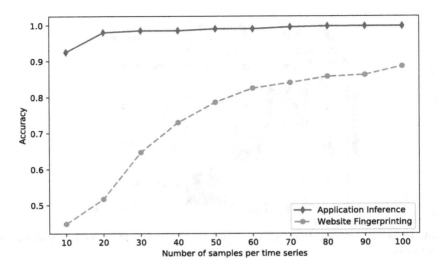

Fig. 6. Webpage and application fingerprinting with shorter interrupt time series.

classification strategies were tested: the first to train two ResNet models for the "noisy" and "clean" (free of noise) data, respectively, under an assumption that the two environments could be effectively differentiated (e.g., by observing mouse movement interrupts or by monitoring other side channels like CPU utilization), while the second to train only one model with both types of data mixed.

From Table 6 we can see that when classifying noisy data with mouse clicks as the noise source, F-measure of both strategies only slightly exceeded 54%. These strategies performed better in classifying data with video playing as the noise source, but the resulted F-measures were still only around 68%. Meanwhile, when using one model to classify both types of data, F-measure of classifying clean data is 3% less than that with two different models. Therefore, we consider the robustness against noise a limitation of our attack, which could also be pointing toward a potential mitigation against GPU side-channel attacks.

Table 6. Webpage fingerprinting with/without noise: average F-measure.

	clean data	noisy data	
		mouse induced noise	video induced noise
Dual models	88.2%	54.2%	67.9%
Mixed model	85.2%	54.6%	67.8%

8   Conclusion

This paper systematically studied the possibility of utilizing graphics interrupts as a leakage vector to drive GPU side-channel attacks. We introduced a series of attack scenarios in which graphics interrupt patterns were leveraged to respectively infer webpage opening, GUI application starting, and GUI tasks with the same graphics perception. Being a passive attack strategy, our attacks demonstrated high accuracy in the tested attack scenarios, suggesting that graphics interrupts could indeed leak sensitive information related to user activities.

Acknowledgment. This research/project is supported by the National Research Foundation, Singapore under its AI Singapore Programme (AISG Award No: AISG-100E-2018-004), National Natural Science Foundation of China (Grant No. 61702399 and 61972215) and National Key R&D Program of China (2018YFA0704703). Any opinions, findings and conclusions or recommendations expressed in this material are those of the author(s) and do not reflect the views of National Research Foundation, Singapore and AI Singapore.

References

1. Alexa: The top 500 sites on the web (2019). https://www.alexa.com/topsites
2. Chen, Q.A., Qian, Z., Mao, Z.M.: Peeking into your app without actually seeing it: UI state inference and novel android attacks. In: Proceedings of the 23rd USENIX Security Symposium, pp. 1037–1052 (2014)
3. Diao, W., Liu, X., Li, Z., Zhang, K.: No pardon for the interruption: New inference attacks on android through interrupt timing analysis. In: Proceedings of the 2016 IEEE Symposium on Security and Privacy, pp. 414–432. IEEE (2016)
4. Ismail Fawaz, H., Forestier, G., Weber, J., Idoumghar, L., Muller, P.-A.: Deep learning for time series classification: a review. Data Min. Knowl. Disc. **33**(4), 917–963 (2019). https://doi.org/10.1007/s10618-019-00619-1
5. Felten, E.W., Schneider, M.A.: Timing attacks on web privacy. In: Proceedings of the 7th ACM Conference on Computer and Communications Security, pp. 25–32. ACM (2000)
6. Gay, R., Mantel, H., Sudbrock, H.: An empirical bandwidth analysis of interrupt-related covert channels. Int. J. Secure Softw. Eng. **6**(2), 1–22 (2015)
7. Hayes, J., Danezis, G.: k-fingerprinting: A robust scalable website fingerprinting technique. In: Proceedings of the 25th USENIX Security Symposium, pp. 1187–1203 (2016)
8. He, K., Zhang, X., Ren, S., Sun, J.: Deep residual learning for image recognition. In: Proceedings of the 29th IEEE Conference on Computer Vision and Pattern Recognition, pp. 770–778 (2016)
9. Hwu, W.M.W.: GPU Computing Gems, Emerald edn. Elsevier (2011)
10. inaz2: Abusing interrupts for reliable windows kernel exploitation (2015). https://www.slideshare.net/inaz2/abusing-interrupts-for-reliable-windows-kernel-exploitation-en
11. Jana, S., Shmatikov, V.: Memento: learning secrets from process footprints. In: Proceedings of the 2012 IEEE Symposium on Security and Privacy, pp. 143–157. IEEE (2012)

12. Kotcher, R., Pei, Y., Jumde, P., Jackson, C.: Cross-origin pixel stealing: timing attacks using CSS filters. In: Proceedings of the 2013 ACM SIGSAC Conference on Computer & Communications Security, pp. 1055–1062. ACM (2013)
13. Lee, S., Kim, Y., Kim, J., Kim, J.: Stealing webpages rendered on your browser by exploiting GPU vulnerabilities. In: Proceedings of the 2014 IEEE Symposium on Security and Privacy, pp. 19–33. IEEE (2014)
14. Lukan, D.: Hooking the system service dispatch table (SSDT) (2014). https://resources.infosecinstitute.com/hooking-system-service-dispatch-table-ssdt
15. Luo, C., Fei, Y., Luo, P., Mukherjee, S., Kaeli, D.: Side channel power analysis of a GPU AES implementation. In: Proceedings of the 2015 33rd IEEE International Conference on Computer Design, pp. 281–288. IEEE (2015)
16. Mantel, H., Sudbrock, H.: Comparing countermeasures against interrupt-related covert channels in an information-theoretic framework. In: Proceedings of the 20th IEEE Computer Security Foundations Symposium, pp. 326–340. IEEE (2007)
17. Miller, J., Osmani, A.: Rendering on the web (2019). https://developers.google.com/web/updates/2019/02/rendering-on-the-web
18. Naghibijouybari, H., Khasawneh, K.N., Abu-Ghazaleh, N.: Constructing and characterizing covert channels on gpgpus. In: Proceedings of the 2017 50th Annual IEEE/ACM International Symposium on Microarchitecture, pp. 354–366. IEEE (2017)
19. Naghibijouybari, H., Neupane, A., Qian, Z., Abu-Ghazaleh, N.: Rendered insecure: GPU side channel attacks are practical. In: Proceedings of the 2018 ACM SIGSAC Conference on Computer and Communications Security, pp. 2139–2153. ACM (2018)
20. Nvidia: Security notice: Nvidia response to "rendered insecure: GPU side channel attacks are practical" - November 2018 (2018). https://shorturl.at/efJO6
21. Olson, L.E., Power, J., Hill, M.D., Wood, D.A.: Border control: sandboxing accelerators. In: Proceedings of the 2015 48th Annual IEEE/ACM International Symposium on Microarchitecture, pp. 470–481. IEEE (2015)
22. Panchenko, A., et al.: Website fingerprinting at internet scale. In: Proceedings of the Network and Distributed System Security Symposium 2016 (2016)
23. Pietro, R.D., Lombardi, F., Villani, A.: Cuda leaks: a detailed hack for cuda and a (partial) fix. ACM Trans. Embedded Comput. Syst. 15(1), 15 (2016)
24. Qian, Z., Mao, Z.M., Xie, Y.: Collaborative TCP sequence number inference attack: how to crack sequence number under a second. In: Proceedings of the 2012 ACM Conference on Computer and Communications Security, pp. 593–604. ACM (2012)
25. Tang, X., Lin, Y., Wu, D., Gao, D.: Towards dynamically monitoring android applications on non-rooted devices in the wild. In: Proceedings of the 11th ACM Conference on Security & Privacy in Wireless and Mobile Networks, pp. 212–223. ACM (2018)
26. Van Bulck, J., Piessens, F., Strackx, R.: Nemesis: studying microarchitectural timing leaks in rudimentary CPU interrupt logic. In: Proceedings of the 2018 ACM SIGSAC Conference on Computer and Communications Security, pp. 178–195. ACM (2018)
27. Van Goethem, T., Joosen, W., Nikiforakis, N.: The clock is still ticking: timing attacks in the modern web. In: Proceedings of the 22Nd ACM SIGSAC Conference on Computer and Communications Security, pp. 1382–1393 (2015)
28. Wang, Z., Yan, W., Oates, T.: Time series classification from scratch with deep neural networks: a strong baseline. In: Proceedings of the 2017 International Joint Conference on Neural Networks, pp. 1578–1585. IEEE (2017)

29. Yao, Z., Ma, Z., Liu, Y., Amiri Sani, A., Chandramowlishwaran, A.: Sugar: Secure GPU acceleration in web browsers. In: ACM SIGPLAN Notices, vol. 53, pp. 519–534. ACM (2018)
30. Zhang, K., Wang, X.: Peeping tom in the neighborhood: keystroke eavesdropping on multi-user systems. In: Proceedings of the 18th USENIX Security Symposium, vol. 20, p. 23 (2009)
31. Zhou, X., et al.: Identity, location, disease and more: Inferring your secrets from android public resources. In: Proceedings of the 2013 ACM SIGSAC Conference on Computer & Communications Security, pp. 1017–1028. ACM (2013)
32. Zhou, Z., Diao, W., Liu, X., Li, Z., Zhang, K., Liu, R.: Vulnerable gpu memory management: towards recovering raw data from gpu. Proc. Privacy Enhan. Technol. **2017**(2), 57–73 (2017)

Malware Analysis

Why Current Statistical Approaches to Ransomware Detection Fail

Jamie Pont$^{(\boxtimes)}$, Budi Arief , and Julio Hernandez-Castro

University of Kent, Canterbury, UK
{jjp31,ba284,jch27}@kent.ac.uk

Abstract. The frequent use of basic statistical techniques to detect ransomware is a popular and intuitive strategy; statistical tests can be used to identify randomness, which in turn can indicate the presence of encryption and, by extension, a ransomware attack. However, common file formats such as images and compressed data can look random from the perspective of some of these tests. In this work, we investigate the current frequent use of statistical tests in the context of ransomware detection, primarily focusing on false positive rates. The main aim of our work is to show that the current over-dependence on simple statistical tests within anti-ransomware tools can cause serious issues with the reliability and consistency of ransomware detection in the form of frequent false classifications. We determined thresholds for five key statistics frequently used in detecting randomness, namely Shannon entropy, chi-square, arithmetic mean, Monte Carlo estimation for Pi and serial correlation coefficient. We obtained a large dataset of 84,327 files comprising of images, compressed data and encrypted data. We then tested these thresholds (taken from a variety of previous publications in the literature where possible) against our dataset, showing that the rate of false positives is far beyond what could be considered acceptable. False positive rates were often above 50% and even above 90% on several occasions. False negative rates were also generally between 5% and 20%, numbers which are also far too high. As a direct result of these experiments, we determine that relying on these simple statistical approaches is not good enough to detect ransomware attacks consistently. We instead recommend the exploration of higher-order statistics such as skewness and kurtosis for future ransomware detection techniques.

Keywords: Ransomware · Anti-ransomware · Statistical tests · Randomness · Entropy · Chi-square

1 Introduction

Ransomware is a strain of malware which, upon compromising a victim's machine, denies access to a user's resources. Typically, this is achieved through the use of a hybrid cryptosystem, where user data is encrypted using symmetric keys. These keys are then encrypted using asymmetric cryptography, such as

W. Susilo et al. (Eds.): ISC 2020, LNCS 12472, pp. 199–216, 2020.
https://doi.org/10.1007/978-3-030-62974-8_12

RSA, and the private key is held by the attacker on their *Command & Control* (C&C) infrastructure [12]. In this scenario, the attacker would hold the encrypted data for 'ransom', demanding a payment (typically via a cryptocurrency such as Bitcoin) from the victim in order to restore their data. This type of ransomware is known as *Crypto-Ransomware* [16], and is the main scope of this analysis.

Ransomware is an ever-growing threat and continually causing widespread disruption. Alarmingly, we have recently observed more targeted attacks, i.e. ransomware attacks aimed at specific organisations with the intention of causing maximum damage [2]. For example, the Spanish company Everis was hit by the BitPaymer ransomware in 2019. It was shown that the ransom note deployed was specifically aimed at Everis, and the extension used for encrypted files was .3v3r1s [5]. Additionally, Norsk Hydro was hit by ransomware in 2019 and despite huge disruption to their production lines, they refused to pay the ransom. They were able to recover from the attack through use of trusted backup servers, whilst consulting paper documentation to continue business throughout the recovery process. This manual recovery process cost Norsk Hydro £45 million [24], but the company correctly refused to fund the cybercriminal economy.

Thankfully, we have also witnessed an increase in anti-ransomware research. One such avenue of research covers the development of techniques and tools aimed at the early detection and recovery from ransomware attacks. A recurring approach to detecting ransomware is the use of statistical tests for randomness, because properly encrypted data should appear completely random to anyone not in possession of the key. Therefore, the problem of detecting ransomware can be (somewhat simplistically) reduced to the problem of detecting random data being written to the filesystem. However, this assumption can be problematic.

Motivation. Whilst the use of statistical tests to detect ransomware has shown promise in the literature, it also raises issues. Most notably, the processing of random data on a machine does not automatically imply that it is under attack by ransomware. It is common for perfectly benign data on the filesystem to appear random and this happens with various image formats (e.g. JPEG and PNG), as well as frequently after the use of compression tools. Additionally, even if the presence of randomness is the result of encryption taking place, that does not necessarily imply that the encryption is malicious (i.e. the result of a ransomware attack).

In this work, we explore the former of these issues by investigating both popular image formats and types of compression commonly in use today. After collecting a representative dataset of JPEG, PNG and WebP images, and compressing and encrypting files from the Govdocs corpus [4], we ran them through Ent [26], a battery of statistical tests for randomness. We compared their output to various thresholds in use by current state-of-the-art anti-ransomware tools, and show our findings in Sect. 5. We show that the thresholds in use by these tools often result in too many false positives, which leads to unencrypted data in the filesystem being incorrectly labelled as encrypted by a ransomware attack.

Contributions. Firstly, we highlight the issue that one of the most popular approaches to detecting ransomware is potentially flawed. This weakness could present a serious problem to many anti-ransomware tools. We also provide insights into statistics beyond those that are currently used in this context, in order to illustrate the fact that the approach of using statistics to detect ransomware needs improving in general. We would like to stress that this *does not* mean that there are underlying problems with the statistical tests themselves. The problem is with using the tests in this context (i.e. for ransomware detection).

Secondly, we provide a number of recommendations for future work in light of our results. We highlight that the statistics which show the most promise in this context are chi-square and serial byte correlation. However, we believe that the research community should also look more carefully to alternatives such as variance, standard deviation, skewness and kurtosis. Finally, in the interests of scientific reproducibility, we have made all of the code we used freely available and open-source, as well as the datasets we used in our analysis.

The rest of the paper is structured as follows. In Sect. 2, we discuss some of the major uses of statistics to identify ransomware, as well as previous works which analyse this approach. In Sect. 3, we provide some intuition as to why these tests are used in ransomware detection. Section 4 explains the methodology we followed in our experiments, and Sect. 5 presents and analyses our results. In Sect. 6, we discuss what these results mean for anti-ransomware development, and we provide some recommendations for ransomware detection moving forwards. Finally, in Sect. 7, we conclude our work.

2 Related Work

The use of statistical approaches to detect ransomware was the second most common approach to detecting ransomware in 2019, according to an analysis of the academic anti-ransomware landscape [20]. Genç et al. classify *measuring entropy inflation* as one of the main *behavioural analysis* approaches to defending against ransomware [7], and Al-Rimy et al. highlight the use of entropy in their analysis of ransomware research [1]. There are some potential reasons as to why statistical approaches may be so popular in this context. For example, it is quite logical to consider using randomness tests to detect encryption (since the process of encryption results in data that is effectively random). The relative ease with which these randomness tests can be implemented may also be a contributing factor. We expand more on this in Sect. 3.

Several anti-ransomware tools use a statistical approach. ShieldFS calculates the entropy of data written to the filesystem and uses this as a machine learning feature to help detect ransomware attacks [3]. ShieldFS implemented a Windows Filesystem Minifilter Driver [17] to observe filesystem *write* operations, including the data buffer over which the entropy could be calculated. In fact, the approach of computing the entropy over filesystem *write* operations is a popular approach. To evaluate the validity of a detection, UNVEIL calculates the entropy value over the data buffer of both *read* and *write* operations [10]. If there is a significant increase in entropy between a *read* and a *write*, random data has likely been written and so a ransomware attack may have occurred.

Similarly, Redemption looks at the difference in entropy between a *read* and its subsequent *write* [11]. If there was an increase, the "malice score" of the associated process is increased, highlighting that there is a greater chance that this is a ransomware process.

CryptoDrop also uses entropy to help with ransomware detection [21]. This tool relies on the fact that ransomware will continually make highly-entropic *writes* to the filesystem, and takes weighted entropy averages to ensure that the low-entropy *writes* resulting from writing ransom notes do not confuse the system. CryptoDrop also looks at the delta between a *read* and its subsequent *write* to determine the change in entropy to a specific file. Furthermore, a small delta (0.1) is used as the threshold, to help cater for the small entropy increase that occurs when a file that is already highly-entropic (such as compressed data) is encrypted by ransomware. RWGuard also measures entropy as an indicator of a ransomware attack; if the entropy of a *write* request to the filesystem results in a value greater than 6, the metrics recorded for the specific file are analysed further due to the increased possibility of a ransomware attack [15].

To the best of our knowledge, Data Aware Defence (DaD) is the only ransomware detection tool that uses chi-square, rather than entropy, as its detection method [19]. In fact, detection is solely achieved using chi-square. Similarly to the above-mentioned tools, this statistic is computed over the data buffer of filesystem *write* operations, and a sliding median over the last 50 *writes* is used as a basis for this calculation.

Other work has explored the robustness of using statistical approaches to detecting ransomware. McIntosh et al. conclude that the use of entropy to detect ransomware should be stopped altogether in future anti-ransomware work [14]. Two methods by which ransomware could implement encryption in such a way as to avoid entropy-based detection measures are presented, using techniques including Base64 encoding and partial encryption. Interestingly, the work presented tackles the same problem explored in this paper, although primarily from the perspective of false negatives rather than false positives.

3   Randomness for Anti-Ransomware

To provide some explanation of the applicability of using randomness tests to detect ransomware, consider data (such as *writes* made to the filesystem, as well as the content of files) purely as streams of bytes (i.e. values between 0 and 255). Random (or encrypted) data should comprise of an approximately equal number of each byte, distributed across the data in an unpredictable way. Therefore, it is possible to apply widely-used tests for randomness across these byte distributions to identify the presence of random data. This may then indicate the presence of encryption, and possibly a ransomware attack.

However, some filetypes are comprised of data which, from the perspective of statistical tests such as entropy, actually appears random. Calculating the entropy of a JPEG typically results in values of 7.8 and higher. Considering the highest possible value is 8 bits per byte (i.e. completely uniform), it is clear

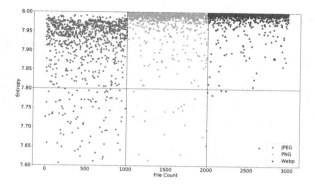

Fig. 1. Entropy values of 3,004 images found in the wild

that an unencrypted file can look as if it has been encrypted. Figure 1 shows the entropy values of 1,004 JPEG files, 1,000 PNG files and 1,000 WebP files that we found in the wild (discussed in more detail in Sect. 4) compared with a threshold of 7.8 (shown as a red horizontal line). This shows the consistency with which these types of files contain highly entropic data, which raises an issue: files like these will frequently cause false positives in anti-ransomware tools heavily reliant on this statistic. We explore this in more detail in Sect. 5.

Below, we expand on some of the main statistical tests used to detect the presence of a ransomware attack. Entropy and chi-square are currently used by the academic state-of-the-art in ransomware detection. However, we analyse three additional tests. Whilst these are not currently used by anti-ransomware tools, the ease with which they can be implemented may make them the next logical step for anti-ransomware developers so we felt it important to preemptively examine their accuracy in this context.

3.1   Shannon Entropy

In the context of ransomware detection, entropy can be seen as a measure of a given input's level of uncertainty. In this case, the input would be a series of bytes typically representing either a file's contents or the contents of a *write* request made to the filesystem. The equation for Shannon Entropy ($H(X)$) can be seen below for a random variable X [22]:

$$H(X) = -\sum_{i=0}^{255} P(x_i) log_b P(x_i)$$

In this case, the summation is between 0 and 255 as there are 256 possible values. Additionally, $b = 2$ allows the representation of bits, and $P(x_i)$ is $\frac{F_i}{totalbytes}$ where F_i is the observed frequency of byte i. This equation returns a value between 0 and 8, where 0 represents totally predictable data and 8 highly uncertain data.

3.2 Chi-Square

The chi-square (χ^2) test is a popular statistical test generally used to determine if an observed distribution is statistically similar to an expected distribution [6]. In the case of perfectly random data on the filesystem, we would expect an equal occurrence of each byte value. Therefore, for ransomware detection, we use equal frequencies of byte values for the expected distribution, and use the following formula to check if the observed distribution is similar:

$$\chi^2 = \sum_{i=0}^{255} \frac{(F_i - f_i)^2}{f_i}$$

Here, there are again 256 possible values for a given byte. F_i and f_i represent the observed and expected frequency of byte i, respectively.

As there are 256 possible categories that a given byte could be, the degrees of freedom for our chi-square test is set to 255 (i.e. *number of categories* -1). This allows us to refer to a chi-square distribution table and find what results we should expect at a given significance level. Researchers often use significance levels of 1%, 5% or 10% [23], and 5% is used in Data Aware Defence [19]. We state as the null hypothesis that our observed input is random. After computing the chi-square, we compare it with a distribution table at a 5% significance level. If our value is higher than the value in the table, this situation would only occur 5% of the time for a perfectly random distribution. Our observed distribution is therefore unlikely to be random, so we reject the null hypothesis.

3.3 Other Statistical Tests

In our experiments we used Ent, a Pseudorandom Number Sequence Test Program [26] which quickly calculates various statistics. In addition to entropy and chi-square, Ent provides the following statistics which we have not yet seen used to detect ransomware:

- **Arithmetic Mean.** This metric is calculated by summing all of the individual byte values and dividing by the total number of bytes. In the event of random data, or a ransomware attack, we would expect a result close to 127.5, i.e. halfway between 0 and 255.
- **Monte Carlo value for Pi.** For this statistic, every sequence of six bytes is used to calculate X and Y coordinates inside a square. For a circle inscribed within this square, the percentage of generated points that fall within the circle can be used to calculate the value of Pi. With sufficiently long and random data streams (for example due to a ransomware attack), the result will be close to the value of Pi.
- **Serial Correlation Coefficient.** Considering a byte stream of length n, it is possible to compare byte 0 with byte 1, byte 1 with byte 2 and so on up until byte n in order to calculate the correlation coefficient of this data. This is typically measured as a value between -1 and 1. The closer the value is

to one of the extremes (i.e. −1 or 1), the stronger that type of correlation is. Random data (for example from a ransomware attack) should be highly uncorrelated. This approach was explored by Pont et al. [20] as a potential ransomware detection technique.

4   Methodology

In the following section, we first detail our data collection process. This covers the collection of JPEGs, WebPs, PNGs, compressed and encrypted data. Following this, we detail how we prepared our dataset for graph generation, and finally discuss the creation of our threshold values.

4.1   Dataset Creation

After noticing the popularity of statistical tests to detect ransomware [20], we began by collecting a large dataset on which we could calculate these statistics for ourselves. Other works have noted that in the case of some filetypes, such as images and compressed data, their data is naturally highly entropic [11,13,21]. We therefore focused on these filetypes as we believed they would cause false positives in state-of-the-art anti-ransomware tools. Most of our data came from Digital Corpora's Govdocs [4]. This is a large corpus of real files from .gov domains that are freely available for research purposes. We first downloaded the entire JPEG image corpus, containing 109,282 JPEG images. This was downloaded as a single compressed directory approximately 36.8 GB in size (about 37.5 GB when decompressed). Within this directory were 961 subdirectories, each containing a number of JPEGs. In order to build a dataset of around 1,000 JPEGs in a way that is easily reproducible, we selected the first 15 of these subdirectories, providing us with a dataset of 1,004 JPEGs (about 145.4 MB).

We then used ImageAssisstant Batch Image Downloader (a Firefox addon which unfortunately seems to have been removed from the addon marketplace) to collect 1,000 WebP images using the Google search engine. Hurley-Smith et al. show that WebP files are frequently reported as random by Ent and the FIPS 140-2 randomness tests [9], so we felt it an important filetype to include in our experiments. We have yet to come across an anti-ransomware tool that includes this filetype as part of their dataset, which is concerning due to its rising popularity. In fact, WebP is in use by approximately 20,000 of all websites on Alexa website rankings, with uptake steadily on the increase [25].

We obtained these files by searching for a keyword followed by the `filetype:` operator. As an example, we searched for `mountains filetype:webp`, then used the Firefox addon to download a selection of the results in bulk. After repeating this process for 15 arbitrarily chosen keywords, we completed our collection of 1,000 WebP images (at approximately 77.1 MB in size). We include these keywords (along with the images themselves) in our dataset, although using different keywords for future experiments may be a good way to corroborate our findings. We repeated this process to collect 1,000 PNG images (at approximately

Table 1. The breakdown of our image files dataset

Filetype	Quantity	Size (MB)
JPEG	1,004	145.4
WebP	25,048	6100.1
PNG	1,000	778.0
LZMA	19,750	5,772.0
Gzip	17,775	5,527.0
Bzip2	17,775	5,351.0
AES Encrypted	1,975	951.7
Total	84,327 Files	24,625.2 MB

Table 2. Statistical thresholds to identify randomness

Statistic	Randomness threshold
Entropy	≥ 7.99
Chi-square	≤ 293.25
Arithmetic Mean	$126.23 \leq \text{value} \leq 128.78$
Monte carlo value for pi	$3.11 \leq \text{value} \leq 3.17$
Serial correlation coefficient	$-0.01 \leq \text{value} \leq 0.01$

778 MB in size). This time, only 14 keyword searches were required to reach the desired quantity of 1,000 images. These two lists of keywords were kept mutually exclusive to ensure as diverse a dataset as possible.

To complete our image collection, we took our JPEGs and PNGs and used the command line utility `cwebp` to convert them to WebP at various quality levels. This was achieved using a bash script which takes every JPEG and PNG, runs `cwebp` at quality levels 0, 25, 50, 75, 80 (the typical quality level used according to the tool itself) and 100, and stores the output in our WebP directory. We repeated this process with the `-lossless` option to include lossless WebPs.

We then moved towards compressed data, whose tendency to generate false positives has been noted in the literature [7,15]. We compressed data from the Govdocs *threads*, which are mutually exclusive sets of approximately 1,000 files. We chose Thread 4 and Thread 5 due to their larger size (containing 986 files (311 MB) and 989 files (295 MB) respectively). We used a bash script to call the Gzip, BZip2 and LZMA command line utilities to compress each file separately at each compression level (0 through 9 for LZMA, otherwise 1 through 9). A detailed breakdown of our dataset is presented in Table 1.

Baseline Dataset. In order to provide an idea of the statistics we would expect for data that really has been encrypted, we encrypted each file in Thread 4 and Thread 5 separately using `openssl`, a command line utility on Linux allowing the use of encryption algorithms [18]. We used the AES symmetric encryption algorithm with a 256-bit key and the CBC mode, as ransomware variants typically implement a hybrid encryption model where user data is encrypted with symmetric encryption (such as AES), and the symmetric keys are encrypted with asymmetric encryption (such as RSA) [16].

4.2   Dataset Preparation

To calculate the statistics described in Sect. 3, we wrote a Python script to call ent on the command line for each file in our dataset. Using the terse mode (-t) option, we were able to generate output in .csv format for easy processing. These steps provided us with the five statistics we needed for each file. We acknowledge that anti-ransomware tools often process individual filesystem operation buffers [3,10], however by processing entire files we are providing the tests with more data in order to increase accuracy. We then created the graphs in this work using Matplotlib [8], a data visualisation library for Python.

4.3   Threshold Creation

Of the five statistics we have looked at in this paper, to the best of our knowledge, only two (entropy and chi-square) are actively being used by anti-ransomware tools. Whilst, for entropy, the absolute threshold values used by the current state-of-the-art in anti-ransomware do not seem to be widely reported, an overall indication is given as to what can be considered as highly entropic data. For example, in ShieldFS, an entropy value of 0.948 (recorded on a scale between 0 and 1 – when scaled up to a scale of 0 to 8, this becomes 7.584) is considered as "very high" [3]. We set our entropy threshold as 7.99 to ensure that only the most uncertain of data is considered as encrypted. The threshold for chi-square was taken based on consulting a chi-square value table at 255 degrees of freedom with a significance level of 5%, as discussed in Sect. 3. This gives us a threshold of 293.25, the same value that was used in Data Aware Defence [19].

For the three remaining tests (arithmetic mean, Monte Carlo value for Pi, and serial correlation coefficient), we defined thresholds based on a 1% error margin. We consider any values calculated that fall within 1% of the baseline values to be random. The baseline values for arithmetic mean, Monte Carlo value for Pi and serial correlation coefficient are: 127.5, 3.14 and 0.00, respectively. Values within this range are treated as cases that would be detected as ransomware (i.e. a false positive for our images and compressed data, and a true positive for our encrypted data). Table 2 summarises the thresholds we used in our experiments.

5   Results and Analysis

We break the analysis of our results down into two main parts: an analysis of 'false classifications', and general observations. Many academic anti-ransomware tools are not open-source or available for use, so in our experiments we were unable to determine false classification rates of the tools themselves. Self-reported results of these anti-ransomware tools are summarised in [20], although interestingly this work highlights that many *false positive rates* (FPRs) are not reported. Below, we investigate the statistics introduced in Sect. 3.

Minimal FPRs are vitally important for real-time ransomware detection tools that always run in the background to prevent a user from instinctively dismissing alerts (putting them at risk of dismissing a real attack) or stopping using the tool altogether. Where the thresholds are not made available, we set our own, as described in Sect. 4. We analyse the percentage of our dataset that falls above and below these thresholds, providing an indication into the FPRs summarised in Table 3 and Table 4.

We also included an analysis of *false negative rates* (FNRs), as shown in Table 5. This would mean truly encrypted data that is incorrectly classified as being unencrypted. We acknowledge that these are devastating to a user, however minimising FNRs is beyond the scope of this paper – it is something that the authors of the respective tools themselves aim to minimise.

5.1 False Classification Analysis

False Positives Rates (FPRs). Table 3 and Table 4 summarise the FPRs we saw in our experiments across our images and compressed data, respectively. For each quality level used (shown as a percentage on the left), we include the number of files detected as a false positive, alongside the percentage of our dataset that this number equates to (i.e. the FPR). We also highlight the highest FPRs from our experiments in bold. We note that in Table 4, we only show the results for the three compression algorithms (BZip2, GZip and LZMA) at three levels of compression rate (1, 5 and 9). This was in the interest of creating a more succinct and readable table. Our complete set of results and graphs are available on GitHub (https://github.com/anti-ransomware/stats-tools-research).

Focusing first on the entropy and chi-square of our image dataset, we see a range in FPRs from 0% with chi-square to 83.90% using entropy. At first glance, this reinforces the idea that chi-square is better at distinguishing between encryption and JPEG compression [13]. However, analysing further, it quickly becomes clear that using chi-square is not necessarily the complete solution to the problem. For example, we see FPRs in the range of 43.13% to 76.69% when analysing lossy WebP files which have been converted from JPEGs at various quality levels. To top this off, when analysing WebPs found in the wild, we still see an FPR of 45.40%, indicating that almost half of this part of our dataset would cause a false positive. We believe this is a serious issue due to the rising popularity of WebP images in the wild [25].

Looking at entropy and chi-square overall, it does appear, however, to be the case that chi-square is in general a better indicator of ransomware (at least for images). Chi-square outperformed entropy (i.e. achieved a lower FPR) in almost all of our batches of data. Interestingly, however, entropy outperformed chi-square for the case of Lossy WebPs which had been converted from JPEGs.

Table 3. False positive analysis for images

Data	Entropy Count	Entropy %	Chi-Square Count	Chi-Square %	Mean Count	Mean %	Pi Count	Pi %	Correlation Count	Correlation %
JPEG	3	0.30%	0	0%	178	17.73%	231	23.01%	92	9.16%
PNG	468	46.80%	2	0.20%	519	51.90%	478	47.80%	74	7.40%
WebP	677	67.70%	454	45.40%	839	83.90%	726	72.60%	668	66.80%
WebP (from JPEG) Lossless 0%	193	19.22%	0	0%	241	24.00%	342	34.06%	4	0.40%
WebP (from JPEG) Lossless 25%	187	18.63%	0	0%	226	22.51%	312	31.08%	5	0.50%
WebP (from JPEG) Lossless 50%	397	39.54%	3	0.30%	396	39.44%	483	48.11%	9	0.90%
WebP (from JPEG) Lossless 75%	403	40.14%	5	0.50%	391	38.94%	477	47.51%	8	0.80%
WebP (from JPEG) Lossless 80%	411	40.94%	5	0.50%	398	39.64%	481	47.91%	8	0.80%
WebP (from JPEG) Lossless 100%	417	41.53%	3	0.30%	389	38.75%	484	48.21%	4	0.40%
WebP (from JPEG) Lossy 0%	18	1.79%	433	43.13%	373	37.15%	300	29.88%	286	28.49%
WebP (from JPEG) Lossy 25%	267	26.59%	759	75.60%	736	73.31%	505	50.30%	582	57.97%
WebP (from JPEG) Lossy 50%	383	38.15%	764	76.10%	839	83.57%	583	58.07%	669	66.63%
WebP (from JPEG) Lossy 75%	458	45.62%	770	76.69%	878	87.45%	641	63.84%	729	72.61%
WebP (from JPEG) Lossy 80%	505	50.30%	749	74.60%	873	86.95%	654	65.14%	782	77.89%
WebP (from JPEG) Lossy 100%	798	79.48%	569	56.67%	916	91.24%	742	73.90%	895	89.14%
WebP (from PNG) Lossless 0%	335	33.50%	2	0.20%	450	45.00%	474	47.40%	25	2.50%
WebP (from PNG) Lossless 25%	357	35.70%	5	0.50%	424	42.40%	482	48.20%	34	3.40%
WebP (from PNG) Lossless 50%	546	54.60%	21	2.10%	555	55.50%	586	58.60%	84	8.40%
WebP (from PNG) Lossless 75%	569	56.90%	18	1.80%	566	56.60%	605	60.50%	96	9.60%
WebP (from PNG) Lossless 80%	571	57.10%	18	1.80%	559	55.90%	593	59.30%	96	9.60%
WebP (from PNG) Lossless 100%	609	60.90%	25	2.50%	619	61.90%	644	64.40%	93	9.30%
WebP (from PNG) Lossy 0%	39	3.90%	202	20.20%	392	39.20%	374	37.40%	294	29.40%
WebP (from PNG) Lossy 25%	408	40.80%	501	50.10%	761	76.10%	600	60.00%	586	58.60%
WebP (from PNG) Lossy 50%	543	54.30%	546	54.60%	839	83.90%	671	67.10%	659	65.90%
WebP (from PNG) Lossy 75%	620	62.00%	515	51.50%	863	86.30%	732	73.20%	696	69.60%
WebP (from PNG) Lossy 80%	665	66.50%	507	50.70%	884	88.40%	737	73.70%	710	71.00%
WebP (from PNG) Lossy 100%	839	83.90%	417	41.70%	928	**92.80%**	826	82.60%	850	85.00%

Table 4. False positive analysis for compressed data

Data		Entropy Count	Entropy %	Chi-Square Count	Chi-Square %	Mean Count	Mean %	Pi Count	Pi %	Correlation Count	Correlation %
BZip2	1	373	37.83%	56	5.68%	395	40.06%	377	38.24%	113	11.46%
BZip2	5	382	38.74%	62	6.29%	394	39.96%	405	41.08%	143	14.50%
BZip2	9	384	38.95%	63	6.39%	395	40.06%	403	40.87%	142	14.40%
GZip	1	418	42.39%	235	23.83%	446	45.23%	348	35.29%	409	41.48%
GZip	5	401	40.67%	250	25.35%	464	47.06%	356	36.11%	428	43.41%
GZip	9	400	40.57%	259	26.27%	471	47.77%	377	38.24%	446	45.23%
LZMA	1	526	53.35%	913	**92.60%**	868	88.03%	667	67.65%	731	74.14%
LZMA	5	511	51.83%	910	92.29%	863	87.53%	664	67.34%	730	74.04%
LZMA	9	509	51.62%	907	91.99%	853	86.51%	663	67.24%	726	73.63%

The remaining FPRs were calculated based on our own thresholds, as discussed in Sect. 4. Arithmetic mean in general seems to be a poor indicator based on the fact that at its best, it still had an FPR of 17.73% and at its worst it had an FPR of 92.80%. This FPR level would be absolutely unacceptable in any context. The situation is similar for the value of Pi, which at its best achieved an FPR of 23.01% and at its worst, 82.60%. Interestingly, for both arithmetic mean and Pi, the best cases were achieved for JPEG, and the worst cases were on Lossy WebPs converted from PNGs at 100% quality.

Serial correlation coefficient, at its best, achieved an FPR of just 0.40%. This was for lossless WebPs converted from JPEGs at 0% quality. We believe this kind of FPR would be more palatable to the average end user. However, at its worst, it had an FPR of 89.14%, higher than the worst case of Pi.

Figure 2a and b show the chi-square distributions of our image and compressed dataset, respectively. The threshold of 293.25 is also included for reference (shown as a red horizontal line). For clarification, we have divided the graph into each of the major sub-divisions of our dataset. Within these sub-divisions are further divisions represented by a change in the corresponding point's colour. These separations represent the different quality levels used in the conversion process (0%, 25%, 50%, 75%, 80% and 100%, respectively). The same is true for the graphs representing the other statistics we calculated, for example those which can be found on GitHub.

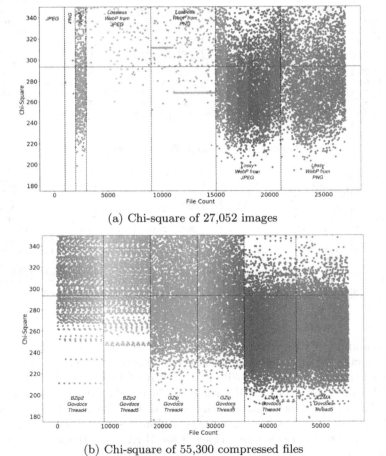

(a) Chi-square of 27,052 images

(b) Chi-square of 55,300 compressed files

Fig. 2. Chi-square of our dataset (Color figure online)

Table 5. False negative analysis for encrypted data

Data	False Negatives									
	Entropy		Chi-Square		Mean		Pi		Correlation	
	Count	%	Count	%	Count	%	Count	%	Count	%
AES Thread4	230	23.33%	48	4.87%	51	5.17%	184	18.66%	115	11.66%
AES Thread5	241	**24.37%**	49	4.95%	50	5.06%	174	17.59%	133	13.45%

We consider data points that fall *below* this line as false positives. We also note that some points are not visible on the graph due to chi-square values much higher than our axis limits. The only data type to achieve zero false positives is JPEG. The false positive count of PNG is low (i.e. 2), but all other data types have a high number of false positives. An interesting point to note is the huge number of false positives received for WebP when lossy compression is used. Our experiments show much lower FPRs when lossless compression is used. However, the FPR of our WebPs "from the wild" (i.e. 45.40%) suggest that the most common type of WebP compression in use is lossy. In fact, when cross-referencing the FPR of all WebPs from Table 3, it seems the most common type of WebP are those from PNGs and using lossy conversion.

Shifting to look at the compressed data, FPRs for both entropy and chi-square unfortunately do not look very promising. As discussed in Sect. 4, compressed data is often highlighted as a potential cause of false positives, so we hope our results reaffirm this serious issue. Looking at Table 4, the FPR for entropy is consistently within the range of 37.83% and 53.35%. Whilst these rates are generally more promising than those of our image dataset, we still deem them to be far beyond the realms of acceptability. Kharraz et al. conduct usability testing in [11], which may be a crucial step going forward to identify an acceptable FPR from a user's perspective. Interestingly, the range of FPRs for chi-square is much larger. At its best, chi-square had an FPR of 5.68%, which is closer (although still not satisfyingly enough) to what could be considered acceptable. However, at its worst, we observe an FPR of 92.60%. This is almost the highest FPR observed across all of our experiments, topped only by using arithmetic mean on lossy WebPs from PNGs at 100% quality.

Moving on to the three remaining statistics, FPRs are again far too high to be considered acceptable. The best performance we see is for BZip2 at a level 1 compression rate. Using correlation, we see an FPR of 11.46%. However, FPRs for these statistics are generally in the range of 40 to 60%, even reaching 88.03% in the case of using arithmetic mean for data compressed using LZMA at level 1 compression rate.

False Negative Rates (FNRs). Table 5 summarises the FNRs we saw in our experiments for the individual statistics. As with the above tables, we provide the number of files detected as a false negative, alongside the FNRs, whilst highlighting the highest FNR in bold. In this context, this represents data that has been encrypted but has incorrectly been classified as not encrypted. In a real life scenario, this would represent ransomware encrypting a user's files without any active protection mechanisms alerting the user to some form of malicious activity.

Whilst this is not the focus of our paper, we thought it would still be relevant to report our findings. The best case we saw was an FNR of 4.87% when using the chi-square statistic over Thread 4. Conversely, the worst case we saw was an FNR of 24.37% when using entropy over Thread 5. Thankfully, we recorded no FNR higher than this, although we still believe that these rates are too high to be acceptable. In this case, almost a quarter of encrypted files go undetected.

An important point we would like to mention is that it was our choice to consider this encryption as malicious. We wanted to include this data to represent what data would look like from a statistical point of view if it had been encrypted by ransomware. However, the presence of encryption on a system does not automatically imply that a ransomware attack is underway. For example, benign applications may use encryption for communication, or a user may wish to encrypt their files for privacy.

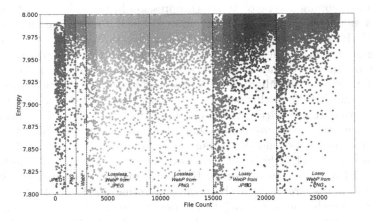

Fig. 3. Entropy of 27,052 images

5.2   General Observations

Figure 3 shows the entropy values calculated for our image dataset, which accurately summaries the patterns we saw for the majority of our other statistics. Within each major sub-division of the dataset, it is clear how – as we progress from left to right through the different conversion quality levels – the dispersion of entropy decreases. In other words, as both JPEGs and PNGs are converted to WebPs at higher quality levels, the resulting entropy of the data is increased. For this reason and that a similar pattern can be observed for the other statistics, we believe investigating the variance, standard deviation and higher-order statistics such as skewness and kurtosis could be a step towards detecting consistently random data, but this would require more experimentation.

Due to the uncertainty as to which filetypes any given user may have on their computer, we do not believe the solution is as simple as picking the statistics that achieve the lowest FPR and FNR. It may be the case that whilst this works well for some users, it does not work at all for others. For example, the obvious choice would be using chi-square or serial correlation coefficient due to their lower FPRs and FNRs in general, but they don't always perform well.

We believe that these results highlight a serious flaw in the current state-of-the-art in ransomware detection. Whilst the tools are generally excellent at detecting ransomware, more effort needs to be put into reducing FPRs. We acknowledge that these tools often use statistics as part of a wider detection mechanism, for example behavioural analysis such as in ShieldFS [3]. Despite this, it is very common for these tools to place heavy reliance on the results of statistical tests. We believe this is worrying due to their susceptibility to errors, as shown by our results. We would again like to stress that this *does not* mean that there are underlying problems with these tests; the problem is with using them for ransomware detection.

6   Recommendations and Future Work

As discussed in Sect. 2, McIntosh et al. recommended that future research should avoid the use of entropy for ransomware detection [14]. This was due to the relative ease by which ransomware could implement encryption without triggering any entropy thresholds in place. We come to a similar conclusion from the perspective of false positives rather than false negatives. The immediately obvious recommendation would be to avoid the *sole* use of entropy to reliably and consistently detect a ransomware attack. The frequency of false positives in our results show that an average user would be plagued by false alarms, ending in a practically unusable system. However, our results also show that the problem is not just with entropy but for all of the statistics we tested. Whilst some statistics (entropy, chi-square and serial correlation coefficient) performed extremely well in certain cases (e.g. FPRs of around 0% to 0.5%), they did not perform this well consistently across our experiments. We are therefore unable to recommend a single statistic as the optimal way of detecting ransomware reliably.

Due to their lower FPRs whilst still achieving the lowest FNRs, we believe chi-square and serial correlation coefficient deserve the most attention going forwards. To the best of our knowledge, Data Aware Defence is the only tool so far that has used chi-square for ransomware detection [19].

The statistics we calculated were for single files at any one given time. An improved approach would be to identify deltas in these statistical values over time for a given set of files. This idea has been explored by Redemption [11] and CryptoLock [21]. It should be immediately obvious when ransomware writes to a file by identifying a significant change in (for example) the entropy value of the *read*, followed by the subsequent *write*. This approach may still be susceptible to false positives, for example if a file is highly structured before the encryption takes place (like much of the data used in our dataset).

As discussed in Sect. 5.2, we believe it would be worthwhile for the anti-ransomware community to investigate variance and standard deviation of the previously discussed statistics. We would expect highly random data to be written to the filesystem *consistently* during a ransomware attack. By calculating the statistics of these *writes* for a given time window, the variance and standard deviation could be calculated in order to determine spread and dispersion from central tendency. We expect a low variance and standard deviation in the case of consistent highly random *writes* to the filesystem, but a high variance and standard deviation in the case of normal system usage. It may also be possible to apply this technique using higher-order statistics such as skewness and kurtosis, although this would require further experimentation.

7   Conclusion

In this paper, we have highlighted the very serious issue that in the context of ransomware detection, popular file formats in use by typical computer users can cause frequent false positive alerts when analysed with various statistical tests for randomness. We analysed a dataset of 84,327 files (at 24.6 GB) consisting of JPEG images, PNG images, WebP images, compressed data (using BZip2, GZip and LZMA), and encrypted data (using AES in CBC mode with a 256-bit key). On this dataset, we calculated values for entropy, chi-square, arithmetic mean, Monte Carlo value for Pi and serial correlation coefficient (using the command line tool Ent). We compared these values against thresholds that were both found in and based on the literature (using a 1% error margin where no thresholds were available) to determine their false classification rates.

We observed FPRs of up to 92.80%, with a large proportion of our dataset attaining FPRs of over 80%. Only an extremely small proportion achieved rates that could be considered acceptable (i.e. below 0.5%). In addition, the lowest FNR we saw was still 5.06%, with the highest being 24.37%. This shows that even in the best case for our dataset, approximately five out of 100 files could be maliciously encrypted without being recognised by these tests.

Some of these tests are in use by many of the state-of-the-art tools in ransomware detection. We believe our results indicate that testing of these anti-ransomware tools has not been sufficient. We therefore believe future anti-ransomware tools should be tested on much larger and representative datasets, particularly including lots of images (especially WebP files) and compressed data, to ensure FPRs and FNRs are as accurate and realistic as possible. This, combined with a detailed analysis and visualisation of these results, would help to highlight the true accuracy of these tools. Finally, experimenting with the use of variance, standard deviation and higher-order statistics such as skewness and kurtosis may help to classify ransomware attacks more accurately and consistently.

References

1. Al-rimy, B.A.S., Maarof, M.A., Shaid, S.Z.M.: Ransomware threat success factors, taxonomy, and countermeasures: a survey and research directions. Comput. Secur. **74**, 144–166 (2018)
2. Constantin, L.: More targeted, sophisticated and costly: Why ransomware might be your biggest threat (February 2020). https://www.csoonline.com/article/3518864/more-targeted-sophisticated-and-costly-why-ransomware-might-be-your-biggest-threat.html
3. Continella, A., et al.: Shieldfs: a self-healing, ransomware-aware filesystem. In: Proceedings of 32nd Annual Conference on Computer Security Applications, pp. 336–347 (2016)
4. Digital Corpora: (2018). https://digitalcorpora.org
5. Esparza, J.M., Blueliv: spanish consultancy everis suffers bitpaymer ransomware attack: a brief analysis (November 2019). https://www.blueliv.com/cyber-security-and-cyber-threat-intelligence-blog-blueliv/research/everis-bitpaymer-ransomware-attack-analysis-dridex/
6. Pearson, F.R.S.K.: X. on the criterion that a given system of deviations from the probable in the case of a correlated system of variables is such that it can be reasonably supposed to have arisen from random sampling. London Edinb. Dublin Philos. Mag. J. Sci. **50**(302), 157–175 (1900). https://doi.org/10.1080/14786440009463897
7. Genç, Z.A., Lenzini, G., Ryan, P.Y.A.: Next generation cryptographic ransomware. In: Gruschka, N. (ed.) NordSec 2018. LNCS, vol. 11252, pp. 385–401. Springer, Cham (2018). https://doi.org/10.1007/978-3-030-03638-6_24
8. Hunter, J.D.: Matplotlib: a 2d graphics environment. Comput. Sci. Eng. **9**(3), 90–95 (2007). https://doi.org/10.1109/MCSE.2007.55
9. Hurley-Smith, D., Patsakis, C., Hernandez-Castro, J.: On the unbearable lightness of FIPS 140–2 randomness tests. IEEE Trans. Inf. Forensics Secur. (2020)
10. Kharraz, A., Arshad, S., Mulliner, C., Robertson, W., Kirda, E.: UNVEIL: a large-scale, automated approach to detecting ransomware. In: 25th USENIX Security Symposium (USENIX Security 16), pp. 757–772 (2016)
11. Kharraz, A., Kirda, E.: Redemption: real-time protection against ransomware at end-hosts. In: Dacier, M., Bailey, M., Polychronakis, M., Antonakakis, M. (eds.) RAID 2017. LNCS, vol. 10453, pp. 98–119. Springer, Cham (2017). https://doi.org/10.1007/978-3-319-66332-6_5
12. Kharraz, A., Robertson, W., Balzarotti, D., Bilge, L., Kirda, E.: Cutting the gordian knot: a look under the hood of ransomware attacks. In: Almgren, M., Gulisano, V., Maggi, F. (eds.) DIMVA 2015. LNCS, vol. 9148, pp. 3–24. Springer, Cham (2015). https://doi.org/10.1007/978-3-319-20550-2_1
13. Mbol, F., Robert, J.-M., Sadighian, A.: An efficient approach to detect Torrent-Locker ransomware in computer systems. In: Foresti, S., Persiano, G. (eds.) CANS 2016. LNCS, vol. 10052, pp. 532–541. Springer, Cham (2016). https://doi.org/10.1007/978-3-319-48965-0_32
14. McIntosh, T., Jang-Jaccard, J., Watters, P., Susnjak, T.: The inadequacy of entropy-based ransomware detection. In: Gedeon, T., Wong, K.W., Lee, M. (eds.) ICONIP 2019. CCIS, vol. 1143, pp. 181–189. Springer, Cham (2019). https://doi.org/10.1007/978-3-030-36802-9_20
15. Mehnaz, S., Mudgerikar, A., Bertino, E.: RWGuard: a real-time detection system against cryptographic ransomware. In: Bailey, M., Holz, T., Stamatogiannakis, M., Ioannidis, S. (eds.) RAID 2018. LNCS, vol. 11050, pp. 114–136. Springer, Cham (2018). https://doi.org/10.1007/978-3-030-00470-5_6

16. Micro, T.: Ransomware (September 2016). https://www.trendmicro.com/vinfo/us/security/definition/ransomware
17. Microsoft: kernel-mode driver architecture design guide (June 2017). https://docs.microsoft.com/en-gb/windows-hardware/drivers/kernel/
18. OpenSSL Software Foundation: Openssl. https://www.openssl.org
19. Palisse, A., Durand, A., Le Bouder, H., Le Guernic, C., Lanet, J.-L.: Data aware defense (DaD): towards a generic and practical ransomware countermeasure. In: Lipmaa, H., Mitrokotsa, A., Matulevičius, R. (eds.) NordSec 2017. LNCS, vol. 10674, pp. 192–208. Springer, Cham (2017). https://doi.org/10.1007/978-3-319-70290-2_12
20. Pont, J., Abu Oun, O., Brierley, C., Arief, B., Hernandez-Castro, J.: A roadmap for improving the impact of anti-ransomware research. In: Askarov, A., Hansen, R.R., Rafnsson, W. (eds.) NordSec 2019. LNCS, vol. 11875, pp. 137–154. Springer, Cham (2019). https://doi.org/10.1007/978-3-030-35055-0_9
21. Scaife, N., Carter, H., Traynor, P., Butler, K.R.: Cryptolock (and drop it): stopping ransomware attacks on user data. In: 36th International Conference on Distributed Computing Systems (ICDCS), pp. 303–312. IEEE (2016)
22. Shannon, C.E.: A mathematical theory of communication. Bell Syst. Tech. J. **27**(3), 379–423 (1948)
23. Stat Trek: Chi-square test for independence (2020). https://stattrek.com/chi-square-test/independence.aspx
24. Tidy, J.: How a ransomware attack cost one firm £45m (June 2019). https://www.bbc.co.uk/news/business-48661152
25. W3Techs: Usage statistics of webp for websites (2020). https://w3techs.com/technologies/details/im-webp
26. Walker, J.: Ent (2008). https://www.fourmilab.ch/random/

A Framework for Estimating Privacy Risk Scores of Mobile Apps

Kai Chih Chang$^{(\boxtimes)}$, Razieh Nokhbeh Zaeem , and K. Suzanne Barber

The University of Texas at Austin, Austin, TX 78712, USA
{kaichih,razieh,sbarber}@identity.utexas.edu

Abstract. With the rapidly growing popularity of smart mobile devices, the number of mobile applications available has surged in the past few years. Such mobile applications collect a treasure trove of Personally Identifiable Information (PII) attributes (such as age, gender, location, and fingerprints). Mobile applications, however, are many and often not well understood, especially for their privacy-related activities and functions. To fill this critical gap, we recommend providing an automated yet effective assessment of the privacy risk score of each application. The design goal is that the higher the score, the higher the potential privacy risk of this mobile application. Specifically, we consider excessive data access permissions and risky privacy policies. We first calculate the privacy risk of over 600 PII attributes through a longitudinal study of over 20 years of identity theft and fraud news reporting. Then, we map the access rights and privacy policies of each smart application to our dataset of PII to analyze what PII the application collects, and then calculate the privacy risk score of each smart application. Finally, we report our extensive experiments of 100 open source applications collected from Google Play to evaluate our method. The experimental results clearly prove the effectiveness of our method.

Keywords: Mobile applications · Privacy · Privacy policy · Permissions · Natural language processing

1 Introduction

In recent years, portable smart devices have rapidly spread, bringing a large number of mobile applications to various users. For example, as of May 2020, Google Play has more than 3 million Apps, which is three times the number in 2013, and these numbers are still growing rapidly. Due to the prosperous development of the smart application industry, the functions of smart devices have been extensively expanded and innovated to meet the needs of diverse users. However, the types of mobile applications are ever-changing, and their contents and architecture are often difficult to understand. Questions about their activities and functions related to privacy and security are endless. In fact, in order to improve the user experience, more and more advanced mobile applications

W. Susilo et al. (Eds.): ISC 2020, LNCS 12472, pp. 217–233, 2020.
https://doi.org/10.1007/978-3-030-62974-8_13

are inclined to gather user data to provide personalized service. These services usually involve access to sensitive personal information such as location.

However, such intelligent mobile Apps may result in potential security and privacy risks for users. So much Personally Identifiable Information (PII) is hidden in a smartphone, such as What We Are (e.g., fingerprints), What We Have (e.g., credit card information), What We Know (e.g., email password), and What We Do (e.g., location history) [29]. We call these PII attributes identity assets. In addition, emerging technologies of IoT (Internet of Things) bring new forms of user interfaces, such as wearable devices, which also pose greater challenges to user privacy. Therefore, it is important to study what identity assets are collected by these mobile applications.

A privacy policy is one of the most common methods of providing user notifications and choices. The purpose of a privacy policy is to inform users how the application collects, stores and discloses users' identity assets. Although some service providers have improved the intelligibility and readability of their privacy policies, not everyone reads them. As of 2019, only 24% of people read the privacy policy [15].

Another potential privacy risk for mobile applications is basically caused by excessive data access permissions of mobile applications. As mentioned earlier, the current mobile applications provide a variety of innovative services, and these services involve various data access permissions. Sometimes these permissions are necessary, sometimes not. Therefore, in this paper we propose to leverage the requested permissions and privacy policies for detecting the potential privacy risk of each mobile App.

To create a comprehensive list of PII, we utilize our longitudinal study of 6,000 identity theft and fraud news stories reported over the past 20 years. This database–named Identity Threat Assessment and Prediction or ITAP [30,31]– is a structured model of PII, manually extracted by a team of modelers from identity theft and fraud reports in the online news media. We take advantage of ITAP to evaluate the risk score of each identity asset in order to estimate the privacy risk score of the set of identity assets that a mobile App collects.

This paper makes the following contributions:

1. We map an independently built, comprehensive list of identity assets to privacy polices and data access permissions in order to evaluate the privacy risk score of mobile apps.
2. We use Natural Language Processing (NLP) methods to automatically parse privacy policies to find the identity assets mentioned in them.
3. Having access to UT CID probabilistic models and Bayesian inference tool Ecosystem [21], we take advantage of Bayesian inference to help calculate privacy risk score of mobile apps.
4. We demonstrate how our approaches can work on 100 popular open-source Android mobile Apps in Google Play and compare our results to other researchers' work.

2 Data and Methodology

In this section, we briefly introduce the dataset that we are using and also the details of our privacy risk measurements.

2.1 UT CID ITAP Dataset

The Identity Threat Assessment and Prediction (ITAP) [30, 31] is a research project at the Center for Identity at the University of Texas at Austin that enhances fundamental understanding of identity processes, valuation, and vulnerabilities. The purpose of ITAP is to identify mechanisms and resources that are actually used to implement identity breach. ITAP cares about the exploited vulnerabilities, types of identity attributes exposed, and the impact of these events on the victims.

Between years 2000 and 2019, about 6,000 incidents have been captured [3]. ITAP gathers details of media news stories (e.g., the identity assets exposed, the location and date of the event, the age and annual income of the victims, and the perpetrators' methods) about identity theft with two methods. First, it monitored a number of Web sites that report on cases of identity theft. Second, it created a Google Alert to provide notifications when any new report of identity theft appears. By analyzing these cases, ITAP has generated a list of identity attributes with each of them being assigned identity-related vulnerabilities, values, risk of exposure, and other characteristics depending on their properties, such as, whether or not an attribute is unique to a person, whether or not an attribute is widely used, how accurately it can be verified, etc. To date, ITAP has generated a list including over 600 identity assets, which is the list of identity assets we are referring to in this research.

Each identity asset in the UT CID ITAP dataset has a group of properties, including, but not limited to the following properties:

Risk: indicates the probability of this identity asset being misused in identity theft and fraud incidents.

Value: indicates the monetary value of this identity asset when misused in identity theft and fraud incidents.

2.2 Identity Assets Collection from Apps

Privacy risks are essentially caused by the data collections of Apps. Thus, an intuitive approach for measuring the privacy risks of Apps is to directly check each of the identity asset they collect/request. In this work, we divide data collection into two parts: (1) the privacy policy of each apps and (2) the Android manifest XML file of each apps.

Privacy Policy. Privacy policies help users understand what portion of their sensitive data would be collected and used or shared by a specific mobile application. By reading the privacy policy of an app, we should know what information this application collects, how this app uses the information, and what information this app shares. A privacy policy discloses all the information an app actively and passively collects, for example, information actively entered when registering for an account or passive HTTP logs and Internet usage.

The *bag-of-words* (BoW) model is a simplifying representation used in natural language processing and information retrieval. We construct a BoW model and take the privacy policy as input to generate a list of words and map it to the ITAP dataset to see what identity assets this privacy policy collects. In our model, we manually map each *word* to different identity assets so that after feeding our model with the privacy policy, we can generate a set of identity assets that this app collects. Table 1 shows some example of BoW mapping. We define the set of identity assets of app S that includes N identity assets as

$$Set_{BoW}(S) = \{x_i\}_{i=1:N} \tag{1}$$

where x_i denotes the identity asset in UT CID ITAP dataset.

Table 1. Examples of privacy policies mapping to ITAP dataset.

Words	Correlated identity assets
Email	Email_Address
Name	User_Name
Phone	Phone_Number
Location	GPS_Location

XML File. To access the personal data in users' Android mobile devices, the permission system will convey users to grant corresponding data access permissions for each mobile app. Actually, these data access permissions may enter some sensitive resources in mobile users' personal data, such as their locations or contact lists. Table 2 shows some example of permissions. We can see that these listed permissions contain potential security risks. For example, an App, which requests READ_CALENDAR permission, may access users' personal calendar which could make users like businesspersons feel uncomfortable due to leaking their schedules. In this work, we construct a program in which we manually map each Android permission to identity assets in UT CID ITAP dataset. This program takes Android manifest file as input and generate a set of identity assets that this app collects. Table 3 shows some mapping example of permissions. We define the set of identity assets of app S that includes N identity assets as

$$Set_{XML}(S) = \{x_i\}_{i=1:N} \tag{2}$$

where x_i denotes the identity asset in UT CID ITAP dataset.

Therefore, we can define a dataset of identity assets for app S as

$$ID_S = Set_{BoW}(S) \cup Set_{XML}(S) \tag{3}$$

Table 2. Examples of Android permissions.

Type	Permission name	Description
String	ACCESS_BACKGROUND_LOCATION	Allows an app to access location in the background
String	NFC_TRANSACTION_EVENT	Allows applications to receive NFC transaction events
String	READ_CALENDAR	Allows an application to read the user's calendar data
String	READ_CALL_LOG	Allows an application to read the user's call log

Table 3. Examples of Android permissions mapping to ITAP dataset.

Permission name	Correlated identity assets
ACCESS_BACKGROUND_LOCATION	GPS_Location
NFC_TRANSACTION_EVENT	Transaction_Records
READ_CALENDAR	Calendar_Information
READ_CALL_LOG	Call_History

2.3 Estimating Risk Scores for Identity Assets

Generally speaking, the risk score should reflect the security level of an identity asset. The higher the score is, the more dangerous when the identity asset is exposed. Dangerous here means the danger of monetary loss one could have encountered when the identity asset of this person is exposed. Recall that ITAP associates monetary values to identity assets.

We have two approaches to calculate the risk score of identity assets. Among those properties, we first choose *risk* and *value* for measuring the risk score of each identity asset.

Basic Measurement. Given N identity assets in UT CID ITAP dataset, each identity asset A_i is labeled with a monetary value $V(A_i)$ and a prior probability $P(A_i)$ of it getting exposed on its own. We define the expected loss of an identity asset A_i as

$$Exp(A_i) = P(A_i) \cdot V(A_i) \tag{4}$$

such that $1 \leq i \leq N$.

Dynamic Measurement. We have another way for calculating expected loss. Instead of using only intrinsic values of identity assets in UT CID ITAP dataset, we leverage two more parameters which we introduced in previous work [6] to refine risk and value of identity assets.

We first provide a high level introduction to our UT CID Identity Ecosystem [6–8,18,21,24]. The UT CID Identity Ecosystem developed at the Center for Identity at the University of Texas at Austin is a tool that models identity relationships, analyzes identity thefts and breaches, and answers several questions about identity management. It takes UT CID ITAP dataset as input and transforms them into identity assets and relationships, and performs Bayesian network-based inference to calculate the posterior effects on each attribute. We represent UT CID Identity Ecosystem as a graph $G(V, E)$ consisting of N identity assets $A_1, ..., A_N$ and a set of directed edges as a tuple $e_{ij} = <i,j>$ where A_i is the originating node and A_j is the target node such that $1 \leq i, j \leq N$. Each edge e_{ij} represents a possible path by which A_j can be breached given that A_i is breached.

The first parameter we reuse from our previous work is called *Accessibility*. In the calculation of a respective identity asset's accessibility, we analyzed its ancestors (in the UT CID Identity Ecosystem graph) to assess the probability and likelihood of discovering this node from other nodes. These "discovery" probabilities on edges in the UT CID Identity Ecosystem graph are calculated using UT CID ITAP dataset representing how criminals discovered identity assets using a respective identity asset. Low values of accessibility indicate that it is more difficult to discover to this attribute from others. An identity asset with low accessibility is harder to breach or discover (discoverability). Since accessibility is the change in risk of exposure, we can calculate new risk of an identity asset A_i as

$$P'(A_i) = P(A_i) + AC(A_i) \tag{5}$$

where $AC(A_i)$ denotes the accessibility of A_i.

The second parameter we obtain from our previous work is called *Post Effect*. For a target identity asset, we analyze its descendants in the UT CID Identity Ecosystem graph. If an identity asset is breached, the post effect measure gages how much the respective identity asset would influence others. The low value of post effect of an attribute indicates that the damage or loss one would encounter is smaller after this identity asset is accessed by fraudsters. Since post effect is also the monetary value, we can calculate new value of an identity assets A_i as

$$V'(A_i) = V(A_i) + PE(A_i) \tag{6}$$

where $PE(A_i)$ denotes the post effect of A_i.

Hence, for dynamic measurement, we define expected loss of identity asset A_i as

$$Exp(A_i) = P'(A_i) \cdot V'(A_i) \tag{7}$$

Since the range of the expected loss in UT CID ITAP dataset is from 0 to 10^7, which is quite wide, in order to rank each identity asset based on expected loss, we apply natural logarithm on each identity asset's expected loss which can be shown as $ln(Exp(A_i))$. As we mentioned at the beginning of this section, the higher the score is, the more dangerous when the identity asset is exposed. To achieve this goal, we find the maximum value of expected loss after applying natural logarithm and use it to calculate the risk score of each identity asset. Thus, we define the risk score of an identity asset A_i as

$$score_{risk}(A_i) = \frac{ln(Exp(A_i))}{Max} \tag{8}$$

where Max denotes the maximum value of expected loss after applying natural logarithm. Hence, the risk score becomes a value that is normalized between 0 and 1.

2.4 Ranking for Mobile Apps

Then, we can compute risk scores of mobile apps with risk scores of identity assets. Given an app S that collects N identity assets, by our data collection approach, we can derive an identity asset dataset $ID_S = \{x_i\}_{i=1:N}$. For all of the members of app S, we can estimate the total risk score of the collected dataset:

$$Privacy_s = \frac{1}{Total} \sum_{i=1}^{N} score_{risk}(A_i) \tag{9}$$

where $Total$ denotes the sum of risk score of the entire UT CID ITAP dataset. Thus, the privacy risk score becomes a value that is also normalized between 0 and 1.

Therefore, we can also calculate the privacy risk score of one's mobile devices by adding up privacy risk scores of apps that one's device have installed.

3 Experimental Results

In this section, we empirically evaluate our app privacy ranking approaches with real-world Android apps.

3.1 Experimental Apps

In order to perform data collection analysis on manifest XML files, we target Android apps that are open-source. We found 100 Android apps that have privacy policies on Google Play and the source code of each of them is available on GitHub. Most of them are still actively maintained. Figure 1 illustrates some statistics of the application dataset. It shows the number of Apps and the average number of requested permissions by each App in different categories. In this figure, we can observe that Apps in categories "Communication", "Business" and "Travel & Local" request more permissions and that we have more Apps in categories "Tools" and "Productivity" in this dataset.

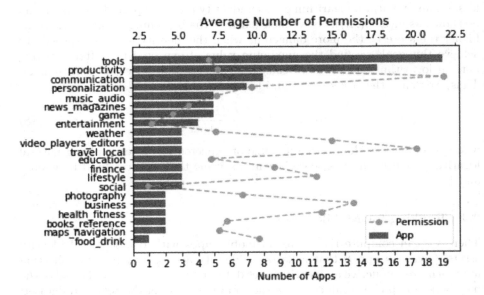

Fig. 1. The number of Apps and the average number of requested permissions by each App in different categories.

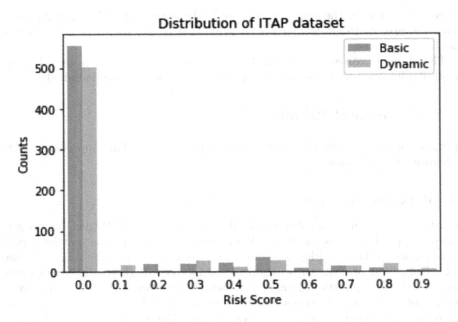

Fig. 2. The value of each rank and the number of identity assets with that rank.

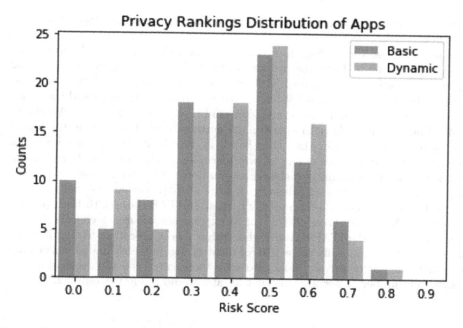

Fig. 3. The ranking distribution of basic and dynamic measurements on Android Apps.

3.2 Evaluation of App Privacy Risk Scores

Here, we evaluate the effectiveness of estimating App risk scores and compare our methodologies with previous work.

General Results. Figure 2 shows the histogram of how many identity assets have a given rank value, according to both basic and dynamic methods of calculation. There are many identity assets that have the monetary value 0 reported from ITAP, because the monetary loss of the identity asset's exposure was not reported in the ITAP news stories. As a result, the number of identity assets in the lowest rank is relatively higher than the rest of ranks. As we mentioned in the methodology section, we apply the dynamic method in order to refine value and risk of identity assets. The dynamic measurement has reduced around 10% (50 identity assets) of the number of identity assets in the lowest rank and those 10% of identity assets have spread into different ranks due to their accessibility and post effect.

Figure 3 shows the score distribution of the experimental Apps. In this figure, we observe that it has lots of numbers concentrated in the middle of the range, with the remaining numbers trailing off on both sides which is close to a normal distribution. The average risk score of the experimental dataset is 0.4469 or 44.69%. The identity asset that has highest risk score (which means it is most dangerous in the ITAP dataset) according to both approaches is "Social Security Number".

Like what we did in Fig. 1, we also analyze risk score with different App categories. Figure 4 shows the average score of different categories of basic and dynamic measurements. From Fig. 1 we know that category of "Communication", "Business" and "Travel & Local" request more permissions and these categories also have the highest average scores in Fig. 4. Also, category of "Weather" and "Food & Drink" do not request many permissions but are still in the higher tier of average score. On the other hand, in Fig. 5, it shows the correlation between risk score of apps and number of permissions they request. Even though not dramatically, according to the regression lines, when the number of permissions increases, the value of privacy risk score slightly increase as well.

Last but not least, we map identity assets in ITAP dataset to both privacy policy and XML file. Overall, the entire experimental dataset collects 70% of identity assets in the ITAP dataset while privacy policies collect 67% of identity assets and XML files only have 10% of identity assets which makes sense since we parse the entire privacy policy to map identity assets and meanwhile the maximum number of permissions that an app would request is only 32.

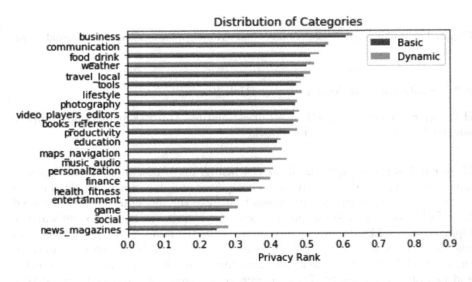

Fig. 4. The average score of different categories of basic and dynamic methods.

Evaluation of Ranking App Risk. We adopt two baselines to evaluate the effectiveness of our approaches in terms of ranking App risks. The first work was introduced in 2019 by O'Loughlin et al. [22]. They evaluated the presence and quality of a privacy policy of apps with questions that aim to assess comprehensiveness of an app's documentation in describing data collection and storage practices and policies. By answering their questions in their work, they divided the score of the privacy policy into three ranks: "Acceptable", "Questionable", and "Unacceptable". In this section, we denote this approach as "OLoughlin".

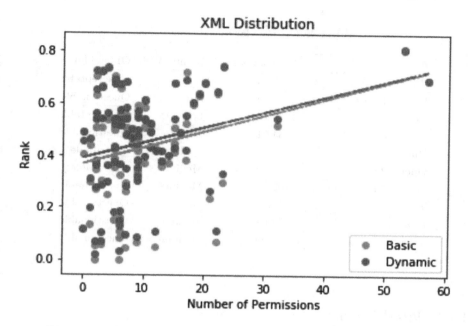

Fig. 5. The scatter diagram of number of permissions and risk score.

The other tool that we use in this comparison as baseline is the ImmuniWeb®Mobile App Scanner [2] (short for ImmuniWeb). It is a tool that develops Machine Learning and Artificial Intelligence technologies for Application Security Testing and Attack Surface Management. Their automated tests reveal several security risk flaws and weaknesses that may impact the application. We pick tests that are related to privacy and data access like *Exposure of potentially sensitive data*. The level of each risk that has been detected can be divided into four ranks: "High", "Medium", "Low", and "Warning". "High" denotes the red light which indicates that this App has higher risk with respect to the according weakness or flaw.

We pick the most popular apps in our experimental dataset to compare our dynamic approach to different measurements. Each of the popular apps has over 5 million downloads in Google Play [1]. Table 4 shows the value of each popular App returned by each approach. The table is sorted by the value of our dynamic approach. We can see that almost every app in the first half of the table are being labeled as "Low" in ImmuniWeb. First 5 apps also have higher risk scores than others in the table. Therefore, we can see that our measurement is promising. The interesting thing is that in OLoughlin, as long as the privacy policy of this app does not mention whether its server encrypts users' information or not, this app is labeled as "Unacceptable". *Duckduckgo* and *OpenVPN*, which are located in the middle of the table, are the only two apps that are labeled as "Acceptable" in OLoughlin.

Table 4. The popular open-source Apps.

App	Dynamics(%)	ImmuniWeb	OLoughlin
Wiki	43.63	Low	Unacceptable
Firefox Focus	47.99	Low	Questionable
Kodi	48.79	Low	Unacceptable
QsmAnd	54.51	Low	Questionable
Duckduckgo	67.39	Medium	Acceptable
OpenVPN	68.92	Medium	Acceptable
Signal Private Messenger	69.32	Medium	Questionable
Ted	71.82	Low	Questionable
Blockchain Wallet	73.67	Medium	Questionable
Telegram	73.99	Medium	Questionable

4   Related Work

Generally speaking, research on mobile privacy risk can be divided into three categories: mobile App's permission analysis, mobile App's privacy policy analysis, and mobile security and privacy framework.

For the first category, mobile App's permission analysis, several works have been published. More and more mobile applications are providing novel services by requesting bunch of access permissions of user's sensitive information. To understand this, for example, Au et al. [5] surveyed the permission systems of several popular smartphone operating systems and taxonomize them by the amount of control and information they provide users and the level of interactivity they require from users. Felt et al. [11] built a tool to determine the set of API calls that an application uses and then map those API calls to permissions. It generates the maximum set of permissions needed for an application and they compared them to the set of permissions actually requested.

However, these approaches are very hard to implement in practice. On the other hand, some researchers have dug into this area by constructing machine-learning-based researches. Wijesekera et al. [26] built a classifier to make privacy decisions on the user's behalf by detecting when context has changed and, when necessary, inferring privacy preferences based on the user's past decisions and behavior. It grants appropriate resource permission requests without further user intervention, denies inappropriate requests, and only prompts the user when the system is uncertain of the user's preferences. Li et al. [17] introduced Significant Permission IDentification (SigPID), a malware detection system based on permission usage analysis to cope with the rapid increase in the number of Android malware. They used several levels of pruning by mining the permission data to identify the most significant permissions. Then, they constructed machine-learning-based classifiers to classify different families of malware and benign apps.

Even so, users often do not fond of security software that frequently scan their devices. Therefore, Zhu et al. [32] introduced the techniques to automatically detect the potential security risk for each mobile App by exploiting the requested permissions. Then, they designed a mobile App recommendation system with privacy and security awareness which can provide App recommendations by considering both the Apps' popularity and the users' security preferences. However, these approaches do not take the identity assets that Apps collect. Privacy risk exists because of insecure data access. Therefore, in this work we map each permission requested by mobile Apps to several identity assets and build our own privacy risk score software.

The other category is about mobile App's privacy policy. Privacy policies help users understand what portion of their sensitive data would be collected and used or shared by a specific mobile application. However, not every application has a privacy policy. For example, Dehling et al. [9] surveyed popular medical health Apps in Apple iTunes Store and Google Play to assess the quality of medical health App's privacy policies. They found out that of the 600 most commonly used apps, only 183 had privacy policies. Liu et al. [19] examined web sites of the Fortune 500 and showed that only slightly more than 50 percent of Fortune 500 web sites provide privacy policies on their home pages. With the lack of taking user's privacy into concern, some works provide guidelines for building software and privacy policies. Harris [14] issued recommendations for mobile application developers and the mobile industry to safeguard consumer's privacy. This work provided guidance on developing strong privacy practices, translating these practices into mobile-friendly policies, and coordinating with mobile industry actors to promote comprehensive transparency.

Researchers have also begun to explore techniques for mitigating digital privacy risk. Zaeem et al. [20,27,28] proposed a technique that parses privacy policies and automatically generating summaries. They used data mining models to analyze the text of privacy policies, train their model with 400 privacy policies, and answer 10 basic questions concerning the privacy and security of user data. O'Loughlin et al. [22] reviewed data security and privacy policies of 116 mobile apps for depression. They constructed a list of questions and answer them by reviewing privacy policies. They showed that only 4% of privacy policies of mobile Apps are acceptable. Harkous et al. [13] proposed an automated framework for privacy policy analysis (Polisis). They built it with a novel hierarchy of neural-network classifiers and trained their model with 130k privacy policies. They provided PriBot which is a program that can answer users questions related to those privacy polices they have. Within 700 participants, PriBot's top-

3 answers is relevant to users for 89% of the test questions. Nevertheless, these works do not look up what sets of identity assets are being collected by those privacy policies. Our work not only map permissions but also privacy policies to identity assets.

The last category is about security and privacy frameworks for mobile Apps. People have proposed scoring framework on social media. Petkos et al. [23] proposed a privacy scoring framework for Online Social Network (OSN) users with respect to the information about them that is disclosed and that can be inferred by OSN service operators and third parties. It took into account user's personal preferences, different types of information, and inferred information. To fight against malwares, many works have been published to address data leakage problem. Rao et al. [25] presented Meddle, a platform that leverages virtual private networks (VPNs) and software middleboxes to improve transparency and control for Internet traffic from mobile systems. By controlling privacy leaks and detecting ISP interference with Internet traffic they found identity assets leaked from popular Apps and by malwares. Enck et al. [10] proposed a malware detection system named TaintDroid. "Taint" values can be assigned to sensitive data and their flow can be continuously tracked through each app execution, raising alerts when they flow to the network interface. Hornyack et al. [16] introduced AppFence. They implemented data shadowing, to prevent applications from accessing sensitive information that is not required to provide user-desired functionality, and exfiltration blocking, to block outgoing communications tainted by sensitive data. Gibler et al. [12] presented AndroidLeaks, a static analysis framework for automatically finding potential leaks of sensitive information in Android applications on a massive scale. AndroidLeaks drastically reduces the number of applications and the number of traces that a security auditor has to verify manually.

Indeed, breaches of personal sensitive information can lead to gigantic damage to uses. To understand why such significant data leakage has occurred, Zuo et al. [33] designed tools for obfuscation-resilient cloud API identification and string value analysis, and implemented them in a tool called LeakScope to identify the potential data leakage vulnerabilities from mobile apps based on how the cloud APIs are used. On the other hand, Agarwal et al. [4] proposed ProtectMyPrivacy (PMP), a crowd sourced recommendation engine, to analyze manual protection decisions, and use them to provide iOS App privacy recommendations. It detects access to private information and protects users by substituting anonymized data based on user decisions. However, all the above recommendation approaches do not take consideration of the potential identity assets collected by mobile Apps, which motivates our novel work with awareness of permissions and privacy policies, which actually covers first and second categories.

5   Conclusion

In this paper, we sought to understand the privacy risk of the set of Personally Identifiable Information (PII), or identity assets, collected, used and shared by mobile applications. Each mobile App has a set of data access permissions and a privacy policy. Therefore, we sought to estimate the privacy risk score of each mobile App by investigating the set of identity assets that each mobile App collects, according to its privacy policy and data access permissions.

Our approaches leveraged the identity assets collected from these mobile apps and cross-referenced these PII to a list of over 600 identity assets collected in the Identity Theft Assessment and Prediction (ITAP) project at The University of Texas at Austin. The ITAP project investigates theft and fraud user stories to assess how identity asset is monetized and the risk (likelihood) of respective identity assets to be stolen and/or fraudulently used. From these mobile apps, our results indicate that 67% of the over 600 reference identity assets were being collected by our sample dataset of 100 Android apps.

In this work, we proposed two approaches to estimate the privacy risk score of each mobile App. First approach is called Basic Measurement. It utilized the intrinsic characteristics of each identity asset to calculate the privacy risk score of each identity asset. The second approach is called Dynamic Measurement. It utilized two parameters that resulted from UT CID probabilistic models and Bayesian inference tool to refine the original risk of exposure and value of monetary loss. Our comparison with other researchers' work showed that our approaches are promising.

This work was the first to study privacy policies and permissions of mobile apps in terms of the identity assets collected, used and shared. We further studied those identity assets in the context of a personal data reference model built by the UT CID Identity Ecosystem and ITAP projects. This research provided a program to generate privacy risk score of each open-source mobile App and gave an empirical study of 100 open-source mobile Apps in different categories.

Acknowledgments. This work was in part funded by the Center for Identity's Strategic Partners. The complete list of Partners can be found at the following URL: https://identity.utexas.edu/strategic-partners.

References

1. Google Play. https://play.google.com/store
2. Immuniweb® Mobile App Scanner. https://www.htbridge.com
3. Itap Report 2019. Tech. rep., Center for Identity, University of Texas at Austin (2019)
4. Agarwal, Y., Hall, M.: ProtectMyPrivacy: detecting and mitigating privacy leaks on iOS devices using crowdsourcing, pp. 97–110 (June 2013). https://doi.org/10.1145/2462456.2464460
5. Au, K., Zhou, Y., Huang, Z., Gill, P., Lie, D.: Short paper: a look at smartphone permission models. In: Proceedings of the 1st ACM Workshop on Security and Privacy in Smartphones and Mobile Devices (October 2011). https://doi.org/10.1145/2046614.2046626
6. Chang, K.C., Zaeem, R.N., Barber, K.S.: Enhancing and evaluating identity privacy and authentication strength by utilizing the identity ecosystem. In: Proceedings of the 2018 Workshop on Privacy in the Electronic Society, pp. 114–120. ACM (2018)

7. Chang, K.C., Zaeem, R.N., Barber, K.S.: Internet of Things: securing the identity by analyzing ecosystem models of devices and organizations. In: 2018 AAAI Spring Symposium Series (2018)
8. Chen, C.J., Zaeem, R.N., Barber, K.S.: Statistical analysis of identity risk of exposure and cost using the ecosystem of identity attributes. In: 2019 European Intelligence and Security Informatics Conference (EISIC), pp. 32–39. IEEE (2019)
9. Dehling, T., Sunyaev, A., Taylor, P.L., Mandl, K.D.: Availability and quality of mobile health app privacy policies. J. Am. Med. Inform. Assoc. **22**(e1), e28–e33 (2014). https://doi.org/10.1136/amiajnl-2013-002605
10. Enck, W., et al.: TaintDroid: an information-flow tracking system for realtime privacy monitoring on smartphones. ACM Trans. Comput. Syst. **32**(2), 5:1–5:29 (2014). https://doi.org/10.1145/2619091
11. Felt, A.P., Chin, E., Hanna, S., Song, D., Wagner, D.: Android permissions demystified. In: Proceedings of the 18th ACM Conference on Computer and Communications Security, CCS 2011, pp. 627–638. Association for Computing Machinery, New York (2011). https://doi.org/10.1145/2046707.2046779
12. Gibler, C., Crussell, J., Erickson, J., Chen, H.: AndroidLeaks: automatically detecting potential privacy leaks in Android applications on a large scale. In: Katzenbeisser, S., Weippl, E., Camp, L.J., Volkamer, M., Reiter, M., Zhang, X. (eds.) Trust 2012. LNCS, vol. 7344, pp. 291–307. Springer, Heidelberg (2012). https://doi.org/10.1007/978-3-642-30921-2_17
13. Harkous, H., Fawaz, K., Lebret, R., Schaub, F., Shin, K.G., Aberer, K.: Polisis: automated analysis and presentation of privacy policies using deep learning. In: 27th USENIX Security Symposium (USENIX Security 2018), pp. 531–548. USENIX Association, Baltimore (August 2018). https://www.usenix.org/conference/usenixsecurity18/presentation/harkous
14. Harris, K.D.: Privacy on the go. Tech. rep., California Department of Justice (2013)
15. Hart, K.: Privacy policies are read by an aging few. Tech. rep. (2019)
16. Hornyack, P., Han, S., Jung, J., Schechter, S., Wetherall, D.: These aren't the droids you're looking for: retrofitting android to protect data from imperious applications. In: Proceedings of the 18th ACM Conference on Computer and Communications Security, CCS 2011, pp. 639–652. ACM, New York (2011). https://doi.org/10.1145/2046707.2046780
17. Li, J., Sun, L., Yan, Q., Li, Z., Srisa-an, W., Ye, H.: Significant permission identification for machine-learning-based Android malware detection. IEEE Trans. Ind. Inform. **14**(7), 3216–3225 (2018)
18. Liau, D., Zaeem, R.N., Barber, K.S.: Evaluation framework for future privacy protection systems: a dynamic identity ecosystem approach. In: 2019 17th International Conference on Privacy, Security and Trust (PST), pp. 1–3. IEEE (2019)
19. Liu, C., Arnett, K.P.: An examination of privacy policies in fortune 500 web sites. Am. J. Bus. **17**(1), 13–22 (2002). https://doi.org/10.1108/19355181200200001
20. Nokhbeh Zaeem, R., Barber, K.S.: A study of web privacy policies across industries. J. Inf. Priv. Secur. **13**(4), 169–185 (2017)
21. Zaeem, R.N., Budalakoti, S., Barber, K.S., Rasheed, M., Bajaj, C.: Predicting and explaining identity risk, exposure and cost using the ecosystem of identity attributes. In: 2016 IEEE International Carnahan Conference on Security Technology (ICCST), pp. 1–8. IEEE (2016)
22. O'Loughlin, K., Neary, M., Adkins, E.C., Schueller, S.M.: Reviewing the data security and privacy policies of mobile apps for depression. Internet Interv. **15**, 110–115 (2019). https://doi.org/10.1016/j.invent.2018.12.001. http://www.sciencedirect.com/science/article/pii/S2214782918300460

23. Petkos, G., Papadopoulos, S., Kompatsiaris, Y.: PScore: a framework for enhancing privacy awareness in online social networks. In: 2015 10th International Conference on Availability, Reliability and Security, pp. 592–600 (2015)
24. Rana, R., Zaeem, R.N., Barber, K.S.: Us-centric vs. international personally identifiable information: a comparison using the UT CID identity ecosystem. In: 2018 International Carnahan Conference on Security Technology (ICCST), pp. 1–5. IEEE (2018)
25. Raoa, A., et al.: Using the middle to meddle with mobile. Tech. rep., Northeastern University (2013)
26. Wijesekera, P., et al.: The feasibility of dynamically granted permissions: aligning mobile privacy with user preferences. In: 2017 IEEE Symposium on Security and Privacy (SP), pp. 1077–1093 (2017)
27. Zaeem, R.N., Barber, K.S.: The effect of the GDPR on privacy policies: recent progress and future promise. ACM Trans. Manag. Inf. Syst. (2020). to Appear
28. Zaeem, R.N., German, R.L., Barber, K.S.: PrivacyCheck: automatic summarization of privacy policies using data mining. ACM Trans. Internet Technol. **18**(4), 1–18 (2018). https://doi.org/10.1145/3127519
29. Zaeem, R.N., Manoharan, M., Barber, K.S.: Risk kit: highlighting vulnerable identity assets for specific age groups. In: 2016 European Intelligence and Security Informatics Conference (EISIC), pp. 32–38. IEEE (2016)
30. Zaeem, R.N., Manoharan, M., Yang, Y., Barber, K.S.: Modeling and analysis of identity threat behaviors through text mining of identity theft stories. Comput. Secur. **65**, 50–63 (2017)
31. Zaiss, J., Nokhbeh Zaeem, R., Barber, K.S.: Identity threat assessment and prediction. J. Consum. Aff. **53**(1), 58–70 (2019). https://doi.org/10.1111/joca.12191
32. Zhu, H., Xiong, H., Ge, Y., Chen, E.: Mobile app recommendations with security and privacy awareness. In: Proceedings of the 20th ACM SIGKDD International Conference on Knowledge Discovery and Data Mining, KDD 2014, pp. 951–960. Association for Computing Machinery, New York (2014). https://doi.org/10.1145/2623330.2623705
33. Zuo, C., Lin, Z., Zhang, Y.: Why does your data leak? Uncovering the data leakage in cloud from mobile apps. In: 2019 IEEE Symposium on Security and Privacy (SP), pp. 1296–1310 (2019)

On the Struggle Bus: A Detailed Security Analysis of the m-tickets App

Jorge Sanz Maroto, Haoyu Liu, and Paul Patras[✉]

School of Informatics, The University of Edinburgh, Edinburgh, UK
paul.patras@ed.ac.uk

Abstract. The growing shift from private to public transportation and the increasing use of smartphones have lead to the development of digital transport ticketing systems. Such systems allow transport operators to enhance their services and income, therefore are important assets that require secure implementation and protocols. This paper uncovers a range of vulnerabilities in the m-tickets app used by Lothian Buses, one of the leading transport operators in the United Kingdom (UK). The vulnerabilities identified enable attackers to predict, reactivate and modify tickets, all of which can have damaging consequences to the operator's business. We further reveal poor implementation of encryption mechanisms, which can lead to information leakage, as well as how adversaries could harness the operator's infrastructure to launch Denial of Service attacks. We propose several improvements to mitigate the weaknesses identified, in particular an alternative digital ticketing system, which can serve as a blueprint for increasing the robustness of similar apps.

Keywords: Mobile app security · Reverse-engineering · Information leakage

1 Introduction

As of 2020, 3.5 billion smartphones have been produced [12], equivalent to 45.1% of the world population. The transportation industry is catching up with this trend and transitioning from cash-based ticketing systems to digital tickets. In a market that was estimated to be worth $500 billion in 2017 [13], the economic impact of public transport ticketing apps is ever-growing. As these systems become more widespread, it is vital that their operation cannot be tampered with for illicit purposes and user data remain protected.

This paper investigates the security and robustness of **m-tickets**, a popular local transport ticketing app deployed among others by Lothian Buses. Lothian Buses manages the majority of public transport operations in Edinburgh, UK, and the Lothian region; it is also the biggest public municipal bus company in the UK, serving approximately 2.3 million passengers per week with a fleet of over 840 buses, and has a daily revenue of approximately £440,000 [9]. We use this as a case study to reveal multiple weaknesses public transport ticketing apps suffer

© Springer Nature Switzerland AG 2020
W. Susilo et al. (Eds.): ISC 2020, LNCS 12472, pp. 234–252, 2020.
https://doi.org/10.1007/978-3-030-62974-8_14

from, including the prediction of tickets and availability issues. Additionally, we propose solutions to the problems identified, in order to improve the security of such systems, whilst maintaining the intended functionality of the official apps.

Prior Work. One of the most notable vulnerabilities in the UK public transport ticketing system was discovered by two Dutch security researchers in 2008 [15]. By exploiting the fact that the older version of the London transport system's Oyster card used Mifare 1k chips, the researchers were able to extract an Oyster card's encryption key and use this to clone and modify other cards as desired. This led to a swap of all Oyster cards in circulation with newly developed, encrypted cards, despite the massive cost incurred.

In terms of transport apps, *get me there*, which can be used for purchasing tickets valid in the Greater Manchester Metrolink tram system, was recently compromised, allowing hackers to create free tickets and defraud operators [14], while posting the methodology used on Reddit [11]. The group explained how they were able to extract the private keys used to build the ticket QR codes directly from the source code, making the findings public without responsible disclosure. The app was developed by *Corethree*, the same company that developed the app in used by Lothian Buses, which we scrutinise in this study.

Contributions. To the best of our knowledge, there are no scientific papers undertaking a formal security analysis on public transportation apps. This paper aims to fill this important gap and stimulate further research on this topic. As such, we make the following key contributions:

1. We reverse-engineer the m-tickets app, revealing an exploit that enables to predict valid tickets for any future date; additionally, we devise a method to modify the characteristics of any given ticket.
2. We design a simple app that works side by side with the official one, to reactivate old, expired tickets, thereby converting a single ticket purchase into an unlimited source of tickets.
3. We propose an alternative system to fix all the vulnerabilities identified and preserve the intended app functionality.

Responsible Disclosure. Prior to the submission of this manuscript, we contacted both the transport operator using this app and the company developing the app, to disclose the vulnerabilities found. The developers are now aware of the problems we discovered and are working towards fixing these vulnerabilities.

2   The M-Tickets App

Lothian Buses is a company primarily owned by The City of Edinburgh Council (91% ownership), which operates the majority of bus services that run in Edinburgh and some throughout the surrounding Midlothian, East Lothian and West Lothian counties. The so called *Lothian City* division provides the local bus operations with an extensive network of routes that are active 24 h/day, 365

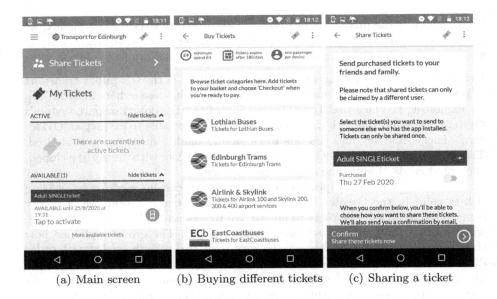

(a) Main screen   (b) Buying different tickets   (c) Sharing a ticket

Fig. 1. Screenshots of the functionality of the m-tickets app.

days/year. In addition, the company owns four other divisions with a focus on sightseeing, private services, and commuter routes.

Given the size of its customer base and the rapid uptake of mobile technology, the company has adopted a mobile app to offer a ticket purchasing and storage service to users. The m-tickets app is developed by *Corethree*, an award winning company [1] specialised in solving the ticketing challenges faced by public and private transport companies. Some of the apps in the company's portfolio serve Transport for Greater Manchester, Transport of London, Northern Link Ferries, Translink, and many more. The m-tickets app is compiled from the same source code for both Android and iOS platforms, has over 200,000 downloads, and we estimate 20%–35% of these correspond to active users [16]. Using the number of weekly customers, we expect the Lothian Buses app accounts for 12.2%–21.3% of the tickets purchased on a daily basis, generating between £19.5 and £34.2 million in revenue per year. Even though this is clearly an important asset for the company, the app was known to have several connectivity and availability problems [6], which we investigate in depth in this paper.

In this work, we focus on the Android version of the app, specifically version 9.7 released on the 17th of July 2019, which at the time of writing is the latest version. Once the app is opened, the user is greeted with a screen displaying the number of tickets available or active (see Fig. 1a). The user has the option to buy (Fig. 1b) or share (Fig. 1c) tickets displayed next to the available ones. Ticket sharing is performed by asking the user for the recipient's email address. The recipient will receive an email containing a hyperlink that, once clicked, adds the sent tickets to their respective list of available tickets. Both sharing and buying of tickets are not available without Internet access.

3   Adversary Model

We expect an attacker to already have a copy of the Android app and have basic understanding of the Android app ecosystem. Additionally, we expect the adversary to have some reverse-engineering knowledge and the appropriate tools to intercept traffic from and to the app. Lastly, the attacker would have basic networking and programming knowledge, enough to identify vulnerable code.

Parts of the app that may be prone to attacks and possible scenarios include:

1. **Financial Interest.** The app's main purpose is to provide tickets to users; however, this has an implied given cost. An attacker may attempt to exploit this application to overcome the financial burden, by figuring out a way of obtaining valid tickets without paying.
2. **Denial of Service.** Attackers may attempt to take control of the resources used by the transport operator and seek to disrupt the standard behavior of the app or servers. This may involve flooding target victims with unsolicited messages, which in the process can also harm the reputation of the operator, as the source of the hijacked resources would be attributed to them.
3. **Reputation Damage.** In addition, hacktivists may seek to publish on dedicated platformed (e.g. Pastebin) information about how to obtain free tickets, simply due to a certain ideology.
4. **Privacy Breach.** Attackers may also seek to leak databases or files containing information about the users of the m-tickets app. This would be done for financial gains or, again, to harm the company's reputation.

4   Methodology

4.1   Vulnerability Analysis

To study the app, we employ both **Static Analysis**, reverse-engineering and code auditing whilst the app is *not* running, and **Dynamic Analysis**, which covers any activity and tests done whilst the app *is* running.

Static Analysis: We first reverse-engineer the Android application package (APK) of m-ticket by using *dex2jar*[1] and *jd-gui*.[2] *dex2jar* is a tool that decompiles the .dex file inside the APK to a .jar file, which is a combination of Java

---

[1] dex2jar Github, https://github.com/pxb1988/dex2jar.
[2] Java Decompiler, http://java-decompiler.github.io/.

classes aggregated as a single file; *jd-gui* further unpacks a .jar file into separate .class files. Some degree of obfuscation is inherently implemented during the compilation of the APK, which means our reverse-engineered code loses all the method and property names. However, given the fact that Java is a static strong typed language, class names are still well preserved, which can reveal sufficient information for subsequent analysis.

A careful analysis reveals that no functionality is implemented in Java per se. Instead a NOTICE file indicates that the core functionality is implemented using the *Xamarin* cross-platform C# application development tool,[3] which allows creating a single application in C# that can be compiled into Android, iOS, and Windows apps. Indeed, C# code was compiled with MonoVM to shared objects and the Java code is responsible for linking the classes in the shared objects and constructing the overall functionality of the app.

Knowing that the overall functionality lies in the shared objects, we extract the C# code from these objects, seeking to understand the functionality of the app and reverse-engineer its features. Shared objects built with Xamarin act as wrappers of Dynamic-Link Libraries (DLLs), which hold the actual functionality of the app. We extract these DLLs using a small script [2]. Lastly, we use *JetBrains dotPeek*[4] to decompile DLLs and retrieve the original source code.

Overall, the app consists of 88 DLLs with a total of 9,990 classes. However, the main functionality of the app is within the *Core* DLL, with 282 classes.

Dynamic Analysis: We split the dynamic analysis into two different phases: one concerning the communications between the app and the server, and the second focusing on analysing the internals of the app and what is stored in the phone once the app is installed.

Phone Internals: Android is a mobile operating system based on the Linux kernel. The default installation restricts the access to multiple files, in order to prevent novice users from deleting/modifying critical functionality. However, this also means that the default version of Android does not allow a user to view the files any app uses/creates. Therefore, in order to further analyse the behaviour of the app, we use a rooted Android phone. *Rooting* is the process of allowing Android smartphone users to attain privileged control of the operating system; this can be done by asking the manufacturer of the phone to provide a code to de-activate the smartphone's protections. With a rooted phone, we can see what files our target m-tickets app would use upon execution. All the app-related information is stored in the **/data/data** folder as shown below:

---

[3] Xamarin, https://dotnet.microsoft.com/apps/xamarin.

[4] dotPeek – Free .NET Decompiler and Assembly Browser, https://www.jetbrains. com/decompiler/.

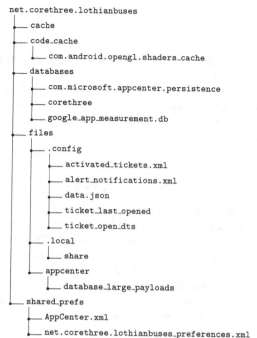

```
net.corethree.lothianbuses
├── cache
├── code_cache
│   └── com.android.opengl.shaders_cache
├── databases
│   ├── com.microsoft.appcenter.persistence
│   ├── corethree
│   └── google_app_measurement.db
├── files
│   ├── .config
│   │   ├── activated_tickets.xml
│   │   ├── alert_notifications.xml
│   │   ├── data.json
│   │   ├── ticket_last_opened
│   │   └── ticket_open_dts
│   ├── .local
│   │   └── share
│   └── appcenter
│       └── database_large_payloads
└── shared_prefs
    ├── AppCenter.xml
    └── net.corethree.lothianbuses_preferences.xml
```

We are now able to read and analyse all information the app saves and how information storage is handled. Nevertheless, to be able to modify this information, we first need to disable *Security-Enhanced Linux*, a kernel security module that provides a mechanism for supporting access-control security policies. In this case, it would not allow the execution of any program, if there was any tampering of the files by an external process. This avoids malicious apps from stealing data from other apps. In order to disable SE-Linux, it is sufficient to obtain a root shell via the Android Debug Bridge (adb), and type `setenforce 0`.

Additionally, there are occasions where the behaviour of the app may be unexpected, therefore we also use *Frida*[5] to trace events. Frida is a dynamic code instrumentation toolkit that allows the injection of snippets of JavaScript or own library into native Android apps. We use this tool to trace the files being opened at certain points or which functions were triggered at certain times.

Communications: Modern day apps consist of two main parts: the app itself and the server with which it communicates. On the app side, we perform static analysis and examine the phone internals. However, the extraction of information from the server is not straightforward and we can only attempt "black box" penetration testing. This consists of performing a vulnerability analysis without access to any of the server's source code. As such, we can observe what messages go to and come from the server, but not the server's inner logic, which makes it hard to identify flaws.

---

[5] Fida analyzer, https://frida.re/docs/android/.

For this part, we built a man-in-the-middle (MITM) setup, using an Alfa Atheros AR9271 Wi-Fi adaptor to set up a controlled hot spot on a laptop, to which the phone connects. We then route the traffic from the adaptor to Burp,[6] an integrated platform for performing security testing of web applications. Additionally, we install Burp certificates on the phone, so that the phone would trust the communications. Finally, the laptop connects to the Internet using its integrated Wi-Fi adopter, thereby allowing to intercept and modify whatever the app running on the phone sends and receives from the server.

We notice the phone compresses requests prior to transmission, hence we load a dedicated module into Burp to decompress requests for inspection.

4.2   Connectivity and Availability Analysis

A key concern for Lothian Buses app users is the app's availability. It has been reported that in some cases the app would stop working and require Internet connection in order to start, or would take too long to launch even when a connection is available [7]. Therefore, we analyse the minimum Internet connection speed required and the amount of bandwidth consumed when the app launches.

To this end, we use *BradyBound*,[7] an app that throttles the phone's Internet connection speed down to a user-defined value. Furthermore, we track the amount of data consumed by simply accessing *Settings>Apps>m-tickets>Data_usage* before and after starting the application, and calculating the difference. We execute all tests with a Motorola Moto G (3rd Generation) running Android v6.0.1.

5   Security Analysis

In this section we describe in detail the vulnerabilities found using the methodology described previously. Most weaknesses are exploited when the phone is off-line, taking advantage of the fact that the app can work without Internet access. We reveal how to predict, duplicate, and modify tickets as explained next. We also describe several functionality problems encountered in the app.

5.1   Generation of Tickets

One of the main goals of our study is to assess how securely ticket generation is handled and how difficult it would be for an attacker to craft valid tickets while evading payment. In order to accomplish this, we first need to understand how the app generates a legitimate ticket.

Once a ticket is purchased, the user has the option to activate it whenever they board the bus. An activated ticket has a certain expiration time, which depends on ticket type (e.g. single ticket, day ticket, etc.), which bus drivers can check when presented with a view of the running app, as exemplified in Fig. 2. The ticket comprises several distinctive elements:

---

[6] Burp analyzer, https://portswigger.net/burp.

[7] BradyBound, https://m.apkpure.com/bradybound/com.oxplot.bradybound.

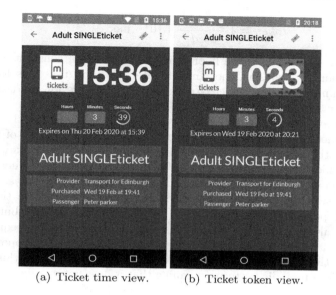

(a) Ticket time view.   (b) Ticket token view.

Fig. 2. Screenshots of an active ticket, alternating between a view of the current time (left) and the daily token (right).

- *Top Title* – Describes the ticket type at the top of the ticket.
- *Watermark* – Visible in the central part of the ticket, comprising the m-tickets logo and a dynamic text block showing the current time and a numeric **token** on a changing background, in an alternating fashion. The numeric token is the same for all tickets activated during the same day, i.e. it is not unique to a ticket.
- *Remaining time* – Small countdown in the centre showing the remaining time until the ticket becomes invalid.
- *Lower body* – Shows information including ticket type, ticket provider, date of purchase, and passenger's name.

One implementation decisions made by the app developer is the activation and generation of tickets without Internet connectivity. The downside to this is that the app itself is in charge of generating the ticket, and not the server. This means an attacker with access to the source code could attempt to understand and replicate the process of generating tickets. Clearly, the numeric token is what bus drivers check in order to decide whether a ticket is valid. Hence, understanding how valid numeric tokens are obtained can compromise the underlying mechanism.

Analysing the source-code, one particular function stands out, namely `Gener- ateWatermark()`, located inside the `Core.Utilities` module. This function will be called whenever a ticket is activated, performing the following computation:

$$token = \left\lfloor \frac{(x-c)^2}{seed} \times 10^4 \mod 10^4 \right\rfloor, \tag{1}$$

where $\lfloor \cdot \rfloor : \mathbb{R} \to \mathbb{Z}$ denotes the floor function, c is a date constant with value 01/01/1990 and x represent the current date. The app uses this formula to create the numeric tokens, which are displayed to drivers for validation when the passenger is boarding the bus.

To accurately predict a token, it is necessary to understand how the *seed* variable is obtained. By performing a text pattern search through all of the app's files, we identify a particularly interesting string, namely ``Ticket.Seed'': ``71473'', located in `files/.config/data.json`. Creating numeric tokens with the logic shown above and this *seed* value across different days, and comparing against tokens for the same days embedded in legitimate tickets, the values match perfectly. This means that the alleged *seed* is nothing but a hidden hard-coded value, rather than an actual seed of a pseudo-random sequence.

Besides, although the existence of the modulo and the floor operations in Eq. 1 makes this computation irreversible, we show in Fig. 3 that this function exhibits obvious periodic patterns, meaning that it does not qualify as a one-way function.

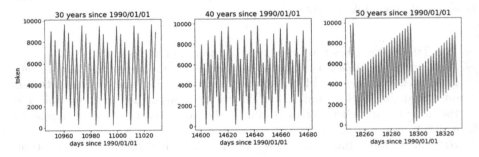

Fig. 3. Graphical illustration of token values, as the time since 01/01/1990 grows.

As shown in Fig. 3, the mapping between current date x and the token value presents a period-like relation, and the period gradually becomes longer as more time elapses from the fixed referenced date c. Thus an attacker can simply modify the system date and collect some data to recover the underlying function through trial and error.

Finding: An attacker can retrieve the procedure and relevant variables (which are unfortunately hard-coded) from the app source code, easily generate a valid numeric token for the current day, and embed that into a Graphics Interchange Format (GIF) image that resembles a genuine ticket, thereby evading payment. We also conclude that reverse-engineering of the application is not necessarily needed to predict the token of any future date, since the token generation algorithm reveals naive periodic patterns.

5.2   Re-activation of Expired Tickets

If one can already predict tickets, what would be the purpose of reactivating expired tickets? Predicting a ticket is one thing, but generating animated images on a phone is not straightforward. An attacker may need to replicate the layout of the official app to perfection and build a new app from scratch in order to exploit the vulnerability discussed in the previous subsection.

Therefore, we investigate whether it may be possible to reactivate an expired ticket, by analysing how the app saves the state of tickets. To this end, we examine the changes made on the app whenever a ticket is activated, first saving all the files in the home directory of the app prior to the activation of a ticket, then comparing them against those changed after the ticket expired.

```
1  try {
2      Runtime.getRuntime().exec("su -c rm -rf /data/data/net.corethree.
           lothianbuses");
3      Runtime.getRuntime().exec("su -c rm /sdcard/.storage/atl.txt");
4      Runtime.getRuntime().exec("su -c cp -rp /data/data/tickets /data/data
           /net.corethree.lothianbuses");
5      Toast errorToast = Toast.makeText(MainActivity.this, "Tickets
           restored!", Toast.LENGTH_SHORT);
6      errorToast.show();
7  } catch (IOException e) {
8      Toast errorToast = Toast.makeText(MainActivity.this, "Was not
           successfull!", Toast.LENGTH_SHORT);
9      errorToast.show();
10 }
```

Fig. 4. Source code of demo app exploiting ticket re-activation vulnerability uncovered.

Most files seem to be modified, however the app would not make any requests over the Internet connection. All of the modified files are inside the net.corethree.lothianbuses folder, except for a small /.storage/atl.txt file created after the activation of the first ticket. After analysing the decompiled app code, it is clear that this file is just a back up of activated_tickets.xml, a file used to store the serialised activated tickets. This means that the content of net.corethree.lothianbuses is the representation of the state of the app. Hence, we can save its contents, activate as many tickets as previously purchased, and then swap the saved folder with the one used by the app, thereby restoring all the tickets as if the app was never opened in the first place. To facilitate repeated testing of this vulnerability and demonstrate the simplicity of the attack, we build a small app, which exploits this process, as detailed in Fig. 4.

In the above, we save the state of net.corethree.lothianbuses into a folder called tickets, and then use the app to substitute the files in the official app with those saved in this folder. However, it appears that after one week of testing, the vulnerability can no longer be exploited. Since our exploit would return to the state of the app after purchasing the tickets, from the apps point of view we

```
1  DateTime universalTime = app.CheckInLastSuccessfulTimestamp.ToUTCDateTime
       ().ToUniversalTime();
2          if (universalTime < DateTime.UtcNow.AddDays(-5.0))
3              app.CheckIn_BlockSession = true;
4          else if (universalTime < DateTime.UtcNow.AddDays(-3.0))
5              app.CheckIn_ShowWarning = true;
```

Fig. 5. Code snippet mitigating the reactivation of expired tickets.

had not been connected to the Internet for more than 5 days, which is one of the security measures that Corethree seem to have implemented. However, by the very fact that this is a response to a certain event, we expect to find the relevant implementation in the app's source code. Indeed, the code checks if the value CheckInLastSuccessfulTimestamp minus 5 days is less than 0, as shown in Fig. 5, where CheckInLastSuccessfulTimestamp was extracted from the timestamp saved as CILST in the net.corethree.lothianbuses_preferences.xml file, as shown in Fig. 6 (see line 4).

```
1  <?xml version='1.0' encoding='utf-8' standalone='yes' ?>
2  <map>
3  ...
4    <string name="CILST">2020-03-02 14:47:50Z</string>
5  <string name="ShowVouchersDownloadedNotifications">True</string>
6  <string name="NSSC">b0cc9f95ba012d9c3cca728af8379307</string>
7  ...
8  </map>
```

Fig. 6. Excerpt from XML file containing m-tickets app preferences.

However, the app does not check whether CILST is larger than the current time, meaning that an attacker can set the CILST to year 2030, and the exploit would work for the next 10 years.

Finding: By restoring the application state prior to ticket activation and modifying the XML file containing the app preferences, an attacker can reactivate expired tickets, which stay valid for any specified duration.

5.3   Modification of Tickets

Being able to re-activate tickets, next we explore the different type of tickets the app offers and whether these could be modified by an adversary. Excluding the fact that the app offers different tickets for different routes, there are 2 main type of tickets: *Single-Adult* and *All-day* tickets. We purchase both types and activate them on the same day, to understand the technical difference between them. Perhaps unsurprisingly, the two are virtually the same, except that a user has 5 min to use a *Single-Adult*, whilst the *All-day* ticket can be used for 24 h.

```
 1   ...
 2   "Name":"Adult SINGLEticket",
 3   "Subtitle":"Purchased Wednesday, 19 February 2020",
 4   "SortOrder":"0",
 5   "TTL":"3600",
 6   "Language":"",
 7   "TimeStamp":"2020-02-19T19:41:49.436Z",
 8   "CommonChildType":"Node",
 9   "AncestorIDArray":["pXTloFK","tgadTUCW_paymentsuccess"],
10   "ComparisonHash":"3f484560fc614c438f194b5f419b88be",
11   "Lifetime":5,
12   "Interval":0,
13   "Tags":{"Voucher.TypeID":"792c-56f8-403d-aed1-8e11af0",
14   ...
15 }
```

Fig. 7. JSON fragment of an Adult Single ticket.

Knowing this, we analyse how the app identifies and stores different type of tickets, and find that the majority of ticket data is stored in the `data.json` file. The file is relatively large, containing information such as the app's layout, user tokens, URLs from where to download images and, most importantly, the characteristics of purchased tickets, as exemplified in Fig. 7.

Examining Fig. 7, note that tickets are defined by a JSON structure, which encompasses their characteristics. Therefore, our first attempt is to change the values of a *Single-Adult* ticket to those of an *All-day* ticket. However, after modifying `data.json`, the app would not open without an Internet connection, suggesting a security provision was implemented to prevent this exploit. We then use the Frida framework to trace precisely what happens internally when the app blocks the modified `data.json`. The trace reveals that both `data.json` and `lothianbuses_preferences.xml` are opened at program execution start. Reviewing the code again and identifying where these files are being used, it appears `data.json` is hashed with `ContentRoot` and the devices GUID, which are given in the `lothianbuses_preferences.xml` file. The hash is then compared with the value stored into NSSC (line 6 in Fig. 6). This procedure is illustrated in Fig. 8. Therefore, an attacker aiming to modify anything in the app, should change the hash stored in NSSC for a new one that passes the checks.

```
1  function onStart(context){
2    content_root = extract_from_preferences("ContentRoot");
3    nssc = extract_from_preferences("NSSC");
4    data_json_str = read_file("data.json");
5    md5 = MD5(data_json_str + "|" + content_root + "|" + context.guid);
6    if (md5 == nssc){ parse_tickets(); }
7    else{ delete_history(); }
8  }
```

Fig. 8. Pseudocode of procedure implemented by the m-tickets app to avoid modification of ticket characteristics. By reversing the hashing applied and retrieving key variables stored by the app, this can be circumvented.

```
1  salt = "3497788798ffff545zhif8";
2  shared_secret = "b70f578f-974d-4efd-a93a-43c8b4f6cd9d";
3  function encrypt(plaintext){
4      prs = HMACSHA1(shared_secret, salt); # pseudo-random string
5      key = prs[: key_size / 8];
6      IV = prs[: block_size / 8];
7      cipher = AES(IV, key, plaintext);
8      ciphertext = base64_encode(cipher);
9      return ciphertext;
10 }
```

Fig. 9. Encryption logic implemented by the m-tickets app.

Since the hash is crafted based on values that we already have, we can write a small C# script to replicate the creation of the hash and use it to modify the app. We are now able to change any of the characteristics of a ticket. For example, we could make a single Adult ticket last for months, if we changed the ticket's "Lifetime" property.

Finding: By replicating the hashing mechanism applied to the tickets data store and overwriting key variables in the m-tickets preferences file, an attacker can extend the lifetime of tickets at will.

5.4   Hard-Coded Keys and Tokens

After decompiling the app, we notice that some of the information being stored is encrypted, since the developers included custom cryptography classes in addition to imported C# crypto libraries. Although our proposed attacks do not exploit any encrypted information, it is still worth analysing the encryption algorithms, so as to understand if any potential weakness may exist once new functionalities or features are integrated into m-ticket.

The app adopts the Advanced Encryption Standard with Cipher Block Chaining (AES-CBC), a block cipher encryption scheme commonly used to provide strong confidential guarantees [4]. This algorithm uses three key instruments to ensure secrecy: a salt, an Initialisation Vector (IV), and a key. The salt is used to avoid brute-force attacks against the resulting cipher-text, the IV ensures semantic security, and the key is used to encrypt the actual plain-text. This algorithm by design is robust against both passive and active adversaries, but unfortunately, our analysis reveals that it is not utilised correctly, resulting in possible information leakage.

As shown in Fig. 9, both the key and IV are derived from a salt and a shared secret, which turn out to be hard-coded right above the encryption function (lines 1–2). That is to say, as long as an attacker obtains these strings, any encrypted information can be easily deciphered on Android phones. Whilst it is obvious that the seeds and secrets have to be stored locally for the program to work in an offline environment, the developers should have been mindful of how easy it is to decompile apps.

Finding: Although state-of-the-art encryption is adopted, key elements aimed at ensuring secrecy are hard-coded in the m-tickets app. Hence cipher-text is straightforward to reverse.

5.5   Root Checker Bypass and Enabling Screenshots

A key step in exploiting the re-activation and modification of tickets is the ability to have full control of the phone (root access), while maintaining full use of the app. For this reason, checking whether the app has a root checker was one of our first priorities after decompiling. Corethree implement a root checker function that looks for certain files or binaries, denying access to the app if found, as revealed in Fig. 10. Unfortunately, having a rooted phone, the system is not to be trusted. In this case the app asks the system to look for certain files, but since an attacker controls the system, they can manipulate the response stating that the relevant files do not exist. To showcase this, we use *Magisk hide*, a module of the Magisk manager,[8] which hides the root files from whatever app it is instructed to.

```
1  public bool isDeviceRooted(Context context)
2      {
3        return  tags.Contains("test-keys") ||
4            File.Exists("/system/app/Superuser.apk") ||
5            executeCommand(check_su_binary) != null ||
6            isPackageInstalled("eu.chainfire.supersu") ||
7            findBinary("su");
8      }
```

Fig. 10. m-tickets root checker function.

Another feature Corethree implemented in the app is the inability to take screenshots whilst the app is in use, so as to prevent users from sharing screenshots of purchased tickets. However, if an attacker has root access to their phone, they can disable the permission granted to apps to block screenshots. In our case we used the *smali patcher* module from the Magisk rooter.

Finding: The app root checker can be bypassed, thereby enabling reverse-engineering and modifying of the original app functionality.

5.6   Password Reset Issues

The majority of vulnerabilities found up to now were in the app source code. However, one part of the ticketing ecosystem we do not have access to is the source code of the server logic. Hence, we carry out a "black box" analysis, by which we intercept the network traffic towards/from the server and seek to

---

[8] Magisk, https://magiskmanager.com/.

make sense of the back-end. In particular, we uncover two main problems with the password reset procedure.

To understand the vulnerabilities, let us first examine the standard behavior of a password reset. After requesting a password rest, the user would receive a URL of the form https://passwordreset.corethree.net/<11upper-lower-casecharacters>. This link would expire within 75 min after the reset request. However, it appears the user could request a password reset as may times as desired and the server would send a new link to reset the password, without invalidating the old one. This means that an attacker could request many resets and increase the probability of guessing the victim's password reset link. Arguably, the probability of brute-forcing a valid URL online is relatively small. For instance, assuming a brute-force rate of 10^5 attempts/s and a reset password rate of 10^5 requests/s, the probability of guessing a valid URL is

$$p_{guess} = \frac{(10^5 \times (60 \times 75))^2}{52^{11}} = 2.69 \times 10^{-4}.$$

However, any further increase in compute power could lower the work factor.

Aside from this threat, the fact that the server allows a user to request as many password resets as desired, creates an opportunity for malicious actors who may exploit this weakness to launch Denial of Service (DoS)/Email flood attacks towards other companies or individuals, using the Lothian Buses server resources, further damaging the transport operator's reputation in the process.

Finding: Poorly implemented password reset mechanisms lowers the barrier to brute-forcing user credentials and launching DoS/Email flood attacks using the transport operator's computing infrastructure.

5.7 Availability

The main purpose of an e-ticket app for public transport is to enable users to purchase tickets and use them at any point in time. The service must be thus available at all times. Following recent reports about app availability issues [5], we decide to run a network test and analyse the Internet connection needed to run the app and amount of data exchanged over this. Unsurprisingly, during 10 tests whereby we open and close the app, the average amount of data consumed is 45 kB and the time required to load the app did not vary with download speeds of 19 kB/s and above. However, examining the source code again, we notice that whenever the app is opened and any error occurs for whatever simple reason, the app closes and all information is erased, as when a tamper attempt is detected. As a result, the app has to re-download all data and validate it before displaying it to the user when re-opened. This leads to a 400 kB increase in data consumption and approximately 12 s boot-up time with an un-throttled connection.

To avoid this nuisance, modern programming languages force the user to implement `try-catch` statements, which permit a program to continue executing even if a small part of it encounters an exception. However, the m-tickets app is peppered with `try` instructions that are not followed by an appropriate `catch` logic. This leads to frequent occasions where the program crashes or gets stuck.

Findings: A combination of aggressive error handling practice and inappropriate use of `try-catch` statements leads to a history of poor app availability. Occasional users will always be forced to have an Internet connection.

6   Recommendations

Given the security vulnerabilities identified in the m-tickets app, we propose a set of solutions that can be deployed to address the exposed problems. We also explain why some of the implementation decisions made by Corethree are insecure, and suggest simple alternatives.

6.1   Tickets

Clearly, the whole purpose of the app is the secure purchase and use of tickets. Security is largely an abstract concept that is not straightforward to measure [17]. However, in essence it should reflect how hard it is for an attacker to read or modify information they are not authorised to. Taking a look at the current design of an e-ticket in the m-tickets/Lothian Buses app and the weaknesses described in Sect. 5–5.3, to begin with, the validation of a ticket should not rely on the bus driver. This is because the process is prone to error, as the driver may fail to recognise the difference between a valid and a crafted ticket. Indeed, previous studies show that humans are the weakest link in information security [3].

Secondly, users can be selfish and app decompiling is increasingly accessible. Therefore, the process of ticket generation should not be client-side, to avoid users tampering with it in order to circumvent payment. Instead, this process should be entirely server-based, whereby the user receives a valid ticket upon purchase, but remains unaware of how it was created.

Thirdly, there is currently no way of knowing whether active e-tickets are being re-used. The task of deleting a used ticket is handled by the app, yet as shown in Sect. 5.2, a user can control the app's behaviour on their phone. The same applies to the illicit modification of the characteristics of tickets (Sect. 5.3). Once again, to circumvent these problems, the user should be provided with a ticket generated on the server side and which cannot be modified by the app.

Alternative Ticketing System: Strengthening the ticketing system may require a complete redesign. In what follows, we propose a simple alternative, which although arguably not flawless, mitigates the vulnerabilities identified. The proposed system consists of (1) a QR code validation protocol that substitutes driver-based visual validation; (2) an additional private app that bus drivers would use to validate tickets; and (3) an RSA signature algorithm to safely maintain the tickets.

We illustrate the envisioned alternative ticketing system in Fig. 11 and summarise its operation below.

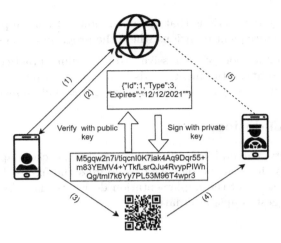

Fig. 11. Blueprint of proposed secure alternative ticketing system.

Step 1: User sends a payment for some amount of tickets of certain type, which they want to purchase.

Step 2: Server crafts each ticket in JSON format, which contains all the information needed to identify the ticket, including a *Unique_id* to avoid ticket reuse; *Ticket_type* to specify if the ticket is Adult Single, All day, etc.; an *Expiry_date* to verify that the ticket is still valid. Once the JSON is crafted, the server would use a private key k_{prv} to sign the JSON and send the result to the app.

Step 3: When the user wants to activate a ticket, the app builds a QR representation of the encrypted ticket and displays it on the phone's screen.

Step 4: The bus driver uses their app to scan the QR code. The app contains a public key k_{pub}, which is used to verify that the ticket has not been tampered with. It also checks that the unique ID was not used in the past. If the ticket appears valid, the app indicates approval and stores the ticket's unique ID.

Step 5: Periodically, the bus driver's app connects to the server and sends the unique IDs that were scanned. At the same time, it is updated with information of other valid/invalid unique IDs that have changed recently.

The downside to this system is that every bus driver must have a smartphone, which increases CAPEX. The advantages might out-weight the cost, since (1) the user only holds signed tickets and cannot craft tickets while subverting payment; (2) the public key could be made available to anyone, since it only serves in verifying if a ticket was tampered with; (3) the ticket duplication weakness is removed, since an attacker would have almost no time to use a copy of a ticket due to the unique IDs; and (4) modification of tickets becomes infeasible, since digital signatures are proven to be secure [8].

6.2   Hard-Coding and Availability

Having a flawless program is almost impossible. However, historically communities have come together to create standards, so that users/developers have the means of checking the correctness of their programs. A widely-known security standard is the OWASP Secure Coding Practices [10], which lays out practices developers should follow to make a program secure. Hard-coding and Availability issues we found in the m-tickets app are covered in these standards. Hence we recommend following these checklists when developing future versions of the app, to avoid the same or other pitfalls.

6.3   Password Reset

Not limiting the number of password resets a person can request has implication on (1) user account security (as it simplifies brute-forcing); (2) can facilitate DoS attacks towards third parties; and (3) can damage the reputation of the app provider. To avoid these, developers could enforce, e.g. a 10-s restriction between each password reset. This would be unnoticeable to the user, since it is roughly the time it takes to check email, while adversarial actors would be unable to perform any of the attacks discussed in Sect. 5.6. Additionally, it is good practice to disable the last password reset link after issuing a new one for the same account.

7   Conclusions

In this paper analyse the security and robustness of the m-tickets system used by Lothian Buses, a leading UK transport operator. We identify a range of vulnerabilities pertaining to ticket generation and life-cycle, app functionality, and back-end logic. To mitigate these, we provide design recommendations which Corethree, the developer, should implement, especially given that parts of older highly-vulnerable versions of the ticketing app remain in use and suggest other iterations of the system might be at risk. This includes those sold to other transport companies in the UK. Lastly, we present the blueprint of an alternative ticketing system, which should help in the development of future secure apps supporting public transport worldwide.

References

1. Corethree Website. https://www.corethree.net/
2. Unpacking Xamarin mono DLL from libmonodroid_bundle.app.so. https://reverseengineering.stackexchange.com/a/17330
3. Accenture: Why humans are still security's weakest link (May 2019)
4. Doomun, R., et al.: AES-CBC software execution optimization (August 2012)
5. Edinburgh News: Edinburgh commuters face more ticket app failures (September 2018)

6. Edinburgh Trams: TfE mtickets (August 2018). https://edinburghtrams.com/news/tfe-mtickets
7. Google Play Store: Lothian buses m-tickets
8. Lindenberg, C., Wirt, K., Buchmann, J.: Formal proof for the correctness of RSA-PSS. IACR Cryptology ePrint Archive (January 2006)
9. Lothian Buses Limited: Consolidated financial statements 2018, 1st edn. (2019)
10. OWASP: Secure coding practices. https://owasp.org/www-pdf-archive/OWASP_SCP_Quick_Reference_Guide_v2.pdf
11. Reddit: Activists release code to generate free public transportation tickets (2019). https://www.reddit.com/r/manchester/comments/cyefu5/activists_release_code_to_generate_free_public/
12. Statista: Number of smartphone users worldwide from 2016 to 2021. https://www.statista.com/statistics/330695/number-of-smartphone-users-worldwide/
13. The Business Research Company: Transit and ground passenger transportation (public transport) global market briefing 2018, 1st edn. (2018)
14. The Telegraph: Public transport apps hacked to create free tickets and defraud operators (September 2019)
15. Wired: Hackers crack London tube's ticketing system (June 2008). https://www.wired.com/2008/06/hackers-crack-1/
16. Xu, Q., Erman, J., Gerber, A., Mao, Z., Pang, J., Venkataraman, S.: Identifying diverse usage behaviors of smartphone apps. In: ACM SIGCOMM IMC (2011)
17. Zalewski, J., et al.: Can we measure security and how? In: Proceedings of the Annual Workshop on Cyber Security and Information Intelligence Research (2011)

Network and System Security

ELD: Adaptive Detection of Malicious Nodes under Mix-Energy-Depleting-Attacks Using Edge Learning in IoT Networks

Zuchao Ma[1], Liang Liu[1], and Weizhi Meng[2(✉)]

[1] Nanjing University of Aeronautics and Astronautics, Nanjing, China
[2] Technical University of Denmark, Lyngby, Denmark
weme@dtu.dk

Abstract. Due to the distributed framework, Internet of Things (IoT) is vulnerable to insider attacks like energy-depleting attack, where an attacker can behave maliciously to consume the battery of IoT devices. Such attack is difficult to detect because the attacker may behave differently under various environments and it is hard to decide the attack path. In this work, we focus on this challenge, and consider an advanced energy-depleting attack, called mix-energy-depleting attack, which combines three typical attacks such as carousel attack, flooding attack and replay attack. Regarding the detection, we propose an approach called Edge Learning Detection (ELD), which can learn malicious traffic by constructing an *intrusion edge* and can identify malicious nodes by building an *intrusion graph*. To overcome the problem that it is impractical to provide labeled data for system training in advance, our proposed ELD can train its model during detection by labeling traffic automatically. Then the obtained detection results can be used to optimize the adaptability of ELD in detecting practical attacks. In the evaluation, as compared with some similar methods, ELD can overall provide a better detection rate ranged from 5% to 40% according to concrete conditions.

Keywords: IoT network · Malicious node · Insider attack · Edge learning · Mix-energy-depleting attack

1 Introduction

Internet of Things (IoT) has become a popular infrastructure to support many modern applications and services, such as smart homes, smart healthcare, public security, industrial monitoring and environment protection. It allows devices to collect information from surroundings, i.e., control units can gather information from other devices to make better strategies.

However, there is a growing concern about energy-depleting attacks on IoT networks, like battery-deplete attacks [2,20] and vampire attacks [21]. For these attacks, once some internal devices are compromised, cyber-criminals can send

© Springer Nature Switzerland AG 2020
W. Susilo et al. (Eds.): ISC 2020, LNCS 12472, pp. 255–273, 2020.
https://doi.org/10.1007/978-3-030-62974-8_15

more packets to other devices (target devices) or request them to forward packets to consume the energy of target devices, via the infected devices. It is more difficult to detect energy-depleting attacks as compared with traditional data-oriented attacks (e.g., tamper attack or drop attack). This is because data-oriented attacks cause damaged data (e.g., tampered data or lost data) that can be identified clearly, while for energy-depleting attacks, the energy consumption caused by attacks cannot be defined explicitly. In addition, it is hard to locate malicious devices as one malicious device can create malicious traffic spreading in the whole network and leading to the complexity of intrusion path. Hence it is very important to design an effective security mechanism for detecting malicious nodes under energy depleting attacks in IoT networks.

In the literature, most existing studies mainly focus on a single and unique attack in an IoT environment, but an advanced intruder may perform several different types of attacks at the same time. In this work, we thus focus on a more powerful attacker, who can control some nodes illegally in an IoT network and launch a *mix-energy-depleting attack* (MEDA) by combining carousel attacks, flooding attacks and replay attacks. The selection is based on their versatility and popularity. In particular, carousel attacks aim to consume energy by generating forwarding loops. These three typical attacks can be performed separately or simultaneously, resulting in an advanced insider attack scenario.

For detecting malicious nodes under energy depleting attacks, most of existing schemes are designed based on the assumption about attacks. That is, the supposed threshold of extra received packets or extra energy consumption caused by attacks. For example, Cong [13] introduced an approach based on received packet threshold by using the count of received packets to judge whether a node is affected by attacks or not. However, the threshold can be easily affected by concrete attack environments and devices. In addition, some research work [18,20] believe that malicious nodes should be those who broadcast messages frequently and have a higher battery energy as compared to other nodes. In fact, there is no guarantee that malicious nodes have higher battery energy. Therefore, we believe that a better solution could be guided by the assumption at the beginning, while the assumption should be updated periodically according to the detection result. On the other hand, many studies attempt to apply anomaly detection for detecting insider attacks, whereas some strong machine learning classifiers cannot be deployed in an IoT device, due to the limited resources. Further, traditional supervised learning requires labeled data or traffic in advance, which might be difficult in some network conditions.

Contribution. Motivated by the above observations, we propose an approach called Edge Learning Detection (ELD) to detect MEDA. ELD focuses on learning the malicious traffic caused by multiple types of attacks instead of using different protocols to handle various attacks. In this case, the deployment of ELD does not need to make any changes on network protocols. ELD can also use a parameter to control the adaptability of detection based on specific environments, in which the parameter can be adjusted automatically to optimize the detection according to current detection results. That is, ELD could improve its adaptability to detect practical attacks based on the feedback from practical environments. For deployment, ELD can gather traffic logs from IoT nodes without knowing the details of transferred packets or other information from neighbors, and can execute the detection on base station or gateway within the network. More importantly, ELD does not need to collect practical malicious traffic to train its model in advance. Instead, the training can be performed during the detection. Our contributions can be summarized as below.

- We propose an approach of Edge Learning Detection (ELD) to defeat MEDA through extracting main features from traffic. For energy efficiency, we use traffic logs (lightweight) to record the received packets and request IoT nodes to send these logs to base station regularly. The system models like attack model and traffic log model can refer to Sect. 3
- For detection, ELD first identifies damaged nodes (suffered from MEDA) and labels their traffic as malicious based on traffic logs. Then ELD constructs intrusion edges and trains a random forest model to identify malicious traffic. These intrusion edges enable ELD to generate intrusion graphs for finding malicious nodes. In addition, the obtained detection results can be used to update the settings of ELD.
- In the evaluation, we compare ELD with two similar schemes of Hard Detection (HD) [8] and Perceptron Detection with enhancement (PDE) [7]. Our results demonstrate that ELD could overall achieve better performance, i.e., offering a better detection rate by around 5% to 40% according to concrete conditions.

Organization. The remaining parts are organized as follows. Section 2 introduces related work on how to detect security threats. Section 3 presents the system model. Section 4 describes the workflow of ELD in detail. Section 5 discusses our experimental settings and analyzes evaluation results. Finally, Sect. 6 concludes our work.

2   Related Work

Energy-related attacks can increase the workload of nodes through sending useless data packets. Besides, electromagnetic emissions can also be used to cause errors and force packet retransmissions, which can increase traffic and energy consumption [6].

Energy-Depleting Attacks. For this kind of attacks, malicious nodes can pretend to be benign and continuously send packets to other nodes, in order to cause additional traffic [5]. Carousel attack is a typical form of energy-depleting attacks [19], in which a node can send corrupted data leading to routing loops. Such attack is difficult to locate, as one malicious node can affect the whole network [21]. For flooding attack, intruders can continuously make a new connection request to consume the resources for all network nodes [11]. For replay attack, an adversary can repeat a valid transmission in the network [17], aiming to fool other nodes by convincing them that the repeated messages contain a new message exchange.

Detection Strategies. For carousel attack detection, Vasserman et al. [21] proposed a protocol to detect and mitigate malicious nodes by routing through the network only for legitimate packets, and verifying that consistent progress is made by packets towards the destination. To locate malicious nodes, some detection methods like [7] need to change existing protocols to provide provenance information. In their work, the network protocol has to be modified in order to deploy the detection system and the content of transmission needs to be checked. In our work, ELD focuses on recording information of traffic without considering the content of transferred packets or changing the network protocol.

In addition, some research studies like [18,20] attempt to detect energy-depleting attack by searching those nodes with high battery and the frequent broadcast behavior. In comparison, ELD does not adopt a certain assumption about attacks which could change its adaptability based on the feedback from the real network environment. Bhunia et al. [3] proposed an SDN-based secure IoT framework called SoftThings to detect abnormal behaviors and mitigate flooding attacks. Rughoobur et al. [15] then proposed a lightweight and reliable framework, which uses a combination of universally unique identifier, timestamp and a self-learning battery depletion monitor to detect and mitigate replay attacks. The main limitation of these studies is that they only consider single attack, but our ELD considers a more advanced insider attack.

Detection Schemes. Intrusion detection is an essential and important solution to protect the security of IoT networks, but there are some major concerns. 1) Many studies like [4,9,16] figured out that traditional anomaly detection schemes are not practical to be deployed in IoT devices due to the constrained resources. To mitigate this issue, our ELD uses traffic logs (a kind of lightweight data structure) to record the received packets without the need of analyzing the content. 2) Existing centralized detection schemes (detection is deployed in a strong node, e.g., base station or gateway of network) usually cannot perceive the communications among end-devices. This makes detection of malicious nodes difficult since the attack path is hard to be examined [4]. To solve this issue, ELD constructs an intrusion graph based on malicious traffic to help locate malicious nodes. 3) Most anomaly detection schemes with supervised learning need to train their own model in advance, but it is hard to get enough labeled data in a real network. By contrast, our ELD can perform training during the detection and use the detection results to update its settings.

3   System Model

3.1   Attack Model

We assume advanced attackers have the ability to invade IoT devices to turn them into malicious nodes and use these nodes to launch their attacks. We consider a more harmful attack, called mix-energy-depleting attack, consisting of three typical malicious actions - with a probability to make carousel attacks, flooding attacks and replay attacks. These attacks can be performed separately or simultaneously in many IoT networks, including but not limited to smart home, wireless sensor network and robot network, as shown in Fig. 1.

- **Carousel Attack.** In this attack, malicious nodes receive packets and send the packets to a node which out of the original path to create a series of loops to drain the energy of these nodes. An example is shown by the case of wireless sensor network in Fig. 1, where a packet is supposed to pass $<n_1, n_3, n_4, base\ station>$; n_3 is invaded by attacker and it redirects the packet to n_2 maliciously and requests n_2 to transfer the packet to base station. According to the route, n_2 has to send the packet to n_1, then the packet is transferred in loop $<n_1, n_3, n_2, n_1, n_3, n_2 ...>$ and the energy of n_1 and n_2 will be wasted.

- **Flooding Attack** In this attack, malicious nodes generate a huge number of spoofed packets, which can result in the channels to be overloaded. All nodes in the channels may suffer from this attack and waste their energy. An example is shown by the case of smart home in Fig. 1, where d_1 generates spoofed packets sent to d_2 to consume the energy of it (assuming d_1, a door lock, works cooperatively with d_2, a monitor camera). Besides, in the case of robot network, r_5 is the leader of r_4 and r_4 is the leader of r_3. An attacker invades r_3 and uses it to generate spoofed packets sent to the gateway to have a report by passing $<r_3, r_4, r_5, gateway>$, therefore the energy of r_4 and r_5 is wasted.

- **Replay Attack** In this attack, a malicious node can copy the packet and send redundant packets to the next node when it receives a packet. An example is shown by the case of wireless sensor network in Fig. 1, where n_6 sends a packet to the base station by passing $<n_6, n_5, n_4, base\ station>$ and n_5 copies the packet to create redundant packets sent to n_4 in order to waste the energy of it.

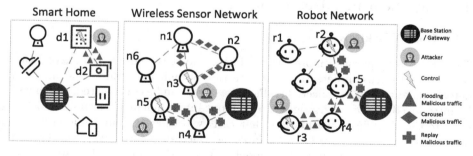

Fig. 1. Energy exhausting attacks

To sum up, it is hard to detect malicious nodes in a multiple-hop IoT network like wireless sensor network or robot network, especially when the scale of the network is big, due to malicious traffic will pass many nodes of the network and it is difficult to locate the origin of malicious traffic. Therefore, for existing traffic detection based anomaly detection systems, they may realize malicious traffic but cannot locate malicious nodes.

3.2 Traffic Log Model

Traffic logs are used for recording the information of traffic in IoT node side and finally these logs are sent to base station or gateway of network for detection. In every certain period (e.g., half an hour), IoT nodes save its traffic logs temporarily and send these logs to base station at the end of period. A traffic log that records the information about a packet received by a node, can be formalized as $log = <sender, receiver, timestamp, dataSize, serviceType>$ where $sender$ is the sender of the packet; $receiver$ is the receiver of the packet; $timestamp$ is the time when the packet is received by the node; $dataSize$ is the size of the packet; $serviceType$ is the service type that the packet is used to request.

The following is an example of implementing a traffic log: we use 7 bits to encode $sender$ and $receiver$ respectively and it can support a network with 2^7 IoT nodes; assume the detection system collects traffic logs in every 30 min, so the $timestamp$ whose unit is second can be encoded by 11 bits; assume the size of packets transferred in network is from 1 Byte to 1024 Bytes and $dataSize$ can be encoded by 10 bits; $serviceType$ is encoded by 4 bits so it can support 2^4 types. Therefore, the log can be encoded by $7 + 7 + 11 + 10 + 4 = 39$ bits and the overall size of log can be 5 Bytes. That is, during 30 min, even if an IoT node receives 100000 packets, the node can only use the space of 500 KB to save all logs without any compress, which is light-weight in saving. On the other hand, these logs can be easily transferred to base station. The cost of saving and transferring can be reduced further if some efficient compress schemes are adopted.

4   Edge Learning Detection

4.1 Core Workflow

To present our approach more clearly, Fig. 2 shows the core workflow of ELD, consisting of intrusion detection and detection of malicious nodes. For intrusion detection, according to collected traffic logs, edges can be constructed, which will be introduced in Sect. 4.2. Edges can be input into a machine learning model to execute the classification and after that ELD will execute damage node identification (refer to Sect. 4.3) to guide labeling edges automatically. These labeled edges will be used for training the model and after the training all edges will be classified by the model again. For detecting malicious nodes, those edges classified to be intrusive are called intrusion edges, which will be used for generating intrusion graphs to identify malicious nodes. This will be introduced in Sect. 4.5.

4.2   Intrusion Detection

Traffic Features. The extracted traffic features are important for detecting an intrusion. Based on the literature and some widely available datasets like UNSW-NB15 dataset [10], we select some features relevant to the characteristics of carousel attack, flooding attack and replay attack. These features include: *dur*, *service*, *srcip*, *dstip*, *ct_srv_src*, *ct_srv_dst*, *ct_dst_ltm*, *ct_src_ltm*, *Stime*, *Ltime*, *Spkts*, and *sbytes*.

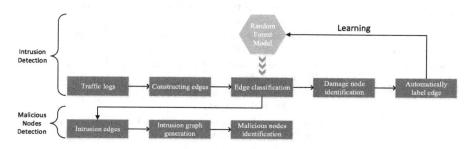

Fig. 2. Core workflow

These features can be extracted from an IoT network, but they cannot be used directly because some of these features are extracted from a single connection (e.g., *Spkts*, *service*) or from the statistics of a connection set (e.g., *ct_srv_src*, *ct_srv_dst*, *ct_src_ltm*). In addition, some features may involve the detail of the whole connection (e.g., *dur*, *sbytes*), which would bring extra cost when analyzing traffic logs. That is, it is not efficient to extract these features directly from traffic logs. In this work, the final accepted features are shown in Table 1.

Edge. The use of edge aims to record the direction of main traffic and edge is the data structure used for training model and being predicted. When the traffic becomes malicious, an edge would be an intrusion edge. Considering a scenario that the packets from multiple senders in a certain time period, the sender that brings most packets can be selected as the pointer of edge and the receiver of the traffic can be selected as the pointee. During the same time period, each node is pointed by only one pointer. In this case, an edge records the direction of main traffic instead of all traffic, which is helpful to simplify traffic analysis and generate an intrusion graph.

Assume that the timestamp of the first traffic log is s_stamp and the timestamp of the last traffic log is e_stamp, then $(s\_stamp + e\_stamp)/2$ can be defined as the timestamp of an edge. Figure 3 shows the process of edge generation, where $N2$ sends most packets to $N1$ according to the traffic log in $N1$. Thus $N2$ becomes the pointer of the edge, $N1$ becomes the pointee, and $(Packet1.timestamp + Packet5.timestamp)/2$ is the timestamp of the edge. Here the edge can be modeled as $edge = <pointer, pointee, timestamp, dur\_aver, dur\_std, ser\_std,$

Table 1. Designed features

Feature [type]	Description ([c]:continuous, [d]:discrete)
dur_aver [c]	In the traffic of a certain period, a sender n is given; from the timestamp of the first packet sent by n to the timestamp of the last packet sent by n (number of seconds) is called the connection duration of n. For all senders of the traffic, the average of their connection duration is called dur_aver
dur_std [c]	For all senders of traffic, the standard deviation of their connection duration is called dur_std
ser_std [c]	The standard deviation of the number of packets that are used to request the same service type is called ser_std
bytes_aver [c]	The average of the size of packets in traffic (bytes) is called bytes_aver
bytes_std [c]	The standard deviation of the size of packets in traffic (bytes) is called bytes_std
land [d]	In the traffic of a certain period, it is 1 if all packets come from the same sender; 0 otherwise
count_aver [c]	In the traffic of a certain period, a sender n is given; the number of packets coming from n is called the count of n. For all senders of traffic, the average of their counts is called count_aver
count_std [c]	For all senders of traffic, the standard deviation of their counts is called count_std
	Note: The following features refer to the connection of the same sender that owns the max count
same_ser_rate_std [c]	The standard deviation of % of requests to the same service
same_bytes_rate_std [c]	The standard deviation of % of packets with the same size
same_count_aver [c]	The average of number of packets with the same size
same_count_std [c]	The standard deviation of number of packets with the same size

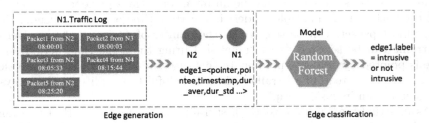

Fig. 3. Edge generation and classification

bytes_aver, bytes_std, land, count_aver, count_std, same_ser_rate_std, same_bytes_rate_std, same_count_aver, same_count_std>, where *pointer* is the pointer of the edge; *pointee* is the pointee of the edge; and *timestamp* is the timestamp of the edge. The rest attributes can refer to Table 1.

Random Forest Based Learning. To detect an intrusion edge via learning features of edges (including intrusion edges and benign edges), this work adopts a classifier of random forest. It is one commonly used algorithm to solve classification problem and has been proved to work effectively in intrusion detection [14]. For example, Ahmad et al. [1] indicated that random forest model can perform well in analyzing huge traffic data. The random forest model is an ensemble of decision trees, and the classification prediction is based on the majority votes of the predicted values using the decision trees. It is noted that only part of attributes of an edge can be used to train the random forest model and perform prediction, while *edge.pointer*, *edge.pointee* and *edge.timestamp* are removed.

Edge Classification. In ELD, edge classification can be executed in every certain period (e.g., half an hour), and the traffic logs can be split by their timestamps - the interval used to split traffic logs depends on the length of a time period. Based on these split traffic logs, edges can be generated and classified by the random forest model. An example is shown in Fig. 3, where the length of a time period is half an hour, thus the traffic logs of N during the period of $(08:00:01, 08:30:00)$ are used to generate $edge1$. The timestamp of $edge1$ is $(08:00:01 + 08:25:20)/2 = 08:12:40$. If we input $edge1$ to the random forest model, then it can be predicted as intrusive or not intrusive.

4.3 Damaged Node Identification

As discussed earlier, our ELD can train its model during the detection without the need of labeled data in advance. This makes ELD practical in a real scenario, as in many cases, there are no labeled data beforehand. While ELD can be adaptive to the real network environments by labeling the traffic to support its learning. ELD works with the knowledge learned from intrusion edges, therefore something must guide ELD to understand what is an intrusion edge. That is, enabling ELD to label edges automatically to provide itself with training data. In this work, we use the information of damaged nodes (by energy-depleting attack) as the tutor. As heterogeneous IoT nodes may have different battery capacity and various energy overhead, it is impractical to use uniform energy consumption metric to determine whether a node is damaged or not. Therefore, we detect damaged nodes according to their abnormal speed of receiving packets.

In each certain period (e.g., half an hour), the base station of an IoT network collects a batch of traffic logs to execute the detection. According to these logs, the average speed of receiving packets of each node can be obtained (the size of received data/the length of certain period). We denote $AverRecvSpeed$ as the average speed, and when the speed is larger than R, it could be detected as abnormal speed of receiving packets and this node is a damaged node. R (varies from 0 byte/s to the bandwidth of an IoT network) is the parameter to control the sensibility of detecting whether a node is damaged. With the increase of R, the sensibility decreases gradually, implying a reduction of both recall of damaged nodes and false alarm rate.

It is worth noting that R should be different in IoT nodes. This is because in an IoT network, some nodes may receive more packets than others, e.g., nodes on the main route of a network (most packets need to pass them to be delivered) or nodes having more neighbors (most packets need to be forwarded). For detection, assuming there are a set of nodes $n_1, n_2, ...n_t$ and a set of R for each node as $RS = R_1, R_2, ...R_t$, where R_i is the R for n_i. For a given route, e.g., $p = <n_1, n_2, n_3, base\,station>$, we can name n_i as the pre-node of n_{i+1}. RS can be initialized based on the assumption that nodes having more pre-nodes should be set with a higher R. Thus, we define the initialization of n_i as $R_i = \begin{cases} 0 & \text{if } n_i \text{ does not have pre-nodes} \\ \sum(R_{pre(i)} + Send_{pre(i)}) & otherwise \end{cases}$ where $pre(i)$ represents the pre-nodes of n_i; $Send_i$ is an estimated value about the average speed of sending packets of n_i. For example, if a sensor node n_i needs to send a packet to base station to report sensing data every minute and the data size varies from 5 bytes to 10 bytes, then we can estimate the speed $Send_i$ to be 10 bytes/min $= 0.167$ bytes/s. For a route example in Fig. 4. In this route, assuming $Send_i$ is 0.167 bytes/s, then we have $R_1 = 0$, $R_2 = R_1 + Send_1 = 0.167$ bytes/s, $R_3 = R_1 + Send_1 = 0.167$ bytes/s, $R_4 = R_2 + Send_2 = 0.334$ bytes/s, $R_5 = R_3 + Send_3 = 0.334$ bytes/s.

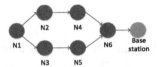

Fig. 4. Route

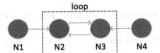

Fig. 5. Loop in an intrusion path

When ELD detects the appearance of damaged nodes, the detection will be executed for certain rounds to improve the accuracy of model. Note that edge classification can be executed in every certain period (e.g., half an hour) and intrusion detection only runs if damaged nodes or intrusion edges appear. In the first round of detection, the edge pointing to damaged node will be labeled as intrusion edge automatically, because before the first round ELD does not have the knowledge about intrusion edge and it can only label edge with the initial RS. However, in next rounds of detection, RS could be optimized based on obtained detection results. This will be introduced later.

4.4   Adaptability Optimization

There are two important steps to improve the adaptability of ELD. 1) To improve the adaptability of identifying damaged nodes (refer to Sect. 4.3), and 2) To improve the adaptability of determining whether traffic is malicious.

Here we explain the whole learning process of ELD as follows. After deploying ELD into a practical environment, it requires a time period (e.g., adaption period) to learn normal traffic of the IoT network. This is common for most existing security solutions like anomaly detection. During this period, if we assume there is no energy-depleting attack, then all edges constructed from traffic logs can be labeled as not-intrusive and relevant training model is called *base model*. After this adaptation period, ELD can work based on its initial knowledge including the initial damaged node identification and the base model. When damaged nodes are detected, ELD can perform multiple rounds of detection. Note that in the first round of detection, the intrusive label of an edge depends on whether the pointee of the edge is a damaged node. That is, in the first round of detection, if the pointee of an edge is damaged, then the edge label can be intrusive and this edge can be used to train the model of random forest. Essentially, identifying some damaged nodes can guide ELD to label more malicious traffic automatically. After learning intrusion edges, ELD can use its model to classify all edges constructed in that round of detection and have the final classification result of that round.

When the next batch of traffic logs is collected (e.g., half an hour later), ELD can perform the next round of detection. From the second round, ELD first uses the pre-round model to classify all edges. There are four cases or conditions of a node: a) the node is identified as damaged and it is pointed by an intrusion edge; b) the node is identified as not-damaged and it is pointed by an intrusion edge (potential damaged); c) the node is identified as damaged and it is not pointed by an intrusion edge, and d) the node is identified as not-damaged and it is not pointed by an intrusion edge.

For case b), we have to decrease R (refer to Sect. 4.3) to enable the identification of these nodes correctly. In a real network, some potential damaged nodes might not be detected at once, under the current setting of RS (refer to Sect. 4.3). If they are pointed by intrusion edges, they may have a high probability to be damaged. In this case, we may notice that RS is not optimized. Thus RS should be adjusted to enable the identification of these potential damaged nodes correctly. For example, in Fig. 4, if malicious traffic exists in $<N2, N4>$ and $<N4, N6>$, then there are intrusion edges $(N2 -> N4)$ and $(N4 -> N6)$. If we set R of $N6$ too high, then $N6$ may not be detected as damaged node.

For case c), there might be two reasons for this conflict: i) R is set too low (false alarm); and ii) there are novel attacks that are not learned by the pre-round model. To handle this issue, we consider both possibilities and create two branches (branch A and branch B). For branch A, we increase R of these nodes until they can be identified as not-damaged. For branch B, we label those edges pointing to these nodes to be intrusive, i.e., each branch contains the corresponding model and RS individually. Note that if there is no node in case c), then no branch will be needed.

Then the same as the first round, ELD learns intrusion edges and uses its model to classify all edges again. It is worth noting that ELD can obtain different RS and different models in different rounds of detection.

4.5 Malicious Nodes Detection

Intrusion Graph Generation. To locate malicious nodes based on intrusion edges, one important step is to construct an intrusion graph by considering joined edges according to their timestamps. Essentially, an intrusion graph consists of many intrusion paths built by linking intrusive edges, which means that the first node of an intrusion path is very likely to be malicious. As the timestamp of each edge could be different, we consider the following two principles to construct an intrusion graph.

1) For an edge e, if other edges can be joined with e, their timestamp ts must obey $|e.timestamp - ts| <= the\ length\ of\ certain\ period$;

2) For an edge e, it will always select one edge of other nodes that has the closest timestamp (i.e., $min(|e.timestamp - ts|)$).

The generation details can refer to Fig. 6, where the length of a certain period is half an hour. For $edge11$, as $|edge11.timestamp - edge21.timestamp| = 00 : 02 : 00 <= 00 : 30 : 00$, then $edge21$ is closer to $edge11$ as compared to $edge22$. In this case, $edge11$ and $edge21$ can construct $Graph1$. $Graph2$ and $Graph3$ in the same way.

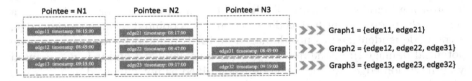

Fig. 6. Graph generation

Malicious Node Identification. Based on the intrusion graph, ELD can link malicious traffic from different malicious nodes. Intuitively, for a flooding/reply attack, packets are transferred via intrusion paths of an intrusion graph, and the first node would be the attacker. In some cases of multiple flooding attacks or multiple replay attacks, different intrusion paths could have an overlap with each other, which may create loops as well. For example, there is an intrusion path $p1 = <n_1, n_2, n_3>$ and $p2 = <n_4, n_3, n_2>$; $p1$ and $p2$ may have an overlap with each other like n_2 and n_3, thus there is a loop $<n_2, n_3, n_2>$, which is shown in Fig. 5. While for a carousel attack, an intrusion path could also contain a loop. We adopt two detection principles as below.

1) The first node of an intrusion path can be identified as malicious;

2) For each node of a loop, if there is another intrusion edge pointing to this node, and the pointer of the edge is not in the loop, then the node should be identified as benign; otherwise, it should be malicious.

For example, given two intrusion paths of $p1 = <n_1, n_2, n_3>$ and $p2 = <n_4, n_3, n_2>$, and a loop of $<n_2, n_3, n_2>$. For n_2, suppose there is an edge $<n_1, n_2>$ but n_1 is not in the loop. For n_3, suppose there is an edge $<n_4, n_3>$ but n_4 is not in the loop. Thus, we can classify n_2 and n_3 as normal.

For each round of detection, we repeat the above steps to identify malicious nodes. As there might be multiple branches with continuous detection, we define, in the final round of detection, malicious nodes detected by a branch are the malicious set of this branch. For example, if we have four rounds of detection, then in the final round there could be 2^3 (maximum) branches and eight malicious sets. Note that only those malicious nodes appeared over half of malicious sets (e.g., four malicious sets) can be determined as final malicious nodes, i.e., the final detection result of ELD.

5   Our Evaluation

In this section, we introduce the comparison schemes, present our experimental setup and discuss the impact of variables on the detection performance.

5.1   Comparison Scheme

As existing detection schemes mainly focus on identifying malicious traffic, it is hard for them to locate malicious nodes in multiple hop IoT networks. Thus we adopt the following detection schemes of malicious nodes in the comparison. Table 2 shows the environmental settings in the evaluation.

- Hard Detection (HD) [8] is a mathematical method to detect malicious nodes that can perform a tamper attack. As the focus of HD is not fully the same as this work, we tune HD to make it workable in a mix-energy-depleting attack environment. In particular, we added a module in HD to help detect duplicated packets corresponding to replay attack, and enabled HD to search replay-attack malicious nodes.
- Perceptron Detection with enhancement (PDE) [7] is a detection scheme that uses both perceptron and K-means method to compute IoT nodes' trust values and detect malicious nodes accordingly. It also adopts an enhanced perceptron learning process to reduce the false alarm rate.

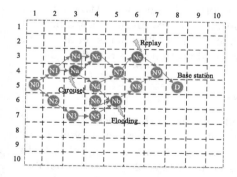

Fig. 7. A distribution of IoT nodes (Color figure online)

Table 2. Environmental settings

Item	Description
CPU	Intel Core i7-4700MQ, 2.4 GHz, 4Core (8 threads)
Memory	Kingston DDR3L 8 GB * 2
OS	Ubuntu 18.04 LTS
Python	3.6.8
Scikit-learn	0.20

5.2 Experimental Setup

In our environment, all IoT nodes were deployed in a $100 \times 100\,\mathrm{m}^2$ rectangle area discretely, and each node's communication range is from $10\,\mathrm{m}$ to $30\,\mathrm{m}$. Our IoT network is generated randomly but has a feature: for each node, there is at least one path from the node to base station, ensuring IoT devices can be connected. Figure 7 depicts an example of the distribution, where the green node is base station, blue nodes are normal nodes and red nodes are malicious nodes - N_a is carousel-malicious, N_b is flooding-malicious, and N_e is replay-malicious.

Simulation. As there is no suitable IoT traffic dataset regarding mix-energy-depleting attack in the research community, we decide to simulate different networks to generate traffic. In our simulation, IoT nodes and base station can communicate with each other randomly in every fifteen seconds (i.e., a node sends a packet to either other nodes or base station). The size of transferred data varies from 1 byte to 100 bytes, and the network bandwidth is $10\,\mathrm{kb/s}$. We set 10 types of service packets and set attacks to vary randomly all the time, in order to explore the adaptability of ELD.

We set all malicious nodes to launch attacks with a probability called attack probability. For carousel attacks, a malicious node can forward malicious packets to the neighbor of its sender with attack probability. For example, if there is a packet transferred in $p = <n_1, n_2, n_3, n_4, base\ station>$ and n_3 is a malicious node, then it can forward the packet received from n_2 to n_1 or to the neighbors of n_2 (assuming n_2 can communicate with them by extending its transmit power). The number of loops caused by carousel attack can vary from 20 to 50. For flooding attacks, malicious nodes can send 50 to 80 packets (one time) to other nodes or base station in every 15 min with attack probability. For replay attacks, the number of replayed packets can vary from 10 to 20, when a replay attack happens with attack probability. In the network, nodes can generate traffic logs and send these logs to base station in every 30 min.

To avoid bias, our simulation repeated in 10 rounds with 10 different networks for each experiment. Then the average value is selected to represent the final experimental result. In particular, we used Python to implement all algorithms, and the random forest classifier was extracted from scikit-learn [12], which is a widely used and open-source machine learning tool library. The *n_estimators* parameter of Random Forest Classifier is set as 10000. If damaged nodes appear, ELD will execute its detection for 3 rounds.

5.3 Impact of the Number of Nodes

To explore the impact of the number of nodes on the performance of HD, PDE and ELD in detecting mix-energy-depleting attack, we consider a typical IoT network, with the number of nodes as 7, 12, 17, 22 and 27, respectively. In this experiment, we set the number of passing packets as 2000; the probability of attack is 0.5; and the percentage of malicious nodes as 0.3. The results are shown in Fig. 8.

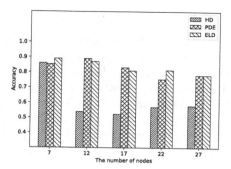 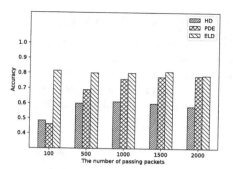

Fig. 8. The impact of the number of nodes on detection accuracy

Fig. 9. The impact of the number of passing packets on detection accuracy

It is observed that when the scale of IoT networks is small, all schemes can reach a high accuracy rate, i.e., ELD can reach a rate of 0.9. With the increase of nodes, the accuracy of HD has an obvious decrease while the accuracy of ELD can decrease much slowly. This is because when the network scale is small, the possible paths are limited so that malicious nodes can be easily identified by HD. When the number of nodes reaches 10 or more, the network topology would become complicated and the increasing complexity of attacked paths could cause many false alarms. As PDE can apply perceptron for reducing false alarms, it can achieve similar performance as ELD, i.e., PDE can reach better performance when the node number is 12 and 17, while ELD is better when the node number is 7 and 22.

5.4   Impact of the Number of Passing Packets

To examine the impact of passing packets (the normal packets generated to be transferred in the network) on the detection performance of HD, PDE and ELD, we set the number of passing packets to be 100, 500, 1000, 1500 and 2000, respectively. In this experiment, we set the number of nodes as 27; the probability of attack as 0.5; and the percentage of malicious nodes as 0.3. The obtained results are described in Fig. 9.

It is found that when the number of passing packets is small, our ELD could achieve an accuracy rate of 0.8, whereas HD and PDE could only reach around 0.5. With the increase of packets, the performance of HD and PDE can be improved. It is worth noting that the performance of ELD is stable and can outperform the other two schemes in all cases. This is because each scheme works differently. For HD and PDE, passing packets indicate the probability of malicious nodes, which could be used for calculating the trust values of nodes. That means the bigger number of passing packets, the more accurate reputation can be computed by HD and PDE. By contrast, ELD focuses mainly on whether there are malicious packets and would not be affected by the number of passing packets.

5.5   Impact of Attack Types

In this experiment, we aim to examine the impact of different attacks on the detection performance, including carousel attack, flooding attack, replay attack and mix-energy-depleting attack. In particular, we set the number of nodes as 27; the number of passing packets as 2000; the probability of attack as 0.5; and the percentage of malicious nodes as 0.3. Our observations are shown below.

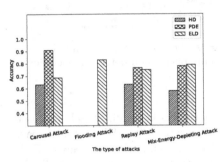

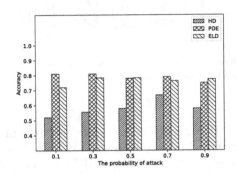

Fig. 10. The impact of the type of attacks on detection accuracy

Fig. 11. The impact of the probability of attack on detection accuracy

- For carousel attacks, as the loop of carousel attack can be recorded by both HD and PDE, they can achieve good performance. PDE can outperform ELD by benefitting from the low false alarm rate; however, as HD suffers a high false alarm rate, ELD still outperformed the performance of HD.
- For flooding attacks, HD and PDE were failed since a flooding attacker only sends useless packets with normal format and these packets cannot be recognized by HD and PDE. Thus, there is no information that could be used by HD and PDE to compute the attack probability of malicious nodes. Under such environment, ELD is more effective.
- For replay attacks, PDE performed a bit better than ELD. For ELD, each malicious node can be the first node of an intrusive path (e.g., flooding attack), but the number of intrusive paths is lower than that in a carousel attack, hence the accuracy of detecting replay attacks is lower than the accuracy of detecting flooding-malicious nodes.

Figure 10 shows that ELD could achieve better performance than HD in all cases, while ELD and PDE have their own merits. Overall, for a mix-energy-depleting attack, ELD could still outperform the other two approaches.

5.6   Impact of Attack Probability

To explore the impact of attack probability on the detection performance, we set the probability of mix-energy-depleting attack to be 0.1, 0.3, 0.5, 0.7 and 0.9, respectively. In this experiment, we set the number of nodes as 27; the number of passing packets as 2000; and the percentage of malicious nodes as 0.3. The results are shown in Fig. 11.

Similarly, ELD could outperform HD in all cases. For ELD, a high attack probability means that it could be easier to detect abnormal traffic and locate malicious nodes. In contrast, for HD, malicious nodes have to be identified based on the path reputation. For example, if there is a node with extremely high attack probability in a path, the path reputation may be very low and it is hard to analyze the reputation of all nodes in this path. In short, HD is not good at handling the scenario of high attack probability. For PDE, it can use the perceptron to help reduce false alarms so that it can reach similar performance as ELD, i.e., ELD is better when the probability is 0.5 and 0.9.

Discussion. Based on the above results, it is observed that our ELD could outperform HD in almost all cases. PDE and ELD have their own merits but PDE cannot detect flooding attacks as it cannot recognize flooding packets. By considering all these aspects, we consider our proposed ELD is overall better than PDE, and these two schemes can complement each other in practice.

6   Conclusion

With the rapid development of IoT networks, there is a significant need to design proper security mechanisms in identifying insider attacks like energy-depleting attacks. Most existing studies mainly consider a single attack, but we notice that an advanced intruder may launch some attacks simultaneously and cause a more harmful impact. In this work, we focus on an advanced energy-depleting attack, which combines carousel attack, flooding attack and replay attack with a possibility. We then propose an approach called Edge Learning Detection (ELD), which can build intrusion graphs to detect malicious nodes and provide adaptability by learning from the obtained detection results. Our experimental results demonstrate that ELD can provide a better detection rate by around 5% to 40% as compared with similar schemes in different conditions.

As our work is an early study in applying edge learning, there are some limitations and open challenges that can be considered in our future work. For instance, we assume that all traffic logs collected by base station are credible in current attack model, but some malicious logs may be sent by malicious nodes. In future work, this issue can be solved by comparing the sent packet logs (from sender) with the received packet logs (from receiver). Also, ELD can consider some more information to locate carousel-malicious nodes, i.e., recording all the paths that a packet may bypass. This can further help reduce the false alarm rate and improve the detection accuracy.

Acknowledgments. This work is supported by the National Natural Science Foundation of China under Grant No. 61402225 and the Science and Technology Funds from National State Grid Ltd. (The Research on Key Technologies of Distributed Parallel Database Storage and Processing based on Big Data).

References

1. Ahmad, I., Basheri, M., Iqbal, M.J., Rahim, A.: Performance comparison of support vector machine, random forest, and extreme learning machine for intrusion detection. IEEE Access **6**, 33789–33795 (2018)
2. Akhil Dubey, V.J., Kumar, A.: A survey in energy drain attacks and their countermeasures in wireless sensor networks. Int. J. Eng. Res. Technol. **3**, 1206–1210 (2014)
3. Bhunia, S.S., Gurusamy, M.: Dynamic attack detection and mitigation in IoT using SDN. In: 27th International Telecommunication Networks and Applications Conference (ITNAC), pp. 1–6. IEEE (2017)
4. Du, Q., Wei, Y., Mao, Y.: Distributed deployment of anomaly detection scheme in resource-limited IoT devices. In: IEEE ICCT, pp. 323–329. IEEE (2019)
5. Geethanjali, N., Gayathri, E.: A survey on energy depletion attacks in wireless sensor networks. Int. J. Sci. Res. **3**(9), 2070–2074 (2014)
6. Gelenbe, E., Kadioglu, Y.M.: Energy life-time of wireless nodes with network attacks and mitigation. In: 2018 IEEE ICC Workshops, pp. 1–6. IEEE (2018)
7. Liu, L., Ma, Z., Meng, W.: Detection of multiple-mix-attack malicious nodes using perceptron-based trust in IoT networks. Future Gener. Comput. Syst. **101**, 865–879 (2019)
8. Liu, X., Abdelhakim, M., Krishnamurthy, P., Tipper, D.: Identifying malicious nodes in multihop IoT networks using diversity and unsupervised learning. In: 2018 IEEE ICC, pp. 1–6. IEEE (2018)
9. Luo, T., Nagarajan, S.G.: Distributed anomaly detection using autoencoder neural networks in WSN for IoT. In: IEEE ICC, pp. 1–6. IEEE (2018)
10. Moustafa, N., Slay, J.: UNSW-NB15: a comprehensive data set for network intrusion detection systems (UNSW-NB15 network data set). In: 2015 Military Communications and Information Systems Conference (MilCIS), pp. 1–6. IEEE (2015)
11. Nguyen, T., Ngo, T., Nguyen, T.: The flooding attack in low power and lossy networks: a case study. In: International Conference on Smart Communications in Network Technologies (SaCoNeT), pp. 183–187. IEEE (2018)
12. Pedregosa, F., et al.: Scikit-learn: machine learning in Python. J. Mach. Learn. Res. **12**, 2825–2830 (2011)
13. Pu, C.: Energy depletion attack against routing protocol in the Internet of Things. In: IEEE CCNC, pp. 1–4. IEEE (2019)
14. Resende, P.A.A., Drummond, A.C.: A survey of random forest based methods for intrusion detection systems. ACM Comput. Surv. (CSUR) **51**(3), 1–36 (2018)
15. Rughoobur, P., Nagowah, L.: A lightweight replay attack detection framework for battery depended IoT devices designed for healthcare. In: Proceedings of ICTUS, pp. 811–817. IEEE (2017)
16. Sedjelmaci, H., Senouci, S.M., Al-Bahri, M.: A lightweight anomaly detection technique for low-resource IoT devices: a game-theoretic methodology. In: IEEE ICC, pp. 1–6. IEEE (2016)
17. Sharma, V., Hussain, M.: Mitigating replay attack in wireless sensor network through assortment of packets. In: Satapathy, S.C., Prasad, V.K., Rani, B.P., Udgata, S.K., Raju, K.S. (eds.) Proceedings of the First International Conference on Computational Intelligence and Informatics. AISC, vol. 507, pp. 221–230. Springer, Singapore (2017). https://doi.org/10.1007/978-981-10-2471-9_22
18. Singh, S., Jain, P.: Detection and prevention for avoidance of energy draining vampire attack in MANET. Int. J. Adv. Res. Comput. Sci. Softw. Eng. **7**(5), 966–970 (2017)

19. Singh, S.R., Narendra Babu, C.R.: Improving the performance of energy attack detection in wireless sensor networks by secure forward mechanism. Int. J. Sci. Res. Publ. **4**, 367 (2014)
20. Soni, M., Pahadiya, B.: Detection and removal of vampire attack in wireless sensor network. Int. J. Comput. Appl. **126**(7), 46–50 (2015)
21. Vasserman, E.Y., Hopper, N.: Vampire attacks: draining life from wireless ad hoc sensor networks. IEEE Trans. Mob. Comput. **12**(2), 318–332 (2011)

Minimal Rare-Pattern-Based Outlier Detection Method for Data Streams by Considering Anti-monotonic Constraints

Saihua Cai, Jinfu Chen[✉], Xinru Li, and Bo Liu

School of Computer Science and Communication Engineering, Jiangsu University,
Zhenjiang 212013, China
{caisaih,jinfuchen}@ujs.edu.cn

Abstract. In the collected associated data streams, some potential outliers are often fixed with the normal data instances, thus, it is necessary to accurately detect the outliers to improve the reliability of the data streams. In real life, people are more concerned about whether some outliers existed in the small scale data instances that satisfy their constraints, rather than in the huge entire datasets. However, the existing association-based outlier detection methods were proposed to detect the outliers from the entire data streams, thus, the time consumption is very long. To content with the existence of the constraints, this paper proposes an efficient constrained minimal rare pattern-based outlier detection method for data streams, namely AMCMRP-Outlier, to process the succinct and convertible anti-monotonic constraints. In the pattern mining phase, the matrix structure is used to quickly mine the minimal rare patterns that satisfy the constraints, thus providing the pattern basis for the outlier detection. In the outlier detection phase, two deviation indices are defined to measure the deviation degree of each transaction, and then the transactions having large deviation degrees are determined as the outliers. Finally, extensive experiments on one synthetic dataset and two public datasets verify that the AMCMRP-Outlier method can accurately detect the outliers with less time cost.

Keywords: Outlier detection · Minimal rare pattern mining · Deviation indices · Data streams · Anti-monotonic constraints

1 Introduction

Outlier detection [10] aims to find potential, rarely appearing data instances (aka transactions) that deviate much from most data elements, thus improving the quality of the collected data. It can be widely used in fraud detection [14], intrusion detection [8], sensor network detection [1], social network detection [12]. In recent years, numerous outlier detection methods have been proposed to effectively detect the outliers, and they

This work was partly supported by National Natural Science Foundation of China (NSFC grant number: U1836116), and the project of Jiangsu provincial Six Talent Peaks (Grant number XYDXXJS-016).

were roughly divided into: clustering-based method [7], distance-based method [9, 11], density-based method [13] and association-based method [2–6]. In addition to the static datasets, data streams also become the processing objects of the outlier detection, while the characteristics of the data streams (such as generating quickly and continuously) make the processing speed of the outlier detection should be as quickly as possible, thus catching up the generating speed of the data streams. In many applications, the data instances in the collected data streams are associated, thus, it is necessary to consider the associations between the data instances when detecting the potential outliers from associated data streams, so as to improve the detection accuracy. However, the associations between the data instances are not considered as the detection basis in the clustering-based, distance-based and density-based methods, thus, these categories of the outlier detection methods cannot effectively detect the outliers from associated data streams. The association-based methods solve this problem well, where the outliers are detected through mining the associations between the data instances, including mining the frequent patterns [5], closed frequent patterns [4], maximal frequent patterns [2] and minimal rare patterns [3, 6].

In real life, users only care about a small scale data streams they are interested rather than the huge scale data streams. For example, sales staff is more concerned about the items having a total sales price exceeds $100. Thus, it is not necessary to wait for a long period of time to process the huge entire data streams, out of which only a tiny fraction may be interesting to users. This leads to constrained processing, which aims to process the data streams that satisfy the user-specified constraints. However, the existing association-based outlier detection methods are proposed to detect the potential outliers from entire data streams, they cannot effectively process the constrained data streams. It will consume long time to obtain the final detection results, while most time is consumed on the data streams that they are not interested in. Thus, it is necessary to design an outlier detection method to accurately detect the outliers from the data streams that satisfy user-specified constraints.

In this paper, we propose an efficient minimal rare-pattern-based outlier detection approach, namely AMCMRP-Outlier, to quickly and accurately detect the outliers from the data streams that satisfy the user-specified succinct and convertible anti-monotonic constraints. The main contributions of this paper are summarized as follows:

1. We propose a matrix-based minimal rare pattern mining method to process two different kinds of anti-monotonic constraints, including: succinct anti-monotonic constraint and convertible anti-monotonic constraint, thus quickly mining the minimal rare patterns that satisfy the user-specified constraints from the data streams.
2. Through considering more factors that will influence the determination of the outliers, we design two deviation indices to measure the deviation degree of each transaction based on the mined minimal rare patterns that satisfy the user-specified constraint, and then propose the anti-monotonic constrained minimal rare pattern-based outlier detection method, namely AMCMRP-Outlier, to accurately detect the potential outliers.

The remainder of this paper is organized as follows. Section 2 reviews the related works of association-based outlier detection methods. Section 3 provides some preliminaries. Section 4 introduces two constrained minimal rare pattern mining methods and anti-monotonic constrained minimal rare pattern-based outlier detection method. Section 5 tests the performance of the proposed method. Section 6 summarizes the full text and gives the direction of the future work.

2   Related Works of Association-Based Outlier Detection Methods

In 2005, He et al. proposed the first association-based outlier detection method, namely FindFPOF [5], to detect the outliers from static datasets based on the mining of frequent patterns, where the deviation index (that is, the ratio of the *count* value of the contained frequent patterns to the total number of all mined frequent patterns) is designed to measure the deviation degree of each transaction. Because the designed deviation index is very simple, thus, its detection accuracy is not very high. In addition, the basis of the FindFPOF method is the frequent patterns, thus, the time cost on the outlier detection phase is very long.

To reduce the scale of the patterns used in the outlier detection phase, the closed frequent pattern-based outlier detection method FCI-Outlier [4] and the maximal frequent pattern-based outlier detection method MFPM-AD [2] are proposed to quickly detect the outliers. In these two methods, more factors that have the possibility to influence the determination of the outliers are considered in the designing of the deviation indices, thus, the detection accuracy of these two methods is obviously increased.

In addition, based on the idea that the rare patterns (represent the patterns that appearing rarely) are more match to the characteristics of "rarely appearing" of the outliers, the minimal rare pattern-based outlier detection method, namely MIFPOD [6], is proposed to accurately detect the potential outliers from data streams. In the MIFPOD method, three deviation factors are defined to accurately measure the deviation degree of each transaction. Although the MIFPOD method can accurately detect the potential outliers from the data streams, but the time efficiency is not very high. To effectively process the uncertain data streams, through considering the existence probability, the MiFI-Outlier method [3] is proposed based on the mining of minimal rare patterns. When the threshold *min_sup* is set slightly large, the detection accuracy of the MIFPOD and MiFI-Outlier methods are very high, but these two methods cannot effectively detect the outliers when the *min_sup* is set small.

3   Preliminaries

Assume that $P = \{p_1, p_2, ..., p_n\}$ is a set of items, where each item is an object with some attributes, such as: *price, weight, length*, etc. Data streams (*DS*) are composed of continuous transactions (that is, $DS = \{T_1, T_2, ..., T_n\}$), where each transaction is composed of several items from P (that is, $T_i = \{p_1, p_2, ..., p_i\}$). Pattern P_i in the transaction T_i is composed of some items existing in T_i, and pattern P_i is called an

n-pattern if the length of P_i is n. For two patterns P_a and P_b, if all items in P_a are existed in P_b but some items in P_b are not existed in P_a, then P_a is called the subset of P_b and P_b is called the superset of P_a. In the data streams environment, the sliding window model is often used to effectively process the data streams, where only k transactions can be processed in the sliding window each time and k is the size of sliding window (denoted as $|SW|$). For a pattern P_i, its appearing times in the sliding window is called *count*, P_i is a frequent pattern if its *count* is not less than the given threshold *min_sup*, otherwise, P_i is a rare pattern. Given a constraint C, if pattern P_i satisfies the specified constraint C (that is, $C(P_i) = $ true), P_i is a constrained pattern.

To describe the pattern mining process and outlier detection process, we provide a detailed example of data streams, and it is shown in Table 1. And then, we provide two SQL-style specified anti-monotonic constraints: $C_1 \equiv \max(P_i.price) < 15$ and $C_2 \equiv \text{sum}(P_i.price) \le 24$. In this example, the size of sliding window ($|SW|$) is set to 6, and the threshold *min_sup* is set to 3.

Table 1. An example of data streams with constraints

TID	Transactions	TID	Transactions	TID	Transactions
01	$\{A, B, D, E, F\}$	02	$\{A, B, C, F\}$	03	$\{A, B, F\}$
04	$\{B, C, D, F, G, H\}$	05	$\{A, B, C, D, E, F, G\}$	06	$\{A, B, C, G, H\}$
...	......	...	......	...	......
item	price	item	price	item	price
A	10	B	6	C	8
D	12	E	5	F	20
G	26	H	16		

Definition 1. *Anti-monotonic constraint: For a specified constraint C, when a pattern P_i violates C, and any superset of P_i also violates C, then constraint C is an anti-monotonic constraint.*

Definition 2. *Succinct constraint: For a specified constraint C, if all patterns that satisfy C can be directly and accurately generated without generating any pattern that violates C, then constraint C is a succinct constraint.*

Definition 3. *Convertible constraint: For a specified constraint C, if it can be converted to the succinct constraint through some ways, then constraint C is a convertible constraint.*

The anti-monotonic constraint can be subdivided into: succinct anti-monotonic constraint and convertible anti-monotonic constraint, where the convertible anti-monotonic constraint can be converted to the weaker succinct constraint, such as constraint $C_2 \equiv$ sum$(P_i.price) \leq 24$ can be converted to $C_2' \equiv$ max$(P_i.price) \leq 24$.

Definition 4. *Constrained frequent pattern (CFP): For a pattern P_i, if it satisfies the specified constraint C and its count is not less than the threshold min_sup, then, P_i is a CFP. That is, pattern P_i is a CFP if $\{P_i \mid sup(P_i) \geq min\_sup \& C(P_i) = true\}$.*

Definition 5. *Constrained rare pattern (CRP): For a pattern P_i, if it satisfies the specified constraint C and its count is less than the threshold min_sup, then, P_i is a CRP. That is, pattern P_i is a CRP if $\{P_i \mid sup(P_i) < min\_sup \& C(P_i) = true\}$.*

Definition 6. *Constrained minimal rare pattern (CMRP): For a pattern P_i, if it is a CRP and any subset of P_i is not a CFP, then, P_i is a CMRP.*

Definition 7. *Outlier: For the transaction T_i in the sliding window, if the deviation degree of T_i is not less than the given deviation threshold DT, then, T_i is an outlier.*

4   Anti-monotonic Constrained Minimal Rare Pattern-Based Outlier Detection (AMCMRP-Outlier)

For the association-based outlier detection methods, they detect the potential outliers through two phases, including: mining the associations between the data instances (such as: frequent patterns, rare patterns) and calculating deviation degree of each transaction based on the designing deviation indices. Similar to the traditional association-based outlier detection methods, the anti-monotonic constrained minimal rare pattern-based outlier detection method detects the outliers through mining the minimal rare patterns that satisfy user-specified constraint and the calculating of deviation degrees of the transactions.

4.1   Constrained Minimal Rare Pattern Mining (CMRP-Mine)

Constrained minimal rare pattern mining is the basis of the entire outlier detection process, it provides the patterns basis for the outlier detection phase. To accurately detect the outliers from the data streams that satisfy the user-specified constraints, this subsection first introduces two minimal rare pattern mining methods for two anti-monotonic constraints, including: succinct anti-monotonic constrained minimal rare pattern mining method and convertible anti-monotonic constrained minimal rare pattern mining method.

Succinct Anti-monotonic Constrained Minimal Rare Pattern Mining. It can be known from the anti-monotonic property [3] that if the *count* of the pattern is less than the threshold *min_sup*, then any superset of this pattern will be the rare pattern. Thus, for both the anti-monotonic constraint and the convertible anti-monotonic constraint, the first operation is to seek for the rare 1-patterns that have no meaning to be further extended, thus reducing the scale of extensible patterns. For the rare 1-patterns, they are divided into the rare 1-patterns that satisfy the constraint and the rare 1-patterns that violate the constraint, where the rare 1-patterns that satisfy the constraint are *CMRPs* and they are stored into the constrained minimal rare pattern library (CMRPL), the rare 1-patterns that violate the constraint are stored into the violate constraint pattern library (VCPL). Then, if the frequent 1-patterns violate the specified constraint, then any superset will also violate the constraint, thus, it is not necessary to extend the frequent 1-patterns that violate the constraint and they are stored into the VCPL. And then the frequent 1-patterns that satisfy the user-specified anti-monotonic constraint are as the basic patterns to participate in the further "pattern extension" operations.

After obtaining the frequent 1-patterns that satisfy the user-specified anti-monotonic constraint (called valid 1-patterns), the matrix structure is used to store the specific information of these valid 1-patterns, thus reducing the scan times of the data streams. The size of matrix is $n*(m + 1)$, where n is equal to the number of the valid 1-patterns and m is equal to the size of sliding window, and the $(m + 1)$ row store the *count* value of the valid 1-patterns. And then, the valid 1-patterns are fetched from the matrix to conduct the "pattern extension" operations. Once the *count* value of the extended 2-patterns is less than the *min_sup*, then the 2-patterns are *CMRPs* and they are stored into the CMRPL, where the *count* value is calculated by multiplying the probability in the column vector in which the two extended patterns are located. After obtaining the *CMRPs* with the length of 2, the valid 2-patterns are used as the basic elements to perform the further "pattern extension" operations, where the "pattern extension" operation means to "right connect" one k-pattern with other k-pattern to form the $(k + 1)$-pattern, note that the two extended k-patterns have the same prefix with the length of $(k - 1)$. Because the patterns are extended by the patterns that satisfy the specified succinct anti-monotonic constraint, thus, it is not necessary to judge whether the extended patterns satisfy the constraint.

For the valid k-patterns ($k \geq 2$), each two k-patterns with the same $(k - 1)$ prefix are fetched to conduct the "pattern extension" operation, thus forming the $(k + 1)$-pattern, and then the *count* value of the generated $(k + 1)$-pattern is calculated using the above manners to determine whether they are the rare patterns that satisfy the user-specified constraint or valid k-patterns. For the mined rare k-patterns that satisfy the constraint, it is necessary to conduct the "minimal checking" operation to seek for the minimal rare patterns that satisfy the predefined constraints, where the "minimal checking" operation is to check whether there is any subset of the k-pattern with the length of $(k - 1)$ is the *CMRP*. If any subset of the k-pattern is the *CMRP*, then the extended k-pattern is discarded, otherwise, the extended k-pattern is the *CMRP* and it is stored into the CMRPL. Recursively perform the above operations until no longer pattern can be further extended, and the patterns that stored into the CMRPL are outputted as the final *CMRPs*.

Convertible Anti-monotonic Constrained Minimal Rare Pattern Mining. The difference of the constrained pattern mining process under the convertible anti-monotonic constraint and the succinct anti-monotonic constrained pattern mining can be summarized as follows: (1) it cannot directly generate the full patterns that satisfy the user-specified convertible anti-monotonic constraint; (2) whether the extended patterns satisfy the constraint should be checked in the mining process. To solve the first difference, it is necessary to convert the convertible anti-monotonic constraint to the tight succinct anti-monotonic constraint, thus making it can generate the complete supersets, where the principle of the conversion is to ensure the pattern mining operation will not appear the situation of false mining based on the converted constraint. And then, scan the data streams to distinguish the 1-patterns, where the rare 1-patterns that satisfy the converted constraint are *CMRPs* and they are stored into the CMRPL, and the 1-patterns that violate the converted constraint are stored into the VCPL. For the frequent 1-patterns that satisfy the converted constraint, they are as the basic patterns to participate in the further "pattern extension" operations.

And then, the valid 1-patterns are fetched from the matrix to conduct the "pattern extension" operations, where the first fetched pattern is arranged by their decrease *price* values, and the second fetched pattern is arranged by their increase *price* values. Therefore, once the extended pattern that prefix by $\{p_i\}$ is not satisfying the converted constraint, it is not necessary to further conduct the "pattern extension" on $\{p_i\}$. With this manner, the time cost on the pattern mining process is obviously reduced. After obtaining the extended 2-patterns, their *count* value is also calculated like the succinct anti-monotonic constrained minimal rare pattern mining method. However, the difference is that whether the extended 2-patterns satisfy the original constraint should be determined, thus accurately mining the rare patterns that satisfy the convertible anti-monotonic constraint. Recursively perform the "pattern extension" operations on the valid k-patterns like the above method and check whether the extended patterns satisfy the original constraint, and then perform the "minimal checking" operation to check whether there is any subset of the k-pattern with the length of $(k - 1)$ is the *CMRP*. With the above operations, the minimal rare patterns that satisfy the user-specified convertible anti-monotonic constraint can be accurately mined.

The detailed process of succinct and convertible anti-monotonic constrained minimal rare pattern mining method is shown in Algorithm 1.

Algorithm 1: CMRP-Mine
Input: Data streams, *min_sup*, *C* (constraint)
Output: *CMRPs*

```
01:if C is C_CAM then
02:   convert the C_CAM into tight C_SAM
03:else //C is C_SAM
04:   foreach 1-pattern {p_i} in the sliding window do
05:     if count(p_i)<min_sup then
06:       if C_SAM(p_i)=true then
07:         {p_i}→CMRPL
08:       else
09:         {p_i}→VCPL
10:       end if
11:     else
12:       if C_SAM(p_i)=false then
13:         {p_i}→VCPL
14:       else
15:         {p_i}→matrix
16:       end if
17:   end for
18:end if
19:foreach 1-pattern {p_a} and {p_b} in matrix do
20:   extend them to 2-pattern {p_a,p_b}
21:   if count(p_a,p_b)<min_sup then
22:     if C(p_a,p_b)=true then
23:       {p_i}→CMRPL
24:     end if
25:   else
26:     if C(p_a,p_b)=true then
27:       {p_a,p_b} is the basic element for "pattern extension"
28:     end if
29:   end if
30:end for
31:k=2
32:foreach two valid k-patterns with the same prefix of length (k-1) do
33:   extend them to (k+1)-pattern
34:   if count((k+1)-pattern)<min_sup then
35:     if C((k+1)-pattern)=true then
36:       perform "minimal checking"
37:       CMRP→CMRPL
38:     end if
39:   else
40:     if C((k+1)-pattern)=true then
41:       (k+1)-pattern is the basic element for "pattern extension"
42:     end if
43:   end if
44:end for
45:k++
46:go to 32
47:return CMRPs
```

4.2 Outlier Detection Method

The designing of the deviation indices is very critical to the detection accuracy, thus, we paid more attention to the following factors in the designing of the deviation indices to improve the detection accuracy.

(I) The length and the *count* of the mined minimal rare patterns that satisfy the user-specified constraint. The longer of the constrained minimal rare patterns indicates that less rare patterns can be extended by them, thus, this factor is negative correlation to the determination of the outliers. In addition, the small *count* value of the constrained minimal rare patterns indicates that the patterns are appearing more rarely, thus, this factor is also negative correlation to the determination of the outliers. (II) The number of the contained 1-patterns that violate the user-specified constraint and the number of the contained minimal rare patterns that satisfy the user-specified constraint. The large number of the contained these two categories of the patterns means that more patterns in the transaction are not satisfying the user-specified constraint, thus, the transaction is more easily to be determined as the outliers. This factor is positive correlation to the determination of the outlier. (III) The length of the transaction. For two transactions that with different length $(len(T_i) < len(T_j))$, and the contained 1-patterns that violate the user-specified constraint and the contained minimal rare patterns that satisfy the user-specified constraint are the same. It is obviously that the larger ratio of patterns in T_i are not required by the user, thus, transaction T_i is more like the outlier than transaction T_j. This factor is negative correlation to the determination of the outliers.

Through fully considering the above three factors, the following two complete deviation indices are designed to measure the deviation degree of each transaction.

Definition 8. *Constrained minimal rare pattern deviation index (CMRPDI): For transaction T_i, its length is $len(T_i)$. In transaction T_i, the contained constrained minimal rare pattern is {X}, its length is $len(X)$ and its count value is $count(X)$. Then, CMRPDI is defined as:*

$$CMRPDI(T_i) = \sum_{X \in T_i} (min\_sup - count(X)) \times 2^{len(T_i) - len(X)} \tag{1}$$

Definition 9. *Transaction Deviation Index (TDI): For transaction T_i, its length is $len(T_i)$. In transaction T_i, the number of contained 1-patterns {Y} that violate the constraint is $n(Y)$ and the number of contained minimal rare patterns {X} that satisfies the constraint is $n(X)$. Then, TDI is defined as:*

$$TDI(T_i) = \frac{\sum_{X \in T_i, Y \in T_i} (CMRPDI(T_i) + n(Y) \times (len(T_i) - 1)) \times (n(Y) + n(X))}{len(T_i)} \tag{2}$$

TDI is the deviation index to measure the deviation degree of each transaction in the data streams that satisfy the user-specified constraint, and the bigger $TDI(T_i)$ value of transaction T_i means it is more like an outlier.

Based on the designing of the deviation indices and the mined patterns, we propose an efficient minimal rare-pattern-based outlier detection method for data streams by considering anti-monotonic constraints, namely AMCMRP-Outlier, for accurately detecting the potential outliers from the data streams. The AMCMRP-Outlier method detects the potential outliers through mining the minimal rare patterns that satisfy the user-specified constraint and calculating the deviation degree of each transaction in the data streams. And then, the transactions are sorted with the decreasing order of their $TDI(T_i)$ values, and the transactions whose $TDI(T_i)$ value is not less than the given deviation threshold DT are judged as the outliers. The detailed process of the proposed AMCMRP-Outlier is shown in Algorithm 2.

Algorithm 2: AMCMRP-Outlier

Input: Data streams, min_sup, constraint, DT

Output: Outliers

01: Mine $CMRPs$ //call Algorithm 1
02: $CMRPDI(T_i)$=0, $TDI(T_i)$=0
03: **foreach** T_i in the sliding window **do**
04:   **foreach** $CMRP$ $\{X\}$ in T_i **do**
05:
$$CMRPDI(T_i) = \sum_{X \in T_i} (min\_sup - count(X) + 1) \times 2^{len(T_i) - len(X)}$$

06:   **end for**
07:   **foreach** 1-patterns that violate the constraint $\{Y\}$ in T_i **do**
08:
$$TDI(T_i) = \frac{\sum_{X \in T_i, Y \in T_i} (CMRPDI(T_i) + n(Y) \times (len(T_i) - 1)) \times (n(Y) + n(X))}{len(T_i)}$$

09:   **end for**
10: **end for**
11: sort the transactions using decreasing $TDI(T_i)$ values
12: **if** $TDI(T_i) \geq DT$ **then**
13:   $T_i \rightarrow outlier$
14: **end if**
15: Output $outliers$

---

5 Experiment Results

To evaluate the detection accuracy and the time cost of the proposed AMCMRP-Outlier method, a synthetic dataset [3] and two public datasets[1] *Lymphography* and *Satimage-2* are used in this experiment, where each element is added a *price* randomly selected from $\{10, 12, 14, 16, 18, 20, 25, 30, 35\}$. In this experiment, the FCI-Outlier [4], MFPM-AD [2] and MIFPOD [6] are used as the compared methods. All the methods compared in this paper are implemented using the Python language (Python 3.6), and all experiments are performed on a PC with 3.30 GHz CPU, 8 GB RAM and Windows 10OS.

5.1 Detection Accuracy of the AMCMRP-Outlier Method

To test the detection accuracy of the proposed AMCMRP-Outlier method, the experiment is conducted under different sizes of sliding window and different min_sup values. For the C_{SAM}, the used constraints are $C_{SAM1} \equiv \max(X.price) \leq 20$ and $C_{SAM2} \equiv \max(X.price) \leq 25$. For the C_{CAM}, the used constraints are $C_{CAM1} \equiv \text{sum}(X.price) \leq 50$ and $C_{CAM2} \equiv \text{sum}(X.price) \leq 80$. The experimental results on the synthetic dataset are shown in

---

[1] http://odds.cs.stonybrook.edu/.

Fig. 1 and Fig. 2, where the X-axis (No. of sliding window) means the concrete number of the sliding window and the Y-axis (Detection accuracy) means the ratio of the number of true outliers to the total number of retrieved transactions when all true outliers are identified. And the experimental results on two public datasets are shown in Table 2 and Table 3.

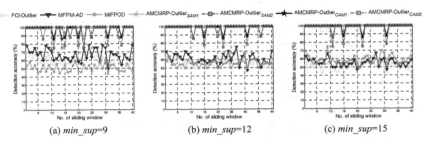

(a) *min_sup*=9   (b) *min_sup*=12   (c) *min_sup*=15

Fig. 1. Detection accuracy of the AMCMRP-Outlier method when |SW| is 30

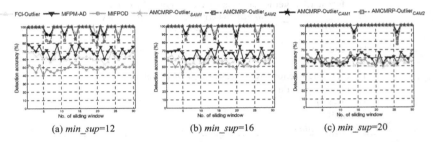

(a) *min_sup*=12   (b) *min_sup*=16   (c) *min_sup*=20

Fig. 2. Detection accuracy of the AMCMRP-Outlier method when |SW| is 40

Table 2. Detection accuracy of the AMCMRP-Outlier method on the dataset *Lymphography*

min_sup	Methods						
	FCI-Outlier	MFPM-AD	MIFPOD	AMCMRP-Outlier$_{SAM1}$	AMCMRP-Outlier$_{SAM2}$	AMCMRP-Outlier$_{CAM1}$	AMCMRP-Outlier$_{CAM2}$
29.6	46.15%	66.67%	15.79%	75%	75%	75%	75%
37.0	37.5%	60%	17.14%	85.71%	75%	75%	75%
44.4	35.29%	60%	18.75%	85.71%	75%	85.71%	75%
51.8	31.58%	50%	20.69%	85.71%	75%	85.71%	75%
59.2	26.09%	40%	25%	85.71%	85.71%	85.71%	75%
66.6	26.09%	35.29%	28.57%	85.71%	85.71%	85.71%	85.71%
74.0	23.08%	33.33%	35.29%	85.71%	85.71%	85.71%	85.71%

When the size of sliding window is set to 30, the detection accuracy of the proposed AMCMRP-Outlier method under different *min_sup* values is shown in Fig. 1. For the

Table 3. Detection accuracy of the AMCMRP-Outlier method on the dataset *Satimage*-2

min_sup	Methods						
	FCI-Outlier	MFPM-AD	MIFPOD	AMCMRP-Outlier$_{SAM1}$	AMCMRP-Outlier$_{SAM2}$	AMCMRP-Outlier$_{CAM1}$	AMCMRP-Outlier$_{CAM2}$
580.3	58.68%	65.74%	27.63%	82.56%	77.17%	79.78%	76.34%
725.325	57.72%	63.39%	30.34%	84.52%	78.02%	79.78%	77.17%
870.45	56.35%	62.28%	32.57%	85.54%	80.68%	81.61%	78.89%
1015.525	55.47%	59.66%	33.65%	88.75%	80.68%	82.56%	79.78%
1160.6	54.2%	57.72%	35.86%	87.65%	82.56%	84.52%	80.68%
1305.675	52.99%	56.35%	38.38%	88.75%	83.53%	84.52%	81.61%
1595.825	51.08%	55.47%	42.51%	91.03%	87.65%	85.54%	83.53%

AMCMRP-Outlier method, its detection accuracy always higher than that of the three compared methods, and the detection accuracy shows an obviously increase trend with the increase of the *min_sup* values. The reason for appearing this situation is that the number of mined minimal rare patterns that satisfy the user-specified constraint is much larger under the large *min_sup* values, thus, more patterns can be used as the pattern basis for the outlier detection phase. When the kind of the constraint is constant, the detection accuracy of the proposed AMCMRP-Outlier method shows a decrease trend when the constraint is set much loose, the reason for appearing this situation is that the less 1-patterns that violate the user-specified constraint can be mined under loose constraint, thus, it cannot provide the strong support for the determination of the outliers. For the compared association-based outlier detection methods, with the increase of the *min_sup* values, the detection accuracy of the rare pattern-based method MIFPOD shows an increase trend, but the detection accuracy of the frequent pattern-based methods FCI-Outlier and MFPM-AD shows a decrease trend.

When the size of sliding window is set to 40, the detection accuracy of the AMCMRP-Outlier method under different *min_sup* values is shown in Fig. 2. When the *min_sup* value is set to 12, the false detection of the AMCMRP-Outlier method is appearing in eight windows of the thirty windows, but the false detection of the AMCMRP-Outlier method is appearing in five windows when the *min_sup* is set to 16, while the false detection is only appearing in two windows when the *min_sup* is set to 20. When the *min_sup* value is set slightly small, the detection accuracy of the MIFPOD method is much lower than that of the FCI-Outlier and MFPM-AD methods, but when the *min_sup* value is set slightly larger, the detection accuracy of the MIFPOD method is higher than that of other two methods in more windows.

It can be seen from Table 2 and Table 3 that on the two public datasets, the detection accuracy of the proposed AMCMRP-Outlier method under two kinds of anti-monotonic constraints is higher than that of other three compared methods, including: FCI-Outlier, MFPM-AD and MIFPOD. When the kind of the constraint is constant, the detection accuracy of the AMCMRP-Outlier method is higher under the tight constraint, such as the detection accuracy under C_{SAM1} is slightly high than that under C_{SAM2}. Similar to the situation on the synthetic dataset, the detection accuracy of the AMCMRP-Outlier method on the two public datasets shows an increase trend with the increasing of the *min_sup* values, it is also owing to that more minimal rare patterns that satisfy the user-specified constraint can be effectively mined under the large *min_sup* values, thus more patterns can provide the pattern basis for the outlier detection phase. For the three compared methods, the detection accuracy of the FCI-Outlier and MFPM-AD methods shows a decrease trend with the increasing of the *min_sup* values, and the detection accuracy of the MIFPOD method shows an increase trend with the increasing of the *min_sup* values. When the *min_sup* value is set slightly larger, the detection accuracy of the MIFPOD method exceeds other two compared methods.

In general, regardless of the kinds of the anti-monotonic constraints, the detection accuracy of the AMCMRP-Outlier method on both the synthetic dataset and the public datasets is higher than that of the three compared association-based outlier detection methods. In addition, for gaining the better detection accuracy when using the AMCMRP-Outlier method, the *min_sup* value should set slightly larger.

5.2   Time Cost of the AMCMRP-Outlier Method

This subsection evaluates the time cost of the proposed AMCMRP-Outlier method and other three association-based methods, where the different *min_sup* values and different sizes of sliding window are also considered in the experiment. Each experiment is performed for 50 times and the average time cost is calculated to form the final experimental results. The experimental results on the synthetic dataset are shown in Fig. 3 and Fig. 4, and the result on the public datasets is shown in Fig. 5.

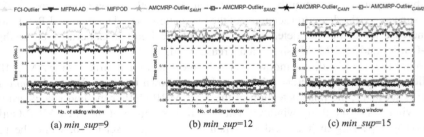

(a) *min_sup*=9   (b) *min_sup*=12   (c) *min_sup*=15

Fig. 3. Time cost of the AMCMRP-Outlier method on the synthetic dataset when |SW| is 30

It can be seen from the Fig. 3, 4 and Fig. 5 that on the synthetic dataset and public datasets, the time cost of the proposed AMCMRP-Outlier method is much shorter than that of the three compared association-based outlier detection methods, while the time cost of the FCI-Outlier method is the longest, it is owing to that only a small amount of patterns are pruned before the "pattern extension" operations, thus, the pattern mining phase consumes very long time, and the time cost of the MIFPOD method and MFPM-AD method is very close to each other. When the size of the sliding window is constant, the time cost of the AMCMRP-Outlier method shows a decrease trend with the increase of the *min_sup* values, the reason for appearing this situation is that more

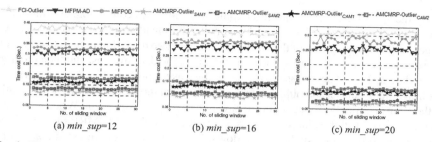

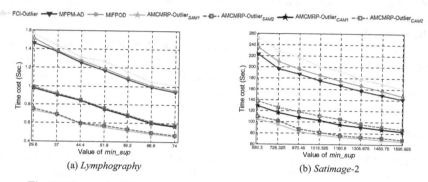

Fig. 4. Time cost of the AMCMRP-Outlier method on the synthetic dataset when |SW| is 40

(a) *min_sup*=12 (b) *min_sup*=16 (c) *min_sup*=20

(a) *Lymphography* (b) *Satimage-2*

Fig. 5. Time cost of the AMCMRP-Outlier method on two public datasets

patterns are rare patterns under the large *min_sup* values, thus, the number of extensible patterns is reduced, which results the time cost on the time consuming "pattern extension" operations is also greatly reduced. Compared with the succinct anti-monotonic constraint, the time cost on the entire outlier detection process under the convertible anti-monotonic constraint is much longer, the reason for appearing this situation is that whether the extended patterns satisfy the user-specified constraint should be checked in the pattern mining. When the kind of constraint is constant, the time cost of the proposed AMCMRP-Outlier method under the loose constraint is much longer, it is owing to that the scale of the patterns that satisfy the loose constraint is obviously increased when the user-specified constraint is slightly loose, thus, more patterns can be participated into the further "pattern extension" process. Thus, it is necessary to set the *min_sup* value slightly larger to obtain a high time efficiency.

6   Conclusions

In this paper, we propose an efficient minimal rare pattern-based outlier detection method, namely AMCMRP-Outlier, to detect the potential outliers from the data streams that satisfy the user-specified anti-monotonic constraint through two phases. In the pattern mining phase, with the use of the matrix structure, we proposed two constrained minimal rare pattern mining methods to effectively mine the minimal rare patterns that satisfy the specified succinct anti-monotonic constraint and convertible anti-monotonic constraint. In the outlier detection phase, through considering more factors that will influence the determination of the outliers, we design two deviation indices to effectively measure the deviation degree of each transaction in the data streams, and then the transactions having largest deviation degrees are judged as the outliers. Extensive experiments on the synthetic dataset and public datasets confirm that the proposed AMCMRP-Outlier method can accurately detect the outliers with less time consumption. When the threshold *min_sup* is set slightly large, the detection accuracy of the AMCMRP-Outlier method can reach to 100% in most sliding windows. However, when the threshold *min_sup* is set small, the detection accuracy of the proposed AMCMRP-Outlier method is not so competitive and its time cost is also very long. That is, when the *min_sup* is set small, the AMCMRP-Outlier method is not an ideal choice for accurately detecting the potential outliers from the data streams.

In the future, we prepare to improve the proposed AMCMRP-Outlier method to make it can effectively process the set of constraints (that is, each constraint is combined using logical operations like "and" and "or"). In addition, we also want to apply the proposed method to some practical applications.

References

1. Branch, J.W., Giannella, C., Szymanski, B., Wolff, R., Kargupta, H.: In-network outlier detection in wireless sensor networks. Knowl. Inf. Syst. **34**(1), 23–54 (2013)
2. Cai, S., Sun, R., Li, J., Deng, C., Li, S.: Abnormal detecting over data stream based on maximal pattern mining technology. In: Sun, Y., Lu, T., Xie, X., Gao, L., Fan, H. (eds.) ChineseCSCW 2018. CCIS, vol. 917, pp. 371–385. Springer, Singapore (2019). https://doi.org/10.1007/978-981-13-3044-5_27
3. Cai, S.H., Li, S.C., Yuan, G., Hao, S.B., Sun, R.Z.: MiFI-outlier: minimal infrequent itemset-based outlier detection approach on uncertain data stream. Knowl.-Based Syst. **191**, 105268 (2020)
4. Hao, S., Cai, S., Sun, R., Li, S.: FCI-Outlier: an efficient frequent closed itemset-based outlier detecting approach on data stream. In: Sun, Y., Lu, T., Xie, X., Gao, L., Fan, H. (eds.) ChineseCSCW 2018. CCIS, vol. 917, pp. 176–187. Springer, Singapore (2019). https://doi.org/10.1007/978-981-13-3044-5_13
5. He, Z.Y., Xu, X.F., Huang, J.Z., Deng, S.C.: FP-Outlier: frequent pattern based outlier detection. Comput. Sci. Inf. Syst. **2**(1), 103–118 (2005)
6. Hemalatha, C.S., Vaidehi, V., Lakshmi, R.: Minimal infrequent pattern based approach for mining outliers in data streams. Expert Syst. Appl. **42**(4), 1998–2012 (2015)
7. Huang, J., Zhu, Q., Yang, L., Cheng, D., Wu, Q.: A novel outlier cluster detection algorithm without top-n parameter. Knowl Based Syst **121**, 32–40 (2017)
8. Iraqi, O., Bakkali, H.E.: Application-level unsupervised outlier-based intrusion detection and prevention. Secur. Commun. Networks **5**, 1–13 (2019)
9. Kontaki, M., Gounaris, A., Papadopoulos, A.N., Tsichlas, K., Manolopoulos, Y.: Efficient and flexible algorithms for monitoring distance-based outliers over data streams. Inf. Syst. **55**, 37–53 (2016)
10. Li, X.J., Lv, J.C., Yi, Z.: Outlier detection using structural scores in a high-dimensional space. IEEE Trans. Cybern. **50**(5), 2302–2310 (2020)
11. Radovanović, M., Nanopoulos, A., Ivanović, M.: Reverse nearest neighbors in unsupervised distance-based outlier detection. IEEE Trans. Knowl. Data Eng. **27**(5), 1369–1382 (2015)

12. Sharma, V., Kumar, R., Cheng, W.H., Atiquzzaman, M., Srinivasan, K., Zomaya, A.: NHAD: neuro-fuzzy based horizontal anomaly detection in online social networks. IEEE Trans. Knowl. Data Eng. **30**(11), 2171–2184 (2018)
13. Tang, B., He, H.: A local density-based approach for outlier detection. Neurocomputing **241**, 171–180 (2017)
14. Vanhoeyveld, J., Martens, D., Peeters, B.: Value-added tax fraud detection with scalable anomaly detection techniques. Appl. Soft Comput. **86**, 105895 (2020)

Towards Transparent Control-Flow Integrity in Safety-Critical Systems

Don Kuzhiyelil[1]([✉]), Philipp Zieris[2][iD], Marine Kadar[1], Sergey Tverdyshev[4][iD], and Gerhard Fohler[3]

[1] SYSGO GmbH, Mainz, Germany
{Don.Kuzhiyelil,Marine.Kadar}@sysgo.com
[2] Fraunhofer AISEC, Munich, Germany
philipp.zieris@aisec.fraunhofer.de
[3] TU Kaiserslautern, Kaiserslautern, Germany
fohler@eit.uni-kl.de
[4] Mainz, Germany
s.tv@me.com

Abstract. Protecting safety-critical Cyber-Physical Systems (CPS) against security threats is becoming a growing necessity. Due to the high level of network integration, CPS pose new targets to remote code-reuse attacks, such as Return-Oriented Programming (ROP). An effective mechanism to detect code-reuse attacks is Control-Flow Integrity (CFI). However, because of the intrusiveness of most current CFI solutions, i.e., their requirement for program instrumentation and run-time interference, we cannot directly apply them to safety-critical CPS. To the best of our knowledge, there is no CFI solution designed for CPS; and more specifically, we are not aware of any solution that fully monitors the forward-edges and backward-edges of an application's control-flow, while providing *independence* and *freedom from interference* guarantees. Hence, for the first time, we propose a safety certifiable, separation kernel-based partitioning architecture to integrate CFI monitoring in a safety-critical system to protect applications with real-time constraints. Our solution leverages ARM CoreSight to transparently enforce both forward-edge and backward-edge CFI for an application at run-time. Despite imposing a significant overhead on the overall system, our approach reliably protects the control-flow of the monitored application, while guaranteeing its real-time constraints. We evaluate our solution by analyzing its timing impact and discussing the resulting considerations for the integration and practical deployment in a safety-critical CPS.

Keywords: Safety-critical cyber-physical systems · Code-reuse attacks · Control-flow integrity · ARM CoreSight

1 Introduction

In modern networked safety-critical Cyber-Physical Systems (CPS) like automotive, railway, and avionics, the industry's trend is the integration of multiple functions on the same hardware platform in order to cope with the non-functional

© Springer Nature Switzerland AG 2020
W. Susilo et al. (Eds.): ISC 2020, LNCS 12472, pp. 290–311, 2020.
https://doi.org/10.1007/978-3-030-62974-8_17

requirements related to size, weight, and power. Due to the highly networked nature of these systems, remote control-flow hijacking attacks pose a serious threat [24, 42].

From the safety certification perspective, modern networked CPS are typically built from components with different criticality or assurance levels and, as such, are identified as mixed-critical systems [12]. The low-critical components in such a system typically implement connectivity (e.g., black channel[1]) for safety components, security functions for safety [44], or user-experience functions such as touch interfaces. Even though the low-critical components don't have any safety function to perform, they are important for availability, user-experience, and preserving confidentiality. A security vulnerability in such low-critical components may even open up the path for an attacker to manipulate safety-critical functions [36]. Thus, low-critical components also play an important role for the commercial success of a product.

While the high-critical components in mixed-critical systems are developed and verified using rigorous software engineering methods, it is common to see low-critical components being developed using less rigorous methods or even with the support of off-the-shelf libraries (e.g., OpenSSL). Due to the large code base and use of less rigorous development methods, memory errors can sustain in low-critical components and, with their direct exposure to the network, open up a large attack surface for an adversary to exploit the entire system. Exploiting memory corruptions is the most prevailing form of initiating remote control-flow hijacking attacks [51]. In particular, code-reuse attacks represent a subtype of such exploits, which consist of manipulating a victim program's execution flow by reusing legitimate code from within its address space in order to perform malicious actions (e.g., privilege escalation). Because of their popularity [24, 42, 51, 54], we identify code-reuse attacks [10, 15, 46] as dangerous and likely exploits in the context of safety-critical CPS.

Control-Flow Integrity (CFI) [1, 13] prevents code-reuse attacks by enforcing the execution flow of the protected application to conform to a pre-defined Control-Flow Graph (CFG). CFI enforcement identifies deviations from the baseline CFG as malicious control-flow transitions. For monitoring a program's control-flow, CFI approaches require instruction-level knowledge of the program including forward-edge and backward-edge CFG branches. For this, CFI implementations commonly require source code [4, 23, 25, 29, 37, 52, 57] or binary instrumentation [1, 3, 20, 38, 39, 55, 56] in order to check the validity of control-flow transitions during run-time. In the context of safety-critical systems, especially in multi-supplier product development, these constraints prohibit a straightforward deployment of CFI.

For safety-critical system requiring certification, the system developer has to ensure *freedom from interference* and *independence* between components to prevent fault propagation and to enable easy verification. For the deployment of CFI in safety-critical system, this means the resource usage (e.g. memory, CPU time) of CFI checking shall be deterministically upper-bounded at run-time. For the

---

[1] See IEC 61508 Part 2.

industrial deployment of CFI, it shall also use commonly available hardware assistance features, such as CFI solutions based on Intel Processor Trace (PT) [22,35] and ARM CoreSight [31]. Although these alternative solutions demonstrate a substantial improvement, they still don't address all aspects of safety-critical deployment and oftentimes even sacrifice complete CFG protection: They only perform partial edge protection [22,31] or discontinuous/punctual monitoring [35]. However, because of the safety-critical essence of our deployment context, we believe a complete CFI enforcement is crucial.

To the best of our knowledge, there is no work addressing the deployment of CFI in the context of safety-critical CPS. More specifically, we are not aware of any CFI monitoring solution for safety-critical CPS fully covering both forward-edges and backward-edges of an application's control-flow, while simultaneously providing freedom from interference and independence.

With this work, we make the following contributions: First, we validate the applicability of instruction tracing of ARM CoreSight to realize transparent, state-of-the-art CFI monitoring. Our solution protects the monitored application's baseline CFG at run-time. It fully covers backward-edges by maintaining a shadow stack [1,14] and considerably reduces the set of authorized forward-edges by employing a type-based policy generated at compile-time [37,52]. Second, we propose a separation kernel-based partitioning architecture to integrate our CFI monitoring solution in safety-critical CPS. We evaluate the temporal interference of CFI monitoring on the monitored application and the system as a whole by analyzing the performance impact for a worst-case and nominal-case scenario. We further discuss the system design considerations to integrate our CFI solution in a safety-critical system and identify optimization strategies to reduce the overhead of our CFI solution.

2   Problem Statement

A major source of control-flow hijacking attacks on CPS are vulnerabilities in their software, such as a buffer overflow corrupting a code pointer in memory. As software for CPS is primarily written in the C and C++ programming languages, which omit enforcing strong type and memory safety in favor of efficiency and flexibility, programming errors are prone to result in such memory corruptions. Unfortunately, modern CPS are highly distributed and interconnected devices, causing these vulnerabilities to become a serious attack surface for remote adversaries.

2.1   Code-Reuse Attacks

The most prevailing form for an adversary to gain access to a remote system are code-reuse attacks [51]. These attacks allow the adversary to execute arbitrary code even on systems that deploy memory isolation measures [6,16,17,28,30,40,50]. However, in the presence of a software vulnerability, an adversary gaining access to a code pointer in writable memory is still able to divert execution to an arbitrary location in executable memory. By repeatedly diverting execution to different locations, the adversary is able to perform his intended malicious behavior, while only repurposing legitimate code already available in the software.

Code-reuse attacks were first introduced with Return-Oriented Programming (ROP) [46] by utilizing function returns to combine arbitrary instruction sequences—so called gadgets—for malicious intent. Later, Jump-Oriented Programming (JOP) [10,15] extended code-reuse attacks to utilize indirect jumps and indirect function calls as well. Both techniques were initially devised on the X86 architecture, but rapidly adapted to various architectures in the embedded systems domain [11,21], including the ARM architecture [15].

2.2 Threat Model

We aim to protect applications on safety-critical systems against remote code-reuse attacks. We assume that the application contains memory errors resulting in exploitable, input-controlled vulnerabilities known to the remote adversary. Further, we presume the adversary has prior knowledge about the application's code layout and is able to identify suitable gadgets that can carry out his malicious intent. The goal of our adversary is to alter a code pointer in the target application's data memory and subsequently achieve the execution of the gadgets identified before. On the system, we assume higher privileged components, i.e., the Separation Kernel (SK), are trusted and operating correctly. The SK does not provide memory layout randomization, but does employ memory isolation. Hence, during an attack, the adversary is confined to the target application's address space, but otherwise able to infer the memory layout and gain arbitrary read access on executable memory and arbitrary read-write access to data memory.

3 Background

In a successful code-reuse attack, the adversary deviates the execution of an application from its predefined Control-Flow Graph (CFG). A CFG abstractly represents the application's execution, in which edges represent control-flow transfers between nodes, and nodes represent uninterruptible instruction sequences that end in a branch instruction, also called basic blocks. Basic blocks connected through jumps and function calls form *forward* edges, while function returns form *backward* edges. To prevent code-reuse attacks, a countermeasure must ensure that during an application's entire execution, no other edges than the legitimate and pre-defined forward and backward edges of the CFG are taken.

3.1 Control-Flow Integrity

A well-known approach to ensure that the execution of an application conforms to the legitimate CFG is enforcing Control-Flow Integrity (CFI) [1]. CFI considers the edges of a CFG to be vulnerable to an attack, if they represent indirect control-flow transfers. An adversary gaining access to a code pointer used to determine a basic block's successor is able to divert control to any other basic block in the graph. Edges representing direct control-flow transfers are considered safe, as CFI builds on the assumption that the application's code in memory is not writable (i.e., memory isolation is in use), resulting in the adversary being unable to inject malicious code of his own. In general, implementations of CFI first compute a representation of the application's legitimate CFG and then validate indirect control-flow transfers against their CFG metadata at run-time. With structural differences in this metadata, variating granularities in enforcing the application's CFG can be achieved.

CFI solutions generally directly instrument CFG enforcement into protected applications. However, this integration requires the metadata to be hidden within or isolated from the application's memory, so that an adversary—controlling the memory—is unable to alter it as part of his attack. An alternative approach is the strict separation of the CFI enforcement and the protected application by means of passively and transparently monitoring the application. This separation requires a secure channel between the CFI monitor and the application in order to pass control-flow information to the monitor at run-time. In our work, we utilize ARM CoreSight to provide that channel.

3.2 ARM CoreSight

CoreSight [7] is a hardware feature in ARM Systems on a Chip (SoCs) intended for the debugging and tracing of executed applications in real-time. Each core on the System on a Chip (SoC) is attached to an Embedded Trace Macrocell (ETM) responsible for trace collection. The traces from multiple ETMs are merged and stored in an Embedded Trace FIFO (ETF) queue. When the queue reaches a configurable threshold, the ETF can raise a signal directed to a core as an interrupt or to an external debugger. The software or external debugger can use this trigger to copy/flush the traces from the ETF queue to system memory or to external pins. CoreSight collects traces in form of *packets*, either containing branch decisions for direct control-flow transfers (i.e., branch taken or not taken) or the target address for indirect transfers. Packets additionally include per-thread Unique Identifiers (UIDs) that enable precise execution tracking of different (potentially multi-threaded) applications. Based on the packets provided by CoreSight and with additional binary information about the executed application, it is possible to reconstruct the entire execution control-flow including the exact sequence of branches taken. For our work, we use CoreSight to trace the program execution and perform transparent CFI monitoring.

3.3 Partitioned Architecture Based on Separation Kernel

As introduced in Sect. 1, modern safety-critical CPS combine mixed-critical components on one hardware. For preventing cascading failures (i.e., a failure in one component causing a failure in another one), all safety certification standards prescribe fault containment requirements. Different standards use different terms to describe the fault containment concept. The automotive standard ISO 26262 specifies[2] *freedom from interference* as a requirement to prevent cascading failures. The industry safety standard IEC 61508 requires[3] *sufficient independence* between safety and non-safety functions when they are running on the same hardware to prevent faults from non-safety functions causing failure in the safety-related functions. The avionics standard DO-178 explicitly states[4] *partitioning* as the means to prevent one component from contaminating another component's code, input/out, or data.

For achieving the freedom from interference and sufficient independence between components, we use a *partitioned architecture* [26], in which the components are executed in spatially and temporally separated sandboxes, called partitions, and communication between components is limited to explicitly defined communication channels. This architectural approach is also called Multiple Independent Levels of Security (MILS) [5,43,53]. The cornerstone of this partitioned architecture is a software SK [43], which is a special type of operating system often based on the microkernel approach [33]. Its primary functionality is to provide separated partitions and secure communication channels. SKs (such as PikeOS [50]) typically also offer the execution of virtualized operating systems inside their partitions, in which case they also act as a hypervisor.

Spatial separation is achieved by resource partitioning in which system resources, such as main memory, CPU cores, and I/O devices, are partitioned and assigned to entities called resource partitions. Components are mapped to different resource partitions and will be limited to the assigned resources at run-time. Temporal separation is achieved by using time partitioning in which a certain CPU time quota is assigned to partitions and the applications are guaranteed to get the time quota assigned to their partitions at run-time. Temporal separation for an application doesn't necessarily require a monopolized CPU usage during a certain period of time, instead, it can also be achieved if the application is guaranteed to get enough CPU time to meet its timing requirements (deadlines) in spite of possible worst-case interference, such as preemptions by a higher priority task.

On safety-critical systems, the resources (e.g., memory or CPU time) required for the nominal operation of an application are determined by the application developer during design-time. The methods used for resource estimation and the pessimism in the estimation depend on the criticality levels of the application [9]. The system integrator, at design-time, allocates the estimated resources to partitions inside which the applications run. During run-time, the SK ensures that this resource allocation is not violated, thus preserving the freedom from interference between applications.

Hence, for securing safety-critical CPS, we choose a partitioned architecture in combination with a SK to strictly separate the CFI monitoring from the monitored application. This design is well suited for the safety-critical domain

---

[2] See ISO 26262 Part 3, Annex D.
[3] See IEC 61508 Part 3, Annex F.
[4] See DO-178 Sect. 2.4.1.

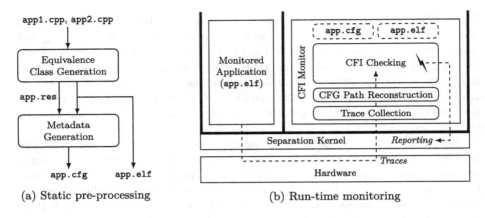

(a) Static pre-processing   (b) Run-time monitoring

Fig. 1. Transparent CFI monitoring design.

because of two reasons: (i) the adversary is not able to interfere with the CFI monitoring due to the separation, and (ii), at run-time, the CFI monitoring tasks and other safety-critical tasks are restricted to their allocated resources, thereby ensuring their independence and freedom from interference.

4   CFI Monitoring using ARM CoreSight

We now present our CFI monitor, a non-invasive and transparent solution for protecting CPS against code-reuse attacks. We specifically target SK-based CPS running on ARM SoCs with CoreSight support. Our monitor is strictly isolated from the monitored applications and periodically collects and verifies control-flow traces from CoreSight.

The architecture of our CFI monitoring solution is shown in Fig. 1. During *run-time monitoring*, after a stream of traces has been collected by the monitor, the current CFG path of the monitored application thread is reconstructed by decoding the trace packets into the sequence of executed basic blocks. Using the reconstructed path and the trace's per-thread identifier, the monitor maintains per-thread shadow stacks for backward-edge CFI enforcement. For the protection of forward edges, the monitor validates that the source and destination addresses of transitions between basic blocks belong to the same pre-computed equivalence class. We compute the per-application equivalence classes according to a type-based approximation of the CFG during a dedicated *static pre-processing* phase and load them into our CFI monitor as metadata before starting the monitored application.

For our work, we assume the SK does not randomize the memory layout of monitored applications and statically inferred addresses are still valid during run-time[5]. To ensure the security provided by our solution, we implement the forward-

---

[5] This is not a limitation of our CFI monitoring solution, as providing randomization details to the monitor would suffice to support memory layout randomization.

edge and backward-edge CFI policies according to [52] and [1], respectively. Both policies are well-established and known to thwart code-reuse attacks effectively [13,14].

4.1 Static Pre-processing

The pre-processing phase statically computes a type-based approximation of the CFG based on the concept of equivalence classes. We generate equivalence classes only for indirect jumps and calls, but handle calls to ordinary functions, calls to virtual methods (C++ only), and intra-function jumps differently.

For ordinary functions, we define equivalence as the signature of a call site matching the signature of the called function, where the signatures are defined as a combination of the function's return type and parameter types. Hence, two functions `int add(int a, int b)` and `int sub(int a, int b)` are considered equivalent by our CFI monitor and may be called from any indirect call site having the same signature. For virtual methods, we define equivalence analogously with the addition of taking class hierarchies into account. Two functions `int Math.add(int a, int b)` and `int Math.sub(int a, int b)` are considered equivalent if and only if they belong to the same class `Math` or any derived or base class of `Math`. Lastly, for simple jumps, we define equivalence based on code locality, i.e., restricting jumps to the switch statement or function body they belong to.

In our final metadata, we store the equivalence classes as a simple lookup table indexed by the addresses of branch targets. For every branch target within the table, we store the list of call site addresses allowed to branch to the that target—effectively representing the equivalence class the target belongs to. Hence, for the two functions `add()` and `sub()`, the table contains two identical entries specifying all call sites allowed to branch to `add()` and `sub()`.

We generate the metadata in a two-step process during the compilation of the application. We adopt this process, as computing equivalence classes at compile-time is more precise than a binary-only computation [55]. Figure 1a depicts the compilation and generation of the binary `app.elf` and the metadata `app.cfg` for an application consisting of two source code files `app1.cpp` and `app2.cpp`.

Step 1: Equivalence Class Generation. The first step is built upon the LLVM compiler infrastructure and computes the equivalence classes for indirect calls to ordinary functions and virtual methods. During this step, we essentially generate a version of our metadata containing descriptive identifiers instead of actual address locations. Branch targets (i.e., functions and virtual methods) are represented as string literals by their names and call sites by the offset into their parent functions. Indirect jumps do not require compile-time information and are only processed during the second step.

For the generation of equivalence classes, we utilize the type metadata mechanism already present in LLVM[6]. The mechanism computes the equivalence

---

[6] https://llvm.org/docs/TypeMetadata.html.

classes according to [52] and as required by our definitions above. Because the type metadata is only available in LLVM's Intermediate Representation (IR), we deploy a custom LLVM pass that passively collects and stores the equivalence classes to a temporary file app.res. To resolve the equivalence on an application-wide level, this step must be performed on a combined version of the application's IR (i.e., in our example, simultaneously for app1.cpp and app2.cpp) or during link-time optimization. The data extracted by our LLVM pass is already represented in the form of our metadata, i.e., for every branch target, we have a list of possible call sites. Because the extracted data still contains equivalence classes represented as string literals, we translate the data into actual address locations in the following, second pre-processing step.

Step 2: Metadata Generation. The second step generates the final metadata file app.cfg based on a binary analysis of the compiled application app.elf and the extracted equivalence classes app.res. We use Capstone[7] to inspect the application binary and translate the string-based equivalence classes to address-based equivalence classes. The extracted data represents equivalence classes in form of a lookup table indexed by function and virtual method names, i.e., the targets of indirect call sites. Each entry in the table contains a list of call sites allowed to branch to that function or virtual method. The call sites are identified by the name of their parent function and their offset within the function. Looking up the function names and virtual methods in the disassembled application binary, we are able to translate the entire lookup table into actual address locations.

As the first pre-processing step only generates equivalence classes for ordinary functions and virtual methods, we still have to generate legitimate branch targets for indirect jumps. For this, we use the binary inspection to identify the type of indirect jumps (e.g., a switch statement) and then extract all addresses of legitimate jump targets within the scope of the identified type. Like this, a switch statement is only allowed to perform jumps within the switch body. Unfortunately, for some indirect branches, the target addresses cannot be identified statically, because, for example, they are inferred from program input during run-time. In such cases, like for other state-of-the-art forward-edge CFI solutions, we refrain from generating metadata, leaving those branches unchecked during run-time. Note that indirect jumps to functions, as generated by tail call optimizations, are handled the same way indirect calls are handled.

4.2   Run-Time Monitoring

After the pre-processing phase, the application is ready to be executed normally with our CFI monitor passively verifying its indirect control-flow transfers. We decompose the monitoring process in five stages.

Initialization. To start monitoring an application, the generated CFG metadata file together with the application binary are loaded into the monitor. The monitor itself first initializes the CoreSight subsystem by configuring the ETMs to

---

[7] https://www.capstone-engine.org/.

generate traces whenever threads of the monitored application are schedule on the corresponding cores (CoreSight does not trace applications by default). Next, the monitor invokes the application, which then gets initialized and scheduled by the SK as usual. At this point, our monitor moves into a waiting state until the first traces are ready to be processed. As shown in Fig. 1b, processing traces is done in three distinct steps, the *trace collection*, *CFG path reconstruction*, and *CFI checking*.

Trace Collection. During execution of the monitored application, tracing is performed automatically by the ETM connected to the core the application is scheduled on. For every control-flow changing instruction executed by the core, i.e., direct and indirect branch instructions, the ETM generates a CoreSight trace and stores it into the ETF queue. Once the ETF queue reaches a threshold configured by the monitor during initialization, the CoreSight subsystem interrupts execution of the application, flushes the queue to system memory, and lastly notifies our monitor of the traces ready for validation. Note that interrupting the application during the flushing of the ETF is required by CoreSight, as traces cannot be collected while the ETF queue is transfered to system memory. After the ETF has been fully flushed, the application can be resumed while our monitor is executed in parallel.

CFG Path Reconstruction. The traces generated by the ETM and received by our monitor include common data such as the application thread's Unique Identifier (UID) and the virtual address of the recorded instruction. Additionally, traces of indirect branches include the destination address, while direct branches omit the address and only include the branch decision, i.e., whether the branch was taken or not. Other data in the traces is not relevant to our CFI monitor.

We use the data provided in the traces to reconstruct the path taken by the application through the CFG. For this, our monitor utilizes the OpenCSD library[8] that takes the application's binary as input and generates a sequence of basic blocks resembling the application's execution path. A basic block is identified by its start and end address, as taken from the application's binary. The end address of a basic block always points to a set of control-flow instructions such as direct or indirect branch (including function returns). The reconstruction also preserves the UIDs and attaches them to basic blocks so that our monitor is able to enforce CFI on a per-thread granularity. Finally, the reconstruction sequentially emits the basic blocks to the CFI checking, where CFG conformity is validated.

CFI Checking. With the sequence of executed basic blocks, our monitor is able to perform per-application forward-edge and per-thread backward-edge CFI checking. For forward-edge CFI, the monitor consults the CFG metadata provided through the pre-processing phase. For every basic block terminating in a direct or indirect function call, the monitor looks up the next basic block's start address

---

[8] https://github.com/Linaro/OpenCSD.

in the metadata. This lookup yields a list of call site addresses that are allowed to branch to the next basic block. To validate CFG conformity, the monitor verifies that the current basic block's end address (i.e., the call site address) is present in the list. If the address is not found, a CFI violation has been detected.

For backward-edge CFI, the monitor does not rely on static metadata, but maintains a per-thread shadow stack. The monitor first evaluates the UID attached to a basic block and then looks up the shadow stack corresponding to the identifier (i.e., the thread). Next, for every basic block terminating in a direct or indirect function call, the call's return address is pushed onto the shadow stack. For every basic block terminating in a function return, the following basic block's start address is compared against the top-most address stored on the stack. If the addresses are not equal, a CFI violation has been detected. Otherwise the return is valid and the top-most address is removed from the stack. To cope with tail call optimization or otherwise shortened return sequences (e.g., longjmp), where the top-most address on the shadow stack is not equal to the next basic block's start address, the monitor pops addresses from the stack until a match is found or the bottom of the stack is reached. Like this, the monitor is able to ignore all return addresses skipped by the longjmp.

CFI Violation Reporting. Finally, if our monitor detects a CFI violation, it notifies the SK, which then is able to react accordingly, e.g., stop or restart the monitored application, or notify the system administrator. In this paper, we do not further elaborate on possible and adequate reactions to detected CFI violations.

5   Timing Overhead Analysis

In this section, we analyze the timing overhead of our CFI monitoring solution based on a prototype implementation on top of the PikeOS SK [50] running on an ARM Juno platform [8]. We map the stages of CFI monitoring described in Sect. 4.2 to the following tasks: trace collection T_{tc}, CFG path reconstruction T_{cfg}, and CFI checking T_{cfi}. These tasks are running inside PikeOS partitions that are separated from the monitored application T_u. For our prototype, we implemented T_{cfg} and T_{cfi} inside a Linux virtual machine using non-optimized libraries. We have implemented T_{tc} as an optimized task directly running on top of the PikeOS SK. As explained in Sect. 4.2, for loss-free tracing, the monitored application only has to be interrupted during T_{tc}, while T_{cfg} and T_{cfi} can be executed in parallel to the monitored application. Hence, the optimized implementation of T_{tc} allows us to identify the minimum timing interference caused by our CFI solution on the monitored application.

For the analysis, we compute the worst-case slowdown any application can suffer (Sect. 5.2) and the nominal slowdown when monitoring a certified IP stack of PikeOS called ANIS (Sect. 5.3). We also measure the execution time of the non-optimized CFG path reconstruction T_{cfg} and CFI checking T_{cfi} (Sect. 5.4).

Listing 1.1. Worst-Case Program

```
ADDR:  branch ADDR
```

5.1   Modeling the Trace Collection Task

We can model T_{tc} as a sporadic task defined by a tuple (p_{tc}, e_{tc}, d_{tc}), where p_{tc} is the minimum inter-arrival time, e_{tc} the Worst-Case Execution Time (WCET), and d_{tc} the deadline relative to the task release. Once the collected traces in the ETF reach a certain threshold, T_{tc} is scheduled by the SK. Hence, the minimum inter-arrival time p_{tc} depends on the trace generation rate, which in turn depends on the number of monitored cores and the monitored application's characteristics (i.e., frequency of branches). To avoid the loss of traces, T_u is interrupted during trace collection and re-scheduled thereafter. In such a scheduling scheme, we can consider d_{tc} to be equal to e_{tc}. The slowdown suffered by T_u due to the inclusion of T_{tc} in the system can be computed as:

$$r_{tc} = \frac{e_{tc}}{p_{tc}}$$

For copying the full ETF (64 KiB) queue to system memory, we have measured an execution time of 1.9 ms with 99% of confidence from 1000 measurements. We use 1.9 ms as a representative[9] WCET e_{tc} for the trace collection task.

5.2   Worst-Case Slowdown Experienced by Any Application

For a given number of monitored cores, the minimum inter-arrival time p_{tc} of the trace collection task T_{tc} depends on the monitored application's characteristics: the ratio $c = \frac{B}{I}$, between the number of branch instructions B and the number of total instructions I executed since application start-up. As branch instructions are included in the total number of instructions, $0 \leq c \leq 1$, and $c = 0$ corresponds to a program composed of a single basic block (one linear sequence of instructions), whereas $c = 1$ represents the worst-case, in which every instruction is a branch (see Listing 1.1). When monitoring such a worst-case program running on a single core, the ETM associated with that core generates traces at the maximum rate and correspondingly releases the monitoring task with a worst-case p_{tc}. As shown in Table 1, we have observed a p_{tc} of $3487\mu s$ for such a program, which correspond to an approx. slowdown of 55% due to monitoring.

5.3   Slowdown for ANIS IP Stack in a Nominal Operation

We evaluate the application slowdown for a nominal operation of a safety-certified IP stack, called ANIS, running in the user-mode of PikeOS. The ICMP

---

[9] Note: In the industry, WCET computation is performed using sophisticated static analysis tools such as aiT from Absint that give tight bounds on the computed values.

Table 1. Experiment results for worst-case and nominal case operations, from 1000 measurements with 99% confidence.

	Worst-Case Scenario		Nominal Scenario	
	Minimum	Maximum	Minimum	Maximum
e_{tc} (μs)	1914	1917	1914	1920
p_{tc} (μs)	3487	3490	541768	581990
r_{tc} (%)	54.84	54.98	0.33	0.35

service of the IP stack is stimulated at run-time via an external agent, which sends ping requests (we treat this as a representative nominal operation). Since we want to observe the worst-case stimulation for this setup, the external agent floods the IP stack with requests. The results from Table 1 show a drastically lower average overhead, compared to measurements of the worst-case scenario's slowdown. During the nominal operation of this application, the buffer is filled more than 150 times slower than during the infinite empty loop (i.e., Listing 1.1). As a result, the monitored application experiences an approx. slowdown of only 0.3% due to monitoring.

5.4 Overhead for CFG Path Reconstruction and CFI Checking

As mentioned in the beginning of this section, T_{cfg} and T_{cfi} can be decoupled from T_{tc} and executed in parallel to the monitored application. After T_{tc} copies the batch of traces (64 KiB) from the ETF to system memory, these two task are invoked by the SK. We measured the time taken by the tasks to process 64 KiB of trace data to be approx. $1s$ (between $[0.92s, 1.10s]$ with 99% confidence). In our observations, 95% of the overhead is contributed by the CFG path reconstruction, while the CFI checking only requires 5%. CFI checking takes approx. between $[1.3ms, 1.5ms]$ for forward edges and $[51.7ms, 61.6ms]$ for backward edges, both with a 99% confidence. This huge overhead for the CFG path reconstruction directly stems from the use of non-optimized libraries and the overhead in the Linux VM that hosts these two tasks. In Sect. 6.4, we describe design strategies to reduce this overhead for a real-world deployment.

6 System Design Considerations for the Integration of the CFI Monitor in a Safety-Critical CPS

Having looked at the partitioned CFI monitoring architecture and its timing overhead analysis, we now focus on the design considerations for the practical deployment of our solution in a safety-critical CPS with real-time constraints. In particular, we discuss methods for guaranteeing the freedom from interference between monitored applications and monitoring tasks, applicability in multi-supplier product development, scalability aspects, and design options to decouple slow paths in our solution.

6.1   Freedom from Interference and Independence Considerations

When deploying CFI monitoring in safety-critical CPS like avionics or automotive, we have to ensure the freedom from interference and the independence between monitored applications and monitoring tasks. We use the separation mechanisms provided by the SK to create a partitioned architecture, where monitored applications and monitoring tasks are separated in space and time.

Spatial separation is achieved by assigning the monitoring tasks and monitored applications in different partitions having statically defined system resources as show in Fig. 1b. By restricting the access of monitoring tasks to this defined set of resources, no fault from the monitoring tasks will propagate to the rest of the system, including the monitored applications. For example, if the CFI checking task is implemented using a third party library, which contains a memory corruption leading to unbounded memory usage, this fault will not cause a memory starvation for the monitored applications in our partitioned architecture.

As we have mentioned in Sect. 5, the monitored applications should be interrupted during trace collection (task T_{tc}) to not lose any traces. So, when integrating our CFI solution with a real-time application, the temporal interference caused by the scheduling of T_{tc} shall be considered during the schedulability analysis. There exist extensive techniques in the real-time literature to perform offline schedulability analysis to determine if a set of tasks (consisting of periodic, aperiodic, or sporadic tasks) can meet their deadlines at run-time when scheduled with a certain scheduling policy. In fixed priority scheduling policies, such as Rate Monotonic [34], the task priority is fixed at design-time, and all instances of the task (jobs) inherit the task priority. In dynamic priority scheduling policies, the priority of each task instance (job) is computed at run-time based on task parameters; e.g., the relative deadline in the case of Earliest Deadline First (EDF) [34] scheduling.

In Sect. 5 we have seen that T_{tc} can be modeled as a sporadic task with the WCET e_{tc} and the minimum inter-arrival time p_{tc} known at design-time. For scheduling sporadic tasks along with periodic tasks, aperiodic server-based algorithms are used. Examples of aperiodic servers with fixed-priority scheduling are polling servers, deferrable servers [32,49], and sporadic servers [48]. An example of an aperiodic server with dynamic scheduling is the constant bandwidth server [2]. The goal of an aperiodic server is to limit the temporal interference caused by misbehaving sporadic tasks to the worst-case behavior of some periodic task. In this way, the worst-case behavior of sporadic tasks can be replaced with equivalent periodic tasks in the schedulability analysis. For example, in the case of a sporadic server, Sprunt et al. [48] have shown that the sporadic server can be replaced with a periodic task with a period equal to the minimum inter-arrival time and the capacity equal to the WCET of the sporadic task in the schedulability analysis. We can use such aperiodic servers implemented inside the SK to integrate the task T_{tc} with the real-time tasks of the monitored application. By servicing T_{tc} in an aperiodic server, we are effectively limiting the CPU time it can take in such a way that the guarantees of other real-time tasks are not violated. Hence, misbehavior such as T_{tc} requiring more time than e_{tc} and T_{tc} arriving at a higher rate than p_{tc} will not affect the timing guarantees of the real-time tasks of the monitored application. In this way, temporal separation of the monitoring tasks from the monitored application is achieved.

When the instances of T_{tc} arriving at a higher rate than p_{tc} are not serviced, the CFI checking for a part of the application's control-flow is effectively disabled. An attacker could leverage this to circumvent the CFI checking simply by changing the nominal behavior of an application (e.g., by increasing the load on a network stack). So, we have to implement a monitoring routine to detect whether T_{tc} is arriving faster than the nominal inter-arrival time. To minimize the monitoring overhead, the routine shall be implemented in the low-level interrupt service routine and the overhead when T_{tc} is arriving at the worst-case shall be considered by the system integrator while allocating CPU time for the monitored applications. Once a deviation is detected during run-time, it should be treated as anomalous application behavior and countermeasures such as restarting/stopping the system, switching to a fail-safe mode (disabling non-vital functions and executing minimal safety functions), or migrating the monitored applications should be applied.

6.2   Transparent CFI Monitoring and Its Applicability in a Multi-supplier Product Development

Our CFI solution is transparent to the monitored application, since it does not require source code or binary instrumentation. For monitoring an application, in addition to the application binary, we only require CFI metadata, which is generated during an offline pre-processing phase by the application developer and stored separately from the application. This makes our solution suitable for use in a multi-supplier product development, as practiced in the automotive, railway, and avionics domains.

For the certification of complex safety and security critical systems built with components from multiple suppliers, typically, a compositional certification methodology [45] is used. Here, the lower-level component developers (e.g., application developers) perform evaluation for their components and provide the evidences to the higher level developers (e.g., system integrator, operators), who then reuse those artifacts to certify the system as a whole. The practice of reusing low-level evaluation evidence is also reflected in standards such as Common Criteria [47], ISO 26262 [27], and IEC 62443[41]. As our monitoring solution does *not* require modification at the source code or binary level, when the system integrator wants to enable monitoring of a component, there is no need to regenerate the evaluation evidence for that component, which eases the reuse.

6.3   Scalability for Monitoring Multiple Applications

In Sect. 5, we simplified the analysis by monitoring one (multi-threaded) application running on a single core. To extend the CFI monitoring to multiple applications, it is possible to include the application UID in addition to the thread UID in the context of CoreSight traces. When scheduling the threads of a different application, the scheduler has to save the tracing context of the outgoing application and restore the one of the incoming application. The tracing context includes the thread and application UIDs, monitored virtual address ranges, and monitoring task parameters (e.g., nominal inter-arrival time). This can be extended to monitoring applications running in virtualized OS by using the Virtual Context Identifier (VMID) register (set by the hypervisor) and ContextID (set by the guest OS) to uniquely identify the VM, application, and thread in the trace stream. As we rely on the ContextID set by the SK scheduler running in supervisor-mode, our solution cannot monitor applications with user-space thread scheduling.

When monitoring multiple applications running from different cores, the instruction traces from all cores are collected on the same ETF and all monitored applications (from all cores) shall be paused during the trace collection. This creates a timing interference between the monitored applications, which might otherwise be independent from each other. Also, when multiple cores are generating traces at a high rate, the overhead for the trace collection might be a limiting factor for the multi-core scalability of our solution. We can see in Table 1 that when monitoring a *worst-case program* with only branches running from one core, the trace collection task arrives at $3490\,\mu s$ and it takes $1917\,\mu s$ to copy traces from the ETF to system memory. So, if all cores (e.g., 6 cores on Juno) are generating traces at such a rate, there will be a huge overhead on the monitored applications. In such a case, we might have to rely on an external accelerator or an FPGA to process the traces (similar to the solution from Lee et al. [31]).

6.4 Strategies for Decoupling Trace Collection from the CFG Path Reconstruction and the CFI Checking

If the combined execution time of the CFG path reconstruction (task T_{cfg}) and CFI checking (task T_{cfi}) is shorter than the nominal inter-arrival time p_{tc} of the trace collection (task T_{tc}), we can run them in parallel to the monitored applications using an intermediate buffer to store the collected traces (whose size equals to the size of the ETF queue, i.e., 64 KiB). However, when the execution of T_{cfg} and T_{cfi} is slower, such as in our case, the monitored applications accumulate more traces than can be analyzed in the available time frame. Checking all the traces for an unlimited time would require an unlimited intermediate buffer. To avoid such unrealistic resource requirements, we can apply the following strategies:

– **Accelerating CFI path reconstruction and CFI checking** so that $e_{cfg} + e_{cfi} \leq p_m$, where p_m is the nominal inter-arrival time of the monitored applications. This can be achieved by (i) optimizing the implementation, (ii) offloading the tasks to an accelerator such as an FPGA, or (iii) dedicating multiple cores to these tasks.

– **Dropping traces** and therefore limiting the coverage of the CFI monitor. We can employ several methods for selecting whether a batch of traces must be checked or can be dropped. The intuitive idea is for tasks T_{cfg} and T_{cfi} to run whenever traces are located in the transient memory buffer in RAM. When the buffer is full, the solution can either ignore newly generated trace batches or overwrite stored data with new upcoming batches. The buffer design depends on the strategy for prioritizing traces to analyze: i.e., recent traces first with FIFO or synchronous analysis via a ring buffer. However, every time traces are dropped, the monitor must reinitialize the current backward-edge and forward-edge CFI status.

7   Related Work

Control-flow hijacking attacks and defenses have been an active research topic for over two decades. A vast proportion of this research has focussed on the enforcement of varying CFI policies. However, most CFI defenses are less applicable in the safety-critical domain, as they either require compile-time instrumentation [4,25,29,37,52,57], binary rewriting [1,56] or run-time instrumentation [20,39,55]. Thus, our discussion focusses on related work leveraging hardware features that potentially enable the transparency of a CFI defense.

In Table 2, we compare our solution to recent state-of-the-art hardware-assisted and hardware-based CFI defenses, taking the following three criteria (see Sect. 6) into account:

CFI enforcement: A solution *should* enforce both forward-edge and backward-edge CFI.

Transparency: A solution should be transparent to the monitored program, i.e., it *should not* require compile-time instrumentation, binary rewriting, or run-time instrumentation.

Safety suitability: A solution should be suitable for the integration in safety-critical systems, i.e., it should be transparent and *should not* impose any interference on the monitored application.

As shown in Table 2, most solutions already support backward-edge CFI, while comparatively less defenses protect forward control-flow transfers. Also, in many solutions, the freedom from interference between the monitored application and monitoring application is not addressed, making them not applicable for safety deployment. Hence, our CFI monitoring solution appears as the first transparent and complete forward-edge and backward-edge CFI implementation, with the freedom from interference criteria addressed and making it usable in the safety-critical domain.

While PT-CFI [22] implements backward-edge CFI utilizing Intel PT, Flow-Guard [35], based on the same hardware, provides complete forward-edge and backward-edge CFI, thus rendering it the closest implementation to our work. Both PT-CFI and FlowGuard achieve transparent CFI monitoring by performing a dynamic analysis of execution traces at run-time. They speed up CFI checking

Table 2. Comparison of our solution to other hardware-assisted and hardware-based CFI monitoring approaches. Solutions marked with '∼' are suitable for safety-critical deployment, but require custom hardware or additional processing elements (such as an FPGA).

Solution	Forward-edge CFI	Backward-edge CFI	Transparency	Safety suitability
PT-CFI [22]	–	✓	✓	–
FlowGuard [35]	✓	✓	✓	–
μCFI [23]	✓	–	–	–
Lee et al. [31]	–	✓	✓	∼
HAFIX [18]	–	✓	✓	∼
CaRE [38]	✓	✓	–	–
C-FLAT [3]	✓	✓	–	–
Our solution	✓	✓	✓	✓

by learning legitimate CFG transitions from previous observations. The solutions are light-weight, since they perform CFI checks at predefined endpoints (such as system calls) on a fixed sequence of the most recently recorded traces. In that regard, PT-CFI and FlowGuard diverge from our solution, which provides continuous CFI enforcement. Further, while both solutions are transparent to the monitored program, they have not evaluated the compatibility for the deployment in safety-critical systems. There is no mechanism to upper bound the time when the monitored program is paused during the CFI checking.

With μCFI, Hu et al. [23] enforce a precise forward-edge CFI policy based on leveraging Intel PT and compile-time analysis. During compile-time, they recursively identify constraining data (i.e., non-control data used in control-flow instructions) and insert routines at locations where these data are written, in order to dynamically trace their values at run-time. With this method, μCFI is able to enforce exactly one possible target for every forward-edge transition. In comparison to our forward-edge CFI policy, this approach is more precise. However, achieving this precision requires an intrusive modification of the monitored program, which is different from our solution and not possible for safety-critical systems.

Lee et al. [31] utilize the ARM CoreSight hardware extension on an FPGA-based SoC to transparently enforce a precise backward-edge CFI policy. The authors build a dedicated FPGA soft core processor that is capable of extracting control-flow information from CoreSight traces and using that information to maintain and enforce a shadow stack. Based on this processor, the authors are able to fully separate the CFI enforcement from the monitored program— identical to our work. From a technical point of view, this enables their solution to be applicable in the safety-critical domain. However, in contrast to our work, their solution lacks forward-edge CFI enforcement and can only be deployed on special SoCs with an on-chip or externally connected FPGA.

Another hardware-based solution for embedded systems, presented by Davi et al. [18,19] as HAFIX, implements a hardware function call stack to enforce an imprecise backward-edge CFI policy. The policy deployed by HAFIX forces function returns to target any call-preceded instruction residing within any function currently recorded on the function call stack. To implement the function call stack and CFI enforcement, Davi et al. develop new processor instructions on the fully synthesizable Intel Siskiyou Peak and SPARC LEON3 microprocessors. This enables their solution to be applicable in the safety-critical domain. However, in comparison, our CFI monitor is based on the widely available ARM platform and further enforces precise state-of-the-art CFI policies for both forward and backward edges.

Nyman et al. [38] present CaRE, a binary rewriting solution that deploys imprecise forward-edge and precise backward-edge CFI utilizing the ARM Trust-Zone hardware extension. In particular, CaRE secures indirect function calls by restricting target addresses to a list of valid function entry points, generated during a static pre-processing phase. To protect function returns, CaRE maintains a shadow stack securely isolated in the ARM TrustZone. In comparison to our work, CFI enforcement for backward edges is equally precise, while CaRE only applies a weak approximation of the CFG for forward edges. Furthermore, CaRE is not transparent to the protected software and therefore less suitable for deployment in the safety-critical domain.

C-FLAT [3], another solution utilizing the ARM TrustZone, defines a remote attestation protocol, in which a (bare-metal) embedded system proves its correct execution to a remote verifier. A cumulative hash chain is computed over the target addresses of indirect branches taken by the embedded system. The hash chain is calculated and stored securely within the ARM TrustZone. The final hash value is transmitted to the verifier and compared to a list of valid hash values gathered during a dynamic pre-processing phase. When performing continuous attestation, C-FLAT achieves complete conformance to the legitimate CFG. However, C-FLAT requires a dynamic pre-processing phase, which has to identify every benign path in the embedded software—a non-trivial task. Furthermore, C-FLAT requires instrumentation of the software being attested, rendering an application in the safety-critical domain less suitable.

8   Conclusion

In this work, we presented a CFI solution to monitor applications in safety-critical CPS. Our solution demonstrates the applicability of instruction tracing with the ARM CoreSight hardware extension to perform transparent CFI monitoring. We experimentally evaluated the worst-case and nominal slowdown on the protected application, and considered system design aspects for deploying the solution in a safety-critical system. In its current state, our solution induces a significant timing overhead on the system to be mitigated in future work.

Acknowledgement. We thank Philipp Gorski, Alez Züpke, and Holger Blasum, as well as the anonymous reviewers for their helpful comments and suggestions. This work was partially funded by the EU H2020 under the FORA project with the Marie Skłodowska-Curie grant agreement no. 764785 and under the ADMORPH project with grant agreement no. 871259. In addition, this work was supported by the German Federal Ministry of Education and Research (BMBF) under the IUNO Insec project with grant agreement no. 16KIS0933K.

References

1. Abadi, M., Budiu, M., Erlingsson, U., Ligatti, J.: Control-flow integrity: principles, implementations, and applications. In: CCS. ACM (2005)
2. Abeni, L., Buttazzo, G.: Integrating multimedia applications in hard real-time systems. In: RTSS. IEEE (1998)
3. Abera, T., et al.: C-FLAT: control-flow attestation for embedded systems software. In: CCS. ACM (2016)
4. Almakhdhub, N.S., Clements, A.A., Bagchi, S., Payer, M.: μRAI: securing embedded systems with return address integrity. In: NDSS. Internet Society (2020)
5. Alves-Foss, J., Oman, P.W., Taylor, C., Harrison, S.: The MILS architecture for high-assurance embedded systems. Int. J. Embed. Syst. 2(3/4), 239–247 (2006)
6. Arm Holdings: Mbed OS MPU management. https://os.mbed.com/docs/mbed-os/v5.15/apis/mpu-management.html. Accessed 10 Sep 2020
7. Arm Holdings: ARM CoreSight SoC-400 Technical Reference Manual (June 2016)
8. Arm Holdings: Juno ARM Development Platform SoC Technical Reference Manual (June 2016)
9. Baruah, S.K., Burns, A., Davis, R.I.: Response-time analysis for mixed criticality systems. In: RTSS. IEEE (2011)
10. Bletsch, T., Jiang, X., Freeh, V.W., Liang, Z.: Jump-oriented programming: a new class of code-reuse attack. In: ASIACCS. ACM (2011)
11. Buchanan, E., Roemer, R., Shacham, H., Savage, S.: When good instructions go bad: generalizing return-oriented programming to RISC. In: CCS. ACM (2008)
12. Burns, A., Davis, R.: Mixed criticality systems–a review. Department of Computer Science, University of York, Technical Report (2013)
13. Burow, N., et al.: Control-flow integrity: Precision, security, and performance. ACM Comput. Surv. (CSUR) 50(1), 1–33 (2017)
14. Burow, N., Zhang, X., Payer, M.: SoK: shining light on shadow stacks. In: S&P. IEEE (2019)
15. Checkoway, S., Davi, L., Dmitrienko, A., Sadeghi, A.R., Shacham, H., Winandy, M.: Return-oriented programming without returns. In: CCS. ACM (2010)
16. Clements, A.A., et al.: Protecting bare-metal embedded systems with privilege overlays. In: S &P. IEEE (2017)
17. Clements, A.A., Almakhdhub, N.S., Bagchi, S., Payer, M.: ACES: automatic compartments for embedded systems. In: USENIX Security. USENIX Association (2018)
18. Davi, L., et al.: HAFIX: hardware-assisted flow integrity extension. In: DAC. ACM (2015)
19. Davi, L., Koeberl, P., Sadeghi, A.R.: Hardware-assisted fine-grained control-flow integrity: towards efficient protection of embedded systems against software exploitation. In: DAC. ACM (2014)

20. Davi, L., Sadeghi, A.R., Winandy, M.: ROPdefender: a detection tool to defend against return-oriented programming attacks. In: ASIACCS. ACM (2011)
21. Francillon, A., Castelluccia, C.: Code injection attacks on harvard-architecture devices. In: CCS. ACM (2008)
22. Gu, Y., Zhao, Q., Zhang, Y., Lin, Z.: PT-CFI: transparent backward-edge control flow violation detection using Intel processor trace. In: CODASPY. ACM (2017)
23. Hu, H., et al.: Enforcing unique code target property for control-flow integrity. In: CCS. ACM (2018)
24. Humayed, A., Lin, J., Li, F., Luo, B.: Cyber-physical systems security-a survey. IEEE Int. Things J. **4**(6), 1802–1831 (2017)
25. Jang, D., Tatlock, Z., Lerner, S.: SafeDispatch: securing C++ virtual calls from memory corruption attacks. In: NDSS. Internet Society (2014)
26. John, R.: Partitioning in avionics architectures: Requirements, mechanisms, and assurance. Technical Report, SRI International Computer Science Laboratory (1999)
27. Kath, O., Schreiner, R., Favaro, J.: Safety, security, and software reuse: A model-based approach. In: RESAFE. Springer (2009)
28. Kim, C.H., et al.: Securing real-time microcontroller systems through customized memory view switching. In: NDSS. Internet Society (2018)
29. Kuznetsov, V., Szekeres, L., Payer, M., Candea, G., Sekar, R., Song, D.: Code-pointer integrity. In: USENIX OSDI. USENIX Association (2014)
30. Kwon, D., Shin, J., Kim, G., Lee, B., Cho, Y., Paek, Y.: uXOM: efficient eXecute-only memory on ARM Cortex-M. In: USENIX Security. USENIX Association (2019)
31. Lee, Y., Heo, I., Hwang, D., Kim, K., Paek, Y.: Towards a practical solution to detect code reuse attacks on ARM mobile devices. In: HASP. ACM (2015)
32. Lehoczky, J.P., Sha, L., Strosnider, J.K.: Enhanced aperiodic responsiveness in hard real-time environments. In: Unknown Host Publication Title. IEEE (1987)
33. Liedtke, J.: On micro-kernel construction. ACM SIGOPS Oper. Syst. Rev. **29**(5), 237–250 (1995)
34. Liu, C.L., Layland, J.W.: Scheduling algorithms for multiprogramming in a hard-real-time environment. J. ACM (JACM) **20**(1), 46–61 (1973)
35. Liu, Y., Shi, P., Wang, X., Chen, H., Zang, B., Guan, H.: Transparent and efficient CFI enforcement with Intel processor trace. In: HPCA. IEEE (2017)
36. Miller, C., Valasek, C.: Remote exploitation of an unaltered passenger vehicle. Black Hat USA **2015**, 91 (2015)
37. Niu, B., Tan, G.: Per-input control-flow integrity. In: CCS. ACM (2015)
38. Nyman, Thomas., Ekberg, Jan-Erik., Davi, Lucas, Asokan, N.: CFI CaRE: hardware-supported call and return enforcement for commercial microcontrollers. In: Dacier, Marc, Bailey, Michael, Polychronakis, Michalis, Antonakakis, Manos (eds.) RAID 2017. LNCS, vol. 10453, pp. 259–284. Springer, Cham (2017). https://doi.org/10.1007/978-3-319-66332-6_12
39. Payer, Mathias., Barresi, Antonio, Gross, Thomas R.: Fine-grained control-flow integrity through binary hardening. In: Almgren, Magnus, Gulisano, Vincenzo, Maggi, Federico (eds.) DIMVA 2015. LNCS, vol. 9148, pp. 144–164. Springer, Cham (2015). https://doi.org/10.1007/978-3-319-20550-2_8
40. Real Time Engineers Ltd.: FreeRTOS memory protection unit (MPU) support. https://www.freertos.org/FreeRTOS-MPU-memory-protection-unit.html. Accessed 10 Sep 2020
41. Rico, J.E., Bañón, M., Ortega, A., Hametner, R., Blasum, H., Hager, M.: Compositional security certification methodology. Zenodo (2018)

42. Rubio, J.E., Alcaraz, C., Roman, R., Lopez, J.: Current cyber-defense trends in industrial control systems. Comput. Secur. **87**, 101561 (2019)
43. Rushby, J.: The design and verification of secure systems. In: Eighth ACM Symposium on Operating System Principles. ACM (1981)
44. Schlehuber, C., Heinrich, M., Vateva-Gurova, T., Katzenbeisser, S., Suri, N.: Challenges and approaches in securing safety-relevant railway signalling. In: EuroS & PW. IEEE (2017)
45. Schulz, T., Gries, C., Golatowski, F., Timmermann, D.: Strategy for security certification of high assurance industrial automation and control systems. In: SIES. IEEE (2018)
46. Shacham, H.: The geometry of innocent flesh on the bone: return-into-libc without function calls (on the x86). In: CCS. ACM (2007)
47. Sinnhofer, A.D., Raschke, W., Steger, C., Kreiner, C.: Evaluation paradigm selection according to common criteria for an incremental product development. In: MILS@HiPEAC. Zenodo (2015)
48. Sprunt, B., Sha, L., Lehoczky, J.: Aperiodic task scheduling for hard-real-time systems. Real-Time Systems **1**(1), (1989)
49. Strosnider, J.K., Lehoczky, J.P., Sha, L.: The deferrable server algorithm for enhanced aperiodic responsiveness in hard real-time environments. IEEE Transactions on Computers **44**(1), (1995)
50. SYSGO GmbH: PikeOS hypervisor webpage. https://www.sysgo.com/products/pikeos-hypervisor/, retrieved September 10, 2020
51. Szekeres, L., Payer, M., Wei, T., Song, D.: SoK: Eternal war in memory. In: S&P. IEEE (2013)
52. Tice, C., Roeder, T., Collingbourne, P., Checkoway, S., Erlingsson, U., Lozano, L., Pike, G.: Enforcing forward-edge control-flow integrity in GCC & LLVM. In: USENIX Security. USENIX Association (2014)
53. Tverdyshev, S., Blasum, H., Langenstein, B., Maebe, J., De Sutter, B., Leconte, B., Triquet, B., Müller, K., Paulitsch, M., Söding-Freiherr von Blomberg, A., Tillequin, A.: MILS architecture. Zenodo (2013)
54. van der Veen, V., Andriesse, D., Stamatogiannakis, M., Chen, X., Bos, H., Giuffrdia, C.: The dynamics of innocent flesh on the bone: Code reuse ten years later. In: CCS. ACM (2017)
55. van der Veen, V., Göktaş, E., Contag, M., Pawoloski, A., Chen, X., Rawat, S., Bos, H., Holz, T., Athanasopoulos, E., Giuffrida, C.: A tough call: Mitigating advanced code-reuse attacks at the binary level. In: S&P. IEEE (2016)
56. Zhang, M., Sekar, R.: Control flow integrity for COTS binaries. In: USENIX Security. USENIX Association (2013)
57. Zieris, P., Horsch, J.: A leak-resilient dual stack scheme for backward-edge control-flow integrity. In: ASIACCS. ACM (2018)

Blokchain

BlockVoke – Fast, Blockchain-Based Certificate Revocation for PKIs and the Web of Trust

Abba Garba[1], Arne Bochem[2][✉], and Benjamin Leiding[2]

[1] School of Electronics Engineering and Computer Science,
Peking University, Beijing, China
abbaggumel@pku.edu.cn
[2] Institute of Computer Science,
University of Goettingen, Goettingen, Germany
arne.bochem@cs.uni-goettingen.de, benjamin.leiding@tu-clausthal.de

Abstract. A reliable certificate revocation mechanism is crucial, as illustrated by the recent revocation of 1.7 million certificates issued by the Let's Encrypt certificate authority. It is just as essential to get revocation information to users in an efficient and timely manner without impacting their privacy. Existing approaches such as Certificate Revocation Lists (CRLs) or the Online Certificate Status Protocol (OCSP) fail with respect to either of those metrics, while approaches that try to mitigate both, such as OCSP-Staple and Must-Staple suffer from soft-failure modes and meager adoption rates. To address these issues, we propose the *BlockVoke* scheme, which decentralizes revocations, allowing certificate owners as well as CAs to revoke certificates, and distribute revocation information rapidly. Our approach furthermore allows the revocation of CA root certificates, which is not possible with traditional approaches. The use of a blockchain as an underlying layer ensures the continued availability and immutability of revocation information. *BlockVoke* interacts favorably with approaches such as CRLite and Certificate Revocation Vectors (CRV), allowing organizations to update revocation filters with as little delay as required by their security policies. We also demonstrate the cost-efficiency of our approach in comparison to other approaches such as CRLs, showing its high feasibility.

Keywords: PKI · Blockchain · Certificate · Revocation · Web of Trust

1 Introduction

Nowadays, Internet services and applications, such as e-commerce websites and e-mail communication or messaging services, are not only essential to our daily life, but also become more common and popular due to the progressing digitization of society, e.g., [21] and [46]. X.509 certificates are used to secure those web applications and ensure their authenticity, integrity, and confidentiality. Public

© Springer Nature Switzerland AG 2020
W. Susilo et al. (Eds.): ISC 2020, LNCS 12472, pp. 315–333, 2020.
https://doi.org/10.1007/978-3-030-62974-8_18

key infrastructures (PKIs) ensure the correct association between a certificate and its owner. The trust model of PKIs relies on hierarchically structured central authorities [39], whereas the PGP Web of Trust (WoT) builds on a decentralized structure [27]. The vulnerability induced by the centralized and intransparent structure of CAs regularly results in security incidents [4,9]. Meanwhile, the PGP WoT is decentralized and does not suffer from these vulnerabilities. Yet, the PGP WoT does neither provide sufficient certainty that the information stated in a public key (certificate) is correct, since users do not carefully verify them due to missing incentives or lack of punishments, nor is it resilient to Sybil node attacks [33].

Certificates expire after a pre-determined lifetime. However, security incidents or other events require a certificate revocation before its expiry date. A certificate may be revoked after its corresponding private key is compromised, the identification of a flaw in the underlying cryptographic system, or due to issues related to internal PKI processes.

Recently, the non-profit CA Let's Encrypt (LE) announced the revocation of 3,048,289 certificates due to a bug in their Certification Authority Authorization (CAA) software – the so-called LE CAA rechecking bug [10,24,25]. Ultimately, only 1,706,950 certificates were revoked, and the remaining certificates were left to expire within the subsequent 90 days.

Even though WoT revocations do not depend on a CA, any revocation has to be propagated within the network. This is done by a set of distributed peer-to-peer (P2P) keyservers which synchronize with each other. However, due to their limited number and reoccurring reliability issues, they potentially pose risks to organizations relying on them [20,28].

Several mechanisms for certificate revocation exist such as Certificate Revocation Lists (CRLs) [14], the Online Certificate Status Protocol (OCSP) [43], or OCSP extensions such as OCSP stapling [15] and OCSP Must-Staple [19]. Nonetheless, due to their centralized nature, these revocation mechanisms inherit the same security concerns as the general PKI concept itself, e.g., single point of failure (SPOF).

Alternative decentralized and more transparent alternatives – for both, PKIs in general as well as the WoT – exist and are being tested, e.g., [12,18,30,45], but are not widely used yet and suffer from different disadvantages such as scalability issues, privacy leaks, efficiency deficits or low security guarantees.

Relying on CAs or WoT keyservers as gatekeepers to crucial information such as certificate revocation data poses a risk not only to the everyday user, but especially to big organizations with large IT-systems and thousands of users. For them, a secure and timely revocation notification channel for X.509 certificates that does not impact user privacy is important. Therefore, a research gap exists with respect to the design of such a system. This work fills the detected gap and investigates the research question of how to enable secure, timely and privacy preserving certificate revocation. Our proposed scheme is, in addition, also decentralized, transparent, scalable and efficient. The proposed *BlockVoke* scheme addresses these issues by rapidly distributing revocation information and decentralizing revocations, allowing certificate owners as well as CAs to revoke certificates.

An instantiation of our scheme is explained using the Bitcoin blockchain and 1-of-2 threshold multi-signature addresses [1], which, once created using certificate specific public keys from both the certificate owner and the CA, will allow either party to create a transaction on the blockchain revoking the certificate.

The remainder of this paper is structured as follows: Sect. 2 introduces supplementary literature and related work. Section 3 focuses on the functional details of *BlockVoke* as a transparent and accountable certificate revocation mechanism, while Sect. 4 details specific properties as well as engagement processes. Afterwards, Sect. 5 evaluates *BlockVoke* and discusses the findings. Finally, Sect. 6 concludes this work and provides an outlook on future work.

2 Supplementary Literature and Related Work

This section provides background information, supplementary literature, and also introduces related work with previous approaches to solving the issue of certificate revocation.

2.1 Certificate Revocation Mechanisms

Certificates expire after a pre-determined lifetime. However, security incidents or other events may require a certificate revocation before its expiry date, e.g., after its corresponding private key is compromised, the identification of a flaw in the underlying cryptographic system, due to an insecure key length, or due to issues related to internal PKI processes [24]. Compromised PGP keys or X.509 certificates enable an attacker to access initially secured data or perform MITM attacks [45]. CAs revoke certificates by issuing a signed revocation statement – as a cryptographic proof – using their private key. Additionally, the CA ensures the distribution of the revocation statement. In the context of the WoT, revocations do not depend on a CA. Instead, the certificate owner revokes the certificate and posts a corresponding revocation message to the PGP keyservers.

The most common X.509 certificate revocation mechanisms are illustrated in Fig. 1 and described in subsequent sections.

Certificate Revocation Lists (CRLs) are signed records of all revoked – but not expired – certificates of a specific CA based on the certificates' serial number [14]. Certificates listed in a CRL are not trusted by any browser. However, CRLs are criticized as not being efficient at dispersing the revocation information for several reasons: First, clients are only interested in the validity of a single certificate – yet, they have to download the complete CRL. Second, each CA maintains its own CRL instead of a single global CRL for all CAs. Third, delays occur between certificate revocation and adding the certificate to the CRL, resulting in browsers trusting the certificate despite its revocation. Fourth, large numbers of revocations, as illustrated by our initial Let's Encrypt incident example, result

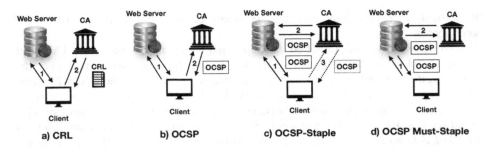

Fig. 1. Certificate Revocation Mechanisms: [a] CRLs: The browser retrieves a signed list of revoked certificates from the CA during the SSL/TLS negotiation; [b] OCSP: The client requests the revocation status of a single certificate from the CA; [c] OSCP stapling: The web server communicates with the CA to periodically receive signed statements which prove that the corresponding certificate has not been revoked yet. Alternatively, [b] serves as a fallback; [d] OCSP must-staple enforces [c] by removing the fallback option [b]. If no valid OCSP response is available, the browser discards the certificate; – Based on [13] and [45]

in large CRLs, which lead to additional latency and communication overhead while loading websites [36].

Online Certificate Status Protocol (OCSP) addresses the CRL overhead issue by allowing clients to query the CA directly and requesting the status of a particular certificate instead of downloading the whole CRL [43]. The CA responds by sending a signed response along with the current certificate's status (revoked, not-revoked, or unknown) along with the validity period of the certificate. Even though OCSP reduces the amount of transferred data, it still results in additional overhead since the CA has to be queried before trusting the certificate [13]. Moreover, delays between revoking a certificate and listing the certificate as revoked still occur [3].

In addition to the previously known issues, OCSP introduces a privacy issue. The CA can profile clients by correlating their browser activities based on the IP address with the requested certificates.

OCSP Stapling – also known as *TLS Certificate Status Request* – addresses OCSP's communication overhead with the CA as well as the privacy issue mentioned above [15]. Instead of the client sending an OCSP request to the CA, the web server serving a certificate periodically requests the most-recent certificate revocation status updates from the CA. The CA responds with a signed statement for the certificates of the requesting web server, additionally stapling a cryptographic proof to the certificate, which is then presented to a client during the TLS/SSL negotiations. The CA's signed statement is only valid for a pre-defined period and thus cannot be used indefinitely by a malicious web server. As a result, OCSP stapling reduces communication overhead and addresses the

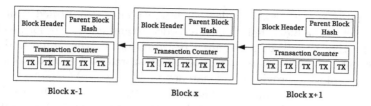

Fig. 2. General Blockchain Structure – Based on [37]

issue of CAs profiling clients based on their browsing activities. In case a web server cannot provide an OCSP staple proof, the client can still fallback to normal OCSP.

Nevertheless, OCSP stapling still does not solve all issues of certificate revocation. For example, CAs operate using a hierarchical trust model where a root CA signs the certificate of a sub-ordinate CA, and so on. Neither OCSP nor OCSP stapling incorporates the revocation status for the end-entity certificate. An extension proposal exists to address this limitation by allowing the server to incorporate multiple certificate statuses in a single response, although this approach is not widely adopted [40].

Finally, the OCSP stapling *Must Staple Extension* enforces the existence of a valid OCSP response to be presented by the web server – otherwise, TLS/SSL negotiations are aborted. Furthermore, the OCSP protocol also enforces the *Must Staple Extension* and addresses attack scenarios where an attacker is able to block clients' OCSP requests or web server OCSP requests forcing them to fallback to less secure certificate validation mechanisms. However, according to [13], out of 500,000,000 certificates tested in 2018 only 0.02% supported the OCSP *Must Staple Extension*.

2.2 Blockchain Technology

Figure 2 presents the general structure of a blockchain and subsequently blocks as used by, e.g., the Bitcoin [37], or Ethereum blockchains [47]. A blockchain consists of a sequentially ordered number of blocks that record transaction events, e.g., transfer of a cryptocurrency from one person to another. Transactions are cryptographically signed and represent an incremental list of records, consistent over the network, time-stamped, and verifiable [37]. Blocks are linked by hashes of their previous ancestor block, thereby chaining all blocks together. As a result, changing information in one block, results in a hash mismatch of the succeeding block. Thus, tampering with one block requires the recalculation of all succeeding blocks. Blocks are publicly available and synchronized via a global, distributed, and decentralized P2P storage system.

The technological foundations of blockchains result in properties relevant for secure, transparent, efficient, and decentralized certificate revocation. *i*) Decentralization: Data is stored and processed in a decentralized and distributed manner. Consensus is determined by the majority of network participants based on the conformity of the network rules. *ii*) Immutability: Confirmed transactions are appended to the blockchain. Once recorded, transactions cannot be changed later on. Furthermore, they are tamper-resistant and prevent unnoticed manipulation of data. *iii*) Transparency: Information stored on a public blockchain is globally available and provides transparency to all users. *iv*) Openness: The P2P network is open; anyone can join or leave the network at any time. *v*) Security: Security of blockchains is achieved based on cryptographically signed statements and information in conjunction with the distributed and decentralized consensus mechanism as well as redundant and transparent P2P data storage.

2.3 Related Work

Besides the general revocation mechanisms presented in the previous section, many more exist and have been proposed in earlier research. In the context of traditional PKI-related revocation, systems such as Certificate Revocation Trees [29] and Certificate Revocation Systems [38] exist, while non-research organizations and entities proposed solutions such as CRLset [23]. Especially the latter two suffer from bandwidth and latency problems and require the client to fetch revocation details from pre-defined servers [22].

Larisch et al. [31] propose CRLite, a revocation mechanism that "aggregates revocation information for all known, valid TLS certificates on the web, and stores them in a space-efficient filter cascade data structure" [31] based on Bloom Filters. The system is implemented in Firefox nightly and is distributed to all browsers with small (580KB) daily updates. However, the system is prone to single point of failure attacks since it relies on a centralized system design. Due to being updated daily, there is also a certain amount of latency between the revocation of certificates and users receiving these revocations.

Besides the classical centralized approaches, various decentralized solutions using blockchain technology emerged in recent times. CertLedger [30] is a blockchain-based PKI which records the complete SSL/TLS certificate lifecycle on the blockchain, including issuance, validation, and revocation of certificates, thereby circumventing SPOF issues as well as transparency-related drawbacks of previous systems. However, CertLedger operates its specialized blockchain, which incurs significant growth in storage (ca. 512GB per year), resulting in storage and network communication overhead. Moreover, clients do not store the complete blockchain and only access block headers. Thus, they cannot confirm whether they receive a proof referring to the most recent revocation state of a certificate without making a request to a full node, which might lie. Finally, operating their special-purpose blockchain implies that CertLedger cannot leverage security guarantees of established public blockchain platforms.

Yakubov et al., [48] and Fromknecht et al. [18], propose further blockchain-based models for issuing, revoking, and validating X.509 digital certificates. The proposed models manage the entire certificate lifecycle via a blockchain. While Yakubov et al. rely on Ethereum-based smart contracts, Fromknecht et al. use Namecoin, which is based on Bitcoin. Similarly, CertChain [12] implements a X.509 digital certificate self-audit and operation service on a blockchain. It stores the entire certificate history from registration to revocation. The proposed system makes entire revoked certificates publicly visible, while CertChain leverages the advantages of blockchain to provide decentralized tamper-evident public certificates.

Despite their decentralized nature, these systems require users/clients to either download the complete blockchain or rely on full nodes to provide the relevant information to clients, which results in network structures that are still prone to manipulation. Also, the proposed methods do not provide efficient methods for clients with storage constraints to query certificate revocation statuses.

3   BlockVoke – Blockchain-Based Certificate Revocation

Traditional PKI systems are based on trusted CAs that sign certificates, maintain CRLs, and provide OSCP proofs for certificates they issued. As previously mentioned, the current mechanisms of certificate revocation are subject to SPOF [2] risk as well as other security and privacy issues, while the WoT suffers from disadvantages of its own. In this section, we describe the lifecycle of a certificate using the blockchain-based *BlockVoke* certificate revocation system. The lifecycle consists of three main parts. First, a certificate signing request is made by the future certificate owner, which is subsequently used by the CA to create the certificate. Finally, the certificate either expires or is revoked prematurely.

Throughout this section, we assume an instantiation of our scheme on the Bitcoin blockchain, using 1-of-2 multi-signature addresses, which allow spending with either of two different public keys. The general structure remains the same even when instantiated on other blockchain platforms or through smart contracts. First, we describe the *BlockVoke* scheme as it applies to the revocation of SSL/TLS certificates. After that, we describe its applicability to WoT-based systems, such as PGP. An overview of the whole process is given in Fig. 3.

3.1   Certificate Signing Request

Creating a CSR generally follows the procedure of creating any regular SSL/TLS CSR. Our approach, however, requires the addition of a new attribute, which contains the public key corresponding to a Bitcoin address owned by the certificate owner – illustrated as step 1 in Fig. 3.

3.2   Certificate Creation

Again, the creation and signing procedure of the certificate follows that of any regular SSL/TLS certificate. In addition, using the public key corresponding to a Bitcoin address, the CA uses its own Bitcoin public key and the certificate owner's key to create a 1-of-2 multi-signature address, which can be spent from with either of the two public keys. The resulting address is added to the certificate as an extension field. If the CA publishes Certificate Revocation Vectors (CRV)

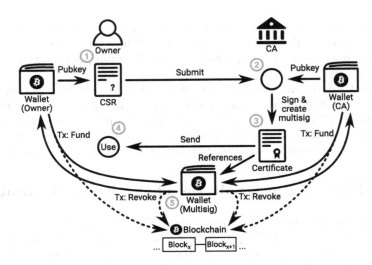

Fig. 3. Overview of the certificate lifecycle, from creation to blockchain based revocation.

as described in [45], it also adds its own public key to the field. These are steps 2 and 3 in Fig. 3.

Once the certificate owner receives the certificate, it is used as any other certificate, as indicated by step 4 in Fig. 3.

3.3 Revocation

The extension field allows users attempting to validate the certificate to look up past transactions originating from this multi-signature address. If any such transaction exists, the certificate is considered revoked. The creation and the process of adding this transaction to the blockchain (the so-called mining process) are indicated by step 5 in Fig. 3.

The actual revocation is performed either by the certificate owner or the CA. To revoke a certificate, the party performing the revocation creates a Bitcoin transaction, sending a small amount into the multi-signature address specified in the extension field of the certificate. After transmitting this transaction, they create a second transaction, spending the funds they just sent to the multi-signature address back to their wallet. This transaction also contains an OP_RETURN script opcode containing necessary information concerning the revocation. During this step, it is not necessary to wait for the first transaction to be confirmed since Bitcoin allows the spending of unconfirmed change. For both transactions, a sufficient miners' fee should be added to ensure the timely confirmation of both transactions.

The OP_RETURN script opcode allows embedding arbitrary information in Bitcoin transactions, with a limited size of up to 40 Bytes. The first ten of these bytes are specified to be *BlockVoke* followed by a zero byte. As a result, it easy to scan the blockchain for revocation transactions even for unknown certificates. This is followed by the first 16 Bytes of the certificate's fingerprint, allowing users to confirm that this transaction actually pertains to the certificate they are trying to validate. It is then followed by a four-byte integer indicating the certificate's date of issuance in days since 2020-02-02. One additional byte encodes the reason for the revocation, following the RFC 5280 [14] revocation codes as given in Table 1.

If the CA that issued the certificate is publishing CRVs, the last nine bytes contain first a three-byte unsigned integer for the revocation number (RN) and finally six bytes containing a unique identifier for the CA. This information is added only in case the CA revokes the certificate, as can be confirmed through the public key that was added to the certificate's extension field.

As revocation information is instantly broadcast over the Bitcoin P2P network, users and entities building their own revocation lists or filters can instantly update their filters to include the newly revoked certificate. Examples of such entities may include companies, universities, or other organizations, which have stringent security requirements that demand a higher update rate than, e.g., the daily updates provided by the CRLite [31] implementation currently being tested by Mozilla in Firefox Nightly builds [26].

We estimate that a revocation transaction on Bitcoin using a single input and output, plus an OP_RETURN operation has a size of up to 283 Bytes, depending on the OP_RETURN payload's size.

3.4   CA Root Certificates

Usually, the revocation of CA root certificates poses difficulties as they are self-signed, and there exists no key that is eligible to revoke them. With our scheme, a separate key tied to a blockchain address is used for revocation. Therefore, the *BlockVoke* revocation mechanism applies as well to CA root certificates, making it possible to revoke them in case of compromise or other reasons.

3.5   Web of Trust Keys

In the WoT, no central authorities exist to provide trust in cryptographic keys. Instead, users mutually sign their keys after, ideally, carefully confirming each others' identities. Users then determine how much they trust other users' keys by checking whether there is a path of transitively trusted signatures leading up to it [33].

The *BlockVoke* scheme for certificate revocation is also applicable to keys in the WoT with minor modifications. Since there is no certificate authority, only the key owner can publish a revocation. Due to this, a regular Bitcoin address can be used instead of a multi-signature address. The key owner directly generates a Bitcoin address and stores it in a User Attribute Packet [11] that is part of an OpenPGP key. From there on, a revocation is performed as specified above for SSL/TLS certificates.

Table 1. Certificate revocation codes according to RFC 5280 [14].

Code	Reason	Code	Reason
0	Unspecified	6	Cessation of operation
1	Key compromise	7	Certificate hold
2	CA compromise	8	Remove from CRL
3	Affiliation changed	9	Privilege withdrawn
4	Key compromise	10	AA compromise
5	Superseded		

4   Analysis

In this section, we give an analysis of various properties of the *BlockVoke* scheme. First, we detail the security properties of our scheme.

4.1   Basic Security Properties

The primary security properties of certificates using our scheme remain unaffected as *BlockVoke* is only concerned with the revocation process. It does this by announcing and preserving revocations through a blockchain platform. Thus, it is possible to also employ traditional revocation publication methods such as OSCP or CRLs in parallel, where required.

The fingerprint provided in revocation transactions allows users to confirm that the transaction is intended to revoke the specific certificate, while the fact that the transaction originates from the address specified within the certificate guarantees that the revocation is legitimate. Allowing for fingerprint verification mitigates the possible scenario that an attacker gains access to the wallet keys of a certificate owner and attempts to randomly revoke their certificates as a form of Denial-of-Service attack, without actually knowing which certificates belong to a particular certificate owner.

4.2   Timeliness of Revocations

In contrast to many other blockchain-based schemes, *BlockVoke* does not require its users to wait until revocation transactions are confirmed before acting on them. The transactions themselves are sufficient to allow the corresponding certificate to be added to revocation lists or CRLite-based filters without delay. The purpose of adding them to the blockchain is to ensure the global and continued availability of these revocations, as the lifetime of transactions that exist merely in the transaction pool of the Bitcoin P2P network is limited.

Because revocations can be processed as soon as they are broadcast through the network, attacks on the underlying blockchain also have only a limited impact on *BlockVoke*. If the transactions do not get mined before falling out of the transaction pool, revocations may be lost at some point in the future, unless the CA or another party rebroadcasts them.

4.3   Comparison with CertLedger

CertLedger moves the entire certificate lifecycle onto a new, special-purpose blockchain [30]. While presenting a comprehensive solution to certificate issuance and revocation, the approach has certain drawbacks.

First, the use of a custom blockchain means that is not possible for the scheme to inherit the security properties of existing public blockchains. In the case of *BlockVoke*, the computational effort spent on securing the Bitcoin blockchain by miners also guarantees the future persistence of revocations on this blockchain.

Another issue concerns the privacy-preserving aspect of CertLedger. The state of a certificate changes to *revoked* by triggering a state update operation in a smart contract. Only full nodes are able to see these updates directly as most clients only download block headers, which are then used to verify certificate state proofs generated by full nodes. CertLedger claims to preserve client privacy as a state proof can be sent to the client together with the certificate when establishing a connection. This way, no request regarding this certificate has to be made to any third party. However, if an attacker takes control of a domain and compromises the key, a situation which certificate revocation should remedy, the attacker can bundle an outdated certificate state proof as long as clients do not check with a third party full node to ensure that the received state proof is up to date.

4.4   Fees

When storing data on a blockchain, the size of transactions and the fees they incur are important factors to consider. Table 2 shows the costs of *BlockVoke* revocation transactions on the Bitcoin as well as the Ethereum platform.

As described in Sect. 3.3 and presented in Table 2, we estimate an optimal revocation transaction in the Bitcoin network to have a size below 283 bytes with a payload size of 40 bytes. As our approach does not depend on fast transaction processing, it is not necessary to gain a very high mining priority for our revocation transactions by paying high fees. Based on data for March 2020, the cost for a transaction average around $0.001751 per byte. Thus, a *BlockVoke* revocation transaction of 283 bytes on the Bitcoin platform costs $0.496.

The costs for an Ethereum transaction are calculated as illustrated in Eq. 1, where 21000 gas are the fees paid for any transaction, and each byte of payload costs 68 gas. Based on the 40-byte payload of a *BlockVoke* revocation, the overall transaction results in an Ethereum gas demand of 23720. As shown in Table 2 and based on the average Ether price for March 2020, this results in a price of ca. $0.07 per *BlockVoke* revocation transaction on the Ethereum platform. Thus, it is seven times cheaper than the Bitcoin platform.

$$\text{Fee} = 21000 \text{ gas} + 68 \text{ gas} * \text{size\_of\_txdata\_in\_bytes} \qquad (1)$$

The size of a minimal Ethereum transaction is 107 bytes, in addition to the up to 40-byte payload of *BlockVoke* data [35, 47].

In addition to the costs for the revocation transaction, there has to be a transaction funding the *BlockVoke* address. This transaction is usually smaller and therefore costs less. However, Ethereum multi-signature transactions are implemented using smart contracts and therefore require two transactions to be made – first, the transaction triggering the smart contract; second, the transaction of the smart contract that transfers the funds. Therefore, we need two 107-byte funding transactions.

We further analyze the impact of transaction size and fees in Sect. 5.

Table 2. Transaction fee comparison between Bitcoin and Ethereum based on the average transaction fee prices per byte for Bitcoin and the average gas price for Ethereum in March 2020 – Sources: [5–7] and [16,17,35,47]

Platform	Min. TX Size	Avg. TX Cost
Bitcoin	283 bytes	$0.496
Bitcoin (Funding)	193 bytes	$0.338
Ethereum	147 bytes	$0.070
Ethereum (Funding)	2 × 107 bytes	$0.124

4.5 Privacy

Privacy can be considered from two perspectives: The privacy of the certificate owner who might be revoking their certificate and the privacy of users who attempt to verify whether a certificate is still valid.

Certificate Owner. The privacy impact on certificate owners is not commonly considered, but we will shortly explore the topic in the following. In the context of *BlockVoke*, the only time a transaction is made on the blockchain is when a certificate is revoked. Therefore, unless the certificate is revoked, our scheme has no impact on certificate owner privacy. If a certificate is revoked, we can again consider two separate aspects. The first aspect is the data contained within the revocation transaction's payload. It contains the fingerprint of the certificate, the date of issuance, and the certificate authority. This information should have little impact on the privacy of the certificate owner. It can only be matched to a certificate when the certificate and thus its fingerprint is already known. The only additional information gained from it is the revocation reason, which is intended to be known by users attempting to use the certificate.

Another aspect is the issue of general blockchain privacy. Revoking a certificate using our scheme requires the creation of a transaction on a blockchain. Therefore the usual considerations about transaction traceability apply [42].

User. Our scheme has no impact on user privacy. Users running a full node receive all revocations without leaking information about which certificates they might be interested in. Users downstream of organizations building, e.g., CRLite filters based on revocations from our scheme, will experience no privacy impact from the use of *BlockVoke*.

4.6   Auditability

Auditability is given as all revocations are publicly stored on the blockchain.

5   Evaluation and Discussion

The following sections focus on evaluating the *BlockVoke* protocol. In Sect. 5.1 and Sect. 5.2, we analyze storage size and costs for different certificate revocation scenarios in the context of PKIs and the WoT on the Ethereum and Bitcoin blockchain.

Bit first, we discuss how fast a *BlockVoke* revocation statement propagates through the system. After revoking a certificate – for both cases, PKI and WoT – the revocation statement is posted to the blockchain in the form of a transaction. The revocation transaction is pushed to the pool of pending transactions before being mined into the next block of the Bitcoin or Ethereum blockchain. Technically, a revocation transaction does not have to be mined to be valid in the context of *BlockVoke*. Therefore, the lower boundary of time that it takes to publish a revocation transaction is almost instantly. However, an upper bound depends on the confirmation time of transactions in both networks.

The Bitcoin network aims to publish a new block every ten minutes (the so-called block time). The larger the transaction fee attached to a revocation transaction, the higher the probability that a miner will pick up the transaction as soon as possible to include it into the next block to receive the transaction fee for doing so. A Bitcoin transaction is usually considered confirmed after six consecutive blocks, i.e., after 60 min. However, the median transaction confirmation time for transactions that include sufficient fees varies between five and thirty minutes for the first block [8].

The Ethereum network aims to publish a new block every 12–15 s and is therefore much faster than the Bitcoin network. A 2018 study suggests that less than 1% of all transactions take more than ten minutes to be confirmed, while 72% are confirmed within 30 s, or less [44].

Next, we present three case study examples to evaluate cost, efficiency, and storage requirements of *BlockVoke* in different real-life scenarios. The calculations are based on the transaction cost and storage size estimates presented earlier in Sect. 4.4.

5.1   Case-Study I – Let's Encrypt CAA Bug March 2020

In Sect. 1, we presented the Let's Encrypt CAA bug, which forced LE to revoke 3,048,289 of its certificates. 1,706,950 were actually revoked while the remainder was left to expire within the next 90 days. Table 3 presents the costs and storage size requirements of revoking the 1,706,950 LE certificates via *BlockVoke*. Assuming a Bitcoin-based implementation, *BlockVoke* needs ca. 812.5 MB of storage for the revocation and funding transactions as well as roughly $1,423,596 in transaction fees. Given a block time of ten minutes and a block size limit of one megabyte, all 1.7 million certificates could have been revoked in less than 136 h – ignoring any further regular transactions which are processed in parallel. An Ethereum-based implementation requires only 616 MB and costs around $331,148 in fees. Due to the shorter block time (12–15) and a transaction limit which is imposed by a gas limit (10,000,000 gas at the time of writing this work), Ethereum could handle the complete set of revocations in less than 47 h – again, ignoring any further regular transactions.

Table 3. *BlockVoke* revocation and funding fees as well as storage size requirements for revoking 1,706,950 certificates involved in the Let's Encrypt CAA Bug of March 2020.

Platform	Min. BlockVoke TX Size	Avg. BlockVoke TX Cost	Storage Size	TX Cost
Bitcoin (Revocation)	283 bytes	$0.496	483.07 MB	$846,647.20
Bitcoin (Funding)	193 bytes	$0.338	329.44 MB	$576,949.10
Ethereum (Revocation)	147 bytes	$0.070	250.92 MB	$119,486.50
Ethereum (Funding)	2 × 107 bytes	$0.124	365.29 MB	$211,661.80

Table 4 goes even one step further and assumes the compromise of the LE root certificate which requires to revoke all existing LE certificates. On March 31, 2020 LE listed around 124.533 million active and valid certificates [34]. Revoking all of them at once results in ca. 59.28 GB of storage and $103.8 million in fees on the Bitcoin, and 44.96 GB of storage and $24.159 million in fees on the Ethereum platform.

Table 4. Transaction fees and storage size requirements for the hypothetical scenario of revoking all 124.533 million valid LE certificates as of March 31, 2020.

Platform	Min. BlockVoke TX Size	Avg. BlockVoke TX Cost	Storage Size	TX Cost
Bitcoin (Revocation)	283 bytes	$0.496	35.24 GB	$61,768,386
Bitcoin (Funding)	193 bytes	$0.338	24.03 GB	$42,092,154
Ethereum (Revocation)	147 bytes	$0.070	18.31 GB	$8,717,310
Ethereum (Funding)	2 × 107 bytes	$0.124	26.65 GB	$15,442,092

It is necessary to put the calculations above into context. Even though the time, storage, and transaction costs seem to disqualify blockchains as foundations for PKIs, it is important to keep in mind that the two scenarios presented above are extreme cases. Revoking 1.7 million – yet alone 124.5 million certificates – never happened before and is thus not comparable with day-to-day operating costs. Moreover, the cost of $24.159 million to safely revoke all compromised certificates of a complete CA is cost-efficient, given the size and potential security implications. As a point of comparison, the US-company Cloudflare estimated that they spend $400,000 per month to distribute their growing CRL [41,45]. This also leaves aside the fact that *BlockVoke* allows the direct revocation of the root certificate, making it even less likely that such a high number of certificates ever needs to be revoked.

Moreover, despite the timespan to add all transactions to the blockchain, the approach is also very time-efficient. As mentioned at the beginning of this section – a revocation is already valid once a revocation transaction is posted to the transaction pool. Adding it to a valid blockchain block is only required for subsequent actions. Nevertheless, adding several gigabytes of data to a blockchain with a public consensus mechanism and slow block times is a tedious process. Finally, due to a limited maximum lifetime of certificates, full nodes do not have to process all past transactions anymore since their content becomes irrelevant after some time (e.g., at the latest after two years) and only remains relevant in the context of maintaining the underlying blockchain's security guarantees.

5.2 Case-Study II – Revoking the Web of Trust

Our second case study scenario concerns key revocation in the context of the WoT. Unfortunately, no statistics exist with regards to the daily, weekly, or monthly amount of revoked certificates. However, [32] performed an analysis of the WoT based on a snapshot from October 2014 and found 2,966,965 keys, which were neither expired nor revoked. Similar to the root certificate compromise of LE, we calculated the storage requirements and transaction fees for the scenario of revoking the complete WoT. The results are presented in Table 5. Again,

Table 5. Transaction fees and storage size requirements for the hypothetical scenario of revoking all 2,966,965 valid WoT keys existing in October, 2014.

Platform	Min. BlockVoke TX Size	Avg. BlockVoke TX Cost	Storage Size	TX Cost
Bitcoin (Revocation)	283 bytes	$0.496	839.65 MB	$1,471,614.64
Bitcoin (Funding)	193 bytes	$0.338	572.62 MB	$1,002,834.17
Ethereum (Revocation)	147 bytes	$0.070	436.14 MB	$207,687.55
Ethereum (Funding)	2 × 107 bytes	$0.124	634.93 MB	$367,903.66

the same considerations regarding time, storage size, and overall costs for this operation apply as presented in the previous section.

6   Conclusion and Future Work

Relying on CAs or WoT keyservers as gatekeepers to crucial information such as certificate revocations poses a risk not only to the everyday user but especially to organizations with large IT-systems and thousands of users. Existing revocation mechanisms such as Certificate Revocation Lists (CRLs), the Online Certificate Status Protocol (OCSP), and further OCSP extensions are subject to various security and privacy challenges. CRLs are being criticized as being an inefficient method of disseminating revocation information; OCSP faces critical privacy concerns, and its extensions such as OCSP-staple and Must-staple have minimal adoption rates. On the other hand, the WoT is subject to various security challenges of its own.

BlockVoke addresses these issues by utilizing blockchain technology to enable secure, transparent, efficient, and decentralized certificate revocation using the Bitcoin or the Ethereum blockchain. The scheme relies on a three-stage lifecycle. First, a certificate signing request is made by the future certificate owner, which is subsequently used by the CA to create the certificate in the second step. Finally, the certificate either expires or is revoked prematurely. The *BlockVoke* scheme is applicable to the revocation of X.509 certificates as well as OpenPGP keys used in the context of the WoT.

Usually, the revocation of CA root certificates poses difficulties as they are self-signed and there exists no key that is eligible to revoke them. *BlockVoke* ties a separate key to a blockchain address, which enables the revocation of such certificates. Revocation information is stored as part of revocation transactions on the Bitcoin or Ethereum network by embedding payload data into the transaction. Our payload is limited to the size of up to 40 bytes and thus very storage efficient. As revocation information is instantly broadcast over the corresponding P2P networks, users and entities building their own revocation lists or filters instantly receive updates for their filters to include the newly revoked certificate.

Furthermore, we detail the protocol parameters and various properties of our scheme related to security, timeliness, cost, efficiency, and auditability. Likewise, we discuss upper- and lower-bounds of revocation times. Finally, we evaluate *BlockVoke* in different real-life case-studies and provide estimates on storage size and revocation costs for these scenarios as well as a proof-of-concept implementation of the protocol for the Bitcoin and Ethereum platform.

For future work, we plan to implement and deploy the *BlockVoke* protocol on the Bitcoin as well as Ethereum blockchain and evaluate real-world use-cases. Moreover, we will further analyze the option to invoke smart contracts instead of plain blockchain transactions. Finally, we will research implementations on alternative blockchain platforms with faster transaction processing times as well as lower transaction fees.

References

1. Bitcoin Wiki - Multisignature (2019). https://en.bitcoin.it/w/index.php?title=Multisignature&oldid=67043. Accessed 1 Sept 2020
2. Baldi, M., Chiaraluce, F., Frontoni, E., Gottardi, G., Sciarroni, D., Spalazzi, L.: Certificate validation through public ledgers and blockchains. In: Proceedings of the First Italian Conference on Cybersecurity, ITASEC 2017, pp. 156–165 (2017)
3. Basin, D.A., Cremers, C., Kim, T.H., Perrig, A., Sasse, R., Szalachowski, P.: Design, analysis, and implementation of ARPKI: an attack-resilient public-key infrastructure. IEEE Trans. Depend. Secure Comput. **15**(3), 393–408 (2018)
4. Berkowsky, J.A., Hayajneh, T.: Security issues with certificate authorities. In: 2017 IEEE 8th Annual Ubiquitous Computing, Electronics and Mobile Communication Conference (UEMCON), pp. 449–455. IEEE (2017)
5. Blockchain Explorer - Blockchain.com: Bitcoin - Average Block Size (MB) (2020). https://www.blockchain.com/charts/avg-block-size. Accessed 1 Apr 2020
6. Blockchain Explorer - Blockchain.com: Bitcoin - Average Transactions per Block (2020). https://www.blockchain.com/charts/n-transactions-per-block. Accessed 1 Apr 2020
7. Blockchain Explorer - Blockchain.com: Bitcoin - Fees per Transaction (USD) (2020). https://www.blockchain.com/charts/fees-usd-per-transaction. Accessed 1 Apr 2020
8. Blockchain Explorer - Blockchain.com: Bitcoin - Median Confirmation Time (2020). https://www.blockchain.com/charts/median-confirmation-time. Accessed 1 Apr 2020
9. Bugzilla: Bugzilla #1311713 - Comodo: CA Comodo used broken OCR and issued certificates to the wrong people (2016). https://bugzilla.mozilla.org/show_bug.cgi?id=1311713. Accessed 19 Mar 2020
10. Bugzilla: Bugzilla #1619179 - Let's Encrypt: Incomplete revocation for CAA rechecking bug (2020). https://bugzilla.mozilla.org/show_bug.cgi?id=1619179#c7. Accessed 18 Mar 2020
11. Callas, J. and PGP Corporation and Donnerhacke, L. and IKS GmbH and Finney, H. and PGP Corporation and Shaw, D. and Thayer, R.: OpenPGP Message Format. IETF RFC4880, November 2007. Accessed 24 Mar 2020
12. Chen, J., Yao, S., Yuan, Q., He, K., Ji, S., Du, R.: CertChain: public and efficient certificate audit based on blockchain for TLS connections. In: IEEE INFOCOM - IEEE Conference on Computer Communications, pp. 2060–2068. IEEE (2018)
13. Chung, T., et al.: Is the web ready for OCSP must-staple? In: Proceedings of the Internet Measurement Conference 2018, pp. 105–118 (2018)
14. Cooper, D., Santesson, S., Farrell, S., Boeyen, S., Housley, R., Polk, W.: Internet X.509 Public Key Infrastructure Certificate and Certificate Revocation List (CRL) Profile. IETF RFC5280, May 2008. Accessed 18 Mar 2020
15. Eastlake, D.: Transport Layer Security (TLS) Extensions: Extension Definitions. IETF RFC6066, January 2011. Accessed 18 March 2020
16. Etherscan.io: Ether Daily Price (USD) Chart (2020). https://etherscan.io/chart/etherprice. Accessed 31 Mar 2020
17. Etherscan.io: Ethereum Average Gas Price Chart (2020). https://etherscan.io/chart/gasprice. Accessed 31 Mar 2020
18. Fromknecht, C., Velicanu, D., Yakoubov, S.: A Decentralized Public Key Infrastructure with Identity Retention. IACR Cryptology ePrint Archive, p. 803 (2014)

19. Hallam-Baker, P.: X.509v3 Extension: OCSP Stapling Required - Draft-hallambaker-muststaple-00 (2012). https://tools.ietf.org/html/draft-hallambaker-muststaple-00. Accessed 18 Mar 2020
20. Hansen, R.J.: SKS Keyserver Network Under Attack (2019). https://gist.github.com/rjhansen/67ab921ffb4084c865b3618d6955275f. Accessed 25 Mar 2020
21. Horst, H.A., Miller, D.: Digital Anthropology. A&C Black, London (2013)
22. Hu, Q., Asghar, M.R., Brownlee, N.: Checking certificate revocation efficiently using certificate revocation guard. J. Inf. Secur. Appl. **48**, 102356 (2019)
23. ImperialViolet: Revocation Checking and Chrome's CRL (2012). https://www.imperialviolet.org/2012/02/05/crlsets.html. Accessed 26 Mar 2020
24. Hoffman-Andrews, J.: Let's Encrypt - 2020.02.29 CAA Rechecking Bug (2020). https://community.letsencrypt.org/t/2020-02-29-caa-rechecking-bug/114591. Accessed 18 Mar 2020
25. JamesLE: Let's Encrypt - Revoking Certain Certificates on March 4 (2020). https://community.letsencrypt.org/t/revoking-certain-certificates-on-march-4/114864. Accessed 18 Mar 2020
26. J.C. Jones: CRLite: Speeding Up Secure Browsing (2020). https://blog.mozilla.org/security/2020/01/21/crlite-part-3-speeding-up-secure-browsing/. Accessed 19 Mar 2020
27. Khare, R., Rifkin, A.: Weaving a web of trust. World Wide Web J. **2**(3), 77–112 (1997)
28. Klafter, R., Swanson, E.: Evil 32: Check Your GPG Fingerprints (2014). https://evil32.com/. Accessed 25 Mar 2020
29. Kocher, P.C.: On certificate revocation and validation. In: Hirchfeld, R. (ed.) FC 1998. LNCS, vol. 1465, pp. 172–177. Springer, Heidelberg (1998). https://doi.org/10.1007/BFb0055481
30. Kubilay, M.Y., Kiraz, M.S., Mantar, H.A.: CertLedger: a new PKI model with certificate transparency based on blockchain. Comput. Secur. **85**, 333–352 (2019)
31. Larisch, J., Choffnes, D., Levin, D., Maggs, B.M., Mislove, A., Wilson, C.: CRLite: a scalable system for pushing all TLS revocations to all browsers. In: 2017 IEEE Symposium on Security and Privacy (SP), pp. 539–556. IEEE (2017)
32. Leiding, B.: Link topological analysis of the PGP web of trust. Bachelor's Thesis, University of Rostock, Rostock, Germany (2015)
33. Leiding, B., Cap, C.H., Mundt, T., Rashidibajgan, S.: Authcoin: validation and authentication in decentralized networks. In: The 10th Mediterranean Conference on Information Systems - MCIS 2016, Paphos, Cyprus, September 2016
34. Let's Encrypt: Let's Encrypt - Statistics (2020). https://letsencrypt.org/de/stats/. Accessed 06 Apr 2020
35. Song, L.: Signing an Ethereum Transaction the Hard Way (2018). https://lsongnotes.wordpress.com/2018/01/14/signing-an-ethereum-transaction-the-hard-way/. Accessed 06 Apr 2020
36. Liu, Y., et al.: An end-to-end measurement of certificate revocation in the web's PKI. In: Proceedings of the 2015 Internet Measurement Conference, pp. 183–196. ACM (2015)
37. Nakamoto, S.: Bitcoin: A Peer-to-Peer Electronic Cash System (2008). https://bitcoin.org/bitcoin.pdf. Accessed 15 Mar 2020
38. Naor, M., Nissim, K.: Certificate revocation and certificate update. IEEE J. Sel. Areas Commun. **18**(4), 561–570 (2000)
39. Perlman, R.: An overview of PKI trust models. IEEE Network **13**(6), 38–43 (1999)
40. Pettersen, Y.: The Transport Layer Security (TLS) Multiple Certificate Status Request Extension. IETF RFC6961, June 2013. Accessed 22 March 2020

41. Prince, M.: The Hidden Costs of Heartbleed (2014). https://blog.cloudflare.com/the-hard-costs-of-heartbleed/. Accessed 1 Sept 2020

42. Ron, D., Shamir, A.: Quantitative analysis of the full bitcoin transaction graph. In: Sadeghi, A.R. (ed.) FC 2013. LNCS, vol. 7859, pp. 6–24. Springer, Heidelberg (2013). https://doi.org/10.1007/978-3-642-39884-1_2

43. Santesson, S., Myers, M., Malpani, A., Galperin, S., Adams, C.: X. 509 Internet Public Key Infrastructure Online Certificate Status Protocol - OCSP. IETF RFC6960, June 2013. Accessed 18 Mar 2020

44. Singh, H.J., Hafid, A.S.: Prediction of transaction confirmation time in Ethereum blockchain using machine learning. In: Prieto, J., Das, A., Ferretti, S., Pinto, A., Corchado, J. (eds.) BLOCKCHAIN 2019. AISC, vol. 1010, pp. 126–133. Springer, Cham (2020). https://doi.org/10.1007/978-3-030-23813-1_16

45. Smith, T., Dickinson, L., Seamons, K.: Let's revoke: scalable global certificate revocation. In: 27th Annual Network and Distributed System Security Symposium, NDSS 2020. The Internet Society (2020)

46. Su, K., Li, J., Fu, H.: Smart city and the applications. In: International Conference on Electronics, Communications and Control (ICECC), pp. 1028–1031. IEEE (2011)

47. Wood, G.: Ethereum Yellow Paper: A Secure Decentralized Generalised Transaction Ledger - BYZANTIUM VERSION 7e819ec - 2019–10-20 (2019). https://ethereum.github.io/yellowpaper/paper.pdf. Accessed 06 Apr 2020

48. Yakubov, A., Shbair, W., Wallbom, A., Sanda, D., et al.: A blockchain-based PKI management framework. In: The First IEEE/IFIP International Workshop on Managing and Managed by Blockchain (Man2Block) Colocated with IEEE/IFIP NOMS 2018, Tapei, Tawain 23–27 April 2018 (2018)

Formalizing Bitcoin Crashes with Universally Composable Security

Junming Ke[1], Pawel Szalachowski[2], Jianying Zhou[2], and Qiuliang Xu[1(✉)]

[1] School of Software, Shandong University, Jinan, China
junmingke1994@gmail.com, xql@sdu.edu.cn
[2] Singapore University of Technology and Design, Singapore, Singapore
{pawel,jianying_zhou}@sutd.edu.sg

Abstract. Bitcoin has introduced an open and decentralized consensus mechanism which in combination with an append-only ledger allows building so-called blockchain systems, often instantiated as permissionless cryptocurrencies. Bitcoin is surprisingly successful and its market capitalization has reached about 168 billion USD as of July 2020. Due to its high economic value, it became a lucrative attack target and the growing community has discovered various flaws, proposed promising improvements, and introduced contingency plans for handling catastrophic failures. Nonetheless, existing analysis and contingency plans are not formalized and are tailored only to handle a small subset of specific attacks, and as such, they cannot resist unexpected emergency cases and it is hard to reason about their effectiveness and impact on the system. In this work, we provide a formalized framework to help evaluate a variety of attacks and their mitigations. The framework is based upon the universal composability (UC) paradigm to describe the attacker's power and the system's security goals. We propose the system in the context of Bitcoin and to the best of our knowledge, no similar work has been proposed previously. Besides, we demonstrate and evaluate our model with case study from the real world. Finally, we signal remaining challenges for the contingency plans and their formalization.

Keywords: Blockchain security · Bitcoin · Contingency plans · Attacks

1 Introduction

Satoshi Nakamoto's Bitcoin [32] is the first decentralized system which does not rely on a trusted party to reach consensus in a large set of mutually untrusting nodes. Up to now, Bitcoin is the most popular cryptocurrency. Every Bitcoin node replicates the public ledger, called the blockchain, and tries to extend it by generating a new block pointing to the previous block and aggregating received transactions. The process of generating a new valid block is called mining and

---

J. Ke—This work has been done while at SUTD.

W. Susilo et al. (Eds.): ISC 2020, LNCS 12472, pp. 334–351, 2020.
https://doi.org/10.1007/978-3-030-62974-8_19

nodes (called miners) are incentivized to run the protocol as each added block rewards its finder with a block reward and transaction fees included.

With the increasing success of Bitcoin, there have been proposed multiple blockchain systems with different capabilities [19, 21, 31, 33]. Consequently, the blockchain security has received increasing attention by researchers analyzing various aspects of blockchain platforms [2, 7, 14, 15, 34, 37]. Since these systems promise to significantly change multiple sectors and businesses their security is critical. Interestingly, their inherent properties, like decentralization and openness, do not help with the security life cycle known from traditional platforms and applications. These systems are difficult to be updated and patched and this limitation is strongly manifested while considering hypothetical catastrophic crashes, like a broken cryptographic primitive, that may affect most of the blockchain users.

Unfortunately, we can predict that it is only a matter of time when a catastrophic failure happens to a popular cryptocurrency like Bitcoin. For instance, an implementation of a privacy-oriented cryptocurrency Zerocoin [25] had a critical bug found by noticing irregular coin spends on the 19 April 2019. Subsequently, the developers tried to replace the core element of the system by another protocol as an ad-hoc contingency plan [23]. To mitigate the effects of such events, Bitcoin developers maintain the documentation of Bitcoin contingency plans [35]. However, these plans cover only a small subset of possible failures in their limited scope. Moreover, these plans are based rather on predictions and speculations, and are not supported by any rigorous formal reasoning.

In this paper, we propose a methodology and framework that helps to formally reason about crashes in Bitcoin. In particular, we aim to answer the following questions:

- What component failures may be particularly harmful to the protocol?
- How could we respond if these components fail (i.e., propose contingency plans)?
- Can we provide a uniform framework for modeling crashes and contingency plans of blockchain systems?

Due to the uncertainty of the adversary's power and strategies, it is not an easy task to formulate possible crashes and contingency plans. One promising direction is to use abstraction and model the Bitcoin functionality. In short, the main application of the bitcoin protocol is as a decentralized currency system with a payment mechanism, which is what it was designed for. An important question is then: what functions does Bitcoin achieve and under what assumptions? To formally answer this question we propose to use the universally composable (UC) paradigm [4] that has been proved to be a successful methodology reasoning about such complex systems [3].

Contributions

In this work, we aim to analyze the Bitcoin security via the UC blockchain protocol [3] and formalize the Bitcoin crashes through the meticulous investigation. More specifically, our contributions are as follows:

- Firstly, we propose a general framework for the Bitcoin system in order to analyze, detect, and mitigate adversarial behaviors. Our framework takes the given attacks as input, while handling the detection method as well as a contingency plan as output. To the best of our knowledge, there is no any similar prior work.
- Secondly, thanks to the UC treatment of the Bitcoin protocol, we illustrate the basic structure of our formalized security model as well as its analysis by extracting the functionality of each protocol. Our security model could help the framework to generate contingency plans.
- Finally, we illustrate the feasibility of our framework by demonstrating and analyzing it with use case. We also identify remaining challenges for the contingency plans modeling.

2   Related Work

The Bitcoin design and its rationale are mostly described in its whitepaper [32]. The document is not formal and does not dive into system details or its analysis, however, multiple papers have focused on analyzing the underlying concepts and techniques related to Bitcoin and the blockchain technology [1,6, 16]. Due to the immaturity of the Bitcoin protocol at the beginning, a lot of attacks have been found, such as selfish mining [1,2,15], where a miner adopts a deviated (malicious) mining strategy to increase its reward. Other attacks include double-spending attacks [29], network-level split attacks [9], forking the public blockchain to invalidate the target transactions [26], or eclipse attacks isolating victims from other peers in the peer-to-peer network [13,24]. With all recent interest in blockchain systems, surprisingly, only little research effort has been devoted to blockchain catastrophic events and contingency plans [35]. Giechaskiel et al. [10] first present the systematic analysis of the effect of broken primitives in Bitcoin. Their analysis reveals that some breakage causes serious problems for Bitcoin, whereas others seem to be inconsequential.

Recently, the simulation-based UC framework [4] is becoming the standard technique for demonstrating that a protocol is "secure". Since its introduction, the framework has been extended and modified. Katz et al. [18] proposed a novel approach to defining synchrony in the UC framework by introducing functionalities exactly meant to model, respectively, bounded-delay networks and loosely synchronized clocks. No constant-round asynchronous MPC protocols based on standard assumptions are known at that time, Coretti et al. [5] realized the synchronous and asynchronous models have to a large extent developed in parallel with results on both feasibility and asymptotic efficiency improvements in either track and they close this gap by providing the first constant-round asynchronous MPC protocol that is optimally resilient (i.e., it tolerates up to 1/3 corrupted parties), adaptively secure, and makes black-box use of a pseudo-random function.

Based on the assumption that the computational puzzle is modeled as a random oracle, Pass et al. [27] proved that the blockchain consensus mechanism satisfies a strong form of consistency and liveness in an asynchronous network with adversarial delays that are a-priori bounded, within a formal model allowing for adaptive corruption and spawning of new players. Concurrently, Garay et al. [7] proposed and analyzed applications that can be built "on top" of the backbone protocol, specifically focusing on the Byzantine agreement (BA) and on the notion of a public transaction ledger. Garay et al. [8] subsequently extend this work to provide the first formal analysis of Bitcoin's target calculation function in the cryptographic setting, i.e., against all possible adversaries aiming to subvert the protocol's properties.

From those points of view, Kiayias et al. [20] modeled the ideal guarantees as a transaction-ledger functionality in the context of universal composition framework. Subsequently, Badertscher et al. [3] put forth the first UC (simulation-based) proof of the Bitcoin security and the functionality allows for participants to join and leave the computation and allows for adaptive corruption.

3 Preliminaries

3.1 Functionalities

In contrast to weaker property-based notions, that only guarantee security in a standalone setting [17] or under sequential composition [11], a UC-secure protocol maintains all security properties even when run concurrently with arbitrary other protocol instances.

The basic idea of the security proofs in the UC model is the real and ideal worlds paradigm [4]. First, we should define a cryptographic task to be achieved in the real world, namely, a distributed protocol that achieves the task across many untrusted processes. Then, to show that it is secure, we compare it with an idealized protocol in which processes simply rely on a single trusted process to carry out the task for them (and so security is satisfied trivially). The program for this single trusted process is called an ideal functionality as it provides a uniform way to describe all the security properties we require from the protocol [22]. We assume a protocol π realizes an ideal functionality F (i.e., it meets its specification) if every adversarial behavior in the real world can also be exhibited in the ideal world. The steps to prove a protocol secure can seem as follows:

1. Specification: for a given ideal functionality F in the ideal world, we should design a protocol π in the real world which achieves the task in the ideal world.
2. Construction: we must provide a simulator S that translates any attack A on the protocol π into an attack on F.
3. Security proof: we need to show that running π under an attack by any adversary A (the real world) is indistinguishable from running F under attack by S (the ideal world) to any distinguisher Z called the environment.

In particular, Z is an adaptive distinguisher, meaning that it interacts with both the real world and the ideal world, and the simulation is sound if no Z can distinguish between the two. The primary goal of the UC model is composability. Suppose a protocol π is a protocol functionality that realizes a functionality F, and a protocol P relies on F as a subroutine, in turn realizes an application specification functionality G. Then, the composed protocol P $\circ$ π, in which calls to F are replaced by calls to π, also realizes G. Instead of analyzing the composite protocol consisting of P and π, it suffices to analyze the security of P itself in the simpler world with F, the idealized version of π.

This paper focuses on the functionalities in the ideal world. Because we base on a secure proof of Bitcoin's UC model from the previous research [3], for every attack we consider only the functionality it breaks, i.e., the attacker's behavior could threaten or break nothing but the functionality assumptions. In such a case, we fix the protocol by "recovering" the functionality, what then can be specified as a contingency plan.

3.2   Notation

The Bitcoin system can be seen as a protocol run by each participant (i.e., node) P_i among the Bitcoin network. We treat each functionality in the Bitcoin protocol as the functionality F providing some functions which are needed for the node P_i. Before we define the security goal of the blockchain, we introduce the basic components of the model.

Algorithm 1. Functionality Random Oracle F_{RO}

Input: x. It maintains a table T_1 (initially $T_1 = \{\}$).
Output: (x, y).
1: **if** no pair of the form $(x, \_)$ is in T_1 **then**
2:     Sample a value y uniformly.
3:     Add (x, y) to T_1.
4: **end if**
5: Get (x, y) from T_1.
6: Return (x, y)

- **Functionality** denotes the process algorithm which could accept a query and respond to the query. In our model, we treat each composable function in the UC model as the functionality.
- **Protocol** in the real world achieves the task in the ideal world, the UC paradigm treats protocol as the real world.
- **Node** represents each user $P_i \in P$ who has access to query a functionality. In Bitcoin, each participant is a node, and the Bitcoin network intends to allow each node to process functionalities correctly.
- **Environment.** In our model, all regular processes are within the environment. An attacker A can observe the environment and launch adaptive attacks, e.g., change the functionality output (we will define the malicious behavior later).

Algorithm 2. Functionality Chosen-format Bounded Pre-image Oracle $\mathsf{F_{CBRO}}$

Input: (a, b, y_l, y_h, i). It maintains a table T_2 (initially $T_2 = \{\}$).
Output: (x, y).

1: Find x to satisfy $y_l \leq h(a||x_i||b) \leq y_h$.
2: add (x, y) to T_2.
3: Return (x, y).

To model the Bitcoin protocol, we need to define its (sub)protocols that will be run to facilitate access to the Bitcoin network resources and to provide its security. The main question in that context can be formulated as what functionality can the blockchain provide to cryptographic protocols? For a simple presentation, in this work we do not present all functionalities and protocols of the Bitcoin protocol, and we refer readers to the work we base on [3].

4   Formalizing Bitcoin Crashes

4.1   Motivation

Bitcoin is a complex decentralized system that combines network, consensus, computation, game theory and other aspects from different areas. This paper does not intend to model the Bitcoin system, however, we base on the prior work [3] to extract some useful constructions and assumptions. As a large-scale protocol, Bitcoin can be divided into functionalities. A functionality is part of the features to be implemented by the Bitcoin system (it is modeled like an algorithm executed by a trusted third party). Functionalities represent action goals the protocol aims to achieve in the ideal world. For example, a simple functionality is the hash query, which provides a random number y for each input x – it is commonly recognized as the random oracle (RO) model as presented in Algorithm 1.

However, with aging hash functions and their implementations the RO assumption may not hold and such an event would "modify" this functionality. Giechaskiel et al. [10] present the first systematic analysis of the effects of the broken hash mechanism on Bitcoin. They summarize different types of breakage into a chosen-format bounded pre-image oracle as in Algorithm 2, and they discuss potential migration pitfalls of the breakage and the contingency plans.

Inspired by this approach, this work aims at another promising direction, namely to analyze every functionality of the Bitcoin system and to find out corresponding formalized contingency plans. Unlike previous work, we give a framework allowing to reason about entire crash classes and contingency plan of each functionality of the protocol (within the considered UC model). Using the above example, we use the modified functionality $\mathsf{F'_{CBRO}}$ to represent an adversary. The modified functionality $\mathsf{F'_{CBRO}}$ corresponds to the adversary with the ability to access not only the $\mathsf{F_{RO}}$, but also the F_{CBPO}. As shown in Algorithm 3, the adversary could access the random mapping y of arbitrary input x

Algorithm 3. The modified functionality Chosen-format Bounded Pre-image Oracle F'_{CBRO}

Input: x or $(,, y, y, 0)$.
Output: (x, y).
1: **if** receive x **then**
2:     Send x to F_{RO} and receive (x, y).
3: **end if**
4: **if** receive $(,, y, y, 0)$ **then**
5:     Send $(,, y, y, 0)$ to F_{CBRO} and receive (x, y).
6: **end if**
7: Return (x, y).

---

and could also determine x of arbitrary input y (if the input y does not have corresponding pre-image x, return ϕ). Such a modeling corresponds to reasoning about the Bitcoin's hash function being broken in the real world, allowing the adversary to find a pre-image of the input y.

Interestingly, the Bitcoin documentation considers the case of the hash function being broken and the following contingency plan is proposed: a) Every participant should be informed about the breach. b) A new secure hash algorithm should be deployed. c) The old blockchain state (i.e., the unspent coins) should be hardcoded and protected by the new secure hash algorithm.

The first and third steps are introduced to eliminate losses and to maintain the state before the breakage. From our perspective, the second step is quite interesting as we can view it as denying the functionality F_{CBRO} for the adversary, i.e., if the broken hash function is replaced, she has no access to the functionality F_{CBRO} anymore.

When the hash function is broken, the adversary has access to F'_{CBRO}. F'_{CBRO} is the combination of F_{CBRO} and F_{RO}, for an adversary, she could invoke F'_{CBRO}, then F'_{CBRO} could access the F_{CBRO} or F_{RO} with inputs, namely, x or $(,, y, y, 0)$, F'_{CBRO} receives the outputs from F_{CBRO} or F_{RO} and finally returns the results to the adversary. Thus a contingency plan could be specified as follows: if the adversary obtains access to F_{CBRO}, we need to restrict this access by replacing (recovering) F_{CBRO} by F_{RO}.

This simple example provides the main intuitions behind our framework. In short, we represent an adversary by parts of the protocol she can affect. Then we build the extracted functionality to analyze the advantage that the adversary is obtaining while attacking the system. The change to the functionality that restricts such an advantage is proposed as a contingency plan.

4.2   Methodology

We aim to analyze and mitigate attacks and crashes, however, in practice it is infeasible to enumerate all possible attacks due to the protocol complexity and the huge attack vector space. On the other hand, omitting an attack in the analysis could result in incomplete analysis or non-functional contingency plans. Therefore, to maximize the effectiveness of our framework, we take an approach where entire attack classes are considered (instead of single attack vectors). Our core observation is that abstractions introduced by the UC model significantly help our approach to capture and handle the protocol's complexity in a formalized way.

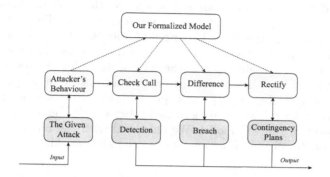

Fig. 1. Our methodology to cope with attacks.

Our framework is illustrated in Fig. 1.

1. For a given attack, we first extract the attacker's behavior as the basis of our process. The process goes as follows, firstly we put the attacker's behavior into our formalized model and we intend to find the attack's pattern and the broken parts. We can verify the broken parts through invoking a special function (i.e., a check call), which can be seen as a detection module.
2. Secondly, from the attacker's behavior, we can find the difference between the base protocol (that we want to achieve) and the broken protocol (i.e., after the attack). This difference characterizes the breakage of the protocol (i.e., its specific affected components).
3. Finally, because we identified the breakage (i.e., the difference between the base and broken protocol), we can rectify the deviation from the model's view and this rectification can be mapped in the contingency plan in the real world.

To sum up, the framework imports the given attack as the input, and exports the detection, the breakage, and the contingency plans as the output. In the following we sketch our framework as shown in Fig. 2.

To realize our methodology, in the first place we need to formalize the protocol by defining what are the properties of the ideal protocol (i.e., what properties should be achieved when the protocol functions correctly). We adopt the UC model of Badertscher et al. [3] as the base model for the correct Bitcoin protocol. Once an attack is launched by an attacker, the real world's process could be harmed more or less, this event will be modeled as a deviation from the base Bitcoin protocol, i.e., some functionalities or protocols will not work as expected which can be seen as replacing this functionality by the attacker.

For example, the Bitcoin protocol requires a solution to a cryptographic puzzle as part of the block generation. This solution is found by finding a partial pre-image of a hash function (i.e., proof-of-work, PoW), requiring enormous computation of the Bitcoin network. However, if the adversary finds a way to solve the hard puzzle without finding a pre-image, the PoW mechanism would be replaced by a simple computation in our model (modeling the adversary breaking the hash functionality). This would imply that the Bitcoin protocol is partially modified by the attacker. In our model, we define such a replacement as an attack and we are able to give the contingency plans to restore the Bitcoin protocol in such a case. Moreover, another advantage in adopting the UC methodology is that when a property is proved under some assumptions, we do not need to consider the adversary's behavior beyond the Bitcoin protocol, i.e., the environment in the UC model. We only deal with the replacement or the modification of the affected functionalities in the ideal world.

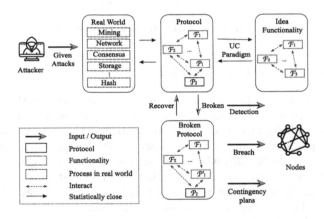

Fig. 2. High-level overview of our framework.

Moreover, although we focus on Bitcoin, our framework could also be deployed in other cryptocurrencies as long as the basic protocol has been proved to be secure in the UC model.

4.3   Adversary Model

Firstly, we assume an adversary able to change some outputs or change the functions of the functionalities. In addition, the adversary can delay the output or does not execute the process. Secondly, the adversary can change the environment which is out of the functionality, due to the security proof of the UC framework, the breakage of the environment will not influence the security of each functionality, thus the security of the individual node will be guaranteed. Finally, we also inherit one of the core assumptions of the blockchain, i.e., the majority of the nodes are honest (i.e., do not launch any attacks) and the attacker's computing power is not larger than 50% of the total computing power in the Bitcoin network. We emphasize, that our adversary model captures also bugs or misconfiguration that can be introduced unintentionally.

Attack. For a Probabilistic Polynomial Time (PPT) attacker, the protocol is secure if and only if the output of the protocol is indistinguishable from the output of the ideal functionality. We define that the attacker can break the protocol if and only if the output of the protocol targeted by the attacker can be distinguished from the output of the ideal functionality.

4.4   Security Goals

We have the following security goals. First of all, for any party $P_i \in P$, any feasible behavior or any potential change from an adversary A should be visible, i.e., the P_i should have the ability to aware of the attacker's potential behavior. This security goal indicates that some detection method is established in the real world. Second, the difference between the broken protocol and the desired protocol should be pointed out, which would help any node aware of the breach of the protocol. Besides, the party P_i should have the ability to solve the problem (e.g., by installing a new software patch or configuring some settings). This objective is in fact, similar to the goals of contingency plans in the real world. Some attacks might not have a contingency plan, i.e., a totally broken function or protocol, and in this scenario we also would like to give insights on why the contingency plans do not work.

4.5   Analysis

It should be noted that the universal composable Bitcoin protocol actually consists of other functionalities which are also composable, including the random oracle functionality, a network functionality, and a clock functionality. The adversary tries to undermine not only the Bitcoin core functionalities, but also its dependencies and (sub)protocols.

The security of our framework can be split into two parts. The first one is the UC security, which is related to the functionality, protocol, node, and environment, and this part is securely guaranteed by the UC framework proof. The second part is the channel's security, which is related to the communication between the nodes and functionality. In a UC protocol, node interactions with a functionality or protocol are assumed to be secure and atomic. In our framework, the node cannot access the functionality which is controlled by the adversary, that means the node's channel is not secure, thus we need to make an assumption necessary to detect an adversarial behavior.

In our model nodes detect attacks by finding a difference between the original protocol and its broken modification. However, such a detection would be infeasible if the protocol is attacked in a way that nodes cannot detect it. Therefore, to model node actions in the face of a functionality or protocol compromise we need to make one assumption. We assume that there exists a functionality that will never be corrupted by the adversary. This functionality only responds to one question: Is any functionality corrupted? The functionality usually does not need to be invoked, unless all of the channels have been corrupted. It should be noted that any other functionality should be prepared to receive a query and return the status of its state (i.e., original or corrupted). In the ideal world, the standard protocol should be preserved, thus the protocol could compare itself with the standard protocol to notice the differences between them.

Although we are aware that in practice attack detection is challenging and the assumption may seem strong, without this functionality attacks can stay undetected, thus rendering contingency plans useless. Interestingly, Bitcoin developers in their contingency plans [36], make a similar (although informal) assumption that there should be at least one operational communication channel while the attack is being launched. As we have a communication channel available, the attack would be noticed by the participants at some points, thus they could apply the contingency plan to fix the attack. The communication channel is actually taking the role of the query acceptance in reality, without the base channel like this, Bitcoin or other cryptocurrencies could be effectively blocked via a severe attack censoring any information exchange between participants. An important difference between an available communication channel and the detection functionality is that the former is rather for notification than for detection.

With the above assumption, we can use the following theorem as a premise to support our methodology.

Theorem 1. *The attacker can break the protocol π_{ledger} if and only if the protocol is modified so as to be distinguishable from the ideal functionality.*

Proof. To prove this theorem, we should prove that the attacker can not break ideal functionality G_{ledger}. The ideal world's functionality in the ideal world is the function that we want to realize. In the event of the breach in the ideal world, we could modify the ideal functionality and try to find another protocol to realize the functionality. Recently, the previous research [30] has proved that protocol π_{ledger} is statistically close to the ideal functionality G_{ledger} under the UC standard assumptions. Thus for any PPT adversary, the output from the protocol π_{ledger} and the output from the functionality G_{ledger} are indistinguishable. That implies that as long as the attacker can not break the protocol π_{ledger}, the original protocol remains secure under various of the attacks. However, if the protocol is modified by the attacker, the modified protocol is not statistically close to the ideal functionality, the attacker could break the modified protocol naturally. Therefore the recovery of the attacker's modification is the key point of our analysis and contingency plans.

We emphasize that all attacks could be handled in our framework as long as the underlying security model is proved (i.e., has a formal proof in the UC framework). Every attack can be modeled as a replacement of functionality in Bitcoin protocol, and if the emerged attack does not relate to the replacement of the functionality, then the protocol remains secure under certain assumptions.

5 Case Studies

Our framework allows adversaries to damage not only the functionality but also a protocol, from the protocol's point of view, we analyze the consequences of the breach and try to find contingency plans to respond to it.

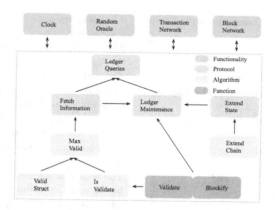

Fig. 3. The ledger queries in the Bitcoin protocol.

The mining process is the key component of the Bitcoin protocol and the considered UC model. It is critical for the stability and security of Bitcoin, therefore, mining is often a subject of detailed analysis and studies. In the model, the mining process is related to ledger queries in as shown in Fig. 3. In this section, we discuss attacks on each part of the mining process (as modeled) and their consequences.

Mining Process in Bitcoin. The underlying concept of Bitcoin is to maintain a decentralized ledger by a group of nodes and selecting a leader is the essential procedure to add new blocks (and transactions, consequently). The Bitcoin system uses a proof-of-work scheme to determine the leader in each round, roughly speaking, every node tries to find a solution of a cryptographic puzzle. These nodes are called miners, and a puzzle solver for a round is its leader able to propose a new block.

Each party can create new transactions, stores a copy of a blockchain (*Valid Struct*), and maintains a transaction buffer to store transactions received from other nodes (*Is Valid State*). At the beginning of a new state (*Ledger Maintenance*), every miner obtains the current blockchain state and its transaction buffer (*Fetch Information, Max Valid*), then the miners try to find a solution for a given puzzle (*Extend Chain*). The miner who discovers a new solution becomes the round leader who sends the solution to other nodes (*Extend State*). Other nodes receive the solution and accept it after the validation event. All of the above processes constitute the mining process in Bitcoin (*Ledger Queries*).

Table 1. The breaches of the mining process. Bold lines are the potential causes of selfish mining.

Mining Process Breach	Effect	Breach description
Ledger Queries	Transaction submission	The node can not submit the transaction
	Fetching the state	The node can not start fetching the state
	Mining start	The node can not start mining
Fetch Information	**Fetching the blocks**	The node can not fetch the block after invoking fetch information
	Fetching the transactions	The node can not fetch the transactions after invoking fetch information
	Handling new party	The node can not join the protocol while the protocol is already executed
	Max Valid	The node can not start verifying the blocks and the transactions
	Valid Struct	The node can not verify the blocks after invoking fetch information
	Is Valid State	The node can not verify the transactions after invoking fetch information
Ledger Maintenance	**Voting the state in the updating round**	The nodes can not reach consensus at the updating round
	Pretreatment of mining process	The node can not fetch the current clock information (block height) before mining; The node can not pack the transactions and blockify the blocks; The new party who join the protocol while the protocol is already executed can not get the latest information about the blockchain
	Voting the state in the working round	The nodes can not reach consensus at the working round
	Fetch the information at the end	The node can not fetch the information after reaching consensus
Extend State	**Extend Chain**	The node can not mining locally by using random oracle

Modeling Mining Process Breach. As defined, a breach means that at least one component of the attacked procedure is replaced by the adversary, thus the entire procedure does not work as intended. Each replacement can seem like a breach, and an attack can be combined as several different replacements. We analyze the consequences of each replacement separately but the attack's final effect (if more components are affected) can be seen as a sum of several partial effects. We, however, note that the framework does not handle the breach beyond the UC model, for example, money fraud, hijacking, private key disclosure, or other attacks related to operations security.

Consequences of the Breach. The consequences of the mining process breach are summarized in Table 1. Due to the page limit, we omit the detailed description of each of those consequences.[1]

Contingency Plan. Any kind of the breach in the mining process would cause the damage to nodes. Unfortunately, nodes are usually distributed in the network and there are no "official" communication side channel proposed, thus it may be challenging to detect a breach in the system by all nodes quickly. The attacker may target a group of victims who would be unaware and respond to the malicious behavior. In this setting, a non-compromised communication channel is however required to prevent the adversary, and once the node realized he is likely to be attacked, the following actions should be taken immediately: a) The nodes should stop submitting transactions and blocks. b) The nodes should stop receiving transactions and blocks actively or passively. c) The nodes should stop mining and any related behaviors. d) The node should verify the recent transactions and blocks carefully, rollback to the previous states if necessary. e) The new node should stop attempting to join the network.

Selfish Mining. Selfish mining attack occurs when a node or a mining pool attempts to withhold a successfully validated block from being broadcast to the rest of the bitcoin network as shown in Table 1. The selfish miner withholds their successfully mined block and continues to mine the next block, resulting in the selfish miner having mined more valid blocks compared to other miners. This allows the selfish miner to claim the block rewards while the rest of the network accepts "malicious" block solutions and abandons their "honest" fork.

In our model, selfish mining can be modeled as a modification of the *Extend State* protocol. The original behavior is broadcasting every newly mined block immediately, but the modified behavior is withholding the newly mined block. Then the attacker modifies also the *Fetch Information* protocol. The original behavior is to update to the latest blockchain view, while the modified adversarial behavior is to monitor the Bitcoin network, and if the attacker wins, the attacker would not take the action; otherwise, the attacker broadcasts the mined block invalidating the work of honest nodes. Finally, the attacker modifies the protocol

---

[1] The extended version of this paper will be publicly available as a preprint.

ledger maintenance, such that the attacker can start mining without applying honest updates, thus it will not lead to reaching the consensus phase (in the adversarial view).

Because the modification of *Extend State* is actually not the key point of the selfish mining, withholding proof-of-work means the attacker can not earn the reward from the blockchain. By focusing on *Fetch Information* and *ledger Maintenance* modifications, the following contingency plans can be suggested.

- A stale block can not be accepted by other nodes. Thus the attacker can not withhold the newly mined block, the attacker should fetch the information from outside if he withholds a block. This suggestion is focusing around *Fetch Information*.
- The protocol should forbid the attacker to mine the next block if the attacker has not published the newly mined block. The feasible procedure is that the valid block should have the majority of the nodes' signature after verifying it, and the next block should contain the hash of these signatures. This suggestion is focusing on *ledger Maintenance*.

The contingency plan guarantees that the messages transmitted by honest miners are delayed maximally by Δ rounds,[2] to formally state the intuition behind the above contingency plans, we first present an useful observation about the protocol's observation.

Lemma 1. *Let P_i and P_j be miners, and let the round $r \geq 0$. Assume P_i is honest in round r, and its local state has length l. Then for any honest miner P_j in round $r + \Delta$ who is registered in the network before round r, the miner P_j must have at least length l.*

Proof. We have the assumption that the messages transmitted by honest miners are delayed maximally by Δ rounds. Thus, if an honest miner receives a state which has length l, then all of other miners will receive the state within the next Δ rounds. Hence, the other honest miners will adopt a chain with length at least l.

We define P_j in the above lemma is honest-and-synchronized miner, then we state the relation between time (rounds) and number of new state blocks, i.e., chain growth.

Lemma 2. *In the real world execution, Let P_i be miners, and let the round $r \geq 0$. Assume P_i is honest-and-synchronized miner in round r, and its local state has length l. Then in the round $r + t$ for $t \geq 0$, it holds that for any $\delta > 0$, any honest-and-synchronized miner P_j will has length at least $l + T$ if $T \leq (1 - \delta)t\frac{\alpha_{min}}{1+\alpha_{min}\Delta}$ except with negligible probability. Where α is the honest mining power.*

---

[2] It is essentially assuming a synchronous network.

Proof. (sketch) Generally, for an interval of rounds $r, ..., r + t$, we can guarantee a length increase of $\gamma \cdot t$ with $\gamma := \frac{\tau}{1+\tau\Delta}$ if for all possible subsets S of rounds of size $t' = t(1 - \gamma\Delta)$ of this interval we have $\alpha_S \geq \tau$ except with negligible probability.

Theorem 2. *In the real world execution, assume that in round r, an honest-and-synchronized miner has a state. The probability that a block st mined by the adversary in this state was first accepted before round $r - wt$ with negligible probability, for any constant $0 < w < 1$, where S denotes the interval $r - wt, ..., r$.*

Proof. (sketch) From chain growth and the above lemma, we derive that if an honest-and-synchronized miner adopts a new state that contains a block the adversary obtained by functionality then either this block has been published by the adversary before, or it was mined quite recently by a corrupted party.

The attacker might have the ability to break the assumption, for instance, delay the message for a long time. In this case, the contingency plans aim to restore the corresponding parts in the protocol, it works as a guarantee of the assumption of the above theorem.

Note, that although these suggestions may be insightful for new systems, they actually require major protocol changes. In fact, multiple proposed selfish-mining mitigations are based on similar observations [12,28].

6   Conclusion

We have presented the first formalized contingency plans framework for Bitcoin. Our framework is able to facilitate analysis of entire attack classes, giving detection guides, breakage classification, and contingency plans as the output. Our framework involves a formalized UC model that describes the Bitcoin protocol and its properties as the start point. This approach allows us to formally reason about attacks on the system, by modeling them as changes of the model. Consequently, contingency plans can be proposed as fixes that recover the modified protocol to its secure modification. Moreover, we demonstrated how to apply our framework to different classes of failures and attacks.

Although we believe that this work can be seen as the first attempt towards more complete and formal contingency plans, we are also aware that there is still a substantial amount of future work to be undertaken. In particular, we see limitations of some aspects of UC models and its relation with the real world (e.g., network models). We leave more realistic and practical models as future work.

Acknowledgment. This project is supported by the Ministry of Education, Singapore, under its MOE AcRF Tier 2 grant (MOE2018-T2-1-111), National Natural Science Foundation of China (Grant No. 61632020), and the Major Innovation Project of Science and Technology of Shandong Province under Grant 2018CXGC0702.

References

1. Gervais, A., Karame, G.O., Wüst, K., Glykantzis, V., Ritzdorf, H., Capkun, S.: On the security and performance of proof of work blockchains. In: ACM CCS, pp. 3–16. ACM (2016)
2. Sapirshtein, A., Sompolinsky, Y., Zohar, A.: Optimal selfish mining strategies in bitcoin. In: Grossklags, J., Preneel, B. (eds.) FC 2016. LNCS, vol. 9603, pp. 515–532. Springer, Heidelberg (2017). https://doi.org/10.1007/978-3-662-54970-4_30
3. Badertscher, C., Maurer, U., Tschudi, D., Zikas, V.: Bitcoin as a transaction ledger: a composable treatment. In: Katz, J., Shacham, H. (eds.) CRYPTO 2017. LNCS, vol. 10401, pp. 324–356. Springer, Cham (2017). https://doi.org/10.1007/978-3-319-63688-7_11
4. Canetti, R.: Universally composable security: a new paradigm for cryptographic protocols. In: Proceedings 2001 IEEE International Conference on Cluster Computing, pp. 136–145. IEEE (2001)
5. Coretti, S., Garay, J., Hirt, M., Zikas, V.: Constant-round asynchronous multi-party computation based on one-way functions. In: Cheon, J.H., Takagi, T. (eds.) ASIACRYPT 2016. LNCS, vol. 10032, pp. 998–1021. Springer, Heidelberg (2016). https://doi.org/10.1007/978-3-662-53890-6_33
6. Florian, T., Björn, S.: Bitcoin and beyond: a technical survey on decentralized digital currencies. IEEE Commun. Surv. Tutor. **18**(3), 2084–2123 (2016)
7. Garay, J., Kiayias, A., Leonardos, N.: The bitcoin backbone protocol: analysis and applications. In: Oswald, E., Fischlin, M. (eds.) EUROCRYPT 2015. LNCS, vol. 9057, pp. 281–310. Springer, Heidelberg (2015). https://doi.org/10.1007/978-3-662-46803-6_10
8. Garay, J., Kiayias, A., Leonardos, N.: The bitcoin backbone protocol with chains of variable difficulty. In: Katz, J., Shacham, H. (eds.) CRYPTO 2017. LNCS, vol. 10401, pp. 291–323. Springer, Cham (2017). https://doi.org/10.1007/978-3-319-63688-7_10
9. Gervais, A., Ritzdorf, H., Karame, G.O., Capkun, S.: Tampering with the delivery of blocks and transactions in bitcoin. In: ACM CCS, pp. 692–705. ACM (2015)
10. Giechaskiel, I., Cremers, C., Rasmussen, K.B.: On bitcoin security in the presence of broken crypto primitives. IACR Cryptology ePrint Archive 2016:167 (2016)
11. Goldreich, O., Micali, S., Wigderson, A.: How to play any mental game. In: ACM STOC, pp. 218–229. ACM (1987)
12. Heilman, E.: One weird trick to stop selfish miners: fresh bitcoins, a solution for the honest miner (poster abstract). In: Böhme, R., Brenner, M., Moore, T., Smith, M. (eds.) FC 2014. LNCS, vol. 8438, pp. 161–162. Springer, Heidelberg (2014). https://doi.org/10.1007/978-3-662-44774-1_12
13. Heilman, E., Kendler, A., Zohar, A., Goldberg, S.: Eclipse attacks on bitcoin's peer-to-peer network. In: USENIX Security, pp. 129–144 (2015)
14. Eyal, I.: The miner's dilemma. In: IEEE S&P, pp. 89–103. IEEE (2015)
15. Eyal, I., Sirer, E.G.: Majority is not enough: bitcoin mining is vulnerable. Commun. ACM **61**(7), 95–102 (2018)
16. Bonneau, J., Miller, A., Clark, J., Narayanan, A., Kroll, J.A., Felten, E.W.: SoK: research perspectives and challenges for bitcoin and cryptocurrencies. In: IEEE S&P. IEEE (2015)
17. Katz, J., Lindell, Y.: Introduction to Modern Cryptography. Chapman and Hall/CRC, Boca Raton (2014)

18. Katz, J., Maurer, U., Tackmann, B., Zikas, V.: Universally composable synchronous computation. In: Sahai, A. (ed.) TCC 2013. LNCS, vol. 7785, pp. 477–498. Springer, Heidelberg (2013). https://doi.org/10.1007/978-3-642-36594-2_27
19. Kiayias, A., Russell, A., David, B., Oliynykov, R.: Ouroboros: a provably secure proof-of-stake blockchain protocol. In: Katz, J., Shacham, H. (eds.) CRYPTO 2017. LNCS, vol. 10401, pp. 357–388. Springer, Cham (2017). https://doi.org/10.1007/978-3-319-63688-7_12
20. Kiayias, A., Zhou, H.-S., Zikas, V.: Fair and robust multi-party computation using a global transaction ledger. In: Fischlin, M., Coron, J.-S. (eds.) EUROCRYPT 2016. LNCS, vol. 9666, pp. 705–734. Springer, Heidelberg (2016). https://doi.org/10.1007/978-3-662-49896-5_25
21. King, S., Nadal, S.: PPCoin: peer-to-peer crypto-currency with proof-of-stake. Self-published 19 2012
22. Liao, K., Hammer, M.A., Miller, A.: ILC: a calculus for composable, computational cryptography. Cryptology ePrint Archive (2019). https://eprint.iacr.org/2019/402
23. Mack, S.: Update on Zerocoin spends (2019). https://zcoin.io/update-on-zerocoin-spends/. Accessed 20 Apr 2019
24. Marcus, Y., Heilman, E., Goldberg, S.: Low-resource eclipse attacks on Ethereum's peer-to-peer network. IACR Cryptology ePrint Archive 2018:236 (2018)
25. Miers, I., Garman, C., Green, M., Rubin, A.D.: Zerocoin: anonymous distributed e-cash from bitcoin. In: IEEE S&P, pp. 397–411. IEEE (2013)
26. Miller, A.: Feather-forks: enforcing a blacklist with sub-50% hash power (2013). https://bitcointalk.org/index.php?topic=312668.0. Accessed 24 Aug 2019
27. Pass, R., Seeman, L., Shelat, A.: Analysis of the blockchain protocol in asynchronous networks. In: Coron, J.-S., Nielsen, J.B. (eds.) EUROCRYPT 2017. LNCS, vol. 10211, pp. 643–673. Springer, Cham (2017). https://doi.org/10.1007/978-3-319-56614-6_22
28. Pass, R., Shi, E.: FruitChains: a fair blockchain. In: ACM PODC, pp. 315–324. ACM (2017)
29. Pinzón, C., Rocha, C.: Double-spend attack models with time advantage for bitcoin. Electron. Not. Theor. Comput. Sci. **329**, 79–103 (2016)
30. Samiran, B., Sushmita, R., Kouichi, S.: Bitcoin block withholding attack: analysis and mitigation. IEEE TIFS **12**, 1967–1978 (2017)
31. Ben Sasson, E., et al.: Zerocash: decentralized anonymous payments from bitcoin. In: IEEE S&P, pp. 459–474. IEEE (2014)
32. Nakamoto, S.: Bitcoin: a peer-to-peer electronic cash system (2008)
33. Sun, S.-F., Au, M.H., Liu, J.K., Yuen, T.H.: RingCT 2.0: a compact accumulator-based (linkable ring signature) protocol for blockchain cryptocurrency Monero. In: Foley, S.N., Gollmann, D., Snekkenes, E. (eds.) ESORICS 2017. LNCS, vol. 10493, pp. 456–474. Springer, Cham (2017). https://doi.org/10.1007/978-3-319-66399-9_25
34. Courtois, N.T., Bahack, L.: On subversive miner strategies and block withholding attack in bitcoin digital currency. arXiv (2014)
35. Bitcoin Wiki. Contingency plans (2019). https://en.bitcoin.it/wiki/Contingency_plans. Accessed 20 Apr 2019
36. Bitcoin Wiki. IRC Channels (2019). https://en.bitcoin.it/wiki/IRC_channels. Accessed 3 Mar 2019
37. Yujin, K., Dohyun, K., Yunmok, S., Eugene, V., Yongdae, K.: Be selfish and avoid dilemmas: fork after withholding (FAW) attacks on bitcoin. In: ACM CCS. ACM (2017)

Characterizing Erasable Accounts
in Ethereum

Xiaoqi Li[1], Ting Chen[2], Xiapu Luo[1(✉)], and Jiangshan Yu[3]

[1] Department of Computing,
The Hong Kong Polytechnic University, Hong Kong, China
csxqli@gmail.com, csxluo@comp.polyu.edu.hk
[2] Center for Cybersecurity,
University of Electronic Science and Technology of China, Chengdu, China
brokendragon@uestc.edu.cn
[3] Faculty of Information Technology, Monash University, Melbourne, Australia
jiangshan.yu@monash.edu

Abstract. Being the most popular permissionless blockchain that supports smart contracts, Ethereum allows any user to create accounts on it. However, not all accounts matter. For example, the accounts due to attacks can be removed. In this paper, we conduct the first investigation on erasable accounts that can be removed to save system resources and even users' money (i.e., ETH or gas). In particular, we propose and develop a novel tool named GLASER, which analyzes the State DataBase of Ethereum to discover five kinds of erasable accounts. The experimental results show that GLASER can accurately reveal 508,482 erasable accounts and these accounts lead to users wasting more than 106 million dollars. GLASER can help stop further economic loss caused by these detected accounts. Moreover, GLASER characterizes the attacks/behaviors related to detected erasable accounts through graph analysis.

Keywords: P2P system security · System maintainability · Ethereum

1 Introduction

Being the largest blockchain that supports smart contract, Ethereum has two kinds of accounts: EOA (Externally Owned Account) and contract account [17]. As a permissionless blockchain system, Ethereum allows any user to create many EOAs through their private keys. Deploying a smart contract to Ethereum will produce a contract account that contains the contract's runtime bytecodes. Every node must synchronize blockchain data, which includes blocks and StateDB (State DataBase) [3]. The StateDB stores all the accounts' state information, such as ETH balance, transaction number, runtime bytecodes, and so on [3].

However, not all accounts should be kept. In particular, we identify three kinds of erasable contract accounts that are produced due to contracts' programming errors or attacks, and two kinds of erasable EOAs that are produced

© Springer Nature Switzerland AG 2020
W. Susilo et al. (Eds.): ISC 2020, LNCS 12472, pp. 352–371, 2020.
https://doi.org/10.1007/978-3-030-62974-8_20

due to contracts' deployment failure or DoS (Denial of Service) attacks. Such erasable accounts not only waste system resources and affect the efficiency of blockchain, but also easily waste users' money (i.e., ETH or gas). For example, one empty account (Address: 0x6e55..) discovered in this paper was created due to contract deployment failure. It wasted user's 137,552 gas when it was called because the contract's runtime bytecodes were not stored in this account, whose information is shown in Fig. 1. We regard the worthless accounts that deserve to be removed without affecting the normal operations of users and other accounts as erasable accounts.

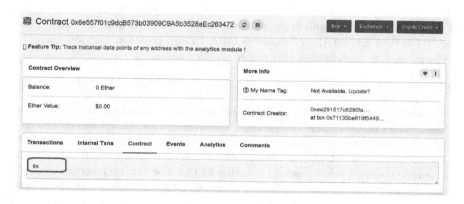

Fig. 1. One empty account detected by GLASER.

Unfortunately, there lacks a systematic study on the erasable accounts that can be removed. Although some studies [10, 11] use call graph analysis to measure the control flow between contracts, their purposes are different from ours. Our work focuses on the erasable accounts that exist in Ethereum, and some of our analyzed accounts (e.g., DoS contracts) are related to interaction between contracts. There also exist some other research analyzing different kinds of security issues for smart contracts [13] or Ethereum architecture [15]. These research mainly focus on security issues on the contract-level and system-level of Ethereum, whose contents and purposes are different from ours.

To fill the gap, we design and implement a novel tool named GLASER (detectinG erasabLe AccountS in EtheReum) to discover erasable accounts by analyzing the StateDB of Ethereum. It is worth noting that marking an account as erasable just according to its liveness and balance value is improper, because an account might contain useful runtime bytecodes or its private key is owned by external user so that it cannot be removed even if it has not been used for a long time and stores no ETH. Instead, GLASER analyzes accounts' contents and states stored in Ethereum StateDB. In detail, it leverages program analysis techniques to discover contract accounts with worthless runtime bytecodes, and employs state field and transaction analysis to discover EOAs that no one owns their private keys. The accounts discovered by GLASER are worthless and deserve to be removed without affecting the normal operations of other accounts/users.

Applying GLASER to all Ethereum accounts, we discovered 508,482 erasable accounts, and more than 99.9% of them are still stored in Ethereum. These erasable accounts have wasted users more than 106 million dollars and can be removed through executing SELFDESTRUCT operation in their runtime bytecodes by users, or removed forcibly by Ethereum officials. For example, one erasable contract account (Address: 0xa30B..) can be removed through transaction sent by any user, and some empty account created due to DoS attacks were already removed forcibly through hard fork by Ethereum officials [1]. This paper mainly focuses on erasable accounts' detection to help users identify erasable accounts and remind users not to call them to save money, and erasable accounts' characterization to interpret their behaviors/attacks and creation reasons.

The main contributions of this paper are as follows:

(1) To the best of our knowledge, we conduct the *first* systematic investigation on erasable accounts in Ethereum. We propose and define five kinds of erasable accounts, i.e., three kinds of erasable contracts and two kinds of erasable EOAs.
(2) We design a novel approach to analyze the Ethereum StateDB, and implement the idea in a tool called GLASER, which can discover and characterize erasable contract accounts and erasable EOAs. For contract accounts, leveraging static analysis and symbolic execution, GLASER analyzes runtime bytecodes of contracts to detect three kinds of erasable contract accounts. For EOAs, GLASER analyzes their state-related attribute fields and historical transactions to discover two kinds of erasable EOAs. GLASER also characterizes erasable accounts through call graph and creation graph analysis.
(3) We conduct experiments to evaluate and characterize the detected erasable accounts. We analyze the 508,482 detected erasable accounts' creation time distributions. More than 99.9% of them are still stored in Ethereum, and their transactions wasted users more than 106 million dollars. GLASER can remind users not to call erasable accounts and help stop further economic loss of users caused by them. Furthermore, the graph analysis of erasable accounts interprets their creation reasons, i.e., attacks, programming errors, or deployment failure.

2 Background

2.1 Ethereum

Supporting smart contracts, Ethereum records not only transactions but also state transitions that occur in blockchain. Ethereum contains two types of accounts, i.e., EOA and contract account [17], which are all indexed by 20 bytes length of addresses.

Account's Creation and Usage: Ethereum is a permissionless blockchain system, and users can create their own EOA and store ETH (native cryptocurrency in Ethereum). Users can initiate transactions by the private key corresponding to the EOA address, including ETH transfers and contract calls. The contract accounts are created by EOAs or other contract accounts. In addition to storing ETH, the contract account also holds the runtime bytecodes of smart contract. There are two types of bytecodes in Ethereum: runtime bytecodes stored in contract account, and deployment bytecodes used for contract runtime bytecodes' deployment. The contract account is not controlled by the user's private key, but by the contract's runtime bytecodes' logics.

Account's Removal: Users can only remove contract account through executing SELFDESTRUCT in its runtime bytecodes. All EOAs and contract accounts without SELFDESTRUCT in runtime bytecodes cannot be removed by users. In addition, all erasable accounts can be removed forcibly by Ethereum officials. Although some discovered erasable accounts in this paper cannot be removed by users, our results can remind users not to call them to save money.

StateDB: The StateDB stores the world state of Ethereum based on accounts. For every account a, its state $\sigma[a]$ consists of four fields [3]: If a is an EOA, $\sigma[a]_n$ stores the number of external transactions *sent from* this account. If a is a contract account, $\sigma[a]_n$ stores the number of contracts created by this account. $\sigma[a]_b$ stores the balance value (in Wei) of account a. $\sigma[a]_s$ stores the root hash of Merkle tree which encodes the storage contents of the account. $\sigma[a]_c$ stores the runtime bytecodes of account a. Note that the main difference between EOA and contract account is whether its code field is empty [3].

2.2 Smart Contract

In Ethereum, each node runs an EVM (Ethereum Virtual Machine), and the runtime bytecodes of contract are executed in EVM. Smart contract can be developed through several Turing complete languages, such as Solidity (the recommended language), Serpent, and Vyper [17].

Execution: When a smart contract is deployed in Ethereum, users can invoke its external functions through transactions. Note that we describe transactions sent from EOAs as external transactions, and message-calls sent from contract accounts as internal transactions in this paper. Gas is the basic unit of resource consumption for transactions in Ethereum [6]. Before users initiate transactions, they all need to pay a certain amount of gas. When the smart contract is running in EVM, each opcode corresponds to a certain amount of gas, whose value is defined in the Ethereum Yellow Paper [3]. To prevent DoS attacks, Ethereum has modified the gas value of some specific opcodes, such as SELFDESTRUCT's value was modified from 0 to 5,000 in EIP-150 (Ethereum Improvement Proposal) [6].

Data: The smart contracts' execution in EVM involves three forms of data, namely storage, memory, and stack [7]. The storage data is stored in StateDB of Ethereum in the form of key-value pairs, and both key's length and value's length are 256 bits [17]. Storage is persistent and will not be released as transaction execution ends. Storage data is stored and read through two opcodes, i.e., SLOAD and SSTORE. Memory is the temporarily allocated space when smart contracts are executed in EVM, which is automatically freed as the transaction execution finishes. EVM is a 1,024 depth stack-based virtual machine, and the contracts' opcodes are all executed around the stack [16].

3   Erasable Accounts

3.1   Erasable Contract

The main difference between EOA and contract account is whether its code field is empty[3]. Below we introduce erasable contracts with runtime bytecodes.

Meaningless Contract: We analyze two kinds of meaningless contract, i.e., MC-S (Meaningless Contract with STOP) and MC-RS (Meaningless Contract with REVERT or SELFDESTRUCT).

MC-S refers to one particular kind of meaningless contract, whose first opcode in its runtime bytecodes is STOP. There exist MC-S because users incorrectly use runtime bytecodes to deploy contracts, whose creation and behavior will be analyzed in Sect. 5. When the MC-S is called, STOP will halt the transaction's execution immediately. Therefore, these contracts are controlled by STOP, which is meaningless and may waste user's gas or ETH.

MC-S Example: One MC-S (Address: 0x2Ab7..) was called with input data three times, which waste users' gas. Their input data were not processed before the related transactions were halted by STOP. Furthermore, this meaningless contract was transferred ETH through transactions twice. Because the MC-S is controlled by STOP, the total of more than 0.042 ETH stored in this account can never be transferred out, which results in users' money waste.

MC-RS refers to contract that has REVERT or SELFDESTRUCT opcode in its first basic block. A basic block means a series of sequential opcodes without any control flow operation (e.g., JUMP, STOP) [6]. The first basic block is the program entrance and every call to the contract will execute it. Most MC-RS are deployed by malicious contracts through internal transactions (i.e., sent from contract). However, MC-RS is meaningless because any call to MC-RS will invoke REVERT or SELFDESTRUCT. REVERT ends runtime bytecodes' execution and reverts state changes of the call. SELFDESTRUCT removes the contract account from blockchain.

MC-RS Example: The snippets of two MC-RS are shown in Fig. 2. There are only three operations in the first MC-RS (Address: 0xa30B..). This contract can be exploited by attacker to steal ETH through setting his own EOA address in the call data. However, this contract is meaningless. Because any call to it will invoke SELFDESTRUCT and transfer out the ETH stored in it. The second MC-RS (Address: 0x7770..) will invoke REVERT during any call to it. Furthermore, the operations after its first basic block will never execute. Any call to the contract will execute operations from 0x0 to 0x8, which is meaningless and waste gas.

```
0x0   PUSH1 0x00  //MC-RS-1
0x2   CALLDATALOAD  //get the first 32bytes call data
0x3   SELFDESTRUCT  //destruct the contract

0x0   PUSH1 0x80  //MC-RS-2
0x2   PUSH1 0x40
0x4   MSTORE  //save 0x80 to memory
0x5   PUSH1 0x00
0x7   DUP1
0x8   REVERT //end execution and revert state changes
0x9   STOP
0xa   LOG2  //other basic blocks
......  ......
```

Fig. 2. Snippets of two MC-RS (i.e., with **REVERT** or **SELFDESTRUCT** in first basic blocks).

Stack or Opcode Error Contract: EVM is a virtual machine based on 1,024 depth stack, and the stack will definitely overflow (push more than 1,024 items into stack) or underflow (pop item from empty stack) if the stack error contract is called. Before EIP-150 increased the gas cost of **CALL** from 40 to 700, the attacker may exploit stack overflow through recursive call depth attack [17]. Nowadays, although stack overflow is hard to occur, stack underflow still exists due to program writing errors.

Stack Error Contract Example: One transaction (Hash: 0x9518..) encountered "Stack Underflow" error and exhausted its gas, due to its contract deployment-related codes. Moreover, runtime bytecodes' contents may be related to some uncontrollable factors, which may also produce stack error contracts. One example of stack error contract's deployment bytecodes is shown in Fig. 3 (Related transaction: 0xf7db..). In program counter 0x5, it returns runtime bytecodes to deploy, whose first byte is related to the current block's timestamp (in program counter 0x0 to 0x1). At last, one stack error contract (Address: 0x7A03..) was deployed, and its first operation in runtime bytecodes is **DIV**, which will result in stack underflow.

```
0x0 TIMESTAMP //get the block's timestamp
0x1 CALLVALUE
0x2 MSTORE8 //save byte to memory
0x3 CODESIZE
0x4 CALLVALUE
0x5 RETURN //return bytecodes to deploy
```

Fig. 3. The deployment bytecodes of one stack error contract.

Developers can use high-level languages or directly write bytecodes to develop smart contract. However, due to programming errors, some runtime bytecodes deployed in blockchain cannot be disassembled to correct opcodes. If there exist unknown opcodes that cannot be recognized by EVM, it will encounter "Bad Instruction Error". Opcode error contract refers to contract that has unknown opcode in the first basic block, which will encounter error during any call to it.

Opcode Error Contract Example: The first two bytes of one contract's runtime bytecodes are 0xd929, which cannot be correctly disassembled to opcodes of EVM. Because the unknown opcodes exist in its first basic block, all transactions calling to it encountered "Bad Instruction Error" (Address: 0x5266..). The transaction with "Bad Instruction Error" exhausts gas, halts execution and reverts state changes [3].

DoS Contract: We analyze two kinds of DoS related contracts: attacked Parity wallets, and malicious contracts exploited for DoS attacks. If contract A hardcodes and calls contract B's address to execute, and B is removed, A will be a dependency error contract without normal service. In November of 2017, the attacker escalated his privilege and removed Parity's multi-sig library contract (Address: 0x863d..), which caused all Parity wallets that depend on it out of service. Note that calling to a removed contract will just return 1 (means no error or exception), and users cannot verify if it is out of service through return value. If users knew in advance that their wallets were out of service, they would not use them anymore to deduce financial losses. Etherscan only marks part of attacked Parity wallets, we attempt to detect more of them.

In 2016, the attacker exploited malicious contracts to initiate DoS attack for Ethereum [17]. The attacker executes massive particular operations (e.g., EXTCODESIZE, DELEGATECALL), which consume low gas but high system resources. The DoS attack leads to low nodes' data synchronization and transaction execution. The Ethereum official modified many operations' gas values in EIP-150 [17] to repair related vulnerabilities.

Malicious DoS Contract Example: We analyze the malicious DoS contracts and discover that they have similar patterns. These malicious contracts just have one basic block in their runtime bytecodes. In the basic block, there are many particular operations that consume low gas but high system resources. For example, one malicious DoS contract's snippets are shown in Fig. 4 (Address: 0x7922..) with 200 EXTCODESIZE in the only basic block of the contract.

```
0x00 PUSH20 0x42a119d24fd64362f3892815d310c83edcb61b88
0x15 EXTCODESIZE
0x16 POP
0x17 PUSH20 0xdfccc8e473dc262cfc6ddb4092946b66baadf88b
0x2c EXTCODESIZE //its gas was modified from 20 to 700
0x2d POP
0x2e PUSH20 0xd96b74abd2ded0b7f2873202a2f3bb562b22b2ef
0x43 EXTCODESIZE
0x44 POP
```

Fig. 4. Snippets of one malicious DoS contract.

3.2   Erasable EOA

Empty Account: The empty account has the following features: ❶zero value balance, ❷zero value nonce, and ❸empty code. Whether the account has code is the main difference between contract account and EOA, and we classify empty accounts into erasable EOA. Ethereum officials have only cleaned up the empty accounts created during the DoS attack exploiting SELFDESTRUCT [1]. However, there still exist empty accounts due to contract deployment failure. Before EIP-2, it will create an empty account if the contract deployment transaction does not succeed (e.g., out of gas). After EIP-2, it will fail with error and do not create empty accounts anymore. The creation process of empty accounts denotes that they are not controlled by runtime bytecodes or external users, which results in their uselessness. The empty account may result in gas waste, because users may incorrectly think runtime bytecodes are deployed in these accounts.

Example: One empty account (Address: 0x6e55..) has been called many times, which wastes users' gas. We analyze all the input data of the related transactions, whose first four bytes are all function signatures. That is to say, all these transactions were intended to invoke the functions in runtime bytecodes.

DoS EOA: The DoS EOA has the following features: ❶1 Wei value balance, ❷zero value nonce, ❸empty code, ❹zero historical external transaction, and ❺one historical internal transaction without error. The differences between empty account and DoS EOA are their balance value and creation process. DoS EOAs are created through internal transactions sent from contracts. Massive DoS EOAs were created during the DoS attack in 2016, whose creation will be analyzed in Sect. 5.1. The attacker created DoS EOAs through smallest financial cost (i.e., 1 Wei), and all of these accounts' addresses were generated through computation in runtime bytecodes, whose process denotes their uselessness (detail in Sect. 6). The existence of massive DoS EOAs increases the StateDB size, resulting in the waste of disk resources and nodes' difficulty in syncing data.

Example: One transaction (Hash: 0x1aa8..) detected by GLASER created ten DoS EOAs through internal transactions. Note that 1 Wei (1 ETH $= 10^{18}$ Wei) is the smallest cryptocurrency unit in Ethereum, which cannot even buy 1 gas. The recommended gas price is 61 GWei [2] (1 GWei $= 10^9$ Wei), which can be set in transaction by users.

4   GLASER

To analyze the StateDB, we synchronize the blockchain with "fat-db = on" option through Parity client, which can build appropriate information to allow enumeration of all accounts. Then we export the StateDB as plain text file through Parity and leverage GLASER to traverse StateDB data to detect erasable accounts. The overview of GLASER's architecture is shown in Fig. 5, which mainly consists of three modules:

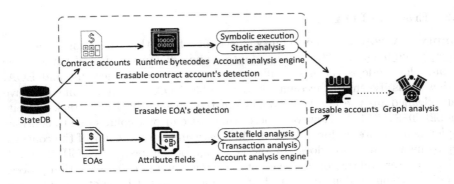

Fig. 5. Overview of GLASER's architecture.

(1) Erasable contract account detection. In this module, GLASER detects three kinds of erasable contract accounts: meaningless contracts, stack/opcode error contracts, and DoS contracts. According to their respective characteristics, we leverage different techniques, which mainly include runtime bytecodes' static analysis and symbolic execution.

(2) Erasable EOA detection. In this module, GLASER detects two kinds of erasable EOAs: empty accounts, which are produced due to contract deployment failure; and DoS EOAs, which are produced due to DoS attacks. We mainly leverage state field and transaction analysis to discover erasable EOAs.

(3) Graph analysis for erasable accounts. For the detected erasable accounts, GLASER characterizes their behaviors/attacks through call graph analysis and creation graph analysis, whose details will be described in Sect. 6.

4.1 Erasable Contract Detection

Meaningless Contract: GLASER leverages runtime bytecodes' static analysis to detect two kinds of meaningless contract, i.e., MC-S and MC-RS. Static analysis refers to techniques that examine codes without attempting to execute them [12]. GLASER statically analyzes contracts' runtime bytecodes to detect MC-S. In detail, it intercepts runtime bytecodes' first byte to judge whether it is 0x00, which is the hex code for STOP. If one contract starts with 0x00 byte in its runtime bytecodes, it will be tagged as MC-S. GLASER also statically analyzes contracts' runtime bytecodes to detect MC-RS. First, it disassembles contract's runtime bytecodes to acquire the opcodes. Second, it splits the opcodes into different basic blocks, which end with specific control flow operations (i.e., STOP, JUMP, JUMPI, RETURN, SELFDESTRUCT, REVERT). Third, it analyzes the first basic block. If REVERT or SELFDESTRUCT exists in the first basic block, it will tag the contract as MC-RS.

Stack or Opcode Error Contract: GLASER leverages symbolic execution and runtime bytecodes' static analysis to detect stack/opcode error contracts.

Symbolic execution uses symbolic values as inputs to simulate the process of program execution [18]. The detection process of stack error contract is divided into three steps. First, GLASER acquires the opcodes of contract's runtime bytecodes. Second, it splits the opcodes into different basic blocks and extracts the runtime bytecodes corresponding to the first basic block. Third, it symbolically executes the extracted runtime bytecodes leveraging OYENTE [18], which is a symbolic execution engine. If the symbolic execution process encounters "Stack Underflow", it will tag the contract as stack error contract. For opcode error contract, GLASER disassembles contract's runtime bytecodes into opcodes and split them into basic blocks. Then GLASER detects whether there exist unknown opcodes in its first basic block. If unknown opcode exists in its first basic block, the contract will be tagged as opcode error contract.

DoS Contract: GLASER leverages symbolic execution and runtime bytecodes' static analysis to detect DoS contracts. GLASER detects attacked Parity wallet contracts leveraging symbolic execution techniques. GLASER analyzes four related operations for contracts' interaction, i.e., CALL, CALLCODE, DELEGATECALL, STATICCALL. If the symbolic execution encounters anyone of these operations, it extracts the second item of the stack $\mu_s[1]$, which is used as the address of contract being called. If $\mu_s[1]$ is a real value that matches the address of removed Parity multi-sig library, it will tag this contract as attacked Parity wallet. For malicious DoS contract, GLASER disassembles contract's runtime bytecodes into opcodes and split them into basic blocks. Then GLASER analyzes the number and content of basic block. If one contract has only one basic block and has more than 100 DoS related operations, GLASER will tag it as malicious DoS contract. We analyze seven DoS related operations: EXTCODESIZE, EXTCODECOPY, BALANCE, CALL, DELEGATECALL, CALLCODE, SELFDESTRUCT.

4.2   Erasable EOA Detection

Empty Account: GLASER leverages account state field analysis and transaction analysis to detect empty accounts. The detection process of empty accounts is divided into two steps. First, GLASER analyzes the account attribute fields to detect possible empty accounts, which should satisfy the three features described in Sect. 3.2. Second, GLASER analyzes the historical transaction of the detected empty accounts in the first step, to verify that they are created due to contract deployment failure. In detail, it analyzes the oldest transaction related to the accounts detected in the first step. If one account's oldest transaction is used for contract deployment, GLASER will tag it as erasable empty account.

DoS EOA: GLASER leverages account state field analysis and transaction analysis to detect DoS EOA. Similar to the detection of empty accounts, detection process of DoS EOAs is divided into two steps. First, GLASER analyzes the account attribute fields to detect possible DoS EOAs, which should satisfy the first three features described in Sect. 3.2. Second, GLASER analyzes the historical transaction of the detected DoS EOAs in the first step, to verify that they are created through internal transactions sent from contracts. In detail, we set relatively strict conditions to verify DoS EOAs in this step. GLASER analyzes their historical external transactions and internal transactions. If one account has no external transaction and only one internal transaction without error (i.e., sent 1 Wei to create this account), we can conclude that it is an erasable DoS EOA. There might exist massive internal transactions with "Out of Gas Error", which were used for DoS attacks.

5   Evaluation

We carry out experiments to answer the following research questions: RQ1 Quantity: How many each kind of erasable accounts can be detected through GLASER? RQ2 Accuracy: To what extent can GLASER accurately detect erasable accounts? RQ3 Waste: How much money lost due to erasable accounts?

5.1   RQ1 Quantity

In this section, we evaluate the quantity statistics of erasable accounts detected through GLASER. Furthermore, we analyze the creation time distribution of the detected erasable accounts.

Table 1. Quantity statistics of erasable accounts detected through GLASER.

Cat.	Taxonomy	Quantity	Erasable accounts	Quantity
❶	Erasable contract	481,087	Meaningless contract	479,153
			Stack/opcode error contract	150
			DoS contract	1,784
❷	Erasable EOA	27,395	Empty account	195
			DoS EOA	27,200

We have exported the StateDB of Ethereum and detect erasable accounts leveraging GLASER, whose quantity statistics are shown in Table 1. We discover 481,087 erasable contracts and 27,395 erasable EOAs respectively. All the five specific kinds of detected erasable accounts' addresses are published on https://figshare.com/articles/dataset/11516694. For the 1,784 DoS contracts, we detect 658 different contracts hardcode and call the removed Parity multi-sig library, while Etherscan only tags 153 of them. Because most users leverage high-level languages to develop contracts, there exists a small quantity of stack/opcode error contracts. Because Ethereum officials have already repaired the bug of empty account's creation due to contract deployment failure, the discovered empty accounts' quantity is small.

To measure the number of erasable accounts at different time, we analyze their historical transactions to acquire their creation time. The analysis of accounts' creation time is divided into two steps. First, we crawl all the historical transactions related to the detected erasable accounts through Geth RPC APIs. Second, we filter out the oldest transaction of each account and acquire the timestamp of this transaction, which is the creation time of this account.

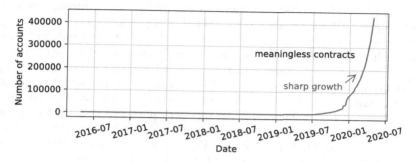

Fig. 6. Cumulative quantity distribution of meaningless contracts.

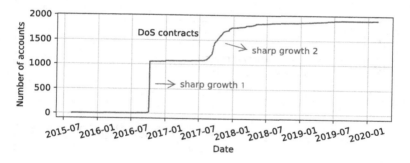

Fig. 7. Cumulative quantity distribution of DoS contracts.

The cumulative quantity distribution of meaningless contracts at different time is shown in Fig. 6. Before July of 2019, the quantity of meaningless contracts is small. Because most meaningless contracts are MC-S and they are directly created by users through EOA. For example, one user (Address: 0x3ff5..) created 9 MC-S with totally same runtime bytecodes around February of 2018. When the user realized his irrational behavior, he did not create MC-S any more. After November of 2019, some active malicious contracts are massively called, which leads to the quantity sharp growth of meaningless contracts (i.e., MC-RS). For example, one Ponzi contract (Address: 0x7C20..) created many MC-RS before April of 2020 through internal transactions (i.e., sent from contract account). Because most users leverage high-level languages to develop contracts, there exists a small quantity of stack/opcode error contracts. Their deployment time distribution does not have clear trends or characteristics.

The cumulative quantity distribution of DoS contracts at different time is shown in Fig. 7. There are two sharp growth periods for DoS contracts. The first period is around October of 2016, the attacker deployed more than 1k malicious DoS contracts and sent massive transactions to them, leading to external transactions' slow execution. The second period is around November of 2017, the Parity's multi-sig library contract was attacked and removed during this period, which produced 658 dependency error wallets without service.

The cumulative quantity distribution of empty accounts at different time is shown in Fig. 8. Because the Ethereum officials have repaired the bug of empty accounts' creation due to contract deployment failure and cleaned up the empty accounts produced due to DoS attacks, the growing of their cumulative quantity is halted around March of 2016. The cumulative quantity distribution of DoS EOAs is shown in Fig. 9. There is a sharp growth period of DoS EOAs' quantity around November of 2016. According to analysis, the attacker (One exploited account: 0xeec2..) created massive DoS EOAs during/after the DoS attacks of empty accounts' creation exploiting SELFDESTRUCT [1].

Answer to RQ1 (Quantity): We have discovered 508,482 erasable accounts, whose quantity distributions at different time reflect their creation reasons.

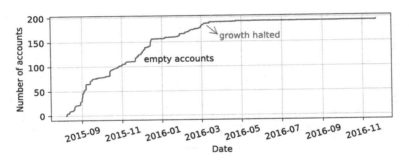

Fig. 8. Cumulative quantity distribution of empty accounts.

5.2   RQ2 Accuracy

In this section, we evaluate the accuracy of erasable accounts detected through GLASER, whose statistics are shown in Table 2. We evaluate the accuracy of erasable accounts in two primary aspects. First, we analyze whether the detected erasable accounts are still stored in Ethereum. Second, we analyze their transactions to verify their uselessness.

Storage: Because it is difficult to traverse accounts in its changing StateDB, we export the StateDB to offchain and execute GLASER on it. Therefore, there exists possibility that the detected erasable accounts are already removed or

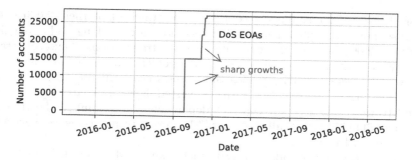

Fig. 9. Cumulative quantity distribution of DoS EOAs.

cleaned up in the newest StateDB. We leverage Etherscan, which is a real-time Ethereum block explorer, to verify their existence. We discover that 99.9% (479,150/479,153) detected erasable contract accounts still store runtime byte-codes. 3 MC-RS contracts are removed through executing SELFDESTRUCT. All the 195 empty accounts can be still normally retrieved without special tagging, and all the 27,200 detected DoS EOAs still store ETH. Therefore, more than 99.9% of the detected erasable accounts are still stored in the latest StateDB.

Table 2. Statistics of erasable accounts' accuracy and waste evaluation.

Erasable account	Quantity	Storage	Ext. tr.	Int. tr.	Gas	ETH
❶ DoS contract	1,784	100% ✓	26,474	7,707,646	50,497,619,162	515,035.16ETH
❷ Meaningless contract	479,153	99.9% ✓	2,080	490,611	36,996,614,413	274.97ETH
❸ Stack/opcode error cont.	150	100% ✓	141	157,513	854,099,555	0
❹ Empty account	195	100% ✓	237	5	79,786,061	0
❺ DoS EOA	27,200	100% ✓	0	1,163,763	1,180,693,660	27,200 Wei

Uselessness: In the following, we analyze the detected erasable accounts' transactions to verify their uselessness. All the below analyzed transactions' data is published on https://figshare.com/articles/dataset/11518017.

For the 1,784 DoS contracts, we crawl all of their 26,474 external transactions and 7,707,646 internal transactions. According to the timestamp of Parity multi-sig library's removal (Transaction hash: 0x47f7..), we extract 920 external transactions of attacked Parity wallets that occurred after the attack. Apart from pure ETH transfers, there are 789 external transactions calling wallets' functions. Because calling to a removed contract does not result in failure or exception, we debug these transactions for analysis. We acquire these transactions' execution traces through Geth API debug_traceTransaction. All these transactions called the removed library through DELEGATECALL, which wasted users' gas or ETH. For malicious DoS contracts, there are 1,128 external transactions used for contract deployments. All the other transactions (15,334 external transactions and 7,700,836 internal transactions) executed with "Out of Gas Error" were exploited for DoS attacks.

For the 479,153 meaningless contracts, we crawl all of their 2,080 external transactions and 490,611 internal transactions for checking and debugging. Apart from 2,002 contract deployment's external transactions, 7 external transactions were halted by the first executed operation STOP before their data fields were processed, which verifies their uselessness. All the other 71 external transactions were executed with "Reverted Error". Apart from 489,890 internal transactions used for contract deployment or compulsive ETH transfer through SELFDESTRUCT, all the other 721 internal transactions were executed with "Reverted Error".

For the 150 stack/opcode error contracts, we crawl all of their 141 external transactions and 157,513 internal transactions for analysis. Apart from 150 transactions used for contract deployment and 337 transactions used for compulsive ETH transfer through SELFDESTRUCT, all the other 157,167 transactions were encountered "Bad Instruction Error" or "Stack Underflow Error".

For the 195 empty accounts, we crawl all of their 237 external transactions and 5 internal transactions. Apart from 195 contract deployment's transactions, we analyze other 47 transactions. All of these 47 transactions transferred ETH or called the empty accounts with function signatures in their data fields, which denotes that they were intended to call a function of contract. However, all of their data fields were not processed because the accounts were empty, which denotes their uselessness. For the 27,200 DoS EOAs, we crawl all of their 1,163,763 internal transactions, and there does not exist external transaction. In 27,200 internal transactions, the attacker created DoS EOA through transferring 1 Wei, which is the smallest financial cost for the attacker. All the other 1,136,563 internal transactions were executed with "Out of Gas Error", which were used for DoS attack (analyzed in Sect. 3.2).

Answer to RQ2 (Accuracy): All the detected erasable accounts' related transactions are useless, and more than 99.9% of the detected erasable accounts are still stored in Ethereum.

5.3   RQ3 Waste

In this section, we evaluate the money lost due to erasable accounts. We analyze the gas and ETH consumed in erasable accounts' transactions, whose statistics are shown in Table 2. For DoS contracts, 733,583,247 gas were consumed during calling Parity wallets before they were attacked. Therefore, these gas are not wasted. We analyze all the DoS contracts' balance values and 515,035.16 ETH transferred to them are permanently locked in DoS contracts, which are wasted. For meaningless contracts, all their consumed gas are wasted. However, 272.77 ETH attached to their transactions were returned to users due to "Reverted Error", which are not wasted. For category ❸ to ❺, all their gas and ETH are wasted. According to the gas prices set in transactions and ETH price (204.36\$/ETH) on May 25 of 2020 [2], 106,360,910\$ is totally wasted due to these erasable accounts.

Answer to RQ3 (Waste): About 89 billion gas and 515,037 ETH are wasted due to erasable accounts, which are worth 106,360,910$.

6 Graph Analysis

We analyze attacks/behaviors related to discovered erasable accounts to answer the question: How are erasable accounts behaved and created in reality?

GLASER's graph analysis module can be divided into two parts, i.e., call graph and creation graph. First, through symbolic execution, we analyze DoS contract's runtime bytecodes to generate call graph from erasable accounts to other accounts. According to the definitions (in Sect. 3) of erasable accounts, only DoS contracts can call other accounts. During symbolic execution, we analyze the operands of DoS related operations (in Sect. 4). If the target address of one operation is a real value, we can conclude that the DoS contract interacts with another account and we add an edge into the call graph. Second, through transaction analysis, we generate creation graph for erasable accounts. We analyze the account creation related transactions of erasable accounts and filter out their source addresses, which constructs the nodes of creation graph. The creation related transactions construct the edges of creation graph. If the erasable account is created through contract account, we also analyze which user (i.e., EOA) calls the contract. Furthermore, we also analyze the creation source address's transactions to see whether it creates other accounts.

Call Graph: According to their features, the DoS contracts can be divided into two types, i.e., Many-to-One DoS contract and One-to-Many DoS contract, whose topology graphs are shown in Fig. 10. We only show the first three bytes of contracts' addresses for better display.

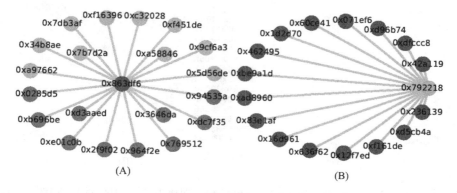

(A)   (B)

Fig. 10. (A): Call graph of Many-to-One DoS contracts (best viewed in color). The center contract has been removed (in red color), and some of its dependency error contracts (in deep grey) still have ETH balance. (B): Call graph of One-to-Many DoS contract. The malicious contract (in grey) executes massive EXTCODESIZE to external contracts, which have all been removed. (Color figure online)

For Many-to-One DoS contract, one center contract's address is hardcoded and interacted with many other contracts. Some Many-to-One DoS contracts detected through GLASER are shown in Fig. 10 (A). In this example, the center contract (Address: 0x863D..) is Parity's multi-sig library, which was attacked in 2017. The center contract is removed, all its dependent wallet contracts become out of service (i.e., dependency error). GLASER has discovered 658 contract accounts calling the removed library. We only show 20 attacked Parity contracts in the figure for better display, and the nodes in deep grey color represent that these erasable contracts still store ETH.

For One-to-Many DoS contract, one DoS contract hardcodes and interacts with many other contracts. One example of One-to-Many DoS contract detected through GLASER is shown in Fig. 10(B). In this example, GLASER has discovered that one malicious DoS contract (Address: 0x7922..) hardcodes and interacts with 200 different external contracts, which have all been removed. We only show 16 removed contracts in the figure, and the malicious DoS contract (in light grey) is still stored in StateDB. Both types of DoS contracts might be called, which will result in waste of gas or ETH. For example, one DoS contract (Address: 0x4184..) shown in Fig. 10 has been transferred ETH in 57 transactions, which can be avoided if its account was detected/alerted in time.

Creation Graph: According to their features, the creation graphs can be divided into two types: erasable account created by EOA, and erasable account created by contract.

Erasable accounts were created by EOAs due to programming error or deployment error, and we explain their creations through one meaningless contract example, whose creation graph is shown in Fig. 11 (A). The user (in red color) called one deployed contract (Address: 0x2Ab7..) and realized that it was mean-

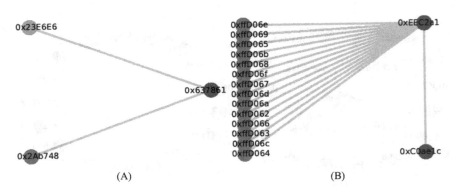

(A)   (B)

Fig. 11. (A): Creation graph of one meaningless contract. After the user (in red) realized the uselessness of the deployed contract (in grey), he redeployed another correct contract (in green). (B): Creation graph of DoS EOAs. The attacker (in red) created 14 different DoS EOAs in one transaction. We show the last three bytes of the DoS EOAs' addresses. (Color figure online)

ingless due to deployment error. The user incorrectly used runtime bytecodes to deploy the contract and transferred ETH to it. Then the user redeployed another correct contract (in green color), whose runtime bytecodes are just same with the data field of the transaction deploying the previous meaningless contract. Note that these types of erasable accounts' creation can be avoided, and it is better to first test and deploy contracts in private/public Testnet before they are deployed in Mainnet.

Erasable accounts were created by contracts due to some attacks, and we explain their creations through one DoS EOA example, whose creation graph is shown in Fig. 11 (B). The attacker exploited one EOA (Address: 0xc0ae..) to call a malicious contract (Address: 0xeec2..), creating 14 different DoS EOAs through internal transactions (Hash: 0xefc6..). Exploiting one storage variable, the malicious contract can generate different addresses in different transactions. These addresses were calculated and generated in runtime bytecodes, and only the last three bytes of them are different. The attacker totally created 12,204 different DoS EOAs leveraging this malicious contract, resulting in the waste of system resources and nodes' difficulty in syncing data.

7 Related Work

Frowis et al. [14] constructed call graph for smart contracts deployed in Ethereum and discovered contracts calling to removed contracts. Note that they focus on measuring the control flow immutability between contracts, whose purpose is different from our work. Kiffer et al. [15] measured smart contracts' creation and interaction with each other, which interpreted how are smart contracts being used. However, they do not analyze erasable contracts that exist in Ethereum. There are some other research leveraging symbolic execution [5], static analysis [4,9], and formal methods [19] to analyze different kinds of security issues for smart contracts. Kiffer et al. [15] measured the overall usage of Ethereum, which interpreted how is Ethereum being used. They discovered that SELFDESTRUCT's usage rose sharply during DoS attacks in 2016. However, they do not measure or analyze erasable accounts produced during DoS attacks. Chen et al. [8] proposed an adaptive gas cost mechanism for Ethereum to defend against under-priced DoS attacks. They do not analyze real accounts in Ethereum that are related to these attacks. Wang et al. [20] proposed an optimization storage engine to reduce nodes' storage volume, which can improve the scalability of blockchain systems. They do not analyze the erasable accounts which are already stored in StateDB. Angelo et al. [13] analyzed contract deployment code patterns which were exploited by attackers, and they described three related attack scenarios in reality appeared in the middle of 2018, whose contents and purposes are different from ours. They focus on the vulnerabilities and attacks leveraging skillfully crafted deployment codes, while we detect erasable accounts due to programming or deployment errors.

8   Discussion and Conclusion

Discussion: We discuss validity threats, limitations, and future work. (1) GLASER can not only discover erasable accounts that already exist in Ethereum, but also erasable accounts that might be created in future. Some kinds of accounts analyzed by GLASER might also be created in future, and GLASER might discover more erasable accounts. (2) For the discovered erasable accounts, only part of meaningless contracts can be destructed by ordinary users. Because some MC-RS have SELFDESTRUCT in their first basic blocks, which can be invoked through transactions by users. Although most of discovered erasable accounts cannot be easily destructed by users, our results can remind users not to call them, which can help users save money. (3) Path explosion and timeout exception are common threats for the symbolic execution techniques leveraged in this paper. However, we use some methods to reduce these threats. During detecting stack error contracts, we first extract runtime bytecodes corresponding to the first basic block and then symbolically execute them. During detecting attacked Parity wallets, we first filter out contracts without external call operations and then symbolically execute them. (4) As GLASER focuses on five kinds of erasable accounts in Ethereum, we will detect more kinds of erasable accounts in future. We will also analyze erasable accounts in other blockchain systems.

Conclusion: We have conducted the first work that systematically characterizes erasable accounts in Ethereum, i.e., erasable contract accounts and erasable EOAs. We have implemented GLASER to analyze the StateDB, which can detect erasable accounts leveraging bytecodes' static analysis, symbolic execution, transaction analysis, and state fields analysis. Furthermore, we have analyzed attacks/behaviors related to erasable accounts through graph analysis. Extensive experiments are also conducted to evaluate the quantity, accuracy, and waste of the detected erasable accounts.

References

1. Empty Accounts and the Ethereum State. https://bit.ly/2YVcL58
2. Etherscan. https://etherscan.io/
3. The Yellow Paper: Ethereum's Formal Specification. http://bit.ly/35Cmkpt
4. Brent, L., et al.: Vandal: a scalable security analysis framework for smart contracts. arXiv (2018)
5. Chang, J., Gao, B., Xiao, H., Sun, J., Yang, Z.: sCompile: critical path identification and analysis for smart contracts. arXiv (2018)
6. Chen, T., et al.: GasChecker: scalable analysis for discovering gas-inefficient smart contracts. IEEE Trans. Emerg. Top. Comput. (2020)
7. Chen, T., Li, X., Luo, X., Zhang, X.: Under-optimized smart contracts devour your money. In: Proceedings of the SANER (2017)
8. Chen, T., et al.: An adaptive gas cost mechanism for Ethereum to defend against under-priced DoS attacks. In: Liu, J.K., Samarati, P. (eds.) ISPEC 2017. LNCS, vol. 10701, pp. 3–24. Springer, Cham (2017). https://doi.org/10.1007/978-3-319-72359-4_1

9. Chen, T., et al.: Towards saving money in using smart contracts. In: Proceedings of the ICSE (2018)

10. Chen, T., et al.: Understanding Ethereum via graph analysis. In: Proceedings of the INFOCOM (2018)

11. Chen, W., Zhang, T., Chen, Z., Zheng, Z., Lu, Y.: Traveling the token world: a graph analysis of Ethereum ERC20 token ecosystem. In: Proceedings of the WWW (2020)

12. Chess, B., McGraw, G.: Static analysis for security. In: IEEE S&P (2004)

13. Di Angelo, M., Salzer, G.: Collateral use of deployment code for smart contracts in Ethereum. In: Proceedings of the IFIP NTMS (2019)

14. Fröwis, M., Böhme, R.: In code we trust? In: Garcia-Alfaro, J., Navarro-Arribas, G., Hartenstein, H., Herrera-Joancomartí, J. (eds.) ESORICS/DPM/CBT -2017. LNCS, vol. 10436, pp. 357–372. Springer, Cham (2017). https://doi.org/10.1007/978-3-319-67816-0_20

15. Kiffer, L., Levin, D., Mislove, A.: Analyzing Ethereum's contract topology. In: Proceedings of the IMC (2018)

16. Li, X., Chen, T., Luo, X., Zhang, T., Yu, L., Xu, Z.: STAN: towards describing bytecodes of smart contract. In: Proceedings of the QRS (2020)

17. Li, X., Jiang, P., Chen, T., Luo, X., Wen, Q.: A survey on the security of blockchain systems. Future Gener. Comput. Syst. **107**, 841–853 (2020)

18. Luu, L., Chu, D.H., Olickel, H., Saxena, P., Hobor, A.: Making smart contracts smarter. In: Proceedings of the CCS (2016)

19. Sergey, I., Kumar, A., Hobor, A.: Temporal properties of smart contracts. In: Margaria, T., Steffen, B. (eds.) ISoLA 2018. LNCS, vol. 11247, pp. 323–338. Springer, Cham (2018). https://doi.org/10.1007/978-3-030-03427-6_25

20. Wang, S., et al.: ForkBase: an efficient storage engine for blockchain and Forkable applications. In: Proceedings of the VLDB (2018)

An Accountable Decryption System Based on Privacy-Preserving Smart Contracts

Rujia Li[1,2], Qin Wang[3], Feng Liu[1], Qi Wang[1(✉)], and David Galindo[2,4(✉)]

[1] Guangdong Provincial Key Laboratory of Brain-inspired Intelligent Computation,
Department of Computer Science and Engineering,
Southern University of Science and Technology, Shenzhen 518055, China
wangqi@sustech.edu.cn, liuf2017@mail.sustech.edu.cn
[2] University of Birmingham, Edgbaston, Birmingham B15 2TT, UK
rxl635@student.bham.ac.uk, d.galindo@cs.bham.ac.uk
[3] Swinburne University of Technology, Melbourne, VIC 3122, Australia
qinwang@swin.edu.au
[4] Fetch.AI, St John's Innovation Center, Cambridge CB4 0WS, UK

Abstract. Accountability is a fundamental after-the-fact approach to detect and punish illegal actions during the execution of a warrant for accessing users' sensitive data. To achieve accountability in a security protocol, a trusted authority is required, denoted as *judge*, to faithfully cooperate with the rest of the entities in the system. However, malicious judges or uncooperative protocol participants may void the accountability mechanism in practice, for example by fabricating fake evidence or by refusing to provide any evidence at all. To provide remediation to these issues, in this paper we propose *Fialka*, a novel accountable decryption system based on privacy-preserving smart contracts (PPSC). The neutrality that is inherent to a secure blockchain platform is inherited by PPSC which are then used in our approach as an accountable key manager as well as a transparent judge. To the best of our knowledge, we present the first PPSC-based accountable decryption system to increase the transparency of warrant execution with formal definitions and proofs. Furthermore, we provide and evaluate a prototype implementation using the PPSC-enabled platform Oasis Devnet, which additionally demonstrates the feasibility of Fialka.

Keywords: Accountability · Privacy-preserving smart contract · Blockchain

1 Introduction

Accountable cryptographic protocol is increasingly crucial in sensitive personal data protection. We focus on the following scenario. Law enforcement or intelligence agencies may demand access to personal encrypted data held by service providers, and sometimes even require access to the communication metadata

© Springer Nature Switzerland AG 2020
W. Susilo et al. (Eds.): ISC 2020, LNCS 12472, pp. 372–390, 2020.
https://doi.org/10.1007/978-3-030-62974-8_21

that is closely related to sensitive information of individuals. In most cases, a granted warrant is needed from a legal authority. However, data owners have no way to know when and how law enforcement collects and accesses their sensitive data. In particular, abuses of granted warrant of decryption may easily happen since the overseers cannot verify whether the practical investigation activities match the scope permitted in the document. Therefore, accountability mechanisms is a critical *after-the-fact* remediation technique to deter investigators, since it provides an instant evidence to detect malicious or deviant behaviors, which increases the transparency of warrant execution.

However, achieving accountability is tricky, and requires additional roles involved. The investigators cannot autonomously convince others of the accountability of their actions. They need to resort to one or more neutral trusted parties, usually named *judge(s)*, to audit their actions. More specifically, an accountability mechanism requires each investigator to generate evidence on their warrant execution. This evidence is then examined by the judge to detect dishonest behaviors or declare the examined participant compliant. This approach relies heavily on faithful cooperation of the judge and the investigator, as a malicious judge or dishonest investigator may undermine the accountability mechanism. If the investigator rejects to cooperate with the judge in order to provide the required evidence, or if the judge themselves examine fake evidence or apply the wrong examination procedure, outsides cannot audit investigators' decryption actions. In this paper, we generalise the above example as a standard case, in which an investigator obtains an order from a court, and his access of users' data needs to be audited by the judge. The discussed challenges lead to the following research question:

Is it possible to design an accountability mechanism guaranteeing that (1) the judge honestly checks the evidence; (2) the investigator does not refuse to provide the evidence trail of their actions?

Based on the previous discussion, the answer would intuitively be "NO". Firstly, it is difficult to guarantee that a judge will always be secure and reliable. Even if the judge claims to be neutral, she faces the threat of being attacked or provided with misleading evidence. Once the judge is compromised, the accountability mechanism fails as it cannot be applied. Undoubtedly, multiple judges may mitigate such concerns, but the judge collusion issue cannot be effortlessly overcome. Secondly, asking the investigator to neutrally create a piece of honest evidence also confronts difficulties. The isolated local execution environment makes it potentially easy and profitable for the investigator to generate fake evidence while incurring a low risk of being detected. Several proposals [3,9] employed a certain trusted hardware to aid the evidence generation. Intuitively, physical hardware is more secure and reliable since the evidence logic and its measurement are hardcoded in non-volatile storage. However, the risk of compromised hardware still exists [17].

Blockchain-based smart contracts [26,27] have been used in [4,14,23] as a building block to implement the judge. Roughly speaking, a smart contract is composed of a set of protocols to be automatically executed in a distributed network, which naturally guarantees the neutrality and behaviour of the judge thus obtained. However, the input/output data of the smart contract is transparent to the public, which limits its usage in some scenarios. For instance, private key-dependent protocols such as decryption are executed in an isolated local environment. A transparent smart contract cannot prevent the investigator from producing fake evidence if it does not have access to the secret key material. But in the latter case, the secrecy of the private key material would be compromised. Privacy-preserving smart contracts (PPSC) [6,13,16,25,29] inherit the security, availability and neutrality benefits of smart contracts while additionally protecting the privacy of the contract data. It naturally could act as a high-level cryptographic primitive to aid in the evidence generation involving local protocol executions. For example, PPSC could be used to implement a private key manager to make decryption accountable.

In this paper, we propose *Fialka*, a novel transaction-triggering accountability framework using PPSC to make investigators accountable for executing decryption calls. Our framework prevents the decryption queries evidence from being maliciously generated (e.g. hidden) while guaranteeing the authenticity of the evidence. More precisely, *Fialka* combines PPSC with an IND-CCA secure public key encryption (PKE) scheme [15] at the protocol level to construct an accountability mechanism. PPSC cryptographically hides a secret random number used as an additional decryption key, where external investigators have to interact with PPSC for the execution of decryption warrant. The secret key will be extracted by invoking the decryption-related smart contract, which consequently generates a transaction-based evidence as an on-chain record. After that, another smart contract plays the role of the judge who transparently checks the transaction to decide whether the decryption is legal in a specific setting. The accountability is thereby achieved. Additionally, our framework inherits the benefit of high availability from the underlying blockchain protocol. This further improves reliability of the PPSC-based judge. Our contributions are summarized here:

- We propose an accountable decryption system called *Fialka* that combines the techniques of PPSC and PKE.
- We formally define our system and provide a security analysis of its accountability properties, namely *fairness* and *completeness*.
- We provide a prototype implementation based on the PPSC platform Oasis Devnet [1,8], and evaluate its running time and gas cost.

The rest of our paper is structured as follows. Some related studies are discussed in Sect. 2. Definitions and building blocks are detailed in Sect. 3. In Sect. 4, we present the formal model with its property definitions. In Sect. 5, we provide the design of Fialka. Both the proof and security analysis are presented in Sect. 6. Implementations and evaluations are discussed in Sect. 7 and Sect. 8. Finally, Sect. 9 presents summaries and future work.

2   Related Work

The smart contract-based accountability approach has been studied comprehensively recently. Xu *et al.* [28] proposed a remotely decentralized data auditing scheme for network storage service, where accountability is achieved by involving smart contract as a third-party auditor to notarize the integrity of outsourced data. Azaria *et al.* proposed MedRec [4], in which an Ethereum [27] smart contract is used as a meta-data agent to manage the permission of data usage, making patients' choices accountable. Neisse *et al.* [23] proposed a blockchain-based framework for data accountability and provenance tracking. However, a pure smart contract does not provide a complete accountable protocol, since it cannot guarantee the authenticity of the input (i.e. the submitted evidence). In other words, even if the smart contract is neutral and trustful, a client may provide fake evidence to the smart contract without being detected.

Several solutions have been proposed to ensure the authenticity of the submitted evidence. Among them, equipping entities with secure hardware devices [3,17,24] is an attractive approach. Alder *et al.* [3] employed Intel SGX [10] to produce a verifiable measurement of the resource usage in each function invocation. Luo *et al.* [21] applied the Intel SGX with blockchain to a data sharing scheme, where the decryption process also relied on the confidentiality of secure hardware devices. The hardware-based approach is intuitively reliable and robust, since trusted hardware devices cannot change the evidence generation rules once loaded. However, the security cannot be guaranteed when adversaries successfully attack the hardware. The approach using multiple hardware may mitigate such security concerns to a certain extent. Unfortunately, the efficiency issue and incentives issue cannot be easily overcome. Another promising approach is directly employing the protocol execution result as the evidence, such as using the ciphertext and the private key as evidence. A typical example is accountable identity-based encryption [11,12,19], where a judge can decide whether a PKG is malicious by showing cryptographic proofs that contain the decryption key. However, such an approach lacks practicality.

Privacy-preserving smart contract (PPSC) is a special contract that aims to make the contract state private. The techniques on PPSC have been studied extensively in the recent years. Enigma [29] provided a decentralized confidential computation platform by employing multi-party computation. Hawk [16], Zether [6] and Zkay [25] realized privacy-preserving smart contract by heavily relying on zero-knowledge proofs. Ekiden [8] and Microsoft Coco framework [22] employed Intel SGX to achieve confidential smart contracts. Essentially, PPSC is a decentralized confidential computing technology, which inherits the benefit of transparent execution from a smart contract while additionally protecting the privacy of contract data. Our accountable system leverages the main benefits of PPSC. The transparent execution of smart contracts ensures the judge honestly checks the evidence, and the trigger mechanism of contract execution enforces investigators to invoke PPSC through transactions, which ensures investigators neutrally provide the evidence.

3 Preliminaries

Let λ be the security parameter, and $negl(\lambda)$ be a negligible function. The challenger and adversary are represented as $\mathcal{C}$ and $\mathcal{A}$, respectively. We use the notation $\eth$ to denote the game in security deduction, adv to represent the advantage that the adversary holds, and the notation "$\approx$" to show these two games are computationally indistinguishable. The message space is denoted as $\mathcal{M}$.

3.1 Privacy-Preserving Smart Contract

Smart contract was first proposed by Nick Szabo [26] and further developed by Ethereum [27] in the blockchain system. A blockchain-based smart contract consists of two mutually interacting components: contract state and operational code [27]. The contract state covers the input and output of the operational code, while operational code specifies operations/commands to store or transfer the contract state. The intuitive target for a privacy-preserving smart contract is to make the contract state private. However, purely protecting the privacy of the state against the public is not sufficient, especially when multiple entities are involved in one contract to finish complex cryptographic tasks. The state in a contract is required to reach a new consensus view after the execution of operational codes, in which this rule is followed by PPSC projects such as Zether [6], Ekiden [8] and *Oasis Devnet* [1]. Thus, we capture two main PPSC principles: **P.1** the contract state should be protected against the public; **P.2** the authorized entities should see the same private data view.

PPSC-Based Accountability. The initial contract state and the operational code will reach consensus after the successful deployment. After that, two approaches can trigger the execution of the operational code: the internal schedule code and the external message call. The first approach allows the operational code to execute periodically. However, it cannot complete a complex task due to massive gas consumption [27]. Thus, to trigger the execution, an external message call with sufficient gas is crucial. PPSC inherits the state triggering mechanism from smart contracts, namely, the state-changing is based on external message call. For example, *Oasis Devnet* [1] requires an external caller to firstly build a secure channel with the TEE-protected smart contract, and then the transition of the private state is accomplished through this channel when a transaction call is provided. *Origo Network* [2] reveals the private input to an off-line executor and then allows the executor to provide a ZKP-proof transaction for online state transferring. Zether [6] funds the Zether tokens (ZTH) by sending some Ethereum [27] tokens (ETH) and converts ZTH back to ETH by sending a ZK-proof transaction. In summary, a transaction is required to trigger the execution and obtain the state from PPSC. Therefore, by tracing the sender who sends the transaction, the auditor implicates the wrongdoing of the contract caller. Based on the above analysis, we give a formal definition of PPSC.

Definition 1. ($\widetilde{PPSC}$) *A Privacy-Preserving Smart Contract (PPSC) is a private state machine built on top of a blockchain system and can be modeled by*

5-*tuple* $(\mathcal{S}, \mathcal{S}', \mathcal{T}, \mathsf{s}, \mathbb{B})$ *and a transition function* $f : \mathcal{S} \otimes \mathcal{T} \xrightarrow{\mathbb{B}} \mathcal{S}'$, *where* $\mathcal{S}$ *repre-sents a set of private state with the initial state* s, $\mathcal{S}'$ *is the new state set after the specified operations,* $\mathcal{T}$ *means the publicly visible transactions that can trigger the execution of a contract, and* $\mathbb{B}$ *represents the blockchain oracle which provides the execution environment.*

- **Deploy** $<$ bytecode $> \otimes$ Tx $\rightarrow$ ($<$ opcode $>$, $<$ reqcode $>$, s): The deployment is triggered by a transaction Tx, where Tx $\in \mathcal{T}$. It takes the binary code $<$ bytecode $>$ as input, and outputs the private state s. The contract is compiled into $<$ opcode $>$ and $<$ reqcode $>$, where $<$ opcode $>$ specifies the operation set to be executed and $<$ reqcode $>$ defines the conditions depending on which the operation of $<$ opcode $>$ can be conducted.
- **Transfer** $<$ input $> \otimes \mathcal{S} \otimes$ Tx $\xrightarrow{\mathbb{B}} \mathcal{S}'$: By sending a transaction Tx with the input $<$ input $>$, the current private state $\mathcal{S}$ is transited to the new private state $\mathcal{S}'$ under the blockchain oracle $\mathbb{B}$. The new state $\mathcal{S}'$ returns only when Tx satisfies the condition defined in $<$ reqcode $>$, *i.e.*, Tx $\in <$ reqcode $>$.
- **Access** $\mathcal{S} \otimes$ Tx $\xrightarrow{\mathbb{B}} \mathcal{S}$: By sending a query transaction Tx through the blockchain oracle $\mathbb{B}$, the private state returns only when Tx satisfies the condition predefined in $<$ reqcode $>$, *i.e.*, Tx $\in <$ reqcode $>$.

Based on the above syntax, we provide four PPSC security properties: *state-privacy, state-consistency, transaction-transparency* and *transaction-unforgeability*. The state-privacy guarantees that the state is protected against the public (Principle **P.1**). Only the caller who satisfies the predefined conditions can learn the state. Meanwhile, the state-consistency ensures that a smart contract shares the same data view after operational code is executed (Principle **P.2**). The transaction-transparency ensures that transactions triggering the execution of PPSC can be freely queried, while the transaction-unforgeability guarantees the transactions (as evidence) are reliable and authentic without being forged or cheated. PPSC is secure when these four security properties are all satisfied.

Definition 2. *PPSC achieves state-privacy, if for all PPT adversaries* $\mathcal{A}$, *there exists a negligible function* $negl(\lambda)$ *such that* $adv^{\partial privacy}_{\mathcal{A},ppsc}(\lambda) < negl(\lambda)$, *where* $adv^{\partial privacy}_{\mathcal{A},ppsc}(\lambda)$ *is the advantage that* $\mathcal{A}$ *successfully obtains the private state without satisfying the condition predefined in* $<$ reqcode $>$.

Definition 3. *PPSC achieves state-consistency, if for all PPT adversaries* $\mathcal{A}$, *there exists a negligible function* $negl(\lambda)$ *such that* $adv^{\partial cons}_{\mathcal{A},ppsc}(\lambda) < negl(\lambda)$, *where* $adv^{\partial cons}_{\mathcal{A},ppsc}(\lambda)$ *is the advantage that* $\mathcal{A}$ *obtains a valid state* $\mathcal{S}^*$ *through the algorithm* **Transfer** *in which* s^* *does not belong to the state set* $\mathcal{S}$, *i.e.,* $\mathsf{s}^* \notin \mathcal{S}$.

Definition 4. *PPSC achieves transaction-transparency, if for all PPT adversaries* $\mathcal{A}$, *there exists a negligible function* $negl(\lambda)$ *such that* $adv^{\partial tran}_{\mathcal{A},ppsc}(\lambda) < negl(\lambda)$, *where* $adv^{\partial tran}_{\mathcal{A},ppsc}(\lambda)$ *is the advantage that* $\mathcal{A}$ *successfully obtains a transaction* Tx* *through calling the algorithm* **Transfer** *with the condition* Tx$^* \notin \mathcal{T}$.

Definition 5. *PPSC achieves transaction-unforgeability, if for all PPT adversaries* $\mathcal{A}$*, there exists a negligible function* $negl(\lambda)$ *such that* $adv_{\mathcal{A},ppsc}^{\partial unforg}(\lambda) <$ $negl(\lambda)$*, where* $adv_{\mathcal{A},ppsc}^{\partial unforg}(\lambda)$ *is the advantage that* $\mathcal{A}$ *successfully forges a transaction* $\mathsf{Tx}^\star$ *and obtains the state through* $\mathsf{Tx}^\star$*.*

3.2 Decision Linear Assumption

Decision Linear Assumption [5,15] is based on the Linear Problem. Due to limitation of space, we skip a full definition and refer to Appendix A for details.

4 General Construction

4.1 System Overview

Our system consists of four entities (see Fig. 1.a): common users (sender/receiver), investigator, key management smart contract (PPSC-KM), and auditor smart contract (PPSC-AD). PPSC-KM is used to manage investigators' decryption keys. PPSC-AD is employed as a "judge" to decide whether the event of the investigator's decryption is conducted under the court-issued order. A detailed workflow is shown as follows. The sender encrypts messages with a random number, which is hidden in PPSC-KM, and then it sends the encrypted message to the receiver. The receiver decrypts the ciphertext as normal. Meanwhile, the investigator who obtained a court-issued order decrypts the ciphertext by fetching the random number from PPSC-KM. When a query is sent to PPSC-KM, the actions will be recorded through a transaction as the evidence. Next, PPSC-AD will check the evidence to report malicious decryption. In our protocol, PPSC-KM and PPSC-AD are, respectively, abbreviated as $\widehat{c}_{km}$ and $\widehat{c}_{ad}$ for simplicity. Formally, we provide the general construction as follows.

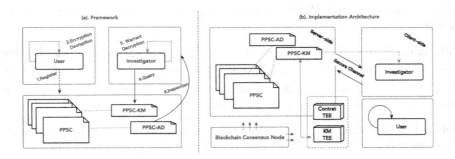

Fig. 1. System Framework & Architecture

Setup $(pms, \widehat{c}_{km}, \widehat{c}_{ad}) \leftarrow \mathsf{Setup}(1^\lambda, codes)$. The algorithm takes as input a security parameter λ and binary codes *codes*, and returns public parameters *pms* and two contracts $\widehat{c}_{km}, \widehat{c}_{ad}$.

Key Generation $(pk, sk, tk) \leftarrow$ KeyGen(pms). The algorithm takes as input pms, and returns receiver's key pair (pk, sk), and a secret tag key tk.

Registration s $\overset{\mathbb{B}}{\leftarrow}$ Register($tk, \check{P}$). The algorithm takes as input a master key tk and accountability policies $\check{P}$, and returns an initial state s $\in \mathcal{S}$. The tk and policies $\check{P}$ are added to $\widehat{c}_{km}$ and $\widehat{c}_{ad}$, respectively.

Encryption $ct \leftarrow$ Encrypt(tk, pk, m). This algorithm takes as input tk, pk, and a message m, and then returns a ciphertext ct.

Decryption $m \leftarrow$ Decrypt(sk, ct). The algorithm takes as input sk, ct, and returns $m \in \mathcal{M}$.

Warrant Decryption $(m, \mathsf{Tx}) \overset{\mathbb{B}}{\leftarrow}$ WDecrypt(r, r_1, s, ct). This algorithm takes as input a random number r, r_1, and s (including tk) calls the algorithm **Transfer** described in Sect. 3.1, and returns $m \in \mathcal{M}$.

Inspection true/false $\overset{\mathbb{B}}{\leftarrow}$ Inspect($\mathsf{Tx}, \check{P}$). This algorithm takes as input $\check{P}$ and Tx, and returns the inspection result. The result true indicates that the authorized decryption is legitimately executed under the warrant, and vice versa.

The procedure of **Decryption** represents normal decryption run by offline users, whereas **Warrant Decryption** is run by the investigators who are forced to leave evidence each time of decryption. Meanwhile, the access control conditions in $\widehat{c}_{km}$ and the accountability policies in $\widehat{c}_{ad}$ are set as the same. We notice that the logic of **Warrant Decryption** might be confusing: the $\widehat{c}_{km}$ has defined the access control conditions for investigators. Is the accountability necessary for investigators' decryption? We clarify that access control and accountability in our system play different roles. The access control condition in $\widehat{c}_{km}$ is similar to an order issued by the court, which describes the actions that an investigator should do but not yet, whereas the accountability policies in $\widehat{c}_{ad}$ are responsible for checking the actions an investigator has done (e.g., whether an investigator has executed the decryption under a warrant). We define *malicious decryption* as: the investigator's decryption does not match the actions permitted in the issued orders.

4.2 Security Definitions

Our *Fialka* system is denoted by Π, and above algorithms are abbreviated as: Set, Gen, Reg, Enc, Dec, WDec, and Insp, respectively. We assume an investigator has already obtained a warrant from a court, and his access to users' plaintext needs to be audited by the judge. Inspired by [18], the investigator should obtain fair treatment, neither being framed for the legitimate investigation nor being escaped from the punishment for wrongdoings. We captures two properties *w.r.t* accountability: *fairness* and *completeness*.

Fairness. This property prevents the judge from framing honest investigators. An honest investigator should follow the pre-defined policies and return true. We consider the adversary $\mathcal{A}$ who imitates an honest investigator, and then maliciously executes the warrant/order attempting to frame him.

Definition 6 (Fairness). *Fialka satisfies fairness, if for all PPT adversaries* $\mathcal{A}$, *there exists a negligible function* $negl(\lambda)$ *such that* $adv_{\mathcal{A},\Pi}^{\Game_{fair}}(\lambda) < negl(\lambda)$ *where* $adv_{\mathcal{A},\Pi}^{\Game_{fair}}(\lambda)$ *is the advantage of* $\mathcal{A}$ *wins the game* $\Game_{fair}$ *defined as,*

- **Initialization***. The system configures the parameters $pms = \bot$, and creates $\widehat{c}_{km}$ and $\widehat{c}_{ad}$ by running the algorithm Set. Then, $\mathcal{C}$ generates the secret key tk by running the algorithm Gen. Next, $\mathcal{C}$ registers the tk and decryption policies $\check{P}$ to the $\widehat{c}_{km}$ and $\widehat{c}_{ad}$, respectively.
- **Actions***. At each round, the adversary $\mathcal{A}$ and the challenger $\mathcal{C}$ execute the following algorithms. (1) $\mathcal{A}$ generates the key pair (sk_a, pk_a) by running the algorithm Gen. (2) $\mathcal{C}$ inputs the public key pk_a, message m, a random numbers r and a secret key tk, and then obtains the ciphertext ct by running the algorithm Enc. (3) $\mathcal{C}$ runs the algorithm **Transfer**, and then returns r_2 and Tx to the $\mathcal{A}$. (4) $\mathcal{A}$ inputs r_2, the ciphertext ct, and outputs the message m by running the algorithm WDec. (5) $\widehat{c}_{ad}$ executes the algorithm Insp with the input Tx, and return the inspection result.
- **Challenge**. Assume that $\mathcal{A}$ executes above actions at most for l times, and obtains a set $\mathcal{T} = \{Tx_0, Tx_1, ..., Tx_l\}$. $\mathcal{A}$ wins if $\mathcal{A}$ generates a transaction $Tx^\star$ satisfying the conditions: false $\leftarrow$ Insp$(Tx^\star, \check{P}) \wedge Tx^\star \notin \mathcal{T}$.

Completeness. This property guarantees that the judge always punishes the users who misbehave. To define *completeness*, we consider an adversary $\mathcal{A}$ aims to evade the responsibility of illegally executing the authorized decryption.

Definition 7 (Completeness). *Fialka satisfies completeness, if for all PPT adversaries* $\mathcal{A}$, *there exists a negligible function* $negl(\lambda)$ *such that* $adv_{\mathcal{A},\Pi}^{\Game_{comp}}(\lambda) < negl(\lambda)$, *where* $adv_{\mathcal{A},\Pi}^{\Game_{comp}}(\lambda)$ *is the advantage of* $\mathcal{A}$ *wins* $\Game_{comp}$ *defined as,*

- **Initialization** and **Actions**. The steps are same with that in fairness game labeled with $(\star)$.
- **Challenge**. Assume that $\mathcal{A}$ executes the above action at most for l times, and then obtains a set of ciphertext-transaction tuple $\{\mathcal{C}, \mathcal{T}\} = \{(ct_0, Tx_0), (ct_1, Tx_1), ..., (ct_l, Tx_l)\}$. $\mathcal{A}$ wins if $\mathcal{A}$ successfully generates a new tuple $(ct^\star, Tx^\star)$ that satisfying the conditions: true $\leftarrow$ Insp$(Tx^\star, \check{P}) \wedge$ WDec$(r, s, ct^\star) = m^\star \wedge (ct^\star, Tx^\star) \notin \{\mathcal{C}, \mathcal{T}\}$.

5   Concrete Instantiation

In this section, we present an instantiation of *Fialka* based on Kiltz's PKE protocol [15] and the Oasis Devnet [1,8]. Kiltz's PKE is an efficient and IND-CCA secure scheme with a tight security reduction, while Oasis Devnet is an SGX-backed PPSC platform with a rigorous security proof under the Universal Composability (UC) framework [7]. In this instance, PPSC-KM manages a secrete random number as the investigator's decryption key and its access permission through the SGX enclave, and the PPSC-AD audits the transactions, and then reports the investigator's malicious decryption. Specifically, a decryption key using for investigation is loaded in PPSC-KM and hidden in an enclave, which forces the outside investigator to fetch it, and further leaves the transaction-based evidence that will be audited by PPSC-AD. Note that SGX-based PPSC is an example by hiding the secret key inside the hardware, and other approaches can also achieve the same goal, such as cryptographically hiding secret key by ZKP. Our framework is compatible with various aforementioned PPSC technologies [6,13,16,25,29]. Importantly, our construction can easily be extended to other accountable PKE protocols without significant modifications.

Setup $(pms, \widehat{c}_{km}, \widehat{c}_{ad}) \leftarrow \mathsf{Setup}(1^\lambda, codes)$. The algorithm takes as input a security parameter λ, and returns public parameters including the multiplicative cyclic group $\mathbb{G}$ with prime order p. Then, it chooses two collision resistant hash functions $\mathcal{H}_1 : \{0,1\}^\star \rightarrow \mathbb{Z}_p$ and $\mathcal{H}_2 : \mathbb{G} \times \mathbb{G} \rightarrow \mathbb{Z}_p$. Next, it takes as input contract binary codes, and calls the algorithm **Deploy** (defined in Sect. 3.1), and finally returns two contracts $\widehat{c}_{km}$ and $\widehat{c}_{ad}$.

Key Generation $(pk, sk, tk) \leftarrow \mathsf{KeyGen}(pms)$. The algorithm is run by the sender and receiver. The receiver runs the algorithm to generate her key pair (pk, sk), and the sender runs the algorithm to obtain a secret tag key tk.

$$tk, x_1, x_2, y_1, y_2 \leftarrow \mathbb{Z}_p^*;$$
$$\text{Choose } (g_1, g_2, z) \in \mathbb{G}, \text{ satisfying } g_1^{x_1} = g_2^{x_2} = z;$$
$$u_1 \leftarrow g_1^{y_1}; u_2 \leftarrow g_2^{y_2}; pk \leftarrow (\mathbb{G}, p, g_1, g_2, z, u_1, u_2); sk \leftarrow (x_1, x_2, y_1, y_2).$$

Registration $s \xleftarrow{\mathbb{B}} \mathsf{Register}(tk, \breve{P})$: The algorithm is run by the sender. It takes as input tk and policies $\breve{P}$, and outputs contract initial state s. In particular, the tag key tk is registered into $\widehat{c}_{km}$. The policies $\breve{P}$ are added to $\widehat{c}_{ad}$ by the means of external message calls (see Sect. 3.1). The privacy of tk and s are protected by the SGX enclave. More details can be found in our implementation.

Encryption $ct \leftarrow \mathsf{Encrypt}(tk, pk, m)$. This algorithm is run by the sender. It takes as input tk, pk, and a message m, returns a ciphertext ct.

$$pk = (\mathbb{G}, p, g_1, g_2, z, u_1, u_2); r_1, r \leftarrow \mathbb{Z}_p;$$
$$r_2 \leftarrow \mathsf{H}_1(tk|r); C_1 \leftarrow g_1^{r_1}; C_2 \leftarrow g_2^{r_2}; \tau \leftarrow \mathsf{H}_2(C_1, C_2); V \leftarrow r_1;$$
$$D_1 \leftarrow z^{\tau r_1} u_1^{r_1}; D_2 \leftarrow z^{\tau r_2} u_2^{r_2}; K \leftarrow z^{r_1 + r_2}; E \leftarrow mK;$$
$$ct \leftarrow (C_1, C_2, D_1, D_2, E, V).$$

Decryption $m \leftarrow \mathsf{Decrypt}(sk, ct)$. This algorithm is run by the receiver. It takes as input the receiver's secret key sk, the ciphertext ct, and returns $m \in \mathcal{M}$.

$$\text{Parse } ct \text{ as} (C_1, C_2, D_1, D_2, E, V);$$
$$s_1, s_2 \leftarrow \mathbb{Z}_p; \tau \leftarrow \mathsf{H}_2(C_1, C_2);$$
$$K' \leftarrow \frac{C_1^{x_1 + s_1(\tau x_1 + y_1)} C_2^{x_2 + s_2(\tau x_2 + y_2)}}{D_1^{s_1} D_2^{s_2}}; m \leftarrow E(K')^{-1}.$$

Warrant Decryption $(m, \mathsf{Tx}) \xleftarrow{\mathcal{B}} \mathsf{WDecrypt}(r, r_1, \mathsf{s}, ct)$. This algorithm is run by the investigator. It takes as input r, r_1 and the private state s (including tk), and then calls the **Transfer** algorithm to execute the function $r_2 \leftarrow \mathsf{H}_1(tk|r)$ in an isolated environment provided by the SGX. This calling progress is represented in the form of a transaction Tx.

$$Parse\ ct\ as(C_1, C_2, D_1, D_2, E, V);$$
$$r_2, \mathsf{Tx} \leftarrow \textbf{Transfer}(\mathsf{s}, r);$$
$$K'' = z^{r_1+r_2};\ m \leftarrow E(K'')^{-1}.$$

Inspection true/false $\xleftarrow{\mathcal{B}} \mathsf{Inspect}(\mathsf{Tx}, \check{P})$. This algorithm is run by $\widehat{\mathsf{c}}_{\mathsf{ad}}$. It takes as input $\check{P}$ and Tx, and returns inspection result. The true indicates the warrant decryption satisfying the policies, and vice versa.

Here, the **correctness** of our construction is easy to check as we have

$$K' = \frac{C_1^{x_1+s_1(\tau x_1+y_1)} C_2^{x_2+s_2(\tau x_2+y_2)}}{D_1^{s_1} D_2^{s_2}} = C_1^{x_1} C_2^{x_2} \left(\frac{C_1^{\tau x_1+y_1}}{z^{tr_1} u_1^{r_1}} \right)^{s_1} \left(\frac{C_2^{\tau x_2+y_2}}{z^{\tau r_2} u_2^{r_2}} \right)^{s_2}$$
$$= C_1^{x_1} C_2^{x_2} \left(\frac{g_1^{r_1(\tau x_1+y_1)}}{g_1^{r_1(x_1\tau+y_1)}} \right)^{s_1} \left(\frac{g_2^{r_2(\tau x_2+y_2)}}{g_2^{r_2(x_2\tau+y_2)}} \right)^{s_2} = g_1^{r_1 x_1} g_2^{r_2 x_2}.$$

Note that the random numbers s_1 and s_2 are used for implicitly testing if the ciphertext is consistent with tag τ [15]. We see that $K = z^{r_1+r_2} = g_1^{x_1 r_1 + x_1 r_2} = g_1^{x_1 r_1} g_2^{x_2 r_2}$. Then, we observe that $K = K' = K''$. Thus, both the receiver and investigator can obtain the message m by

$$\mathsf{Dec}(sk, ct) = E(K)^{-1} = mK(K)^{-1} = m.$$

6 Security Proof

Theorem 1 (Fairness). *Assume that the SGX-based PPSC is secure, our construction Fialka satisfies the property of fairness.*

Proof. Suppose that there exists an adversary $\mathcal{A}$ who wins the fairness game ∂_{fair} with a non-negligible advantage. Then, we transform an adversary $\mathcal{A}$ against *Fairness* into adversaries against PPSC security. Next, we describe a sequence of games to finish the proof.

Lemma 1 (SGX-based PPSC [8,20]). *Our SGX-based platform is a secure instantiation of PPSC whose protocols match the ideal functionality in the UC framework. More details can be found in [8].*

Game ∂_0. This is an unmodified game. Trivially, the winning probability of this game equals the advantage of $\mathcal{A}$ against fairness game, namely, $adv_{\mathcal{A},\Pi}^{\partial_{\mathsf{fair}}}(\lambda)$.

Game $\eth_1$. In this game, when $\mathcal{A}$ calls $\mathcal{C}$, we disallow $\mathcal{C}$ to call contract $\hat{\mathsf{c}}_{\mathsf{km}}$.

Game $\eth_2$. In this game, when $\mathcal{A}$ calls $\mathcal{C}$, the transaction-based evidence is not allowed to be given to the $\hat{\mathsf{c}}_{\mathsf{ad}}$. Instead, the evidence is randomly selected for auditing.

Obviously, the winning probability of the game $\eth_2$, denoted as $adv_{\mathcal{A},\Pi}^{\eth_2}(\lambda)$, is negligible, since the transaction-based evidence is randomly selected. Next, to find out the differences between these games, we define the following events.

- $\mathbb{E}[a1]$: forging an evidence. The event $\mathbb{E}[a1]$ implies that the adversary $\mathcal{B}_1$ forges a valid transaction Tx^* without update $\hat{\mathsf{c}}_{\mathsf{km}}$, denoted as $\neg\mathbf{Transfer}$.

$$\left.\begin{array}{c} r_2, \mathsf{Tx}^* \xleftarrow{\mathbb{B}} \neg\mathbf{Transfer}(\mathsf{s}, r) \wedge \\ \mathsf{WDec}\left(r, r_1, \mathsf{s}, \mathsf{Enc}(tk, pk, m)\right) = m \wedge \\ \mathsf{false} \xleftarrow{\mathbb{B}} \mathsf{Insp}(\mathsf{Tx}^*, \check{P}) \end{array}\right] \Rightarrow \mathbb{E}[a1].$$

- $\underline{\mathbb{E}[a2]}$: forging an inspection result. The event $\mathbb{E}[a2]$ implies that the adversary $\mathcal{B}_2$ forges an inspection result, where the originally "true" in the algorithm $\mathsf{Inspect}$ is modified to be "false".

$$\left.\begin{array}{c} r_2, \mathsf{Tx} \xleftarrow{\mathbb{B}} \mathbf{Transfer}(\mathsf{s}, r) \wedge \\ \mathsf{WDec}\left(r, r_1, \mathsf{s}, \mathsf{Enc}(tk, pk, m)\right) = m \wedge \\ \mathsf{false} \xleftarrow{\mathbb{B}} \mathsf{Insp}(\mathsf{Tx}, \check{P}) \end{array}\right] \Rightarrow \mathbb{E}[a2].$$

Game $\eth_0 \approx$ **Game** $\eth_1$. The winning condition for $\eth_0$ is equal to the winning condition for $\eth_1$ if and only if the event $\mathbb{E}[a1]$ does not happen. The probability of $\mathbb{E}[a1]$ happening is identical to the advantage of breaking the promise of transaction-unforgeability. Thus, we have

$$|\Pr[\eth_0] - \Pr[\eth_1]| = \Pr[\mathbb{E}[a1]] = adv_{\mathcal{B}_1,\Pi}^{\eth_{\mathrm{unforg}}}(\lambda).$$

Game $\eth_1 \approx$ **Game** $\eth_2$. The winning condition for $\eth_1$ is equal to the winning condition for $\eth_2$ if and only if the event $\mathbb{E}[a2]$ does not happen. We consider the possibility of $\mathbb{E}[a2]$, and it is identical to the advantage of breaking the promise of state-consistency. Thus, we obtain

$$|\Pr[\eth_1] - \Pr[\eth_2]| = \Pr[\mathbb{E}[a2]] = adv_{\mathcal{B}_2,\Pi}^{\eth_{\mathrm{cons}}}(\lambda).$$

Putting everything together, we conclude that

$$adv_{\mathcal{A},\Pi}^{\eth_{\mathrm{fair}}}(\lambda) \leq \Pr[\mathbb{E}[a1]] + \Pr[\mathbb{E}[a2]] + adv_{\mathcal{B},\Pi}^{\eth_2}(\lambda)$$
$$\leq adv_{\mathcal{B}_1,\Pi}^{\eth_{\mathrm{unforg}}}(\lambda) + adv_{\mathcal{B}_2,\Pi}^{\eth_{\mathrm{cons}}}(\lambda) + adv_{\mathcal{A},\Pi}^{\eth_2}(\lambda) \leq negl(\lambda).$$

Theorem 2 (Completeness). *Assume that SGX-based PPSC is secure and Kiltz's full PKE scheme [15] is secure against chosen-ciphertext attacks, Fialka satisfies completeness.*

Proof. The concrete proof can be found at Appendix B.

7   Implementation

In this section, we discuss the implementation[1] of our instantiation based on the SGX-based PPSC platform Oasis Devnet [1,8] (version 2.0). Our implementation (see Fig. 1.b) has two components: the *client-side* and the *server-side*. The client-side is run by the sender, receiver and investigator, while the server-side is run by the PPSC platform. The client-side covers four algorithms: Set, Gen, Enc, Dec. They are implemented by 1000+ lines of Javascript codes in total, containing the packages of client and client-connector. The client implements basic operations executed by end-users at local, while client-connector builds a bridge between the client-side and the server-side. The server-side consists of two pieces of privacy-preserving smart contracts: PPSC-KM and PPSC-AD. PPSC-KM covers the algorithms CGen, Reg and Trans[2], while PPSC-AD includes the algorithm Insp. Both of them are implemented in Rust. PPSC-KM protects private decryption keys by using the enclave technology from Intel SGX [10], while PPSC-AD determines whether the decryption is legal or not by checking the security policies.

To be specific, after a successful deployment of the contract PPSC-KM and PPSC-AD, the evidence inspection algorithm Insp and the investigator's key generation algorithm (by revoking Trans) as well as their access conditions, will be compiled as the binary codes and replicated to the enclaves [10] in SGX-powered blockchain nodes. Then, an encrypted contract state containing the investigator's key $H_1(tk|r)$ reaches an agreement across distributed blockchain nodes. After that, to obtain the key from PPSC-KM, two requirements must be fulfilled: (1) a transaction with the input satisfying access conditions should be provided; (2) An encrypted and authenticated channel connected to enclaves should be established (after a successful attestation [1,8,10]). Then, an invoked progress will be executed in the form of a transaction, and remains visible and immutable which could be publicly accessed. Each entity is able to see/witness the progress of obtaining the investigator's key, but no entity except the contract caller, knows the exact output (key) of the smart contract. Subsequently, PPSC-AD audits the transactions through an internal query to detect suspicious activities. Essentially, the privileges of the Trans algorithm are protected and managed in a CPU-level by Intel SGX. Only designated investigators should be allowed to access this secret key. We also notice that our implementation only provides one-off auditing, since it can only trace the records when the first time an investigator extracts the secret key. Our implementation provides a prototype to demonstrate the feasibility.

8   Evaluation

We first provide the performance evaluation on average CPU-time, representing the consumed time since the operation starts. The evaluation contains all the

---

[1] A demo site and reference source code are accessible at http://www.fialka.top.

[2] Trans (**Transfer** algorithm) calculates the investigator's key and it belongs to WDec.

algorithms, and the testing environment is set as follows. The client-side runs on a Dell precision 3630 Tower with 16 GB of RAM and one 3.7 GHz six-core i7-8700K processors running Ubuntu 18.04. The server-side runs on a blockchain node, which is provided by Oasis SDK [1,8].

Table 1. The average CPU-time, Gas cost and Latency of Operations.

Operations	CPU-time/ms	Cost/gas	Latency/ms
Set	1.16	–	–
Gen	50.04	–	–
CGen[†]	0.0880	5129943	5683
Reg	0.0104	494553	3960
Enc	102.35	–	–
Dec	64.86	–	–
Trans	0.0325	342514	3643
Insp	0.0027	251971	2450

†: CGen means contract generation

CPU-time. The evaluation results illustrate some critical points. The offline operation Enc is the most time-consuming operation since the encryption covers the seven exponentiations. The offline operation Dec takes approximately half the time of that in encryption because it processes four exponentiations. On the contrary, blockchain-related operations CGen, Reg, Trans and Insp take much less than offline operations, since they do not have group mathematics computation. In particular, the operation Insp is the fastest operation, which indicates the efficiency of our accountability protocol. However, CPU-time is close to testing environment, inefficient to convince that our framework is practical. Therefore, we provide further evaluations on *gas cost* and *latency* for real-world scenarios.

Gas Cost. The gas cost measures the amount of computational effort that a blockchain takes to execute an algorithm. The gas cost evaluation includes the operations of CGen, Reg, Trans and Insp. The operation CGen costs the most gas among all since the initial configuration of a smart contract has to be loaded. Fortunately, this bottleneck can be ignored, because each contract is created only once and can be reused multiple times. The cost of Reg is relatively high, since the public parameters are needed to store on smart contracts. The cost of Trans and Insp are relatively low due to simple online calculations, which indicates that our accountability protocol is financially feasible[3]. In a real-world setting, different investigators may call the functions in a same PPSC for decryption and auditing simultaneously. To demonstrate the practicability of our system,

---

[3] Estimates on real value of gas cost are omitted, since the Oasis token has not been officially released at the time of writing.

we simulate a distributed environment by increasing the number of invocations from different investigators. Specifically, we test the gas cost of Trans and of Insp along with a maximum 1000 invocations simultaneously. As shown in Fig. 2, the outputs remains relatively stable under the variations, and the average cost of Trans reaches approximately 340k while Insp is about 250k. It matches our intuitive expectation, since the gas cost is theoretically independent with the number of investigators. Based on such results, our accountability framework is practically affordable which could be widely adopted.

Latency. Our latency test covers all the blockchain-related operations including CGen, Reg, Trans and Insp. Among them, CGen is the most time consuming, as the contract codes need to be compiled into the blockchain. The operation Reg also takes a long time because all parameters have to be configured into contracts. In contrast, the operations Trans and Insp are in low latency, due to the fact that they do not have sophisticated on-chain computations. We also provide a simulation by increasing the invocations in a distributed environment. Our simulation includes the most two frequently used functions in PPSC, namely Trans and Insp. As shown in Fig. 2, the results turn out that the latency stably increases along with the growing number of invocations. Theoretically, numerous invocations will impose a heavy burden onto the distributed network, which may even cause the network failure or transaction stuck. We set an upper bound of invoking transactions with 1000 users at the peak. The testing results confirm our expectations.

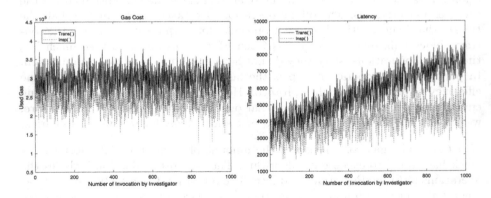

Fig. 2. Gas and latency evaluation

Weakness. The average latency of the operation Trans reaches approximately five seconds, which is the primary drawback of our implementation. Frankly speaking, our system, at least built on the current version of Oasis Devnet (version 2.0), cannot compatibly support the applications that require fast decryption, due to the latency constraints. However, it is worth noting that the execution of warrant focuses on finding criminal evidence, which is latency insensitive.

9   Conclusion

In this paper, we propose *Fialka*, a novel transaction-triggering accountable decryption system based on the privacy-preserving smart contracts. Our system utilizes PPSC to trace and detect the decryption evidence, which makes warrant execution accountable. To the best of our knowledge, we present the first PPSC-based accountability mechanism with formal definitions and proofs. The security analysis shows that our system holds the accountability properties of fairness and completeness. The implementation based on Oasis Devnet with the detailed evaluation indicates that our system is feasible and applicable.

Future Work. Fialka is a composite framework containing PKE and PPSC. The definition and proof of our instantiation are complete and sound. However, SGX-based PPSC and its underlying blockchain are inherently hybrid systems with a sophisticated mechanism, making our assumption inevitably strong. The possibility to weaken the assumption will be further explored.

Acknowledgments. R. Li, F. Liu and Q. Wang were supported by the National Science Foundation of China under Grant No. 61672015 and Guangdong Provincial Key Laboratory (Grant No. 2020B121201001). D. Galindo was partially supported by the European Union's Horizon 2020 research and innovation programme under grant agreement No. 779391 (FutureTPM).

A   Appendix: Linear Problem

Definition 8. (Linear Problem [5,15]). *Let $\mathbb{G}$ be a cyclic multiplicative group with prime order p, and g_1, g_2, g_3 be generators of $\mathbb{G}$. Given $g_1, g_2, g_3, g_1^a, g_2^b, g_3^c \in \mathbb{G}$, decide whether $a + b$ equals to c. If $a + b = c$, outputs true, or false otherwise. The advantage of an algorithm $\mathcal{A}$ in deciding the linear problem in $\mathbb{G}$ is*

$$adv_{\mathcal{A}}^{LP} = \left| \begin{array}{l} Pr[\mathcal{A}(g_1, g_2, g_3, g_1^a, g_2^b, g_3^{a+b}) = true: \\ \qquad\qquad\qquad g_1, g_2, g_3 \leftarrow \mathbb{G}, a, b \leftarrow \mathbb{Z}_p] \\ -Pr[\mathcal{A}(g_1, g_2, g_3, g_1^a, g_2^b, \eta) = true: \\ \qquad\qquad\qquad g_1, g_2, g_3, \eta \leftarrow \mathbb{G}, a, b \leftarrow \mathbb{Z}_p] \end{array} \right|,$$

with the probability taken over the uniform random choice of the parameters to $\mathcal{A}$ and over the coin tosses of $\mathcal{A}$.

Assumption 1 (Decision Linear Assumption). *No adversary $\mathcal{A}$ succeeds in deciding the Linear Problem in $\mathbb{G}$ with a non-negligible advantage.*

Lemma 2. *Assume H_2 is a target collision-resistant hash function, under the Decision Linear Problem, Kiltz's full PKE scheme [15] is secure against chosen-ciphertext attacks.*

B   Appendix: Completeness

Proof (Theorem 2: Completeness). Suppose that there exists an adversary $\mathcal{A}$ who wins the completeness game ∂_{comp} with non-negligible probability. Then, we transform an adversary $\mathcal{A}$ against *Completeness* into adversaries against PPSC security and IND-CCA security of Kiltz's PKE scheme. We describe a sequence of games to conduct the proof.

Game ∂_0. This is the unmodified completeness game. The winning probability equals the advantage of $\mathcal{A}$ against *Completeness* game, namely, $adv_{\mathcal{A},\Pi}^{\partial_{\mathrm{comp}}}(\lambda)$.

Game ∂_1. In this game, when the adversary calls the $\mathcal{C}$, we disallow contract $\widehat{c}_{\mathrm{ad}}$ to execute the algorithm Insp, and then $\widehat{c}_{\mathrm{ad}}$ outputs true to the adversary.

Game ∂_2. In this game, we disallow $\mathcal{A}$ calls $\mathcal{C}$, and thus **Transfer** in $\widehat{c}_{\mathrm{km}}$ cannot be executed, indicating $\mathcal{A}$ cannot obtain secret key from blockchain.

Clearly, without querying smart contract, the adversary's advantage of winning ∂_2 equals the advantage of breaking the CCA security of PKE. The adversary against security of Kiltz's PKE scheme $adv_{\mathcal{B},\Pi}^{\partial_{\mathrm{CCA}}}(\lambda)$ is negligible, and the proof is given in Lemma 2. To find out the difference between these games, we define the events: (1) $\mathbb{E}[b1]$: blocking the transaction-based evidence. The adversary $\mathcal{B}_1$ fetches the key from the blockchain, and successfully hides the transaction Tx^* that used for validation in the algorithm Insp. (2) $\mathbb{E}[b2]$: forging an inspection result. The adversary $\mathcal{B}_2$ forges an inspection result by executing $\neg\mathsf{Insp}$, where $\neg\mathsf{Insp}$ means the malicious behaviors of inspection and it modifies the false result as true. (3)$\mathbb{E}[b3]$: breaking the security of PPSC. The adversary $\mathcal{B}_3$ obtains a valid private key without invoking the blockchain.

Game $\partial_0 \approx$ Game ∂_1. The winning conditions for ∂_0 equals the winning conditions for ∂_1 if neither event $\mathbb{E}[b1]$ nor event $\mathbb{E}[b2]$ happen. Thus, we have $|\Pr[\partial_0] - \Pr[\partial_1]| = \Pr[\mathbb{E}[b1]] + \Pr[\mathbb{E}[b2]]$. We then consider the happening probabilities of the $\mathbb{E}[b1]$ and $\mathbb{E}[b2]$. The happening of $\mathbb{E}[b1]$ implies that the adversary $\mathcal{B}_1$ hides the transaction evidence, which contradicts the assumption of the transparency properties. Thus, the wining advantages of $\mathbb{E}[b1]$ is identical to breaking the promise of transaction-transparency. If the event $\mathbb{E}[b2]$ happens, indicating that the adversary $\mathcal{B}_2$ breaks the state-consistency of PPSC, the possibility is identical to the advantage of breaking the promise of state-consistency. Thus, we have $\Pr[\mathbb{E}[b1]] = adv_{\mathcal{B}_1,\Pi}^{\partial_{\mathrm{tran}}}(\lambda)$ and $\Pr[\mathbb{E}[b2]] = adv_{\mathcal{B}_2,\Pi}^{\partial_{\mathrm{cons}}}(\lambda)$.

Game $\partial_1 \approx$ Game ∂_2. The winning condition for ∂_1 is equal to the winning condition for ∂_2 if and only if event $\mathbb{E}[b3]$ does not happen. The possibility of $\mathbb{E}[b3]$ is identical to the advantages of breaking the promise of state-privacy. Thus, $|\Pr[\partial_1] - \Pr[\partial_2]| = \Pr[\mathbb{E}[b3]] = adv_{\mathcal{B}_3,\Pi}^{\partial_{\mathrm{privacy}}}(\lambda)$.

Combining everything together, we obtain that

$$adv_{\mathcal{A},\Pi}^{\partial_{\mathrm{comp}}}(\lambda) \leq \Pr[\mathbb{E}[b1]] + \Pr[\mathbb{E}[b2]] + \Pr[\mathbb{E}[b3]] + adv_{\mathcal{B},\Pi}^{\partial_{\mathrm{no\text{-}query}}}(\lambda)$$
$$\leq adv_{\mathcal{B}_1,\Pi}^{\partial_{\mathrm{tran}}}(\lambda) + adv_{\mathcal{B}_2,\Pi}^{\partial_{\mathrm{cons}}}(\lambda) + adv_{\mathcal{B}_3,\Pi}^{\partial_{\mathrm{privacy}}}(\lambda) + adv_{\mathcal{B},\Pi}^{\partial_{\mathrm{CCA}}}(\lambda) \leq negl(\lambda).$$

References

1. Oasis labs: A safer way to use data (2020). https://www.oasislabs.com/
2. Origo: the privacy preserving platform for decentralized applications (2020). https://origo.network/
3. Alder, F., Asokan, N., et al.: S-FAAS: Trustworthy and accountable function-as-a-service using intel SGX. In: CCSW 2019, pp. 185–199 (2019)
4. Azaria, A., Ekblaw, A., Vieira, T.: Medrec: using blockchain for medical data access and permission management. In: OBD 2016, pp. 25–30. IEEE (2016)
5. Boneh, D., Boyen, X., Shacham, H.: Short group signatures. In: Franklin, M. (ed.) CRYPTO 2004. LNCS, vol. 3152, pp. 41–55. Springer, Heidelberg (2004). https://doi.org/10.1007/978-3-540-28628-8_3
6. Bünz, B., Agrawal, S., Zamani, M., Boneh, D.: Zether: Towards privacy in a smart contract world. In: FC 2020 (2020)
7. Canetti, R.: Universally composable security: a new paradigm for cryptographic protocols. In: FOCS 2001, pp. 136–145. IEEE (2001)
8. Cheng, R., et al.: Ekiden: a platform for confidentiality-preserving, trustworthy, and performant smart contracts. In: EuroSP 2019, pp. 185–200. IEEE (2019)
9. Contractor, D., Patel, D.R.: Accountability in cloud computing by means of chain of trust. IJ Network Secur. **19**(2), 251–259 (2017)
10. Costan, V., Devadas, S.: Intel SGX explained. IACR Cryptol. ePrint Archive **2016**(086), 1–118 (2016)
11. Goyal, V., Lu, S., Sahai, A., Waters, B.: Black-box accountable authority identity-based encryption. In: ACM CCS 2008, pp. 427–436. ACM (2008)
12. Guo, H., Zhang, Z., Xu, J., Xia, M.: Generic traceable proxy re-encryption and accountable extension in consensus network. In: Sako, K., Schneider, S., Ryan, P.Y.A. (eds.) ESORICS 2019. LNCS, vol. 11735, pp. 234–256. Springer, Cham (2019). https://doi.org/10.1007/978-3-030-29959-0_12
13. Juels, A., Kosba, A., Shi, E.: The ring of GYGES: investigating the future of criminal smart contracts. In: ACM CCS 2016, pp. 283–295. ACM (2016)
14. Kaaniche, N., Laurent, M.: A blockchain-based data usage auditing architecture with enhanced privacy and availability. In: NCA 2017, pp. 1–5. IEEE (2017)
15. Kiltz, E.: Chosen-ciphertext security from tag-based encryption. In: Halevi, S., Rabin, T. (eds.) TCC 2006. LNCS, vol. 3876, pp. 581–600. Springer, Heidelberg (2006). https://doi.org/10.1007/11681878_30
16. Kosba, A., Miller, A., et al.: Hawk: the blockchain model of cryptography and privacy-preserving smart contracts. In: IEEE S&P 2016, pp. 839–858. IEEE (2016)
17. Kroll, J.A., Zimmerman, J., Wu, D.J., Nikolaenko, V., Felten, E.W.: Accountable cryptographic access control. In: Workshop, CRYPTO 2018, vol. 2018 (2018)
18. Küsters, R., Truderung, T., Vogt, A.: Accountability: definition and relationship to verifiability. In: ACM CCS 2010, pp. 526–535. ACM (2010)
19. Lai, J., Tang, Q.: Making *Any* attribute-based encryption accountable, efficiently. In: Lopez, J., Zhou, J., Soriano, M. (eds.) ESORICS 2018. LNCS, vol. 11099, pp. 527–547. Springer, Cham (2018). https://doi.org/10.1007/978-3-319-98989-1_26
20. Li, R., Galindo, D., Wang, Q.: Auditable credential anonymity revocation based on privacy-preserving smart contracts. In: Pérez-Solà, C., Navarro-Arribas, G., Biryukov, A., Garcia-Alfaro, J. (eds.) DPM/CBT -2019. LNCS, vol. 11737, pp. 355–371. Springer, Cham (2019). https://doi.org/10.1007/978-3-030-31500-9_23
21. Luo, Y., Fan, J., Deng, C., Li, Y., Zheng, Y., Ding, J.: Accountable data sharing scheme based on blockchain and SGX. In: CyberC 2019, pp. 9–16. IEEE (2019)

22. Microsoft: The coco framework: Technical overview, May 2019. https://github.com/Azure/coco-framework/
23. Neisse, R., Steri, G., Nai-Fovino, I.: A blockchain-based approach for data accountability and provenance tracking. In: ARES 2017, p. 14. ACM (2017)
24. Ryan, M.D.: Making decryption accountable (Transcript of Discussion). In: Stajano, F., Anderson, J., Christianson, B., Matyáš, V. (eds.) Security Protocols 2017. LNCS, vol. 10476, pp. 99–108. Springer, Cham (2017). https://doi.org/10.1007/978-3-319-71075-4_12
25. Steffen, S., et al.: zkay: specifying and enforcing data privacy in smart contracts. In: ACM CCS 2019, pp. 1759–1776. ACM (2019)
26. Szabo, N.: Smart contracts: building blocks for digital markets. EXTROPY: J. Transhumanist Thought, 18(16), 2 (1996)
27. Wood, G., et al.: Ethereum: a secure decentralised generalised transaction ledger. Ethereum Project Yellow Paper 151(2014), 1–32 (2014)
28. Xu, Y., et al.: Blockchain empowered arbitrable data auditing scheme for network storage as a service. IEEE TSC 13(2), 289–300 (2019)
29. Zyskind, G., Nathan, O., Pentland, A.: Enigma: Decentralized computation platform with guaranteed privacy. arXiv preprint arXiv:1506.03471 (2015)

Security Applications

PvP: Profiling Versus Player! Exploiting Gaming Data for Player Recognition

Mauro Conti(ID) and Pier Paolo Tricomi(✉)(ID)

University of Padua, Padua, Italy
conti@math.unipd.it, tricomipierpaolo@gmail.com

Abstract. Video games Industry generated 150$ billion (approx. two times Facebook revenue) and involved one-third of the world population, in 2019 only. It is not hard to imagine how this attracted cyber-criminals, e.g.: 77 million PlayStation Network accounts were compromised in 2011; in 2015 Steam reported more than 70 thousand victims of scam monthly; cyberbullism events are also frequently reported. Being able to recognize gamers leveraging their gaming data could help to mitigate these issues, e.g., harmful players that are banned could be found again in all the other profiles they own. On the other side, this capability could be a further tool in the hand of cyber-criminals.

In this paper, we are the first to demonstrate that players can be recognized based on their play-style. In particular, we observe the play-style through gaming data and use a Deep Neural Network for recognition. Our solution addresses games in which players control a character, and generic features are used to make our system possibly applicable to other games as well. To demonstrate the feasibility of our proposal, we run a thorough set of experiments based on players of Dota 2, which counts more than 10 million monthly active users. Our results show the efficiency and feasibility of the proposal, achieving 96% accuracy with only two minutes of gaming data.

Keywords: Video games · Security · Privacy · User recognition

1 Introduction

Video games are an important and often present part of modern society. As of July 2018, almost a third of people on Earth are gamers [11]. The video game evolution is glaring: increasingly new technologies led to more performing gaming platforms, going from Arcade Console a Nintendo64 to PlayStation 5 and Nintendo Switch, potentially involving Augmented Reality (AR). In 2019, the video game market generated around $150 billion in revenue [30], approximately two times Facebook ones [26]. Nevertheless, the large diffusion of online video games opened up a plethora of new paths for fraud. In-game purchases are incredibly common nowadays, and one-click payments are becoming the trend, i.e., users'

© Springer Nature Switzerland AG 2020
W. Susilo et al. (Eds.): ISC 2020, LNCS 12472, pp. 393–408, 2020.
https://doi.org/10.1007/978-3-030-62974-8_22

payment information is centralized and accessible through the accounts. There is no surprise that account takeovers are a primary aim for hackers. A recent study [19] showed that about half of all console gamers spend money in-game, and at least one fifth has been the victim of payment fraud. In 2011, the PlayStation Network registered more than 77 million accounts being compromised [3]. In 2015 Valve, Steam's developer, stated that more than 70 thousand account were stolen monthly, and mitigated the problem with a two-factor authorization method [29]. In 2018, the popular League of Legends (LOL) and Fortnite faced serious account takeovers problems. LOL was targeted with several phishing attacks [2], while in Fortnite several players discovered many unauthorized payments in their bank movements [5]. Very often, such scammers add the victims on friends list, then start chatting sending malicious links or offering favorable trades. To be more credible, the scammers usually add the victims after a game played together. Even if scammers can be reported and banned, they can easily create new accounts and continue with their malicious actions.

The problems of account takeovers and scams could be reduced being able to uniquely recognize a player, regardless of the account they plays in (i.e., profiling a player[1]). An in-game payment could be blocked if the purchaser is not recognized as the owner. At the same time, if dangerous user are banned, they could be banned again every time they make or use another profile. The same approach could be used to reduce harassment and cyberbullying that often appears in video games [9]. In our opinion, a powerful way to carry out such player recognition is by using the player's play-style, i.e., in-game data. The intuition behind this work is that players have their own way to play, and this could potentially be a "biometric" factor.

The mentioned gaming data can be retrieved by exploiting matches replays and tracking websites, tools that derived from the growing popularity of *Electronic Sports* (or *e-sports*). The replays availability and their analysis brought up the birth of tracking websites, i.e., web applications that gather players data to expose their entire careers and personal statistics. However, such data are public, visible to anyone, without any exception, and the possibility of recognizing a player starting from in-game data might lead to serious privacy issues.

In this paper, we are the first to demonstrate that players can be recognized and distinguished using their in-game data as features. If this could help to reduce the aforementioned problems, it could also boost harmful behaviors. If a cyberbullying victim decides to create a new account to stop being bothered by bullies, they can chase them down analyzing new players' play-styles and finding a correlation. Thus, we are also spreading awareness about these possible attacks.

Contributions. Our contribution is twofold: (1) we give the first demonstration of player recognition using in-game data extracted from replays, and (2) we show the current panorama of online gaming and discuss potential issues and consequences arising from (1).

---

[1] The title of the paper, Profiling vs Player, has the same acronym (PvP) of Player vs Player, a term used in video games to express battles between gamers.

Organization: Section 2 overviews related work, while Sect. 3 provides a panorama of online gaming and Dota 2 background. Section 4 shows the data collection procedure we used. Next, Sect. 5 describes the model used for the recognition system, followed by experiments and results in Sect. 6. Discussions follow in Sect. 7 and Sect. 8 concludes the paper.

2 Related Work

Video games, privacy, and deep learning fields have been widely explored in the literature, although they have been treated together only recently. We restrict the discussion to these three main areas related to video games: effects and impacts on gamers, security and privacy issues, and studies carried out using machine learning techniques, especially on Dota 2.

One of the main interests researchers have in the video games field is to understand the benefits of playing video games and their impact on society. In [13] Gong et al. conducted a study over 27 "expert" players of League of Legend and Dota 2, showing that playing video games increases the amount of grey matter and promotes better connectivity in a person's brain. Despite the video game influence on child health is usually perceived to be negative, [17] proved that children who play more video games may be more likely to develop good social skills and to build better relationships. Granic et al. demonstrated in [14], that children who played strategy-based games usually improved their problem-solving skills, getting better grades in the next school year. Studies have tried to analyze the correlation between violence and video games [10], while or to understand the learning potential of such means [25].

Privacy issues in video games are a recent concern. In [21] Newman et al. evidence of how companies gather their players' data through consoles using several different sensors. Players' voice, physical appearance or geographical location are the main interesting and private features that are usually collected. Moreover, players' psychographic information can be obtained starting from their in-game interactions. In [24], a full overview of how modern games aligns with information privacy norms and notions is given. Furthermore, it analyzes how users, in particular child gamers, may be affected by data practices and technologies specific to gaming. Many means have been used to recognize users, such as movements information published on a social network in [15] and laptop power consumption in [4], but video games were never used before, to the best of our knowledge. Deep learning techniques have been applied in several fields of recognition, such as Human Action Recognition [1] or Speech Recognition [6].

Classic machine learning techniques have been applied to video games for several reasons. In 2009, Drachen et al. utilized an unsupervised learning approach to construct models of players [7] of "Tomb Raider: Underworld". One year later, on the same game, different supervised learning algorithms were trained on a large dataset of player behavior data, to predict when a player will stop playing and the time to complete the game, if the player does it [18]. Müller et al., in 2015, classified player behavior in Minecraft using PCA, focusing on how much

Table 1. Comparison between most played online video games.

	Monthly players	Age Range	Release Year	Free to Play	Revenue	Tracking Websites	Replays Availability	Replays easy to get	Replay Parsers
Minecraft	112M (2019)[1]	5-50	2011	✗	$110M (2018)[7]	✓	Low	✗	✗
Fortnite	250M (2019)[2]	6-54	2017	✓	$2.4B (2018)[8]	✓	Medium	✗	✓
League of Legends	115M (2019)[3]	11-50	2009	✓	$1.5B (2019)[9]	✓	Medium	✓	✓
PUBG	227M (2018)[4]	10-50	2017	✗	$1.3B (2019)[10]	✓	Medium	✗	✓
CS:GO	17M (2019)[5]	13-40	2012	✓	$414M (2018)[11]	✓	Medium	✓	✓
Dota 2	11M (2019)[6]	12-50	2013	✓	$406M (2017)[12]	✓	High	✓	✓

[1] https://tinyurl.com/minec-pl   [2] https://tinyurl.com/fortn-pl   [3] https://tinyurl.com/league-pl
[4] https://tinyurl.com/plunk-pl   [5] https://tinyurl.com/countst-pl   [6] https://tinyurl.com/dota2-pl
[7] https://tinyurl.com/minec-re   [8] https://tinyurl.com/fortn-re   [9] https://tinyurl.com/league-re
[10] https://tinyurl.com/plunkn-re   [11] https://tinyurl.com/countst-re   [12] https://tinyurl.com/dota2-re

time players put in actions such as building, mining, exploring and fighting [20]. Different studies have been conducted on Dota 2 during the years. In [12], Gao et al. used different classifiers to detect hero roles from IDs, achieving a 75% accuracy, and hero positioning with more than 85% accuracy. Eggert et al. continued the work in [8] achieving 96.15% test accuracy using Logistic Regression. Finally, OpenAI et al. [22] used deep reinforcement learning to create OpenAI Five, a Dota 2 team composed by five bots trained for over ten months, which was the first artificial team able to defeat world champions at an esports game, demonstrating that self-play reinforcement learning can overcome a difficult task with superhuman performance.

3   Background

In this section we first give a wide overview of the Online Gaming scenario, to let the reader understand the impact our research could have on the society (Sect. 3.1). Second, we explain more in details the game Dota 2, the one we chose for the project (Sect. 3.2).

3.1   Online Gaming Panorama

As of July 2018, there are approximately 2.2 billion gamers on Earth, and 1.2 billion of those plays on a PC [11]. We gathered data to create a panorama about the most played online multiplayer games. The list includes Minecraft, Fortnite Battle Royale, League of Legends, PlayerUnknown's BattleGrounds (PUBG), Counter-Strike: Global Offensive (CS:GO) and Dota 2. Table 1 shows many characteristics of the mentioned video games, such as monthly users, age ranges and revenues. We also evaluated the availability of tracking websites and replays, considering if they were available, easy to get for a casual player and the existence of parsers. The reported data come from our estimate, which did not follow any specific procedure. We considered official reports, forum discussions, survey results, and other online resources.

Each video game has at least 10 Million monthly players, with a huge spike in Fortnite Battle Royale with 250 Million users. The age ranges are incredibly wide, with games such as Minecraft and Fortnite involving very young children. This fact emphasizes the critical impact of being able to recognize a user given this very young audience. The revenue data shows the huge influence video games have on the economy and society.

All the considered games have websites held by third parties that track their players, while the replays availability is limited in some games (e.g., only some typologies of matches are available). All of them, except for Minecraft, have good replay parsers and keep updating their replay systems to make matches replays available for all the players, especially professional matches, since watching replays is a good way to learn and improve in the game. Overall, Dota 2 has the more complete replay system, and replays of any player are very easy to obtain. Every player can search and download any match using the match ID, and different perspectives can be selected to watch the replay. Dota 2 also has different parsers and tracking websites, thus we chose it as the game for our case study. For the rest of the paper, we will use Dota 2 features to recognize players. However, we selected general features that can be possibly found in other video games, or easily replaced by characteristics of such video games likely to be "biometric". Section 7 discusses on applicability of the presented system to other games.

3.2   Dota 2

Dota 2 is a Multiplayer Online Battle Arena (MOBA) video game. Released by Valve Corporation in 2013 and available on Steam for free, it is currently one of their most played multiplayer game, with more than 400,000 unique players every day. Two different teams of five players, the Radiant and the Dire, fight each other to destroy the enemy base, defending their own one at the same time. Each player controls a single character, called "hero", with unique abilities.

Tracking Websites. Tracking Websites are web applications that automatically analyze players' matches to produce individual statistics as well as general trends about the game. Each player career, i.e., all the matches they played, is publicly exposed. The main Tracking websites for Dota 2 are Dotabuff[2] and Opendota[3]. Players allow data collection to such websites enabling an option in the game client. Players not giving consent to such websites are not visible to them, but their matches are still public and easy to get using the match ID.

Replay Parsing. Parsing a replay means going over it and extract useful information. In Dota 2, replays are basically event streams, involving players' orders, spawn of unities, combat logs and so on. For this project we used the replay

---

[2] https://www.dotabuff.com.
[3] https://www.opendota.com.

parser Clarity[4] written in Java, which is also used by Opendota. We will give more details about what data we used in our system in Sect. 5.

4 Our Data Collection

We now illustrate the data collection procedure. We used an online survey to gather players willing to help with our research, with the details presented in Sect. 4.1. The survey results with considerations are given in Sect. 4.2. Finally, the survey allowed us to retrieve players' IDs and download their replays as shown in Sect. 4.3.

4.1 Dota 2 Online Survey

We found participants for our research using an online survey. The survey was anonymous, and fulfilling it users gave us the consensus to use their data (from the survey answers and from Dota 2) related to a Steam ID. The purpose of the survey was twofold: (1) retrieving the Steam ID to download players' replays and statistics, (2) having a general idea about the Dota 2 community and to understand if problems such as virtual scams and harassment were still actual problems. We gathered this information in two different sections.

We spread the survey in different places, i.e., Facebook groups, Reddit, Discord groups, and private messages on different platforms. The estimated time to complete the survey was 4 min, and we organized a prize draw for valid participants. To be validated, users had to be visible on tracking websites and the answers had to be coherent.

We know that the conducted survey cannot be a complete representation of the Dota 2 community, but we do believe it was enough for a qualitative assessment.

4.2 Survey Results

We received a total of 625 answers. 16 answers were considered invalid, while 43 participants were not visible by tracker websites. 37 players did not have recent matches in the last three months, so a total of 529 active users from 62 different countries were considered for the research. 502 of them were males while only 27 were females. Most of the players were students (47.5%), followed by workers (30.8%), working student(11.7%) and a small fraction of unemployed (10%). The age ranges from 13 from 46, with the majority between 16 and 28. 35% of them declared to have multiple accounts, but they answered providing their most used one. We also asked their experience about scams and virtual harassment in Dota 2. 429 players were never scammed, while 94 were scammed at least once and 6 three or more times. However, 55% of them was contacted by strangers suspecting a scamming attempts multiple times (3 or more), while 20%

---

4 https://github.com/skadistats/clarity.

was contacted one or two times, and 25% never had this risk. Finally, 56.5% of the players were never harassed in game through chat or weird behaviour during matches, while 22.8% was harassed very few times (1–2), and 20.6% was harassed multiple times.

According to these results, we do believe our research tackles a big problem in online games. A lot of players have multiple accounts, and the risk of being scammed or harassed is pretty high.

4.3   Players Data

After we collected all the players' ID from validated answers, we downloaded all the matches replays of such players for one month. We used Steam APIs and Opendota to retrieve the download link of the matches. We also used Opendota APIs[5] to retrieve player's statistics, using the last three months as of date filter.

5   Model Selection for Player Recognition

In this section, we show the model we created to identify a player using gaming data, i.e., the data extracted from replays. We start showing the data creation, what data we collected and how in Sect. 5.1. In Sect. 5.2 we present the first model we built along the consideration to create the definitive one. Section 5.3 reports the model selection phase.

5.1   Dataset Creation

To create our dataset, we followed a four-step procedure. We firstly selected the number of players to recognize due to computational resource limitation(*Players Selection*). Then, in the *Features Selection* phase, we identified the features that could be used to represent the user play-style. Next, we parsed all the replays focusing on the selected features (*Replay Parsing*). Lastly, we aggregated the output of the parsed replays (*Data Aggregation* phase), to have multivariate time-series representing the matches.

Players Selection. For the 529 users, we downloaded more than 30000 matches of ~45 mb each. Analyzing all these replays would have been extremely expensive in terms of time and resources. We then reduced the number of players to analyze: we selected the first 50 players with a higher number of played matches. Since a player can be Radiant or Dire, which means playing in the opposite parts of the map for most of the time, we randomly selected 50 Radiant matches and 50 Dire matches, for a total of 100 matches per player and 5000 matches in total. A balanced dataset is very important to achieve good and explanatory accuracy. Balancing the matches played on the different sides of the map, as well the number of matches per player, would surely help our model to learn better.

---

[5] https://docs.opendota.com/.

Features Selection. To identify players, we wanted to use general features possibly available in other video games, to make the research transferable to other games as well. Features such as gold or experience per minute were too related to the game. Instead, information such as the cursor movements, the camera movements (what the player sees), hero positions and the actions a player can do are more likely to be found in games similar to Dota 2. In detail, the cursor is defined by X and Y coordinates, while the camera is defined by a cell and a vector, both together giving the exact position, and each of them is defined over the three axis X, Y and Z. For cells, we did not consider the Z axis since it does not vary. The same approach of cells and vectors is used to represent a hero position. Actions, instead, are the orders a player can give to the controlled hero. We used only the most common actions as features to reduce the dimensionality of the problem. Some actions can also have X and Y coordinates of the target. The type and values of considered features are given in Table 2.

Table 2. Initial set of features considered for the task.

Type	Values	Aggregated features
Cursor, Camera Cell, Hero Cell, Hero Vector	X,Y	X_mean, X_std, X_changes Y_mean, Y_std, Y_changes
Camera Vector	X, Y, Z	X_mean, X_std, X_changes Y_mean, Y_std, Y_changes Z_mean, Z_std, Z_changes
Action: Move_to_position	occurred, X, Y	n_occurs, X_mean, X_std, Y_mean, Y_std
Action: Move_to_target	occurred	n_occurs
Action: Attack_move	occurred, X, Y	n_occurs, X_mean, X_std, Y_mean, Y_std
Action: Attack_target	occurred	n_occurs
Action: Cast_position	occurred, X, Y	n_occurs, X_mean, X_std, Y_mean, Y_std
Action: Cast_target	occurred	n_occurs
Action: Cast_target_tree	occurred	n_occurs
Action: Cast_no_target	occurred	n_occurs
Action: Hold_position	occurred	n_occurs
Action: Drop_item	occurred, X, Y	n_occurs, X_mean, X_std, Y_mean, Y_std
Action: Ping_ability	occurred	n_occurs
Action: Continue	occurred	n_occurs

Replay Parsing. A replay is organized in ticks, with 30 ticks per second. At every tick, information about entities (heroes, players, ...), players' orders, etc. are saved. We used the parser to get, at every tick, the features we showed above, i.e., related to the cursor, the camera, the hero and the actions. In this way, a replay became a sequence of states (cursor, camera, hero positions) and actions.

Data Aggregation. Since a game is usually 45 min long, the number of data points for a single game would have been definitely too much to be analyzed, in terms of computational resources. Thus, we aggregated the ticks' information to have a data point every 0.5 s, i.e., 15 ticks. For every spatial feature, we kept the average, the standard deviation and the number of changes that happened over every axis. For actions, we counted the number of occurrences. Thus, a replay became a sequence of states every 0.5 s, each of them expressing the spatial information and the number of occurrences for every action. We ended up with a total of 61 aggregated features, shown in Table 2.

5.2   Preliminary Model and Considerations

Since the game involves a high level of randomness, which depends on hero choices, allies and enemies, strategies and so on, we reduced the identification problem considering only the first 10 min of the game, in which players usually remain in the same part of the map, even if their behavior can still be very different depending on the heroes they selected and their allies or enemies. This is a good choice for two reasons: it is very unlikely that a game ends before 10 min, and we want to identify a player as soon as possible. We then split the 10 min into sub-sequences, since it was better if we could recognize a player in less time. The problem then became a sequence classification problem, with 50 classes.

Training, Validation, Test Sets Split. Not knowing a priori the best sequence length to work with, we set the maximum acceptable length to 2 min (with no overlap), and split the sequences even further afterward, to study the correlation between length and accuracy. In this way, we could also create the training-validation-test sets and not contaminating them (when shuffling) during the model selection phase. Thus, we formed the dataset creating 25000 sequences (5 sequences per match * 100 matches * 50 players), each one with 240 data points (120 s/0.5 s) assigning each of them the player they came from as the target class. We then shuffled the dataset and proceeded with the training-validation-test split of 80%-10%-10%. For the first try, we split our sequences of 2 min in sequences of 20 s, which was a possibly good amount of time to recognize players. Finally, we standardized each feature in the training set (i.e., makes the values have zero-mean and unit-variance), and we applied that standardization to the validation and test set.

First Model. Working with sequences, and being the time information relevant, for the task we used a Recurrent Neural Network, in particular a Long Short Term Memory (LSTM), which has been proven to work well in these situations [27]. In LSTM, information persists over time, allowing it to learn time-dependent patterns. In our case, the way a player moves the mouse or the camera is exactly the kind of pattern an LSTM can learn. For instance, to move from a point A to B, a player could click one time in B, or two times in B, or do it in whatever way. Our intuition was that the way of moving, as well as controlling the camera, is in some way "biometric", i.e., every human has their own different way to do so.

For the model, we used two LSTM layers (which are usually enough to solve even tough problems [23]) with *tanh* activation function, a fully connected layer with *RELU* activation, and a *softmax* output layer since we are classifying sequences. We started with a standard value of 64 units in both LSTM and dense layers. We used a batch size of 256, 100 epochs and the categorical cross-entropy loss function. As optimizer, we used Adam, which was proven to be one of the best optimizers so far [16], with a learning rate = 0.001. For the implementation, we used the Keras library with Tensorflow backend.

Feature Elimination. From the first run of the model over our dataset, the model was not able to learn: the noise was surely hiding the signal. We then removed some features that could cause this problem. Information such as the hero positions might introduce a lot of noise, since it could strongly depend on the selected hero. The coordinates relative to some actions could also introduce noise, since they might be very specific and varying a lot from each match. Instead, we kept the coordinates for the movement actions, since it could tell us how a player is used to move into the map (e.g., how many clicks to go from point A to point B). Thus, from the features listed in Table 2 we completely removed `Hero Cell` and `Hero Vector`, and the X and Y coordinates from `Attack_move`, `Cast_position`, `Drop_item`.

5.3   Model Selection

Training the model with the new set of features, it was definitely able to learn and generalize on the validation set: we achieved 83.6% of accuracy. It was a promising result, but we thought a problem could be related to the length of the sequences. 20 s were probably too few to recognize a player very accurately. We then tried different sequence lengths before moving on. Intuitively, a longer sequence would help in better recognizing a player. We also used shorter

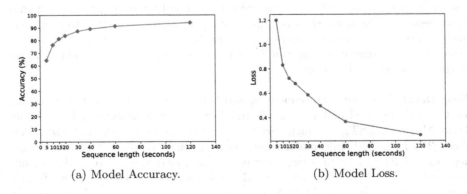

(a) Model Accuracy.   (b) Model Loss.

Fig. 1. Model performance for difference sequence lengths.

sequences to better understand the relationship between sequence length and accuracy. We tried sequences of 5, 10, 15, 20, 30, 40, 60 and 120 s with the same architecture as before. The accuracy and loss graphs are shown in Fig. 1.

Our intuition was confirmed: longer sequences mean better accuracy, and accordingly, smaller losses. With sequences of 5 s, the accuracy was about 65%, and near to 80% with 10 s. Sequences of 15, 20 and 30 s all scored an accuracy between 80% and 90%. An accuracy of 90% was almost reached with 40 s and slightly surpassed with 60 s, while 120 s scored definitely higher, 94%. The losses followed the same trend, with a significantly lower value for sequences of 120s. According to these results, to find the best model to solve our problem we used a sequence length of 120 s, a reasonably good amount of time to recognize a player from a match. Figure 2 shows epoch accuracy and epoch loss for training and validation sets using the sequences of 120 s. From this first graph, we could see that our model was definitely not overfitting (the validation loss remained constant), and it was not really learning after ∼70 epochs. Thus, in the future, we could potentially stop the learning around ∼70 epochs to reduce computational expenses.

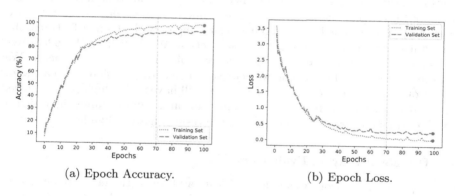

(a) Epoch Accuracy.   (b) Epoch Loss.

Fig. 2. Model performance for training and validation sets.

Before applying a grid search approach to find the best model, we tried another run using Adam optimizer setting the learning rate to 0.01, and we noticed the model converged around ∼35 epochs, with no risk of overfitting (i.e., training and validation losses stabilized after 35 epochs). With this new information, we applied a grid search approach to find the best hyperparameters for our model, i.e., the number of neurons in each hidden layer and the learning rate of Adam optimizer. Since there is not a fixed rule to choose the number of units in a hidden layer, we used the common rule of thumb that suggests a starting point of $N\_train\_samples/(2 * (Input + Output))$, that in our case yields $20000/(2 * (37 + 50)) = 115$. We then used the closest power of 2 (128), the next one (256) and the first we used (64). We tried a learning rate of 0.01 and 0.001. The number of epochs was set to 50 for learning rate of 0.01 and to 75 for learning rate of 0.001, according to previous experiments.

6   Results and Further Experiments

Based on the results of the grid search, we selected the model that performed the best on the validation set. Such model (accuracy = 96.48%, loss = 0.179) had 256 neurons for both LSTM layers and 128 neurons on the dense layer, with a learning rate of 0.001. We then trained the selected model using both training and validation set, and tested it on the test set, with a final accuracy of 96.32% and a loss of 0.198: our model is able to generalize very well, recognizing a player with very high accuracy. To better evaluate our model, we conducted further experiments: we investigated in Sect. 6.1 if we could recognize a player even with less features, and consideration of recognizing "unknown" players are discussed in Sect. 6.2.

6.1   General Features Evaluation

Many of the action features were related to Dota 2, such as casting a spell or dropping an item. We believe these kinds of actions can be replaced in other games with different actions. For instance, in an FPS, you could have the action "shot" or "recharge", and their occurrence frequencies could be "biometric" for a player. However, we tried to train our model using only the Cursor features, the Camera features, and the Move_to_position action. We do believe these features are almost always available in a game where a player controls a character. We used the same split as before, and we achieved an accuracy of 95.6% and a loss of 0.162. Compared with the previous result, we still have a very high performance, using features that can be found in almost all online video games in which a player controls a character, which makes the result highly valuable.

6.2   Unknown Players Evaluation

Our Deep Neural Network was able to classify a player with very high accuracy. However, we wanted to study how it could face players that were not used in the training phase. Neural Networks do not perform very well with open-set problems, and there is still not a very effective solution. To evaluate our algorithm, we tried two approaches: using a background class, and using a sort of threshold for the last layer.

In the first case, we created an "unknown" background class, using 45 unseen users, perfectly balanced with the known ones. Additional 5 unseen users were put in the test set. Analyzing the confusion matrix after the testing phase, only 4 sequences of the new users were correctly classified as "unknown". This is understandable, since the unknown users belong to the same domain of the known ones, i.e., matches sequences. The network was probably trying to find the most similar player for the unseen sequences.

In the second case, we assigned a player to a match only if at least 4 sequences out of the 5 of the match were assigned to the same player. We used 50 unseen players for the purpose, each one with two games of 5 sequences (the first 10 min). Out of the 100 games, 28 were assigned to a known player, obtaining a

72% of success. Considering instead the two games together, i.e., two matches were assigned to a player only if both matches were assigned to the same player, only 8 unseen players were assigned to a known player, with a success rate of 84%. Even if the system did not reach very high accuracy, we showed that we have some possibilities to reduce misclassification.

7   Discussions

Many consequences arise from our results. As we already mentioned, a well-known issue is the presence of scammers. The victim must accept a scammer friends request to be at risk. Usually, people do not accept requests from low-level profiles, but the situation changes if the request comes from a good player after a game won together. This means that scammers should be players of the game to have a higher success rate. As we showed before, if a scammer is reported, we could ban them from all the accounts they plays with.

More serious problems, such as cyberbullying or stalking, are usually involved in online games. As the survey's participants stated, almost 50% of them were harassed in the game at least once. Bullies or stalkers usually try to chase their victims, even if their account are banned. Using our system, all the accounts where those mean people play can be banned. Nevertheless, the system might also have negative feedback, since it could allow stalkers to chase the victim more effectively, recognize them even if they creates a new account. However, a known problem is easier to tackle than an unknown one.

A particular consequence, proven that the play-style is "biometric", is that the system can be used for authentication. It can be useful to prevent account stealing, or to allow in-game purchases only to real owners. Even if the play-style could be potentially reproduced by deep learning techniques as well, but we do believe it is not an easy task, and the attack ranges would be definitely reduced.

The game community could benefit from this finding as well. Smurfing, boosting and account selling are current problems in Dota 2 [28]. A "smurf" is a high-skilled player who creates a new account to be matched against inexperienced players for easy wins. This inevitably ruins the matches for the players in those skill brackets. Boosting is a similar concept: low-skilled players pay a high-skilled player to boost their accounts, i.e., win a lot to reach a higher rank. Selling an account can cause both smurfing or boosting consequences, since buyers could ruin other people game's if they are not in the right skill bracket. With our system, severe punishments can be taken against smurfs or booster players. Since we are able to recognize players from their play-style, we would be able to find the main account of a smurf or a booster, and ban that one. Usually, high-rank players have a lot of expensive items in their account, so getting banned would be an amazing repellent for the problem.

System Permanence. Concerns can arise about the *permanence* of the presented system, i.e., whether the "biometric" (the play-style) remains consistent over long term. Events like replacing the mouse with a different one or improvements of the player in the game might influence their play-style, resulting in the system not being able to recognize the player anymore. While more studies should be conducted in this direction, we strongly believe these two factors are not a threat for our system. First of all, gaming mice are built to last long, some of them for more than 60 million clicks[6], so these changes are very rare in our opinion. Moreover, if controllers are used instead of mice, these devices are usually standard for a console, thus replacing them will not be a problem. Finally, the number of clicks or the actions issued by the player, as well as camera movements controlled by keyboard keys, are not device-dependent, thus most of our features will remain the same. Speaking about players' improvements, they usually happen slowly, step by step, since learning requires some time. The idea of the system is to keep training the model adding new matches, so that small improvements of players are considered to not be an obstacle. Anyhow, this recognition system is not intended to be the only method used by producers to authenticate or detect malicious users, but to improve and support their current techniques.

Applicability to Other Games. Although this system was designed for Dota 2 and uses some of its specific features, we expect the idea of this research can be applied to other games in which a player controls a character. As we demonstrated, the play-style can be considered "biometric" in the way a player moves the controlled unit, issues orders, or "looks around" in the virtual world. Cursor and camera movements are almost always available in such video games, and using a deep neural network to recognize a player in the way we did, once the actions in the game are identified, should be straightforward. If such data are not recorded into replays, they can be implemented by the publisher for the purpose. From an attacker's perspective, if such data are not available, ideally, it would be possible to "reconstruct" the cursor movements, using supervised learning techniques, starting from the character movements, the direction it is looking to, and so on. Moreover, replays, instead of being parsed, could be directly used as input for computer vision models, probably obtaining similar results. The generality of features we used let us believe that, once movement and action orders are identified into a video game, the players' play-style can be analyzed and used to recognize them.

8   Conclusion and Future Works

In this paper, we showed that deep learning algorithms are able, using sequences of two minutes, to recognize a player by exploiting their play-style, which is unique with respect to our dataset. The presented method has a wide range of adoption. It could be used to try recognizing scammers or harmful players in every account they own. The features used in this case study are very generic and can be easily found or replaced in other games, so the idea of this research could be applied to other games as well. Also, authentication systems could be

---

[6] https://steelseries.com/gaming-mice, accessed: 15th July 2020.

built on such recognition, enhancing the security offered by a simple password-based method. For instance, this recognition could be asked before an in-game payment, reducing the damages when an account is stolen.

In this work, we conducted our experiments on Dota 2. A natural continuation of the project could involve different games, trying transfer learning approaches to better evaluate if the biometric play-style is game-dependent or not. Moreover, more sophisticated models could be used to reduce the sequence length needed to recognize a player, or other means could be found for the purpose. Also, a better solution should be found to face unknown player recognition. Finally, we expect that online-gaming data may also reveal more information about a player. Such data could be used for several purpose, for instance, to find and study categories of players or inferring some kind of private information.

References

1. Baccouche, M., Mamalet, F., Wolf, C., Garcia, C., Baskurt, A.: Sequential deep learning for human action recognition. In: Salah, A.A., Lepri, B. (eds.) HBU 2011. LNCS, vol. 7065, pp. 29–39. Springer, Heidelberg (2011). https://doi.org/10.1007/978-3-642-25446-8_4
2. Blog, A.: League of legends gamers targeted by phishing scam — avast (2018). https://securityboulevard.com/2018/10/league-of-legends-gamers-targeted-by-phishing-scam-avast/. Accessed 8 Mar 2020
3. Chung, E.: Playstation data breach deemed in 'top 5 ever'. CBC News (2011)
4. Conti, M., Nati, M., Rotundo, E., Spolaor, R.: Mind the plug! laptop-user recognition through power consumption. In: Proceedings of the 2nd ACM International Workshop on IoT Privacy, Trust, and Security, pp. 37–44 (2016)
5. D'anastasio, C.: What's really going on with all those hacked fortnite accounts (2018). https://kotaku.com/whats-really-going-on-with-all-those-hacked-fortnite-ac-1823965781. Accessed 10 March 2020
6. Deng, L., Hinton, G., Kingsbury, B.: New types of deep neural network learning for speech recognition and related applications: an overview. In: 2013 IEEE ICASSP, pp. 8599–8603. IEEE (2013)
7. Drachen, A., Canossa, A., Yannakakis, G.N.: Player modeling using self-organization in tomb raider: underworld. In: 2009 IEEE Symposium on Computational Intelligence and Games, pp. 1–8 (2009)
8. Eggert, C., Herrlich, M., Smeddinck, J., Malaka, R.: Classification of player roles in the team-based multi-player game dota 2, pp. 112–125 (2015)
9. Fryling, M., Cotler, J.L., Rivituso, J., Mathews, L., Pratico, S.: Cyberbullying or normal game play? impact of age, gender, and experience on cyberbullying in multi-player online gaming environments: Perceptions from one gaming forum. J. Inf. Syst. Appl. Res. 8(1), 4 (2015)
10. Funk, J.B., Baldacci, H.B., Pasold, T., Baumgardner, J.: Violence exposure in real-life, video games, television, movies, and the internet: is there desensitization? J. Adolescence 27(1), 23–39 (2004)
11. Gaimin.io, A.: How many gamers are there? July 2018. https://gaimin.io/how-many-gamers-are-there/. Accessed 7 2020
12. Gao, L., Judd, J., Wong, D., Lowder, J.: Classifying dota 2 hero characters based on play style and performance. University of Utah Course on ML (2013)

13. Gong, D., et al.: Enhanced functional connectivity and increased gray matter volume of insula related to action video game playing. Sci. Rep. **5**, 9763 (2015)
14. Granic, I., Lobel, A., Engels, R.C.: The benefits of playing video games. Am. psychol. **69**(1), 66 (2014)
15. Jedrzejczyk, L., Price, B.A., Bandara, A.K., Nuseibeh, B., Hall, W., Keynes, M.: I know what you did last summer: risks of location data leakage in mobile and social computing, pp. 1744–1986. Department of Computing Faculty of Mathematics, Computing and Technology The Open University (2009)
16. Kingma, D.P., Ba, J.: Adam: A method for stochastic optimization. arXiv preprint arXiv:1412.6980 (2014)
17. Kovess-Masfety, V., et al.: Is time spent playing video games associated with mental health, cognitive and social skills in young children? Social Psychiatry Psychiatric Epidemiol. **51**(3), 349–357 (2016). https://doi.org/10.1007/s00127-016-1179-6
18. Mahlmann, T., Drachen, A., Togelius, J., Canossa, A., Yannakakis, G.N.: Predicting player behavior in tomb raider: Underworld. In: Proceedings of the 2010 IEEE Conference on Computational Intelligence and Games, pp. 178–185, August 2010
19. McDonald, E.: ACI and newzoo whitepaper: turning players into payers — understanding the gaming payments experience. https://newzoo.com/insights/articles/aci-and-newzoo-whitepaper-turning-players-into-payers/ (2018). Accessed 8 March 2020
20. Müller, S., et al.: Statistical analysis of player behavior in minecraft. In: Proceedings of the 10th International Conference on the Foundations of Digital Games. Society for the Advancement of the Science of Digital Games (2015)
21. Newman, J., Jerome, J.: Press start to track privacy and the new questions posed by modern video game technology. AIPLA QJ **42**, 527 (2014)
22. OpenAI, Berner, C., et al.: Dota 2 with large scale deep reinforcement learning (2019). https://arxiv.org/abs/1912.06680
23. Reimers, N., Gurevych, I.: Optimal hyperparameters for deep lstm-networks for sequence labeling tasks. arXiv preprint arXiv:1707.06799 (2017)
24. Russell, N.C., Reidenberg, J.R., Moon, S.: Privacy in gaming. Fordham Intell. Prop. Media & Ent. LJ **29**, 61 (2018)
25. Shaffer, D.W., Squire, K.R., Halverson, R., Gee, J.P.: Video games and the future of learning. Phi Delta Kappan **87**(2), 105–111 (2005)
26. Statista.com: Facebook's annual revenue from 2009 to 2019 (2020). https://www.statista.com/statistics/268604/annual-revenue-of-facebook/. Accessed 4 March 2020
27. Sutskever, I., Vinyals, O., Le, Q.V.: Sequence to sequence learning with neural networks. In: Advances in Neural Information Processing Systems, pp. 3104–3112 (2014)
28. Team, D.: Matchmaking update for the next ranked season, September 2019. http://blog.dota2.com/2019/09/matchmaking-update-for-the-next-ranked-season/. Accessed 6 March 2020
29. Valve: Security and trading. https://store.steampowered.com/news/19618/ (2015). Accessed 11 March 2020
30. Wilson, J.: Newzoo: U.S. will overtake china as no. 1 gaming market in 2019 (2019). https://venturebeat.com/2019/06/18/newzoo-u-s-will-overtake-china-as-no-1-gaming-market-in-2019/. Accessed 9 March 2020

Privacy-Preserving Computation
of the Earth Mover's Distance

Alberto Blanco-Justicia[(✉)] [iD] and Josep Domingo-Ferrer [iD]

Department of Computer Engineering and Mathematics, Universitat Rovira i Virgili,
UNESCO Chair in Data Privacy, CYBERCAT-Center for Cybersecurity Research
of Catalonia, Av. Països Catalans 26, Tarragona, Catalonia
{alberto.blanco,josep.domingo}@urv.cat

Abstract. The Wasserstein distance, also known in computer science as the *Earth Mover's Distance* (EMD) is a distance metric between two probability distributions. EMD has often been used as a distance metric to compare images and documents, and is central to privacy models such as t-closeness. In this work, we show that, given one-dimensional discrete probability distributions, the computation of EMD can be reduced to the computation of the cardinality of the intersection of two sets. We then use a private matching scheme to create a privacy-preserving computation protocol for EMD: two parties can compute EMD between their privately-owned documents without revealing them to the other party. We demonstrate our proposal by implementing a privacy-preserving reverse image search, where images are kept encrypted at an external server.

Keywords: Secure multiparty computation · Private matching schemes · Searchable encryption · Earth Mover's Distance

1 Introduction

The Wasserstein distance, better known in computer science as the Earth Mover's Distance (EMD), is a distance metric between two distributions that measures the minimum amount of work needed to transform one distribution into the other. If we imagine distributions as heaps of earth—hence the name of the distance,—the cost of transforming one heap of earth into another is equal to the amount of earth we need to move times the distance we need to move it [18]. EMD is a special case of a transportation optimization problem and, for discrete one-dimensional distributions (such as a histogram), there exist efficient algorithms to compute it.

EMD can be used to compare images according to their distribution of colors and textures [18,19], and to semantically compare documents [14,22]. Thus, EMD can be used as a building block to develop databases with reverse search support. EMD has also been used in microdata anonymization: the t-closeness privacy model [15], which is an extension of k-anonymity [21], requires confidential attributes to have a distribution within each k-anonymous class that is close

© Springer Nature Switzerland AG 2020
W. Susilo et al. (Eds.): ISC 2020, LNCS 12472, pp. 409–423, 2020.
https://doi.org/10.1007/978-3-030-62974-8_23

to their distribution on the whole microdata file. This closeness is measured as the EMD.

In this work, we propose a mechanism for privacy-preserving computation of EMD. Two individuals, each of them holding a private file, want to compute the EMD of their files without any of them revealing their own file. Our proposed mechanism is based on two-party computation of the set intersection cardinality [10]. It might be used as a building block for the implementation of searchable encryption schemes for reverse image and document search or to develop distributed anonymization mechanisms.

In Sect. 2, we present the Earth Mover's Distance and give an overview of methods for secure multiparty computation of the cardinality of the intersection of private sets. In Sect. 3 we demonstrate that, for discrete one-dimensional distributions, the computation of EMD can be reduced to the computation of the cardinality of the union or the intersection of two sets. Section 4 presents our experimental work, in which we apply our EMD computation mechanism to a reverse image search service for encrypted outsourced images. In Sect. 5 we summarize the conclusions of the work.

2   Background

2.1   The Earth Mover's Distance

Given two probability distributions A and B, EMD measures the distance between such distributions [18]. In the general case, EMD can be obtained by solving a transportation optimization problem. In the special case of discrete one-dimensional distributions, or relative frequency histograms $A = \{a_0, \ldots, a_{n-1}\}$ and $B = \{b_0, \ldots, b_{n-1}\}$, EMD can be iteratively computed using Algorithm 1.

Algorithm 1: Earth Mover's Distance between two one-dimensional discrete distributions

---

Input: $A = \{a_0, \ldots, a_{n-1}\}$, $B = \{b_0, \ldots, b_{n-1}\}$
Output: $\mathrm{EMD}(A, B)$
1 $w_0 = 0$
2 **for** $i = 1 \rightarrow n$ **do**
3 $\quad | \quad w_i = a_{i-1} - b_{i-1} + w_{i-1}$
4 **end**
5 **return** $\sum_{i=0}^{n} |w_i|$

2.2   Private Computation of the Size of the Intersection of Two Sets

In this section we present an overview of secure multiparty computation protocols for computing the cardinality of the intersection of privately held sets. These mechanisms are called *Private Set Intersection – Cardinality* (PSI-CA) and are a recurring primitive for secure protocols in privacy-preserving data mining. Their main goal is to allow data sharing among entities that do not fully trust each other. Instead of sharing all data held by each of them, the entities can start by sharing information about the data they have in common.

More formally, parties P_1 and P_2, with private inputs x and y, respectively, want to compute a function $f(x, y)$ without revealing any information on x, resp. y, to the other party. In our case, the private inputs x and y are sets of elements in a common universe, and the function f is $|x \cap y|$. A typical security requirement on PSI-CA (but also on general multiparty computation schemes) is that parties P_1 and P_2 do not learn more information about the other party's input than the information they would obtain if a trusted third party collected their inputs, computed f and distributed the output to the participating parties.

An example application of PSI-CA would be several institutions co-operating in searching and detecting fraudulent financial movements of the customers they have in common. Other uses of PSI-CA include searching keywords in outsourced document databases or matching social medial users according to their shared contacts.

One of the most influential works on PSI-CA is that of Freedman, Nissim and Pinkas [10]. This work presents several secure protocols to compute different set operations, including the set intersection cardinality. All of them are based on the same primitive, namely oblivious polynomial evaluation (OPE). One of the parties builds a polynomial whose roots are the elements of her privately owned set. The other party evaluates such a polynomial for all elements in her own set. All elements whose evaluation is 0 are elements that are shared by both parties. Using additively-homomorphic encryption (e.g.. the Paillier cryptosystem [16]), the second party can evaluate the polynomial from its encrypted coefficients. Unfortunately, these protocols require the computation of expensive cryptographic operations and are not suitable for large datasets, although [9] describes some optimizations.

Another frequently used construction in PSI-CA protocols are Bloom filters. Dong, Chen and Wen [6], use modified Bloom filters and oblivious transfer protocols to compute multi-set operations. Pinkas, Schneider and Zohner [17] proposed a scalability improvement of this protocol.

PSI-CA Based on Oblivious Polynomial Evaluation. Next we briefly recall the computation of the size of the intersection of two sets using oblivious polynomial evaluation, as per [10]. Let $\mathcal{C}$ and $\mathcal{S}$ be the two participants in the protocol, with $\mathcal{C}$ bringing in the set $A = \{a_0, \ldots, a_{n-1}\}$ and $\mathcal{S}$ the set $B = \{b_0, \ldots, b_{m-1}\}$. Let Enc be the encryption under the Paillier cryptosystem with $\mathcal{C}$'s public key. The Paillier cryptosystem is additively homomorphic, that is, it satisfies the following two properties:

$$Enc(x) \cdot Enc(y) = Enc(x + y);$$
$$Enc(x)^k = Enc(kx).$$

Protocol 1. *PSI-CA-OPE*

1. $\mathcal{C}$ computes $P(x) = \sum_{i=0}^{n} p_i x^i = \prod_{j=0}^{n-1} (x - a_i)$.
2. $\mathcal{C}$ sends $Enc(p_0), \ldots, Enc(p_n)$ to $\mathcal{S}$.
3. $\mathcal{S}$ chooses random integers $r_j \in \mathbb{Z}_n$ for $1 \leq j \leq m - 1$. $\mathcal{S}$ computes $Enc(r_j \cdot p(b_j) + k)$ for all $1 \leq j \leq |B|$. Next, $\mathcal{S}$ returns these ciphertexts to $\mathcal{C}$.
4. $\mathcal{C}$ decrypts the obtained ciphertexts. The result of each decryption is either k or a random number.
5. The number of obtained k's equals $|A \cap B|$.

This protocol is secure against semi-honest adversaries. After this protocol is executed, $\mathcal{C}$ obtains $|B|$ from the number of ciphertexts received in Step 3, $\mathcal{S}$ obtains $|A|$ from the degree n of $P(x)$, and $\mathcal{C}$ obtains $|A \cap B|$. For $\mathcal{S}$ to also obtain $|A \cap B|$, the protocol has to be run a second time, with $\mathcal{C}$ and $\mathcal{S}$ inverting their roles.

PSI-CA Based on Bloom Filters. We summarize here the properties of Bloom filters and how they are used as a building block of PSI-CA protocols. Bloom filters [2] are a probabilistic data structure used to encode sets that allows membership queries. Membership queries for elements in the original set will test positive with 100% probability, while for elements not in the set there is a fixed probability of false positives.

A Bloom filter is a vector $B \in \mathbb{Z}_2^m$, with all its elements initialized to 0, and equipped with $k \ll m$ hash functions $H_i : \{0, 1\}^* \rightarrow \{0, \ldots, m-1\}$. To insert an element e, we compute a list of indices $(i_0, \ldots, i_{k-1}) = (H_0(e), \ldots, H_{k-1}(e))$ and assign a value 1 to the corresponding positions in B. Similarly, a membership query for element e is resolved by checking whether the corresponding k positions in the vector are all set to 1. The false positive probability for membership queries in a Bloom filter containing n elements is given by the expression $(1-(1-\frac{1}{m})^{kn})^k$, which is the probability that the k indices of the element e that is tested are set to 1 when the element is not encoded in the filter. This may happen if an element $e' \neq e$ shares the same indices of e (which is unlikely if cryptographic hashes are used) or if a combination of other elements set these indices to 1.

The approximate number of elements inserted in a Bloom filter is

$$|A| \approx -\frac{m}{k} \ln \left(1 - \frac{\mathcal{H}(B_A)}{m} \right), \tag{1}$$

where A is the encoded set, B_A is the Bloom filter containing the elements of A, $\mathcal{H}(\cdot)$ is the Hamming weight, m is the length of the Bloom filter, and k is the number of hash functions.

A Bloom filter encoding the union, resp. the intersection, of two (or more) sets can be easily obtained by applying the bitwise $\vee$ (logic "or"), resp. $\wedge$ (logic "and") operation. By applying Expression (1) to the resulting Bloom filters, we obtain an estimate of the cardinality of the union, resp. the intersection, of the sets.

Bloom filters, by themselves, do not offer enough protection to the encoded elements to be directly used in PSI-CA protocols. If both parties share the same universe of elements, any of them might obtain all elements from the other party's Bloom filter with a brute force attack. Using oblivious transfer protocols, one of the parties can request the other party for all indices that are set to 1 in her own Bloom filter and thus obtain the intersection of the sets [6]. An alternative option is to encrypt all the Bloom filter positions with a cryptosystem which is homomorphic for the binary sum, such as Goldwasser-Micali, and sum the filters index-wise. Positions where both filters agree will result in 0 s and the rest as 1 s [13]. Another option is to alter the Bloom filter's values with some probability, as in randomized response [7]. Finally, using keyed hash functions, such as HMAC, we can control who is able to insert elements into the Bloom filter and who is able to query it, which allows us to build indices for symmetric searchable encryption schemes as we do in our experiments.

3   The EMD as a PSI-CA Problem

In this section, we show how the computation of EMD between two discrete one-dimensional distributions A and B can be reduced to operations between the cardinality of two sets that encode such distributions and the cardinality of their intersection. This reduction will allow us to describe a protocol for secure two-party computation of the EMD. To this end, we first show that Algorithm 1 is equivalent to the Manhattan distance between two cumulative distributions.

Theorem 1. *Let $\tilde{A}$ (resp. $\tilde{B}$) be the cumulative distribution, or cumulative sum of A (resp. B). Then, the distance $EMD(A, B)$ can be computed as the 1-norm, or Manhattan distance, of $\tilde{A}$ and $\tilde{B}$:*

$$EMD(A, B) = \|\tilde{A} - \tilde{B}\|_1. \qquad (2)$$

Proof. Given the discrete one-dimensional distribution $A = \{a_0, \ldots, a_{n-1}\}$, the cumulative distribution of A is

$$\tilde{A} = \{\tilde{a}_i = \sum_{j=0}^{i} a_j \ : \ 0 \le i \le n - 1\}. \qquad (3)$$

On the other hand, the 1-norm or Manhattan distance is defined as

$$\|A - B\|_1 = \sum_{i=0}^{n-1} |a_i - b_i|. \qquad (4)$$

By developing line 3 of Algorithm 1, which refers to the computation of w_i, and reordering the factors, we obtain for $i > 0$ and with $w_0 = 0$

$$w_i = a_{i-1} - b_{i-1} + w_{i-1} \tag{5}$$
$$= a_{i-1} - b_{i-1} + a_{i-2} - b_{i-2} + w_{i-2}$$
$$\cdots$$
$$= a_{i-1} - b_{i-1} + a_{i-2} - b_{i-2} + \cdots + a_0 - b_0$$
$$= (a_{i-1} + \cdots + a_0) - (b_{i-1} + \cdots + b_0)$$
$$= \sum_{j=0}^{i-1} a_j - \sum_{j=0}^{i-1} b_j.$$

According to line 5 of Algorithm 1 and using Expressions (3), (4) and (5), we obtain

$$EMD(A,B) = \sum_{i=0}^{n} |w_i| = w_0 + \sum_{i=1}^{n} |w_i| = \sum_{i=1}^{n} |w_i|$$

$$\overset{(5)}{=} \sum_{i=1}^{n} \left| \sum_{j=0}^{i-1} a_j - \sum_{j=0}^{i-1} b_j \right| \overset{(3)}{=} \sum_{i=1}^{n} |\tilde{a}_{i-1} - \tilde{b}_{i-1}|$$

$$= \sum_{i=0}^{n-1} |\tilde{a}_i - \tilde{b}_i| \overset{(4)}{=} \|\tilde{A} - \tilde{B}\|_1.$$

□

Next, we prove that the Manhattan distance can be obtained from the cardinality of the intersection of two sets. This result comes from [1], and we elaborate on it.

First, we define an encoding function f, which takes a list $A = \{a_0, \ldots, a_{n-1}\}$ of nonnegative integers and returns a set of the form:

$$\mathcal{A} = f(A) = \{(i,j) : a_i > 0, \ 1 \le j \le a_i\}.$$

For example, given the list $A = \{2,1,3\}$, the resulting set $\mathcal{A}$ is $\{(1,1),(1,2),(2,1),(3,1),(3,2),(3,3)\}$. Figure 1 shows a graphical example of the encoding function.

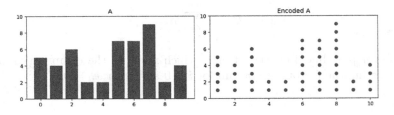

Fig. 1. The encoding function f encodes the histogram A as a set of two-dimensional points $\mathcal{A}$

Theorem 2. *Given the encoding function f, two lists A and B containing the same number n of nonnegative integers, and their respective encodings $\mathcal{A}$ and $\mathcal{B}$, the following holds:*

$$\|A - B\|_1 = |\mathcal{A}| + |\mathcal{B}| - 2|\mathcal{A} \cap \mathcal{B}|.$$

Proof. First, we rewrite the expression of the Manhattan distance between lists A and B as the difference between the sum of the element-wise maximum values minus the sum of the element-wise minimum values of A and B:

$$\|A - B\|_1 = \sum_{i=0}^{n-1} |a_i - b_i|$$

$$= \sum_{i=0}^{n-1} \max(a_i, b_i) - \min(a_i, b_i)$$

$$= \sum_{i=0}^{n-1} \max(a_i, b_i) - \sum_{i=0}^{n-1} \min(a_i, b_i).$$

We also observe that the cardinality of the set resulting from applying the encoding function f to a list equals the sum of the values of such list:

$$|\mathcal{A}| = \sum_{i=0}^{n-1} a_i.$$

The encoding function f also has the following property: the size of the union of the encodings of A and B is the sum of the element-wise maximum values of A and B:

$$|\mathcal{A} \cup \mathcal{B}| = |\{(i, j) : (i, j) \in \mathcal{A} \text{ or } (i, j) \in \mathcal{B}\}|$$
$$= |\{(i, j) : a_i, b_i > 0, \ 1 \le j \le \max(a_i, b_i)\}|$$
$$= \sum_{i=0}^{n-1} \max(a_i, b_i).$$

Likewise, the size of the intersection equals the sum of the element-wise minimum values:

$$|\mathcal{A} \cap \mathcal{B}| = |\{(i, j) : (i, j) \in \mathcal{A} \text{ and } (i, j) \in \mathcal{B}\}|$$
$$= |\{(i, j) : a_i, b_i > 0, \ 1 \le j \le \min(a_i, b_i)\}|$$
$$= \sum_{i=0}^{n-1} \min(a_i, b_i).$$

Figure 2 shows a graphical example of these union and intersection properties. In the top row, we show the encodings of histograms A and B. In the bottom row, we show the sets representing the intersection and the union of the encoded datasets. It can be observed that the resulting sets represent the element-wise minimum and maximum, respectively, of the two histograms.

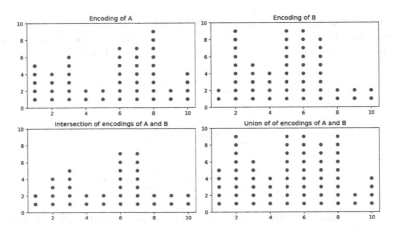

Fig. 2. The intersection and union of $\mathcal{A}$ and $\mathcal{B}$ result in the element-wise minimum and maximum, respectively, of A and B

Therefore, the Manhattan distance between A and B results from the difference $|\mathcal{A} \cup \mathcal{B}| - |\mathcal{A} \cap \mathcal{B}|$. Given the identity $|\mathcal{A} \cup \mathcal{B}| = |\mathcal{A}| + |\mathcal{B}| - |\mathcal{A} \cap \mathcal{B}|$, this results in

$$\|A - B\|_1 = |\mathcal{A}| + |\mathcal{B}| - 2|\mathcal{A} \cap \mathcal{B}|.$$

$\square$

From Theorems 1 and 2 it follows that the computation of EMD can be expressed as

$$EMD(A, B) = |\tilde{\mathcal{A}}| + |\tilde{\mathcal{B}}| - 2|\tilde{\mathcal{A}} \cap \tilde{\mathcal{B}}|. \tag{6}$$

In Expression (6), $|\tilde{\mathcal{A}}|$, $|\tilde{\mathcal{B}}|$ and $|\tilde{\mathcal{A}} \cap \tilde{\mathcal{B}}|$ can be privately computed by both parties holding A and B, respectively, using the PSI-CA protocols discussed in Sect. 2.2, in particular Protocol 1.

3.1   Message Expansion

Let the size of set A be $|A| = n$ and its sum be $s = \sum_{i=0}^{n-1} a_i$. The message expansion of set $\tilde{\mathcal{A}}$, resulting from computing the cumulative sum $\tilde{A}$ and encoding it using function f is:

- In the best case, when $a_0 = \cdots = a_{n-2} = 0$ and $a_{n-1} = s$, $|\tilde{\mathcal{A}}| = s$;
- In the worst, case, when $a_0 = s$ and $a_1, \cdots, a_{n-1} = 0$, $|\tilde{\mathcal{A}}| = sn$;
- In the average case $|\tilde{\mathcal{A}}| = (1 + n)s/2$.

Thus, the spatial complexity of our proposal is $\mathcal{O}(sn)$.

4   Experimental Results

In our experimental work, we simulated a symmetric searchable encryption (SSE) scheme that allows the data owner to conduct reverse image search queries on an outsourced database of encrypted images. We use our proposed scheme to privately compute the EMD between two distributions to build the search index of an SSE scheme. Typical SSE schemes consist of two parts: on the one hand, the information is encrypted using some standard symmetric encryption scheme (e.g.. AES), and, on the other hand, a search index is built such that only the parties holding some private information (i.e. a trapdoor generated with the symmetric secret key) can query it [3–5,12,20]. In this experimental work we focus on the search index to demonstrate the private computation of the EMD.

The experiments were implemented in Python in a Jupyter Notebook, which is available in Github[1]. The images for the experiments were obtained from [8], which contains 9144 images of 101 different categories.

We took half of the images (4572) from the database to build our search index. For each image, we obtained its gray level histogram with $n = 16$ bins of 16 values each, and we re-scaled it so that its cumulative sum was $s = 100$. The maximum number of elements to be included in each of the Bloom filters after encoding the histograms using function f was, as per Sect. 3.1, $sn = 1600$. The implementation of the Bloom filters used keyed hash functions (HMAC) so that only those who owned the key were able to add images to the database and query it. To query the database, we encoded the image to be searched in the same way as the index images, and we computed its EMD with respect to all images in the search index.

We first studied the impact of the Bloom filters' false positive rate on the overall performance of the reverse image search service. The optimal values for m and k can be computed as a function of the maximum number sn of allowed item insertions, and a fixed false positive rate ρ [11]:

$$m = -\frac{sn \ln \rho}{(\ln 2)^2}, \qquad k = \frac{m}{sn} \ln 2. \qquad (7)$$

For a maximum number of $sn = 1600$ elements, the optimal bit-length of the Bloom filters m and number of hashes k with respect to the false positive rate ρ, going from $\rho = 0.0001$ to $\rho = 0.5$, are shown in Figure 3.

The false positive rate, thus, directly affected the size of the search index, from $10.06MB$ for a false positive rate of 50% to $133.73MB$ for a false positive rate of 0.01%. Next, Figure 4 shows how the choice of ρ affected the time to build the search index and the individual query times.

---

[1] https://github.com/ablancoj/privateEMD/blob/master/EMD.

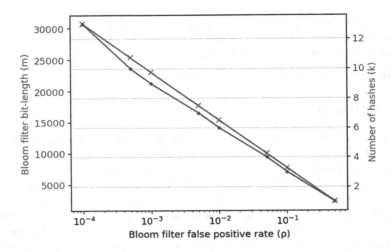

Fig. 3. Size of the Bloom filters (m) and number of hashes (k) as a function of the false positive rate, for a fixed maximum number of elements equal to 1600

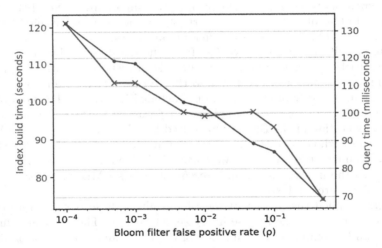

Fig. 4. Index build time and image query time as a function of the false positive rate, for a fixed maximum number of elements equal to 1600

Some error in the computed EMD was to be expected for the following reasons. On the one hand, we forced all gray level histograms to have the same cumulative sum and we could only operate on integer values. Therefore, some error had to come from the rounding of values. On the other hand, the false positive rate of the Bloom filters affects the collisions in the membership queries, and therefore also the computation of the intersection, the estimation of encoded elements and, thus, the computation of the EMD. Figure 5 shows the Mean

Absolute Error of the EMD computed on the cleartext images versus the EMD computed using our mechanism for different values of ρ.

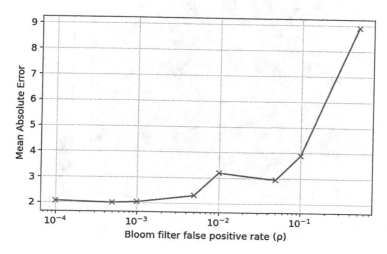

Fig. 5. Mean Absolute Error as a function of the false positive rate, for a fixed maximum number of elements equal to 1600.

The pairwise distances of the first 1024 images in the search index, computed in the clear and using our method with Bloom filters with $m = 8000$, $k = 4$ and $\rho \leq 0.09$ are shown as distance matrices in Figures 6 and 7.

Next, we generated queries for all 9144 images in the original database against the search index including 4572 images. All images whose distance was less than a threshold 10 were returned as the result. All search queries for the 4572 images in the database returned the correct result, although some queries returned more than one result. Figure 8 shows one of such false positives.

Regarding the 4572 images *not* included in the database, a few queries returned a result. Figure 9 shows one such false positive.

Figure 10 shows the ratio of images not in the search index that returned some result and the ratio of images in the search index that returned more than one result, as a function of the Bloom filter's false positive rate ρ.

Additionally, we generated queries on modified images. In particular we applied random anisotropic scaling to images (randomly scaling each of the axes by x0.5 to x1.5) both in the search index and out of it before querying for them. In this scenario, we built a search index consisting of Bloom filters with $\rho = 0.0001$, $m = 30672$, and $k = 13$. The number of bins $n = 16$ and maximum cumulative sum $s = 100$ remained the same. The distance threshold to accept an image in the index as a result was set to 15. The results were as follows:

- For images in the search index, 42.5% returned a correct result.
- For images not in the search index, 8.9% returned some result.

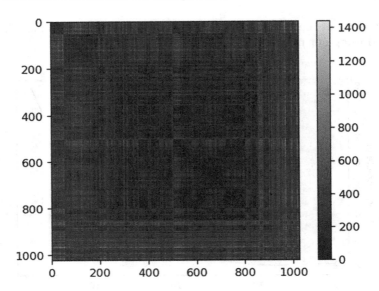

Fig. 6. Pairwise EMD computed from cleartext images

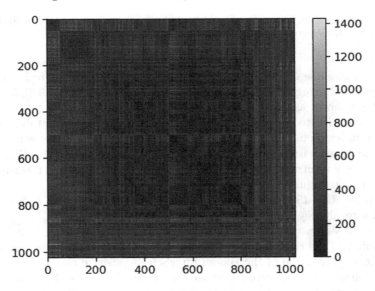

Fig. 7. Pairwise EMD computed using our mechanism

Increasing the maximum cumulative sum to $s = 500$ (which increased the maximum number of elements to $sn = 8000$ and changed the Bloom filter parameters to $m = 115020$ and $k = 9$ for a false positive rate of $\rho = 0.001$) and increasing the distance threshold to 100 improved the matching results to 72.7% correct matches for images in the search index, but increased the false positives for

Fig. 8. False positive: querying for the left image returned both that image and the image on the right

Fig. 9. False positive: querying for the image on the left resulted in the image on the right

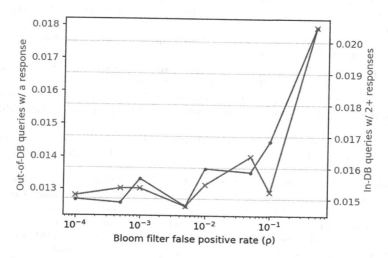

Fig. 10. Left: ratio of queries for images not in the search index that returned some result. Right: ratio of queries for images in the search index that returned more than one result.

images not in the search index to 21%, at the additional cost of increasing the search index size to $500MB$ and the query time to 381 ms.

5   Conclusions

In this work we have proposed a secure multiparty computation scheme to calculate the Earth Mover's distance between one-dimensional discrete distributions. To do so, we have proved that computing EMD in such cases can be reduced to finding the size of the intersection of sets encoding these distributions. From these results, we propose to use existing Private Set Intersection—Cardinality schemes to obtain EMD between two distributions. We have demonstrated our scheme with a symmetric searchable encryption scheme that supports reverse image search.

Acknowledgements and Disclaimer. We acknowledge support from: European Commission (projects H2020-871042 "SoBigData++" and H2020-101006879 "Mobi DataLab"), Government of Catalonia (ICREA Acadèmia Prize to the second author and grant 2017 SGR 705) and Spanish Government (project RTI2018-095094-B-C21). The authors are with the UNESCO Chair in Data Privacy, but their views here are not necessarily shared by UNESCO.

References

1. Blanco, A., Domingo-Ferrer, J., Farràs, O., Sánchez, D.: Distance computation between two private preference functions. In: Cuppens-Boulahia, N., Cuppens, F., Jajodia, S., Abou El Kalam, A., Sans, T. (eds.) SEC 2014. IAICT, vol. 428, pp. 460–470. Springer, Heidelberg (2014). https://doi.org/10.1007/978-3-642-55415-5_39
2. Bloom, B.H.: Space/time trade-offs in hash coding with allowable errors. Commun. ACM **13**(7), 422–426 (1970)
3. Bost, R., Fouque, P.A.: Security-efficiency tradeoffs in searchable encryption. Proc. Privacy Enhanc. Technol. **2019**(4), 132–151 (2019)
4. Bost, R., Fouque, P.A., Pointcheval, D.: Verifiable dynamic symmetric searchable encryption: optimality and forward security. IACR Cryptol. ePrint Arch. **2016**, 62 (2016)
5. Curtmola, R., Garay, J., Kamara, S., Ostrovsky, R.: Searchable symmetric encryption: improved definitions and efficient constructions. J. Comput. Security **19**(5), 895–934 (2011)
6. Dong, C., Chen, L., Wen, Z.: When private set intersection meets big data: an efficient and scalable protocol. In: Proceedings of the 2013 ACM SIGSAC Conference on Computer & Communications Security, pp. 789–800 (2013)
7. Erlingsson, Ú., Pihur, V., Korolova, A.: Rappor: randomized aggregatable privacy-preserving ordinal response. In: Proceedings of the 2014 ACM SIGSAC Conference on Computer and Communications Security, pp. 1054–1067 (2014)
8. Fei-Fei, L., Fergus, R., Perona, P.: Learning generative visual models from few training examples: an incremental bayesian approach tested on 101 object categories. In: 2004 Conference on Computer Vision and Pattern Recognition Workshop, pp. 178–178. IEEE (2004)

9. Freedman, M.J., Hazay, C., Nissim, K., Pinkas, B.: Efficient set intersection with simulation-based security. J. Cryptol. **29**(1), 115–155 (2016)
10. Freedman, M.J., Nissim, K., Pinkas, B.: Efficient private matching and set intersection. In: Cachin, C., Camenisch, J.L. (eds.) EUROCRYPT 2004. LNCS, vol. 3027, pp. 1–19. Springer, Heidelberg (2004). https://doi.org/10.1007/978-3-540-24676-3_1
11. Gerbet, T., Kumar, A., Lauradoux, C.: The power of evil choices in bloom filters. In: 2015 45th Annual IEEE/IFIP International Conference on Dependable Systems and Networks, pp. 101–112. IEEE (2015)
12. Guo, C., Chen, X., Jie, Y., Zhangjie, F., Li, M., Feng, B.: Dynamic multi-phrase ranked search over encrypted data with symmetric searchable encryption. In: IEEE Transactions on Services Computing (2017)
13. Kerschbaum, F.: Outsourced private set intersection using homomorphic encryption. In: Proceedings of the 7th ACM Symposium on Information, Computer and Communications Security, pp. 85–86 (2012)
14. Kusner, M., Sun, Y., Kolkin, N., Weinberger, K.: From word embeddings to document distances. In: International Conference on Machine Learning, pp. 957–966 (2015)
15. Li, N., Li, T., Venkatasubramanian, S.: t-closeness: privacy beyond k-anonymity and l-diversity. In: 2007 IEEE 23rd International Conference on Data Engineering, pp. 106–115. IEEE (2007)
16. Paillier, P.: Public-key cryptosystems based on composite degree residuosity classes. In: Stern, J. (ed.) EUROCRYPT 1999. LNCS, vol. 1592, pp. 223–238. Springer, Heidelberg (1999). https://doi.org/10.1007/3-540-48910-X_16
17. Pinkas, B., Schneider, T., Zohner, M.: Faster private set intersection based on {OT} extension. In: 23rd {USENIX} Security Symposium ({USENIX} Security 14), pp. 797–812 (2014)
18. Rubner, Y., Tomasi, C., Guibas, L.J.: A metric for distributions with applications to image databases. In: Sixth International Conference on Computer Vision (IEEE Cat. No. 98CH36271), pp. 59–66. IEEE (1998)
19. Rubner, Y., Tomasi, C., Guibas, L.J.: The earth mover's distance as a metric for image retrieval. Int. J. Comput. Vis. **40**(2), 99–121 (2000)
20. Sun, S.F., Yuan, X., Liu, J.K., Steinfeld, R., Sakzad, A., Vo, V., Nepal, S.: Practical backward-secure searchable encryption from symmetric puncturable encryption. In: Proceedings of the 2018 ACM SIGSAC Conference on Computer and Communications Security, pp. 763–780 (2018)
21. Sweeney, L.: k-anonymity: a model for protecting privacy. Int. J. Uncertainty, Fuzziness Knowl. Based Syst. **10**(05), 557–570 (2002)
22. Wan, X., Peng, Y.: The earth mover's distance as a semantic measure for document similarity. In: Proceedings of the 14th ACM International Conference on Information and Knowledge Management, pp. 301–302 (2005)

Author Index

Printed in the United States
By Bookmasters